THE URBANIST

Dan Doctoroff and the Rise of New York

Foreword by **Michael Bloomberg**
Introduction by **Paul Goldberger**

ℳ

First Spread: A view down Madison Street toward Lower Manhattan.

Title Page: Dan Doctoroff on the High Line in front of The Shed in construction.

Opposite: New York City metropolitan area photographed by crew members aboard the International Space Station, March 23, 2013.

THE LEGACY OF DAN DOCTOROFF

Daniel L. Doctoroff was only in government for six years, serving as Deputy Mayor for Economic Development and Rebuilding between 2002 and 2007. In that time, he oversaw one of the most profound overhauls of New York's physical environment in the city's history. The plans he set in motion — many of them initiated as part of his bid for the Olympic Games before joining government — included rezoning 40% of the city, creating new economic hubs in all five boroughs, reclaiming the long-derelict waterfront with a series of striking and now iconic parks and new housing, supporting new museums, cultural institutions, and industries as cornerstones of new, vibrant neighborhoods, and reshaping the transportation network, including the first extension of the subway in decades.

Rezoned Areas (2002–2013)

Development Initiatives

1. Bronx Terminal Market
2. The Brooklyn Navy Yard
3. Hunter's Point South Neighborhood
4. Hunts Point Market
5. The Hub
6. World Trade Center

Cultural Initiatives

7. 369th Regiment Armory
8. Barclays Center
9. Citi Field
10. Columbia University Expansion
11. Coney Island Amusement Zone
12. Downtown Brooklyn Cultural District
13. Kings Theatre
14. Museum of Arts and Design
15. Silvercup Studios
16. Steiner Studios
17. The Shed
18. Whitney Museum of American Art
19. Yankee Stadium

Parks

20. Brooklyn Bridge Park
21. Bushwick Inlet Park
22. Calvert Vaux Park
23. East River Waterfront Esplanade
24. Far Rockaway Beach and Boardwalk
25. Flushing Meadows Corona Park Aquatics Center and Ice Rink
26. Fort Washington Park
27. Freshkills Park
28. Governors Island
29. Highland Park/Ridgewood Reservoir
30. Hunter's Point South Park
31. Macombs Dam Park
32. McCarren Park
33. Mill Pond Park
34. Ocean Breeze Athletic Complex
35. Soundview Park
36. The High Bridge
37. The High Line
38. West Harlem Piers

Transit

39. No. 7 Line Subway Extension
40. East River Ferry
---- Select Bus Service (SBS) Routes
— New Bike Lanes

New Jersey

Stapleton Waterfront

Staten Island

Annual Kite Festival, Pier 5,
Brooklyn Bridge Park.

DAN DOCTOROFF

PREFACE

This project began in early 2022, soon after former New York City Deputy Mayor Daniel L. Doctoroff disclosed that he had been diagnosed with ALS, the fatal neurodegenerative disease that took the life of his father and uncle. He vowed to dedicate the rest of his life to raising at least $250 million for research to one day make the disease — which will impact 1 in 400 Americans — survivable.

For those of us who worked with him, Dan's diagnosis sparked a different call to action: documenting the impact of the man who has had a more transformative impact on New York City than any unelected official in the last half century.

We have both worked with Dan on and off for the last two decades; Marc as a senior policy advisor and ultimately chief of staff in City Hall and then as an executive at Sidewalk Labs, Dan's venture alongside Google to improve life in cities and Sophia, who wrote or edited three of his major vision plans, including the Bid Book for the International Olympic Committee, his landmark sustainability blueprint, PlaNYC, and the *Master Innovation and Development Plan* for Sidewalk Labs that outlined a vision for a new kind of city along the Toronto waterfront.

In deciding what to include in this book, we applied the "but for" test: that but for Dan, the project likely would not have happened, or happened so quickly, or happened so well.

That is not to suggest that these projects happened solely because of Dan, who emphatically ascribes the lion's share of the credit for the transformation of New York primarily to Mayor Michael Bloomberg, First Deputy Mayor Patricia Harris, and the many others involved with the initiatives described here.

But those same partners readily point to Dan's catalytic role. Essay after essay tells a similar story: a longtime government employee with an idea, struggling to cut through bureaucratic inertia . . . until sharing that idea with Dan. They recount how Dan didn't accept an idea at face value. He asked question after question, until becoming convinced of the merits — at which point, *everything* changed. Bureaucratic inertia was replaced by newfound momentum, unprecedented interagency coordination, more funding, and — above all — driving intensity from Dan (best evidenced in recurring meetings that began in predawn weekday hours or on weekends, or that stretched well past midnight).

In telling this story, we fear that the breadth of projects included in this book may be too much for some readers to find credible. How is it possible that one man played such a central role in so many undertakings?

We, too, question how it could be possible, but we also know it's true. The contributors to this book are the most authoritative voices — they were at the center of these efforts and led them from idea to implementation. One after another they offer a similar refrain: "We couldn't have done it without Dan."

Equally astonishing is the compressed time period in which Dan helped instigate and make irrevocable most of the projects documented in this book. While he began his Olympic efforts at only 36, he did not acquire the power to advance projects until becoming deputy mayor at 43. He left City Hall six years later at the age of 49. By contrast, the legendary Robert Moses pursued his agenda — for good and for ill — during a career in public office that lasted more than four decades.

While this book comes in at nearly 500 pages, it could easily have been longer; the projects we left out could practically fill another book. This is particularly true for initiatives that don't lend themselves to photography, but that are no less important — for example, Dan's work to reform the city's business incentive programs, grow procurement from minority- and women-owned businesses, diversify the construction industry, and more. And for each of the essayists we invited to participate, there are many more who played integral roles and could testify firsthand to Dan's unique impact.

There are so many more stories we could have included:

The story of how midway through Mike Bloomberg's first term, a group of commissioners assembled at a planning offsite encouraged Dan to narrow the team's focus, arguing that prioritization was necessary to get anything done — only to have Dan reject that advice out of hand. The story of how Dan battled with property owners hellbent on tearing down the High Line. And the story of how Dan navigated project after project through city and state approval processes, finally putting to rest the consensus that in the post-Moses era, New York could no longer do big things.

There is one part of Dan's story that this book can't capture with sufficient richness: the extraordinary personal affection that Dan inspires in those who worked with him. As we contacted contributors, we often found ourselves acting as informal therapists, particularly just after Dan's diagnosis.

Time and again, we heard more stories of Dan's lasting impact not only on New York, but on individuals.

How he set seemingly unreachable standards, and then helped people achieve them.

How he inspired them with an unabashed belief that great things were possible — and worth pursuing.

How he mentored them, not only while working together, but in the years that followed.

How he enabled them to make a lasting contribution to their city.

And in so doing, how he earned for himself their undying loyalty, respect, admiration, and yes, love.

Sophia Hollander
Marc Ricks

New York
June 2023

FOREWORD

When I offered Dan a job in the fall of 2001, he was not a conventional choice for Deputy Mayor for Economic Development and Rebuilding. He had no experience working in government. He had no experience working in economic development. And he had no experience working to rebuild a city after a catastrophe. But, of course, neither did I. And besides: I wasn't looking for a conventional deputy, because I wasn't interested in a conventional mayoralty. I am not even sure whether Dan voted for me. I never asked.

Dan wasn't interested in the job, at first. He was too committed to his effort to bring the Olympics to New York City. As a private citizen, I had supported Dan's Olympic plan, but that's not why I wanted him for the job. It was his creativity and drive in creating and building support for the plan that fit perfectly with what I wanted to bring into city government: people with big, bold, audacious, against-the-odds ideas, and the determination to bring them to life. Dan had those qualities in spades. And he had something else, which allowed me to talk him into taking the job: a deep love of the city and a deep sense of responsibility to it. In the wake of the 9/11 terrorist attacks, as experts doubted the city's future and predicted dark days ahead, how could he resist the challenge — and the once-in-a-lifetime opportunity — of helping to write one of the world's great comeback stories, and to do it while making $1 a year? Thankfully, for all of us, he couldn't.

Hiring Dan sent a message to all of City government, whether people understood it at that time or not: Our administration was not going to be satisfied with bringing New York City back from the brink, and we were not only going to rebuild Lower Manhattan. We were aiming much higher — at remaking the future of all five boroughs for the next several generations.

In the years ahead, while the press focused on the highest-profile and most politically contentious projects, especially the World Trade Center and the West Side of Manhattan, Dan led our efforts across the city to diversify the economy away from the industry we both had come from— finance — and to reimagine and reinvest in New York City's foundational building blocks: vibrant neighborhoods, beautiful parks, cutting-edge cultural centers, and new housing for the dreamers and immigrants we worked to attract and welcome.

At the heart of this work was a landscape that our administration recognized as the city's most underutilized asset: more than 500 miles of waterfront that had been allowed to decay for decades. It was a painful reminder of a postwar economy that had disappeared and taken many good jobs with it. Wire fencing shut out New Yorkers from a shoreline that held shuttered factories, rotting piers, vacant warehouses, and empty lots — all frozen in place by a zoning map that had been largely unchanged since John F. Kennedy sat in the White House.

Dan embraced the promise of the waterfront and led our work to reclaim and revitalize it, opening it to families and visitors. Working closely with Amanda Burden and the Department of City Planning, and many other agencies, Dan played a central role in turning New York into a model of 21st century design, centered not around buildings or vehicles — as past urban planning schemes had been — but instead around people.

That work took its fullest shape in the comprehensive redevelopment effort Dan spearheaded to make New York "greener and greater," PlaNYC. At the heart of PlaNYC was an idea that was still relatively new at the time — more of a catchy buzzword than a governing philosophy: sustainability.

Up to that point, no one had accused either Dan or me of being tree huggers. But Dan came to see that what he had originally conceived of as an infrastructure plan was something much bigger, and much more important. By that time, we had lost out on the Olympics. But here was a challenge even more difficult, and far more significant. Dan had found his next crusade, and he dove into it headfirst.

The problem of global warming had long been known, but efforts at tackling it — and adapting to it — had focused on national governments. A smattering of state and local efforts had been piecemeal, at best. What made PlaNYC so groundbreaking was that it placed cities — which account for the largest share of greenhouse gas emissions — at the center of both the problem and the solution.

It was the world's first truly comprehensive locally-created urban sustainability plan, and it set a new standard for urban planning and design. After we launched it, other cities followed — and soon, hundreds of cities around the world were taking up this work.

PlaNYC, however, wasn't just a global catalyst. It was also a way for us to show New Yorkers how fighting climate change — by reducing air pollution, planting trees, and creating more green spaces to enjoy — would be good for their health, their commutes, their job prospects, and even their property values. Instead of talking about climate change as a matter of sacrificing for the future, we asked New Yorkers to imagine the health and economic benefits that we could reap in the here and now, while also passing them down to our children and grandchildren. Dan understood that fighting climate change was good for economic development and job growth, because cities with cleaner air, less congested streets, and more greenery are places where people want to live and businesses want to invest.

The press expected our second term to be slower and less ambitious than the first. The creation of PlaNYC put that idea to rest — and it did something else. It inspired my passion for fighting climate change. In our second and third terms, we reduced the city's carbon footprint by 19%. And when Congress failed to pass a cap-and-trade bill in 2010, despite having Democratic super majorities in both houses of Congress, our administration expanded our ambitions. In addition, I began devoting a substantial part of my philanthropy to the issue — helping other cities to go green, and helping to retire, in partnership with the Sierra Club, more than two-thirds of all U.S. coal plants, an effort we have since taken global. It all grew out of PlaNYC.

It's no accident that when Dan decided he was ready for a new crusade, Peter Grauer and I decided to hire him as President and CEO of Bloomberg. When I returned to the company six years later, I found it far stronger and larger than when I had left. I wish I could say I was surprised.

4

For all that Dan has accomplished, and this book only scratches the surface of the work he has led, what most stands out to me isn't a collection of buildings, parks, cultural attractions, or even a subway line. Any one of those areas would be accomplishment enough for one lifetime. But what most stands out to me is how the people he has pushed the hardest along the way — his staff — are so deeply devoted to him. He has always inspired the teams around him to be their best — by dreaming the unimaginable and doing the impossible, always reaching higher, working harder, and tirelessly pursuing their shared goal. They would run through a brick wall for Dan. But their loyalty to him isn't really about what Dan sees in the world. It's about what Dan sees in them.

This book is a chance to remind Dan that, today in New York City, we can see him all around us. To walk the waterfront along the East River, Bronx River, and Hudson River, or to walk neighborhoods from Red Hook to Coney Island and St. George to Ocean Breeze, or to take a ferry to Governors Island, is to see a landscape transformed with housing, parks, businesses, art and culture, athletic facilities, and, most of all, people. In all of it, we can see Dan's guiding hand.

Not bad for a guy who didn't want the job.

Mayor Michael Bloomberg announcing the departure of Dan Doctoroff from City Hall, December 6, 2007.

THE URBANIST

Dan Doctoroff remade his adopted city, guided by a desire to make urban life more fulfilling for the people who lived there. In doing so, he advanced a humanist vision of urbanism that enlivened New York's neglected and forgotten corners, masterminding the most profound changes to the city's physical landscape in decades.

Daniel Doctoroff grew up near Detroit, which may seem an unlikely place for the opening chapter of a life that would do as much to transform New York City as any other over the last two centuries. Then again, Frederick Law Olmsted was born in Hartford; John Roebling in Prussia; DeWitt Clinton in upstate Little Britain, New York; Andrew Haswell Green in Worcester, Massachusetts; John D. Rockefeller in rural Richford, New York; Robert Moses in New Haven, and Jane Jacobs in Scranton. There is something to be said for the notion that New York has been shaped most by those for whom it has been an acquired taste, not a birthright. Doctoroff surely did not see New York as his destiny. As a young lawyer he did not want to come to the city at all, and envisioned a life in Boston, where he had gone to Harvard, or in Philadelphia, which struck him as more manageable. He first settled in New York as an accommodation to his wife, Alisa, whose work as a media executive left her fewer geographical choices than Doctoroff, who was expecting to spend his life as a corporate lawyer. He arrived reluctantly and assumed his stay in the city would be brief. He was not, like so many young people of great ambition, convinced that New York was the ultimate stage on which to perform, the most meaningful place in which to prove himself.

In time he would come to think exactly that, but there was never a moment of epiphany, an instant when he moved from skeptic to believer. It was more gradual and had a lot to do with his recognition that the world was complex and difficult, and that New York offered more opportunities to learn than anywhere else, and that it was teaching him things he had never learned in the classroom. He began to wander around a city that had just begun to emerge from the depths of the fiscal crisis of the 1970s, "taking the then-wretched subway to remote stations in the system just to see the neighborhoods above them," he would write many years later. "I began to play a game of guessing how many different nationalities there were among the passengers on the subway cars."

It was a confirmation that New York offers the most to the curious, and Doctoroff was nothing if not curious. Still, in his early years in the city he was less what one would call an engaged resident than an indifferent one. He plunged deeper into the investment banking career that had enticed him to give up the law early on after realizing, he said, that he had a talent not so much for immersing himself in numbers as "for spotting stories in numbers." That quality was not sufficient to get Doctoroff hired by either Goldman Sachs or Salomon Brothers, neither of which had any use for a young lawyer who lacked an obligatory business school degree. But Lehman Brothers thought differently and chose to take a chance on him, largely at the urging of Peter Solomon, then one of the firm's senior partners and the former deputy mayor for economic development under Mayor Edward I. Koch. Solomon had a fondness for candidates with unorthodox backgrounds. "Anyone can buy numbers people," he told Doctoroff, "but investment banking is about interpersonal skills and relationships."

Deputy Mayor Dan Doctoroff in the "bullpen" of City Hall, the large, open room where Mayor Michael Bloomberg, senior administration officials, and staff worked side-by-side in open cubicles during the Bloomberg administration.

Alexander Garvin, NYC2012 Planning Director.

Dan Doctoroff with Jay Kriegel, NYC2012 Executive Director.

Peter Solomon's perception would ultimately mark a turning point not only in Doctoroff's career, but in his entire life, and set the groundwork for him not just to remain in New York, but to become deeply involved with the city for the rest of his life. But this would come slowly, since as Doctoroff began to work the long days and nights that were an expected part of the existence of a young investment banker, it was all he could do to pay attention to his family, let alone the city. "Only very gradually did I begin to appreciate New York," he said. The first hint that he might in time come to view the city as something more than a place with a value somewhere between neutral and intolerable — "when I first began to overcome my strong, negative, reflex reaction to the city," as he would put it later — came early one morning, when he was slumped in the back of a taxi heading home from his job at Lehman Brothers and saw the towers of the Brooklyn Bridge in the glow of the rising sun. "I was completely stunned by how magical it seemed," he said.

But Doctoroff's taxi ride was hardly like the young Lewis Mumford's revelatory walk across the Brooklyn Bridge one evening at twilight, when Mumford saw the towers of the bridge "topped by the golden pinnacles of the new Woolworth Building" and "saw the skyscrapers in the deepening darkness become slowly honeycombed with lights until ... these buildings piled up in a dazzling mass against the indigo sky," as Mumford wrote. "Here was my city, immense, overpowering, flooded with energy and light ... The world, at that moment, opened before me, challenging me, beckoning me ..." Doctoroff's perception, unlike Lewis Mumford's, came in the context of exhaustion, not exhilaration. He went home to sleep, and then back to work, sensing not so much a climactic moment, as the view of the city against the bridge had been for Mumford, as a tiny glimpse of pleasure, an intimation that the city might offer beauty as well as economic opportunity.

Then, bit by bit, he came to see it differently. As he returned from business trips, he began noticing the view of the skyline from the air, and how it gave him the sensation not of being a tourist but of returning home. He became possessive about his neighborhood on the Upper West Side, which in his case meant being unhappy about grime, about homelessness, about prostitutes on the streets. And most of all he began to realize that for all that the city is an amalgam of private places, it is

Pedestrian Plaza, Meatpacking District.

itself a public place, a vast collection of different public places, and that the most important aspect of the city is the public realm that it constitutes.

It was a realization that would grow into the guiding principle of his professional life. His recognition that the city is a public place, and that its greatness comes not just from the accomplishments of its private sector but from the way in which every element in the city supports the public realm, would be his real Brooklyn Bridge moment, and if it came more deliberately than Mumford's, it would be no less lasting in its impact. Doctoroff soon came to see his own career as a problem solver and his innate intellectual curiosity not as separate from his sense of the city, but as intimately intertwined with the very idea of being a part of New York. The more time he spent in the city, the more New York itself seemed to be the problem he wanted to solve.

In time, Doctoroff's accomplishments as a force for change in New York would lead to comparisons with Robert Moses. But for now, it makes more sense to stay with Lewis Mumford, the critic, historian, and public intellectual whose career focused heavily on the purpose and meaning of the city, and whose long career as a moralizing social critic who violently disapproved of the status quo would seem to make him altogether different from a young investment banker with a growing urban consciousness. For all their differences, however, the two men shared a deep earnestness and an innate ability to believe that clear, rational thinking could solve the problems of the city. And both believed, with an almost religious conviction, in the notion that urban life offered the promise of civilization developed to its highest potential.

Mumford could also be high-handed, arrogant, sexist, and humorless, and that, along with his extreme discomfort with high levels of density and his deep fondness for the concept of the garden city as an alternative to crowded cities, surely makes him an inappropriate symbol of the urbanism that the 21st century aspires to achieve. His urban vision was not the same as Dan Doctoroff's, not by a long shot. Still, Mumford's sincere and heartfelt belief in the city as an idea and the enthusiasm with which he acted as a kind of urban evangelist very much foreshadowed what Doctoroff would become. Mumford was the urban prophet of his time; so, to a very different time, would Doctoroff be.

The Olympic effort

It is one of the great historical ironies that Doctoroff's career as a public figure began with a project that by the most obvious measure would be considered a failure: his campaign to bring the Olympic Games to New York City. It began in 1994, when, excited by the spectacle of seeing the World Cup being played at Giants Stadium in the New Jersey Meadowlands, Doctoroff came up with the idea that New York City should host the 2008 Olympics. He did not simply pass the notion along to a few well-connected friends who might be able to do something about it. He set out to educate himself about international sports, he learned about what was required for a city to bid for the Games, and he discovered — and this would be key — that hosting the Olympics could be a catalyst for cities to complete major planning and infrastructure efforts. Planning for the Olympics, Doctoroff concluded, would not just be a way to build some sporting venues; it would be a way for New York to make much broader plans for its future, plans that would have a firm and unmovable deadline and thus would have an urgency that large-scale development in New York hadn't possessed for decades.

And so Doctoroff built an entire Olympics planning organization, on his own, and initially funded it himself. A colleague suggested he read a new book by the planner Alexander Garvin, *The American City: What Works, What Doesn't*, which led to a meeting with Garvin, a Yale professor who was also a member of the New York City Planning Commission, and his invitation to Garvin to join the team as the head planner for the Olympics. Garvin, who knew next to nothing about sports but next to everything about New York City, shared Doctoroff's enthusiasm and earnestness, and the two bonded quickly. Their close working relationship would continue for more than 20 years, supported by the same notion that had led Peter Solomon to recommend Doctoroff be hired as an investment banker: that if instinct and human qualities were the right fit, you could be taught the technical information you needed to know. Garvin, who died in 2021, viewed cities with a mix of idealism and pragmatism much

NYC2012 karate demonstration, Rockefeller Center, July 5, 2005.

Hudson Yards.

Macombs Dam Park, the Bronx.

Flowers in bloom at Hunter's Point South Park with Gaston Lachaise's *Floating Woman* sculpture in background.

Promenade and the Granite Prospect, Brooklyn Bridge Park.

Residential tower, 8 Spruce Street.

like Doctoroff's, and he would help shape Doctoroff's view of cities, functioning not only as the Olympic planner but also as Doctoroff's tutor in urban planning.

Garvin's counterpart was Jay Kriegel, who became Doctoroff's adviser on political and fundraising matters. Kriegel, the former aide to Mayor John Lindsay who was celebrated for his connections with almost every political, business, and cultural leader of New York, would come to manage the Olympic plan, which had shifted to a bid for the 2012 Olympics owing to the United States Olympic Committee's decision not to put forth an American candidate city for 2008.

The specifics of the Olympic bid, both in terms of the extraordinary reach and inventiveness of Garvin's physical plan and the success of Kriegel and Doctoroff's campaign to enlist the support of almost every influential politician and business leader in the city, are amply documented in in the pages that follow. But it is important to mention that the effort would have as much effect on Doctoroff himself as it would ultimately have on New York, since it forced him to understand the entire city in a fine-grained way. He came to know obscure locations in all five boroughs, and his sense of New York both broadened and deepened. The plan that he and Garvin devised, which became known as the "Olympic X" due to its two intersecting transportation axes — one via ferry extending out from the proposed Olympic Village site on the Queens waterfront, the other the New York subway — reflected their determination that the Olympic athletes would have a deep engagement with the city, not be kept apart from it. That alone marked it as enlightened in a way that few other Olympic plans, before or since, have been.

And it led directly to Doctoroff's belief that the waterfront held opportunities for growth and development that had barely begun to be understood — along with his recognition that the entire city would benefit from the sense of urgency that an Olympic deadline would bring. Even though the bid did not ultimately succeed — the 2012 Olympics went to London — Doctoroff's original notion, that a plan to host the Olympic Games could be a catalyst that could mobilize infrastructure and other developments around the city, succeeded beyond expectations. Large-scale housing development on the Queens waterfront and the site of Hudson Yards in Manhattan; the extension of the No. 7 subway, which was not only an achievement of public works but also of creative financing; the Barclays Center in Brooklyn; the Greenpoint-Williamsburg waterfront development; and replacement stadiums for both the Yankees and the Mets — all of these things can be traced, at least in part, to the Olympic plan. So, too, with the renovation of the 369th Regiment Armory in Harlem as a community athletic facility, the replacement of the Bronx Terminal Market with retail and a public park, the construction of a new public pool and ice rink in Flushing Meadows Corona Park, and the conversion of the Fresh Kills landfill on Staten Island into a public park. It would take years, but despite the failure of the city's bid for the Olympics, all these things would happen or are in the process of happening.

Citi Bike riders on Allen Street in Manhattan.

Doctoroff in City Hall

They happened, of course, because early on, the extraordinary energy and commitment that Doctoroff brought to the Olympic effort attracted the attention of Michael Bloomberg, who after his election as the city's 108th mayor in 2001, just weeks after the traumatic events of 9/11, offered Doctoroff the job of Deputy Mayor for Economic Development — or, as the position was titled in the aftermath of September 11th, Deputy Mayor for Economic Development and Rebuilding. When Doctoroff took the job, after a negotiation that permitted him to remain involved in the Olympic bid, he found himself in charge of all the city's planning efforts, including the rebuilding of a devastated Lower Manhattan after the destruction of the World Trade Center.

That was somewhat problematic, since the City technically had no power over the World Trade Center site: the destroyed twin towers had been built by a bi-state agency, the Port Authority of New York and New Jersey, which controlled the land, meaning that the governor of New York, George Pataki, had more control over its future than the mayor of New York or his deputy mayor for rebuilding. Doctoroff, true to form, was not intimidated by the fact that neither he nor his boss had authority over the process; he stepped in anyway, and through sheer force of personality made his views felt. Not the least of them, and one of the ways in which he showed that he was thinking more creatively than anyone else involved in the rebuilding process, was his suggestion that the City and the Port Authority swap the land underneath the two New York City airports, which the City owned and leased to the Port Authority, for the 16-acre World Trade Center site, which would allow the City to control the future of the site on its own.

The land swap never happened — it was a bridge too far for the two bureaucracies to negotiate — but Doctoroff, undaunted, developed a *Vision for Lower Manhattan* beyond the World Trade Center site. It incorporated much of Alex Garvin's thinking, and it made clear that while the State may have had the power, the City, in the person of Doctoroff, had most of the ideas. The "vision" that Mayor Bloomberg articulated in a major speech announcing the plan was classic Doctoroff: earnest, determined, idealistic and at the same time not the slightest bit naïve. It envisioned Lower Manhattan as a "vibrant global hub of culture and commerce, a live-and-work-and-visit community for the world." Doctoroff understood that the World Trade Center had been conceived in the misguided belief that it would strengthen Lower Manhattan's traditional role as the city's financial district, but the opposite had happened: The area had weakened as a commercial center but had become something much healthier, a genuinely mixed-use neighborhood containing housing, public space, and cultural activities, an evolution that Doctoroff wanted to see continued with more of all of these things. By contrast, the State's plan for the former World Trade Center site simply replaced the office space of the original World Trade Center with the same amount of office space spread across several medium-sized towers instead of two huge ones and envisioned no housing at all.

Like the Olympic vision that would ultimately come together without the Olympics, Bloomberg's and Doctoroff's Lower Manhattan vision, too, would be largely realized, thanks to the fact that while the State may have controlled what would happen on the 16 acres that had become known as Ground Zero, the City could influence what happened elsewhere in the neighborhood. And Doctoroff made certain that it did. Today the urban energy that Doctoroff celebrated enlivens a Lower Manhattan that has been reconceived to be less dependent on the financial services industry than ever, with a wide mixture of different kinds of commercial activity, a substantial residential component, and significant investments in public space and culture.

The revival of Lower Manhattan after 9/11, and the extent to which Doctoroff's vision came into being even without the ability to control the rebuilding of the World Trade Center site, was Doctoroff's first challenge as Bloomberg's deputy mayor, but it was only a preview of what was to come. Along with Amanda Burden, who Bloomberg had named as Chair of the City Planning Commission, Doctoroff oversaw a rezoning of much of the city to encourage further development, especially on the Brooklyn

Deputy Mayor Dan Doctoroff and Mayor Michael Bloomberg at City Hall, 2002.

The High Line, looking south from Hudson Yards.

Kayak Launch, Pier 2, Brooklyn Bridge Park.

and Queens waterfronts. He was a strong and early advocate of congestion pricing as a means of limiting the use of private automobiles in Manhattan below 60th Street — an idea that is finally on the cusp of being approved — and he encouraged more sustainable design. He advocated for the notion, somewhat radical at first, that city planning has a direct connection to public health, since the more people walked, the healthier they would be, and he wanted the City to do more to make walking and bicycle riding attractive options. He was closely involved in the development and expansion of Citi Bike, New York's bike-share program. And he played a critical role in the explosion of new and significant investments in public space, including the High Line — perhaps the most acclaimed new public park in New York in generations. The notion of converting an abandoned elevated freight line into a public park was proposed before Bloomberg became mayor, but it was too unorthodox a notion for the previous city administration. Bloomberg and Doctoroff, however, had the sophistication and imagination to be excited about the idea, and Doctoroff set about to make it happen.

He played a similar role with Brooklyn Bridge Park and Governors Island and the Hudson River Park and the East River Park, all projects that would depend on his involvement and benefit from it. Not the least of Doctoroff's gifts was his willingness to champion projects that he had not originated himself, as he had with the Olympic bid; if he thought an idea had value, he would focus his energy on making it happen.

He was both a public advocate and a private negotiator, steering projects through the bureaucracy, which in many cases meant not only dealing with City government but also with his counterparts in State and federal governments and with public agencies like the Port Authority and the Metropolitan Transportation Authority, as well as with private nonprofit groups set up to build and oversee these new parts of the public realm. It was a complex chess game, and he took pride in understanding all the moves.

A holistic approach to city building

He was an unusual public official, not so much a part of the bureaucracy as a force determined to rise above it. He worked intensely and expected his staff to do the same, but he also listened to their ideas, and was willing to entertain proposals from any source. If an idea was new and untried, it became all the more alluring to him, another chance to show that things were being done differently by this administration.

But perhaps what most distinguished Doctoroff's tenure as a public official was not the ease, or the apparent ease, with which he navigated the turbulent waters of the politics of producing public works, but the way in which he was determined to connect the physical form of the city with policy. He did not believe that economic development was a matter of responding to the needs of businesses, or of shaping tax policy, though he was as interested in these things as anyone else who had held his job. It was clear that he wanted "Rebuilding" as part of his portfolio not only because of the challenges facing the city after 9/11 but because he was convinced that construction, infrastructure, housing, and planning went hand in hand with economic development, and that all of it needed to be seen as a totality.

Doctoroff demonstrated his holistic view best, perhaps, in PlaNYC, a comprehensive report issued in 2007 that envisioned the expansion of the city's population by another million residents over the coming two decades; called for significant increases in infrastructure maintenance, repair, and replacement; and set the goal of cutting the city's carbon emissions by 30%. PlaNYC, which included the call for congestion pricing among its recommendations for fighting the effects of climate change, did what reports issued by public officials almost never do, which was to look ahead, far beyond the terms, and in some cases even the lifetimes, of the people in the administration writing the report. PlaNYC, in other words, was not a list of projects that the Bloomberg administration hoped could be accomplished immediately in the hope of earning political points. It was a prescription for the coming decades, a report issued with Doctoroff's full knowledge that he was planning for the long term. If politicians usually look no farther than the next election, Doctoroff looked to the next generation.

Doctoroff remained engaged with building and planning after he left City government to become the president and eventually chief executive of Bloomberg LP — a position he held until the end of Bloomberg's mayoralty, at which point Michael Bloomberg decided he again wanted to run his company himself. Not the least of Doctoroff's accomplishments at Bloomberg was to hire Foster + Partners to design the new European headquarters for Bloomberg in London, a building that would become one of the most acclaimed commercial structures of its era. He was also active on the civic front and became the Founding Chairman of the board of The Shed, the experimental cultural center that he envisioned as a key part of the public realm of Hudson Yards, the immense real estate development on the Far West Side that, as deputy mayor, Doctoroff had helped bring into being.

Doctoroff then went on to start an entirely new chapter in his professional life, founding Sidewalk Labs in 2015 in partnership with Google. They conceived the company as a way to develop the "smart city," by using data technology to improve urban planning

New York Post and *New York Daily News* articles and accompanying editorials announcing the departure of Dan Doctoroff from City Hall.

Dan Doctoroff was the Founding Chairman of The Shed, opposite, which opened in 2019.

and infrastructure. Sidewalk Labs, its very name underscoring Doctoroff's fascination with, and commitment to, a traditional idea of urbanism, was best known for its plans to develop Quayside, a 12-acre neighborhood in Toronto. The ambitious project was intended as a prototype for this new kind of city but was ultimately abandoned in 2020 owing largely to complications of the COVID-19 pandemic.

Quayside was not without controversy. Critics accused Sidewalk Labs of overreach in Toronto, and of giving the project the potential to violate privacy by using technology to track residents' comings and goings, not to mention their utility use, their purchases, and their leisure activities. But it was mostly using data that existed elsewhere; Sidewalk's goal was to aggregate it and to use it to guide the process of managing city services and planning for urban growth.

It is a prospect that, in other hands, might well be troubling: The city that tracks you through data could also be the city that restricts you. In Doctoroff's case, it is hard to believe that the plan was motivated by anything other than enthusiasm, a belief that the more information a wired city possessed, the more services it could deliver to more people more quickly. To Doctoroff, this was all a form of connection, and as urbanity is itself a matter of connections, connecting people through information was not so different from connecting them in physical space. And there was no reason, he believed, that connecting people through data should not support the larger goal of connecting them in real life.

A humanist approach to urbanism

Doctoroff, in the end, is not much of a technocrat; he is more interested in the material reality of urbanism, in the physical form of the real city, than he is in data, which to him is merely a means to an end. In this sense, paradoxically, he is far less of a technocrat than Robert Moses, who did not have the digital technology of the 21st century at his disposal, but who far more than Doctoroff viewed the city as a system that needed to be made more efficient. For Doctoroff, efficiency has never been an end, but only a tool toward the sense of community to which he has always aspired, and which has always excited and moved him.

Doctoroff, at bottom, is a humanist. He is moved by traditional urbanism, by the pleasures of the street, by the activity and diversity of the city, by the surprise that it engenders. He and Moses are surely comparable in the impact they had on New York: They shared an ability to think in broad terms, and to make big things happen to a degree that their contemporaries could only dream of. But they could not have been more different in almost every other way. Moses's arrogance was legion. He planned by fiat, and was famously rigid in his views about every aspect of design and planning. He had the gift of seeing the entire New York region as a vast entity, a canvas on which he could paint a system of physical connections. But it often seems as if that system was almost devoid of people. Moses connected the city's parts but seemed, particularly in the later parts of his career, to be indifferent to the people he was ostensibly connecting, and to have minimal interest in neighborhoods.

Doctoroff acted less as the emperor of planning than as its eager student, sophisticated, earnest, capable of learning and excited by the new. Many of his greatest achievements — The Shed, the cultural center at Hudson Yards where he served as chairman for more than a decade; the program to plant one million trees in New York City; the rezoning of so much of New York; the High Line and the other new parks — were frankly experimental, even radical. If Moses became more conservative as his career went on, Doctoroff seemed to grow ever more enthusiastic about doing things that had never been done before. To Dan Doctoroff, who began his urban awakening by paying more attention to the people he saw on the subway and to the patterns of life in his Upper West Side neighborhood, the vision of the city began at the grass roots, in the essence of the urban fabric. The point was the people, and the places in which they lived. The question Doctoroff asked was not what system city planners could impose on them, but what city planners could do to make their lives better, and to make the city more uplifting, more nurturing, and more fulfilling for the 21st century.

Dan Doctoroff in Times Square promoting
the NYC2012 Olympic bid.

THE CYCLIST

Doctoroff's "virtuous cycle of growth" powered a new urban vision

An avid cyclist, Dan Doctoroff often began his long days as a new deputy mayor with a pre-dawn ride down the West Side Highway to City Hall. The West Side then was a pastiche of existing neighborhoods interspersed with the detritus from a long-gone industrial past including surface parking, gas stations, self-storage, and rail infrastructure. The greener, growing West Side he would ultimately seed, from Hudson Yards to the High Line to the reborn World Trade Center, existed then only in his imaginings, just a small swath of the hundreds of miles of shoreline and the thousands of acres of Gotham his tenacity would transform.

After 9/11, the city was reeling in fear from a central question — would residents and businesses remain in New York City? With echoes of our 1970s collapse still ricocheting, many wondered whether the city could survive, particularly in light of the business exodus we had been experiencing for decades across the river to New Jersey, down the coast to Charlotte, and across the pond to London. Dan knew that our great historical laurels offered illusory rest — people and commerce vote with their feet.

Such dire concerns arose from the worst terrorist attack in American history and the smoldering aftermath it seared into the city's financial core, but the context was broader. Before the murderous attack, the new millennia had already brought new challenges and opportunities. From *Seinfeld* to *Sex in the City*, urban life had become popular again after decades of urban renewal, white flight, the crime and upheaval that resulted, and the *Law and Order* that came in response. Gentrification and displacement, about which too few spoke in the early aughts, was on the rise as a consequence of this rediscovery of the city by the wealthy and white. Tough policing policies had tamed crime, but too often at the expense of Black and brown communities. The triumvirate of New York, London, and Tokyo became the epicenters of global capital — Stamford, Connecticut, not so much.

Instinctually understanding this broader context, Doctoroff, the biking banker, was also a booster, sensing that New York City could leverage this rediscovered love of urban life. He realized before many that 21st century urban policy would center on the ability to attract and retain the best and the brightest, and to do so we would have to compete with cities around the globe for human capital. Seeded by experiences as diverse as the 1994 World Cup, where Doctoroff realized any two countries in the world could compete in the New York area and fill an entire stadium with hometown fans, and Central Park family movie nights, which drew children and their parents out after dark in safe, celebratory gatherings — he realized that New York could not only be a global epicenter, but one that could offer a unique quality of life attractive to families and businesses alike. His consequent conception of the 2012 Olympic bid embodied his faith in New York to convene the world, but competing with it was always his larger economic development pursuit.

For Dan, recovery from 9/11 was never about returning to the status quo of the 20th century. For decades, the city and state's economic development czars had a singular strategy: Throw money at big business to coerce them into keeping their jobs here, much like parents bribing their kids to do their homework, with similarly poor results. Dan was focused on a fundamentally different question — how could we induce growth not through corporate welfare, but through people faring well? How could we convince the world's talent, and the companies that so desperately wanted to hire them, that they wanted to be in New York, particularly in the wake of 9/11?

The cyclist's response was to insist upon an urban revolution, what he still calls "the virtuous cycle of the successful city." His theory was easy to explain, difficult to execute, and even harder to prove. Essentially, Doctoroff believed that for New York City to recover, and for any city to thrive, government had to invest in quality of life, from parks to schools to subways to affordable housing to anything else that created social mobility and urban joy (what I've

Hudson Yards in Manhattan as seen from Hoboken, NJ, 2019.

subsequently described as the "infrastructure of opportunity" in my own writing). From his perspective, bribing companies to stay in New York was beneath us — instead we could invest that money in our physical and social infrastructure to benefit all New Yorkers, but with the underlying goal of making the city irresistible to the world's top talent. Dan was convinced that these investments were worthwhile because they would attract new residents and businesses, which would in turn bolster the municipal tax base, which would allow the City to make more investments, and so on in a virtuous cycle.

Consequently much of New York City's government, including every agency that was under his watch — and an astonishing number that were not, including some of the State's apparatus — was set to the task of identifying, funding, and implementing these quality of life improvements. On a weekly basis we staffers were grilled about where new housing, better parks, and more social

infrastructure could emerge, not just for their own sake, but for the sake of attracting a new generation of New Yorkers and the stabilizing tax base they would bring. This holistic view of cities and city government remains unprecedented in modern history, and was arguably broader and certainly more democratic than the worldview of Robert Moses, to whom Dan is often compared without nuance. Dan's unyielding grip across the apparatus of government, his unstoppable drive, and his unwavering belief in New York as a magnet for the multitudes, made Doctoroff one of the leading — and too often unsung — urban leaders of his or any generation.

Dan understood that revitalizing Lower Manhattan was a multi-front campaign to not only rebuild the World Trade Center site but to reimagine the entire financial district, which had become an office monoculture that was largely lifeless on nights and weekends. Our congressional delegation secured $20 billion of recovery funding, but with that money channeled through a new agency

largely controlled by a governor with presidential aspirations, the City's team led by Dan had to be strategic to maintain his focus on quality of life — particularly in terms of good design — in a city where historically form followed finance.

Rather than focus on the narrow issues of business retention and real estate leases, Dan realized that this was an opportunity to rethink all of Downtown, from river to river, in a comprehensive vision plan that incorporated parks, social infrastructure, streetscapes, and of course, Ground Zero itself. Under Doctoroff's aegis and led daily by our brilliant City Planning Chair Amanda Burden, the team worked tirelessly on the public spaces and waterfronts across Lower Manhattan, particularly the East River Waterfront, all in partnership with the local community. Together we won the battle to reintroduce the street grid on the World Trade Center site against ruthless retail interests, which was critical to connect the area to the broader public fabric of Lower Manhattan as we had envisioned. Governance worked because while we sweated the details and fought for great design outcomes, we always knew that the mayor and the deputy mayor had our back, and would never cower from controversy out of political convenience.

Despite our requisite, round-the-clock focus on Lower Manhattan and its recovery, Dan knew that for his theory of the virtuous cycle to succeed it had to be a citywide effort. The Olympic bid not only undergirded his strategy across all five boroughs, it fueled an education in urbanism for which Dan yearned. In addition to Amanda, Dan learned from the late, indefatigable urbanist, Alex Garvin — who had conceived the "Olympic X" plan — the power of a broad, deadline-driven vision. From the late, great Jay Kriegel, whose extraordinary career spanned serving as chief of staff to

Mayor John Lindsay to becoming the executive director of the Olympic bid, Dan would learn political maneuvering as precisely as Luke learned to wield a lightsaber from Yoda. Simultaneously, grassroots community actors, local institutions, and daring investors cycled through City Hall, informing Dan's strategy as much as his own instincts.

As has been well-documented, Dan's five-borough focus on Olympic planning had a manifold, visible impact across the city, particularly in the creation of parks, housing, and mass transit from Downtown Brooklyn to Long Island City, which he would connect to Manhattan's West Side via an extended No. 7 subway line. We witnessed throughout the outer boroughs the manifestation of Dan's long-held dream to shift development that had for too long focused west across the Hudson River in the opposite direction, across the East River. Today's success of the East River Ferry owes much to the efforts of his day, which initiated the dense multi-nodal city of live, work, and play across the boroughs that has made our economy resilient to this day.

Manhattan will always be the geographic and commercial center of our city's kaleidoscopic quilt, and the thought of being hired to be its planning director in mid-2002 under Dan and Amanda still sends shivers down my spine. At my job interview, I remember Dan asking me to focus on Lower Manhattan for obvious reasons, explaining that other initiatives like the City's massive planning efforts for the West Side were covered by others. That geographic division of labor lasted less than two weeks into my tenure because as I learned, all who toiled under Dan had to walk, chew gum, hop on one leg, and sprint forward, at the same time, all the time. Of the many cycles in which Dan believed, the sleep cycle was not one.

Opposite: The amusement zone at Coney Island had withered to a single block before a 2009 rezoning created a 27-acre amusement and entertainment district, including plans for new housing and infrastructure upgrades. The vision included restoring the historic boardwalk.

Left: The Brooklyn Navy Yard, formerly one of the largest naval shipbuilding facilities in America, had been declining for decades until Deputy Mayor Dan Doctoroff prioritized its revitalization. Today, the Navy Yard is home to more than 500 businesses that employ more than 11,000 workers.

I don't miss a wink of that sleep, particularly the sleep lost over helping to save the High Line, one of the deeply impactful experiences of my life, and I would argue in the administration's tenure. Unlike so many economic development projects, the High Line effort was exceptional in every regard. It was driven by a formidable grass roots organization, Friends of the High Line, led by Robert Hammond and Joshua David. It wove together preservation of the High Line and the galleries that surrounded it, with much needed new housing, groundbreaking architecture and landscape architecture, and a re-conception of what successful public space could be. Early on, those of us committed to saving the High Line were continually told we were nuts — "No one will use it, it will become a security nightmare ... people will get killed up there!" went the retrograde opposition mantra. To the contrary, as the centerpiece of a new urban neighborhood, the High Line now attracts more annual tourism than the Statue of Liberty. It is gobsmacking that the Whitney Museum of American Art, one of our most revered cultural institutions, relocated to be next to the High Line — something that if imagined in the year 2000 would have spawned guffaws across Central Park.

Many have gone on to criticize the High Line's allure for luxury as a fuel for gentrification, along with Hudson Yards, which for some symbolizes the extravagance of the Bloomberg era. It is far too easy for armchair urbanists to now look back and criticize those years. The theory of urban growth to which we adhered wasn't an attempt to displace or gentrify New York City, it was an attempt to ensure the city's survival at a moment when the precariousness of the situation is now too easily dismissed. The fierce urgency of then — which we hopefully feel again now that we are in this pandemic recovery moment — was fueled by the knowledge that cities can fail, as did Detroit, and that when they do, the poor suffer disproportionately in terms of crime, disinvestment, and loss of opportunity.

From this perspective, Dan's theory of the virtuous cycle was wildly successful, culminating with his final major act as deputy mayor, the five-borough economic development and sustainability blueprint, PlaNYC. During the period he was Deputy Mayor of Economic Development and Rebuilding, the municipal budget almost doubled, soaring from $42 billion in 2002 to $60 billion in 2007. Tax revenues soared during this period fueled by intense population growth. By the time Dan left office, New York City was on pace to add nearly one million new people by 2030. Just as importantly, New York's economy diversified during this period in ways that other administrations could only dream about — for decades it had been an article of faith that New York had to shake its economic dependence on the FIRE industries (Finance, Insurance and Real Estate). The City's policies during Dan's tenure, including the expansion of Columbia University and our educational sector more generally, helped to grow the city's tech sector base substantially. Prior to the Bloomberg administration, the city housed few tech jobs, whereas today the largest cache of information workers outside of Silicon Valley resides in New York City. Geographies across the city burgeoned from the World Trade Center to Long Island City, including spectacular new parks such as Brooklyn Bridge Park, Governors Island, and Freshkills Park — along with more than 200 hundred playgrounds.

The success delineated by such metrics were the lingua franca of Mike Bloomberg, but many outside his orbit and culture question this definition of success today. Many have rightful questions about whether the growth of this period fueled gentrification and

displacement. Many question whether growth for growth's sake is wise given global climate change despite the clear ecological advantages of urban life. And while those questions are legitimate, what often gets glossed over is that Dan's virtuous cycle theory wasn't just about growth, it was about growth providing the fuel for the many public services cities must be able to afford to provide for those most in need.

The expansion of the tax base funded the creation of hundreds of acres of new public spaces and 165,000 affordable housing units citywide, not to mention funding the critical daily municipal services New Yorkers rely on from public health, education, sanitation, public safety, and clean water. Given federal disinvestment since President Ronald Reagan, cities now largely fend for themselves to provide municipal services and it is in this context that this cycle of growth should be understood to be virtuous, particularly for our city of immigrants.

As a city that welcomes waves of newcomers, New York exists as an inexorable, beautiful, like-it-or-not, cycle of change. Dan rhapsodized about this often. Wall Street booms and busts. We cycle through eras of great park building, including during the Bloomberg administration. Cycles of geographic and cultural tumult source our immigrant populations, from exiled Jews to Irish and Italian Catholics to Chinese and South Asians to the African and West Indian diasporas. Tragic cycles of climate change will no doubt bring new waves of immigrants to our own fragile shores. Dan is a student and master of these cycles, including sharing the leadership of the "New" New York Panel charged with the post-pandemic

recovery of our business districts. His experience, our experience, says that once again we cannot rest on our laurels. The foundation he laid 20 years ago has given New York economic, cultural, and spiritual resilience. In the face of hybrid work, cities are now more than ever about the people who love them — Dan understood this two decades ago, and we must all now remember it going forward as new generations of urbanists seek to serve and save this city for those who follow.

So it is to Dan we owe our thanks, not only as a great maker of cities, not only as a good man of the people, but also as a gravitational mentor, the person who keeps those of us who had the privilege to serve with him grounded and grateful as we pedal forward, his encouragement forever at our back, our cadence forever inspired by his.

Opposite: Dan Doctoroff oversaw the transfer of Governors Island, a former military base, from the federal government to local control, opening it to New Yorkers for the first time in more than 200 years. In 2022, the Island attracted nearly a million visitors, including New Yorkers from every city zip code.

Above: Dan Doctoroff and Olympians preparing to ride in the Five Boro Bike Tour to support NYC2012, New York's Olympic bid, 2004.

MARIA TORRES-SPRINGER | Deputy Mayor for Economic and Workforce Development, 2022-Present

THE MENTOR

How Dan's unique leadership created the Doctoroff diaspora

I moved to New York City a week before 9/11. That fateful morning the planes crashed into the World Trade Center, I was at a board meeting in Midtown. One of the attendees was desperately trying to make contact with her husband who was in one of the towers. I watched in real time as she grappled with the horror, as all of us struggled to understand what was happening, and then I confronted a blunt logistical problem: I don't even know how to get home. Where do I even go? What is this city that I've moved to?

I wandered from Midtown to my apartment in Brooklyn alongside hundreds of thousands of New Yorkers all walking through the streets in grief, and shock, and fear. That experience — on one hand being a stranger to the city and on the other becoming an instant family in the midst of this tragedy — cemented my identity as a New Yorker and my commitment to this place.

New York was a city of neighbors. People banded together to survive and then to help, feeding and encouraging first responders and supporting each other in endless small, kind ways. That's the New York that I fell in love with — a city home to the most courageous people, with the capacity for acts grand and small, all motivated by a deep and abiding love of this place. I knew that I wanted to devote my career to the city.

I left for graduate school and when I returned to New York, I sought a job in City Hall in the office of Daniel Doctoroff, the deputy mayor charged with rebuilding the city's economy after the attacks. All I knew about him was that he was a larger than life figure, whose agenda was shaped by a quest to bring the Olympic Games to New York City. This vision had led to massive plans to reimagine vast swaths of the city. I didn't know much about the Olympic bid, but I wanted to be part of its impact.

Incredibly, I would only work with Dan for three years. I've worked for many other people for longer periods of time and served the city under three mayoral administrations, but those three years had a profound and enduring impact on me as a person, a leader, a New Yorker, and as a public servant.

As I think about the impact Dan has had on my life, three categories emerge: First, Dan as Boss, second, Dan as Mentor, and finally, Dan as Inspiration, not just for me but for a generation of leaders in different sectors who have become a kind of Team Doctoroff diaspora filling civic and political leadership roles across New York and the rest of the country.

Dan as boss

It wasn't an auspicious beginning. I joined Dan's staff as a policy analyst, a junior position, in June 2005 — just weeks before the International Olympic Committee (IOC) was scheduled to make its decision on the host city for the 2012 Olympic Games.

I barely saw him. Dan had staked the city's entire development agenda on the Games. So, in those frantic few weeks, he was flying around the world lobbying members of the IOC. I moved into my

basement office and tried to become as familiar as I could with the projects I assumed I would be helping to implement.

Then we lost the bid to London. I remember a frenzy, hushed voices; above all I recall that everyone was incredibly tired. I didn't know anyone; I hadn't contributed to the effort or felt the full pain of the loss. When I imagined my life in City Hall, I had been excited about the significance and glamour of working in the heart of this important and historic building every day. Now I sat in a dingy basement, surrounded by heartbroken co-workers, our plans in shambles. Those weren't the easiest first days.

After the defeat, Dan took a few days to recover. Then he summoned us all to a meeting. In what I would quickly come to think of as a quintessential Dan moment, he spoke to all of us and reminded us

New York City is at an important inflection point

Pre-COVID-19, New York City's economy was strong and growing...

4.6M jobs in NYC in 2019, a record-high

8.8M resident population in NYC according to the 2020 Census, another record

...but COVID-19 introduced new challenges, while exacerbating existing inequities

38% current NYC office occupancy rate as a share of pre-pandemic levels

6.3% unemployment rate among total NYC workforce as of March 2022 (vs. 3.0% in Jan. 2020)

1_ nemployment ra ack workers as (vs. 6.3% C workforce)

Source: U.S. Bureau of Labor Statistics, Moody's Analytics, https://www.soc... icms, Office of the NYS Comptroller, Fede...

Dan Doctoroff co-chaired the "New" New York Panel, formed to guide New York's economic recovery after the COVID-19 pandemic, alongside Richard R. Buery, Jr. (far left). The committee was overseen by Deputy Mayor for Economic and Workforce Development Maria Torres-Springer (at podium), who began her government service career as a policy analyst for Doctoroff.

of our purpose. We had work to do, he told us. We weren't going to sit on our hands. Even though we had lost, we were still going to aggressively pursue the Olympic development agenda as part of a mission to remake the city. As only Dan can do, he rallied us and reset the team. It was nonstop from that point forward.

One of the first projects I worked on was Willets Point, where we were aiming to turn an area known for junkyards and pollution into a thriving neighborhood. None of the things we were trying to do had playbooks — they were types of development interventions that had never been done before. Until we did them. And they were challenging — we faced lawsuits, difficult land-use processes, contentious public meetings, political clashes, and funding shortfalls.

But it was worth the difficulty because the questions we were trying to engage through these projects were so urgent. The Olympic bid put a spotlight on the idea that New York City couldn't just be about nostalgia — it had to evolve to remain the greatest city in the world. We asked, how do we make the most of what makes New York City great? What can New York City, or cities in general, represent at a global level? How can cities tackle those underlying challenges of growth and affordability, economic diversity, quality of life? The Olympic bid was a vessel to tackle those issues, but when the bid campaign ended, those questions remained. The city still needed answers. More than individual deals and plans, that's what we were working toward.

Rendering of Greeley Square prepared for the "New" New York Panel as part of its effort to reinvigorate the city's business districts.

Only an extraordinary leader could have united a team to supply those answers. As boss, Dan taught me several essential lessons that I've carried forward through today.

First and foremost, perhaps: There's such a thing as 'not good enough.' This wasn't always an easy lesson to learn. Dan had unapologetically high standards for the products that the team presented and for the work ethic of each team member — from the font of the memos to the efficiency of our meetings. I remember one instance, in particular, when I presented some promotional materials for the Coney Island rezoning project. This was a fairly minor component of the project as a whole, and it was basically fine. But Dan hated it, and he made that known. I had to do better.

He wore his own emotions on his sleeve — his feedback could be intense, but you always knew where you stood; you didn't need wayfinding with Dan. And that provided a clarity of direction that benefited the projects. Especially in government, it can be rare to have that culture of high expectations. Dan would always say, "no lazy meetings" — you should always be moving the ball forward. That has stuck with me to this day, and I hold my own team to that standard.

I'd like to say that all of those conversations with Dan were done in a very gentle way. That was not always the case. Dan had a reputation for losing his temper at times but I know from personal experience that he was always committed to resolving the conflict with compassion. After one particularly difficult conversation, I needed time away from my desk. When I came back, he was standing there waiting for me. He apologized and we talked through it. On one hand, it was not a great experience. On the

other hand, it showed that he's human and — in another leadership lesson — that he was often the first to acknowledge when he made a misstep.

The second lesson is the importance of being proactive, a strategy enabled by structured, sustained collaboration. At the City, Dan believed in offense — bold ideas to pursue beyond the crush and heave of the day — and that structured collaboration was the key to success. He convened a regular meeting of close to two dozen agencies, called the Economic Development Advisory Council (EDAC) so that the agencies under his portfolio — and some that weren't — could meet regularly to share ideas and projects. These meetings became an incubator for some of the most exciting, ambitious work in the city. They weren't just bureaucratic box-checking: they mattered. Agencies spent weeks preparing for their presentations and scouring their staff for the best ideas to impress the group. Citywide initiatives came out of those presentations, like when the City's chief demographer suggested that New York City would be gaining one million new people and Dan realized we needed a citywide plan to respond (PlaNYC). Or when the Parks Department presented the startling return on investment of street tree plantings, and the MillionTreesNYC initiative was born. Nearly every meeting generated a new groundbreaking idea that drew on multiagency support. I've tried to replicate that kind of collaborative structure at City Hall.

The third lesson is never taking no for an answer — and we encountered nearly endless versions of no. The path of least resistance in government is to say, "Well, we've never done that before," or, "That's impossible," or "They'll never let you do that." If you accept these answers, then you don't get very far. Instead, what I learned from Dan is that you have to throw out conventional

Maria Torres-Springer.

thinking, push past the routine excuses, and expand your field of vision to actually drive real change. I've tried to cultivate that mindset in every team I've led since then.

The fourth lesson is supporting your team when they need you. We always knew that if we needed Dan's support, he would be there to back us up. This confidence inspired a velocity of action and the type of risk-taking that is uncommon in government but necessary to propel our most difficult projects forward. That was a real lesson that I've carried with me — what it means to nurture a team and create an environment where people feel like they can push for things, advance really transformative projects, and know that you will be there to support them when things inevitably go south. It also taught me how there are few things in your career that provide more fulfillment than watching your team shine as they themselves overcome seemingly intractable issues.

Fifth, and perhaps most importantly, he modeled a commitment to family that I've taken with me throughout my career. It was clear from the very beginning that Dan is a family man. Seeing how Dan's commitment to family could coexist with his dedication to the work has been critical to me as I made my own career decisions over the years. Dan would always pick up when his family called, no matter what important project or crisis was unfolding, and he would shift gears immediately, giving them his complete focus. What that taught me — and that what that gave me license to do — was to say that I could be relentless in the work and also unapologetic about putting my family first.

When I was appointed to head the Department of Small Business Services under Mayor Bill de Blasio, I was just a couple weeks from my due date for my second child. My experience watching Dan

helped me believe that it was possible to raise a family, spend time with my family, be devoted to my family and also get the job done. That was the most precious gift that Dan gave me, likely without even knowing it.

Dan as mentor
The number of people who passed through Dan's office and still feel great loyalty towards one another is a great testament to Dan's unfailing commitment to his team. Seventeen years later, we still do a big reunion, almost annually, for anyone who can attend. Dan nurtured that bond in big and small ways, inside and outside of the office. We would do off-site team building activities together, or he would invite us to his home. He let us see his vulnerable side — he talked about his family, the diets he went on, how he felt about growing older. I remember a lot of dad jokes.

Dan created these moments and spaces that allowed us to see how much he cared about the team and how much responsibility he felt toward us. He didn't care about us because we were helpful to him in moving forward a project when he was deputy mayor. He is still just as available to us, years after we stopped being his direct reports. That, too, has become a kind of a lesson for me in what it means to be invested in people.

At critical moments of my career, whenever I've asked to see him or asked for his advice he gives it freely. He has never said, "I don't think you could do that job," or even any version of, "Oh, that's a growth opportunity." There has always been an unflinching confidence and belief that I could do it. That's how he makes all of us feel — that we can be super human, larger than life, in whatever role we are considering. He has always made us all believe we have the capacity to do anything.

Above: Deputy Mayor for Economic and Workforce Development Maria Torres-Springer speaks at the Astoria Ferry Landing in New York City, July 2022.

Right: Dan Doctoroff led the reclamation of the High Line during his time at City Hall. Torres-Springer served as Chief Operating Officer of Friends of the High Line from 2012 to 2015.

When I was offered my current job, as Deputy Mayor for Economic Workforce Development, Dan was the first person I called after my family. I was nervous for that conversation, because what if he didn't think I could do it? What if he thought the job was too hard for me? But he was full of joy at the news. I've since asked him for his advice on a number of issues, but in that first call he didn't offer any wisdom. He only told me that he was incredibly happy for me and that I was the perfect choice. It wasn't about him and what he had to impart. It was about his support of me. That's Dan as a mentor.

Dan as inspiration

Dan is still very proud of the work that was done when he was deputy mayor — and he should be. But he's also the first to acknowledge that he didn't get everything right. It takes a certain level of honesty and humility to reflect on your own decisions and say, "maybe we should have done more on affordable housing," or "maybe we missed an opportunity."

That's been a beautiful thing to see and learn from — we all do the best that we can in these roles and we're not going to get it all right. That's a lesson I'm keeping in mind as we move forward now. There needs to be, and can be, a virtuous cycle. But you can't assume that prosperity and the growth will accrue to communities in an equitable fashion. And that's a large part of why I was excited to take this job: Deep down, I wanted to make good on what we started together.

New York post-pandemic has been a cascade of crises. It's a mass casualty event, like 9/11, but it's also a devastating economic event, like the Great Recession. It's the beginning of a long-overdue racial reckoning, on a scale that's unprecedented in my lifetime. There are so many urgent questions — how do we reimagine not just the physical city, but the economy as well, into the future? Of course,

the first person who came to my mind to help lead us towards answers was Dan.

It was not a foregone conclusion that New York City would recover after the terrorist attacks in 2001. Dan led a transformation of Lower Manhattan and the resurgence of the city economically and physically that few believed was possible. And it's not a foregone conclusion that we are going to emerge from the pandemic in ways that make us stronger. But when we put together a "New" New York blue-ribbon panel (a commission formed by the City and State to reimagine the city's postpandemic economy), I asked Dan to leave his retirement and serve as co-chair. New York was in crisis; of course, he accepted.

Everything I remembered about Dan I experienced again on this panel — his ambition for bold solutions, his impatience with obstacles, his drive for details to ground every big idea and make it not just exciting, but actionable. In other words, what I'm seeing again right now in this work are the signature Dan Doctoroff moves both in the why we do this work and the how. We do it for New York; to succeed we have to be rigorous, create a vision, tell a story, build a plan.

I've learned from Dan to not squander an opportunity. We have these roles for a short period of time, and every time one of us takes the baton, the city changes. But the chance to make a difference won't be there forever. The window to do something truly significant is unmercifully narrow.

Despite everything, I'm fundamentally an optimist. And I got a lot of that from Dan: that belief in the city, in government, in New Yorkers. One of my favorite things to do, to the chagrin of my children, is to point out one by one as we travel across the city, all

those New York landmarks that I've had the wild fortune of helping advance — projects that wouldn't exist without Dan's leadership. From the High Line to Coney Island, from Governors Island to Brooklyn Bridge Park to the new skyline of Hunter's Point South, these are the city's new icons. New York wouldn't be what it is today without him — and neither would I.

THE LISTENER

Dan Doctoroff's "magic sauce" was unleashing the pent-up creativity of longtime City employees

Dan Doctoroff had a typical opening question when interviewing people to join his staff at City Hall, which immediately distinguished him from every workaday bureaucratic boss.

"What is the best idea you ever had?" he would ask, both to gauge and galvanize their creativity. "I ask it," Doctoroff later recalled, "because I only want people who can connect unobvious dots."

Running a government — New York's, in particular — typically means that most visionary strategies will be sacrificed to more pressing agendas as the city lurches from crisis to crisis. As the Bloomberg administration's Deputy Mayor for Economic Development and Rebuilding after the terrorist attack on September 11, 2001, Doctoroff was one of those rare officials whose docket spanned the next decade or two instead of just the next day or his mayor's four-year term.

While New York lost its bid for the 2012 Olympic Games, the administration could claim victory because of Doctoroff's brilliant gamesmanship: He dangled the deadline for selecting an Olympic host city as a cudgel to transform what might have been a lesser urban planner's pipe dreams into concrete public works constructed with private partners.

Doctoroff did it his way, which was not always easy or right. Nor did it always work. But it endowed a cadre of City officials with a collaborative, proactive, dynamic, and gratifying experience rarely associated with government bureaucracy — even by the bureaucrats.

"Dan set ambitious deadlines and many people who worked for him did some of their best career work trying to uphold his expectations," said Eric Kober, the former director of housing, economic and infrastructure at the Department of City Planning (DCP) who joined City government in 1979. "He wanted to get things done, not make symbolic political points or advance his own career by pandering to potential political allies."

While the Bloomberg administration became famous for bringing a private sector mentality to City Hall, perhaps their most unheralded achievement — and Doctoroff's in particular — was tapping into the talent of longtime civil servants. They, too, had a long-term vision unencumbered by term limits. In Doctoroff, they found a rare elected official who operated on the same timeline — and wanted to hear their wildest ideas, honed over decades.

Doctoroff set the tone for absurdly ambitious ideas immediately. Take the Olympics. Please.

"There was always something preposterous about overcoming the economic, political, and physical obstacles to landing and pulling off an Olympics in New York," said Sandy Hornick, who joined DCP in 1991 and became its deputy executive director for strategic planning. "But I remember that Dan made sound plausible

something that every bit of my New York City experience drew me to conclude was implausible. From the very first meeting, his agenda was larger. The Olympics would leave a legacy of physical improvements in the city. Of equal importance, it would break the decades-long logjam that not only prevented 'big things' from being done but discouraged people from even thinking such things were possible and worth pursuing."

During Hornick's decades in city government, Doctoroff stood out, he said. "None of the other deputy mayors that I dealt with over the years had Dan's grasp of the biggest possible picture nor how to think outside the box and make it happen."

Doctoroff threw his idea in the ring and invited others to do the same — as long as they had a detailed plan to make it happen. Regina Myer joined DCP in 1984. As the Brooklyn director, she and her team developed plans for Greenpoint-Williamsburg, Downtown Brooklyn and other promising parts of the borough. "I pitched my heart out," she said. "And people were just saying no."

When Doctoroff became deputy mayor, she gamely tried the projects again — and he greenlit them all. "Dan was clearly excited about the breadth of the neighborhood planning and research that we had done," she said. He set up the first standing weekly interagency meeting to coordinate projects Myer had ever experienced in government. "They were listening," she said.

Purnima Kapur joined DCP in 1989 and became director of the Bronx office in 2001. She requested the assignment based on a tenuous hope: that a new administration couldn't possibly be less supportive of the borough than what she had seen before. In her time at DCP "the Bronx was particularly neglected," writes Kapur later in this book. But even she was surprised when Doctoroff wanted to spend a hot summer Saturday walking the length of the South Bronx with her team.

"A deputy mayor spending his Saturday walking through the Bronx with the local City Planning team was the first signal to me that a new kind of management was in place — one I hadn't seen before," she writes. "I learned that Dan might not always agree with a recommendation, but he listened."

Jeffrey Friedlander, who retired as second in command of the city's Law Department in 2015, said that he had met many competent professionals during his 44 years in city government but "none projected Dan's spirit of adventure and exploration of urban possibilities." Friedlander added: "Dan certainly encouraged free expression of ideas. The corollary was also true: He readily accepted pushback on his ideas."

Dormant dreams of rezoning the derelict Hudson Yards were revived by Doctoroff overnight. Planting a million trees to stretch the city's lungs suddenly seemed less audacious. Optimistic population projections by Joseph Salvo, the City's chief demographer, prompted a visionary exercise called PlaNYC to

Deputy Mayor Dan Doctoroff and Department of Environmental Protection Commissioner Emily Lloyd, touring New York City's third water tunnel, 2006.

reimagine and reengineer New York to cope with the anticipated influx years in advance. This is when Doctoroff had the old-time city officials dig deep in their drawers of ideas.

"I remember Eric Kober and Sandy Hornick and Joe Salvo being almost giddy when we engaged them in this initiative," said Joe Chan, one of Doctoroff's senior advisors leading the effort. "They were kind of like, 'finally someone gets it! Someone is listening!' Chan recalled. "One of the things that I really enjoyed was seeing these lifelong civil servants who were so committed, who were so talented and passionate, but at the same time had been kind of brushed off in the past coming to Dan with ideas and Dan being like, 'That's a great idea!'"

Hornick included himself among "these pent-up bureaucrats that Dan unleashed" and added: "To my mind, if he unleashed us, it was because he had the magic sauce to make things happen."

Few committed, untapped, and underappreciated City employees remembered another boss asking them for their best ideas before, much less taking them seriously enough to listen to their answers.

Yes, Doctoroff's dream of a West Side stadium was defeated when he was blindsided naïvely by Assembly Speaker Sheldon Silver's veto. But two decades later, his goal of congestion pricing is nearing reality, another missed opportunity that had been nixed by Albany — but only after Doctoroff had mounted a more constructive campaign, enlisting his colleagues and soliciting the views of affected New Yorkers.

When I asked him what the difference was in how he had approached the two issues, what characterized his growth and successes as deputy mayor, he had a ready answer.

"Maybe I had learned something," he replied. "I listened."

THE STORYTELLER

The power of narrative shaped Doctoroff's big visions — and helped him sell them to the world

The moment I realized Dan Doctoroff never stopped thinking about stories was when he accidentally called me about one on my day off. It was the summer of 2017. We'd been developing a story we called, "Jane Jacobs plus Google." Dan really wanted to talk about it.

"I think it has the potential to be really, really powerful," he said.

The basic premise of "Jane Jacobs plus Google" was that cities could combine the best of Jacobs' incremental urbanism with the best of Google's transformative technology to improve lives in a fundamental way. For example, we could finally achieve Jacobs' desire for personal mass transit by turning Google's self-driving cars into robo-taxi fleets. Extend that logic to her other ideas for better building codes, modular housing, weather-mitigation systems, and more, and we might finally be able to tell the story of how urbanism and technology could combine forces for a brighter future.

In Dan's focus on getting the story right, he'd forgotten I was off work. I reminded him and he apologized and — after a few more minutes when he couldn't help himself — soon got off the phone. But I could tell it would pain him to wait even just three more days to talk again: When Dan got hooked on a story, he couldn't find peace of mind until he figured it out.

Dan has always held a special place in his heart for storytelling. On the second page of his book, *Greater Than Ever* — itself a lively tale of New York's recovery after 9/11 — he writes about working with a famous pollster in college and discovering how to stitch the numbers into a story. He credits that revelation with redirecting his entire school tenure, propelling him from a driftless college kid to an honors student. No doubt Dan would have excelled in any case, but the fact that he attributes the leap to storytelling just reinforces the value he sees in it.

The narrative behind the numbers drove his early career in finance. He may be the only investment banker to enter the field because he loved its storytelling potential. As he'd later tell *Crain's*, great storytelling was essential to preparing an initial public offering, or arranging a merger of two companies, or making a pitch to investors. "You have to be able to tell a coherent and compelling story," he said. "If I look over the course of my career … it's one of the things that's been a consistent advantage to me over time."

These early lessons evolved into the two core tenets of Doctoroff storytelling: "vision plus substance." A story must be inspiring enough to move someone to action but also detailed enough to withstand scrutiny. The substance part came from the numbers. The vision part often took its roots in history — a rhetorical nod to "once upon a time." For Dan the optimist, it was always possible to recapture the best of bygone eras while solving for the unintended outcomes we missed the first time around.

These two elements, vision and substance, were on clear display with the Olympic bid, which was as much a story about the future of New York City as it was a pitch for the Games. That story began by taking us back to the times of *West Side Story*, set in the area that later became Lincoln Center, as a way of showing how neighborhood transformation can propel economic growth. Today, we're more aware of the social setbacks that such change brings, but that's also where the numbers fit into the Olympic story. The more taxes a city can generate through new developments, the more services it can provide for all populations — a virtuous cycle of positive change.

The Olympic story revealed another key storytelling lesson: The narrative process can help force strategic decisions. New York lost the Olympic bid but gained a plan for its future that might never have emerged without the deadline of the story. This insight reached a new level entirely with the story of PlaNYC, a vision for a greener New York backed by 127 data-rich initiatives. Not only did the process of writing that book alter the course of climate action in New York, it provided a blueprint the entire world could use for sustainable urban development.

Therein lies the complete power of Doctoroff storytelling. Done right, it is both a process for shaping a big idea and the product for selling that idea to the world.

All these elements came together at Sidewalk Labs, an Alphabet company that developed innovations to address big urban challenges. The very first thing we did was write a book — a long, yellow book — called, *A City from the Internet Up*. The vision was rooted in history, describing digital advances as a fourth urban revolution with the capacity to transform cities as much as electricity, steam engines, and cars had before it.

The substance was founded on an intense analysis about how such advances might produce quality of life benefits. The strategic insights forced by the storytelling exercise ultimately gave rise to spinoff companies like Cityblock, which began as the yellow book chapter about using technology to deliver better healthcare to diverse local communities. The product of the book itself, with its audience of two (Larry Page and Sergey Brin), was sufficient for Alphabet to keep backing Dan's journey.

We relied so much on storytelling in the early years of Sidewalk Labs, before we had real products in the world, that we (only semi-jokingly) called it Sidewalk Publishing Labs. The fourth urban revolution story, mentioned above, was a mainstay. One stretch of storytelling focused on the "chief engineer," a once-common city job tasked with providing major infrastructure changes that delivered big social advances, like London's 19th century sewer system or Ancient Rome's famous aqueducts. Another story obsession was trying to answer the question about a future city of "what does this place *feel* like?" Inevitably, Dan would turn to pictures of early 19th century streets of Manhattan teeming with life and say *that's* what it needs to feel like. Equally inevitably, any narrative concepts we coined to meet that charge fell short, with the notion of a 21st century "urban village" coming closest.

The length of a story always mattered to Dan. For Sidewalk's initial vision for a future city in Toronto, *A Neighbourhood from the Internet Up*, Dan insisted that we include an entire 171-page appendix on top of the required Request for Proposals (RFP) response elements, because the page requirements prevented us from telling a complete story. The *Master Innovation and Development Plan* for Toronto, delivered in 2019, spanned four volumes and 1,524 pages — the longest book ever produced by the legendary design firm Pentagram, or so they reminded us with every addition we requested.

A long story wasn't indulgent to Dan. While most of us need executive summaries, Dan has the mental capacity to hold a vast story in his head in its entirety. If anything, he finds the abridged version offensive for its removal of the details that make a vision sparkle or a substance sturdy.

More than that, the primary value of a story for Dan was its ability to generate significant momentum for bold projects — enough momentum to keep it moving against the shifting headwinds of political fortune. Public attention wanes. Civic budgets slip. Political will retreats. A good story is the antidote to inaction; a good *long* story offers something for everyone to act upon. It's storytelling not just as product but also as civic engagement. Dan was never scared of the controversy or contention that comes with any big pitch for change. His far bigger fear was indifference.

That Dan saw so much riding on his stories explains the emotional attachment he developed with them. The biggest smile I ever saw Dan crack came when someone from Google told us the Toronto RFP response was "the most impressive document I've seen since our IPO," a smile that I believe had as much to do with the storytelling implications of such a comment as with the financial ones. The angriest I ever saw him get was about a story that failed to convey "what this place feels like" with sufficient force, just a few days before a big presentation. (I later asked Marla Pardee, his longtime assistant, how that outburst ranked on a scale of 1–10, and she paused for a moment before saying: "About a 6.") Even when first diagnosed with ALS, he brought up the idea of telling his story in a way that could rally others to the cause.

As it happened, we only told the "Jane Jacobs plus Google" story once. It was mid-October 2017, just before the public launch of the Sidewalk Toronto project. Dan spoke at an internal town hall at the Google Toronto office. Afterward, he and I discussed what worked and what didn't, with a particular focus on the middle section that drew on the urban ideas of Jacobs. It was too much substance without enough vision — we needed a more emotional kick.

"There *has* to be a better way to tell this story," he said. But I realize now he wasn't really talking about that particular story, or any other. He was talking about why stories mattered in the first place. Stories are to Dan what the green light was to Gatsby: always a little elusive but always worth reaching for, the ultimate symbol of hope.

Sidewalk Labs rendering of Quayside Canoe Cove as part of the Sidewalk Toronto project.

THE HISTORIAN

How a deep understanding of New York's past informed Doctoroff's approach to city building

The Bloomberg administration took office less than four months after the September 11, 2001 terrorist attack on the World Trade Center site. Lower Manhattan was literally smoldering, and more than 2,750 individuals, including 343 firefighters, had perished. Additionally, 13 million square feet of office space, or more than even existed in most American cities, had been obliterated. Many thought New York's future was itself in question.

The newly-elected Mayor Michael Bloomberg asked Daniel L. Doctoroff, a 43-year-old investor who was leading the city's Olympic bid for the 2012 Olympic Games, to take charge of New York's rebuilding effort as the Deputy Mayor for Economic Development and Rebuilding. Neither of them had any prior government experience.

No doubt a confluence of complicated factors yielded the spectacular success that the Bloomberg-Doctoroff team had in reviving New York, a comeback that ranks with the city's greatest triumphs across its four centuries. But let me propose a lesser-known reason: Doctoroff studied New York City history.

This gave him the combination of ambition, confidence, boldness, blithe disregard for daily disasters, and requisite humility needed for the task.

Doctoroff viewed himself as a temporary steward of New York City, one in a long history of New Yorkers who rose to the challenges of a critical moment to make transformative change. This long view freed him from the constraints, pressures, and daily concerns that more typically consume government officials in this unruly city, where various crises are always surfacing and gobbling attention, resources, and time. Instead, it connected him to the sweep of the city's 400 years and prompted him to ask bigger questions — How would these achievements fit in the pantheon of great New York City achievements? How did this moment compare to other crises decades, even centuries earlier — and how had New York solved them before? What could we learn from the past and do differently this time? What would the future learn from us?

In advance of the release of PlaNYC, Mayor Michael Bloomberg, Ashok Gupta of the National Resources Defense Council, and Deputy Mayor Dan Doctoroff discuss *A Plan for New York City,* a master plan developed by the Lindsay administration in 1971. NYC Office of the Mayor Photograph ©2007. City of New York. All rights reserved.

Industry on East River piers adjacent to Brooklyn Bridge, circa 1916.

Brooklyn Bridge Park on East River piers a century later.

This view of our moment, informed and inspired by the history of our city, became his touchstone as he planned out the future.

For every project Doctoroff proposed, he looked to a historical precedent. When he talked about developing Hudson Yards — the transformation of a 50-block underdeveloped swath of Manhattan that had bedeviled planners for decades, which was anchored by 28 acres of exposed rail yards — he pointed to the open rail yards that once pocked Park Avenue.

When Doctoroff talked about the sweeping parks initiatives in PlaNYC, his landmark sustainability plan, he framed them as the third great age of New York City's parks development, after the eras of Calvert Vaux/Frederick Law Olmsted and Robert Moses.

When Doctoroff talked about The Shed, the $500 million striking new cultural facility that shimmies across a Hudson Yards plaza, shrinking and expanding to accommodate an unprecedented range of art forms, performances and exhibitions, he invoked the Met and Lincoln Center as pioneering organizations that reset expectations for what cultural institutions could be and look like and do.

When he oversaw rezonings touching nearly half of the city, in every borough, including reimagining New York's moldering waterfront, which had been largely abandoned once the age of manufacturing ended, Doctoroff framed the initiatives as helping New York transition to the new challenges of a new age, just as the city had successfully evolved many times before.

Later at Sidewalk Labs, the company Doctoroff founded in partnership with Google to merge the work of urbanists and technologists, Doctoroff's historical view broadened out from New York to cities generally. He invariably described digital technology as the fourth great urban technological revolution, after electricity, steam engines, and cars. And his plans for the Toronto waterfront famously referenced images of historic, teeming Lower East Side streets filled with pushcarts. Everything he did to chart a path to the future was viewed in conversation with the past.

It's not an accident that he encouraged new hires to his team at City Hall watch the 14-and-a-half-hour New York City documentary by filmmaker Ric Burns; he wanted to make sure that everyone understood their role as caretakers of this precious history; that

it was their turn to carry it forward and meet the moment just as generations of New Yorkers had before.

Today, with the benefit of nearly two decades sufficient for hindsight, the question now comes to the historians: How did he do on his own test? History is ready to judge. Let me attempt the first answer.

There is no question that Gotham's transformation in physical and psychological terms during the Bloomberg-Doctoroff partnership was astonishing. But to put this accomplishment in broader historical perspective, let us first compare other extraordinary moments in New York's past, and the public servants whose vision and imagination made great changes possible: (1) Peter Stuyvesant (1610-1672), (2) DeWitt Clinton (1769-1828), (3) George B. McClellan, Jr. (1865-1940) and George McAneny (1869-1953), and (4) Fiorello La Guardia (1882-1947) and Robert Moses (1888-1981).

Peter Stuyvesant (1610–1672)

The most important figure in pre-Revolutionary New York was born in the Netherlands in 1610 and lived to become the fourth and last Dutch Governor of New Amsterdam. Working for the large and influential Dutch West India Company, Peter Stuyvesant managed

Peter Stuyvesant, the last Dutch Governor of New Amsterdam, served from 1647-1664 and oversaw efforts to transform the fort and trading post into a bustling city whose population quadrupled from 2,000 to 8,000 during his tenure.

Aruba, Bonaire, and Curacao, all Dutch possessions in the West Indies, before receiving the assignment to lead the West India Company's operations in what would become known as Manhattan Island.

Stuyvesant was autocratic, opinionated, and efficient, and he did not share power with his constituents. But the despotic and opinionated governor transformed what was little more than a fort and a trading post into New Amsterdam, an official city of the Dutch Empire.

Stuyvesant established law and order in the colony, encouraged commercial development, stimulated population growth from 2,000 to 8,000, saw to the construction of a wall (now Wall Street) along the northern edge of the settlement, and made possible the early development of an extraordinarily diverse citizenry. Stuyvesant did oppose the residence of Quakers, Jews, and Catholics in the compact community, but religious diversity prevailed, and the long tradition of toleration in New York was established. When the British Army attacked the harbor, eager to conquer this newly powerful destination, Stuyvesant reluctantly surrendered the city to invaders, which was renamed New York.

DeWitt Clinton (1769–1828)

DeWitt Clinton was the most important public official in New York in the 19th century, thanks to his signature project: leading the construction of the Erie Canal, one of the most important public works projects in American history.

A graduate of Columbia College, Clinton served as a United States Senator before resigning because he thought Washington, D.C., was a miserable place to live. Returning to the booming city at the mouth of the Hudson River, he served three terms as mayor of New York City between 1803 and 1815. He then served as governor of New York from 1817 to 1822 and again from 1825 until his death in 1828.

During much of that time, from 1810 to 1824, Clinton was a member of the Erie Canal Commission and largely responsible for its construction from the eastern shore of Lake Erie to the Hudson River at Troy. Although it was not much more than a ditch with water, its impact on the growth of the United States was immense. Despite being only 363 miles long, it made possible a navigable all-water route from the Great Lakes to the Atlantic Ocean. New York City became the perfect transportation break where goods going or

coming to the New World were loaded onto ships, whether canal boats or other ocean-going vessels.

Many people thought the project was ridiculous and dubbed it "Clinton's Folly." But the canal reduced the cost of transporting goods from Buffalo to New York City by 90%, paying for itself in just a few years. It was so phenomenally successful that cities throughout the East and Midwest rushed to build their own canals to duplicate the success of New York City. Of course, nothing could match the Erie Canal. By the time of the Civil War, Gotham had more than a million inhabitants and by the turn of the 20th century, it was the second-largest city in the world, after London.

In addition to transforming New York into an economic powerhouse, Clinton also had a profound impact on the city's cultural life. He organized the New-York Historical Society in 1804 and was its president; he was president of the American Academy of the Fine Arts between 1813 and 1817; and he was vice president of the American Antiquarian Society between 1821 and 1828. He never viewed commerce and culture at odds and indeed advanced them both to New York's benefit.

George B. McClellan, Jr. (1865–1940) and George McAneny (1869–1953)

George B. McClellan, Jr., son of the famous Union general, would become more successful than his father. For six impressive years (1904-1909), Mayor McClellan presided over a drastic change to the New York City landscape, including the opening of the first subway, the Interborough Rapid Transit (IRT) in 1904, and Chelsea Piers on the Hudson River, which solidified New York's claim to be the world's greatest port. The RMS *Titanic* was on its way to Chelsea Piers when it hit an iceberg in 1912, while the RMS *Lusitania* sailed from Chelsea Piers before it was torpedoed by a German submarine in 1915.

Grand Central Terminal and the New York Public Library were almost finished during his watch. McClellan gave Longacre Square the new name of Times Square in 1904. One new bridge, the Williamsburg, opened during his administration, and another, the Manhattan, was well under way. Unfortunately, Mayor McClellan would become less well-known for those major achievements than for publicity stunts, such as raising the Irish flag over City Hall on St. Patrick's Day or opposing motion pictures as immoral.

DeWitt Clinton, Governor of New York, 1817–1822 and 1825–1828, was largely responsible for the construction of the Erie Canal.

George B. McClellan, Jr., New York City Mayor from 1904–1909, oversaw the opening of the New York City subway system.

Workers digging the subway tunnel for the G line, 1929.

Construction of the No. 7 subway line extension to Hudson Yards, 2011.

McClellan was not a close friend of George McAneny, but the two men were both heavily involved in City Hall politics in the first decades of the 20th century and knew each other well. McAneny served as Manhattan borough president from 1910 to 1913 and as president of the New York City Board of Aldermen from 1914 to 1916. Among his other jobs during these years was secretary of the New York City Civil Service Reform League, executive manager of *The New York Times* (1916-1921), and president of the Regional Plan Association for 10 years. His major accomplishments were in the fields of transit and zoning.

In 1911, McAneny became chairman of a new transit committee of the Board of Estimate. Its task was to work with the private railroad companies and the State Public Service Commission to determine which companies would receive franchises to operate new subways and the routes that those underground and elevated railroads would take. Their decisions, which came to be known as the Dual Contracts, were among the most significant in the long history of the metropolis and led to the opening up of a dozen new IRT and BMT (Brooklyn-Manhattan Transit Company) lines into the outer boroughs of the Bronx, Brooklyn, and Queens.

McAneny's other vital contribution to the New York physical landscape was zoning. Essentially, there was no such thing as zoning when he became the driving force behind the city's 1916 comprehensive zoning resolution. That initiative, since copied by thousands of municipalities around the nation, set up height limits for new construction and separated commercial, residential, and industrial areas. Edward M. Bassett, who served on one of McAneny's committees and later became the full-time director of the zoning office, called McAneny, the "father of zoning in this country."

Fiorello La Guardia (1882–1947) and Robert Moses (1888–1981)

Until Michael Bloomberg served three terms as chief executive early in the 21st century, Fiorello La Guardia was generally acclaimed in New York as "the great mayor." A one-man melting pot, he was the son of an Italian Catholic father and a Jewish mother who became an Episcopalian. He was loud, abrasive, irascible, energetic, and charismatic, with the short and stout shape of a fireplug. He led the city through the Great Depression when New York had the highest unemployment of any big American city, and the dark years of World War II, when Gotham became the greatest port city the world had

George McAneny was the driving force behind the city's 1916 comprehensive zoning resolution.

Mayor Fiorello La Guardia (left) and Robert Moses transformed New York City through an array of major public works projects spanning four decades, from the 1930s to the 1960s.

ever seen. La Guardia was there in the early days of public housing, he expanded and unified the park system, and he reorganized the New York City Police Department. In short, he restored the economy of the great city after crises threatened its foundations.

La Guardia's lasting impact upon Gotham was largely due to his association with Robert Moses, the greatest builder in American history. Indeed, Moses' biographer, Robert A. Caro has opined that the master builder could only be compared to some elemental force of nature, which is another way of referencing God.

Moses never held elective office, but he was adept at circumventing the rules that prohibited persons from holding multiple government positions (eventually he held 12 at the state or municipal level). Just during La Guardia's mayoralty, Moses refurbished Central Park and built 255 playgrounds, 11 huge public swimming pools, Orchard Beach, Jacob Riis Park, the Triborough Bridge, the Whitestone Bridge, and the Belt Parkway. And after La Guardia left office, Moses just picked up speed. Among his creations were the Brooklyn-Queens Expressway, the Cross Bronx Expressway, Stuyvesant Town, the Gowanus Expressway, the New York 1939-1940 World's Fair, the United Nations, a large proportion of the city's public housing stock, the Staten Island Expressway, and Lincoln Center — and this is only a partial list. No one is likely ever to compare with Robert Moses as a builder of New York.

Michael Bloomberg (1942–present) and Daniel L. Doctoroff (1958–present)

In the months following the complete destruction of the World Trade Center on September 11, 2001, predictions were common that few people in the future would want to work in a tall building, or descend into a subway station, or even live in a place which

would likely be a target of future terrorist attacks. The received wisdom in 2002 had it that thousands of families were relocating to the suburbs or to less dense and more distant places like Vermont, New Hampshire, and Maine. As if this were not enough, the administration of Mayor Rudolph Giuliani bequeathed to his successor a multibillion-dollar budget deficit.

The forecasts did not hold true. In fact, the city boomed in the two decades after 2001. The population grew by 800,000, scores of new skyscrapers transformed the skyline, the crime rate continued to plummet, and the city became one of the most popular tourist destinations in the world. Mayor Bloomberg emerged as the finest

Right: Grand Central Terminal during construction, 1905.

Far Right: West Side Rail Yards during the development of Hudson Yards, 2016.

Opposite: Lincoln Center during construction in 1969.

Left: The Shed during construction. The arts center at Hudson Yards opened in 2019.

Los Angeles nearly half a century earlier; a refurbished Bronx Terminal Market, a new campus for Columbia University, a new high-tech campus for Cornell University on Roosevelt Island, the transformation of the Hudson Yards district, anchored by the first expansion of the subway system in 30 years, the rebuilding of Ground Zero, the development of the Downtown Brooklyn Cultural District, world-famous parks like the High Line, Brooklyn Bridge Park, and Governors Island. And this is only a partial list. The accomplishments are astounding. What is less known, is that virtually all of the achievements just listed were conceived or largely executed by Doctoroff and his team.

Like Stuyvesant, as development czar, Doctoroff inherited a city whose economic power was concentrated on the island of Manhattan and created a broader and more formidable metropolis. His citywide economic policy created a slew of new economic centers to power a new generation of growth — in fact, as former *New York Times* reporter, Diane Cardwell writes later in this book, between 2000 to 2015, the number of city businesses grew by 48% in Brooklyn, 33% in Queens, 26% in the Bronx, and 22% in Staten Island — while declining 2% in Manhattan.

Doctoroff's successful economic development initiatives — which focused on improving the city's quality of life as a way to attract more residents and businesses, which in turn would generate tax revenue to fund further public improvements — helped spur a dramatic population increase. Just four years after the attacks of 9/11, City demographers were predicting that New York's population was on track to grow by another million people by 2030. Unlike Stuyvesant, Doctoroff believed the city's diversity was its superpower and celebrated it always.

Like Clinton, many of Doctoroff's boldest plans were derided by critics. The Olympic bid was dismissed by some as a quixotic quest; his projections for the potential of Hudson Yards were deemed absurd by a chorus of critics. And yet, while New York lost to London, the Olympic plan he developed formed a blueprint that has guided the city's development for nearly two decades. Virtually every neighborhood renaissance during the Bloomberg administration owes its revival to the bid, from Greenpoint-Williamsburg and other parts of the Brooklyn waterfront, affordable housing at Hunter's Point South, the city's three new professional sports facilities, Freshkills Park on Staten Island, the reclamation of Coney Island, the revival of land along the Harlem River and the Bronx Terminal Market, new parkland and amateur training facilities in all five boroughs, the High Line, and, of course, Hudson Yards. In 17 years, Hudson Yards has already achieved 80% of the City's initial projections for office space, residential, hotel, and retail development that was expected to take 30 years — and the area has already exceeded projections for hotels and retail. The

executive in the city's long history. Bloomberg was an inspiring and visionary leader who did not owe favors to anyone, thanks to his unparalleled personal wealth which enabled him to forgo campaign contributions and make decisions based on his genuine beliefs in the best outcomes. He made excellent appointments and allowed his department heads the latitude to make important decisions without his approval.

Among the many economic development initiatives accomplished under his watch were new stadiums for the Mets and Yankees and a new arena in Downtown Brooklyn for the Nets, the borough's first professional sports facility since the Dodgers decamped to

extraordinarily rapid success suggests that, if anything, Doctoroff's initial estimates were too conservative.

Like Clinton, Doctoroff also embraced culture as a foundational element of New York's success. In addition to spearheading the development of a new cultural district in Downtown Brooklyn and assisting with Columbia University's most dramatic campus expansion in a century, Doctoroff helped broker the relocation of the Whitney Museum of American Art to a new location along the High Line, secured a new home for the Museum of Arts and Design, and helped found the city's newest major cultural institution, The Shed.

Like McClellan, Doctoroff recognized the power of zoning to shape a city. He spearheaded New York's most ambitious rezoning in nearly half a century, with 78 successful rezonings across all five boroughs covering 6,000 city blocks. Where McClellan coined the phrase Times Square, Doctoroff named Hudson Yards.

Doctoroff also echoed McClellan by establishing the blueprint to reinvent the city's transportation network, including delivering the first subway line extension in 30 years and growing a ferry network along the East River that today carries close to 20,000 riders daily.

Like La Guardia, Bloomberg and Doctoroff led the city out of its greatest crisis in a generation. As the architect of the city's recovery, Doctoroff used his financial background to unstick negotiations around Ground Zero, supported his team, including City Planning Chair Amanda Burden, to stitch Lower Manhattan back into the

surrounding city and foster its growth as a neighborhood where people lived, visited, and worked.

Like La Guardia, Doctoroff drove historic affordable housing initiatives, overseeing the most comprehensive and ambitious municipal affordable housing construction program in American history at that time. The $7.5 billion plan he oversaw spurred the creation or preservation of 165,000 units of affordable housing, including the 5,000-unit development at Hunter's Point South, his generation's answer to Stuyvesant Town.

Did Doctoroff's building achievements in six years match what Moses achieved in more than three decades? Of course not. But I would be remiss if I didn't note that after Moses, a slew of new process checks were put in place designed precisely to prevent another Moses. And it worked. For nearly 40 years, not a single big project survived to completion. For most of that period, City leaders pointed to those process checks as an excuse for why they couldn't get anything done. But Doctoroff showed otherwise, marshaling support in the City Council for virtually all of his initiatives — notwithstanding the heavy requirements of the city's Uniform Land Use Review Procedure, or ULURP. Doctoroff himself offered this assessment in a speech opening an exhibit on Robert Moses I co-curated at the Museum of the City of New York: "ULURP works. The City Council can be a highly effective collaborator if we listen, and respond — with lower densities, more affordable housing, more open space, and a commitment to minority hiring — that in every case have made our plans better. As a result, we have succeeded in

Deputy Mayor Dan Doctoroff and Mayor Michael Bloomberg announcing plans for the redevelopment of Coney Island, 2007.

Manhattan landscape in the mid–19th century, before the construction of Central Park.

Constructing "the Hills" on Governors Island, 2015.

gaining approval of all of our dozens of projects, except that one [the proposed West Side Stadium]."

Then Doctoroff did some things without historical precedent. The population growth inverted the problem he had inherited — a shrinking city with its survival at risk — and posed a new challenge: New York could be swallowed by its own success.

His answer to that question may be his most profound legacy, with global impact that far transcends the city's borders. PlaNYC — part master plan, part sustainability blueprint, vigorous argument for the power of cities and the necessity of change — certainly changed New York.

This comprehensive plan, embraced by Mayor Bloomberg, transformed city government practices, leading to one million new trees, nearly 300 new public playgrounds on refurbished schoolyards, and eight new destination parks spread across all five boroughs. Citywide carbon emissions have fallen by nearly 20% since 2007.

Through PlaNYC, he redefined what transportation meant in an urban environment, outlining a vision that shifted policy focus from cars to people and sustainable public transit. The transportation commissioner he and Bloomberg selected — Janette Sadik-Khan — would go on to implement that vision, developing 400 miles of bike lanes, including the city's first protected lanes; reclaiming acres of streets to create 70 new public plazas and promenades; and implementing 38 miles of a new Bus Rapid Transit system with emphasis on the outer boroughs — a people-first streets movement that has been copied around the world.

The philosophy animating PlaNYC was that New York City should control its own destiny — a shockingly radical proposition in the city's modern history. That included controlling its own energy policy for the first time; establishing the largest air quality survey in the country; overseeing its own brownfield program, and other initiatives. To take brownfields: At the time of PlaNYC, there was not a single city-run brownfield program in the United States.

PlaNYC created one and it quickly became the second-largest program in the country — second only to California.

But PlaNYC did more than that. According to Mark Watts, the current president of C40, the international climate coalition of cities, "The inspiration that Dan and PlaNYC provided is still central to our thinking." PlaNYC pioneered the idea that economic success and environmental responsibility were mutually supporting rather than mutually exclusive, he writes. "The faster cities cut pollution, the greater is their ability to create good jobs, keep energy bills down, and enable residents to live healthier, happier lives."

Its belief in the power of cities catapulted urban centers to the forefront of the climate movement, where they remain today.

It also sparked a passion in Mayor Bloomberg, who had previously come under fire from environmentalists for ending City-provided recycling in the face of budget deficits. After PlaNYC, climate change became a driving passion, fueling his climate philanthropy which in 2019 included a $500 million commitment to eliminate every coal-fired power plant in the United States and in 2022 included $242 million to fund clean energy in 10 developing countries. "It all grew out of PlaNYC," he writes in his foreword to this book.

With Bloomberg's essential backing, Doctoroff brought back big ideas, bold thinking, grand projects — and he did it because he was a student of the city's history. He understood what the city was capable of — because he knew what it had done before and could do again.

In the press release announcing Doctoroff's departure from City Hall, Mayor Bloomberg called Dan's $1 annual salary "one of the greatest bargains for the City since the purchase of Manhattan for $24."

That is a sentiment historians of this great city will agree on for generations to come.

DANIEL L. DOCTOROFF | Deputy Mayor for Economic Development and Rebuilding, 2002–2007

MAKING OMELETS WITHOUT BREAKING EGGS: GETTING THINGS DONE IN THE POST–MOSES ERA

Speech at the exhibit, "Robert Moses and the Modern City: The Transformation of New York" at the Museum of the City of New York, February 1, 2007

"One must wait until the evening to see how splendid the day has been." SOPHOCLES

The Power Broker opens with this line from Sophocles. It is a timeless reminder to us that history takes its time to judge.

This magnificent exhibition, for which we extend our gratitude to its curator, Hilary Ballon, and the Museum of the City of New York, has re-ignited the debate about Robert Moses. It has proven that as far as Moses is concerned, we are not even close to sunset yet.

The conventional wisdom about Moses is based largely on Robert Caro's masterwork. It holds that Moses entered government as an idealistic reformer, who in his early years performed miracles of highway and park construction.

Over time, he became insular and arrogant in his exercise of power. His grand plans reshaped New York — but ultimately left too many devastated communities — especially those inhabited by minorities — in their wake.

The revisionist view is kinder. It tends to excuse many of the actions that today we condemn, like slum clearance and over-reliance on the automobile, as products of their times.

Instead, it is awed by the scope and majesty of Moses's works — from the Triborough Bridge, to Lincoln Center; from the West Side Highway to 658 playgrounds; from the United Nations to 17 major middle-income housing developments — and sees them as indispensable to creating the New York that we love today.

This exhibition will help you form your own judgment about which of these two perspectives is more accurate.

But what no one has ever disputed is that Moses was the single most prolific builder of public works New York has ever known. He got things done.

So, to me, the more interesting — and relevant — question for us today is how did he do it? And what lessons — both good and bad — do we learn from him?

Moses revealed his recipe in a remarkable 23-page, 1974 retort to the 1,246 page, *The Power Broker.*

Paraphrasing Lenin, he exclaimed: "I hail the chef who can make omelets without breaking eggs."

To strain the metaphor just a little bit further, I would argue that the ingredients in his omelet were the following: a vision backed by a concrete plan, concentrated authority, longevity, financial opportunism, and an iron will that led him to disregard nearly everything that stood in his way . . . especially public opinion.

Moses thought deeply about the long-term future of New York. This was a man whose chauffeured car license plate read NY2000 by the early '50s. Although he never learned to drive, he assumed power in the mid-1920's possessed of a clear vision that the future of New York lay in its relationship to the automobile. "We live in a motorized civilization," he wrote.

Needless to say, this was not an original notion in the America of the Model T, and he borrowed a pre-existing blueprint — the Regional Plan of 1929's spiderweb of highways and bridges — to fulfill his vision of connecting the orderly suburbs to the chaotic city throughout his career.

Moses' effectiveness was enhanced by the ever-increasing series of positions he held in both City and State governments — up to 12 at his peak.

This was critical. You may have heard of Metcalfe's Law, which postulates that the value of a communications network is equal to the square of the number of users in the system. Certainly you have heard of Murphy's Law, which says that anything that can go wrong, will.

Doctoroff's Law is a corollary of Metcalfe's and Murphy's Laws. It holds that the degree of difficulty in completing a public project is a mathematical function of the number of governmental entities involved. On a 1 to 100 scale, the degree of difficulty is two times the number of City entities involved, plus four times the number of State agencies involved plus 50 if the Public Authorities Control Board must approve it.

And, if you are trying to build a stadium on the West Side, well, then, you have to add infinity.

When all of these entities are controlled by the same person, needless to say, you can get almost anything done!

A corollary of Doctoroff's Law is that the chance of getting something done is a function of the length of time from conception to construction. Changes in administrations, at both the City and State levels, shifting economic conditions, and external events all play havoc with long-term planning and execution.

Even though by today's standards, Moses moved at lightning speed, his projects still took years. The Whitestone Bridge took nine years to complete; Lincoln Center, 12; and the Verrazano-Narrows, 18. Moses, who served for 44 years, was there to shepherd them through.

Moses has been labeled a "gifted opportunist." In rising above the cacophony of competing priorities and generating the financial resources for his projects, Moses was a genius. In fact, perhaps more than anything else, it was his ability to create or identify new and unique sources of funding that was the basis of his success.

He pioneered bond financings to pay for his parks and parkways. He modeled the Triborough Bridge and Tunnel Authority after the Port Authority and created for himself a permanent source of capital for other highway and bridge projects.

Robert Moses, Roosevelt Island, 1959.

When FDR made manpower and money available through the WPA, Moses was ready with hundreds of park projects. And, shortly after Congress passed Title 1, he announced seven slum clearance projects while his counterparts across the nation were still trying to comprehend the bewildering legislation.

In government, it is all about the money. If you can find it, and no one else can, you can get things done.

The final ingredient in Moses' recipe for success was his determination to break eggs — regardless of the consequences. He was definitely an ends over means kind of guy. This is what he said in response to *The Power Broker:* "There are broad hints that my associates and I were not always ultra-refined in our actions . . . As the city folk ride into the open country we shall, I trust, be forgiven."

Or this: "The cities and second-guessers say we were sometimes rude, arbitrary and high-handed. Maybe so, but suppose we had waited?"

Moses believed that he and his "experts" — the many engineers, architects, and construction executives, who served him — should exclusively determine what was right and how to make it happen. "In the absence of prompt decisions by experts, no work, no payrolls, no arts, no parks, nothing will move," he wrote.

He was certainly right about the ability of experts — guided by a very firm hand — to move things along. But Moses' reliance on his team left him increasingly insensitive to the insights of public opinion and the private market, and led to massive dislocation and lost opportunities.

As Chairman of the Mayor's Committee on Slum Clearance, his vehicle for completing Title 1 projects, Moses was responsible for 17 projects which generated badly needed middle-income apartments and helped to create or expand cultural and educational institutions, including Lincoln Center, NYU, Fordham, and Long Island University.

They were also characterized by "Tower in the Park" designs, which deliberately turned their backs on the surrounding communities, destroying street life and largely limiting any sort of private market reaction to the developments.

Of greater consequence was the dislocation of people. By some estimates, 200,000 or more people were cleared from their homes to make way for Moses' Title 1 efforts.

Moses' hubris ultimately shattered the myth of his omnipotence. Fourteen of his urban renewal projects were never completed. It also led to the ill-fated Mid-Manhattan and Lower Manhattan Expressways, and ultimately his downfall.

For nearly 40 years after Moses lost power, with a few notable exceptions such as Mayor Ed Koch's ambitious affordable housing program, pretty much nothing happened. The waterfront was left to rot, Lower Manhattan continued to slide. We built one new mile of subway in 40 years, a handful of new parks, and no stadiums.

Right: Architectural rendering of McCarren Park Swimming Pool that appeared in the *Brooklyn Daily Eagle* on July 30, 1936. The massive pool, a Works Progress Administration project in Greenpoint–Williamsburg, Brooklyn, opened in 1936.

Opposite: PlaNYC called for the renovation and reopening of McCarren Park Swimming Pool, which had been shuttered for 28 years. The pool reopened in 2012 after a $50 million renovation.

SWIMMING POOL & BATHHOUSE
MC CARREN PARK
BROOKLYN

Then 9/11 happened. Mayor Bloomberg was elected. And everything changed: almost on Day One. The past five years have seen the most prodigious burst of development activity since Moses's heyday. Big projects are once again getting done in all five boroughs.

Hudson Yards. Atlantic Yards. The High Line. New Yankee and Mets stadiums. The revitalization of the Brooklyn and Queens waterfronts, the expansion of the Javits Center. Billions of dollars of public and private investment in Flushing, Long Island City, Harlem, and the South Bronx.

Fresh Kills is being transformed from the world's largest dump to the City's largest park, and that's just one of dozens of park projects that are underway. We are in the midst of the largest local affordable housing program in U.S. history. All the while, the complete rebirth of Lower Manhattan is unfolding before our eyes.

In total, the major initiatives undertaken in the past five years, $19 billion of public investment will leverage an estimated $71 billion in private dollars, producing 54 million of square feet of office space, 77,000 residential units, 2,400 acres of parkland. And all of it to a higher standard of design than ever before thanks to Amanda Burden.

People frequently say that all we learned from Moses was how not to get things done.

What we did for those 40 years was ignore the real lessons of Moses. There was no vision, there was no continuity, agencies and levels of government didn't talk to each other, money was tight and no one figured out how to stretch it.

I believe we have developed a new model for getting things done. One that borrows much from Moses, but differs in important respects too.

Like Moses, we brought to office a fully-formed five-borough development agenda. Ours was called the Olympic X. For the five years before, a team of planners, architects, engineers, and lawyers worked to develop a detailed plan that would use the strict

timetables of bidding for the Olympic Games as a catalyst to get things done.

Unlike the Regional Plan of 1929, it didn't focus on connecting the suburbs to the city by car. Instead, its hallmark was the development of underutilized sections of the city along two mass transit axes — one water, and one rail.

Along those two axes, barren manufacturing, warehouse and waterfront districts, rail yards, former military bases, landfills, and even elevated freight lines — would be reclaimed as homes, offices, parks, and attractions necessary for New York to compete in the 21st century global economy.

Once in office, the administration used the strict bid deadlines to complete planning and secure approvals and financing in record time.

That's why, just five years later, every area targeted by the Olympic Plan is undergoing a renaissance.

With our original agenda well underway, we have set our sights even further. The Mayor's Long-Term Sustainability Plan will look to 2030 and propose a specific agenda to tackle the challenges posed by the enormous growth we foresee for the city, our aging infrastructure, and our increasingly precarious environment. When our successors take office, many of the plans will be in place or the blueprint will be handed to them.

The impacts of "Doctoroff's Law" have been muted by the mayor's decision to have one person oversee all of the fabulous City agencies responsible for economic development and infrastructure. That hasn't been the case in New York City in decades, if ever.

As hard as it is to believe, at five years I am now the longest serving Deputy Mayor for Economic Development (and if you add the Olympic bid, it's been ten years for me).

And our partnership with other governmental agencies has been aided by the relationships forged through the massively complex and emotionally charged rebuilding process at the World Trade

Center site, especially with the Port Authority and its gifted chairman, Tony Coscia, the Empire State Development Corporation, and with the MTA.

Taking a page from Moses, we have found new and creative sources of funding that are enabling us to move things forward. Rather than be bogged down in the decades-long battle over transit priorities, we decided to fund the No. 7 line expansion ourselves to unlock the potential of the Hudson Yards. To do that, we created the world's largest tax increment financing district.

To help fund the Lower Manhattan rail link, we asked the federal government to allow us to "trade-in" for cash $2 billion of unused tax benefits that were part of the 9/11 aid package. We have used density bonuses to build infrastructure and thousands of units of affordable housing in our major developments, and even help to save the High Line.

It also hasn't hurt that the strong economy has filled the city's coffers, which has enabled us to fund many projects ourselves and has enabled us to find new ways to partner with the private sector.

While we do ascribe to the need for vision, continuity, longevity, and financial creativity, we definitely do not believe that you have to break eggs to make an omelet. We have learned, occasionally the hard way, the wisdom of getting out to affected communities and their elected officials early and often.

ULURP [the City's Uniform Land Use Review Procedure] works. The City Council can be a highly effective collaborator if we listen, and respond — with lower densities, more affordable housing, more open space, and a commitment to minority hiring — that in every case have made our plans better. As a result, we have succeeded in gaining approval of all of our dozens of projects, except that one.

Listening has also helped us avoid some of the more egregious impacts of the Moses era. Despite creating 130 million square feet of commercial and residential space, three new sports arenas, a convention center, a new subway line, and 2,400 acres of parks, we will displace only 410 residences and 718 businesses.

So I think it's clear that we've taken the best of Robert Moses's omelet recipe, left out the worst of it, and come up with a recipe all our own that works . . . one that is enabling New York to once again get things done.

In short, we have all learned our lessons.

Or . . . have we?

Earlier I told you that there was only one big project where we failed to win approval. But actually that's not quite right. There's one more.

In 2004, the City joined the United Nations in proposing the creation of a new tower to house UN staff across the street from its main campus. Sure, it was complicated . . . with many City agencies involved with a multinational organization with nearly 200 sovereign members.

All we needed was the alienation of a small, 1.3-acre park. And I use the term "park" loosely, because it was a barren, windswept asphalt lot that was virtually always empty. It was going to be replaced by a landscaped waterfront esplanade nearly three times larger, at no cost to the City.

Surely, in the post-Moses era, we could get this project done.

But we couldn't get it through the State Legislature . . . or we haven't yet. And in a wonderful example of irony, the name of that park we can't get alienated?

Robert Moses Playground.

And the inscription on the playground plaque? A quote from the man himself: "Parks are the outward visible symbol of democracy."

Somehow, the old man got the last laugh on all of us.

THE OLYMPIC CITY

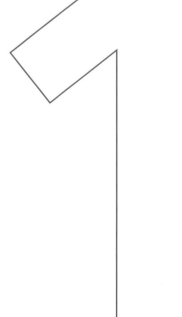

NYC2012 rendering of an Olympic
celebration in Times Square.

"Throughout our history, New York has welcomed people from every nation and creed to pursue their dreams, to be judged on their ability, and to succeed by their determination. In this most competitive yet most accepting of all cities, we live by the Olympic ideals each day."

DANIEL L. DOCTOROFF, JUNE 2002

Runners in Central Park show support for the NYC2012 Olympic bid, June 2005.

AN URBANIST'S OLYMPIC VISION

NYC2012's unconventional approach to Olympic planning prioritized improving the urban experience

It was no surprise to those of us who worked on New York's Olympic bid that our proposal did not look like other cities' plans.

Although the final plan included input from dozens of Olympic experts and met all of the detailed technical requirements established by the International Olympic Committee (IOC), the organizing principles of the plan and the fundamental values embodied within it were developed by a team whose passion for transforming New York — and for shaping a bid around the unique physical presence of the city — was the driving factor.

This made it an outlier. By the late 1990s, when New York's bid was in its early phases, the IOC had begun to codify universal requirements for an Olympic plan. A small but growing sector of the planning, engineering, and construction industry began to market their services to bid cities as a single source provider for comprehensive Olympic planning. Most of these were excellent firms with sterling reputations and deep expertise and experience. Hiring one of these teams would have been a much less complicated approach and would have resulted in a workable plan to host the Olympics in New York.

That type of plan would likely have looked familiar to Olympic observers. Within a decade, most bidding cities were proposing plans that looked essentially the same — they featured a giant "Olympic Park," usually many miles from the city center, that clustered a majority of the sports venues in the same place. The IOC appeared to favor these bids, such as Athens in 2004 and Beijing in 2008, but it was clear to urbanists and economists that these sites were extraordinarily expensive to build and had practically no value or public benefit following the Olympics.

Fortunately, there was a second model for hosting the Olympics that could work. In 1992 Barcelona had hosted an extremely successful Olympics that showcased the city's unique qualities in a series of downtown venues and left a legacy of revived urban areas.

This model of deep engagement with the unique aspects of the host city and a strategy of using the large Olympic investments to shape long-term improvements to the city formed the basis for the New York bid, which was conceived by a 36-year-old investment banker who had recently moved to the city just a decade earlier named Daniel Doctoroff.

Doctoroff, who had no experience with urban planning, sports, politics or managing big events, had attended a World Cup soccer game in 1994 at Giants Stadium between Italy and Bulgaria. He expected to be bored. Instead it was the most electrifying sports event of his life and he stood for the entire game as tens of thousands of Bulgarian- and Italian-Americans shook the stadium with their roars from kickoff to the final whistle. Any country in the world could play here, he realized — and New York could supply enough hometown fans to fill the 80,000-seat stadium for all of

them. It was one of the wonders of his adopted city. There were others. He spent his weekends cycling around New York, taking the subway to the edges of the boroughs. There was nothing else like it. New York had magic and it was a mess — miles and miles of abandoned rotting waterfront; the most famous world icons, the densest business district, intimate, energetic neighborhoods, communities that wove together dozens if not hundreds of cultures from around the world, stores selling every conceivable thing at every conceivable hour, forests, beaches, wastelands.

It had everything, from everywhere — and there was one global event where that mattered. At a New York City Olympics, every country would have a hometown crowd — while the development required to host the Games could catalyze desperately needed transformations. He spent the next 18 months obsessively studying the history of the Games, the geography of New York City, and the strategy of successful bids.

"As I began to better understand New York and the dynamics of hosting the Games, I began to conclude that New York not only could host the Olympics, but that it *desperately* needed to," he wrote in his book, *Greater Than Ever*. New York had struggled to recover from the brink of bankruptcy in the 1970s and the crime wave that carried Rudy Giuliani to victory as mayor in the 1990s. Even as the city grew safer, "there hadn't been time or money to address basic infrastructure and the terrible toll of neglect was still apparent everywhere," he wrote. The city was stuck in an industrial past that wasn't returning, but large-scale ideas for transformation stirred memories of the aggressive tactics of Robert Moses' projects, rousing almost reflexive opposition, which had successfully stalled any bold project for the past 30 years.

"The result was huge swaths of land across the city filled with abandoned factories, wharves and warehouses, many of them littered along the city's 520 miles of waterfront. The potentially beautiful edge along the Hudson River was marred by rotting and abandoned piers. Rail yards and rail lines on the West Side of Manhattan, in Downtown Brooklyn and in Long Island City, Queens, were inhospitable to any form of development," Doctoroff concluded.

Like Barcelona, New York could harness the deadlines, publicity, and power of the Games to achieve a reinvention for the next century. This Olympic vision led Dan to planner Alexander Garvin.

Although I was not present at the time, I've heard the story of Dan's first meeting with Garvin many times (from both Dan and Alex). Garvin taught planning at Yale University, had just released a book about city planning, and had worked in New York City government early in his career. He was a passionate New Yorker from the Upper East Side who took the subway everywhere, wore bow ties to every occasion, and considered the beginning of the Metropolitan

Rendering of proposed Olympic Village at Hunter's Point South, Queens.

Opera's fall season to be the true start of the year. He had likely never attended a sports event in his life.

Dan asked, "Can New York host the Olympics?" to which Alex replied, "Of course, New York can do anything."

"How?" Dan asked.

Alex smiled cheerfully. "I haven't the faintest idea."

He was hired. While this wouldn't seem like the winning argument in a conventional job interview, Dan's approach has never been about finding the easy or conventional approach. It's about asking the right questions, and then finding the people with the passion and talent to work toward answers, wherever they lead. In this case the question he focused on was not "Can New York host a great Olympics?"; it became "How can hosting a great Olympics make New York a better place?" This became the standard by which nearly all decision-making would be measured.

Dan hired Garvin based on the strength of his ideas about cities (as expressed in his book, *The American City*) and specifically for his extensive knowledge about and experience with New York City. I believe it was also partially based on Alex's deep love for, and irrational optimism about New York, which was a perfect match for Dan's feeling about his adopted city.

With Alex leading the planning work, Dan hired Jay Kriegel as the executive director, (Jay joined the John Lindsay administration in 1966 as a whiz kid; talking to him was once described as "putting your finger into an electric light socket"). Jay, a Brooklyn-born Dodgers-turned-Mets fan with wild white hair, rumpled suits, thick-rimmed glasses, and at least two phones pressed against his ears at all times, was quite possibly the most passionate New Yorker who ever lived. He gave a markedly different answer than Alex when Dan first pitched the idea: "That's the stupidest fucking idea I ever heard in my life."

Rendering of proposed Olympic sports cluster along the Harlem River in the Bronx and Upper Manhattan.

But like Alex, Jay had dedicated his life to New York and he found the opportunity ultimately irresistible. Not only was Dan able to convince Jay to join the bid, but Jay became a lifelong friend and political mentor throughout Dan's long public career.

On the planning side of the bid, Alex was able to provide the expertise required to start navigating the challenging world of planning and land use approvals, which was mostly foreign to Dan. On the political side of the bid, which was equally, if not more important, Jay provided the expertise into the intricate, and sometimes arcane, alliances and bureaucracies of the city's municipal and civic leadership. He became Dan's partner and early

guide through that world. It was Jay who tracked down Gertrude Ederle — a New Yorker and former Olympian who was the first woman to cross the English Channel in 1926 and returned home to a ticker tape parade lined with two million spectators. At over 90 years old, she was living in a retirement home in the New York area, all but forgotten until Jay insisted the bid celebrate her story.

I had been a student of Alex at Yale and joined the Olympic planning team in 1999. Having just moved to New York a year earlier, I also had a newcomer's passion for learning about the city, and was extraordinarily lucky to have front row seats to some of the greatest experts. Everyone at the bid shared a constant curiosity to

Rendering of proposed Olympic Stadium in Hudson Yards, Manhattan.

learn more about the city's unique sports history and personalities, international communities and traditions, and physical spaces and capabilities. It was pretty common for staff meetings to get off-track trying to recall the name of an Olympic competitor from Queens from the 1950s or to identify images of New York that could stand in for the Olympic motto, "Faster, Higher, Stronger."

But even among this group, Dan was an outlier. No single moment captures Dan's passion for New York better than the argument over what image would be placed on the cover of the official Bid Book submission to the IOC. Dan loved the majesty of the snow-capped mountains on the cover of Salt Lake City's 2002 Bid Book, and

during a contentious weekend meeting on this topic he announced that ours had to look like that. Everyone was quiet except for Jay, who responded "But Dan, New York doesn't look like that." Dan replied, "It does to me." I knew he wasn't being literal, but Dan's insistence on seeing New York as a place of beauty and magic was a constant challenge for the rest of us to do the same.

The plan we created was the result of a collaboration between these unconventional personalities with unique backgrounds — from the newest arrivals like me to New York veterans who had spent their lives navigating the city's morass of bureaucratic and political hurdles. There were no illusions that it would be easy.

But Dan put together a team that was bound by a common love for New York and by a belief that New York can always be improved. The plan that emerged touched all five boroughs and included a proposal for the reclamation of the East River waterfront with new parks, housing, and transportation, significant investment in existing parks and recreational facilities, transformation of a landfill into an equestrian park, new professional sports venues in multiple boroughs, and a reimagined West Side of Manhattan with public space, commercial buildings, a subway extension, and a new stadium.

Each of these ideas grew out of an ability to envision New York City's next incarnation. Dan's passion for New York was not rooted in how things were but in what they could be.

The Olympic X — invented by Alex and the initial planning team — set nearly all of the venues along a north-south river axis and an east-west rail axis and provided the framework for a larger vision. But at the granular level, each site needed to fit into local goals for the neighborhood, whether it was the need for new parks along the Brooklyn waterfront, additional investment in housing in Queens, or a ferry network that could knit together the city's isolated waterfront. It was this deep New York expertise in planning and politics that allowed the bid to pivot in less than one week after the West Side Olympic Stadium project failed to a new stadium in Queens that would ultimately be built by the Mets.

The focus on improving New York also explains some complex challenges taken on by the Olympic project. Competitions in equestrian sports, mountain biking, and rowing are frequently located at some distance from the host city due to the need for unusual terrain and expensive competition venues. It would have been easy to propose non-city venues for these sports, saving money and headaches. But that wouldn't have made New York City a better place to live or provided New Yorkers with new recreational opportunities. The proposed equestrian and biking venue at a new Freshkills Park — once the largest landfill in the world, which had recently been closed but without a clear path forward — helped to accelerate the creation of that unique public space. The proposal to clean and join the lakes in Flushing Meadows Park for rowing competitions would have yielded an amazing legacy for generations of New Yorkers.

Over the years I have often reflected on Dan's decision to approach the planning for New York's Olympic bid in such an unconventional manner.

I have come to believe that few leaders would have made the decision to place such critical responsibilities in the hands of a team that had never done an Olympic bid. But that's because few leaders would have looked beyond the question of "Can we host a great Olympics?"

By reframing the question to include New York in the equation, the unconventional approach becomes not just a viable path to success, but in fact the only one. And when the bid was lost, the New York half of the equation remained as strong as ever, forming the basis for a true transformation.

FRESHKILLS — EQUESTRIAN CENTER

Before

Olympic Rendering

After

CITI FIELD — OLYMPIC STADIUM

Before

Olympic Rendering

After

HIGH LINE

Before

After

HUNTER'S POINT SOUTH — OLYMPIC VILLAGE

Before

Olympic Rendering

After

369TH REGIMENT ARMORY — BOXING

Before

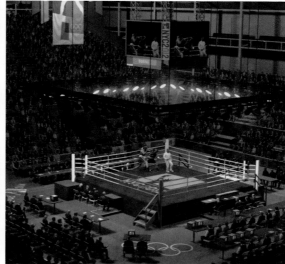

Olympic Rendering

After

YANKEE STADIUM AND HARLEM RIVER — BASEBALL, TRACK CYCLING, AND BOXING

Before

Olympic Rendering

After

THE OLYMPIC X PLAN

The Olympic X plan organized the Games along two intersecting axes, with the Olympic Village at the center. The north–south axis followed the East River and envisioned transporting athletes and spectators using a new network of ferries. The east–west axis traveled along the route of the No. 7 train and commuter rail lines from Flushing, Queens to Manhattan's Far West Side. The plan for the Manhattan Olympic cluster, in a new neighborhood it called Hudson Yards, included a new subway stop, parkland, and an Olympic Stadium on undeveloped rail yards overlooking the Hudson River.

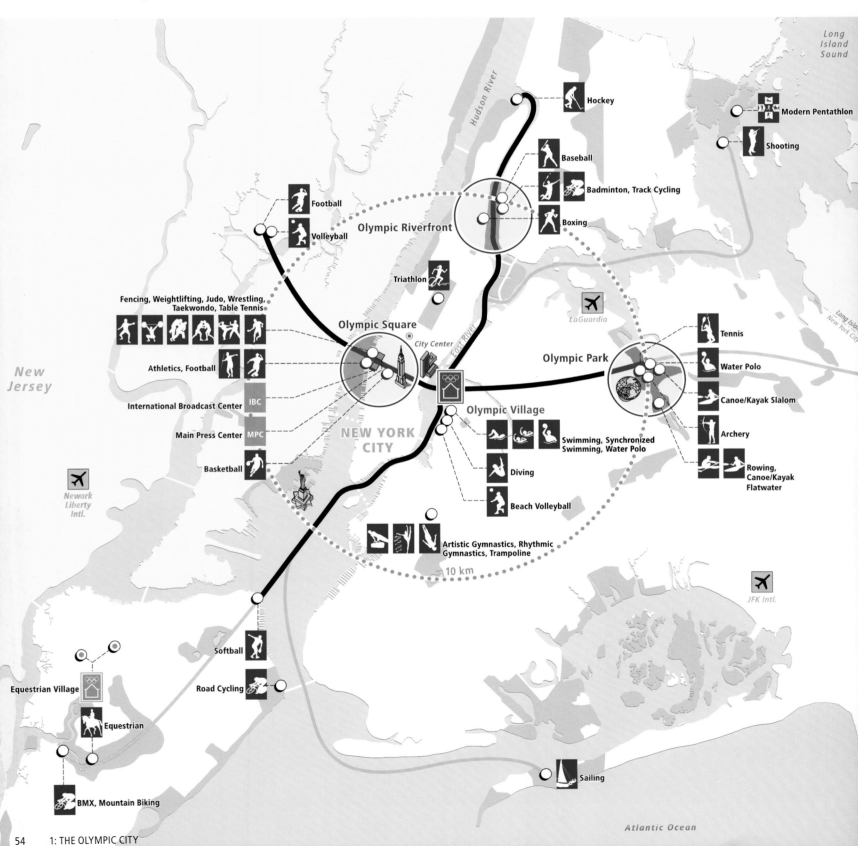

LET THE GAMES BEGIN – IN N.Y.

City poised to pitch itself as site for 2012 spectacle

By EDWARD LEWINE
SUNDAY NEWS STAFF WRITER

Are you ready for the 2012 New York Summer Olympics?

Despite years of trying, New York is one of the few great international cities that has never hosted an Olympiad. Now, the city seems closer than ever to grasping the gold.

"This is the best chance for New York to get the Games in decades," said financier and longtime Olympic promoter Daniel Doctoroff.

"All the planets do seem to be better aligned this time," said Fran Reiter, a former deputy mayor who has worked on bringing the Olympics to the city in the past. "The city is stronger and healthier now, and by 2012, you will probably have put some years between North American Olympics."

Doctoroff's group, NYC2012, is preparing a formal proposal to the U.S. Olympic Committee making the case for New York. The Sunday News has learned key provisions of the 600-page plan, which must be submitted to the committee by Dec. 15, 2000.

The New York Olympics would be financed privately, using no tax dollars, under the proposal.

Based on past Olympics, such as the 1996 Atlanta Games, which grossed $1.7 billion, NYC2012 has estimated that the 16-day New York Games would generate $3.1 billion from television, corporate sponsorships and ticket sales.

With the costs of mounting the Games estimated to be around $1.8 billion, the city would be left a whopping $1.3 billion surplus to fund facilities around the city that could be used for years to come.

These might include a rebuilt pool and park in Astoria, Queens, an East River ferry system and the transformation of the 369th Regiment Armory in Harlem into a multisport complex, according to the proposal.

The Games would pump an estimated $10 billion into the local economy, and the international attention also might inspire the state and city to attend to projects that have languished, such as rail links to the airports, extending the proposed Second Ave. subway and refurbishing the East River waterfront.

Since the 1984 Los Angeles Summer Games, Olympic host cities have reaped ample rewards. Barcelona rebuilt its waterfront. Tokyo constructed a new public transportation system. Atlanta expanded its airport.

Most of the sports venues for a New York Games already are built and would only require touching up. They might include Yankee Stadium for baseball, the Meadowlands for soccer and basketball, Madison Square Garden for gymnastics, the Javits Center for weightlifting, judo and table tennis, and the Astoria Pool in Queens for diving and swimming.

"One of the big advantages of holding the Olympics in New York is that most of the needed infrastructure is already in place," Doctoroff said.

Although NYC2012's plan says the city would not be required to use tax money, its proposal hinges on construction of

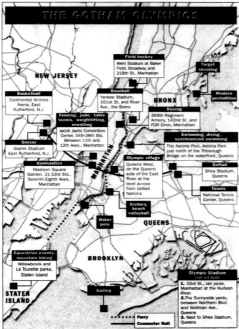

THE GOTHAM OLYMPICS

NEW JERSEY

NEW YORK

BRONX

MANHATTAN

QUEENS

BROOKLYN

STATEN ISLAND

Field hockey
Wein Stadium at Baker Field, Broadway and 218th St., Manhattan

Target shooting

Basketball
Continental Airlines Arena, East Rutherford, N.J.

Baseball
Yankee Stadium, 161st St. and River Ave., the Bronx

Modern pentathlon

Fencing, judo, table tennis, weightlifting, wrestling
Jacob Javits Convention Center, 34th-38th Sts. Between 11th and 12th Aves., Manhattan

Boxing
369th Regiment Armory, 142nd St. and FDR Drive, Manhattan

Soccer
Giants Stadium East Rutherford, N.J.

Swimming, diving, synchronized swimming
The Astoria Pool, Astoria Park just north of the Triborough Bridge on the waterfront, Queens

Gymnastics
Madison Square Garden, 31-33rd Sts., Seventh-Eighth Aves., Manhattan

Olympic village
Queens West, on the Queens side of the East River at the level across from United Nations

Softball
Shea Stadium, Queens

Tennis
National Tennis Center, Queens

Archery, beach volleyball

Water polo

Equestrian events mountain biking
Willowbrook and La Tourette parks, Staten Island

Sailing

Olympic Stadium (not yet built)
1. 33rd St., rail yards, Manhattan at the Hudson River.
2. The Sunnyside yards, between Northern Blvd. and Skillman Ave., Queens
3. Next to Shea Stadium, Queens

— — — Ferry
————— Commuter Rail

a large Olympic stadium — most likely over the 33rd St. rail yards on Manhattan's West Side, in Sunnyside, Queens, or next to Shea Stadium — for track events and opening and closing ceremonies.

Doctoroff is hoping that the tab for a $100 million to $300 million stadium will be picked up by the city and the New York Jets, which would make the stadium their home after the Games. If not, there is an alternative plan to rebuild one of the area's existing stadiums or put up a temporary structure.

Athletes would be housed in a new Olympic Village on the East River in Queens, across from the United Nations. The private-

ly funded Queens West location would be sold as housing after the Games.

Most of the proposed Olympic venues are within a 7.5-mile radius of midtown along a north-south axis and an east-west axis, which would form the basis for an innovative transportation plan for athletes, media and Olympic officials.

A ferry service would ply the waters of the harbor from Staten Island to the northern tip of Manhattan along the East River. And a dedicated rail line using existing facilities would run on Long Island Rail Road and New Jersey Transit tracks from Shea Stadium in Queens to the Meadowlands in New Jersey.

About 500,000 spectators would be expected to converge on the city during each Olympic day. NYC2012 estimates that bus and subway lines could handle the influx, especially in August, when ridership is down 800,000 riders a day from its October peak.

"If they can schedule events around the a.m. rush hour, this could work," said Steven Weber, a transportation expert for the Regional Plan Association, an independent city planning group.

The mayor, the City Council and state officials have agreed to the NYC2012 proposal in principle. So have scores of business and labor leaders, including developer Lewis Rudin,

Loews Hotel President Jonathan Tisch and Transport Workers Union President Willie James.

"We think it is a very promising plan," said mayoral aide Joe Rose. "It makes sense for the Olympics to come here."

Robert Kiley, the president of the New York City Partnership, the premier local business group, also was enthusiastic.

"I think this will get significant support," he said.

Unlike Moscow, Paris, Rome and London, New York has never hosted the Olympics. But that hasn't been for lack of trying.

In 1977, the city lost out in its bid for the 1984 Games to Los Angeles because the U.S. Olympic Committee was worried about the city's soaring crime rates and fiscal instability.

In 1994, Doctoroff decided to make a bid for the 2008 Games after he attended a World Cup soccer match at Giants Stadium and realized that New York is a city uniquely disposed to supporting an international sporting event.

"Around 65% of New Yorkers either were born or have a parent who was born somewhere else," said Doctoroff, 41, who manages money for the powerful Bass family of Texas. "So there is a ready-made fan base for any Olympic sport or participating country."

Despite support from business and political leaders, New York missed out on the 2008 Games because the U.S. committee decided not to sponsor a U.S. city for that year.

The committee was worried that there already were too many North American locations in the Olympic mix. The 1996 Summer Games were held in Atlanta, the 2002 Winter Games will be held in Salt Lake City, and Toronto was a hot prospect for the 2008 Summer Games.

Now Doctoroff has dusted off his Olympic sales pitch for 2012 — and many of the obstacles of the past seem to have evaporated.

New York City is enjoying a falling crime rate, a rising economy and a newfound success as a center of tourism. The Atlanta Games are over, and Beijing has replaced Toronto as the 2008 favorite.

But New York is not yet a shoo-in.

Doctoroff's group must submit its proposal to the U.S. Olympic Committee, which has until 2002 to choose from a field of seven other U.S. cities: Dallas, Houston, Tampa, San Francisco, Los Angeles, Washington-Baltimore and Cincinnati.

The international committee has never been forthcoming about how it makes its selections. And it has been refining its approach to picking a city in

Once the committee selects a city, it will pass along its recommendation to the International Olympic Committee in Lausanne, Switzerland, which will announce the final choice in 2005.

Meanwhile, the international committee is scheduled to announce its choice for the 2008 Summer Games in two years. The 2004 Summer Olympics are scheduled for Athens and the 2000 Games for Sydney, Australia.

"We've never had so many cities looking to have the Games," said committee spokesman Mike Moran.

the wake of bribery scandals that marred the Salt Lake City selection process.

But clearly the committee will be choosing a city that has the best transportation systems, accommodations, communications, security arrangements and sports facilities that can best showcase the Games.

Critics of New York's Olympic aspirations question whether a crowded old city can pull off an Olympic Games — or whether it will fall victim to the traffic jams and security woes that plagued the 1996 Atlanta Games.

"Could this work on paper?" asked an official who is sponsoring an Olympic bid for another U.S. city. "Yes. The question is whether their numbers can withstand scrutiny."

New York's pitch, however, will use its size and age as big advantages.

The city boasts the world's largest police force and transportation system. It is home to the big media companies that will cover the games and has three times the hotel space of earlier Olympic cities.

"I believe that New York best represents what the Olympics are about," Doctoroff said. "This is the city that embodies internationalism, competition and the pursuit of dreams."

Daniel Doctoroff, 41

MILL POND PARK — TRACK CYCLING

Before

Olympic Rendering

After

BARCLAYS CENTER — GYMNASTICS

Before

Olympic Rendering

After

EAST RIVER FERRY NETWORK

BROOKLYN BRIDGE PARK

Before

After

Before

HUDSON YARDS — OLYMPIC STADIUM

Before

Olympic Rendering

After

GREENPOINT–WILLIAMSBURG — BEACH VOLLEYBALL

Before

Olympic Rendering

After

CONEY ISLAND

After

Before

After

THE OLYMPIC LEGACY

When the International Olympic Committee (IOC) awarded the 2012 Olympics to London, many observers thought it was a loss for New York City. Nothing could be farther from the truth.

Planning for New York City's bid to host the 2012 Olympic Games provided a strategic agenda for the city, including many projects that had been under discussion for years, if not decades. Dan Doctoroff's remarkable strength lay in building a coherent, compelling case for how the city could benefit from moving them all forward together and on an accelerated timetable.

His expertise in finance was key to the plans for financing extension of the No. 7 train and construction of the High Line. Doctoroff understood how the skills and resources of the private sector could be harnessed to help achieve major public objectives — at Hudson Yards, in the development of Hunter's Point South, in launching the East River Ferry Service at minimal cost to the city, and on many other projects.

Doctoroff also repeatedly showcased the flexibility that is critical to success in both business and government. When it was clear that some element of the NYC2012 plan was not going to work out, he didn't dwell on it, but instead moved quickly to line up an alternative.

Finally, one of the keys to the long-lasting nature of Doctoroff's impact on the city was his effectiveness as a team-builder. At NYC2012, at City Hall, in Lower Manhattan and elsewhere, he brought together teams of people, both seasoned veterans and promising young professionals, many of whom are still working today to strengthen and improve the City of New York.

The result is that New York City has achieved virtually all of the key elements of the NYC2012 plan without having to hold the Games. Unlike other cities that have hosted the Games and are saddled with heavy debt and abandoned sports facilities, the legacy of New York's bid continues to benefit the city. This reflects both the vision of Daniel Doctoroff and the capacity of the Bloomberg administration to get things done, to plan wisely for the future, and to create new neighborhoods where New Yorkers can work and live.

The bold and visionary NYC2012 plan has strengthened neighborhoods across the city and fostered new public and private investment in long-neglected, underused, industrial corridors. The legacy of the NYC2012 plan is not confined to one project, borough, or community.

For New York City, planning for the 2012 Olympic Games provided a bold agenda that catapulted New York into the 21st century — and continues to shape the future of the city.

MITCHELL L. MOSS AND HUGH O'NEILL

MITCHELL L. MOSS | Henry Hart Rice Professor of Urban Policy and Planning, New York University

HUGH O'NEILL | President, Appleseed, 1993–Present

HOW NEW YORK CITY WON THE OLYMPIC GAMES

New York's Olympic plan became a blueprint for the city's transformation

New York City's bid for the 2012 Olympic Games was never just about the benefits New York could derive from hosting a 17-day global sports festival. It was designed to use the bid process as a catalyst for revitalizing New York City, both physically and economically. Although the International Olympic Committee (IOC) chose London to host the 2012 Games, New York came out a winner when judged by the long-term impact that planning for the 2012 Olympics had on the city's transportation infrastructure, reinvented waterfront, commercial and residential development, and recreational and athletic facilities.

The idea that the bid preparation process could be used to develop and deliver a far-reaching urban revitalization program began with Daniel Doctoroff, then a 36-year-old New York City-based investment banker. In 1994, after attending an exhilarating World Cup soccer match at Giants Stadium between Bulgaria and Italy — and recognizing the city's unique capacity to supply fans to cheer on any country in the world — he began exploring the idea of New York hosting the Olympic Games.

After two years of extensive research, planning, and organizing, Doctoroff presented his plan to then-Mayor Rudy Giuliani. The mayor committed his administration to begin collaborating with Doctoroff's group on a proposal to win the 2008 Olympic Games. When the United States Olympic Committee (USOC) decided to bid for the 2012 Games instead, Doctoroff and the City adjusted to the new deadline and kept planning.

Doctoroff recruited two experienced New York City veterans to help develop the detailed bid plans. Jay Kriegel, a Brooklyn native who had been a top aide to former Mayor John Lindsay, became NYC2012's executive director and Alex Garvin, an urban planner who had worked for several City agencies and taught at the Yale School of Architecture, became the bid's director of planning.

Doctoroff and Garvin took an innovative approach toward identifying the Olympic venues and supporting facilities required for the Games. While proposing to make full use of the city's iconic sports facilities — including Yankee Stadium, Shea Stadium, Madison Square Garden, and the United States Tennis Association National Tennis Center — they also sought to build new sites or to upgrade existing facilities in neighborhoods across New York City.

Top: *New York Daily News,* November 28, 1999.

Opposite: Deputy Mayor Dan Doctoroff and Mayor Michael Bloomberg arrive in Singapore in advance of New York's final presentation to the International Olympic Committee on July 6, 2005.

In particular, they focused on five areas of the city that had untapped development potential and that had not yet made the transition from the old industrial economy to the modern information-based city:

- **FAR WEST SIDE OF MANHATTAN**

- **EAST RIVER WATERFRONT IN BROOKLYN AND QUEENS**

- **HARLEM RIVER IN MANHATTAN AND THE BRONX**

- **FLUSHING, QUEENS**

- **FRESH KILLS, STATEN ISLAND**

Many of these areas had been targeted as potential locations for new development — in some cases for decades — but little progress had been made to bring them to fruition. Doctoroff believed that by locating Olympic sites in these areas, the inflexible deadline, investment, and attention associated with the Games would have a catalytic effect on broader, long-needed development in each neighborhood.

The Olympic X

Virtually all of the proposed venues, both existing and new, would be located along two intersecting axes that Garvin dubbed the "Olympic X," with the two axes crossing at the proposed site of the Olympic Village in Hunter's Point South, Queens on the East River waterfront across from the United Nations. The X featured:

A north/south axis extending from the Bronx and the northern tip of Manhattan, down the Harlem and East Rivers along the Brooklyn and Queens waterfront (passing the Olympic Village), through the harbor, and down to Staten Island; and

An east/west axis that would extend from Flushing Meadows Corona Park in Queens, past the Olympic Village, across the East River, through the center of Manhattan, past the Olympic Stadium, and across the Hudson River to the Meadowlands.

The Olympic X became the basis for the bid's transportation plan. It offered efficient ways to move athletes — even through the dense center of Midtown Manhattan — from the Olympic Village to their venues and efficiently move spectators as well. Most venues on the east/west axis would be accessible by subway and commuter rail, while those on the north/south axis adjacent to the waterfront would be accessible by subway, rail or ferry. In addition, there would be one major new transit line: an extension of the No. 7 subway line from Times Square west to 11th Avenue and then south to the Javits Center and to a new Olympic Stadium at 33rd Street and 11th Avenue.

Coordinating development from City Hall

In December 2001, the link between planning for the 2012 Games and the municipal government's overall agenda for revitalizing New York City was reinforced when newly elected Mayor Michael Bloomberg appointed Doctoroff to be Deputy Mayor for Economic Development and Rebuilding. Bloomberg built a team of leaders that differed from those of prior mayors. His top appointees were notable for the diversity of their experience and for their demonstrated talent and leadership skills.

Bloomberg recognized that rebuilding Lower Manhattan and the city's economy were going to be top priorities in the wake of the September 11th attack on the World Trade Center. As a result, Doctoroff was given a broad portfolio, including redevelopment of Lower Manhattan after 9/11, oversight of the city's Olympic bid, and other major economic development initiatives.

With this appointment, the mayor made the long-term goals and specific projects of the NYC2012 Olympic plan part of his administration's initial planning and development strategy. The Bloomberg administration would use the pressure of the fixed Olympic bid timetable to accelerate the legal and technical review and approval of these projects so that by the time the IOC made its decision in mid-2005, New York would be positioned to go forward regardless of whether the city's bid was successful.

The Olympic catalyst effect

Every country is allowed to nominate one city to compete internationally for the right to host the Olympic Games. In November 2002, the USOC selected New York as its candidate, giving the city two and a half years to prepare for the final IOC vote. As part of the bid evaluation process, the IOC demanded detailed plans and solid evidence that the proposed projects would be completed on schedule.

In the case of New York, it was a reasonable question. The scale of the projects proposed in New York's bid was unique in the city's modern history — and each one required an enormous volume of additional technical work in planning, design, logistics, and financing information to meet the IOC standard. Additionally, the City needed to prepare a full legal analysis of the required approval processes, as well as a financial plan for each venue.

Historically in New York City, massive projects of this scale — requiring community consultation and review, technical analysis, rigorous environmental impact studies, and a series of votes by government bodies — usually take years for full approval. Once the plans and environmental reviews are complete, the city's Uniform Land Use Review Procedure (ULURP) takes an additional seven months. In addition, several Olympic projects also required approval by the state government and, in one case (sailing), the federal government.

Doctoroff concluded that the best, perhaps only, way to demonstrate the feasibility of each project was to complete all of the required approvals before the July 2005 IOC vote. The challenge was to mobilize municipal agencies (and in some cases state agencies) to expedite and coordinate their work to achieve an unprecedented scale of approvals at unprecedented speed.

As deputy mayor, Doctoroff was uniquely positioned to manage this process and execute on its delivery. The fixed Olympic timetable imposed an external absolute deadline, something that is rare for public projects. Since slippage in any one project or venue could jeopardize the entire Olympic bid, it created leverage over the various reviewing agencies; Doctoroff recognized the power of this tool to maintain momentum and used it effectively.

There were setbacks. Doctoroff and his team both at NYC2012 and in city government had to adjust their plans repeatedly. In some cases, this involved changes to particular venues in response to concerns from the IOC or various sports federations. In others, it involved responding to community concerns or suggestions about the location of particular facilities. And in some cases, it meant changing the plan to take advantage of new development opportunities that emerged in New York City after 2002.

The most significant change was a last-minute shift in the proposed location of the Olympic Stadium from the Far West Side of Manhattan to Flushing, Queens where, rather than being linked to the development of a new football stadium for the New York Jets, it would be linked to the development of a new baseball stadium for the New York Mets. The Bloomberg administration developed this remarkably fast revision just one month before the IOC vote in 2005, after the original stadium plan was rejected by the New York State Public Authorities Control Board.

The Olympic city

As it evolved, the Olympic plan considered and imagined different futures for vast swaths of the city. While only a select number made it into the final bid proposal, many of the sites Doctoroff learned about through these Olympic explorations became integrated into a broader vision for the city.

Accordingly, even areas that were ultimately not included in the revised NYC2012 plan, such as Coney Island and Brooklyn Bridge Park, remained priorities of the Bloomberg administration. Coney Island was originally identified as a site for sailing and a new arena. It ultimately became the focus of a major revitalization plan initiated by Doctoroff that included a rezoning, a new amusement district, updated infrastructure, and new housing and community facilities. Pier 1 on the Brooklyn waterfront, originally proposed for diving competitions, became the heart of Brooklyn Bridge Park.

By the end of Mayor Bloomberg's second term, virtually all of the parks, neighborhoods, and waterfront sites identified in the Olympic plan were well on their way to becoming iconic parts of the new and revitalized New York.

> "Mr. Doctoroff, whose formal title is deputy mayor for economic development and rebuilding, has relentlessly pushed his organizing principle: the plans for the Olympics — a world class stadium, expanded subway lines, more hotels — is simultaneously a catalyst for the city's remaking and revitalization."

Opposite: Dan Doctoroff's vision to leverage the Olympic Games to improve New York City received extensive media coverage during the bidding process, including in *The New York Times* and the *New York Daily News*.

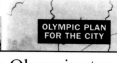

SPECIAL REPORT

CITY'S BID FOR THE OLYMPICS

Ambitious pitch calls for remaking West Side

By MICHAEL R. BLOOD, MICHAEL O'KEEFFE and LUKE CYPHERS
DAILY NEWS STAFF WRITERS

New York's bid to be the host of the 2012 Olympics — and transform the face of the city — leaps from the starting blocks Friday when local planners submit a 600-page proposal to the U.S. Olympic Committee.

The city's efforts to land the Games have as much to do with remolding the West Side and reviving the East River waterfront as with the human drama of athletic competition.

"The Olympics tend to act as a catalyst for getting things done that otherwise wouldn't because the city or state couldn't generate the political will," says Daniel Doctoroff, president of NYC2012, the private group behind the Games bid.

Doctoroff says the city could use the Olympics to improve transit, housing and athletic facilities — and ease an office-space crunch.

Coupled with an expanded Jacob Javits Center that would connect to a retractable domed stadium over the West Side rail yards, the Games could spawn a new stretch of midtown skyscrapers — filled with commuters arriving from new subway and train stops.

The Games could also give rise to housing and waterfront parks across the East River from the United Nations.

"As luck would have it," says an NYC2012 planning document, "what is good for the city is good for the Olympics, and vice versa."

But New York's efforts, backed by business and union leaders and celebrities including Diana Ross, Billy Crystal and Jerry Seinfeld, face tremendous obstacles, among them:

■ BIG BUCKS: Based on figures from NYC2012 documents and state records, the cost of putting on the Games, together with the price tag for a West Side stadium and related transit and convention center improvements, easily could surpass $7 billion. The 2012 committee says all of the costs — except the stadium — could be paid for with TV and corporate-sponsor revenue, proceeds from the sale of development rights for the new business districts and new tax revenue. To open the way, the city wants to overhaul zoning on the West Side, now mostly reserved...

ballpark for years. In Queens, residents are protesting the proposed conversion of two Flushing Meadows Park lakes into a rowing venue, and borough President Claire Shulman has declared war on a proposed Olympic Village in west Queens. "It's a real estate scheme," says urban planner Meta Brunzema, a member of the Hell's Kitchen Neighborhood Association.

■ NATIONAL WOES: Many Olympic watchers say New York has only a middling chance of beating seven other cities for the U.S. bid; competitors such as Dallas have more land to develop

...with school children playing on ballfields that were once brown fields.

For construction unions, the prospect of redeveloping the West Side holds the lure of long-term employment guarantees. Thousands of workers would be needed over many years to erect the Olympic facilities and put up millions of...

OLYMPIC PLAN FOR THE CITY

Daniel Doctoroff, President of NYC2012

COOPER, ROBERTSON & P

HEATHER EATMAN DAILY NEWS

> "The Olympics tend to act as a catalyst for getting things done that otherwise wouldn't because the city or state couldn't generate the political will," says Daniel Doctoroff, president of NYC2012, the private group behind the Games bid.
>
> Doctoroff says the city could use the Olympics to improve transit, housing and athletic facilities — and ease an office-space crunch.

2012 OLYMPICS ROSTER & KEY DATES

U.S. CITIES MAKING BIDS

Cincinnati, Dallas, Houston, Los Angeles, San Francisco, Tampa, Washington/Baltimore, New York.

LIKELY FOREIGN CITIES MAKING BIDS

Rio de Janeiro, Buenos Aires, Paris, Cape Town or Johannesburg, Toronto.

TIMELINE

Friday → U.S. cities submit 600-page bids to U.S. Olympic Committee.

Six months → U.S. Olympic Committee sends back comments, asks for revisions.

Five to nine months → USOC sends technical review team to inspect proposed sites, transit options, security plans.

July 2001 → International Olympic Committee selects 2008 Games host.

January 2002 → USOC chooses three finalists for U.S. nominee.

Fall 2002 → USOC picks U.S. winning bid.

2003-2004 → IOC announces procedures for 2012 selection.

2005 → IOC selects 2012 Games host.

WILD CARDS

■ If Toronto upsets favored Beijing for 2008 Games, "We're dead," says NYC2012 head Dan Doctoroff.

■ Salt Lake City bribery scandal trials next year could embarrass IOC, produce lasting grudges against United States.

■ NBC-TV contract expires in 2008, and the IOC may want to use the lure of hosting Games in a U.S. city to drive up its broadcasting-rights fees.

...d idea 3 years ago

While New York's 2012 Olympic pitch has Pataki's official endorsement, his support has been far more restrained than that of the cheerleading Mayor Giuliani.

"What sort of public monies are going to be asked for?" the governor has asked. "What sort of public benefit will there be? What sort of environmental impact will this have?"

While any games in 2012 would be played almost entirely in city, the Empire State study looked at the potential of a regional bid supported by New Jersey, New York and Connecticut.

"The only way you could ever do this, and do it credibly," says Scheckner, who wrote the bid that brought the 1998 Goodwill Games here, "is to do it regionally."

OLYMPIC DREAM
PART 2 TOMORROW
2012 Games would transform West Side

The Metro Section

The New York Times

SUNDAY, MAY 16, 2004

oN 29

A Traveling Salesman For School Reform

Anthony J. Alvarado is no longer a field commander in the campaign for educational reforms, but he is still spreading the gospel according to Alvarado.

It goes like this: To teach children effectively, you must teach teachers effectively — and constantly — about how to teach children effectively.

From the 1970's to the 1990's, Mr. Alvarado was known in New York City for his teacher-training innovations and other reforms as superintendent of two public school districts in Manhattan, first in East Harlem and then in a district running from Lower Manhattan to the Upper East Side.

To be sure, he was even more wide...

THE NEW YORK TIMES METRO SUNDAY, MAY 16, 2004

A True Champion Of Grand Plans And Tiny Details

With the Zeal of an Athlete, Doctoroff Pursues Olympics

By LIZ ROBBINS and MIKE McINTIRE

Daniel L. Doctoroff has recorded a personal best time of 21 minutes and 3 seconds bicycling from his Upper West Side brownstone to City Hall. He has noted the 22 consecutive days he has not lost his temper, as well as the 615 plants, trees and shrubs that would be affected by his plans to redevelop the West Side of Manhattan.

He makes sure that every document that comes from his office of deputy mayor uses the clean typeface Gill Sans, and that charts are perfectly aligned to the last decimal. All this, of course, has a deliberate purpose.

Mr. Doctoroff has harnessed his obsession with small details to create a blueprint for a sweeping legacy — his and New York City's.

Ten years ago, Mr. Doctoroff, a multimillionaire Michigan native and former investment banker, gave birth to the city's Olympic bid — now aimed at landing the 2012 Summer Games.

Today, at age 45, Mr. Doctoroff has vaulted from that job to become one of the city's most powerful officials, bringing with him his Olympic-inspired vision to reshape the New York economy and physical landscape.

Unelected, and still unknown to many New Yorkers, Mr. Doctoroff has nonetheless been granted extraordinary authority by Mayor Michael R. Bloomberg. He shaped the mayor's speech outlining the future of Lower Manhattan, and oversaw the rezoning of industrial Williamsburg for housing development and the development of a master plan for downtown Brooklyn. And it is Mr. Doctoroff whom Mr. Bloomberg has charged with reinventing a 50-block swath of Manhattan's West Side, transforming it from a collection of tenements and warehouses into the city's third-largest business district, complete with new skyscrapers and a sports stadium.

With the mayor's complete confidence, he has immense ability to promote or derail projects on a moment's notice. Throughout his ef-

Continued on Page 32

> Mr. Doctoroff has . . . become one of the city's most powerful officials, bringing with him his Olympic-inspired vision to reshape the New York economy and physical landscape."

CITY

Deputy Mayor, New York Finds a Champion of Grand Plans and Tiny Details

Continued From Page 29

Mr. Doctoroff, at the Olympic Media Summit on Friday, has an Olympic-inspired vision to resh

> Unelected, and still unknown to many New Yorkers, Mr. Doctoroff has nonetheless been granted extraordinary authority by Mayor Michael R. Bloomberg. He shaped the mayor's speech outlining the future of Lower Manhattan, and oversaw the rezoning of industrial Williamsburg for housing development and the development of a master plan for downtown Brooklyn. And it is Mr. Doctoroff whom Mr. Bloomberg has charged with reinventing a 50-block swath of Manhattan's West Side, transforming it from a collection of tenements and warehouses into the city's third-largest business district, complete with new skyscrapers and a sports stadium.

As New York City recovered from the economic and fiscal crises of the 1970s, public officials and private developers began to focus on the potential for transforming the gritty industrial neighborhood of the Far West Side of Midtown Manhattan into a vibrant residential and commercial community.

A mile removed from Fifth Avenue, this isolated stretch (from 30th to 42nd Streets, Ninth Avenue to the Hudson River) housed a jumble of old industrial buildings, parking lots and garages, approaches to the Lincoln Tunnel, a small smattering of apartment and office buildings, and other underused land.

It was dominated by a massive six-block open pit leading down to the Long Island Rail Road (LIRR) rail storage yards that support Penn Station. While seemingly derelict and not well served by the city's existing transit network, the entire area was close to one of the busiest railroad stations in the United States — Penn Station — and the busiest bus station in North America — the Port Authority Bus Terminal. It was also home to the Javits Convention Center and near Madison Square Garden, the city's premier sports and concert arena.

The Olympic plan sought to take advantage of Manhattan's largest area of underused land — close but not well connected to Midtown and to transportation infrastructure that moves millions of people each day — by putting a transformed Far West Side at the heart of New York's Olympic experience. The plan proposed covering the rail yards with a 26-acre platform to accommodate a new Olympic Stadium that would subsequently be home to the National Football League's New York Jets, about eight acres of public plazas and parks, and millions of square feet of new commercial and residential development. For NYC2012's plans and promotional materials, the new district was called "Hudson Yards."

Doctoroff used the firm deadlines of the Olympic bid to drive this long dreamed of project forward. The scale and speed of these integrated efforts — including a comprehensive rezoning to accommodate about 43 million square feet of new office, retail, and hotel space and 12,600 new housing units; construction of commercial, cultural, and public open space on a deck over the rail yards, the design and financing of a new subway extension into the district; five acres of new parks, the creation or relocation of two major cultural institutions, The Shed and the Whitney Museum of American Art, and saving the High Line — are remarkable, if not unequaled in modern New York history.

New York's Olympic bid proposed an Olympic Stadium on exposed rail yards on Manhattan's Far West Side to catalyze development of a new neighborhood called Hudson Yards. The plan included extending the No. 7 train into the area and creating new public spaces, including the High Line. Right, Hudson Yards, February 2023.

HUDSON YARDS

As early as 1999, Dan Doctoroff — in his capacity as a private citizen heading the city's Olympic bid — had discussions with New York's Department of City Planning (DCP) about the need for rezoning the Far West Side. Under the NYC2012 plan, the Olympic Stadium would be the site of the Opening and Closing ceremonies, athletic events (track and field), and the gold medal match in football (soccer). Sports as diverse as fencing, weightlifting, wrestling, judo, tae kwon do, and table tennis would be contested one block north at an expanded Javits Convention Center. And in the final version of the plan, Olympic basketball would be played at nearby Madison Square Garden.

NYC2012's work on the Far West Side coincided with an effort by DCP to prepare its own rezoning plan that covered largely the same territory. Like the vision articulated by NYC2012, DCP's plans proposed higher-density commercial and residential development, supported by improved transit access, new parks, and other amenities, as well as an expanded Javits Convention Center. At the same time, the report of the Group of 35, created by U.S. Senator Chuck Schumer, called for development of the Far West Side to meet the city's future needs for commercial space.

In 2002, when Doctoroff became deputy mayor, all these efforts were combined in a single drive working with DCP, led by Amanda Burden, to complete the rezoning process before the International Olympic Committee (IOC) met in mid-2005 to make its decision. The product of that joint effort was a proposal to rezone a 50-block area — now widely known as Hudson Yards.

The new Hudson Yards Special Zoning District extended from 28th and 30th Streets on the south to 42nd and 43rd Streets on the north, and from Hudson River Park on the west, to Eighth Avenue (with an extension east to Seventh Avenue to include Madison Square Garden and Penn Station) on the east. After extensive review and public discussion, the New York City Council approved the rezoning in January 2005.

Hudson Yards represented one of the largest and most comprehensive zoning changes in the city's history. As Doctoroff foresaw, connecting the effort to the timetable for submission of the city's bid to the IOC made it possible to accomplish this major action in less than three years, making it one of the most remarkable achievements of the Bloomberg administration.

After several years of delay caused by the global financial crisis of 2008 and the recession that followed, the pace of redevelopment in the Hudson Yards district began to accelerate. As of 2022:

- Nine new buildings with approximately 16 million square feet of office space had been completed or topped out. Additionally, other commercial buildings in the area have seen transformative reinvestment and repositioning such as 450 West 33rd Street (now 5 Manhattan West) and 460 West 34th Street.

- 35 new hotels with over 9,300 rooms had been completed or topped out, and others are in development.

- 32 new residential buildings with a total of more than 12,600 units had been completed or topped out, with others in development.

Planners had eyed the exposed rail yards and derelict lots on Manhattan's Far West Side as potential development sites for decades. Right, the rail yards in 2005.

In January 2005, the City completed a 50-block rezoning, paving the way for 43 million square feet of new development. Above, Hudson Yards, 2018.

In 2019, The Shed, one of the city's most prominent new cultural facilities, opened on 30th Street where the High Line meets the Hudson Yards public plaza. And the transformed Farley Post Office building opened in phases from 2020 to 2022 as the new Moynihan Train Hall along with high-quality office and retail space.

Moreover, the rezoning's impact extended beyond the boundaries of the Hudson Yards District. Between 2002 and 2009, 11 new residential buildings with a total of more than 3,300 units were either completed or scheduled to be completed by 2023 in the area just below the district (from West 27th Street to West 30th Street, and from the West Side Highway to Eighth Avenue).

Also adjacent to Hudson Yards, under a 99-year lease with the United States Postal Service, Tishman Speyer is in the process of

converting about 625,000 square feet of space in the Morgan Annex (on Ninth Avenue) into commercial office space. Columbia Property Trust and L&L Holdings are transforming the historic full-block, Terminal Stores in West Chelsea into 1.2 million square feet of Class A office and retail. In 2022, the State gained approval for the redevelopment of the area around Penn Station.

When it is fully built out — a process expected to take 20 to 30 years — the redevelopment of the entire Hudson Yards area is expected to accommodate nearly 50,000 new residents and more than 150,000 new jobs in an area where, before 2000, only a few thousand people had worked and just a few thousand had lived.

Above: The mosaic, *Funktional Vibrations* which greets people to the No. 7 subway station at Hudson Yards, began as crocheted pieces by fiber artist, Xenobia Bailey. It is among the largest commissioned mosaics in the city's transit network.

Right: Entrance to the No. 7 subway line extension, which opened on September 13, 2005.

NUMBER 7 SUBWAY EXTENSION

Along with the rezoning, improving transit access was probably the most critical factor in the redevelopment of Hudson Yards. Despite its proximity to Penn Station and the Port Authority Bus Terminal, there were no subway lines that directly linked the area to the rest of New York City.

To rectify this, NYC2012 and the City joined with the Metropolitan Transit Authority (MTA) to propose extending the No. 7 subway line from its final stop at Times Square to the proposed Olympic Stadium at 33rd Street and 11th Avenue. During the Games, NYC2012 envisioned that the No. 7 train would form one full axis of the Olympic X, carrying travelers from the Olympic events on the West Side to the hotels, restaurants, and entertainment venues of Times Square and finally to another major cluster of Olympic facilities in Flushing Meadows Corona Park, Queens.

Beyond the benefit to the Olympics, planners and public officials had long understood that extending the No. 7 train was essential to the area's long-term redevelopment. The Department of City Planning had suggested extending the No. 7 train in its 1993 report, *Shaping the City's Future*. The Group of 35 had also argued in its 2001 report that redevelopment of the Far West Side would not be successful unless the subway was expanded to serve the area.

But there would be no MTA funds for the No. 7 extension project for years to come; the MTA capital budget was already under great pressure, especially for the Second Avenue subway and East Side Access projects, each of which still needed billions of dollars and years for completion.

As a result, Doctoroff led a team of financial advisors to devise an innovative financing plan which allowed the City to finance the No. 7 extension itself through the issuance of more than $2 billion in special purpose bonds. These bonds would be repaid from several streams of revenue generated by future development in the Hudson Yards area, including payments in lieu of taxes (PILOTs).

It was the first subway project financed by New York City since the MTA was created. Further, it represented the largest construction project ever to use the creative financing of bonds backed by funds that would be generated by the future development itself, a form of self-financing.

Even after the proposed site for the Olympic Stadium had been moved to Queens — and after the International Olympic Committee selected London to host the 2012 Games — the City moved ahead with its plans for extension of the No. 7 train.

The line began public service in 2015, marking the first new expansion of the New York City subway system since 1989.

Left: A Metropolitan Transportation Authority (MTA) worker prepares for the opening of the No. 7 subway extension. Doctoroff led a team to devise an innovative financing plan for the $2.4 billion, 1.5-mile extension that used special purpose bonds to be repaid by revenue streams generated by the area's future development, making it the first City-funded subway extension since the MTA's creation in 1965.

THE HIGH LINE

The transformation of the High Line into one of the city's premier parks is closely connected to New York's bid for the 2012 Games.

Although the High Line had not been part of the original plan for a new stadium, Doctoroff, the NYC2012 team, and the New York Jets began to understand its potential during the planning process. They realized the High Line could be an innovative above-ground pedestrian walkway that would provide exciting access to the Olympic Stadium, connecting the Meatpacking District, West Chelsea, and the new Hudson Yards neighborhood.

Independent of its connection to the stadium, the Chair of the City Planning Commission, Amanda Burden, was a strong champion of the project and supported the local nonprofit advocacy group, the Friends of the High Line, in its proposal to turn the High Line into an elevated linear park. Doctoroff met with park advocates who used his own logic to argue that repurposing the High Line into a unique community asset could help drive the area's economic development. But according to Doctoroff's own book, *Greater than Ever*, the final impetus for saving the High Line came when the Speaker of the City Council, Gifford Miller, agreed not to oppose NYC2012's plan for a West Side Stadium in return for a commitment from the Bloomberg administration to save the structure and turn it into a park (a commitment he did not honor).

As a result of these factors, in a dramatic reversal of the Giuliani administration's position, the Bloomberg administration began to work with the Friends of the High Line to secure approval by the federal Surface Transportation Board for preservation of the High Line, and to commit millions of dollars in City funds for its preservation and conversion.

Like the Hudson Yards plan, the West Chelsea rezoning was approved in 2005. Thus, the High Line was integrated into the overall Hudson Yards district as part of a network of open spaces that would stretch from Gansevoort Street in the Meatpacking District to West 42nd Street. Under NYC2012's Olympic plan, the High Line was envisioned connecting to a grand Olympic Plaza — the major new public space over the eastern section of the West Side Rail Yards that would host crowds in front of the Olympic Stadium and become a great new gathering place — as well as the Hudson Boulevard, a new avenue designed to create a more walkable neighborhood and enliven street life, and a new park. Many of these public spaces are proceeding, including the park which was subsequently named after Bella Abzug and currently has four of its six segments completed.

Today, the High Line has become one of the city's great public spaces, a major tourist destination and gathering place, a spur to adjacent development, a cultural corridor that connects the new Whitney Museum of American Art building, the arts galleries of West Chelsea, and The Shed, and a sterling example of the adaptive reuse of aging industrial structures, forming the spine of a reimagined West Side.

The High Line converted an abandoned rail line into one of the world's most popular parks, drawing eight million people annually by 2019 — nearly twice the visitorship of the Statue of Liberty — and spurring development in West Chelsea and along Manhattan's Far West Side.

The Olympic plan prioritized the reclamation of the city's decaying and largely abandoned waterfront for recreation, housing, and transportation, reestablishing the historic link between New York and its waterways. It envisioned a series of venues connected to new parks lining the East River in Brooklyn and Queens. This included reviving long-stalled plans to transform the dormant Hunter's Point South neighborhood of Queens into a vibrant residential community as the site of the Olympic Village and integrating scattered proposals to remake the waterfront of Greenpoint and Williamsburg in Brooklyn into a series of new neighborhoods connected by striking waterfront parks.

As was true elsewhere in the city, the Olympic plans for revitalizing the East River waterfront were not all original. Instead, NYC2012 (and later the City under Doctoroff's direction) drew ideas from multiple sources, integrated them into a coherent vision, and by 2005 had greatly accelerated the process of translating that vision into reality.

As deputy mayor, Doctoroff led the Bloomberg administration effort to reclaim one of the city's most historic and important assets and restore it to a central place in New York City's urban experience.

Pier 15, a two-level 50,000 square-foot structure with greenery and seating, is part of the 1.5-mile, $135 million East River Waterfront Esplanade, which transformed a collection of parking lots, salt piles, and empty lots in Lower Manhattan into striking public spaces.

HUNTER'S POINT SOUTH

Located at the western tip of Queens, where Newtown Creek curves into the East River, Hunter's Point was once home to warehouses, factories, vacant lots, railroad tracks, and the current site of the Queens-Midtown Tunnel. In the 19th century, it was the final terminus of trains from Long Island, giving it the feeling of a frontier railroad town. It hosted hundreds of hotels and saloons to support overnight stays by those awaiting the morning ferry. Once the Penn Station tunnels were dug under the East River and completed in 1908, the area began to rely more heavily on its other use: as the site of an early Rockefeller oil refinery along Newtown Creek.

For decades, officials struggled to transform the area — which sits directly across the East River from the United Nations — into a residential neighborhood. In 1983, the Port Authority of New York and New Jersey proposed the construction of apartment towers and office buildings in Hunter's Point, packaged with a similar plan to redevelop the Hoboken waterfront. The New Jersey State Legislature quickly approved the Port Authority's proposal. After extensive negotiations with the administration of Mayor Ed Koch, aimed at ensuring that both the Hoboken and Hunter's Point projects would proceed in tandem, the New York State Legislature also approved the required legislation.

Both the Hoboken and Hunter's Point projects moved slowly, however — in part due to real estate market conditions and the complexities of site assembly, and in part to recurring conflicts in Hoboken over what role the Port Authority should play in the project. In 1991, Governor Mario Cuomo repackaged the Hunter's Point project under the title Queens West and created the Queens West Development Corporation as a subsidiary of the New York State Urban Development Corporation to oversee development. Governor Cuomo offered no new funding for the project, hoping private developers would build on the land. Even when the economy picked up in the mid-1990s, however, progress was slow. Although 15 towers were initially planned for the site, it took 13 years for the first building to break ground. In 1996, the first privately financed building in Hunter's Point, a 42-story apartment tower, began construction.

In 2000, NYC2012 incorporated the southern portion of Hunter's Point into its plan for the 2012 Games as the site of the Olympic Village, with about 5,000 units to be constructed along the shore of Newtown Creek and the East River.

NYC2012 proposed that private developers would finance and construct the Village, which would house 16,000 athletes, coaches, and other team personnel during the Games. After 2012, the Village would become attractive apartments, many at affordable rents, instantly transforming a large waterfront section of Hunter's Point into a fully developed residential neighborhood.

Doctoroff pressed ahead with these plans after the city's Olympic loss, proposing that the City acquire the Village site from the Port Authority to create a major new residential community for working households not well-served by affordable housing programs. The City Council unanimously approved the plan in November 2008, and in June 2009, the City acquired 30 acres of land from the Port Authority and the Empire State Development Corporation.

By 2022, Hunter's Point South included more than 3,500 units of market-rate and affordable housing either completed or under construction (with plans to develop 1,800 additional units), neighborhood retail and community facilities, and an award-winning 11-acre waterfront park.

The proposed Olympic Village site at Hunter's Point South, Queens, was developed into mixed-income housing and an award-winning park.

GREENPOINT-WILLIAMSBURG

Manufacturing dominated the waterfront in the Brooklyn neighborhoods of Greenpoint and Williamsburg for decades. But as the industry declined in the 1970s and 1980s, the waterfront piers began to decay and old factories and warehouses were abandoned. Rising real estate prices in Manhattan led artists and students to move into these aging buildings, often in violation of the area's industrial zoning.

To support residential development along the waterfront, the City needed to amend the zoning code. In 1989, Brooklyn Community Board 1, which covers the two neighborhoods, began to outline its priorities for the waterfront. For the next decade, City officials and community groups debated how to rezone Greenpoint and Williamsburg.

Meanwhile, periodic efforts were also made to open the waterfront to public access. In 1998, the State Legislature earmarked $10 million to acquire a two-block section of an industrial waterfront site between North Seventh and North Ninth Streets in Williamsburg for conversion into a park — a measure that was seen as an alternative to a proposed development of a waste transfer station at the site, which had triggered community outrage.

NYC2012 made redevelopment of this industrial Williamsburg waterfront a major priority. In its 2000 submission to the United States Olympic Committee, NYC2012 proposed a new waterfront park to host the beach volleyball and archery competitions. In 2003, the Bloomberg administration announced plans to rezone major sections of Greenpoint and Williamsburg for both high-rise and low-rise residential construction, along with commercial and mixed-use occupancies, a continuous two-mile-long public esplanade, docks for ferries and water taxis, and a series of waterfront parks.

Responding to community concerns, the 2003 plan extended the proposed Williamsburg waterfront park northward to Bushwick Inlet. NYC2012's Olympic X plan was then revised to shift other sports to the new park, including aquatics (swimming, synchronized swimming, and diving) and the water polo finals, plus beach volleyball.

Two months before the 2005 International Olympic Committee vote, the City Council approved the vast rezoning of a 175-block area of Greenpoint and Williamsburg, which included not only the waterfront but also mixed-use communities inland to encourage residential, commercial, and light industrial activity appropriate to the established neighborhood contexts.

Today, the legacy of the Olympic bid is the transformation of one of the most decayed stretches of waterfront land in New York City into one of the city's most desirable neighborhoods. Between the 2005 rezoning and 2019, the area saw 12,500 new housing units, 11,000 new jobs, and plans were in motion to create 50 acres of new waterfront parks along the East River.

Bushwick Inlet was part of Brooklyn's abandoned industrial waterfront. NYC2012 proposed locating multiple Olympic sports on the site, including aquatics, unlocking years of stalled community efforts to transform the area into a waterfront park. Bushwick Inlet Park became part of the City's 175-block rezoning of Greenpoint-Williamsburg.

EAST RIVER FERRY SERVICE

One of the distinctive features of NYC2012's Olympic bid was the proposed use of ferries to connect many of the competition venues, the Olympic Village, and other sites along the north-south axis of the Olympic X.

As part of their efforts to promote the bid between 2000 to 2005, Doctoroff and other NYC2012 officials took visitors from across the United States and around the world, as well as local officials and the media, on frequent ferry trips along the East River and into New York Harbor. For many, it offered a dramatic new sense of the

city, reminding residents and visitors alike that the city's historic development was a direct result of its great harbor and vast river waterfront and that sites that were seemingly distant by land could be reached quickly and conveniently by ferry.

A few months after the International Olympic Committee selected London to host the 2012 Games, Doctoroff directed the New York City Economic Development Corporation (EDC) and the Department of Transportation (DOT) to begin planning for the development of new, privately-operated ferry services, with a particular focus on

the East River waterfront. As with other aspects of their planning for the Olympics, Doctoroff's team sought to maximize private-sector involvement. They proposed to have the City provide access to waterfront sites and pay for the development of ferry landings, with a private partner managing (and financing) ferry operations.

In 2010, EDC and DOT selected NY Waterway to operate the new East River Ferry. The new service was launched in June 2011, with stops at the Brooklyn Army Terminal, Brooklyn Bridge Park, South Williamsburg, North Williamsburg, Greenpoint, Hunter's Point,

Astoria, East 37th Street and Wall Street; and weekend service from Brooklyn to Governors Island. In 2017, the system expanded under the new name NYC Ferry. Within five years, the network had expanded into all five boroughs and was carrying a weekly average of nearly 120,000 riders.

The Olympic X proposed transporting athletes and spectators by ferries along the East River, catalyzing the development of a new five-borough ferry network. Below, a ferry crossing the East River past Hunter's Point South, Queens.

HARLEM RIVER

Long before the city's Olympic bid, local officials and community residents had spent years trying to redevelop two public facilities along the Harlem River — the historic 369th Regiment Armory in Harlem and the decaying Bronx Terminal Market in the Bronx. The revised bid submitted to the International Olympic Committee in 2004 proposed using both of these sites as venues for Olympic competition. In doing so, it raised awareness of the value of these long-neglected assets and helped set the stage for their redevelopment.

In addition to these facilities, the Olympic bid included a proposal to reclaim portions of the adjacent Harlem River waterfront for competition venues. These areas were later developed into new public parks.

The final piece of the Harlem River Olympic cluster included baseball in a new stadium for the New York Yankees. The Yankees redevelopment project included 55 acres of new public parks, including state-of-the-art track and field facilities, baseball fields, recreational space, and waterfront parks, along with a new Metro-North station.

Mill Pond Park is an 11-acre riverfront park on the Harlem River in the Bronx.

Harlem Children's Zone employees and students meet at the renovated armory in advance of their annual Peace March, 2017.

369TH REGIMENT ARMORY

The historic 369th Regiment Armory is an imposing Art Deco fortress that sits at the upper end of Fifth Avenue along the Harlem River. It was built in 1933 for the 369th Infantry of the New York National Guard — the first African-American unit to fight in Europe during World War I. But over the decades, this historic site fell into disrepair.

In 1985, community activists won landmark status for the building and ultimately secured several hundred thousand dollars for renovations. Despite these efforts, the Armory did not attract public attention or investment. For a time, the City used part of the building as a homeless shelter. The State-owned Armory remained distressed, with Governor George Pataki later describing it as a "decrepit mess."

The Olympic bid — which proposed renovating the Armory to hold Olympic boxing matches — brought the building, its significance, and its need for renovation to prominence as one of Harlem's and the city's great historic sites.

A year after New York lost the Olympic bid in 2005, Doctoroff helped secure more than $6 million in government funding for badly needed renovations — $2.4 million from the City and State and $4 million from the federal government. The renovation provided eight new tennis courts surrounded by 3,000 seats and an electronic scoreboard, three classrooms, a computer room, and a chess lounge.

Today the 369th Regiment Armory serves as a popular community facility offering recreation, coaching, and organized leagues for tennis, volleyball, basketball, martial arts, boxing, gymnastics, and track and field.

The 369th Regiment Armory was originally built in 1933 for the 369th Infantry Regiment, known widely as the Harlem Hellfighters, one of the few Black units in World War I. The renovation created new sports and community facilities while preserving its historic Art Deco facade.

The Bronx Terminal Market, originally built to house food vendors, had been largely abandoned when NYC2012 identified the area as a potential site for multiple Olympic sports. The redevelopment plan spurred by the Olympic bid ultimately resulted in the first modern retail center in the South Bronx and preservation of the building's historic facade.

BRONX TERMINAL MARKET

The Bronx Terminal Market was constructed by New York City in 1935 to house food vendors. For a time, it served as a vibrant facility, first attracting Italian fruit and vegetable sellers, and — beginning in the mid-1960s — Puerto Rican vendors who turned the market into a leading source for tropical fruits and vegetables. Over the decades, however, the building decayed until it stood as a worn out shell covered in graffiti.

In the 1970's, the City entered into a 99-year lease with a private developer, David Buntzman, who was required to renovate and expand the market. But the City and the developer quickly became entangled in a series of disputes over which party was obligated to pay for which improvements. The renovations the City had anticipated never occurred and the market continued to decline. By the mid-1990s, there were only 30 vendors left, compared to 100 during its heyday. Concerns over the structural integrity of the building led to its temporary closure.

New York City's Olympic bid incorporated the Bronx Terminal Market site and surrounding waterfront by proposing to demolish the facility and construct a velodrome for Olympic track cycling and an arena for badminton, along with a food court, broadcast facilities, and parks along the Harlem River.

The need to secure these facilities finally led the City to find a way out of its 20-year stalemate with the developer. In April 2004, the litigation was settled and the Related Companies bought out the remainder of Buntzman's ground lease with the City, pledging to redevelop the market and surrounding area as a retail complex, with a parking garage, park, and waterfront esplanade along the Harlem River.

Under the plan, the historic facade and entrance of the Bronx Terminal Market was preserved. The Related Companies donated the land that would be needed for the proposed velodrome and other facilities to the City. In exchange, the City gave Related the nearby Bronx House of Detention, which had been closed since 2000, to include as part of the redevelopment project.

While New York did not win the right to host the 2012 Games, a comprehensive development plan was now in place with broad community and political support, eliminating the ill-maintained market, and instead bringing much needed modern retail stores to this severely underserved area. In February 2006, the City Council approved the redevelopment plan and the complex opened three years later.

This was the first modern retail center of its kind in the South Bronx. The project provided 1,200 construction jobs plus 2,000 permanent jobs, 60% of which have gone to residents of the Bronx — the county with the highest unemployment rate in New York State.

YANKEE STADIUM AND PARKS

The Yankees and Mets had each lobbied for years for new stadiums. But the State Legislature's rejection of the Far West Side stadium in June 2005 created a crisis for the city's Olympic bid. With the final vote of the International Olympic Committee just weeks away, the Bloomberg administration's discussions with both the Mets and the Yankees were quickly resolved so that the bid could proceed with a viable world-class Olympic Stadium at Citi Field (with the Yankees promising to host the Mets in their new stadium during the 2012 season).

While the City did not win the 2012 Olympic Games, these deals were upheld and work on the two new stadiums began in 2006. Both structures — Citi Field for the Mets, and the new Yankee Stadium — opened on schedule in 2009.

As a condition of the deal with the Yankees, the City agreed to build new parks to replace the acreage lost when Yankee Stadium relocated. This included the new 44-acre Macombs Dam Park and Heritage Field, which included three grass ballfields, a 400-meter track that featured the same surfacing used at the Olympic Games, a turf field with seating for 600 spectators, and basketball and handball courts.

As part of this overall project, the 11-acre, $64 million Mill Pond Park opened on the waterfront just west of the Gateway Center in 2009. It included 16 tennis courts, lawns and trails, and a playground, further helping to realize the Olympic vision of revitalizing neglected waterfront for public use.

In addition to these improvements, the City helped to fund a new Metro-North Railroad station to serve the waterfront district, and provided necessary air and land rights. The station helps to ease vehicle traffic in the neighborhood and provides access to the stadium, parks, and retail center.

Top: The proposed Harlem River Olympic cluster included a new Yankee Stadium, along with new community parks and recreational facilities. These plans advanced even after the Olympic loss.

Right: Mill Pond Park, the Bronx.

Opposite: The new Yankee Stadium opened in 2009.

Flushing was envisioned as one of two major Olympic clusters for the 2012 Games, along with the Far West Side. In the middle of the two clusters sat the proposed site for the Olympic Village. Together, the three sites formed the east-west axis of the X, all connected by the No. 7 train (once it had been extended into Hudson Yards).

The Olympic plan called for Flushing to host eight sports in a mix of new venues and existing facilities, such as the United States Tennis Association National Tennis Center. While not all of the ambitious plans came to pass — most notably, the City never pursued joining and reconfiguring two existing man-made lakes in Flushing Meadows Corona Park to serve as an Olympic rowing course — several did.

The centerpiece of the cluster was a new stadium for the New York Mets that would serve as the Olympic Stadium; Citi Field opened in 2009. The bid also proposed hosting water polo in a long-stalled project to build a new pool complex in Flushing Meadows Corona Park. The Flushing Meadows Corona Park Aquatics Center and Ice Rink opened in 2008.

The Flushing, Queens, Olympic cluster included existing facilities like the United States Tennis Association (USTA) National Tennis Center, a new stadium for the New York Mets that would serve as the Olympic Stadium during the Games, and water polo in a new swimming facility, the Flushing Meadows Corona Park Aquatics Center and Ice Rink.

CITI FIELD

A month before the International Olympic Committee awarded the Games to London, New York State's Public Authorities Control Board declined to approve the financing of the proposed New York Sports and Convention Center, which would have served as both the Olympic Stadium and a football stadium for the New York Jets, and as an extension of the Javits Center's convention and exposition facilities.

The State Legislature's rejection unexpectedly pushed the New York Mets baseball team into the center of the city's planning for the 2012 Games. In a little over 72 hours, city officials came up with an alternative for the Olympic Stadium, entering into an agreement with the Mets to build a new baseball stadium in Queens — to be transformed in 2012 into the Olympic Stadium.

The New York Mets agreed to build — and pay for — a new stadium, estimated to cost $600 million, next to their existing Shea Stadium in Queens, while the City and State agreed to spend $180 million on infrastructure improvements and site preparation. To help reduce the cost of the stadium, the City granted the Mets the right to construct it on City-owned property, foregoing payment for the land.

The proposal for the new stadium — eventually named Citi Field — was approved by the City Council in April 2006, with the Mets pledging to donate 25% of their annual charity spending to groups and programs based in the borough of Queens, to have 25% of stadium construction contracts go to Queens-based firms and workers, and to have a further 25% of construction contracts go to New York City based female- or minority-owned firms. The groundbreaking was in November 2006 and the stadium opened on schedule for the 2009 season.

When NYC2012's initial plans for an Olympic Stadium on Manhattan's Far West Side fell through, the City quickly pivoted and struck a deal with the New York Mets to build a stadium that would host the Games in 2012. Citi Field opened in 2009.

FLUSHING MEADOWS CORONA PARK AQUATICS CENTER AND ICE RINK

Despite having a population of 2.3 million, the borough of Queens has only a few City-run public pools. A pool built for the 1939 World's Fair in Flushing Meadows Corona Park was closed in 1981. After it had been vandalized and used by the homeless as a place to sleep, it was finally demolished by the City in 1996.

Even scarcer than places to swim are places to ice skate. While Rockefeller Center is famous for its winter ice skating rink, the reality is that for a city as large as New York there are few public ice rinks. In the early 2000s, the Queens Museum of Art, located in Flushing Meadows Corona Park, sought to expand by taking over an ice skating rink located within its building. New York City could ill afford to lose this ice skating rink in Queens.

To replace the demolished pool and make room for the museum's expansion, then-Mayor Rudy Giuliani proposed building an indoor ice-skating rink and Olympic swimming pool complex adjacent to the Van Wyck Expressway in the northeast part of Flushing Meadows Corona Park. In 2001, the project broke ground. Work proceeded steadily, with piles driven into the marshy ground to support the building. But in December 2002, work suddenly came to a halt when final bids for the project came in $20 million over the projected budget. Given New York City's budgetary pressures in the wake of the September 11th terrorist attacks, the project seemed doomed.

Instead, Doctoroff revived the pool project by incorporating it into the city's bid as the site for water polo matches. The design was reengineered to be more flexible and cost-effective, including the ability to shift walls to create greater space and expand seating capacity.

Doctoroff helped secure the additional needed funding and the City prepared to resume construction. Despite the end of the Olympic bid in 2005, full funding for the pool and ice rink was now in place, and plans to expand the Queens Museum of Art moved ahead.

A second groundbreaking occurred in September 2005 and the building — known as the Flushing Meadows Corona Park Aquatics Center and Ice Rink — opened in March 2008. Housing an indoor Olympic-sized swimming pool and a National Hockey League-sized ice rink, both of which are fully accessible to handicapped individuals, the facility is the largest recreation building ever constructed in a New York City park. Construction and maintenance problems, however, have limited use of the swimming pool and diving area; after a three-year closure, it reopened in 2023, with more repairs to come.

Like the renovation of the 369th Regiment Armory, the construction of a new swimming and skating complex in Flushing had a history that preceded New York City's bid to host the 2012 Olympic Games — and it similarly had strong support from the local community. But as a result of technical problems, rising costs, and a constrained city budget, the project had been put on hold indefinitely.

Only the pressures of the Olympic bid and its inexorable deadline got the project fully funded, rapidly redesigned, and moving back into construction, so it could become one of the gems of the city's park system and the borough of Queens.

Above: Tennis legend Billie Jean King and Dan Doctoroff escort members of the International Olympic Committee Evaluation Commission through the USTA National Tennis Center in Flushing, Queens.

Opposite: The Flushing complex includes a National Hockey League-sized ice rink.

Top: Plans for a new pool in Flushing, Queens, had stalled when NYC2012 identified the site as a potential host for Olympic water polo matches. The fully accessible Flushing Meadows Corona Park Aquatics Center and Ice Rink opened in 2008.

Top: When completed, the 2,200-acre Freshkills Park on Staten Island will be the second-largest park in New York City. Plans for the site's transformation were accelerated by the city's Olympic bid, which proposed locating equestrian and mountain biking venues inside the new park.

Right: Freshkills Park, formerly the site of the largest landfill in the world, now welcomes everyone from student artists studying the landscape to cyclists taking in the scenery.

FRESHKILLS PARK

In 1999, NYC2012, in partnership with the Giuliani administration, identified Fresh Kills — at that point the largest landfill in the world — as the only location within New York City that could host the Olympic equestrian events. While studying the topography, the Olympic team also determined that a mountain biking facility could be built there as well. The landfill was in the process of being decommissioned and its garbage mounds capped, with a long-term vision to convert the area into a park. The bid team successfully argued that the Olympic deadlines could accelerate these plans.

From 1999 through 2001, Doctoroff and the bid planners developed a plan for hosting the competitions on the site that was consistent with the plans being generated by the Parks Department and the project engineering teams.

The Olympic plan used only a fraction of the site's 2,200 acres, but the venues were conceived of as early trails and facilities that could transform into the first section of a vast new public park.

When Doctoroff entered City Hall, Freshkills Park was one of the Olympic projects that he pushed forward, including accelerating the selection of designers, scoping of the Environmental Impact Statement, and conducting public hearings. After New York lost the bid in 2005, Doctoroff continued to prioritize the project, assigning it to the newly-created Office of Capital Project Development, which coordinated with the Parks Department and the Department of City Planning to accelerate the planning and environmental work — critically important for an environmentally sensitive site.

In 2006, the City released a *Draft Master Plan* and by the end of the Bloomberg administration the City had begun opening sections as public parkland. Today, the plan to restore the entire site for parkland continues with a projected completion date of 2036.

WENDY HILLIARD | Director of Sports, NYC2012, 1999–2005

SPORTS LEGACY: CREATING AN OLYMPIC CITY

People thought we were crazy. You could see it in their faces when we pitched the idea: Hundreds of people diving into the Hudson River and swimming down the West Side of Manhattan as part of the city's first-ever triathlon. They were clearly picturing slime creatures crawling out of the water at the beginning of the course on 99th Street. But as usual, Dan Doctoroff proved the skeptics wrong. The NYC Triathlon started out as one of dozens of improbable feats that the NYC2012 Olympic bid team achieved under Dan's leadership; 21 years and thousands of athletes later, the beloved now-annual event is just one of the ways the bid reshaped the city's sports legacy forever.

I joined the NYC2012 team in 1999 as Director of Sports, overseeing all of the bid's Olympic-related sports initiatives, including youth programming, sports events, and Olympian and Paralympian outreach. At the time, I had recently finished heading up the Women's Sports Foundation, after a career of competing in rhythmic gymnastics and coaching an Olympic athlete. I brought a big network of relationships with other athletes and I had attended four Olympic Games as a commentator but I wasn't really a campaign person. Dan wasn't a sports person. So we both had a steep learning curve.

At the time, New York was not widely perceived as an Olympic sports town. The city has some of the most famous professional sports teams and venues in the world — but if anything, that worked against us in the eyes of the Olympic movement, which celebrates amateurs. Alongside Dan and the bid's executive director, Jay Kriegel, we developed a multi-pronged strategy to combat that misperception.

We started with New Yorkers. New York is a city of subcultures. For any sport you can think of, there's a group working hard somewhere in the five boroughs to stake out a home for it. We charted all the amateur sports communities in the city and reached out to support their work and bring them in on the bid effort, discovering archers in Queens, fencers in Manhattan, wrestlers and weightlifters everywhere.

That was helpful, because we had come late to an unofficial bid process requirement: Hosting national and world championships. Bid cities use these events to prove their ability to stage Olympic-level competitions and win the goodwill of sports federations (whose leadership tends to include multiple voting International Olympic Committee (IOC) members). By the time we started bidding, most of the higher profile sports had already been claimed. The late Setrak Agonian, a local and international wrestling leader, proposed we host the Wrestling World Championships.

This was an opportunity, but at first Dan didn't see it that way. We needed to prove New York City was an Olympic town by hosting a world championship, I told him — and it didn't matter that the sports with the biggest audiences, like track, gymnastics, and swimming, were off the table. We needed to host whatever was left — and no matter what indoor sport we snagged, the finals

U.S. Olympians perform a fencing demonstration on the steps of the New York Public Library to show support for New York's Olympic bid, February 2005.

had to be held at Madison Square Garden. I knew that The Garden cost a (not so) small fortune. I also knew it was essential. So when Dan started yelling, no doubt seeing his hard-won budget evaporating in thin air, I braced myself for a fight.

I stood my ground and explained that the Olympic movement doesn't play favorites as far as the sports are concerned. That every sport mattered equally (at least officially!) — and we could demonstrate our commitment to the Olympic ideals. That New York's best asset was its stage — and wrestlers on the floor of The Garden would be a thrill none of them forgot. It would get us taken seriously.

Dan took a moment to calm down. Then he listened. We drew on New York's amateur sports communities to staff the events and fill the stands for a range of championships, and pulled off some of the most memorable world championships the sports had ever

seen: the World Archery championships in Central Park, World Cup fencing championships, and, of course, wrestling in Madison Square Garden. And when we had to reschedule the wrestling championship — which was scheduled for September 26, 2001 — Dan stayed calm, decisive, and compassionate, keeping us all on track as we canceled, mourned, and rescheduled.

It wasn't easy. New York is many amazing things, but it's not easy — especially given some of the intricate event requirements. For instance, we had to build full saunas off the competition floor in Madison Square Garden to help athletes lose weight before the weigh-ins — when an ounce could be the difference between elimination and qualifying for the Olympics (just add it to the budget!). But — following the tone set by Dan — we approached these events the same way we did every aspect of the bid: We did our homework to master the details and leaned into New York's competitive advantages. That meant executing at the highest level and leveraging the city's iconic sites. Dan had always understood the power of storytelling. Now he was learning how to put that in service of Olympic sports.

He was a dedicated study. One thing about Dan: He always knows what he doesn't know. Just as importantly, and refreshingly, he recognizes that there are people — lots of people! — who know more than he does — and he loves to learn from them. Dan learned about table tennis and badminton and team handball and other sports he had limited experience with before the bid. We traveled together across the world, to Lake Placid to watch the Goodwill Winter Games, to Marrakech for the Olympic Women's conference, Lausanne for International Olympic Committee meetings, Beijing as they prepared for the 2008 Olympics, Sydney, Salt Lake City, and Athens to watch the Games in action, and many more places and he listened as I explained the importance of celebrating diverse athletes, Paralympians, and female athletes at every event. This became a hallmark of our bid.

The Olympians and Paralympians became our best ambassadors and formed the final, and in some ways, most enduring part of our sports strategy. Remarkably, the United States Olympic Committee (USOC) had no records for tracking or reaching former Olympians. So together, Jay Kriegel and I created our own database of athletes who had connections to New York. Ultimately, we connected with over 2,000 current and former U.S. and International Olympians and Paralympians who agreed to support the bid. We brought them together for events, branded them as members of our Circle of Olympians and Paralympians, and celebrated them in ways some hadn't experienced since their competition days. Today, athletes still tell me what it meant to be sought out and reconnected to the community that at times seemed to have left them behind. That's a legacy that lives in them — and it sparked a greater commitment by the USOC and subsequent bid cities to keep in touch with athletes. That effort continues today.

Above: Wendy Hilliard, Director of Sports for NYC2012.

Left: Young gymnasts from the Wendy Hilliard Gymnastics Foundation.

Left: Paralympic athletes perform a sitting volleyball demonstration in Times Square, 2012.

Below: Karate students perform in Rockefeller Center to rally support for NYC2012 in advance of the International Olympic Committee vote on the site of the 2012 Olympic Games.

Above: Cardinal Hayes High School Track & Field team practice at Joe Yancey Track, a state-of-the-art 400-meter track with Olympic-quality surfacing, in Macombs Dam Park, the Bronx, 2010.

Two-time U.S. Olympic fencer, Nzingha Prescod, was born in Brooklyn and studied fencing at the Peter Westbrook Foundation. Right, Prescod training at the New York Fencers Club, 2015.

Ours was also the first bid to include the Paralympic Games as equally important to the Olympic Games and to include Paralympians in the planning. When we had athletes celebrating the ball drop in Times Square, Olympians and Paralympians both participated. We highlighted them in our marketing campaigns and they traveled with us to most international events. That level of respect and community was deeply ingrained into the planning from the beginning — and has continued through bids today.

Transforming New York into an Olympic city meant taking a closer look at ideas that seemed absurd on their surface — like, for instance, putting swimmers in the Hudson River. But Dan was always ready to consider a bold idea and sports were no exception. As a leader, Dan was something like a great coach: tough but fair, expecting excellence from himself and everyone else, but fundamentally valuing his team as people. In terms of intensity, my experience of working on the bid was second only to my training as an athlete. And Dan never held himself above the fray, though he could have. When some swimmers got caught in currents that were stronger than expected during the first triathlon, Dan grabbed my rickety bicycle and rushed down to the dock — to rescue them himself, I think. (Thankfully, in the end, nothing so drastic was needed!)

Like a match that doesn't go your way, the campaign — even though it was "unsuccessful" — still changed so many lives. In addition to ongoing events like the triathlon, there is a legacy of elite level sports facilities — including Icahn Stadium on Randall's Island and the Flushing Meadows Corona Park Aquatics Center and Ice Rink in Queens — that were built as potential Olympic training sites or to capitalize on the Olympic enthusiasm that swelled across the city.

Since the bid, other elite facilities have been integrated into the city's sports landscape (many of them projects championed by Dan), such as the Ocean Breeze Athletic Complex on Staten Island, which became the first indoor track facility in the nation to be certified by the International Association of Athletics Federations and was part of Dan's PlaNYC sustainability plan. Or the championship level ballfields and track facilities at Macombs Dam Park in the Bronx, which were built as part of the Yankee Stadium relocation project (which happened, of course, as a result of the bid). These facilities and others have opened a path to training and competition for New Yorkers that never existed before.

I can personally attest to how the institutions, communities, and spaces developed in the course of the bid have had a lasting impact for sports in the city. Row New York was founded in 2002, during the heart of the city's Olympic push, with the goal of introducing rowing to disadvantaged students across the city and providing them with academic support. According to the rowing website Row2K, it's since become "one of the world's flagship programs for outreach in the sport," and in 2020, the founder, Amanda Kraus, became the CEO of U.S. Rowing, the sport's national governing body.

My own organization, the Wendy Hilliard Gymnastics Foundation, celebrated its 25th year in 2022. We've grown from 10,000 athletes when the bid started to almost 25,000 today. Since the bid began, New York has produced dozens of Olympians and Paralympians, including many from programs we worked with; one of them — Manhattan's Peter Westbrook Foundation — has sent an Olympic fencer to every Games since the year 2000. Now people think about youth sports in this city as a long-term project, with an Olympic finish line.

Dan once said that no city embodies the Olympic spirit more than New York City. It's true. What other people love about the Olympics are the things New Yorkers live with and embody every day: all the different cultures coming together, the ambition, the passion, the excellence. As we used to say on the bid, New York is an Olympic Village every day. Whether it was swimmers in the Hudson or archers in Central Park, bidding for the Olympics amplified the city's essential character. And at its core, New York is, and always has been, an Olympic city.

Dan Doctoroff and others founded the New York City Triathlon in 2001 as part of the city's Olympic bid and it now draws thousands of competitors annually. Triathletes swim through the Hudson River as part of the course.

THE OLYMPIAN PERSPECTIVE

BOB BEAMON | Olympic Champion, Long Jump

Once-in-a-Generation Talent

After my record-setting leap at the 1968 Mexico City Games, some people started using the word "Beamonesque" to describe an athletic feat so superior to previous efforts that it was overwhelming. That's how I feel about Dan Doctoroff.

I'm from New York. I knew we were an Olympic city in our hearts — and I also understood why the Games had never come here before. The vision, willpower, ambition, delusion, and dedication required to pull off a Games in this place — well, just like setting a record that could hold for years, it needed once-in-a-generation talent. That's Dan. I could tell immediately he had the vision, knowledge, and insight into the Five W's — Who, When, Where, What, and Why — to bring this project to fruition. So even though I was living in Miami at the time, I agreed to join the effort, putting in long travel hours with Dan on behalf of the bid. Dan didn't just have a vision — he understood the importance of a team and his enthusiasm, love for the city, respect for our experiences as Olympians (and Paralympians), and passion for the Games motivated us through the finish line. We didn't win. But I loved reconnecting with my hometown, my fellow athletes, the new generation of track and field kids who came to watch us and cheer on the bid at Olympic events we held all over the city.

Dan once told me that he fell in love with the Olympic Games watching me compete in 1968. But competing together, on behalf of New York, was something I'll never forget. And now one of my favorite Olympic legacies is the friendship we share.

Olympian Bob Beamon, Mayor Michael Bloomberg, and Olympian Donna de Varona announce that New York has been selected as one of the International Olympic Committee's (IOC) Candidate Cities for the 2012 Games.

Olympic gold medalist Bob Beamon's record-setting long jump, 29.2 feet (8.9 meters), at the Summer Olympic Games in Mexico City, 1968.

BART CONNER AND NADIA COMANECI
Olympic Champions, Gymnastics

The Perfect Choice

We could tell we liked Dan Doctoroff from the very first moment when we met. His warm smile, strong handshake, and genuine demeanor made us feel welcome and important right away. It was clear to us then that Dan was the perfect choice to spearhead the NYC2012 Olympic bid.

Despite enormous geopolitical odds against New York City hosting the Games, Dan's enthusiasm never wavered. The thing we most remember about working with Dan was the fact that even though he was building a plan to host one of the most challenging and complex events in the world, he always made the athletes feel like they were the absolute center of the equation.

Many bids talk about an "athlete-centered Games." Dan's commitment to give the athletes a chance to play on the world's greatest stage was truly genuine.

It is a great honor to be Dan's friend, and we are grateful for the time that we worked together on events in New York, as well as our eventful trip to Singapore to proudly present New York as a potential host city of the Olympic Games.

Dan insisted that all of the diverse people and neighborhoods of New York City had a chance to feel that they had a crucial role to play in the success of the Games. This was truly an inclusive mindset that, in our opinion, has transformed the bid process and forever improved the value proposition of the Olympic and Paralympic movement.

Top: Olympic gold medalists Bart Conner and Nadia Comaneci, after the NYC2012 presentation to the IOC in Singapore, July 2005.

Above: Nadia Comaneci competing at the 1976 Summer Olympics in Montreal, Canada; Bart Conner at the 1984 Summer Olympics in Los Angeles, California.

DONNA DE VARONA | Olympic Champion, Swimming | Consultant, NYC2012 | Member of the Executive Board, U.S. Olympic & Paralympic Committee

A True Champion

The passion Dan has for the Olympic movement was a gift to New York City and to all of us who he drew into his circle. My regret is that in another time, during another Olympic bidding cycle, Dan could have realized his dream of bringing the Olympics to the Big Apple. He is just what this movement needed, an honest, detail-oriented visionary. A charismatic leader who continues to devote his intellect, time, and passion to his family and his community. He meets every challenge head on while calling on his deep ties to the political, business, philanthropic, sports, and entrepreneurial communities in the city he loves. I was extremely honored to work with Dan and the team he built. His energy was contagious and as we planned and traveled we became a family. Many of us have stayed connected with each other and he to us.

Thank you, Dan, for daring to dream, for continuing to stay involved by serving on the United States Olympic and Paralympic Committee even though New York did not win the bid to host the 2012 Olympics. Thank you for inspiring us all to envision and plan for prosperity beyond the tragedy of 9/11, for sharing your hopes and plans to tackle the setbacks driven by the COVID-19 pandemic. You continue to inspire as you fight your own personal health battle. A true champion meets a setback with a comeback. You are the very definition of a true champion.

Olympic gold medalist Donna de Varona, training in advance of the 1964 Olympic Games in Tokyo.

VICTOR CALISE | Paralympian, Para Ice Hockey | Accessibility Coordinator, Department of Parks & Recreation, 2006–2012 | Commissioner, Mayor's Office for People with Disabilities, 2012–2022

ACCESSIBILITY LEGACY: FROM THE PARALYMPICS TO PARKS

"Our city is so much more accessible because of the catalyst of the bid."

When Victor Calise left city government in 2022, he became the rare commissioner to earn his own editorial in the *New York Daily News*, which urged Mayor Eric Adams to fill his role swiftly with a person of "similar independence." Calise, who led the Mayor's Office for People with Disabilities under three separate mayors, had become known as a fierce advocate of improving the city's accessibility.

It is less widely known that his path to government began with New York City's Olympic and Paralympic bid. The Queens-born Calise, who was paralyzed in an accident at the age of 22, competed in the 1998 Nagano Paralympic Games in sled hockey. When he learned of New York's bid for the 2012 Games, he understood its potential to elevate disability issues. Curious to learn more about the project, he attended an NYC2012 press conference at City Hall with bid founder Daniel Doctoroff — and ended up answering a question about the Paralympics.

When Calise reached out to Doctoroff to discuss the bid further, he "immediately met with me," Calise said. "Hold us accountable," he said Doctoroff told him. "Go out there, don't hold back."

"For me, it was like, I got the blessing," Calise said. He vowed to push on disability issues, knowing he could reach out to Doctoroff if he met resistance. "But I never needed to because Dan must have gotten the message to everybody that this was important."

Calise's work at the bid translated into a career in government transforming New York's accessibility landscape, including accessible playgrounds, beaches, parks — and, famously, hiring Mayor Michael Bloomberg's passionate sign language interpreter to join him for television appearances during Superstorm Sandy, which set a new national standard for emergencies. "It was a great time in my life," Calise said. "I got involved in a bid, and made some considerable change."

I grew up in Ozone Park, Queens and I was a plumber. I was downhill mountain bike riding in Forest Park, Queens, and I flew over my handlebars into a tree. I injured my spinal cord when I was 22 years old. After that, I got immediately involved in adaptive sport. I found sled hockey and was passionate about it, and eventually made the first USA Paralympic sled hockey team that went to Nagano, Japan [in 1998]. Would I make the team today? That's debatable.

After the Paralympic Games, I heard about the [NYC2012] bid. It was a proud moment to be a New Yorker. It was good to see people come together and show that New York pride, and be able to get on the world stage and say, "We have the ability to do this." I knew the impact the bid would bring if people with disabilities were involved. Dan knew what disability was, he got it, and he understood it because of the history of ALS in his family. He knew that people with disabilities needed to have the same access that everyone else did. He was pretty adamant about that and how it meant something to him. So I knew right there I had an ally.

The [United States Olympic Committee] and the bid were presenting to the International Olympic Committee and I was asked to participate. It was at Randall's Island at Icahn Stadium, and I rolled next to this guy. I said, "Hi, I'm Victor Calise." And he goes, "Hi, I'm Adrian Benepe," and I was like, "Pleased to meet you." And then it clicks in my head that it's the Commissioner of the Parks Department, and I'm like, "I'm Victor Calise, *very* pleased to meet you," and I automatically do what I do. I said, "It's sad that other park systems around the country help disabled athletes, and I really don't see much coming from the Parks Department." Adrian and I struck up a very good conversation.

I eventually ended up getting a job at the Parks Department as their first ADA [Americans with Disabilities Act] Coordinator. I mentioned earlier that I was a plumber, so I was able to take my plumbing and my blue collar expertise at the time and really embed it into disability design. The first thing we did was make our beaches accessible. Then we worked on making our indoor and outdoor pools accessible by putting lifts in. Then we slowly worked on bathrooms to make them more accessible throughout the Parks Department. We added wheelchair softball fields, wheelchair football fields. We did them in every borough.

The idea was that, if you're a kid with a disability, you're a parent with a disability or a grandparent, you're able to use this space in a way that is totally accessible to you. I would argue now that New York City is the most accessible park system in the world.

I worked on a lot of different initiatives for the bid. I often think that people forget about the disability aspect and the things that we drove in the architecture. But it was firmly planted. Hudson Yards became fully accessible. There was the redesign of Citi Field. There was the redesign of Yankee Stadium. The old stadiums didn't have accessibility built into them. Citi Field and Yankee Stadium went over and beyond what they needed to do. [The process] was led by people with disabilities and there was real action. It could be something like putting plugs in the seating area, so people can recharge their wheelchairs. I'm pretty sure now they use them for phones. I mean, we didn't even have phones then.

[For Citi Field] we were able to make a station accessible for game day that was never accessible before, and that was all because I was part of the bid, part of the Parks Department.

Then they were building the recreation center in Queens. We were able to build the first sled hockey accessible rink in the country at that time.

I was the first ADA Coordinator in the City of New York. When I moved on to Commissioner, I took the model of the Parks Department and worked to implement that [across] other agencies. I took PlaNYC and turned it into Accessible NYC.

Government was never on my radar — ever. To say that Dan helped me get into government is absolutely fair and true. If it wasn't for Dan, I wouldn't have met Adrian. And if I didn't meet Adrian, I wouldn't have been involved in government and I wouldn't have had the experiences and the life-changing things that I've done for people with disabilities throughout New York City.

If you look at the state of accessibility in the time of the bid, now it's drastically different. Our city is so much more accessible because of the catalyst of the bid.

LESSONS IN LEADERSHIP: AFTER DEFEAT, THE DREAM ENDURED

Two days before Dan Doctoroff flew to Singapore to persuade the International Olympic Committee that New York should host the 2012 games, he called my Senate office and asked if I wanted to join him. I immediately said yes.

Rearranging a highly-managed schedule and flying around the world to support an unlikely Olympic bid might sound foolish, but only if you don't know Dan. He has an extraordinary talent for seeing the bigger picture, for making the impossible seem possible, and for inspiring the people around him to join him in getting to work. When he started championing the idea of bringing the Olympics to New York City in the early 1990s, Dan was one of the few people who thought it was a good idea. And he was right. He saw the once-in-a-generation opportunity to transform the city and catalyze major projects that would bring new investments, good jobs, and economic growth to the Big Apple. I wanted to do whatever I could to help make his vision for New York a reality.

Dan had painstakingly built a credible bid, fulfilled all the preliminary requirements for hosting the Games, and enlisted everyone from Serena Williams and Magic Johnson to President George W. Bush (and my husband!) to record a video of support. He had spent years incorporating expertise from city planners, athletes, and immigrant communities across the five boroughs to develop his plan. His dream was to revitalize underdeveloped areas in the city and ensure that visiting athletes and dignitaries would experience a revitalized, vibrant New York that was recovering from 9/11 but steeped in Olympic excitement.

Everyone was disappointed when we didn't win the bid, but I wouldn't have missed that trip to Singapore for the world, regardless of the end result. I remember talking to Dan on the flight home. He was exhausted and dismayed that this long-shot campaign had ended, but I told him that things have a way of working out in time and in their own way.

And indeed, Dan's vision of the future wasn't gone, it just changed a little. He didn't give up on the development plans he originated for the Olympic bid. Many of them, like the Hudson Yards project, have since changed the face and skyline of New York City. His dream for an Olympic Village in Queens turned into the city's largest affordable housing development since the 1970s. Ferry service on the East River, new parks, and even a new Yankee Stadium, Citi Field, and the Barclays Center in Brooklyn all began with Dan's bid to bring the Olympics to New York.

Over the years, I've watched Dan celebrate many projects he shepherded to completion. But my fondest memories of him are from that trip to Singapore, presenting his utopian idea of a New York City Olympiad — championing a dream he had nurtured for so long, on behalf of a city and country he loved so much.

As he put it in an email to friends during the 2012 Olympics hosted in London, "New York really is an Olympic Village every day." His creativity, resourcefulness, and determination made sure of it — and the nearly nine million people who call the city home are his grateful beneficiaries.

Senator Hillary Rodham Clinton applauds as Mayor Michael Bloomberg and Deputy Mayor Dan Doctoroff celebrate after presenting the NYC2012 plan to the International Olympic Committee in Singapore, July 6, 2005.

Deputy Mayor Dan Doctoroff and Senator Hillary Rodham Clinton arrive in Singapore for New York's final presentation to the International Olympic Committee for the right to host the 2012 Games, July 2005.

Billy Crystal, Mayor Michael Bloomberg, and Deputy Mayor Dan Doctoroff celebrate New York City being selected as the U.S. candidate city to host the 2012 Summer Olympics, November 2, 2002.

BILLY CRYSTAL | Actor and Comedian

A Pitch for the Games

Dan Doctoroff fought tirelessly to bring the 2012 Olympics to the city he loved. I got involved with the effort because of Dan's passion. A passion that echoed my own thoughts imagining the world's greatest athletes performing on the biggest stage in the city where I was born. I remember thinking when he approached me … why me? Dan told me that humor is a great communicator, and, combined with knowledge and facts, it would be a formidable tool. He encouraged me to be unique in my presentation and use my sense of humor and creativity to create an impassioned plea to the U.S. Olympic Committee. It was a thrill to join forces with Dan and Mayor Bloomberg and the entire staff as we tried valiantly to bring the world to New York City for the 2012 Olympic Games.

THE RESILIENT CITY

9/11 Tribute in Light,
September 11, 2020.

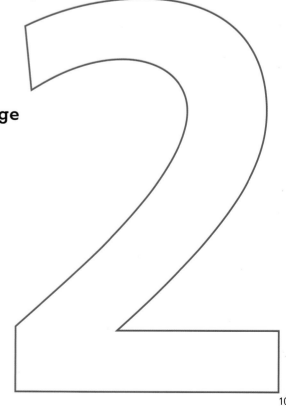

"New York has a rich tradition of stepping up and transforming itself whenever things seem at their worst."

DANIEL L. DOCTOROFF, APRIL 2003

New York Harbor with view of Lower Manhattan and the new One World Trade Center, 2014.

MIKE WALLACE | Historian | Co-Author, *Gotham: A History of New York City to 1898* | Winner of the Pulitzer Prize

A NEW DEAL FOR NEW YORK

Dan Doctoroff led a rebuilding effort that transformed the catastrophe of 9/11 into an opportunity to reimagine and strengthen New York City for new generations

On September 11, 2001, I was happily settling into a year's residency at the New York Public Library's Center for Scholars and Writers. My intention was to work on the history of New York City in the 20th century — a follow-up volume to my previous book, *Gotham: A History of New York City to 1898*. I had just plunged into the Second World War and was reading about U-boat attacks in New York Harbor when the World Trade Center was destroyed.

I pivoted to write an unusual document for a historian: a slim 99-page call to action — less a historical account than an intervention in an urgent public debate — called, *A New Deal for New York*. The book prompted an equally unusual call for me personally: I was invited down to City Hall to speak with the Deputy Mayor for Economic Development and Rebuilding, Daniel Doctoroff. It was the first time I, a historian who had been studying and teaching about New York for more than three decades, had been summoned to confer with the city's political leadership. We discussed my idea that 9/11 was an opportunity to reimagine Lower Manhattan — but also to rethink the city's economy and future, drawing on New York's enduring ability during its 400-year history to turn catastrophe into opportunity, emerging stronger than before.

When I was approached about this current project and had a chance to reflect on the last 20 years, it was clear that Doctoroff agreed with that analysis.

New York's resurgence since the terrorist attacks has indeed become another story to cite in history books — an example of the city's resilience in the face of crisis and ability to reinvent itself when a more timid metropolis might have been lost. When we met, Doctoroff had clearly studied New York's history and understood something eternal in the heart of the city, a spirit of bold reinvention and sense of possibility that he used to guide the City's response. Still, when I left his office, success was far from a foregone conclusion.

September 11th made starkly manifest the interconnecting ties that bind our immensely complicated civic organism. Shock waves juddering out from the blast site set off cascading chains of collateral damage (fear of flying led to a drop in tourism, led to hotel layoffs, led to besieged soup kitchens). "Missing" posters in the subways and capsule biographies in The Times made clear the distances from which people had come to their fatal Downtown rendezvous. Stabbed in Manhattan, we bled in the boroughs and the suburbs, too.

The redeveloped World Trade Center site, as seen from Midtown Manhattan, 2014.

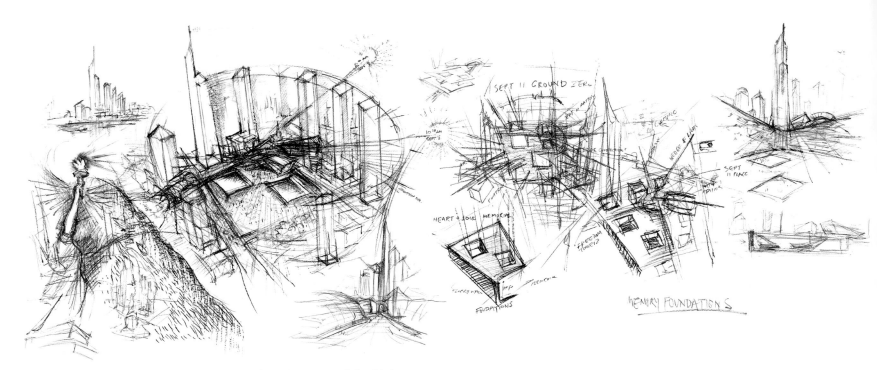

Concept sketches for the World Trade Center site by architect, Daniel Libeskind.

Renewed awareness of, and attention to, our common weal came just in time. September 11th — and the recession it accompanied and exacerbated — yanked to the front burner a host of problems left too long a-simmer. The attack, in making chronic conditions acute, helped galvanize the will to confront them. It also cracked open conventional ways of thinking about how to tackle our dilemmas. For nearly a quarter century, since the so-called fiscal crisis of the 1970s and Reaganism's subsequent triumph on the national scene, reigning mantra-makers had chanted the ineffectuality, indeed the impermissibility, of purposive public action. In the harsh aftermath of the Twin Towers, the fantasy of privateers — that passive reliance on the "free market" cures all ills — suddenly came to seem tired, timid, an altogether inadequate response to challenge.

Starting from Ground Zero, Lower Manhattan, and the immediate imperatives of rebuilding and memorializing, I used my book to consider some of the proposals — many of them splendid and imaginative — that addressed the future of the entire city. I also promised to reevaluate them over time, to assess how far we had — or hadn't — come. Two decades later, and on the eve of the city's 400th birthday, this updated essay represents that effort.

Ground Zero
No sooner had it stopped snowing ghastly ash then some urged rebuilding the Twin Towers, exactly as they had been. This was quickly deemed problematic, partly on prudential grounds. Terrorists had attacked the complex twice, after all, and daring them to take a third shot (while meanwhile hunkering down in bunker mode) seemed pleasingly defiant but seriously impractical. Nor was replication really in the Gotham grain. Warsaw meticulously resurrected itself after World War II, but New York, when wounded, has always opted for new and improved versions of its former self.

With the cloning option set aside, opinion shifted quickly toward wholesale and rapid construction of up-to-date office buildings, enough to replace (or exceed) the 13 million square feet of horribly imploded space. Given that more square footage had been lost

than existed in all of central Atlanta, erecting new towers seemed imperative lest the Financial Center decamp, and the area lose its third-place ranking on the list of America's largest office concentrations, just behind Midtown Manhattan and Chicago. Developers called for mammoth subsidies, and the waiving of zoning and environmental regulations, so that structures could be shot up swiftly. This insistence subsided as awareness set in that, due to recession and relocation, Downtown was awash with millions of square feet of vacant offices.

For a long time, what happened was nothing. Four years after the attacks, the 16 acres remained a ragged gash in Lower Manhattan. Nothing was built — not out of conviction, but because the parties were paralyzed and secretive.

One of the great ironies is that the State controls very few properties in New York City, and if the attack had been against nearly any other site, the local government would have had primary responsibility. But New York City had no legal authority at the World Trade Center site, which was owned by the bi-state entity known as the Port Authority of New York and New Jersey, and controlled by the private developer, Larry Silverstein, who had signed a 99-year lease on the Twin Towers and other parts of the site less than two months before the attacks. As State leadership and Silverstein bickered over insurance payouts and rebuilding plans, the city was left to stare for years at the raw, still, black hole in its heart.

Despite the City's lack of power at the World Trade Center site, Doctoroff managed to exert strong influence over key elements of the rebuilding: First, using his team's financial expertise to understand and then renegotiate a path forward for the rebuilding, and second using his vision and his team's planning expertise to focus rebuilding efforts on Lower Manhattan beyond Ground Zero, where the City had enormous authority.

Doctoroff used the one slim lever the City had — its half of $3.35 billion of tax-free Liberty bonds that had been part of the federal

Despite having no legal authority at the 16-acre site, which is owned by the Port Authority of New York and New Jersey, the Bloomberg administration worked publicly and behind the scenes to unstick negotiations around the redevelopment and new memorial.

recovery package — to force Silverstein to release financial records showing there was not enough money to rebuild. The gap was substantial: by some estimates as much as $6 billion.

Doctoroff then forged an alliance with the New Jersey side of the Port Authority and the New Jersey governor to force Silverstein to renegotiate the deal. With the new terms in place, rebuilding began at once.

In December 2002, Mayor Michael Bloomberg unveiled the *Vision for Lower Manhattan*, crafted by Doctoroff and his team, which focused on public investments in parks, transportation, housing, and schools. At the World Trade Center site, this translated into City support for plans that focused on reweaving the former superblock into the cityscape, replacing the vast and often desolate WTC plaza with New York's traditional gridded streets.

Along these new plowed streets Doctoroff's plan supported a combination of residences, offices, cultural institutions, and the kinds of retail shops once hidden below ground in the WTC's cavernous mall — a mixed set of uses intended to restore vigor and life to a place so marked by death.

In other words, as part of his rebuilding portfolio, Doctoroff began looking beyond the Ground Zero site to the broader challenge of Lower Manhattan.

A new approach to Lower Manhattan

In the 18th century, in the vicinity of today's courthouse complex at Foley Square sat the Collect Pond, a little inland lake hemmed in by hills, sited squarely athwart the pathways heading up-island. The Collect, in turn, drained off east, through swampy wetlands toward the East River, and west, through broad pasture land, swamps, and salt marshes, toward the Hudson. This western stretch (from Duane Street on the south to Spring Street on the north) was known as Lispenard's Meadows. It all but cut Manhattan in two: Small boats could navigate the sluggish stream that ran from pond to river. In 1733, to mitigate the swamp's "unwholesome vapors," the stream was turned into a trench, creating a barrier formidable enough to warrant throwing two stone bridges across it, at Broadway, and today's Greenwich Street.

By 1803, the Collect Pond, long a dumping ground for noxious effluvia from nearby slaughterhouses, tanneries, breweries, and potteries, had become New York's first ecological disaster zone; it was ordered filled with "wholesome earth." To drain the underground springs, the Hudson-bound trench was expanded (by 1811) into an eight-foot-wide, plank-sided canal, flanked by roadways. It, too, became an open sewer, and was converted to a covered one, which runs beneath Canal Street to this day.

If we accept this watery subterranean frontier as Lower Manhattan's outer limit — and there are substantial historical as well as ecological grounds for doing so — then the territory

Lower Manhattan was home to the first colonial settlements, establishing it as the historic heart of New York City. Here St. Paul's Chapel, built in 1766, and One World Trade Center, which opened more than 200 years later, in 2014.

properly includes Chinatown, Tribeca, the City Hall complex and the East River housing projects, not just the Financial Center, whose future dominated most of the early conversations about the area's post 9/11 future.

Yet for all the initial focus on doing whatever it took to keep the Financial Center at the island's southern tip, there was a growing awareness that Lower Manhattan long ago forfeited sole right to that title. Arguably, Lower Manhattan lost its unchallenged predominance back in the 1920s, after Midtown had established direct rail links (Grand Central, Penn Station) to the ever-expanding suburbs. Midtown developers reared their own great office towers, which soon overmatched Downtown's both in height and numbers — a victory symbolized by the triumph of the Chrysler Building (Midtown's champion) over 40 Wall Street (Downtown's contender) in the great race at decade's end to build the city's tallest tower.

After a construction hiatus during the Depression and World War II, Downtown continued to languish while Midtown surged. Part of the problem was that starting in the early 1950s and accelerating in the late 1960s, many corporate headquarters followed the white middle class to the suburbs, relocating near the Westchester, Connecticut, and New Jersey abodes of top executives. This allowed senior staff to escape the ever more grueling commute to the city (and facilitated quick getaways to the golf course). The number of Fortune 500 companies resident in Manhattan plummeted from 140 in 1956 to 98 by 1974.

The roller coaster economy swung upward again in the 1980s — bequeathing Lower Manhattan the World Financial Center and its residential correlative at Battery Park City, among other new structures — but the exodus of corporate headquarters and financial sector jobs continued.

In the late 1980s and early 1990s, the economy lurched downward yet again. Downtown was hardest hit: By the mid-90s, more than 60 million square feet of office space sat empty — a quarter of the total stock, the equivalent of six vacant World Trade Centers.

One City and State response was to offer remaining companies, especially those considering flight, huge financial incentives to stay. Faced with a potential loss of 12,000 commodities exchange jobs, the Dinkins administration (together with the State) set in motion $145 million in tax breaks for the big four exchanges. Similar payouts were arranged for Morgan Stanley, which had been debating moving its headquarters and 4,200 jobs to Stamford ($86 million); for Bear Stearns ($30 million); for Prudential ($106 million); and for many others, even though loss of public revenues sped layoffs of public employees. More proactively, the City tried to convince determined departees to resettle within the five boroughs; in 1988, Mayor Ed Koch gave Chase $235 million — the largest corporate retention deal yet — for moving 5,000 jobs into Brooklyn's MetroTech Center, rather than to Jersey City.

And yet, in 2000, Chase began moving thousands more employees from Lower Manhattan to Sam LeFrak's Newport complex in Jersey City. Awaiting them on the farther shore — now called by some Manhattan's West Bank — were the likes of Goldman Sachs, Merrill Lynch, and PaineWebber.

During this exodus, the Giuliani administration accelerated its corporate retention program, loosing an avalanche of 49 mega-tax breaks that totaled nearly $2 billion. Canny companies with no intention of leaving New York had but to bat their eyes in Jersey's

direction to trigger a handout. Many firms — Bear Stearns, ABC, Bertelsmann — got lucrative abatements without even threatening to relocate; some were previous recipients, back for a second helping. Ruthless to the poor, Rudy rolled over for the powerful, a complaisance culminating in his agreement to provide the New York Stock Exchange with $1.1 billion to stay Downtown (he hailed its December 1998 acceptance of this largesse as "a Christmas gift to the city").

No doubt the $2 billion in tax breaks and subsidies halted some departures, and no doubt city officials were structurally vulnerable to such extortion. But too many expensive concessions went to industries that considered their Manhattan location vital. Claims that giveaways were offset by jobs created and taxes reaped were found suspect. Of 80 aided firms, half later ordered major layoffs, according to a Center for an Urban Future study. Merrill Lynch got $28.5 million in 1997 to create 2,000 jobs and retain 3,888 others, then fired 1,800 people in 2000. (Fortunately, some companies split before slow moving bureaucrats had disbursed their funds). Nor did the City require its recipients to disclose the percentage of employees that lived within the five boroughs: Those few that did volunteer the information revealed that nearly half their workers lived elsewhere. We clearly needed, in the booming 90s, a tougher poker player in City Hall.

That arrived in the form of Mayor Bloomberg and Doctoroff, who immediately analyzed the situation and concluded, "almost always, the companies and their legions of consultants played the City," as Doctoroff wrote in his own book, *Greater than Ever*. They came up with a new policy, he wrote: "We would not pay companies to stay in New York." In particular, Doctoroff concluded that the billion-dollar New York Stock Exchange subsidy, "was a really dumb deal." He and his team advised Bloomberg to reject the giveaway — and the mayor agreed. The New York Stock Exchange fumed and threatened — then stayed in New York anyway.

The question remained: What to do about Lower Manhattan? Even after the violent subtraction of so much office space, Lower Manhattan had a higher vacancy rate than existed before the attack.

The vision Doctoroff embraced was to foster Downtown's ongoing evolution as a 24/7 community, with exchanges, clearing houses, federal agencies, and brokerage firms at the center, surrounded by complementary high-tech information industries, offices, housing, retailing, and a bevy of cultural institutions.

Instead of bribing companies to stay, "we invested in transportation, parks, housing, cultural activities, and other necessary amenities such as schools and health care sites to make neighborhoods more attractive for residents and workers and therefore, employers," Doctoroff wrote in his book.

He followed the recommendation of the Civic Alliance (a coalition of 80 organizations spearheaded by the Regional Plan Association), which preferred to concentrate on enhancing the area's attractiveness as a development site for the next generation of businesses and residents — preparing a sumptuous stage set for players yet unknown, as well as for seasoned veterans.

Doctoroff, moreover, refused to accept as a given that youthful professionals will head for the suburbs once they generate families. Children were in woefully short supply Downtown, a function of insufficient support services, notably public schools; yet it was clear that a multigenerational community in the future could be attained if it was planned for properly.

That's just what Doctoroff did, ensuring that $25 million of the first rebuilding funds were spent on neighborhood parks and playgrounds, supporting the *Vision for Lower Manhattan* plan's aspiration to "see strollers on Wall Street. Picnickers at the World Financial Center. Businessmen kayaking during lunch off South Street. And grandparents cycling on the West Street promenade."

Today, around 64,000 people live in Lower Manhattan. By 2022, the neighborhood had 40 hotels, 1,100 retail shops, restaurants, and bars, and nearly a dozen new or expanded parks and playgrounds.

A new economy for more New Yorkers

Downtown benefited from calming its competitive struggle against what are now considered to be complementary nodes in a larger regional complex, including Downtown Brooklyn and Long Island City.

Realizing the economic potential of the outer boroughs was not a given. Twenty years ago, I wrote that the current bustle of plans and projects was all well and good — and exciting. But I worried that with the understandable focus of attention on Lower Manhattan, resuscitating the rest of the city was getting lost in the shuffle.

My concern was that the hyper-concentration on Wall Street and its immediate surrounds, with even badly wounded Chinatown getting relatively short shrift, was symptomatic of a deeper overattentiveness to, and over reliance upon, our financial sector in general. September 11th drew attention to the fact that wherever the Financial Center is physically located, New York had become dependent on it to an unhealthy degree.

Leading up to 9/11 there was, for example, a steady escalation in the percentage of our income and jobs that flow from the FIRE (finance, insurance, and real estate) sector. The securities industry alone accounted for about 5% of New York City's total employment, but generated 20% of its total wages and salaries — up fourfold since 1969. Of greater concern, the securities sector overwhelmed all others as a source of economic growth: During 1992-1999, according to the Fiscal Policy Institute, it contributed roughly 50% of the Gross State Product.

This was problematic for several reasons. One is the tremendous volatility of the money business: When it's hot, it's hot, and bonuses overflow the land; but when it cools, it sheds load rapidly, pulling associated business and information services down with it.

There was another problem with the skewed nature of that overall economic mix: its maldistribution of rewards. The financial industry downsized or exported many of its middle income jobs, leaving behind very highly and very poorly paid employees. Additional middling positions were lost with the departure of manufacturing and commerce slots, many of which paid relatively well, and afforded climbable career ladders, in large part because they were heavily unionized.

Our economic arrangements thus exerted an overall downward push on the majority's standard of living. The number of jobs here grew vigorously in the 1990s boom. But even with the boom in full swing, the diminution of middle class positions, coupled with the wildly unequal reward structures for professionals and managers (on the one hand) and low-level service employees (on the other), generated enormous inequalities and serious social problems. While the rich did fabulously well, the middle class shrank. And the so-called working poor (their numbers swollen by arriving immigrants and the 350,000 people shoved off welfare) became ever more impoverished, despite ever more arduous labor, pincered as they were between insufficient wages and escalating expenses.

The city's population surged by more than 450,000 in the 1990s, but new housing production reached historic lows. Rising rents forced between a quarter and a third of all New Yorkers to spend over half their income on rent; or to burrow into one of the estimated 100,000 illegal apartments carved out of basements, garages, or subdivided rooms; or to resort to homeless shelters. Lines at soup kitchens and food pantries lengthened even as the boom roared on. By 1999, with irrational exuberance at its peak, one of every four New Yorkers lived below the poverty line, a rate twice the national average. By 2000, the distance between rich and poor — always substantial throughout New York's "sunshine and shadow" history — had grown to outrageous and shameful proportions.

For too long, our primary macroeconomic policy concentrated on assisting big financial and media institutions. Understandable — at times even justifiable — this approach was not a satisfactory approach to civic stewardship. I asserted that it was time to end corporate welfare as we'd known it. Instead of chasing individual companies with a checkbook, I called on the City to do more to cultivate entire economic sectors — including FIRE, to be sure, but also paying far greater attention to its less favored siblings.

Doctoroff apparently agreed. He developed a five-borough economic development strategy that targeted New York's competitive advantages and developed new sectors that included substantial blue collar jobs — such as film and TV production, health care, higher education, and tourism — thus going a long way toward overcoming the city's hyper-reliance on finance, and attendant levels of inequality.

He also vigorously pursued workforce training programs — so spurned by the Giuliani administration that it refused to spend tens of millions of dollars in federal funds given the City under the 1998 Workforce Investment Act, an act of ideological folly that was happily reversed by the new mayor. Doctoroff led a fundamental shift in the City's workforce development approach, recognizing that the City had leverage with many private employers through contracts, loans, grants, tax incentives, and other levers. He sought to use that leverage to connect those companies with job seekers, moving the responsibility for overseeing adult workforce development into one of his own agencies, the Department of Small Business Services (SBS), run by new commissioner, Rob Walsh.

When the Bloomberg administration took office, there was a single Workforce1 Career Center. By the time Doctoroff left government in 2007, there were seven spread throughout the five boroughs and SBS had facilitated more than 25,000 job placements — often by connecting job seekers with development projects such as the Hunts Point Fish Market in the Bronx, new hotels in Manhattan, and retail in Downtown Brooklyn.

Twenty years ago, I wondered how the City could pay for these proposals — investments in social services, parks, culture, new

industries, new business centers. Conventional wisdom said it couldn't. Estimates of the budget shortfall in 2002 hovered around $5 billion. There's no money, people said. We have to cut back, batten down, tighten belts, bite bullets, wait (hope) for the economic revival that surely lurks just around the corner.

At the same time, there was widespread agreement that rampant budget chopping spells municipal disaster. Memories lingered on of the disastrous 1970s cutbacks in maintenance, education, policing, fire protection, health care, and welfare — and their decades-long reverberation in crumpling infrastructure, sagging school performance, crack and murder epidemics, widespread arson, the return of tuberculosis, and soaring poverty rates, among other ills. Felix Rohatyn, a veteran of that crisis, warned that taking the extreme measures required to wipe out the budget gap would permanently damage our social and economic structure.

Doctoroff and Mayor Bloomberg agreed. "Part of the answer," Doctoroff wrote, "was to invest in the city when everyone else was pulling out." Bloomberg had embraced this strategy as a private citizen, investing aggressively in his own company during the recession of the 1980s to great effect. He and Doctoroff both believed, "the condition of the city would improve — it always had," Doctoroff wrote. "We could use the recovery years to plan, so when the upturn came, we would be ready."

Doctoroff also fervently believed in something he called "the virtuous cycle of growth" — that making the city a better place to live, would attract more people, which in turn would generate tax revenues that could be plowed into public services, making the city even more attractive.

With that said, some projects, like subway lines, had been proposed in good times and bad to no effect. There would need to be something more.

I pointed out that a host of urban areas in the U.S. had established Tax Increment Financing (TIF) districts, in which a portion of real estate tax revenues generated within its boundaries were used to

New York's recovery from 9/11 ushered in a period of economic prosperity and development across all five boroughs, leading to projections that the city would grow by nearly one million people by 2030.

back bonds, which allowed financing of the improvements in the first place. Doctoroff used this exact strategy to finance the extension of the No. 7 subway line, the system's first expansion in decades.

A New Deal for New York

If a touch of Jane Jacobs is required in some quarters, others could use a dash of Robert Moses.

Ultimately, I called for a New Deal for New York. The old New Deal — a panoply of 1930s federal interventions aimed at administering life support to a stricken society and collapsed economy — was in large measure devised in New York City. I asked New Yorkers to imagine, then, what a new New Deal might look like. Not an instant replay but a 21st century version — bolder, smarter, more inclusive.

The attack reminded us, if we needed reminding, that our addiction to oil is an extremely expensive habit, both in treasure (at the time we paid more than $5 billion each month for imported oil) and

in blood (it leads us into military ventures to ensure our supply keeps coming). We should kick the habit, I argued, outlining ideas for alternative sources of energy, more sustainable buildings, and smarter infrastructure.

The original New Deal grappled with providing shelter to the ill-housed, pioneering in the provision of public housing. We would need to do the same.

The New York City Works Progress Administration (WPA) employed more people than any private corporation in town, more people than the War Department. It was one of the biggest enterprises in the United States — a veritable army of labor — and it soon transformed the face of the city.

Roughly two-thirds of WPA employees labored on construction and engineering projects. With astonishing rapidity and efficiency, labor battalions helped build the Triborough Bridge, the Lincoln

Tunnel, and the Holland Tunnel; extended the West Side Highway and launched the FDR Drive; and constructed LaGuardia Airport, the single most ambitious and expensive WPA undertaking in the nation. In addition, workers repaired and painted 50 bridges, built or rehabbed 2,000 miles of streets and highways (including Queens Boulevard, Jamaica Avenue, and the Grand Concourse), removed 33 miles of trolley tracks, and built boardwalks along Coney Island and Staten Island's south shore. At the same time, they built or fixed 68 piers, laid 48 miles of sewers and 218 miles of water mains, erected a host of sewage treatment plants, and conducted pollution control research.

WPA workers also built public amenities that allowed millions of New Yorkers access to benefits not available to them in the prosperous 1920s. The New Dealers refurbished and expanded 287 parks (including Jacob Riis and Mount Morris) and laid out 400 additional ones (including Alley Pond and Cunningham). They built 17 municipal swimming pools, Orchard Beach in the Bronx, the 20,000 seat Randall's Island Stadium, a new zoo in Central Park, and 255 playgrounds in residential neighborhoods.

In a little over six years in office, Doctoroff spearheaded PlaNYC — still the most ambitious urban sustainability plan launched by an American city — which transformed New York into a leader on green buildings (including its affordable housing developments), cleaner energy, and cemented cities as the forefront of the climate movement. It established the only municipal cleanup program for brownfields in the United States — which quickly became the second-largest cleanup program in the country, second only to California with 756 properties remediated, 3,000 petroleum tanks removed, and 41,000 tons of hazardous waste removed clearing the way for $15 billion in new capital investment, including 5,200 affordable housing units.

PlaNYC set in motion a green infrastructure program that replaced the need for costly, energy-intensive filtration factories with gardens, trees and grass that could filter water naturally; today New York City's 11,000 such projects also lead the nation. And the Bloomberg administration completed the last 8.5 miles of the essential third water tunnel, a project begun half a century before.

The Bloomberg administration invested $6 billion to set in motion more than 3,000 acres of new and refurbished parks — more than the next 12 largest cities in the United States combined. PlaNYC alone contributed 229 playgrounds, one million new trees — including a new civilian corps of volunteers to help plant and garden — and eight new destination parks spread across all five boroughs, including the restoration of McCarren Park Pool, one of the largest and grandest of the WPA pools that had fallen into disrepair and been shuttered for nearly three decades. Whereas 2.5 million New Yorkers lived more than 10 minutes away from open space in 2006, today the number is 75,000 — meaning that 99% of New Yorkers now live a short walk from open space.

The PlaNYC transportation initiatives included the creation of nearly 400 miles of new bike lanes, including the nation's first parking protected lanes on a city street, 70 pedestrian spaces across the city in spaces seized from cars, and 38 miles of new Bus Rapid Transit. (Not to mention the No. 7 train extension, using the TIF financing method; some worried it would compete with the Second Avenue subway extension, but that has opened new stops, too).

Under Doctoroff's leadership the City rezoned 6,000 blocks — or 40% of the entire city — created 60 miles of accessible waterfront; and rebuilt the Coney Island boardwalk (along with saving the amusement district, installing infrastructure to support the neighborhood's 60,000 residents, and upgrading the aquarium).

His Olympic plan helped spur the construction of new world-class athletic facilities for athletes of all ages, including high school students, including the 5,000-seat Icahn Stadium on Randall's Island; Ocean Breeze, the 135,000-square-foot indoor track and field facility on Staten Island that has seen 18 national records set by athletes from nine different countries, and a fully accessible competition-level pool and ice rink in Flushing, Queens that became the largest building ever constructed in a New York City park — not to mention new baseball stadiums for the city's two Major League teams and an arena that lured a professional basketball team back from the suburbs into the heart of Downtown Brooklyn.

In my research, when Bloomberg took office, the housing advocates were calling for 185,000 units of housing. Doctoroff and his team built 165,000 units — the most ambitious program to date in American history, using creative and underused financing techniques I had highlighted like inclusionary zoning, which to date had funded only a few hundred units in the past two decades. It wasn't enough. But it was more than had ever been done before.

Twenty years ago, I feared the post-9/11 recession could well be a prolonged and nasty affair. It wasn't.

People have often asked me, as an historian, if the Twin Towers attack marked the end of an era, if New York would be utterly transformed in its aftermath. My response was always twofold.

No, because a city 400 years old and eight million strong is a social-historical organism with a fantastic amount of momentum; it cannot so easily be deflected from its path, even by such a horrific event. We ourselves have experienced worse. In 1776, when the city and country rebelled against the English, redcoats invaded New York in history's largest amphibious assault up to that point, which resulted in the fiery destruction of a large part of the town, the flight of almost all its inhabitants, and its occupation for the subsequent seven years. And yet the postwar city rebounded miraculously. Think, too, of other cities around the world — Berlin, Dresden, Tokyo, London, Hiroshima — that survived and transcended unimaginable carnage.

Yes, however, in the sense that so devastating a blow shatters encrusted pieties about what is and is not possible. The opposite side of disaster is opportunity. The events of 9/11 provided us an opening, as a city, to make our own course corrections on the river of history — requiring only the desire, and our ability to summon the will. Doctoroff, charged to lead the city's rebuilding, had both. It would only be the end of an era if we decided to make it one. Instead, under the press of hard blows and hard times, our audacious metropolis again led the nation in recalling our history, reimagining our future, and seizing hold of our collective destiny.

This essay was updated and modified from the book A New Deal for New York.

LYNNE B. SAGALYN | Professor Emerita, Columbia University Business School | Author, *Power at Ground Zero: Politics, Money, and the Remaking of Lower Manhattan*

PUSHING FOR PROGRESS: DAN DOCTOROFF AT GROUND ZERO

The task of rebuilding the site of the World Trade Center after the deadly traumatic terrorist attack on 9/11 had to meet many symbolic aspirations. It needed to embody American values and speak to the world about America's resilience in the face of mass murder. Simultaneously, the effort had to show that local decision makers could "do the right thing" as the world watched. It had to represent strength and determination and reflect deep sensitivity in recognition of the lives lost in the attacks. It had to create an economic future for Lower Manhattan. And it had to protect New York City's status as "the capital of the free world" and assure its global leadership in the 21st century. That was what the mayor promised in his inaugural address on January 1, 2002, and throughout his 12 years in office, Michael Bloomberg would try to act in full accord with that pledge: "We will go forward. We will never go back." The confounding issue, however, was that City Hall was in an especially weak position to influence decisions that would shape the physical and economic landscape of Lower Manhattan for decades to come.

Though these 16 acres were an integral part of its territorial DNA, the City lacked both formal rights to plan what would be built anew and formal powers to control the decisions of those who would take hold of the reins of planning. The Port Authority of New York and New Jersey had owned the site for nearly 40 years; by governing statute, it was free of New York City's regulatory and land-use powers and it reported to two higher levels of government, New York State and the State of New Jersey. After the City's heroic job of cleaning up and stabilizing the site in record time by the end of June 2002, it was effectively shut out; control over the site returned to the Port Authority.

Whereas the Port Authority's "city-within-a-city" position gave the bi-state agency a governmental purpose on the site, the City of New York had no legal jurisdiction there, except for nearly forgotten control over two discontinued and closed stub streets running into the site that had somehow been left out of the Port Authority's original 1960s condemnation transaction and offered little from a real estate perspective. The City's shadow position in the rebuilding process would irritate Michael Bloomberg and Deputy Mayor Dan Doctoroff to no end. Politically, the situation was untenable.

As Deputy Mayor for Economic Development and Rebuilding, Dan was the driving force behind the City's elbowing its way into the contentious and critically important mission of ensuring Lower Manhattan's economic viability beyond the immediacy of rebuilding the WTC site. His visions for the city were large; he was the one, for example, who pushed New York to apply for the 2012 Olympics. At Ground Zero, he wanted the site to be rebuilt as more than just a collection of office buildings. Whether working with the New York congressional delegation to ensure that the city received the many billions President George W. Bush promised, articulating City Hall's position that housing should be a component of the rebuilding project, working to keep Merrill Lynch from relocating out of Lower Manhattan, or structuring agreements for the Port Authority's turnover of the commercial sites to developer, Larry Silverstein, Dan was a forceful presence for furthering City Hall's agenda. Although

he understood the City's ability to impact rebuilding was limited, Dan thrived on finding a way for the Bloomberg administration to play a critical role in defining the future of Lower Manhattan. He did this by maneuvering opportunistically and tactically — and repeatedly — to successfully gain influence.

Doctoroff's first thrust at gaining control at Ground Zero was the proposal to swap the City's ownership of the land beneath LaGuardia and JFK Airports, operated by the Port Authority since 1947 under a series of leases, for the Trade Center site. As a land-to-land transaction, the swap was lopsided — 4,930 acres at JFK plus 680 acres at LaGuardia for the 16 acres of the Trade Center. The idea was attractively simple, but the fiscal math of the potential transaction was complex and did not look promising; it was also laden with technical complications. More significantly, the politics of the site would not allow it. While it was possible that the bold property exchange might have simplified the task of executing on the rebuilding mission, the idea was anathema to government leaders at the state level who saw opportunity for national advancement through their work at the site.

When the land swap failed, Dan told me, he and the mayor knew that they had to try other means. When it came to events taking place — or not, as was often the case — they pursued a series of strategic interventions, assiduously exercising the City's political capital (and the mayor's bully pulpit) in ways calibrated to push the project through bottlenecks and toward tangible progress. In July of 2002, they scotched the first set of master plans for the site. In spring of 2005, they intervened with a deal to keep Goldman Sachs from pulling out of Lower Manhattan. In 2006, they went public with a financial analysis of the commercial rebuilding program at Ground Zero that called into question the developer's financial capacity to meet his responsibility to rebuild all 10 million square feet of lost office space.

Over months of secret negotiations with the New Jersey side of the Port Authority and Governor Jon Corzine, they maneuvered New York Governor George Pataki and developer Larry Silverstein into an agreement that realigned who would build what on the commercial portion of the site. This particular strategic intervention was the first financial watershed of rebuilding; it unlocked the bottleneck and allowed work on the Memorial and Freedom Tower to move ahead.

In May of that year, Dan and the mayor took a similarly forceful position calling into question the ballooning costs of the planned memorial on the site, a crisis that had been simmering since the fall of 2005. The City's push resulted in design modifications that slashed the cost estimate by almost $300 million, nearly 30 percent.

Each of these strategic interventions was designed to get around the formal reins of power at Ground Zero. Through the strength of his relationships with other players at the site, Dan could productively maneuver behind the scenes to further the City's aims. Through the force of his personality and strategic skill, and with the firm backing of the mayor, he was a resolute voice pushing to shape the process of rebuilding in ways that aligned with the economic future of the City of New York. To which New Yorkers, including myself, can only say: Bravo.

ANTHONY COSCIA | Chairman, Port Authority of New York and New Jersey, 2003–2011 | Chairman, Amtrak, 2010–Present

THE UNLIKELY ALLIANCE THAT UNLOCKED THE WORLD TRADE CENTER SITE

When I joined the Port Authority as Chairman in early 2003, the agency was still suffering from the wounds of 9/11. The Port was not just the owner of the 16-acre site where the Twin Towers had stood; it had built the World Trade Center and the site was our headquarters. Eighty-four of our colleagues died in the attacks. After rising to deal with the initial crisis, many at the Port had spent the past two years attending dozens of funerals of co-workers and friends. Some were too traumatized to go back to Lower Manhattan. With the site cleared and stabilized, adrenaline ebbed, leaving grief and trauma in its wake.

Against that backdrop, the Port was struggling to drive the rebuilding of the site when I arrived at the agency. And in fact, even by 2005 not much progress had been made. Beyond the emotional challenges, we faced some extraordinary obstacles. The developer, Larry Silverstein, was arguing with his insurers over how much money he was entitled to receive; without that information, it was impossible to develop a realistic plan.

The most important stakeholders — the families of the victims — were deeply divided over next steps. In meetings, I was called an abject coward and a tool of the terrorists for not rebuilding things exactly as they had been — and cruel and heartless for contemplating building anything at all. I liked when Dan Doctoroff joined me at the meetings because he gave people a sense of optimism that there was a plan to balance our obligation to the families with the imperative to rebuild.

Then there were the staggering geotechnical challenges of the site itself, which featured a "bathtub" holding off the Hudson River on one side and containing a snarl of needs underground, including subway tunnels and train lines. Simply digging from ground level to bedrock was an enormous undertaking.

There was no path to untangling the multiple Gordian knots. And so for years, the site sat empty and still in the heart of Lower Manhattan to the growing frustration of everyone. It was around that time, when spirits were at their lowest, that Dan and I began a remarkable series of discussions.

Prior to 2005, the City's role in rebuilding the World Trade Center was limited thanks to its ownership by the Port, an agency controlled by the governors of New York and New Jersey. It was clear to me that as we were rebuilding a large site in the middle of Lower Manhattan, the City deserved to be part of key decisions. This was not always a widely shared view.

Of course, the City wasn't sitting patiently on the sidelines waiting to be invited into the conversation. Anyone who has spent 10 minutes with either Dan or Mayor Michael Bloomberg knows that would never be the case. Dan made a bold proposal that I readily embraced: to swap the World Trade Center site with the City-owned land beneath Kennedy and LaGuardia airports. That would have given the Port control of two of its most important assets, while allowing the City to control a 16-acre site in its second-largest central business district. I was optimistic about the transaction until the 11th hour, when I received a call from Dan while I was at a Yankees game at Fenway Park, telling me that the State of New York had killed it. I still wonder if the spectators around me thought the stream of profanities that erupted from me was about the game.

The dynamic changed a few months later, when Silverstein applied for more than $3 billion in Liberty Bonds, a federal program that granted the City a formal role in approving the request. Dan used that leverage to demand detailed financials from Silverstein. With the help of experts at Lehman Brothers, the City tore apart the numbers to answer a simple but important question: Would there be enough money to rebuild under the proposed plan?

There had been a lot of fast talking about what could be built, the rents that could be charged, and the profit that would be made — in the hope that nobody ever sat down with a calculator and did the math. Dan and his team did the math.

The report was dire: There was a shortfall of at least $4 billion, largely a result of the fact that the site was underinsured, as nobody had ever anticipated a total loss. In the months that followed, Dan and one of his team members, Seth Pinsky, repeatedly rode the subway to my Midtown office to share the results with me and strategize behind the scenes on what to do about it.

I technically represented the New Jersey side of the Port Authority. As the board chairman, I was not supposed to be deeply involved in the technical details of agency projects. But Dan and I both wanted to give the public what they had been promised: five office buildings, a transit hub, an appropriate and world-class memorial and museum, a performing arts center, and public space. And we both saw that the math just wouldn't work: Silverstein would run out of money long before the project was completed, and the public sector would be left holding the bag.

Those working sessions between Dan, Seth, and myself — held quietly over months as we hashed through not only the analysis but what to do about it — were the catalyst that finally unlocked progress on the site. Armed not only with the City's analysis but a strong partnership with Mayor Bloomberg and Dan, the Port drove a renegotiation with Silverstein that tackled the funding shortfall — including shifting Towers 1 and 5 to Port ownership, shifting Tower 5 from office to residential use, and bringing Port, State, and City employees to the site. After more than four years of stalemate, construction began quickly thereafter.

While public servants across a multitude of agencies can rightly claim credit for delivering the project, it's no exaggeration to say that it was Dan's forceful behind-the-scenes engagement to insist on a plan that was buildable, rather than one that sounded good in a press release, that sparked the rebuilding effort. Dan never encountered a problem he didn't think he could solve. His finance and real estate expertise, along with his understanding of how to work alongside an alphabet soup of government agencies, were critical to our success.

He didn't always do it by playing nice. Sometimes, he and the mayor were publicly rough on the Port and Silverstein. But he was always focused on realizing the vision of a renewed World Trade Center. When I'm at the World Trade Center today and see the vision drawn on paper after 9/11 realized in vibrant reality, I know how much we have Dan to thank.

CARL WEISBROD | Founding President, Alliance for Downtown New York, 1995–2005

BEYOND GROUND ZERO: THE REVITALIZATION OF LOWER MANHATTTAN

When the Bloomberg administration took office at the beginning of 2002, the World Trade Center was still a recovery site covered in rubble. The smell of the September 11th attacks still lingered in the air. But the devastation went far beyond the World Trade Center itself. Canal Street was a dividing line between what passed for normal in New York City and what seemed like a war zone; it was almost like East Berlin vs. West Berlin before the wall came down. Thousands of residents had left their homes in Lower Manhattan. Landline telephone service was nonexistent and cell service was spotty at best. Most offices remained unoccupied.

This was the Lower Manhattan that confronted Dan Doctoroff when he was named Deputy Mayor for Economic Development and Rebuilding.

But in addition to these clear emergencies, Lower Manhattan's challenges ran deeper. The neighborhood's core — the Financial District — had been the leader of the Age of Capitalism during the first half of the 20th century. It was the world's center of the international financial markets, home to the major stock exchanges, the largest banks and financial services companies, and the headquarters of many global corporations. By mid-century, it was strictly a business center, with very few residents and virtually no uses other than commercial ones; there were fewer people living in the area in 1950 than lived there in 1800. Meanwhile, its vaunted commercial status was fading. Lower Manhattan was becoming increasingly outclassed by the vibrant Midtown business district, which had better regional transit connections and more modern buildings. By the mid-1990s, Lower Manhattan had more than 60 million square feet of vacant office space, desolate streets that emptied after dark, and few attractions to reverse the decline.

In 1995, I became the founding President of the Alliance for Downtown New York, which was established by the Lower Manhattan business community to address the seemingly intractable problems of the neighborhood. It instantly became the largest business improvement district in the nation.

Six years later, we had made real progress. The Lower Manhattan of September 10, 2001 — the day before the attacks on the World Trade Center — was experiencing something of a revival. The commercial vacancy rate was finally dropping. A shopping mall at the World Trade Center was commanding top tier rents from national retailers. People — especially young professionals — were moving into the area, thanks to an aggressive program converting outmoded, largely shuttered, commercial buildings to residential use. New restaurants and other retail outlets, including the neighborhood's first supermarket (although it required a subsidy from the Downtown Alliance!) were opening. Nevertheless, it was unclear whether this hopeful picture was the product of just another financial cycle, or indeed something more permanent. After the attacks, many feared the progress we had made would be totally undone, perhaps irrevocably.

It is the legacy of Dan Doctoroff that he recognized the need not only to rebuild the World Trade Center site — whatever that meant — but to reimagine all of Lower Manhattan, replanting and growing the seeds from the previous decade. His *Vision for Lower Manhattan* plan largely embraced the goals of the Downtown Alliance and built on them in order to create a district that could serve as a model for older downtowns throughout the country. His goal was not only to stabilize a community which could survive in good economic times, but to create a new, multiuse neighborhood that would thrive in all times.

The East River Waterfront Esplanade, including Pier 15, above, was part of a broader Bloomberg administration effort to integrate housing, parks, and other amenities into Lower Manhattan as part of the rebuilding effort.

In this, he succeeded. Two decades later, his approach has more than stood the test of time.

Today, Lower Manhattan, despite the pandemic-related setbacks experienced by central business districts across the nation, is a thriving mixed-use business and residential neighborhood. It is less dependent on financial services and more attractive to creative, tech, and other growing companies. Its residential population not only returned and stabilized after the September 11th attacks but over the past two decades has actually grown faster than virtually any other precinct in the city. Lower Manhattan's East River waterfront has been rediscovered.

How did this happen?

First, it is worth noting the significant obstacles that the City, and Dan Doctoroff particularly, had to confront to achieve a better, long-lasting vision for Lower Manhattan — even beyond recovering from the attacks destroying the World Trade Center site.

Dan was viewed suspiciously by the Lower Manhattan community due to his focus on locating multiple Olympic venues in a costly new development called Hudson Yards on the West Side of Manhattan. This was particularly true for the powerful Speaker of the Assembly Sheldon Silver, who represented the Downtown area. Silver saw virtually every proposal to aid the Olympic bid as a potential loss for Lower Manhattan, rather than a win-win for the city. At one point, aware that Silver trusted me, Dan asked if

I would approach the Speaker to find out what Dan — and the City — could do for Lower Manhattan that would enable Silver to drop his opposition to the Hudson Yards development and its proposed Olympic Stadium. I dutifully did so and could hardly get the proposition out of my mouth before Silver threw me out of his office. There was nothing anyone could say that would assuage Silver's suspicions or anger that Hudson Yards was claiming any part of the City's attention. He would become a formidable enemy.

Dan's next challenge: The Port Authority of New York and New Jersey, the owner of the World Trade Center, was resistant to integrating that site into the larger fabric of Lower Manhattan and to the City's efforts to exert more influence. When Dan tried to solve the problem by offering the Port ownership of the land under the City-owned John F. Kennedy and LaGuardia airports in exchange for the land under the World Trade Center site, politics doomed the deal.

Finally, the federal government was making a push to decentralize the location of financial services companies — in other words to reduce the number of major headquarters located in New York City. The effort threatened to destabilize the very foundation of Lower Manhattan's economy.

Despite these headwinds and setbacks, Dan forged ahead undaunted. He made several important decisions that have guided Lower Manhattan's transformation over the past two decades. He terminated the City's efforts to build a new headquarters

for the New York Stock Exchange at the intersection of Wall and Broad Street. This opened several sites for new housing, but more importantly, the decision symbolized that Downtown's future was no longer tethered to a bricks and mortar approach to financial services. He focused on fostering the mixed-use character of the neighborhood by allocating tax-exempt Liberty Bonds to build 10,000 units of new housing south of Canal Street.

Notwithstanding the federal government's push for decentralization, Dan helped assure that the vast majority of companies kept their headquarters in Lower Manhattan, including Goldman Sachs, American Express, AIG, and, at the time, Merrill Lynch. Those few that left the city are, for the most part, no longer in existence (the notable exception being Bank of America). Thanks to the work of City Planning Chair Amanda Burden, Dan was somewhat successful in connecting the redeveloped World Trade Center site to the broader city street grid and enabling the integration of the four quadrants of Lower Manhattan for the first time in half a century: the Financial District, the Civic Center, Battery Park City, and TriBeCa.

Some of Dan Doctoroff's more ambitious visions have not come to pass. There is no train from Lower Manhattan to either JFK or Newark Airport. The connection between Lower Manhattan and Chinatown remains squirrelly. And, all of us missed the boat — and the opportunity — to create significant affordable housing south of Chambers Street. But Lower Manhattan has

nearly doubled its population since 2001, growing from nearly 33,000 people in 2000 to about 64,000 residents today. There is more open space in Lower Manhattan today than two decades ago and the East River waterfront has been opened up with a new esplanade from the Lower East Side to the Battery, for the enjoyment of area residents, workers, and visitors. In 2001, the neighborhood had six hotels; by 2022, there were 40 and the area boasted more than 200 new shops and restaurants.

Beyond the specific programs that have benefitted Lower Manhattan, Dan made a crucial policy shift that has transformed how New York approaches economic development citywide.

From at least the 1960s until the attacks on the World Trade Center, City policy was to provide tax incentives to businesses to keep them in New York. In the wake of 9/11, that shifted dramatically. We have now learned that business follows talent; talent does not follow business. Thanks to Dan Doctoroff, we have made shrewd decisions to invest in the physical and social infrastructure — parks, culture, schools and the like — that grow, attract, and retain human talent in New York City.

That may be his most lasting achievement arising from his work in Lower Manhattan.

ROY BAHAT | Senior Policy Advisor, Office of the Deputy Mayor for Economic Development and Rebuilding, 2002-2003

THE DAN METHOD: CREATING THE LOWER MANHATTAN VISION PLAN

Thirty years ago, Lower Manhattan was a dump. I went to high school there, and the best food option was a Blimpie. A swarm of people in suits — not even nice suits — would wander out of tall buildings and immediately disappear into the subway. Wait until the sun went down, and you could watch tumbleweed blow, even though a few of the intrepid lived in Battery Park City.

So when terrorists destroyed the World Trade Center, they took away one of the few parts of Lower Manhattan that made New Yorkers proud. (It made us proud despite the fact that it was like a brick thrown through a window ... powerful, but destructive to everything around it, a slab of concrete that blocked streets and sidewalks with buildings that made the neighborhood feel desolate. The World Trade Center site was truly part of the mess that Lower Manhattan had become.)

After the attacks, the World Trade Center mattered to more than just New Yorkers — it mattered as a symbol to the world. Proof that the free world couldn't be bullied. And Dan knew it. What kind of city did New York want to become? And how could a renewed Lower Manhattan become an emblem of that resilience?

"In the immediate aftermath of Sept. 11, it seemed almost inconceivable that anyone would ever want to live downtown," *The New York Times* said in 2006. The article quoted Dan's answer: "People invest in an area because they believe in its future, and that requires articulating a vision and a plan that gives people hope."

Lo and behold, a neighborhood that was once a mess became the fastest-growing residential neighborhood in the city. Dan assembled the vision — and the plan — that gave people the hope that induced that transformation.

Our vision for Lower Manhattan reattached the severed limb of the World Trade Center site, weaving it in with streets and connecting the area via new transit to the rest of the city. It called for the rest of Lower Manhattan to come to life — with housing (which New York desperately needed, and was less expensive there than in other neighborhoods), parks, stores, and more. And, on the site itself, we left a welcome mat for new facilities that would add offices, bring in visitors, remind the world what had happened, and celebrate what would come.

Like everything with Dan, the day we started working on the project we already felt like we were running behind. He knew our administration might only have a few short years, which is the blink of an eye in the life of a city. (That feeling, of being short on time, started for me the day I met Dan. One Sunday morning in 2002, Dan called me out of the blue to ask if I wanted to interview for a job in City Hall. When I said I'd love to come in sometime, he told me that if I wanted the job I needed to come over to his house "right now.")

Dan delivered deadlines and we all charged. So Dan only gave us a couple of months to pull together a vision (and, because Dan never does vaporware, a feasible plan to bring that vision to life, including financial estimates and lists of projects to ensure every proposal could be made real).

The street toward implementing that plan ran uphill. To succeed, we would need to align a wide array of constituencies and agencies of different governments. Even getting the city's own agencies to tell their stories using a shared language was a challenge. (The first time we tried to do a public presentation on Lower Manhattan, my teammate Laurel Blatchford and I had to pull an all-nighter just to get all the agencies to use a common PowerPoint format. I bought a

The Bloomberg administration converted "slip streets" — areas where waterfront boat slips carved into the shoreline had been filled in — into pocket parks like Coenties Slip as part of the rebuilding effort.

toothbrush the next morning from one of the many Duane Reades near City Hall.) When you added the other complicating interests (State, federal, Port Authority, realtors, residents, and grieving families), it felt daunting.

Our official government relations person at City Hall told us not to talk with the City Council because "you can't trust them." The representatives from the Lower Manhattan Development Corporation, when we presented them with ideas for a joint plan for rebuilding, asked us whether those ideas would come "out of the City's end or the State's." Nothing was about doing right by the people of New York, everything was one institution negotiating with another.

As part of the rebuilding effort, the Bloomberg administration directed $25 million in federal funds to create parks in Lower Manhattan, including Imagination Playground, above, designed by David Rockwell.

Dan said, "That's not how I do things." He insisted on his own philosophy for doing things — trying to convince people of their common interests and building personal relationships as a way of cementing a foundation of trust that could enable taking risks, together. Even when Dan lacks formal power, he acts like he's in charge. And, more often than not, it works. I've come to think of this as The Dan Method — which I suppose comes from a mix of his family's Michigan roots, his successful professional experiences in what only people in government call "the private sector," and just the observations of a wise person moving through a complicated world trying to drive change.

So we set to work. Gathering plans. Adding up numbers. Enlisting the most imaginative urban planning and architectural minds (the architects who would remake Lincoln Center!) to draw pictures.(Dan taught us that plans had to be visual for people to relate to them.)

Dan made sure our vision was more than just pretty pictures — we needed to account for how we'd pay for it. (He loves to track projects — at one point he wanted his staff to keep a spreadsheet of every economic development project in the city. We played

along for a few weeks but that turned out to be one step too fantastic because of the overwhelming number of projects and their complicated overlaps and intersections that made them hard to separate into discrete efforts.) The corollary was that any idea could fly if the details penciled out — even one as far-fetched as the land swap, where we proposed trading the World Trade Center (which the Port Authority owned and the City wanted) for the New York airports (the land under which the City owned, and the Port Authority wanted).

After a few intense weeks collecting data, aligning the many stakeholders within the City, consulting with urban planning experts like Alex Garvin, who worked with Dan to develop his Olympic X plan, leading thinkers about architecture and urbanism like Paul Goldberger, historians like Mike Wallace, and many others — some of whom had decades of expertise without the city government ever having asked their opinion! — and many late nights, we'd written a vision. And, more than a vision, it was a plan with a financial model — and 38 footnotes, of which Dan was proud (presumably because it was evidence that we'd done

The seasonal ice rink at Brookfield Place in Battery Park City.

our homework and the plan was more than just a pretty rendering). Dan even had a favorite footnote he used to talk about in meetings as a way of illustrating the critical details on which the whole plan might turn; I bet he still remembers which footnote it was (I've long since forgotten).

The mayor supported this vision, in part because he had put his own business in Midtown and knew the challenges Lower Manhattan would have to overcome. He prepared to debut it at a breakfast of the Association for a Better New York. The night before the mayor's presentation, the edits — seemingly from everyone who had ever had an opinion about anything, including Dan and the press release writers in City Hall — came in so fast I got "Blackberry blisters" on the sides of my thumbs.

The next morning, we exhaled. *The New York Times* called the vision "a bracing tonic for anyone dispirited by the future of downtown New York City." And Dan locked into place a process that continued for years to create more housing, better parks, and a belief that Lower Manhattan — with a new symbol at its heart — could keep beating New York's drum. Years later, looking

In 2001, there were six hotels in Lower Manhattan. By 2022, there were 40, including the Beekman Hotel.

Above: Country Dance Night at South Street Seaport is one of the festivals enlivening Lower Manhattan.
Below: The restored Battery Maritime Building includes new restaurants, event space, and a hotel in addition to the ferry access point for Governors Island.

at the legacy of what's happened in Lower Manhattan, I take great pride in seeing that our vision has come to life. Within a decade, there were more than 10,000 units of new housing, dozens of new restaurants, parks, people, streets reconnected, transit to the rest of the city, and a memorial on the World Trade Center site that honors the tragedy that remade this part of New York City. By 2020, the number of residents had doubled to nearly 65,000 (and the percentage of those residents under 18 had also doubled). There were hundreds of new stores and restaurants, and nearly half a billion dollars had been invested in 11 new parks and public plazas.

As I looked up any day from my desk at City Hall, I saw the rest of Dan's team, most of us with too little experience, the good intentions of fresh ideas, and the high pain tolerances needed to bring ideas to life. (That kind of team is another part of The Dan Method.) And everyone else was working on visions and plans as significant to New York's future as the one on which I'd worked. All of us inspired, shepherded — and sometimes maddened — by Dan.

Opposite: In the 20 years since 9/11, the population of Lower Manhattan nearly doubled to 64,000 residents, with striking new housing like the Frank Gehry–designed 8 Spruce Street.

WHY GOLDMAN SACHS STAYED IN LOWER MANHATTAN

I was the chairman and CEO of Goldman Sachs when terrorists attacked the World Trade Center on September 11, 2001. Our global headquarters was at 85 Broad Street — a few blocks south of the Twin Towers. Our people were emotionally devastated by the attack and understandably fearful about their safety and security. It took weeks before many of them were ready to come back into the office.

We were also in the midst of a planning process for a badly needed new headquarters building because we had outgrown 85 Broad Street. We were seriously considering a move to Midtown, New Jersey, or another Downtown site. In the wake of the attack, there was plenty of sentiment to move away from Downtown and the proximity of the World Trade Center.

Ultimately, we made the decision to keep the firm in Lower Manhattan, rebuilding on Ground Zero — in no small part because

we had enormous trust and confidence in Mayor Michael Bloomberg and his outstanding team.

The Bloomberg administration was filled with first-rate people, and Deputy Mayor Dan Doctoroff was a prime example. As a superb professional at Oak Hill Capital Partners, he had already won the trust of Goldman Sachs and other financial institutions and we were confident that he was going to be able to promote New York City's role as the financial capital of the world.

Dan also quickly became an expert on city planning. He had a vision for the future of Lower Manhattan — coupled with the competence to execute that vision. Competence inspires confidence. Mike Bloomberg and Dan Doctoroff had a comprehensive plan for restoring a sense of safety and vitality to the area, which gave us the confidence to build a magnificent new headquarters

building, growing our presence Downtown and contributing to its revitalization. The firm broke ground on its current worldwide headquarters in 2005 at 200 West Street.

In the aftermath of 9/11, it was difficult to contemplate relocating at the site of that devastating attack. But Mike Bloomberg, Dan Doctoroff, and Dan's outstanding team — which included my friend and former partner, Andy Alper, who left Goldman Sachs to report to Dan as president of the City's Economic Development Corporation — exceeded our high expectations for the recovery of Lower Manhattan, ensuring that Wall Street continues to play its historic role. And Mike Bloomberg went on to become one of the best mayors in New York City's history because, like all good leaders, he surrounds himself with best-in-class professionals.

KEN CHENAULT | Chairman and CEO, American Express, 2001–2018

American Express and its Recommitment to Downtown

After the September 11th attacks, American Express was forced to temporarily relocate its Lower Manhattan headquarters across the Hudson River. At the time, there was a widespread fear that major employers would permanently leave Manhattan, hurtling New York back to the 1970s. When newly-elected mayor Mike Bloomberg called me, he delivered a simple message, the same message he was delivering to other business leaders: "You can't leave — the city needs you — and we're going to get Lower Manhattan back on its feet." Mike's business background gave us confidence that he could do it, and his hiring of Dan Doctoroff as Deputy Mayor for Economic Development and Rebuilding proved to be a stroke of genius.

I had first met Dan when he was leading New York City's bid for the 2012 Olympic Games. He immediately impressed me. Dan didn't just conceive of big ideas — he also had incredible attention to the details and an ability to execute. He had the audacity of all great New Yorkers; he pitched American Express for a contribution to the bid — even though one of our biggest competitors was the official Olympic sponsor! We gave it to him, because we believed the Olympics would be great for our home city — and because we believed in him and his passion, which has always been contagious.

As deputy mayor, Dan responded to the short-term needs of American Express in the aftermath of the 9/11 attacks, and he understood the importance of addressing employees' concerns about safety and security. We also talked about the long-term work he and the administration were leading to ensure that Downtown emerged stronger than ever, which only strengthened our belief in the city's future. Thanks to his and Mayor Bloomberg's leadership, we became one of the first big companies to move back to Lower Manhattan, just a few months after the attacks. For our firm and our employees, it was the right decision — and I know how proud our team was to help lead the city's great comeback.

Above: American Express CEO Ken Chenault and Mayor Michael Bloomberg.

Left: The decision by Goldman Sachs to build a more than two-million-square-foot headquarters, shown at far left, across the street from the World Trade Center site was a critical vote of confidence in the Bloomberg administration's vision for a reborn Lower Manhattan.

SETH PINSKY | President, New York City Economic Development Corporation, 2008–2013

DIVERSIFYING THE ECONOMY OF NEW YORK CITY

Between the middle and end of the 20th century, New York City's economy underwent an astonishing transformation that would also prove to be incredibly wrenching. During this time, the city transitioned from a production economy built on manufacturing and industry to an economy that would increasingly be built on the provision of services. As the 21st century dawned, this transformation had basically run its course, with the disappearance of nearly one million industrial jobs across all five boroughs and the emergence of a nearly equal number of service-related jobs, concentrated primarily in the city's central business districts in Manhattan.

Though the city's new service-related jobs would be found in a wide range of sectors, one service sector quickly came to dominate: Finance. In fact, by 2000, while the securities sector comprised approximately 5% of all jobs in the city, it represented 20% of wages paid.

The growth of the financial sector helped fuel a resurgence in the city's economy, driving away memories of the dark days of the 1970s, when New York stood on the brink of bankruptcy and people and businesses fled the city for the suburbs and beyond. New York began to regain a certain hustle and swagger, assured of the fact that — while it had fundamentally changed — the city would nonetheless remain the nation's and, arguably, the world's business capital for the foreseeable future.

That said, not everything about New York's transformation would prove to be positive.

As factories closed, the jobs that they supported were replaced by jobs in office suites. With this shift, large numbers of individuals and families — along with whole communities — found themselves on the losing end of the bargain. Instead of offering employment opportunities at decent wages to workers with a wide variety of educational backgrounds, the city's economy increasingly favored those who had studied in the ivied halls of the nation's elite higher educational institutions, leaving many behind.

In the waning days of the Giuliani administration and on the eve of September 11, 2001, this was the state of our economy. It was, to be sure, robust and growing, but with significant concentration risks, owing particularly to New York's outsized reliance on Wall Street.

Then came the terrorist attack on the World Trade Center.

Of course, its most important impact was on the families and loved ones of those who lost their lives on that horrific morning. The day was one of death and destruction for New York like almost none the city had ever previously experienced.

At the same time, the attacks also had a significant and immediate impact on the city's economy. Overnight, geopolitical uncertainty begat a meaningful economic slowdown, with all industries pulling back on investment and shedding jobs rapidly. While the whole world was impacted by this slowdown, its impact on New York, which was both literally and figuratively "Ground Zero" of the 9/11 attacks, were even more pronounced. City leaders were particularly worried that industries and companies based in New York would question whether keeping so much infrastructure on one small island, Manhattan, was still wise. This was especially true of the financial sector, for which business interruptions of even a few milliseconds could wreak havoc.

It was in this challenging environment that the Bloomberg administration assumed office in January 2002. And it was under these precarious conditions that the economic development team, led by a young and untested deputy mayor, Dan Doctoroff, began to chart the city's emergence from the calamity of September 11th.

While stabilizing the city's finances and restoring confidence in New York's safety were key elements of the administration's recovery plans, from the very beginning, these plans included much more. In particular, they built on Dan's insight that without greater diversification, New York's overreliance on Wall Street — a highly cyclical industry — would doom the city to wide and frequent swings from boom to bust through which it would be difficult to build economic momentum. For this reason, Dan made clear that his goal for New York's recovery was not a return to the city's pre-attack economic model, but a new, more holistic approach that he dubbed his "five-borough economic development plan."

This was not mutually exclusive with continuing to support the Finance, Insurance, and Real Estate (FIRE) sector. Dan recognized that the financial industry had the potential to remain a proverbial goose laying golden eggs capable of providing the City with critical resources to invest in infrastructure and address a wide range of civic challenges, from housing to public education. So, Dan advanced policies that nurtured Wall Street, while also identifying and encouraging the growth of other industries suited to New York's unique strengths. In cultivating these new sectors, Dan saw the opportunity to spread economic growth across all five boroughs (rather than just Manhattan) and to benefit people with a wide variety of skills and a broad range of educational attainment.

I joined the administration in 2003 and stayed for the next 10 years, eventually becoming the president of the New York City Economic Development Corporation (EDC) in 2008. I saw firsthand how starting from the administration's very earliest days, Dan's "five-borough economic development plan" became a blueprint that the City followed closely. Even after Dan's departure from government, I and others in the administration continued to look to the plan as our urtext and guiding light.

And it succeeded.

As EDC would trumpet in 2022, 15 years after Dan's departure from city government:

> When people think about New York, a lot comes to mind. Wall Street. Media. Skyscrapers. Real estate. And it's true that New York is the finance and media capital of the world. But it's so much more than that. NYC is the furthest thing imaginable from a one-industry town. We're a thriving, interconnected ecosystem, with all the ingredients for business success across every sector.

By the end of the Bloomberg administration, New York had the second-most film jobs of any state in the country, which generated $7 billion a year in economic impact.

So what special alchemy did the "five-borough economic development plan" bring to the table? The answer to that question could itself fill several volumes. However, a few illustrative case studies might help give a flavor of the methods and practices that Dan, over time, honed to perfection.

Film and television production

The film and television industry had once been a mainstay in New York. However, as production facilities in New York aged and new facilities were built in nearby cities, much of this work started to dry up. The out-migration of the industry (particularly soundstage work, which employed many more people than location shooting) accelerated as exchange rates moved against U.S. locations. The proverbial nail was driven into the production coffin in 1990, when a devastating seven-month strike drove nearly all soundstage production out of town long enough for the industry to realize that other markets (especially Toronto) were both less expensive and less challenging than New York.

This was the context in which the Bloomberg administration assumed office. Iconic New York-based TV shows such as, *Friends* and *Seinfeld* were being filmed before live audiences in Los Angeles. Feature films set in New York would jet into town for a few days of shooting on the city's streets for authenticity and then would employ hundreds of carpenters, painters, and teamsters in cavernous studio facilities north of the border.

In response, Dan tasked EDC with commissioning a study by Boston Consulting Group to understand what the City could do to reverse its fortunes. The study found that while cities such as Toronto had stolen much of New York's thunder, a good deal of the industry's talent continued to live in New York and preferred to shoot near their homes. While studios wanted to accommodate this talent, the cost premium and administrative burden of doing business in New York had simply become too great. However, if the premium and burden could be reduced, New York might just be able to lure the industry back.

With this better understanding of the environment, we developed a three-pronged plan of attack. First, the City partnered with the private sector to invest in modern soundstages, with a particular focus on Brooklyn (including the new Steiner Studios in the City-controlled Brooklyn Navy Yard) and Queens (including Silvercup Studios and the City-controlled Kaufman Astoria Studios). Second, the Mayor's Office of Film, Theatre and Broadcasting, an agency overseen by Dan and run by a new commissioner, Katherine Oliver, began to eliminate many of the administrative impediments to shooting in the city that had added cost and delay. And finally, in Albany, Katherine and I led an effort to craft a film tax incentive that would encourage local soundstage work, with a goal of maximizing the employment not just of movie stars, but of blue-collar workers who built sets and drove production vehicles.

Alexandria Center for Life Science, New York City's first commercial life science campus, houses one million square feet of lab space for industry leaders like Eli Lilly and Pfizer.

While the three-pronged plan would take several years to come to fruition, its success is unquestionable. Whereas in 2001, New York City had a handful of soundstages, many of them old and outdated, by the time the Bloomberg administration left office, New York's three major film studios — Steiner Studios in the Brooklyn Navy Yard, Silvercup Studios in Long Island City, and Kaufman Studios in Astoria, Queens — had all undergone or were planning major multi-million dollar modern expansions. New York ranked second among states for film jobs in the nation and the industry was generating $7 billion annually, an increase of over $2 billion dollars versus 2002. Today, the film industry continues to expand in the city, with a new studio planned for the Bronx and a second major facility, Wildflower Studios, backed by actor Robert De Niro, planned for Astoria, Queens, which will include 11 soundstages along with 775,000 square feet of carpentry shops and production offices.

Tourism

Another industry Dan and his team focused on was tourism. It was, after all, an industry that could pump billions of dollars in spending into the five boroughs, creating employment opportunities up and down the skills spectrum.

To achieve his goals, Dan relied heavily on a supercharged public-private partnership, NYC & Company, the city's convention and visitor's bureau. In 2006, Dan recruited George Fertitta, a successful former advertising and marketing executive, to run NYC & Company, and charged him with transforming New York from a destination that many feared and shunned to one that everyone from the business traveler, to culture vultures, to young families, could place at or near the top of their list of favorites.

Responding to Dan's charge, NYC & Company opened tourism offices around the world to market New York aggressively and worked closely with the hospitality industry to ensure that the city's hotel stock was ready for growing demand. The City also leveraged attention-grabbing events such as an NFL Kickoff in Times Square and Christo and Jeanne-Claude's The Gates exhibit in Central Park to generate "buzz" and turn New York into a topic of global conversation. And, the administration invested heavily in the city's art, culture, and entertainment infrastructure, making New York not only a more rewarding place in which to live, but also, not incidentally, making it a more exciting place to visit.

Once again, the results would speak for themselves. Over the course of the Bloomberg administration, the number of tourists coming to New York each year would increase from around 35 million to 54.3 million or nearly 54%, while the number of international visitors coming to the city would increase from 5.1 to 11.4 million, an astounding increase of more than 100%.

Commercial life sciences

Still another industry on which we heaped attention under Dan's leadership was the commercial life sciences industry. For years, New York had lagged industry leaders such as the Bay Area, San Diego, and Boston. And yet, New York had so many natural advantages, including more academic medical centers than any other city in America.

Why then, Dan would ask us, were the companies generated within New York's hospitals and universities nearly all growing outside of the city? Eventually, Dan, working with EDC under its President Andy Alper, would conclude that what the industry lacked in New

York was space — or, more particularly, purpose-built space in which life science discoveries could be turned into businesses and then grown to scale.

Dan directed EDC to set about creating life science facilities across the city, with the flagship effort being the Alexandria Center for Life Science on Manhattan's East Side. Built on City-owned land wedged between a shelter for homeless men, the FDR Drive, and, most crucially, NYU Langone Hospital, the facility was developed by California-based Alexandria Real Estate Equities, one of the world's leading builders and operators of commercial life science space, with a long track record of success. By the end of the Bloomberg administration, the facility would contain more than one million square feet of cutting-edge lab space in two state-of-the-art towers and would be occupied by industry leaders, including Bristol Myers Squibb, Eli Lilly, and Pfizer.

Tech

And then there was tech — a sector that had powered so much economic activity in New England and on the West Coast, but had largely bypassed New York. After watching the seeds of sectoral activity in New York almost entirely disappear over the horizon after the dot-com crash of 2001, the sector would rise once again in the city like a phoenix under the Bloomberg administration.

Thanks to groundwork laid during Dan's tenure, by the time the Bloomberg administration drew to a close, the city was viewed by most as the nation's number two tech center, drawing billions of dollars in venture capital investment each year and attracting hundreds of thousands of square feet of office leases from leading companies such as Google, Amazon, and Facebook/Meta.

While the sector's meteoric growth would largely occur following the 2008 financial crisis after Dan's departure from city government, Dan nurtured and taught the team who led that growth.

We followed Dan's playbook to the letter, spending months analyzing the city's strengths and weaknesses, then developing and deploying pilot programs to test emergent hypotheses, and finally doubling down on programs and initiatives that turned out to be most successful to ensure maximum policy impact.

From a network of new business incubators to partnerships with venture capital firms that directed seed capital to local entrepreneurs, step-by-step, the City's efforts built the case that New York was open to and welcoming of the tech industry and that the industry could actually benefit from a New York location.

All of these efforts culminated in our idea for an Applied Sciences Competition, which I initiated during my presidency at EDC. We designed the project to secure a critical mass of applied sciences talent and research and development for New York — the sort of activity at MIT that had powered Boston's start-up scene and at Stanford that had powered Silicon Valley. Eventually, multiple leading universities from around the world participated in the competition, drawing breathless international press attention and signaling to previously skeptical industry leaders that New York had arrived as an "it" location. Among the projects that emerged from the competition were a major expansion of Columbia University's engineering program, the creation of a brand-new engineering center for NYU in Downtown Brooklyn, and the ground-up development of what would eventually become a $2 billion technology campus on Roosevelt Island developed by Cornell University and The Technion of Israel.

The dividends continue

Of course, even after all that Dan did to transform New York, the finance industry would continue to be a major economic driver for New York. But it is irrefutable that thanks to Dan's "five-borough economic development plan" the city's economy became far different from — and far more resilient than — when Dan had first arrived on the scene in 2002.

Perhaps nothing illustrates this point better than the economic crisis of 2008. In that fateful year, the world's financial infrastructure was rocked by the serial collapse or near-collapse of venerable firms such as Bear Stearns, Merrill Lynch, and Lehman Brothers — a recipe that, prior to 2002, surely would have spelled disaster for the city's economy.

Yet, following the crisis, New York's economy confounded the predictions of nearly every expert. In fact, not only did the city enter the Great Recession that ensued well after the rest of the

The Cornell Tech campus on Roosevelt Island was initiated by the Bloomberg administration to support New York's ambition to diversify the economy and bring in new industries, including the technology sector.

country, but it also *emerged* faster and with a stronger recovery than the rest of the country, benefitting from its then-appreciably greater economic diversification — a testament to Dan's foresight and his effectiveness at putting his economic development theories into practice.

Even in 2022, a full 15 years after Dan left City Hall, the economy of New York — the economy imagined and nurtured by Dan — continues to pay dividends. For example, life sciences represents one of the city's fastest growing sectors, and now contributes more than $3 billion annually to the region's gross metropolitan product. And New York's 25,000 tech-enabled start-ups represent the most such start-ups anywhere in America outside of the Bay Area. Of course, in 2022, such statistics are taken for granted. However, the truth is that, prior to Dan, they were virtually unimaginable, and without Dan, they simply never would have come to be.

ANDREW ALPER | President, New York City Economic
Development Corporation, 2002–2006

GROWING JOBS IN THE POST-9/11 ERA

In late 2001 when Dan Doctoroff told me he was leaving his private equity firm to become deputy mayor I questioned his sanity. When he asked if I wanted to join him to run the New York City Economic Development Corporation (EDC), I knew he had lost his mind. I had been at Goldman Sachs for 21 years and I wasn't contemplating leaving. I firmly said, "No thanks." But anyone who knows Dan knows he can be very persuasive. A couple of months later I found myself in the City Hall Blue Room standing next to Mayor Michael Bloomberg while he announced my appointment.

What changed? Several things . . . like many New Yorkers, for me, 9/11 was personal. I had spent my entire career in Lower Manhattan and the destruction was an inconceivable insult. Mike Bloomberg promised that he was beholden to no special interests and that we were free to "do the right thing" to rebuild New York. Most importantly I had enormous respect for Dan. We had gotten to know each other across the negotiating table while I was running Goldman's Financial Institutions Group and Dan was running a private equity fund investing in insurance companies. I quickly realized during those sometimes torturous negotiations that we were both invested in actually getting a deal done; we weren't trying to kill each other. I appreciated Dan's integrity, creativity, and energy and we became close friends. At the City, Dan articulated an exciting vision for New York's future and the opportunity to work closely with him to help realize that vision was too compelling to pass up.

Still, when I showed up at EDC in early 2002, New York City's future seemed bleak. The accepted wisdom, reinforced with daily newspaper headlines, was that the city and especially Lower Manhattan would never recover. There were concerns about further terrorist attacks, the many government stakeholders couldn't agree on priorities, we faced years of disruption from rebuilding, and businesses and their employees were reluctant to commit. More than two decades later, it can be difficult to remember the degree to which people feared that New York's economy would never recover.

Dan and I quickly got to work, deploying many of the skills we'd built in our finance careers to persuade employers to stay and grow in New York. We retained world-class, pro bono advisors to perform detailed analyses of the city's competitive advantages — including a diverse, talented, and resilient workforce, our concentration of key supporting industries like media, law and finance, and our connectedness to the world as a global travel hub. We also carefully assessed the city's weaknesses, including most notably the cost of doing business as compared to alternatives such as New Jersey — and we developed tactics to address those weaknesses, such as carefully deploying incentives like low-cost financing. Dan and I — and the teams we built — had the experience to know not only how to communicate to CEOs, but also to their tax departments. We spoke their language.

But even as we sought to persuade employers to stay in New York, we took a hard line when companies tried to take advantage of our position. Early in the administration, Dan and I met with a lobbyist for an energy project, who showed a glossy PowerPoint

presentation that included financials explaining how successful the project could be. Dan just grilled him on the numbers, and it turned out that he had no idea what they meant. You could just see this poor guy thinking, "Oh boy, this is a different ballgame than what I'm used to."

The best example was our discussions with the New York Stock Exchange (NYSE), which had cut a deal with the prior administration for huge subsidies to stay in New York rather than move to New Jersey. Dan and I dug into the details, and came to the conclusion that the arrangement was just a giveaway with no public benefit. We went to see the CEO of the NYSE in his enormous office, which you could only reach after passing through layers of security (most of which predated 9/11), and that for some reason was heated to what felt like 100 degrees. The whole scene seemed

As part of a new policy cracking down on corporate incentive programs, the Bloomberg administration retracted a $1.1 billion subsidy to the New York Stock Exchange promised by the previous administration. The New York Stock Exchange ultimately stayed in its historic Downtown location anyway.

designed to convey the power of the NYSE, and to intimidate visitors such as Dan and myself. But he couldn't intimidate us, and he couldn't intimidate Mike Bloomberg. We called his bluff, and of course the NYSE stayed put in Lower Manhattan.

Along with the backing of the mayor, the most powerful tool we had was Dan's vision, powerfully rendered in perfect PowerPoint presentations and energetically articulated in countless speeches. Dan's vision for the future of New York got people excited but more importantly, he gave them confidence in that future. The confidence was well placed. Many people are persuasive but few deliver — Dan and the team around him over-delivered.

Today, driving around the five boroughs you can see Dan's vision realized everywhere. From Downtown Brooklyn and Williamsburg, to Hunter's Point South and Long Island City; from the South Bronx to Hudson Yards and, of course, at Ground Zero and the surrounding Financial District — Dan's exciting plans and tireless promotion helped us turn the tide. New York bounced back faster and stronger than anyone imagined possible. I'm grateful that he persuaded me to come along for the ride.

MAUREEN J. REIDY | President and CEO, NYC Big Events, 2002–2007

WELCOME TO NEW YORK: PUTTING THE CITY BACK ON THE WORLD STAGE

The attacks of 9/11 were first and foremost a human tragedy, but more than two decades later it's easy to forget that it was also economically devastating for New York — particularly for the tourism industry. Outsiders saw the city as a terrorist target, and the result was that thousands of New Yorkers in the industry lost their jobs — including men and women just starting their climb up the economic ladder.

In early 2002, I unexpectedly found myself at City Hall being offered a job in the Bloomberg administration by the new Deputy Mayor for Economic Development and Rebuilding, Dan Doctoroff.

The task that Dan outlined was to build a permanent "host committee" to attract high-profile events to New York City that could draw visitors, generate positive media impressions, and make it clear that New York was "open for business." I had previously served as CEO of the Miss Universe Organization and, among other things, was responsible for reviewing host city bids and negotiating the host city agreements, which provided a unique perspective for this new role from the other side of the table.

As the daughter of a New York City firefighter and a public school math teacher, and a lifelong New Yorker, this opportunity immediately felt like more than just a job . . . it was a calling.

We called the new entity NYC Big Events, and our first project was executing an event Dan and his team had already secured: the first-ever NFL Kickoff concert, to be held in Times Square in September — near the first anniversary of the attacks.

Working with Dan's staff and a dozen city agencies, we overcame extraordinary logistical challenges to pull off a concert that *The New York Times* reported attracted a half million people. A year after 9/11, we broadcast to the nation and the world that New York was back. I was just three months into my new role, and our new agency was off and running.

We quickly turned our attention to attracting other marquee events to build on that momentum, using a deliberate strategy to prioritize counterintuitive events that could introduce New York to new audiences and reshape the perception of the city around the nation and the world. Three such events stand out in my memory.

Republican National Convention, 2004
During this time, New York submitted bids to host both the Democratic and Republican National Conventions in 2004. But as Dan wrote in his book, *Greater Than Ever*, the one he really wanted was the GOP — not because he was a Republican (he's not), but because he wanted to introduce New York to audiences who were unlikely to visit otherwise. The Republican Convention included high-spending visitors from all 50 states, many of whom had outdated perceptions of the city; when you added in the global media surrounding the event, it was an irresistible prize.

We won, but planning it was a full-time job and I was consumed with running NYC Big Events and preparing for the 2003 MTV Video Music Awards and the 2004 VH1 Hip-Hop Honors. As a result, initially I cheered on the capable convention Host Committee from afar. When Dan and the mayor later asked me to come on board to simultaneously run the committee's day-to-day operations, I was reluctant to say the least. "This is so much bigger than anything I've ever done before. I'm not sure I can do this," I told him. But Dan was firmly in my corner. He assured me that I could do it, telling me, "You have the smarts, experience, energy, and capability to do this. I know you can do this, and we will all be here for whatever you need." And so, we got to work.

Every Monday over the next year, I joined afternoon meetings with Kevin Sheekey, who led the Host Committee, Dan, Mayor Bloomberg, and First Deputy Mayor Patti Harris as we worked through the complex details of an event with a $150 million budget. Hosting a political convention is an extraordinary undertaking in any city — but in New York in the post-9/11 era, it was herculean. To add a special New York touch and create a happy press corps, at Kevin's suggestion, we hired famed retailer, Barneys to set up a spa in the media center in the Farley Post Office and built a special pedestrian bridge over Eighth Avenue to let them travel easily to the convention at Madison Square Garden without separate security checks.

Dan emphasized how important this opportunity was for New York to dispel negative stereotypes, showcase the best of the city, and change perceptions. And it worked. Even in the face of security concerns and large but mostly peaceful protests, delegates had a great time spending money on Broadway shows, in restaurants, and even at the famed Copacabana night club. In at least one theater, different delegations took turns singing their state songs while waiting for the show to begin (including the Kansas delegation's rendition of "Home on the Range"). If our mission was to bring new audiences to New York, we succeeded beyond our wildest dreams.

Country Music Association (CMA) Awards, 2005
In its nearly 40-year history, the CMA Awards had never once been held outside of Nashville. New York City didn't have a single country music station. Nonetheless, with Dan's guidance in mind, I cold-called the CEO of the CMA, and asked if they would ever consider hosting the CMA Awards in New York. I pointed to the potential to grow the industry's fan base in the country's largest market. It was the longest of long-shot calls. After I made my pitch there was a pause that seemed to last forever; he finally responded in his distinguished southern accent, "Now, that's an idea."

From there we were off and running. In New York, the country music community found an extraordinary welcome, including from a cowboy hat-wearing Mayor Bloomberg. We put together a week-long series of events across the city under the motto, "Country Takes New York City." *People* did a special issue on country music that was so successful, it became a weekly publication. And it created extraordinary moments for fans and artists alike. I vividly remember one event: When the Grand Ole Opry — a century-old Nashville institution — came to Carnegie Hall. Country music

In September 2002, the first-ever NFL Kickoff concert drew half a million people to Times Square around the first anniversary of 9/11.

superstars accustomed to singing before tens of thousands of people walked onto the main stage, wide-eyed, obviously awed at the opportunity to perform in such a historic venue. One female artist quipped after finishing her first song, "That's the first time I've done that one wearing a ball gown but the next song is a ballad and hey — it's Carnegie Hall."

Latin GRAMMY Awards, 2006

Every two weeks, Dan and I would meet at City Hall to strategize, brainstorm, and review the status of our plans. During one such meeting we were discussing the administration's various efforts to raise the profile of the Hispanic-focused media industry in New York (Dan had chartered a Latin Media and Entertainment Commission). Our conversation quickly turned to the Latin GRAMMY Awards, which had previously only been held in Los Angeles and Miami. The next day, I once again placed a cold call, but this time to the CEO of the Latin Academy of Recording Arts & Sciences (LARAS), the organization that produces the Latin GRAMMY Awards.

This time the pause wasn't quite so long. The CEO of LARAS immediately saw the benefit of hosting the Latin GRAMMYs in New York City. Together with the broadcaster, Univision, we hashed out a deal and in November 2006, for the first and only time, the Latin GRAMMY Awards took place in the Big Apple. Working with LARAS, we created Latin GRAMMY Week, which included activities in schools, neighborhood concerts, and more. While the show's finale was a grand tribute to New York's largest Latin community — featuring the renowned Puerto Rican style of salsa music — the show and the events surrounding it celebrated the rich tapestry of Spanish-speaking nationalities represented in the five boroughs.

Country Music Association (CMA) Board of Directors President Kix Brooks (far left) and Maureen J. Reidy (far right) join Mayor Michael Bloomberg to announce that the 2005 CMA Awards will be held in New York City. The event marked the first and only time the event has taken place outside of Nashville.

Dan's crystal-clear vision and faith in me — his refusal to accept the status quo and unprecedented belief in what is possible — gave me a reservoir of confidence that I continue to draw on two decades later. During my time in government, I gave everything I had to New York, but it's nothing compared to what that experience — and Dan himself — gave to me.

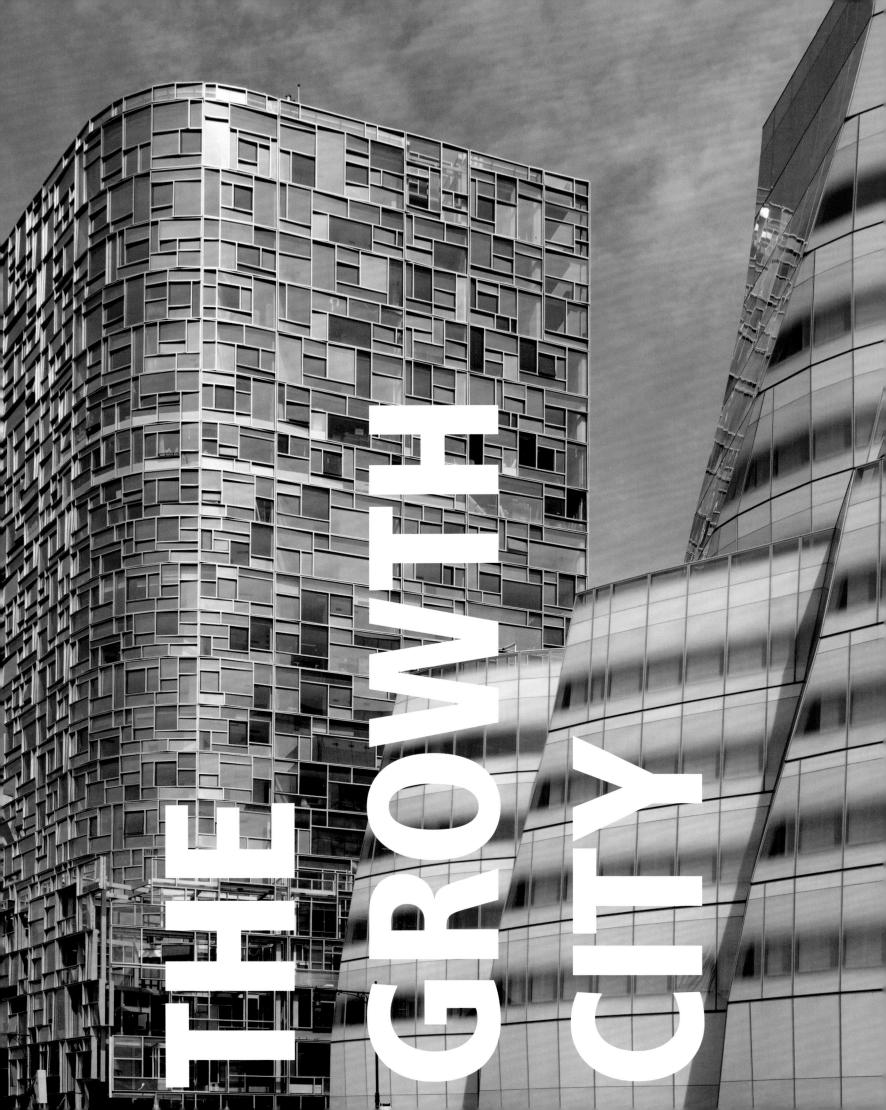

THE GROWTH CITY

Development on Manhattan's
Far West Side, including the Frank
Gehry-designed IAC headquarters
on the right, completed in 2007.

151

"We are a
restless people
and we know
in our hearts that
cities, like people,
must grow
and change."

DANIEL L. DOCTOROFF, NOVEMBER 2003

Pier 2 Uplands,
Brooklyn Bridge Park.

DIANE CARDWELL | City Hall Bureau Chief, *The New York Times*, 2006–2008

DOCTOROFF'S VIRTUOUS CYCLE OF GROWTH

How a five-borough growth strategy reinvigorated New York City

If you walk down DUMBO's Old Fulton Street, named for the man who first established regular steam ferry service between Manhattan and Brooklyn, you'll come to Brooklyn Bridge Park.

Twenty years ago, you would have seen black metal fencing blocking a ribbon of faded cargo piers, cutting off access to the waterfront. Today, you can meander from basketball and pickleball courts to woodlands and lawns, or past the marsh grasses that herald a sandy shoreline with a kayak launch and marina, and to the soccer field and restaurant farther south. It is possible to stay at the park — luxury residences and a hotel sit along its inland edge, controversial sources of revenue that pay for the bulk of the park's upkeep. But you can also Citi Bike over from a digital economy office in DUMBO or a film production job at the Brooklyn Navy Yard for a picnic lunch or a waterfront workout.

The roots of this development stretch to earlier administrations, but the borough's evolution into essentially a thriving, 21st century city was ultimately masterminded and fast-tracked under the direction of Daniel Doctoroff as the Deputy Mayor for Economic Development and Rebuilding in the Bloomberg administration.

From the park's Granite Prospect, a majestic stairway of more than 300 granite stones salvaged from the reconstruction of the Roosevelt Island Bridge that rises some 30 feet, visitors can access a dramatic vantage point and view of New York City that never existed before — Doctoroff's imagination and approach come to life. The panorama sweeps across from Midtown Manhattan and the Brooklyn Bridge to the Statue of Liberty, framing Lower Manhattan and the rebuilt World Trade Center, where the fires that burned for months in the wreckage of the 2001 terror attack still smoldered when Doctoroff came into office. Now that area is much as he promised: a diverse neighborhood where gleaming corporate and residential towers rub against historic homes and commercial buildings, knit together with restaurants, shops, schools, and open spaces.

Also visible across the river is the Victorian splendor of the Battery Maritime Building, which creates a portal to the busy Harbor District that Doctoroff championed, believing — like Fulton before him — that the waterways could be crucial drivers of economic expansion. A network of ferries now connects Manhattan and Brooklyn to Governors Island — a former military outpost Doctoroff helped repurpose as a popular, multiuse park — and provides links to far-flung parts of the city, all the way from Throgs Neck in the Bronx to the Rockaway Peninsula at the southern border of Queens.

Indeed, Brooklyn Bridge Park and its environs are as complete an encapsulation as any of the ambitious and transformative developments Doctoroff devised, resuscitated, or accelerated.

Dan Doctoroff envisioned Brooklyn Bridge Park as a key link in the redevelopment of the postindustrial Brooklyn waterfront. He coordinated City efforts to develop the 85–acre park, which now attracts five million annual visitors. Below, Pier 1, Brooklyn Bridge Park.

Barclays Center in Downtown Brooklyn is home to the Brooklyn Nets, the first professional sports team in Brooklyn since the Dodgers left the borough in 1955. The arena's location, at the intersection of Atlantic and Flatbush Avenues, is where Dodgers owner, Walter O'Malley wanted to build a new ballpark to replace Ebbets Field.

Doctoroff aimed to create completely new ways of life — self-sustaining mini-cities, in essence — in areas of New York he considered neglected, underdeveloped, or otherwise not living up to their potential. The plans and vision he brought to City Hall were guided by the Olympic bid, which gave a terror-ravaged city a sense of hopefulness and the development agenda a sense of urgency. But the result, even with the bid's failure, was a historic reimagining of the built environment that, with its emphasis on attractive public spaces, sidewalks with sleek new newsstands and bus shelters, increasingly diverse transit options, residential density, and vibrant mixed-use districts, continues to reshape people's experience of the urban landscape in all five boroughs.

By the time Doctoroff ended his tenure as development czar in 2007, he had laid the groundwork for 130 million square feet of commercial and residential space, three new professional sports facilities, the city's first subway extension in decades, 2,400 acres of new or renovated parks, and the development of more than 60 miles of waterfront, according to City Hall at the time. Officials had approved 78 rezonings across all five boroughs, affecting more than 6,000 blocks, the most significant changes since the 1960s. Agencies had either completed, begun constructing or funded 65,000 of the 165,000 affordable housing units that they had promised by 2013.

"As the chief architect of our five-borough economic development plan," an unusually emotional Mayor Michael Bloomberg said in announcing Doctoroff's departure near the end of 2007, "Dan Doctoroff has done more to change the face of this city than anyone since Robert Moses."

Five-borough economic plan

Doctoroff frequently inspires such comparisons, and it's likely that no one else came into New York City government armed with as towering an ambition for change since the Moses era. For Moses, though, a central focus was remaking New York for the motor age, easing drivers in and out of the city, whether they were commuting for work or heading out of town for the weekend to a Long Island beach or a vast new state park.

Doctoroff, by contrast, wanted to create a city of enclaves you didn't want to leave, with its own destination parks like Governors Island, Brooklyn Bridge Park, and the High Line. His transportation agenda focused on how to move people through the city efficiently and pleasantly, largely without disturbing the surrounding neighborhoods. Instead of bulldozing streets and houses for new urban highways, Doctoroff oversaw the extension of the No. 7 subway line to 34th Street and 11th Avenue and established plans to improve bus service, add hundreds of miles of bike lanes, and jumpstart the new ferry network.

Much of the growth he championed was conceived as a way to defend against multiple challenges to New York's success. When the Bloomberg administration took office on January 1, 2002, it faced a need to replace office and commercial space destroyed in the terror attack, provide resiliency in the event another disaster struck Manhattan, and reverse the economic outflow to New Jersey, which had been siphoning jobs and back office workers since the 1990s.

Doctoroff also recognized that New York needed new kinds of jobs — the terrorist attacks laid bare the dangers of concentrating the city's financial power in one industry, in a single place. There were more reasons to diversify the economy by sector and geography. When manufacturing dried up as the city's main

industry — leaving swaths of abandoned, contaminated waterfront land — middle and working class jobs had evaporated with it.

The idea was to play off New York's built-in advantages — cultural and educational institutions, a well-developed transit system, miles of waterfront, and historic neighborhoods — to develop new outer borough business centers and expand into new industries. Doctoroff focused on the many places, including waterfront Brooklyn, the Far West Side of Manhattan and West Chelsea, the South Bronx, Willets Point, Hunter's Point South, Flushing, and Jamaica in Queens, and the Homeport, a decommissioned Reagan-era naval station in Staten Island, which all seemed like natural candidates for reinvention.

The virtuous cycle of growth

Underpinning Doctoroff's work as deputy mayor was a conviction, shared by the mayor, that New York would need to do more than just add jobs to survive, let alone thrive in the coming decades: It needed to grow. Even as the city still reeled from the economic devastation of the dot-com bubble collapse and 9/11, New York needed to attract more residents to add to the tax base, more businesses to employ them, and more housing, restaurants, and amusements to keep them — and their spending — in the city.

"The most important metric of a city's health is population growth," Doctoroff wrote in his 2017 memoir, *Greater Than Ever: New York's Big Comeback*. "In my mind, a city was like any other product. It had customers. It had competitors. It had to be marketed. How would you know if you were doing your job successfully? The answer: More people would choose New York over other places to live, and the population would grow."

Population growth, he believed, powers a virtuous cycle for the flourishing metropolis. Most cities in the developed world have already invested tremendous amounts of capital in their infrastructure such as roads, mass transit, power plants, sewers, schools, his thinking went. As long as there is excess capacity in those systems, the marginal tax revenue of adding the average new person will exceed the marginal cost of absorbing them, resulting in a net profit to the coffers. That increased revenue can go to improving quality of life, which then attracts more people and businesses, generating more revenue, allowing the city to become even safer, cleaner, more entertaining, interesting, and convenient, with better housing, greater education and employment opportunities, and so on.

In the absence of population growth, cities are instead sucked into a vicious cycle — a death spiral in which the flight of residents and businesses occasions a loss of revenue, resulting in cuts to core services like education, healthcare, sanitation, and public safety, which further accelerates population and business losses and disinvestment. Doctoroff had observed that downward swirl directly growing up in the suburbs of Detroit during the 1960s and 1970s.

New York experienced a similar cycle during that era when many middle-class and affluent New Yorkers moved to the suburbs and revenues could not keep pace with spending, leading to increased borrowing, sharp reductions in services and, ultimately, the brink of bankruptcy. In fact, when Doctoroff visited the city as a child he developed an instant aversion to its dilapidated buildings and dirty streets. By the time he reluctantly moved near Gramercy Park in 1983, the city's budget had stabilized and the economy was poised to rebound, but New York continued to struggle with economic and social issues and rising crime.

In the 1990s, a tech boom and a spectacular reduction in crime mainly under Mayor Rudolph Giuliani fueled economic and population growth. But 9/11 rekindled fears of a return to the budget cuts and trash-filled, crime-riddled streets that could drive people away and doom the city to decline for at least another generation. Those fears had some grounding in the facts: In the three months after the attack, New York lost around 430,000 jobs and about $2.8 billion in wages, as well as roughly $2 billion in tax revenue.

Historic scale of rezonings

As part of the Olympic bid, Doctoroff and his planning director, Alex Garvin, had identified areas that could support the Games but that were also ripe for dense residential and mixed-use development over the long term, including large waterfront swaths of Williamsburg and Greenpoint in Brooklyn, Long Island City in Queens, and the Metropolitan Transportation Authority (MTA) rail yards on the Far West Side of Manhattan. Much of those areas remained zoned for manufacturing, a relic of New York's last comprehensive zoning resolution in 1961 when planners were looking to retain an industrial economy already in decline. It hadn't succeeded and New York City lost nearly a million manufacturing jobs while leaving the waterfront largely abandoned and constrained by zoning that often limited construction to low-slung industrial buildings.

Once in City Hall, Doctoroff worked with Amanda Burden, the Chair of the City Planning Commission, to spearhead an aggressive land-use program to reassess and rezone these long-neglected areas. Ultimately, they would rezone nearly 40% of the entire city.

A pattern emerged in several of the plans: upzone to increase density and require street level commerce where there were existing (or potential) transit options, infrastructure, and sufficiently wide streets, while capping heights on residential mid-blocks to maintain, at Burden's insistence, neighborhood architectural context. The rezoning of more than 100 blocks of Park Slope in 2003, for instance, largely preserved the charm and scale of the area's three- and four-story Victorian town houses while spurring larger-scale residential development along Fourth Avenue. At the time, its width matched that of Park Avenue in Manhattan yet the avenue was dominated by auto repair shops, gas stations, delicatessens, and three-story walk-ups.

They designed many of the rezonings to achieve 24-7, live-work-play communities, in contrast to traditional "downtown" business districts where vast canyons of buildings went dark at night or cut off the surrounding streetscape — as had been the case with the original World Trade Center development and much of Lower Manhattan. That meant integrating housing, commercial, and retail development into the plans, along with significant public space. But Doctoroff, Burden, and their teams also experimented with more novel, targeted interventions to enliven street life. In the 125th Street rezoning, the City included rules that banks — which typically closed in the afternoons — put most of their operations on the second floor, freeing ground level space for more dynamic commercial operations.

While rezonings occurred in every borough, Doctoroff saw Brooklyn's potential to emerge almost as a separate city. The borough boasted its own transit and energy infrastructures, business core, industry, schools, cultural institutions, leisure hubs, and retail centers. The coordinated suite of Brooklyn rezonings — from the office-driven reinvention of Downtown Brooklyn, the housing-focused reimagining of the Greenpoint-Williamsburg waterfront, and the mixed-use development of Atlantic Yards, anchored by Barclays Center — dovetailed with other efforts to enliven faded parts of the borough and strengthen its natural competitive advantages. That included reviving Coney Island and supporting its long-neglected residential community, creating a new Brooklyn cultural district around the Brooklyn Academy of Music (BAM), one of the borough's established artistic anchors, and building new signature waterfront parks like Brooklyn Bridge Park. The City's investments spurred private developments that are still bringing glassy residential towers to formerly dilapidated waterfronts, as well as upscale hotels, office and apartment buildings, and clusters of restaurants, fitness centers, and stores to the Downtown area and beyond, with a Brooklyn brand known worldwide.

New construction in Port Morris, the Bronx. After years of neglect by prior mayoral administrations, Dan Doctoroff and the broader Bloomberg administration gave the South Bronx renewed focus, resulting in new residential and commercial development.

Planning officials took a similar approach in Long Island City and Hunter's Point South, Queens, upzoning light manufacturing areas for higher density, mixed commercial and residential uses, and sparking a building boom that continues to fill the area with enormous residential and commercial towers in a new Downtown, anchored by an award-winning waterfront park.

And on the Far West Side of Manhattan, Doctoroff used the Olympic catalyst to bring long-simmering plans to fruition, powering through a massive rezoning in 2005 involving the exposed MTA rail yards between 30th and 34th Streets and 10th Avenue to the Hudson River that allowed for 28 million square feet of new commercial space and 12,600 units of housing. In an area once largely populated by auto body shops, parking lots, and warehouses, the redevelopment has plopped corporate skyscrapers, luxury condominiums, restaurants, parks, and a huge shopping mall atop a platform constructed over the yards that allows trains to continue running underneath. After he left city government, Doctoroff spearheaded the effort to give the neighborhood a signature cultural institution — The Shed — where in October 2022,

Ralph Fiennes opened as none other than Robert Moses in a play examining his legacy, *Straight Line Crazy*, by David Hare.

Doctoroff used a variety of strategies to encourage the kind of development he wanted to see: pushing every agency to pony up City-owned land under its control, creating a revolving credit facility for small developers to buy property for affordable housing, instituting a grant program to encourage brownfield remediation, and adopting a voluntary inclusionary zoning policy that allowed developers to build bigger in exchange for providing (or preserving) a portion of onsite or offsite below-market apartments.

By 2010, the Bloomberg administration had added 170,000 housing units since 2000, more than any other city, according to a *New York Times* census analysis. That growth was concentrated in neighborhoods that the administration had targeted for development.

The economy expanded across the city as well, driven by gains outside Manhattan, according to a 2017 report from the city comptroller's office. While the number of businesses overall grew by 16% between 2000 and 2015, it declined by 2% in Manhattan —

The postindustrial Hunter's Point South area was abandoned when Dan Doctoroff and his NYC2012 Olympic planning team identified it as a potential site for the Olympic Village. After New York lost its bid to host the Games, the City moved ahead with plans to develop the land into mixed-income housing and an 11-acre waterfront park. Above, Hunter's Point South Park, showing the circular lawn and seven white phosphorescent mounds that glow at night, features of the award-winning park design.

while increasing by 48% in Brooklyn, 33% in Queens, 26% in the Bronx, and 22% in Staten Island.

As for population, Doctoroff's approach was indeed effective in attracting new people. The city grew by nearly 10%, adding almost 800,000 residents, from 2000 to 2020, according to census figures from the Department of City Planning. Brooklyn gained the most overall, an additional 270,700 residents, with some of the highest growth rates occurring in the rezoned areas of Brooklyn and Queens, especially along the waterfront.

The recovery accelerated so quickly that even Doctoroff and his team were stunned. When City Planning projected in 2005 that New York City was on track to attract another million people by 2030, the shift in Doctoroff's challenge had become explicit. He was no longer seeking to save a city from shrinking in decline after the terrorist attacks of 9/11 — instead, he needed to manage the city's abundant growth before New York was overrun.

How one feels about all this is largely a matter of perspective. If you view the city as a product — a commodity with value to be captured and reinvested — then it's all been to the good: Doctoroff's virtuous cycle attracted newcomers and businesses whose economic activity helped swell the city's purse, which allowed for greater government outlays on amenities and basic services benefitting the general population — which drew more business and newcomers.

According to expenditures reported by the Independent Budget Office, spending under Bloomberg grew faster in the first half of his tenure than under any mayor since the Lindsay administration, despite a diminishing share of state and federal aid, and continued to grow until he left office. This included bigger operating budgets for police, which increased by roughly 30% over his three terms (from about $3.6 billion to $4.7 billion), sanitation, which went up by 43% (from $989 million to $1.4 billion), education, which rose by 59% (from $11.7 billion to $18.7 billion), and parks, which expanded by 83% (from $198 million to $363 million), while the Parks Department capital budget more than doubled from $211 million to $424 million.

All of that churn was clearly good for the property owners and developers who made fortunes as land values soared as well as for the more highly educated and affluent residents who flocked to the buffed and polished neighborhoods, where they supported all manner of restaurants, shops, cultural institutions, and service providers.

But if you were among the longtime, lower income, often minority, apartment dwellers and shopkeepers and customers who found no place amid the upscale grocers, swankier establishments, and glass towers creating new skylines in so many parts of town, you might see things differently. Doctoroff has said that to be progressive, a city must be prosperous, meaning that the government needs to generate enough money to be able to spend on helping those who need it. But he has also acknowledged that the city's runaway prosperity did not result in commensurate progress for all members of society.

A downside to the explosive growth, he wrote, was that the city became more expensive more quickly and that the costs and benefits of his plans were not fairly shared. The city still needs to grow, he told *The New York Times* in 2020, but it also needs,

The redevelopment of Pier 17 at the South Street Seaport into a new concert venue and public space, with its signature lightband, is part of the recently completed 1.5-mile East River Waterfront Esplanade, which the Bloomberg administration initiated more than two decades ago as part of the rebuilding effort from 9/11.

"a more comprehensive, shared prosperity model." The question, he added, "is, what does that mean?"

Subsequent administrations have continued to grapple with that question, making inclusionary zoning mandatory, for instance — to limited effect — and battling stiff opposition to put even one affordable apartment building next to Brooklyn Bridge Park. The market for luxury in neighborhoods like the Upper East and Upper West Sides has become so overheated that developers are building fewer, larger, more expensive units where they could create multiple smaller, less expensive apartments as of right, further exacerbating the affordability crisis.

In 2022, Doctoroff responded to another generational crisis with his answer. He joined Robin Hood CEO Richard R. Buery, Jr. in co-chairing a blue-ribbon panel for Mayor Eric Adams and Governor Kathy Hochul to develop strategies for reviving the city's commercial districts in the wake of the COVID-19 pandemic. The plan, *Making New York Work for Everyone*, is as striking for the breadth of its mission — which places the equitable sharing of the city's prosperity at the center of the economic recovery strategy — as it is for the apparent cooperation of the mayor and governor, a requirement if the plan is to succeed.

A changed city
In the meantime, what Doctoroff started back in the aftermath of 9/11 — when the site was still a yawning chasm of debris and the city was suffused with legitimate worries about its ability to survive — continues to breathe a certain kind of life into spaces in all five boroughs, remaking the landscape and how it functions.

At Brooklyn Bridge Park — as in Williamsburg, Hudson Yards, Long Island City, Downtown Brooklyn or around the High Line — it's getting hard to see how things used to be, hard even to remember what running along the narrow sidewalks of Furman Street from Atlantic Avenue toward the bridge was like in the 1990s: a spooky, exhaust choked affair, affording only the occasional, fleeting glimpse of the river and Lower Manhattan beyond the gated piers, unpeopled, dotted with shipping containers and industrial sheds.

What a difference now, when you can run along the river itself, close enough to watch the seaweed, flotsam, and jetsam drift with the currents. For the average New Yorker, this may be among Doctoroff's most enduring achievements: restoring access to the waterfront, whether for transit, recreation, relaxation, or dwelling, and helping to redefine what and where a spectacular public space can be.

Following Spread: Promenade at Pier 6, Brooklyn Bridge Park.

CHARLES V. BAGLI | Reporter, *The New York Observer*, 1987–1996 | Reporter, *The New York Times*, 1996–2018

ONE PLAN AFTER ANOTHER

Over 20 years I covered how a "kid from Michigan" left a mark on his adopted city

I first sat down with Daniel L. Doctoroff at the ESPN Zone sports bar in Times Square in December 2001, shortly after newly elected Mayor Michael Bloomberg announced that he had selected the curly-headed, whiz kid from Michigan to be his deputy mayor for economic development and rebuilding.

By then, I had been getting reports about Dan for six or seven years from the developers, politicians, hedge-funders, and operators in the world I covered as a reporter, first at *The New York Observer* and later at *The New York Times*. They would tell me about their encounters with this brash former equity manager who implored them to get behind his quest to bring the Olympics to New York City, first in 2008 and later, in 2012.

I admit I shared some of their eye-rolling and the deeply embedded New York indifference — What a hassle! New York doesn't need the Olympics; it already is the greatest city in the world — with which some of them greeted Dan's seemingly quixotic pursuit.

As it turned out, his dream for the 2008 Olympics did not pan out when the United States Olympic Committee decided not to bid that year, but Dan did not disappear, nor did he abandon his dream of bringing the Olympics to his adopted home. Dan is nothing if not tenacious. When Mayor Michael Bloomberg tapped him to be deputy mayor, he did have one condition: that the Bloomberg administration get solidly behind the bid for the 2012 Olympics.

I was never keen on the centerpiece of Dan's Olympic bid: building and subsidizing a multibillion-dollar stadium in one of the most traffic-congested spots in Manhattan, for later use by a team that plays only 10 home games a year and generates a few low-paid, seasonal jobs (aside from the players).

But by my calculation, Dan brought to City Hall something that had been sorely lacking — a broad and ambitious vision for what needed to be done to overhaul the city for the 21st century. He told me in one of our early conversations that many of the projects embodied in the voluminous Olympic proposal were things that needed to be done whether or not New York won the Olympic sweepstakes. I bought it. (Well, maybe not the Equestrian Center on Staten Island, or the Velodrome on the Queens waterfront.)

And just as important, this guy, who was riding his bike from his home on the Upper West Side to City Hall at 6 a.m., was not beholden to the entrenched private interests that held so much sway in New York.

Over my 30 years of reporting in New York, I found that mayors and governors don't often get behind big, long-term projects. That kind of thing can be expensive and controversial. It requires focus, persistence, and political muscle. And bottom line — the politician won't be around years later for the payoff: the ribbon cutting, the grip-and-grin, and the political credit.

Also, in my experience, many deputy mayors for economic development had little interest in zoning, urban planning, or in big thinking about what the city should do to prepare for the future.

They might've had big resumes, but most were small thinkers. They were simply deal makers, who during the Giuliani years especially, were interested solely in providing Bear Stearns, Conde Nast, Travelers, First Boston, the New York Stock Exchange, CBS, The New York Times (my employer for 22 years), and literally dozens of others with oversized tax breaks, otherwise known as corporate welfare.

In contrast, Deputy Mayor Doctoroff unveiled one plan after another for seemingly every corner of the city. Indeed, Mayor Bloomberg gave Dan carte blanche and in the first two years of the administration, Deputy Mayor Doctoroff was the public face of the administration. He worked with a talented group of government officials in planning, economic development, and affordable housing, even if they did not always get along.

There was a proposal for massive office towers, parks, and affordable housing for what became known as the 50-block Hudson Yards neighborhood in Manhattan and the creation of the Life Sciences Center on the East Side. There was a similar mix of development slated for the rusting and dilapidated waterfront of Williamsburg and Greenpoint. The revitalization of Coney Island called for new housing, storefronts, and an upgrade for the famous but aging amusement park. He had the fearlessness needed to extricate the city from an industrial past that had been painfully eclipsed by the global economy.

In the early 2000s, the City and the State also faced a daunting challenge in rebuilding Lower Manhattan after the September 2001 attack on the World Trade Center, when many people feared New York would never recover.

As I got to know Dan, I found him to be laser-focused, a creative thinker, and an indefatigable promoter. He was a shrewd synthesizer who weaved other people's ideas — even if he didn't always give them credit — into what became a 630-page proposal for the 2012 Olympics. That included the Municipal Art Society's yearning for a publicly accessible waterfront along the East River in Queens and Brooklyn, as well as Manhattan's east and west shorelines, or recommendations by Senator Chuck Schumer's Group of 35 — affectionately and not so affectionately known as the Gang of 35 — for the creation of dozens of new office towers for 300,000 new workers through a combination of condemnation, zoning changes, tax breaks, and transit links.

I'll never forgive Dan for popularizing the use of PowerPoint presentations packed with renderings, statistics, and a sweeping narrative. I hated those things; they never had the answers to my questions. Far more important, he was not afraid to clearly state the administration's goals and provide transparent access to data that allowed good government groups, citizens, and reporters to assess the success or failure of each initiative.

The high point for the Olympic Dream probably came at the United States Olympic Committee November 2002 meeting in Colorado Springs, where New York vied with San Francisco to be the U.S. candidate to host the 2012 Olympic Games. I can still see a

City Wants Stock Exchange To Invest More for Complex

BY CHARLES V BAGLI
THE NEW YORK TIMES — MAY 24, 2002

Unified Financial Plan Is Presented for Ground Zero

BY CHARLES V BAGLI
THE NEW YORK TIMES — APRIL 20, 2006

Bloomberg administration and Port Authority Get Closer on Possible Land Swap Deal

BY CHARLES V BAGLI
THE NEW YORK TIMES — APRIL 1, 2003

Plan for Middle-Class on Queens Bank of East River Prompts Ideas and Protest

BY CHARLES V BAGLI
THE NEW YORK TIMES — MAY 16, 2007

City Offers Coney Island Plan That Conflicts With a Developer's

BY CHARLES V BAGLI
THE NEW YORK TIMES — NOV. 9, 200

Deputy Mayor Leaving to Run Bloomberg L.P.

NE CARDWELL AND CHARLES V. BAGLI
W YORK TIMES — DEC. 7, 2007

From Ashes of Olympic bid, a Future Rises for the Far West

Y CHARLES V BAGLI
HE NEW YORK TIMES — NOV. 27, 2011

Redevelopment of Manhattan's Far West Side Gains Momentum

BY CHARLES V BAGLI
THE NEW YORK TIMES — JUNE 19, 2015

beaming Dan Doctoroff as New York's flashy, well-honed proposal outstripped the bid from San Francisco, whose leader was a former Olympic swimmer. "This effort was a catalyst for getting a lot of things going," he told me afterward.

Alas, it was not to be. Three years later in 2005, the International Olympic Committee selected London, not New York, as the host city. New York's poor showing probably had a lot to do with the enormous controversy surrounding the proposed stadium on the West Side of Manhattan.

Dan had fended off advice (until the bitter end) suggesting building the stadium in Queens where it could be used in the future as a new Mets stadium. Critics often decried that Doctoroff always acted as if he was the smartest guy in the room. Truth is, he often was. But that didn't mean he was always right.

Whatever the outcome, Dan eventually returned to City Hall with renewed vigor and plans to turn Lower Manhattan into a 24/7 neighborhood, rather than a district where they rolled up the sidewalks after 6 p.m. He ensured that the site for housing Olympic athletes was turned into a new neighborhood of 5,000 apartments, mostly rent regulated, an 11-acre public park, and shops.

I'm not a fan of public investment in sports facilities, but I would be remiss if I didn't mention that Dan Doctoroff and the Bloomberg administration enabled and subsidized a new Yankee Stadium in the Bronx, the Barclays Center in Brooklyn, and a new stadium for the Mets in Queens.

His plans were not without drama. He had to shove aside developer Joe Sitt in Coney Island, rebuffed the powerful Real Estate Board of New York at Queens West, and clashed with developer Larry Silverstein at what used to be known as Ground Zero.

I wrote an article in *The New York Times* in 2011 — four years after Dan left City Hall — assessing the progress at the Hudson Yards complex, over the rail yards on the Far West Side. The extension of the No. 7 subway train from Times Square to 34th Street and 11th Avenue was nearing completion. After a slow start, 15 towers were beginning to rise in this once low-slung neighborhood of tenements, warehouses, and factories. I noted that "No one expects the Far West Side to look like the office canyons on Avenue of the Americas anytime soon." In 2022, we can say Hudson Yards looks a lot like the Avenue of the Americas.

In contrast with the indifference of the Giuliani administration (with the exception of housing commissioner Jerilyn Perine), Dan and his cohorts in the Bloomberg administration understood the urgent need for affordable housing, increased the capital budget, and pushed the number of affordable units to 165,000, from an initial 65,000. They leveraged the power of the Housing Development Corporation to create new housing in a way that no other city in the country could or did match.

Still, the surging demand for housing, particularly at the lowest income levels, outstripped even those efforts and the income gap widened. But there is no doubt that Dan Doctoroff left his mark in every borough of his adopted city for decades to come.

A HISTORIC REZONING ERA

The Bloomberg administration spearheaded the most significant citywide rezoning program in more than half a century. Many of those initiatives were overseen by Deputy Mayor for Economic Development and Rebuilding Dan Doctoroff in collaboration with City Planning Commission Chair Amanda Burden. Doctoroff saw an opportunity to create new, attractive neighborhoods in all five boroughs that could provide lower-cost office space, increased housing, and establish a new model for central business districts as lively live-work-play communities.

During his tenure, the City successfully executed 78 rezonings across all five boroughs, encompassing more than 6,000 city blocks and reinventing more than 60 miles of dilapidated waterfront — all while displacing only 400 residents. The rezonings balanced neighborhood context with sustainable growth, preserving low-rise character on side streets and concentrating housing and commercial development around transit corridors. They were designed to foster complete communities, with new commercial, residential, cultural, and recreational spaces integrated into revitalized neighborhoods connected by new sustainable transit infrastructure that improved walkability, added bike lanes, ferry stops along the waterfront, and new rapid bus lanes. By 2006, demographers were predicting New York City was on track to grow by one million residents by 2030.

As of 2022, those predictions were being realized, as New York's population grew by 800,000 people — with 35% of its new housing built between 2012 and 2021 occurring in the areas rezoned by the Bloomberg administration.

New York City Rezonings 1970–2021
The Bloomberg administration rezoned more of the city than the previous 30 years and subsequent nearly 10 years combined. While a consistent philosophy animated its rezonings, each borough benefitted from a customized strategy.

Rezoned Areas
1970–2001
2002–2013
2014–2021

MANHATTAN
Doctoroff's original Olympic vision included transforming an underutilized swath of Manhattan's Far West Side into the heart of the Games. Once in office, Doctoroff initiated a dramatic reinvention of the borough's West Side, including a massive 50-block Hudson Yards and the rezoning of West Chelsea, which included the conversion of an abandoned rail line into the High Line. He also oversaw a rezoning of 125th Street to reinvigorate Harlem's historic center of culture and commerce.

New Jersey

Staten Island

STATEN ISLAND
While Staten Island sought to maintain its low-rise character, the Bloomberg administration identified the Stapleton Waterfront as a potential area for growth and investment, completing a rezoning that created new commercial space, waterfront parks, and housing in 2006.

BRONX

Doctoroff envisioned a cluster of Olympic activities in the long-neglected South Bronx, including baseball at Yankee Stadium and track cycling at a new facility along the Bronx River. Upon assuming office, he made the area one of his primary areas of focus for revitalization, overseeing a rezoning that knitted together the neighborhood with new parks, a new Yankee Stadium, new affordable housing, including Via Verde, which set national standards for sustainability, and the redevelopment of the 31-acre Bronx Terminal Market site, which had languished for decades, into a shopping center and riverfront parkland.

QUEENS

The Bloomberg administration identified Jamaica and Flushing as two potential areas of investment. Doctoroff believed that Jamaica, with its proximity to John F. Kennedy International Airport and its history as a thriving commercial center, could become a key business district outside of Manhattan. His office led the 368-block Jamaica rezoning, the largest by area of the Bloomberg administration.

BROOKLYN

Early in his tenure as deputy mayor, Doctoroff began to envision Brooklyn as a competitive response to the increasing economic threat posed by New Jersey. With ample land (including miles of derelict waterfront), a dense transit network and three bridges linking it to the rest of the city, elegant housing stock, a concentration of colleges and cultural institutions, and an independent source of gas that could support electricity and fuel in the case of another attack on Manhattan, Doctoroff believed Brooklyn could emerge as a "a second city," he wrote in his book, "with a mixed-use downtown filled with arts, recreation, and parks at or near the core." Doctoroff oversaw a coordinated set of rezonings in Greenpoint-Williamsburg, Downtown Brooklyn, and Atlantic Yards to complement other economic development initiatives across the borough.

SOUTH BRONX

In the immediate aftermath of 9/11, the Bloomberg administration was confronted with the economic impacts of the horrific attacks, which devastated the city's historic economic base in Lower Manhattan. Upon taking office in January 2002, the new administration immediately moved towards a more diversified economic development model to buffer the city against future disasters. As a result, for the first time, a five-borough economic development strategy became the underpinning of most land-use and planning work.

The Bronx, which had been historically ignored, and especially so by the prior Giuliani administration, was approached with a fresh perspective for the first time since I joined the Department of City Planning in 1989.

For my first decade in city government, New York was still reeling from the aftermath of urban renewal and three decades of disinvestment, creating vacant, often vandalized properties in many areas of Brooklyn, the Bronx, southeastern Queens, and Upper Manhattan. When I joined the Dinkins administration, a major priority was selling off publicly owned sites to developers for almost nothing, just to get the land under some kind of stewardship and encourage development. The focus was less on a comprehensive planning approach, but rather removing these vacant acres from government ownership and transferring them onto the tax rolls.

Four years later, the Giuliani administration came in with a heavy focus on crime reduction. Physical planning was not on the top of any agenda. To the extent there was any proactive planning, it was limited to Manhattan and Staten Island. At the time, I was Deputy Director of the Brooklyn office and saw the borough beginning to emerge as an attractive residential destination as well as a center of creative and non-traditional business enterprise. But though we developed plans for Downtown Brooklyn and the Greenpoint-Williamsburg waterfront that would later become the basis for rezonings in these areas, there was little interest during the Giuliani years in moving these initiatives forward.

During this time, the Bronx was particularly neglected. Then-Borough President Fernando Ferrer and Mayor Rudy Giuliani were political and personal adversaries. As a result, the Bronx, which had always struggled to gain attention and resources from the City, became even more of an afterthought. There had been little investment outside of subsidized housing development as an ad-hoc, uncoordinated stop-gap response to the borough's challenging poverty, high crime, and housing shortages.

And yet — similar to Downtown Brooklyn — the Bronx was a 25-minute subway ride from Midtown Manhattan and only 10 minutes from the Upper East and West Sides, with seven separate subway lines. It was so connected to Manhattan that the street grid continued seamlessly at 132nd Street across the Harlem River.

When the Bronx Planning Director position opened up in the summer of 2001, I applied for the job and joined as the director in July 2001, barely two months before our world was to change forever on 9/11. Although we didn't know at the time who the new

administration would be, I relied on my instinct that things could only get better for the Bronx.

My hopes faltered as I watched the smoke from the Twin Towers billow out far in the distance from my window in the Bronx office that fateful September 11th. The Bronx hadn't received attention before; now with the city in crisis, it seemed even more unlikely. We were as surprised as anyone else when Mayor Michael Bloomberg won the election, adding more uncertainty. He was a complete unknown in political and city circles.

But it quickly became clear this administration was different and had arrived ready to work. We had prepared transition memos, as we did with each new administration — but it was clear that this team had paid attention to them. The new Deputy Mayor of Economic Development and Rebuilding Daniel Doctoroff, had even given us specific direction, asking each borough office for its thoughts on the greatest opportunities within its jurisdiction.

Built near the Bronx transit node known as The Hub, Via Verde is a national model for sustainable housing development. Dan Doctoroff brought multiple city agencies together to create plans for the site.

In my memo, I had argued that the South Bronx was an area of tremendous opportunity worthy of serious attention. Still, when I extended an invitation to his office to walk them through the neighborhoods, I never expected them to take me up on it. Instead, not only was the team interested — Dan himself wanted to come and see the area firsthand.

A walk through the South Bronx

On a sweltering Saturday morning, Dan and a few of his staff members met me and a couple of my team members in the parking lot of McDonald's on Alexander Avenue in Port Morris, curious and ready to listen. No deputy mayor had ever come to walk a neighborhood with me before; on the few occasions when top officials came for a site visit, they frequently begged off quickly, citing other commitments on their busy schedules. It was hot and I worried that Dan would get tired. He preferred to bike, but I had insisted we walk. I had a long list of places I wanted to get to, but I was prepared for the tour to end at any moment.

Hours later, we had visited every site we had identified. I showed him the sights that I thought were potential development opportunities and why, the proximity to subways, the availability of vacant land, and noted city ownership of several key sites. We stopped at gas stations along the way to pick up water, which we needed in the heat.

It's not that he accepted our word as gospel. I learned quickly that he never does. Instead, he peppered us with questions: Why would someone come and build here? What was needed to reach its potential? There weren't easy answers, especially 20 years ago. In Brooklyn, I could point to local developers invested in the borough, willing to take risks. None of that existed yet in the Bronx. I learned that Dan might not always agree with a recommendation, but he listened. You could talk to Dan and you could persuade him if your argument was valid and strong.

New housing rising in
Port Morris, the Bronx.

Port Morris

We started our walk in Port Morris, a nascent mixed-use area
served by the No. 6 train. The area was largely a collection of vacant
or partially vacant lots, open storage areas, and parking. As a
planner and architect, I was trained to envision possible outcomes
for sites that didn't remotely resemble their potential futures. But
Dan's background was in finance. I wasn't sure what he would see,
beyond the scattered vacant lots and derelict buildings. I needn't
have worried: We all agreed on its potential.

In 2005, we passed a new rezoning for light manufacturing and
mid-rise residential development — the first medium density
mixed-use rezoning in the Bronx. It supported 10 to 12 story
apartment buildings and required sophisticated design, including
a base that could activate the street, setbacks to promote light on
the sidewalk and inside the units, and an orientation toward the
water and a new waterfront promenade. These had been standard
features of rezonings along the waterfront for years — but they
hadn't been applied to the South Bronx before.

Then we walked up Third Avenue, a wide street leading to The Hub.

It was a leap of faith for both of us. In my time in New York City
government, none of the top officials had seemed to recognize
there was opportunity in the Bronx. That morning was the first
time that we started talking about it as a place with potential,
where people lived — and might come — by choice. A deputy
mayor spending his Saturday walking through the Bronx with the
local City Planning team was the first signal to me that a new kind
of management was in place — one I hadn't seen before.

I quickly learned that his interest wasn't an aberration — Dan's
vision was rooted in his Olympic planning, which entailed a
reconnaissance of the entire city to discover areas of potential.
This provided the foundation for the Bloomberg administration's
"five-borough strategy" and became the blueprint for much of
the work in the next decade. That meant creating housing in Long
Island City and Hunter's Point South, a shopping center in the South
Bronx, revamping Yankee Stadium, revitalizing the Hunts Point
Food Market, reimagining the Brooklyn waterfront, establishing
the commercial potential of Downtown Brooklyn. It was the kind
of comprehensive look across the city that had not occurred in
decades. One of the biggest beneficiaries was the Bronx.

Since its heyday in the early part of the 20th century, when the
Grand Concourse was, in fact, a "Grand" boulevard with Art
Deco apartment buildings lining its wide, elegantly landscaped
streetscape, the Bronx had experienced a devastating decline.
By 1980, more than 40% of the South Bronx had been burned
or abandoned. In the decades since, its potential had not been
recognized or supported in a significant way.

Over the course of the day, my team and I endeavored to show him
a different perspective.

The Bloomberg administration's *Hunts Point Vision Plan* identified Lafayette Avenue
as a key corridor in the new South Bronx Greenway, connecting pedestrians and
cyclists to mass transit, employment centers, and parks. The redesigned street
included widened sidewalks, sustainable landscaping, cycling infrastructure, and
other quality-of-life improvements.

The Hub, a South Bronx commercial center, sits at the nexus of three subway lines and eight bus lines. As part of a renewed focus on the area, the Bloomberg administration invested in the site to revitalize its retail, and relocated a Department of Finance office to help anchor the development. Today, the Hub hosts the first YMCA in the South Bronx, alongside new housing and commercial development.

The Hub

Dan understood that transit was the key to a successful growth site. The Hub sat at the confluence of the No. 2, No. 3, and No. 5 trains and eight bus lines and had been a historic commercial center in the borough. But it suffered during the devastation that struck the Bronx in the 1970s and for years had sat largely vacant.

The Hub had anchored the borough once and we agreed it could do so again. In 2006, the City brokered efforts to attract a new anchor retail center and committed to move a Department of Finance office to the strip. Today, the neighborhood hosts the first YMCA in the South Bronx, alongside new housing and commercial development.

One of those housing developments was Via Verde, which became an example of how Dan was able to bring multiple city agencies to the table to create more nuanced, creative, and balanced plans.

In my experience, agencies frequently disagreed about priorities and strategies. Dan's personal involvement lent a different dynamic to these interagency conversations. We listened to each other more. We were less likely to shift responsibility to someone else and move

on. In the collegial atmosphere promoted by Dan and his team, if there was a disagreement, the agencies knew they needed to resolve it. For Via Verde, the Department of Housing Preservation & Development (HPD) owned the site and oversaw the construction. City Planning helped to situate the building in neighborhood context and craft height and construction guidelines, while the city's Economic Development Corporation (EDC) helped consider the broader economic impact of this groundbreaking development. Today, Via Verde remains a national model for sustainable affordable housing.

Bronx Terminal Market

We walked to the bleak site of the Bronx Terminal Market. The historic facility had degraded over the decades, with few vendors and deteriorating infrastructure leading to a closure over structural concerns. In the 1970s, the City had entered a redevelopment deal, but the developer had failed to deliver the required upgrades and the two sides had been locked in a stalemate ever since. Meanwhile, the facility continued to decline.

Barretto Point Park, which opened in 2006, converted an abandoned brownfield that was formerly an asphalt plant, into a popular waterfront park, featuring a stone and grass amphitheater, recreational areas, and a seasonal "floating pool."

As part of the development of the new Yankee Stadium, the City built the 44-acre Macombs Dam Park and Heritage Field, with three championship-quality grass ballfields, a state-of-the-art, 400-meter track, and a new all-weather turf field with seating for 600 spectators, along with courts for basketball and handball.

Dan was already familiar with the site from his Olympic planning days, as he hoped it would be converted into a velodrome for Olympic cycling. He brought an urgency to solving the problem, unlocking the puzzle that had been bogging down redevelopment for years. He and his team figured out how to break the lease by bringing on a new developer and worked with EDC to create a new plan for the site featuring a new shopping destination called the Gateway Center and new waterfront parkland.

This development would ultimately be connected to the new Yankee Stadium, a new Metro-North stop, and the redevelopment of historic Yankee Stadium into a public park. These projects slowly began to knit a shattered neighborhood together with amenities, retail, waterfront access, housing, and new jobs.

Hunts Point Market
On the South Bronx's peninsula sits Hunts Point Market. Even then, it was the largest food market in the Northeast, serving the entire metro area with meat, produce, and fish. But the surrounding neighborhood was poor, crime-ridden, and polluted from the delivery trucks that streamed in and out of the facilities all day, idling for hours as they waited for the markets to open, leading to some of the city's worst asthma rates.

It was clear that we needed to find a way to preserve the economic impact of the site while minimizing the harmful neighborhood impacts. Dan encouraged us to work with the Department of Transportation to landscape the streets, slow down traffic, and

create a parking area for trucks with electric plug-ins to reduce the need for idling. He initiated a partnership with the Parks Department to introduce a kayak launch nearby on the Bronx River and supported collaborations with local arts groups like THE POINT to support cultural investments and youth engagement opportunities.

Harlem River waterfront
Linking nearly all these sites was Harlem River, which runs all the way from Port Morris past 145th Street. While some of the redevelopment along the waterfront took place after Dan and I had both left office, the work that laid its foundations started during his time.

A legacy of transformation for a resurgent Bronx
In Dan, we found a partner who was willing not just to listen to us make the case in his office at City Hall, but was ready to roll up his sleeves and put his walking shoes on to see the neighborhood firsthand — and he led a team who was just as committed and engaged.

Dan Doctoroff signaled to other officials that this area was worth attention and that quality-of-life improvements for the neighborhood were worth pursuing, in collaboration with the local community. It is a mandate that continues to guide New York's approach to the resurgent Bronx today.

As part of the Bronx Terminal Market redevelopment, the Bloomberg administration converted an abandoned 11-acre site along the Bronx River into Mill Pond Park. The park includes 16 tennis courts, recreational lawns and trails, a playground, and a renovated power station that now contains the Bronx Children's Museum.

Dan Doctoroff initiated a partnership with the Parks Department to introduce a kayak launch on the 23-mile-long Bronx River.

THOMAS MCKNIGHT | New York City Economic Development Corporation, 2001–2019

CECILIA KUSHNER | New York City Economic Development Corporation, 2015–Present

HUNTS POINT MARKET

The Hunts Point Food Distribution Center served as an economic anchor for the South Bronx since the cluster of facilities began opening in the late 1960s, becoming one of the largest distribution centers in the world. But by the time the Bloomberg administration entered government in 2002, the entire peninsula — which also included a multigenerational residential community and a rich cultural history as the birthplace of Hip Hop — had fallen on hard times, with vacant industrial lots, high unemployment, and poor air quality. While the aging food facilities were still operating, they required substantial repairs and modernization.

Recognizing both a community need and economic development opportunity, Deputy Mayor Dan Doctoroff led a collaborative effort between the City and community to develop the *Hunts Point Vision Plan*. It focused on four categories: land-use and development, access and mobility, traffic and air quality, and workforce development. Since its release in 2005, the Plan has led to more than 14 acres of new parks, 1,000 new jobs, safer streets, remediated 70 acres of land, and improved air quality. These investments, including nearly $150 million which Dan helped secure, spurred the South Bronx Greenway initiative, a project to improve waterfront access, create more open space, connect and expand pedestrian and bike pathways, and strengthen the neighborhood's resiliency. The Plan also led to the Hunts Point Workforce1 Career Center, which has connected hundreds of residents to employment opportunities.

Today, the complex, which includes the relocated Fulton Fish Market, distributes 4.5 billion pounds of food annually. In 2022, the City and community released the *Hunts Point Forward* report to guide future investment in the Hunts Point community.

The redevelopment of the Hunts Point Market was a central element of the 2005 *Hunts Point Vision Plan*, a joint City–community initiative led by Dan Doctoroff that resulted in 14 acres of new parks, 1,000 new jobs, safer streets, 70 acres of remediated land, and improved air quality in the Hunts Point section of the South Bronx.

BOB CATELL | Founding Chair, Downtown Brooklyn Council, 1998-2003 | Co-Chair, Downtown Brooklyn Partnership, 2006-2012

DOWNTOWN BROOKLYN

In 1986, the President of Brooklyn Union Gas, Elwin S. Larson told the *Wall Street Journal* that the company intended to play a leadership role in the development of Downtown Brooklyn as a major business location. The area had been renamed "MetroTech" two years earlier by George Bugliarello, the President of Polytechnic Institute of New York and there was a growing consensus that with the right investment, the rundown area could become a prime location for back-office facilities for large Manhattan financial firms.

Brooklyn Union was founded in 1825 and had played a major role in Brooklyn's economy ever since. Seeking to build on that history and accelerate the future of Brooklyn, Larson signed a lease to relocate its headquarters to Jay Street.

The first financial firm to locate in Downtown Brooklyn was Morgan Stanley, which established a location on Pierrepont Street in 1988. The second was the Securities Industry Automation Corporation, which moved to the MetroTech area behind Jay Street. It was a promising beginning.

But by the time Michael Bloomberg became mayor in 2002, New York City had failed to support or invest in this transition. Although the previous borough president, Howard Golden, had led an effort to establish Brooklyn as the premier "outer borough," he did not have a great relationship with the then-Mayor Rudolph Giuliani, so things didn't progress very far.

With Bloomberg's appointment of Daniel Doctoroff as deputy mayor, a focus was put on the development of Brooklyn, and in particular Downtown Brooklyn.

Doctoroff recognized the opportunity for Brooklyn to be a competitive response to New Jersey, which had been attracting New York business with tax benefits and more affordable office buildings. Brooklyn had miles of unused waterfront and was linked to Manhattan by three bridges and a subway system. Dan saw Brooklyn's emergence as an economic engine for the city as a real possibility, but recognized there was no comprehensive plan for the development of the borough.

He started by doing his homework.

Dan met with me (I had become CEO of Brooklyn Union Gas in 1991), along with other leading political and civic leaders across the borough, including Jim Whelan, executive director of the Downtown Brooklyn Partnership; Don Elliott, former chair of the City Planning Commission; Alan Fishman, chief executive of Independence Community Bank; Harvey Lichtenstein, executive director of the Brooklyn Academy of Music (BAM); and Bruce Ratner, CEO of Forest City Ratner. Everyone was a leader in Brooklyn, but everyone had a different project to promote.

Dan began to see a pattern emerge out of many disparate ideas. He came to believe that Brooklyn should be thought of as a separate city with a mixed-use downtown, filled with arts, recreation, and parks, surrounded by incomparable housing and a newly accessible waterfront — all just a short subway ride from Manhattan.

Dan had a tremendous ally in Marty Markowitz, the new Brooklyn Borough President, who was a major cheerleader for the borough and was obsessed with bringing a new professional team to replace the beloved Brooklyn Dodgers, who left in 1957.

Dan brought the Economic Development Corporation and the Department of City Planning together to do an in-depth study of Downtown Brooklyn as a potential new central business district outside of Manhattan. They concluded that a plan should provide for a large increase in office space, with a mix of retail and high-rise residential.

Just 15 months after taking office, on April 14, 2003, Dan and the mayor held a press conference at City Hall to announce the City was preparing to rezone the downtown area and would commit $100 million toward the revitalization of Downtown Brooklyn over the next decade.

The Bloomberg administration's 2004 rezoning of Downtown Brooklyn resulted in 15 new and renovated office towers and more than 20,000 new housing units.

Planning began for several projects which developed a consistent narrative: Brooklyn was ready to become a new thriving center of economic development, waterfront parks, and new housing. The Downtown Brooklyn rezoning passed in 2004, paving the way for 2.4 million square feet across 15 new and repositioned office towers, more than 20,000 new housing units — including 20% affordable — and the transformation of Downtown Brooklyn into one of the city's most important economic hubs. In fact, while jobs fell in Manhattan between 2000 and 2015, jobs rose in Brooklyn by 48% in that same period, driven by the Downtown Brooklyn rezoning. In 2022, Downtown Brooklyn employed 84,000 people across the public and private sectors.

As we look at Brooklyn today, in particular Downtown Brooklyn, we see a rejuvenated borough where people want to live and work.

It's a place where they can walk to see a professional sports team, the Brooklyn Nets, in the heart of downtown, stay in one of eight new hotels, shop, and eat. Over 2.2 million square feet of retail has been added to the local market. The debut of City Point brought Target, Alamo Drafthouse, Trader Joe's and most recently, Primark, to Downtown Brooklyn. Two food halls at Dekalb Market Hall and Gotham welcomed over 30 local vendors to the neighborhood, while those seeking more high-end dining can visit the historic, reopened landmark Gage & Tollner, which was recently added to the Michelin Guide.

Some of Brooklyn's newest residents offer the ultimate endorsement of the success of Dan's vision 20 years ago: His own children moved there.

JOE CHAN | Senior Policy Advisor, Office of the Deputy Mayor for Economic Development and Rebuilding, 2002-2006

GREENPOINT-WILLIAMSBURG

Any person who has ever worked for Dan Doctoroff has had to answer the now-fabled interview question — "what was your most creative idea?" The premium that Dan places on creativity and innovation, both as an individual and as a manager, is legendary. Second only to carbohydrates, good ideas are a primary fuel source for Dan.

That is why one of my favorite City Hall moments remains the day when the Department of City Planning staff first pitched Dan on the idea of rezoning a large swath of Greenpoint and Williamsburg.

It was early in the Bloomberg administration — March 2002. Dan packed every day with back-to-back meetings, many of them with city agencies, which he mined for ideas that could transform the city's landscape and the way New Yorkers experienced their city. It was amazing to watch Dan at work, analyzing pitches and asking the questions those pitching didn't see coming. It was almost like bearing witness to a municipal version of *Shark Tank*. Some of those pitches went well, some didn't.

I was looking forward to this meeting in particular. The woman doing the pitch, Regina Myer (then Brooklyn Director for City Planning) was a friend. She had previously raised the rezoning concept repeatedly to the Giuliani administration, who had expressed no interest.

Regina had some reason for hope this time around. Dan's plan for the 2012 Olympics had envisioned siting beach volleyball and archery within a new park that would sit in the middle of the waterfront area to be rezoned. So she knew that she was starting with a more motivated subject.

Still, it was with a healthy dose of nervous energy that Regina and her young staffer, Howard Slatkin, pitched the idea to Dan. They sold the opportunity to establish the first public access to a two-mile stretch of North Brooklyn waterfront in over three centuries, highlighting key lots that the City could acquire for parkland while demonstrating how private developers could be required to fund construction and maintenance for a continuous string of open spaces for the remaining stretch. They also showed how rezoning an area that had witnessed a historic exodus of manufacturing could catalyze billions of dollars in private investment and create thousands of new apartments (20% of which were likely to be affordable to low-income families).

When the pitch was done, there was a pregnant pause — Regina and Howard stood by anxiously, as Dan maybe enjoyed the silence too much. Dan finally broke into a grin and said, "That was brilliant. What a historic opportunity — this will be transformative . . ." in his familiar proud and declarative tone.

Over the following weeks, Dan tasked an interagency team, including City Planning, the Department of Housing Preservation & Development (HPD), and the Parks Department to figure out how

Just two months into the Bloomberg administration, Dan Doctoroff approved a proposal by staffers in the Brooklyn office of the Department of City Planning to rezone the Greenpoint-Williamsburg waterfront, setting in motion the second-largest rezoning in New York City history in terms of development capacity. Left, Greenpoint Landing residential development.

The William Vale hotel opened in 2016 in response to the growing dining and nightlife scene in Williamsburg, Brooklyn.

to maximize affordable housing and ensure that the open spaces were impactful and well-maintained. The team met on Wednesday mornings in the Committee of the Whole room at City Hall, the same room where mayors had convened with senior staff and welcomed visiting dignitaries for decades.

Progress on the plan came fast. By the time of the 2002 Five Boro Bike Tour in May, Dan was already taking a victory lap on Williamsburg's Kent Avenue. He proudly noted how compelling a story the resulting transformation would be — and how hard it would be for even the biggest skeptics to say no.

Hello, Community Board One. The community was extremely organized and distrustful of government and industry alike, having spent recent decades fighting to keep waste transfer stations off the East River and advocating for the clean up of Newtown Creek, one of the country's most notorious industrial dumping grounds.

Over the next two years, the plan witnessed more pushback than any other Bloomberg rezoning to date. The local community argued that the affordable housing offering was paltry and worried that low-income units wouldn't be guaranteed. They railed that the open spaces would be the new version of Gramercy Park — fully privatized parks. They even rushed the stage at a Community Board meeting.

Processing the unanticipated response, Dan acknowledged that our brilliant idea clearly needed to get more creative. For every challenge raised, Dan demanded a strong and substantive answer — he insisted that we not let this historic opportunity go to waste.

And the team responded. By the time the rezoning reached the deciding vote in May 2005, a number of great policy ideas (most still in effect two decades later) were added to the plan's offering and delivered to City Council Land Use Chair Melinda Katz. Ideas addressed almost every challenge to the plan — and more.

When tasked by Dan with finding an effective guarantee for affordable housing that developers would actually use, Housing Commissioner Shaun Donovan, his top deputy Rafael Cestero, and their team worked with City Planning to supercharge an arcane zoning tool — inclusionary housing bonuses — into a generator of thousands of affordable units and a "Yes" vote from the City Council.

The bonuses, which on paper allowed developers to build bigger buildings if they committed to set aside a portion of the units located within as permanently affordable, were scarcely used in previous years. HPD suggested strategically combining these bonuses with public funding. City Planning tweaked the zoning to work on both waterfront and inland blocks. Developers ended up taking the bait in Greenpoint-Williamsburg and other rezoned neighborhoods that followed.

HPD identified parking lots and underutilized land at New York City Housing Authority (NYCHA) developments that could be transformed into mixed-income buildings and found underused government-owned sites, including a former hospital and a decommissioned police station, that could be pledged towards the guaranteed creation of hundreds of new affordable housing units.

City Planning and the Parks Department created a zoning-embedded fund where developers could hire the Parks Department to run and maintain private open spaces. Developers of waterfront properties would either have to adhere to a strict set of zoning-based maintenance and operating requirements, or they could opt to outsource operating responsibilities to the City. Either way, the bar would be substantially raised and community concerns meaningfully addressed.

The plan was approved.

Since then, rubble-strewn lots have been reborn into more than 12,500 new housing units as of 2019, with nearly 3,200 new or preserved affordable units and plans are in motion for 50 acres of new waterfront parks, while Williamsburg has become a worldwide brand.

In so many ways, Dan's insistence on good ideas has forever transformed the Brooklyn waterfront and the communities of Greenpoint and Williamsburg. By leveraging creativity into a political streetfight victory, Dan also proved that his clever interview question was also an active management principle.

When I think about what ultimately won both the plan's approval and the front page attention of *The New York Times*, I think about Dan's dogged adherence to valuing the most creative ideas.

I also think about another one of Dan's go-to interview questions — "what adjectives would your coworkers use to describe you."

Speaking for the Greenpoint-Williamsburg team, I would describe Dan as, "Visionary, innovative, tenacious beyond belief, and a pretty good listener."

North Fifth Street Pier and Park is part of 50 acres of waterfront parks set in motion by the 2005 Greenpoint-Williamsburg rezoning.

ATLANTIC YARDS/ PACIFIC PARK

In 1955, the Brooklyn Dodgers suggested relocating their stadium to the corner of Atlantic and Flatbush Avenues in Brooklyn. When the proposal fell through, the team infamously left for Los Angeles and half a century later, the land — dominated by a slash of exposed rail yards — was still largely vacant.

Marty Markowitz, the indefatigable Brooklyn borough president, believed Brooklyn had never recovered from losing its beloved team. He helped convince longtime Brooklyn developer, Bruce Ratner to pitch Doctoroff on a new 18,000-seat professional sports arena at the heart of a new 22-acre, $4.9 billion mixed-use development project to be built at the same intersection the Dodgers had eyed decades earlier. His "passion helped me see Brooklyn as it wanted to be seen," Doctoroff wrote in his book. "As a big league city in its own right."

The project, later renamed Pacific Park, would be built over 8.5 acres of exposed rail yards, echoing Doctoroff's signature project at Hudson Yards. It would reclaim central, but underutilized land in the heart of Brooklyn that was served by exceptional transit access, including nine subway lines, six bus lines, and a Long Island Rail Road stop, consistent with Doctoroff's objectives for sustainable and transit-oriented economic development across New York.

Doctoroff viewed Downtown Brooklyn as New York's best response to intensifying competition for business from the New Jersey waterfront. So perhaps the most poetic triumph of Atlantic Yards was that the anchor tenant for the Barclays Center, the National Basketball Association's Nets, would be swiped from suburban New Jersey, bringing professional sports back to Brooklyn for the first time in nearly 50 years.

But the process, which required significant use of eminent domain and a controversial decision to avoid the city's traditional land-use regulations and allow the State to lead the project (as the State-controlled Metropolitan Transportation Authority owned much of the land), mired the project in nearly a decade of delay, protests, and multiple lawsuits.

"In the face of this intense opposition, it would have been very easy to jettison the whole project," wrote Michael Kalt, Doctoroff's senior policy advisor at the time. "The arena was not part of the original Olympic plan. And given that it was introduced at the height of the West Side stadium debate, Dan could have been forgiven for simply deciding that it was one more problem that he did not need. But he understood that the central thesis of Atlantic Yards was no different from the waterfront rezonings, or from Hudson Yards itself. If we were going to continue creating the capacity for growth, then we needed to keep leaning into transforming underutilized parcels of land, especially when they were in the bull's eye of the path of productive development. For Dan, accepting the status quo and bowing to the loudest voices of criticism in the room was never an option, on this project or any other that he has steered."

Barclays Center opened in 2012, part of a thriving district that includes 16 mixed-use buildings, more than 6,400 new apartments, including 2,250 affordable units, and a thriving retail and restaurant scene. The feared traffic congestion, which drove some of the protests, never materialized — in fact, after a year, *The New York Times* reported "that car use has been even lower than had been projected." And a decade after Barclays Center opened, an impact analysis by *Crain's* hailed the "neighborhood's reinvention."

Pacific Park (formerly known as Atlantic Yards), Downtown Brooklyn. Anchored by Barclays Center, the redevelopment decked over exposed rail yards to create a thriving district that includes 16 mixed-use buildings, more than 6,400 new apartments, and a popular retail and restaurant scene.

ALAN FISHMAN | Board Chairman, Brooklyn Navy Yard Development Corporation, 2002–2013

ANDREW KIMBALL | President and CEO, Brooklyn Navy Yard Development Corporation, 2005–2013

THE BROOKLYN NAVY YARD

"Dan had it in his mind that you had to take some risk . . . These projects were insane and incredibly important for New York."

For more than 150 years, the Brooklyn Navy Yard was one of the largest naval shipbuilding facilities in the United States, producing some of the country's most famous war ships, including the *USS Maine*, the *USS Arizona*, and the *USS Missouri*. During World War II, its efforts were considered so critical that steps were taken to shroud its work from aerial spies. But in 1966, the Department of Defense shuttered the facility and it quickly fell into decline. Although the City bought the massive 300-acre complex from the federal government three years later, and established the nonprofit Brooklyn Navy Yard Development Corporation (BNYDC) in 1981, the property continued to deteriorate.

Three decades later, Deputy Mayor Dan Doctoroff found the troubled development site within his portfolio. "The boatyard was a total train wreck when we showed up," said Alan Fishman, who Doctoroff quickly brought on as board chairman. "Derelict in every respect." Andrew Kimball joined the Navy Yard in 2005 as president and CEO of the Development Corporation and together he and Fishman oversaw a transformation of the site and its surrounding environment.

The challenges were stark: Manufacturing jobs in the city had been declining for more than half a century in New York City. The site required asbestos removal, structural repairs, demolition, and intensive remediation of the piers supporting the waterfront property.

Fishman and Kimball refashioned the Navy Yard to respond to a new age of industry. Manufacturing now included artisans, filmmakers, and other "knowledge-based" businesses. Steiner Studios opened at the Yard in 2004 and has expanded several times. "Large-format manufacturing was largely gone," Kimball said. "What had replaced it was lots of small entrepreneurs who wanted to make something."

Today, the Navy Yard has about 11,000 workers at more than 500 businesses, ranging from food and liquor manufacturing to 3D printing, a technology incubator, a body-armor manufacturer, fashion houses, furniture, even rooftop farming. Pratt Institute's new Research Yard provides onsite collaboration in diverse fields such as robotics and community development. The Brooklyn STEAM Center trains high school students for modern technology and manufacturing careers. The Albert C. Wiltshire Employment Center centralizes jobs at Navy Yard companies, which range from welders to software developers, deckhands, engineers, and accountants. In 2023, Mayor Eric Adams announced another expansion: a $20 million biotech hub.

"I think the Navy Yard drove the Brooklyn brand," Fishman said. "It's a beacon for others to try to emulate."

BACKGROUND

ALAN FISHMAN
The Navy Yard wasn't functioning before we showed up. The level of maintenance, the level of standard of cleanliness, of environmental product, all of that had to get cleaned up. The Yard itself, the piers had to be all redone because they were falling down when we got there. Interestingly the higher water quality [in New York City] created an interesting set of issues because different forms of animal life were living there and creating problems for the old wooden docks.

The Brooklyn Navy Yard, abandoned by the Department of Defense in 1966 and sold to New York City three years later, deteriorated for decades prior to the Bloomberg administration taking office. Deputy Mayor Dan Doctoroff installed new leadership at the site and allocated significant new funding. Today, the Navy Yard is home to more than 500 businesses employing over 11,000 people across a range of industries.

It was every man for himself. There was a sense of community; for survival, they had to hang out together because they were alone there in that crazy world. But it was really random and not thoughtful and not curated and not coherent. There were some cheap rents. Building 77 was rented to a guy who paid 50 cents a foot. In turn, he rented [a] million feet to people that stored big industrial waste, rusted equipment, and rags and paper at $5 a foot. So, the guy was paying 50 cents and making four-and-a-half million bucks for himself. What did he have, 10 jobs in the whole place?

ANDREW KIMBALL
Not many. He only used about a quarter of the building. If you went up the street, it was three blocks to Myrtle Avenue that had been known as Murder Avenue in the 80s and early part of the 90s.

FISHMAN
The streetscape at the Yard was actually worse than the interior of the Yard when we started. Innately Dan understood that. And then obviously Andrew arrived and it all went very, very, very fast.

Steiner Studios, a film and television production facility at the Brooklyn Navy Yard, has expanded several times since opening in 2004.

FIRST PROJECTS

KIMBALL

The Giuliani folks had an RFP [for a new film studio] that came down to Robert De Niro and Harvey Weinstein against a little-known New Jersey real estate family, the Steiners. The Steiners beat out De Niro and Weinstein, and that was a surprise, because they didn't have any experience with film studios. Then, the first thing they did when Bloomberg won was to try to renegotiate the deal that they'd made with the Giuliani administration. Dan pretty forcefully shot that down.

It was the beginning of him being unafraid to work with us to redefine what manufacturing was. Film and television was a new way of thinking about manufacturing and I would say touched every sector that we had there. Instead of it being gritty, old smokestack jobs, it tended to be infused with creative industry, with design, with fashion, with technology. The film studios had all of that.

FISHMAN

There was a tow pound, which was a place where they took the towed cars from all over Brooklyn. It was right across from [public] housing. I went to Dan and said, "We need to get this thing shrunk immediately because it's offensive. It's just a gross intrusion on the neighborhood." In five minutes it was done. We [gave] the Police Department a clean new building to administer the pound in a much smaller, more efficient way. That unlocked a whole side of the Navy Yard, the Sands Street side, just like the Steiner decision unlocked the Kent Avenue side of the Yard. The streetscape was critically important.

KIMBALL

This huge blue wooden structure that said "Brooklyn Tow Pound" sat on top of two beautiful iconic historic structures, which were gate houses on either side of the entrance on Sands Street, right across from Ingersoll Houses [public housing]. Not only did we remove the wooden superstructure but we got the money to renovate both of those beautiful houses. Now, they are leased to Kings County Distillery. It was the beginning of touching every piece of the perimeter of the Yard to make it more inviting to the surrounding community. Not only did those changes make the Navy Yard a more hospitable and successful place for business, but it had an enormous ripple effect on the turnaround of the surrounding areas.

INNOVATIVE APPROACHES

FISHMAN

Every time I dealt with Dan, there was a surprising calmness about him and a relaxed attitude. And I think that stemmed from the fact that he had a vision and a plan of what, generally speaking, he wanted to achieve. So, there was never a lot of angst. He had enormous confidence in the people that he selected. [Dan] trusted Andrew. He trusted the process and what we were trying to do. He never micromanaged this thing, not once.

KIMBALL

We put together a ten-year business plan. [Dan] would ask tough questions, but if you had a reasoned answer, that was it. This really speaks to the overall Bloomberg approach that Dan was such a big part of. You put good people in place and let them manage.

Early in my tenure when I was making the case to renew the use of the dry docks for continued boat repair, he teased me saying: "Are you sure you're not going native?" He said it as a reminder to not just take the easy path. He wanted us to think outside the box. He [would] support us if we made tough short-term decisions for long-term gain.

FISHMAN

Andrew, God bless him, had this vision to take this gigantic machine shop that sat in the middle of the Yard and renovate it. He had a plan in his mind and nobody believed it. If you looked at his spreadsheet, you would've vomited. Today, it is among the most important buildings in the United States in terms of high tech space, the future of manufacturing. The roof alone was so expensive that no rational executive would've done it. And Dan never got in the way of it, because he believed in the project, he believed in the process, and he believed in Andrew. He had it in his mind that you had to take some risk.

KIMBALL

What the world now knows as Newlab was three separate but connected ship repair buildings totaling about 200,000 square feet dating back to WWI. There are amazing historic photos, including one showing an 80-ton crane holding up a captured German U-boat. The buildings had been essentially vacant for decades. It was supposed to be knocked down because it blocked speedy travel through the Yard. But they were spectacular structures. We had to do everything we could to save them.

The first anchor was a company called Crye [Precision]. Two guys from Cooper Union had started [at] the Yard in a small space designing Kevlar vests and body armor for the Army Special Forces. They kept growing, and they were like, "We think we can take 80,000 square feet." That's a massive leap and so we had to take a massive leap of faith [with them].

The other [anchor tenant], David Belt came up with this notion for Newlab, which would be this hub of innovation anchored around design universities, as well as big innovation companies. He could barely pay the bottom range of rent. When I came to [Alan to pitch the idea], he's like, "I think it's a little crazy, but I'll give you the room to do your thing." Now, as he said, it has become a model. People from all over the world come to see Newlab.

FISHMAN
At Building 92, we decided to put a job center in a brand-new building attached to a Marine guardhouse that had nothing but metal straps around it to hold it from falling down when we started. Today, it's a beautiful structure with a museum, a hiring center. These things made no sense if you didn't have a plan and a vision. These projects were insane and incredibly important for New York, incredibly important. And Dan allowed them and encouraged them. And for that, he deserves enormous credit.

KIMBALL
Alan and I worked closely with Dan Conlon [the Chief Financial Officer at the Navy Yards], who had been there through the worst of it and held it together with glue and Scotch tape before we were able to really get City support. He had begun to cut up the spaces into these small units. He saw that leasing strategy working. And we said, "If we see something that's working, let's put it on steroids. Let's cut up several million square feet of space like that."

People kept saying, "Well, aren't you going to create a glut on the market of these small spaces?" [What we found was] a bottomless pit of demand. Really small creatives want to not only make something but be part of a community and particularly, want to be in beautiful old buildings — because the authenticity of that speaks to the history of the past making. [They] want to be connected with the community and doing the right thing around local hiring and creating the next pathway of diverse workers. You saw all those things in Building 77.

SUSTAINABILITY

SUSTAINABILITY

FISHMAN
When we got there, the environmental quality at the boatyard was just not acceptable. It's 300 acres. It's a big ecosystem.

KIMBALL
We kept hearing from the small tenants [that] they cared about sustainability. Many of them make sustainable products. And so, we decided we had this incredible canvas to paint on, let's do some demonstration projects. So, we put the first building-mounted wind turbine on a roof there. It didn't particularly work so well, but it became a symbol of what we were trying to do. We put up lights that were run by both wind and solar, first in the city. We put in green space. We put in solar-powered trash compactors, some of the first in the city.

FISHMAN
There was never any conversation to be at LEED standard [for buildings]. That was just obvious to us because we're working with City money, we're working with public funds. Often, we'd make a deal with our tenants because they were working on sustainable projects and products. The outdoor lights that Andrew referenced were done by a longtime tenant at the Yard.

LEGACY

FISHMAN
I think the regeneration, renovation and rejuvenation of the Navy Yard was an essential part of building the Brooklyn brand. Socially conscious, aggressive, self-confident, can-do, humane, inclusive, sustainably done — if you think about the words that you can associate with Brooklyn, they are all relevant in the Navy Yard context.

KIMBALL
Alan is right. The Navy Yard is a huge part of the Brooklyn comeback and its global brand. And like he did on project after project as deputy mayor, Dan knew how to pick the right people, inspire them to dream big, and then get out of the way.

Building 92, an exhibition and visitors center at the Brooklyn Navy Yard.

HARLEM'S 125TH STREET

The 125th Street rezoning sought to strengthen Harlem's place as a historic cultural destination and develop its potential as an economic corridor. The neighborhood's transit infrastructure, including 10 subway lines along 125th Street from river to river, positioned it as a hub for office, cultural, and housing development.

Deputy Mayor Dan Doctoroff initiated the planning process, "really articulating the vision of strengthening Harlem's importance as a cultural arts and entertainment district and also finding opportunities to create the framework for office towers to be developed once the market was there," said Jennifer Sun, who worked on the project as Doctoroff's policy advisor, and is now executive vice president of planning at the New York City Economic Development Corporation.

At the same time, community leaders advocated for preserving the historic architectural distinction of the neighborhood's brownstones. Harlem's last major rezoning, in 1961, hadn't had to grapple with that issue, said Assemblywoman Inez Dickens, who was the area's councilmember during the rezoning negotiations.

While that "rezoning allowed for any height to be built," Dickens said, it didn't matter because "no one was investing in Harlem at that time."

But Dickens and Doctoroff both foresaw that this time would be different. They negotiated over how to preserve Harlem's historic context, while fostering its economic and cultural potential. "I wanted to protect that in Harlem and I was able to do so through my negotiating with Dan," Dickens said. "I give Dan a lot of credit for understanding where I was coming from."

Although they "started on opposite ends of the table, Dan and I became good friends," she said, noting that they stayed in touch long after the negotiations ended. "Dan is a formidable opponent. He is a brilliant negotiator, a brilliant tactician. He actually made me a better negotiator."

The rezoning incorporated a series of innovative strategies to support the neighborhood's cultural status and promote street life, including limiting banks on the ground floor and testing a zoning bonus for developers that included cultural facilities in their buildings. When the Victoria Towers Residences opened in 2021, it included the preservation of part of the historic Victoria Theater and two black box theaters managed by the Apollo Theater, along with a new hotel and nearly 200 market-rate and affordable units.

"There was a recognition that it was important through the rezoning to provide for more opportunity for new cultural productions and performance space to support the next generation of Harlem artists and performers," Sun said. But Doctoroff and his team also provided technical support, she said. "There was this strategy of both investing in physical space but also investing in the capacity of cultural nonprofits in Harlem to be more financially stable," she said. "A lot of the work was around pairing consultants

Taystee Lab, a West Harlem development for life sciences, arts, commercial, retail, and academic tenants, offers 40,000 square feet of wet and dry lab space for early-stage companies.

with Harlem cultural nonprofit organizations and doing a lot of business planning; taking a hard look at their business model, finding ways to create programming that could also generate revenue while meeting the mission of these cultural nonprofits to serve Harlem children and residents."

The rezoning passed in 2008 — a year after Doctoroff left City Hall and just before the financial collapse. As a result, many projects are only now getting underway, including an expansion of the Apollo Theater and the emergence of a new life sciences cluster in West Harlem, near Columbia University's Manhattanville expansion,

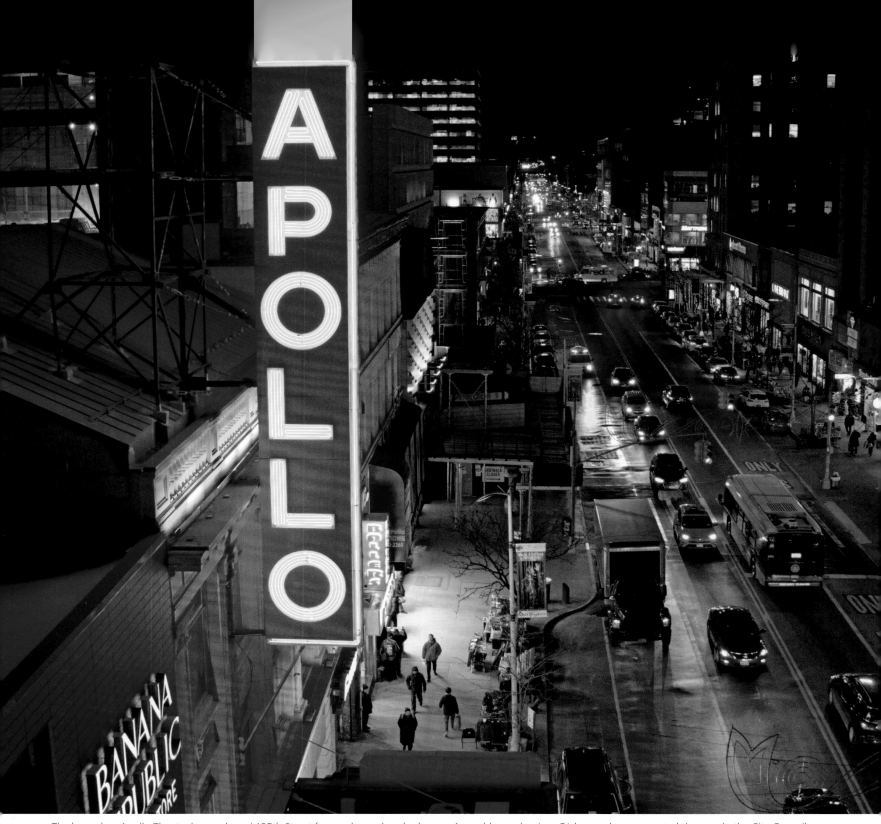

The legendary Apollo Theater has anchored 125th Street for nearly one hundred years. Assemblymember Inez Dickens, who represented the area in the City Council during the rezoning, says of the corridor, "It's just now, in the last 10 or 15 years, being built back up to become the hub that it was in the 40s and 50s."

anchored by the Taystee Lab building, which provides nearly 40,000 square feet for wet and dry lab space for early-stage companies. The National Urban League (NUL) recently began construction on a $242 million, 414,000-square foot Urban League Empowerment Center, which will include the organization's national headquarters, the Urban Civil Rights Museum, the NUL Institute for Race, Equity and Justice, along with offices for community groups, affordable housing, a Trader Joe's, and a Target. The complex fulfills the 2008 rezoning's call for a mixed-use building featuring arts, retail and office uses on the site.

Today, the 125th Street corridor is "a bustling economic hub," Dickens said. "It's just now In the last 10 or 15 years being built back up to become the hub that it was in the 40s and 50s."

The 2008 rezoning set the framework by "looking into the future, not just what was going to be done today," she continued. "I didn't even know if I'd be alive, but I was trying to prepare the community to come into the 21st century."

WEST CHELSEA

Approved unanimously by the City Council in 2005, the West Chelsea rezoning was among the most complex ever undertaken by New York City.

It created the capacity for over 5,500 units of new housing between 10th and 11th Avenues from West 30th Street to West 16th Street, making it the third-largest of the Bloomberg administration (after Hudson Yards and Greenpoint-Williamsburg) in terms of housing production and larger than any area rezoning completed under prior mayors.

In addition to creating housing, it also needed to preserve the midblock art gallery district. But the most challenging aspects of the rezoning came from the nuances associated with the redevelopment of the High Line, which encompassed a mix of city, state, federal, and private jurisdictions.

The 22 property owners whose sites abutted the High Line had an usually prominent seat at the table, because the railroad that owned the structure refused to consent to its transformation into a park without obtaining a variety of legal consents from these owners, all of whom had voiced initial opposition to the project.

For more than three years, Deputy Mayor Dan Doctoroff led an interagency team that combined the rezoning with a Byzantine array of negotiations with the railroad, the property owners, the nonprofit Friends of the High Line advocating to save the structure, and the federal Surface Transportation Board (which regulates rail corridors, as the High Line was prior to its transformation) in order to realize the creation of what has become one of the most popular public open spaces in the world. Through the use of a novel transfer mechanism that allowed the property owners beneath the High Line to create value from air rights sold to adjacent sites, the rezoning was critical to securing the consents required to finally transfer the structure to permanent City ownership.

New and old, juxtaposed along the High Line in revitalized West Chelsea.

HUDSON YARDS

Most New Yorkers associate Hudson Yards with the 13-acre parcel built on a platform over the rail yards between 10th and 11th Avenues and 30th and 33rd Streets. There, a developer created a 7 million square foot complex that includes office, retail, and residential uses, alongside a cultural facility — The Shed — as well as the Heatherwick-designed sculpture, the Vessel.

However, the Hudson Yards name was originally applied by Dan Doctoroff to the roughly 300-acre area running from Ninth Avenue to the West Side Highway, from 30th Street to 41st Street. As a private citizen leading New York's bid for the 2012 Olympics, Doctoroff sought to use the deadline of the Olympic process to catalyze the redevelopment of this underutilized swath of West Midtown. The area would be anchored by a stadium for the Olympics and subsequently the New York Jets. Although a redevelopment of the area had been contemplated for decades, the plans had never advanced.

As deputy mayor, Doctoroff was able to marshal the resources of the City to unlock the potential of the district. Even after the demise of the Olympic bid, the plan moved forward at a speed that was extraordinary by modern standards. In 2005, just three years after the start of the Bloomberg administration, the City Council approved a rezoning to create more than 40 million square feet of space, including 12,600 units of housing, across a 50-block zone that spans virtually the entirety of the area originally envisioned by Doctoroff as part of the bid.

Since then, companies such as Pfizer, BlackRock, and Facebook have rushed to fill the office space afforded by the district's towers, both on the former rail yards, as well as in the Farley Post Office building and the new Manhattan West development along the 34th Street corridor. Today, a series of towers marches north from the rail yards site along the new Hudson Boulevard and Bella Abzug Park built by the City to break up the superblock between 11th and 12th Avenues. While the Hudson Yards name may not yet extend beyond the rail yards site, the new development that Doctoroff contemplated more than two decades ago is already filling the Far West Side.

While most New Yorkers associate the name Hudson Yards with the 10-acre parcel built on a platform over the rail yards between 10th and 11th Avenues and 30th and 33rd Streets, Dan Doctoroff originally applied the label to the roughly 300-acre area running from Ninth Avenue to the West Side Highway, from 30th Street to 41st Street. In 2005, the City completed a rezoning of the entire area to accommodate more than 40 million square feet of new mixed-use development. Right, Hudson Yards, 2018.

ERIC KOBER | Director for Housing, Economic, and Infrastructure Planning, Department of City Planning, 1986-2017

RETURNING TO GROWTH

When the Bloomberg administration, with Dan Doctoroff as Deputy Mayor for Economic Development and Rebuilding, took office in January 2002 there was great uncertainty about the city's future in the aftermath of the 9/11 attacks. Would people and businesses flee a city that had been revealed to be so vulnerable to terrorism?

Savvier observers knew that security was just one of the issues that made the city's economic course precarious in the first decade of the 21st century, to be added to many others. New York's key office-based industries, including finance and advanced business services, had grown in the 1980s and 90s. This kind of office-based employment was expected to be the main driver of growth in the early 21st century, but New York's ability to capitalize would soon be limited: The city's office stock was aging and much of it couldn't meet the needs of contemporary businesses. To compete with other cities, New York needed modern office buildings, with high ceilings, large office floor plates, sophisticated technology, and best-practice environmental sustainability, but the city lacked zoned capacity for more than a fraction of what it should build.

A 2000 report by the Group of 35, civic and business leaders convened by Senator Chuck Schumer, had recommended that the City enact zoning changes in Long Island City, Downtown Brooklyn and the Far West Side of Manhattan to create major new office districts. The outgoing Giuliani administration had secured the Long Island City rezoning in 2001, but the other two areas were still in the planning stages.

Meanwhile, the 2000 U.S. Census had marked an important milestone as the city's population passed eight million for the first time. Economic growth was leading to population growth; the city needed entire new residential districts as well.

The city's waterfront was a postindustrial embarrassment. While northern New Jersey had been redeveloping former industrial sites for housing and public access to the waterfront, the East River waterfront in Brooklyn and Queens was largely a mess of collapsing piers and vacant buildings.

Finally, an unused elevated rail freight line, known as the High Line, stood on the West Side of Manhattan. A group of activists wanted to see it turned into a park, while owners of property under it and nearby wanted to see the hulking structure torn down to facilitate redevelopment.

I entered city government in 1979 and knew that any one of these challenges would have daunted a typical city administration. Dan's response, in contrast, was, "Why don't we solve all of them at the same time?" Astonishingly, he largely did. Likely because of his private equity experience, it seemed perfectly normal to him to have dozens of initiatives underway at once. Some would become big hits, with a big and fast payoff to the city in terms of jobs and tax revenue. Others would have more modest or long-term payoffs. In total, the city's economy and tax base became immensely stronger.

Dan used New York's application to host the 2012 Olympics as the framing device for moving fast on a series of ambitious zoning and infrastructure proposals, many of which I had seen languish for years. But Dan was determined that the Olympics would take place in a city transformed. The centerpiece of these efforts was the Far West Side, which Dan grandly renamed Hudson Yards. In reality, the grim neighborhood around the Javits Convention Center was filled mostly with parking lots and low-scale buildings. The area also included an open-air Metropolitan Transportation Authority (MTA) train storage yard.

The Hudson Yards plan included the air rights of the MTA's rail yards, initially planned as the site of the Olympic stadium and other key facilities, along with blocks north to West 42nd Street and east to Penn Station. These blocks included many potential development sites, which despite the City's past efforts, remained largely rundown and underused.

The proposal built on plans for the Far West Side that had been generated by the previous administration, when Mayor Giuliani proposed a new Yankee Stadium over the western rail yard, served by an extension of the No. 7 subway to 11th Avenue and West 34th Street. The Department of City Planning then undertook an initial planning study, which proposed a midblock park between 10th and 11th Avenues.

Dan's contribution was to move from planning concepts, to a consensus plan, to implementation at lightning speed. It was clear that the community wasn't just interested in office space; the plan had to be a mix of offices, residences, and open space. The final plan reflected this broader vision.

It featured a predominantly commercial office core, across from the Javits Convention Center on 11th Avenue and along the West 34th Street corridor, that would be large enough to meet the city's emerging office needs. Housing was concentrated to the north and east of this core, with a new midblock park to be constructed between 10th and 11th Avenues — just as we had originally envisioned.

The combination of workplaces, residences, and public spaces would create a vibrant, 24-hour community — an early example of what planners today call a "15-minute city" where everything one needs to live is available within a short walkable distance. The final proposal was drawn up by the Cooper Robertson design firm and the City Planning staff rapidly translated it into a workable zoning amendment and other necessary City actions.

At the same time, the MTA had to be brought in as a partner to build the subway extension, despite having no money to do so. Dan made the decision not to apply for federal funding — the timeframes were impossibly long, considering the Olympic deadlines. For example, the Access to the Region's Core (ARC) proposal, a collaboration between the Port Authority and New Jersey Transit to build new commuter rail tunnels under the Hudson, began planning in the mid-1990s and nearly a decade later was still far from federal approval. (The approval didn't come until 2008 and the project was ultimately canceled by New Jersey's then-governor.)

Sketch for 10 and 30 Hudson Yards by Bill Pedersen at KPF Architects. Right, the completed office buildings, which are located on the rail yards site that anchors the broader Hudson Yards district.

Instead, Dan proposed that the subway and the midblock park would be financed by the City from bonds repaid through revenues generated by new development, principally office space. The Office of Management and Budget (OMB) proposed phasing the park, with the second section being constructed once development was more advanced. The final piece of the puzzle was contributed by the City Council's Finance Division staff, who proposed that the City cover bond interest out of annual appropriations in the initial years before development-generated revenues were sufficient.

Everything happened with blazing speed for government work. The zoning was approved in January 2005, along with the subway extension and parks. The special financing entity for Hudson Yards issued bonds in 2006, and again in 2011. The Hudson Yards subway opened in 2015. In more than 30 years in government I never saw anything like it.

Not everything went according to plan. The Olympics were awarded to London and the Cooper Robertson plan has evolved over the decades. The MTA was in charge of development over the rail yards and awarded rights to the highest bidder to support its chronically constrained budget — rather than prioritizing the creation of great urban space. Partially as a result of this decision, which was outside the City's control, the initial eastern phase of that development has been criticized for its upper-income

orientation and its ill-fated central sculptural feature (although given the challenges of building in that location, it's an impressive achievement, nonetheless).

But it is inarguable that today the West Side is transformed. The subway financing plan is a success and the larger Hudson Yards area is a forest of office and residential towers. Beginning at the western rail yard and extending to the south, the High Line is one of the world's great public spaces, flanked by striking new buildings.

The changes to the city during this time can be seen beyond Manhattan. Downtown Brooklyn is also transformed — largely with residential towers and not the office buildings that planners once envisioned. The Greenpoint and Williamsburg waterfronts are also lined with residential developments — which are mixed-income, as a result of innovative inclusionary zoning provisions — and public spaces.

That all this, and more, happened in such a fast time frame is Dan's achievement. He assembled an extraordinary team of collaborators, who made most of the decisions on a day-to-day basis. Dan mobilized the resources they needed to get the job done, set timeframes, tracked progress, and inspired many of the people who worked under him to do the best work of their careers.

DAN AND THE "$60 BILLION"

In 2002, newly appointed Deputy Mayor Dan Doctoroff assembled a team of development and finance professionals, planners, attorneys, and infrastructure experts and charged them to implement his vision for the area he had named the Hudson Yards district (I was the founding president of what became known as the Hudson Yards Development Corporation).

The plan, unveiled a year later, included a subway extension and new public open space, a civic plaza on the rail yards that formed the centerpiece of the area, an expanded Javits Convention Center, a multiuse facility for the 2012 Olympics and the New York Jets, and a rezoning concept that would allow for about 43 million square feet of mixed-use development.

Although the details of the plan were new, it borrowed extensively from studies reaching back to the Regional Plan Association in the 1920s, work by the Metropolitan Transportation Authority

decking over of exposed rail tracks. Dan argued that Hudson Yards could be the latest example of how at key moments the public sector — usually in partnership with private industry — had funded key infrastructure upgrades that enabled New York to grow and evolve in powerful and sometimes unforeseeable ways. Precedents stretched back to the Erie Canal and the New York Central Railroad's planning for the Park Avenue office district around Grand Central Terminal in the early 20th century.

Not everyone was convinced. At community board meetings, City Council hearings, and in newspaper op-eds, vocal opponents emerged. Some believed it was foolish for New York to invest in so much additional office space. Many questioned the scale of the required City investment — pegged at as much as $3 billion — at a time when there were so many other pressing needs and scarce resources.

Right: Trains gather at the northern tip of Manhattan before making their descent into Grand Central Terminal, 1906.

Middle: New York Central railroad tracks north of Grand Central Terminal in the process of being covered over to create Park Avenue. In hundreds of presentations advocating for the Hudson Yards plan, Dan Doctoroff showed these images as a precedent for his plan to build on top of the exposed rail yards on the Far West Side.

Opposite: Grand Central Terminal officially opened in 1913.

(MTA) in the 1980s, Senator Chuck Schumer's Group of 35 Report in 2001, and the Department of City Planning's *Far West Midtown: A Framework for Development,* completed under the Giuliani administration. This integrated vision would support the Olympics, expand Midtown's central business district, and help meet surging demand for housing as the city recovered from the effects of 9/11 and the recession of the early 2000s.

Dan saw Hudson Yards as the latest in a series of transformative investments that redirected the course of the city's history. He began every presentation with historic photos of exposed rail tracks and locomotives belching smoke against a jumbled low-rise cityscape, challenging audience members to guess the location being depicted. Only hard-core planning and transit nerds usually would identify the site as the future Park Avenue, prior to the

Even within government, some questioned Dan's ambitious projections. While all involved agreed that the area had great potential, many thought his outlook was overly optimistic. Some favored funding more immediately pressing priorities rather than seeding a new district of unproven marketability and without a voting constituency. They cautioned that execution on a plan of this magnitude would be a near impossibility, especially since the financing approach would be dependent on unpredictable market cycles and the conflicting and competing interests of heterogeneous developers. What these government leaders and analysts missed — and what Dan understood better than anyone else — was the vast economic potential of the district.

While somewhat blighted, the roughly 300-acre, 50-block area had enormous advantages — a location adjacent to the largest and most dynamic business district in the nation, extraordinary transportation infrastructure that crossed it and provided service at its edges (Port Authority Bus Terminal, Amtrak and Long Island Rail Road, West 39th Street Ferry Terminal), the Javits Center, views of the river, and plentiful, largely vacant land for development. Other nearby neighborhoods were also on the cusp of transformation, particularly the West Chelsea district that would soon explode following the City's rezoning and investment in the High Line, sending a torrent of New Yorkers and tourists strolling north into Hudson Yards.

Dan insisted that the team shout from the rooftops that Hudson Yards would boom with new private development and enable New York's companies to grow, thereby increasing employment and tax revenues. He articulated a virtuous cycle of public investment in infrastructure, parks, and cultural amenities that would spur office, retail, tourism, and new housing, and thus generate tax revenues that the City could deploy to support public services and an improved quality of life for residents across the five boroughs.

We are now just over halfway through the original projected time frame for district build-out and have a chance to re-evaluate the project's progress.

When the rezoning passed in 2005, the district saw an immediate burst of housing and hotel development. In 2015, the opening of the No. 7 subway extension and the first of the new parks spurred strong office and retail construction. Since then, the pace of development has been faster and more diverse than even the team foresaw, with multiple categories already exceeding initial projections.

The original proposal estimated that Hudson Yards would realize about 1.5 million square feet of hotels. By 2022, over 4 million square feet had been completed. About 0.7 million square feet of retail was projected and 1.2 million square feet has already been completed; about 12.6 million square feet of housing was projected and 13.1 million square feet has been completed; and out of the 28 million square feet of office that was projected, about 16 million square feet has been completed.

Ultimately, the team's economists came up with a projection for how much money Hudson Yards would contribute to the City and State's bottom lines over the next 30 years: $60 billion.

The criticism poured in: The development projections were too rosy, meaning the tax revenues would never be sufficient to cover debt service, argued everyone from journalists to the Independent Budget Office. The criticism was renewed after the plan's approval when, during the Great Recession of 2008, the City had to make over $300 million in unanticipated interest payments on bonds that had been issued to pay for the subway extension and other public investments. While those investments were intended to be repaid exclusively by tax revenues generated within the district, the economic downturn had caused delays in office development, forcing the City to cover the temporary shortfall.

In total about 34 million square feet of office, residential, hotel and retail space has been completed in just 17 years (80% of the original projection of 43 million square feet over 30 years). While a fiscal impact estimate has not been undertaken to assess new tax revenues generated in the district, it is clear that it has already achieved a critical mass of new office buildings and retail options, and more-than-expected housing (including over 3,000 affordable units) and hospitality offerings, with more cultural, educational, and social service institutions than initially planned (including The Shed, Signature Theatre, Success Academy, and a new Covenant House).

The area also has room to grow for years to come — including alongside the new Bella Abzug Park and Hudson Boulevard, which the City designated to run for six block-long segments between 11th and 12th avenues. Four segments are already completed, with

Senator Chuck Schumer, Deputy Mayor Dan Doctoroff, and Mayor Michael Bloomberg discuss the expansion of the Javits Convention Center, August 2006. Although the State controlled the building, the Bloomberg administration advocated successfully for significant new funding to allow it to host larger events.

CHUCK SCHUMER | U.S. Senator for New York, 1999-Present

Doctoroff and the Comeback City

New York is a comeback city — always has been and always will be. At a time when so many of us who love our hometown are focused on yet another comeback, it would be wise for all of us to spend some time thinking about, and learning from, a true maestro of NYC comebacks — and my dear friend — Dan Doctoroff.

In the years after September 11th, when others were writing the Big Apple's epitaph, Dan believed that the key to our recovery was big-thinking ambition. I remember sitting with Dan, who was clear-eyed about his five-borough plan, and thinking: He is precisely the leader we need right now. His list of accomplishments — and the economic and job activity they have sparked — is remarkable. The High Line, Brooklyn Bridge Park, the World Trade Center complex, Governors Island, and Hudson Yards. His execution of our original plan to extend the No. 7 line to Manhattan's Far West Side spurred the development of the entire Hudson Yards area, one of the most ambitious economic development projects in our country's history.

Through all of this, it was Dan's drive, his compassion — and most of all his love for and belief in New York City — that really stuck with me. With our next great comeback now underway, it's those qualities that help drive us to do better each day. Even as his work continues, Dan's legacy as a New York City Hall of Famer (or All-Star) is firmly settled.

the final two in the design phase. The area has become home to the New York operations of some of the world's most innovative companies in technology, healthcare, and finance which were looking for the kind of new, amenity-rich office space that can attract talent — particularly in a postpandemic, hybrid work world.

The assumption in the planning stage in the early to mid-2000s was that office rents in Hudson Yards would be lower than Midtown proper. However, now the Far West Midtown/Hudson Yards office subdistrict has the highest average rents of any submarket in New York City — higher than the Plaza District, Grand Central, or the Sixth Avenue corridor. While there certainly are individual buildings on Fifth Avenue or Park Avenue with higher rents, on average Hudson Yards has become established as a premium work, play, and visit location that commands rents second to none.

The wisdom of Dan's view that Hudson Yards could only be financed "off balance sheet" rather than through the city's general obligation bond program, and thus not in direct conflict with other capital funding priorities, can also be seen in the extraordinary success of Hudson Yards' innovative "value capture" financing. The Hudson Yards Infrastructure Corporation (HYIC) was formed to issue bonds backed by pledged future revenues (primarily incremental property taxes produced in the district). HYIC issued $3 billion of bonds to investors, who agreed to take the risk that the bonds would be repaid only by new revenues generated in the district, if the City committed to meet any shortfall in interest payments.

Aside from the brief period when city payments were needed to cover interest, revenues have not only repaid the bondholders, but also generated surpluses for use by the City as part of its general operating budget. Since 2017, HYIC has turned over cash surpluses of more than $662 million to the City — a number that is expected to increase dramatically in the years to come. Not reflected in that number is the array of income, sales, and other taxes that flow directly to the municipal budget, and that made up a significant share of the original $60 billion forecast.

Twenty years ago, Dan assembled a team and directed us to develop and execute a plan that could finally realize the long-held vision for a vast space that was all but ignored near the heart of Manhattan. His unshakable confidence steadied us as we delivered on plans that others had discussed for decades but could not or would not prioritize. And today we have the receipts: Hudson Yards has exceeded what even we, privately, wondered might be wild expectations, helping to drive the city's economy and generate the prosperity needed to fund essential services. Dan's optimism has only ever been matched by his demanding attention to detail. In Hudson Yards, the city is benefitting in ways only he could have foreseen.

Between 10th and 11th Avenues, the City is creating Bella Abzug Park and Hudson Boulevard, a new six-block, four-acre system of streets and open spaces which will make the previously barren area more attractive to both residents and office tenants.

JAMAICA

The Jamaica rezoning — covering 368 blocks — was the largest rezoning plan by area in New York City's history. Deputy Mayor Daniel Doctoroff tasked his team with turning Jamaica into a vibrant commercial center while preserving the area's residential character of low-rise one- and two-story family homes and its diverse culture.

The final plan, developed over four years of extensive consultation with the local community, businesses, and politicians, projected three million square feet of commercial space, almost 10,000 jobs, and more than 5,000 residential units, including approximately 800 subsidized units. It sought to create a regional business district that could become an alternative to Long Island, activate an important transportation hub, which included the AirTrain and the No. 7 subway train, and raise the living standards of almost a quarter million residents who were living below the poverty line. Doctoroff's senior policy advisor, Angela Sun, oversaw the rezoning process during her time at City Hall.

Jamaica had all the ingredients: diverse community, excellent transportation, and its history of being a great shopping and business district. That all needed to be revitalized.

There was nostalgia from people who had lived and worked in Jamaica for many, many decades. There was [a longing] for what it used to be — a great shopping corridor, a lot of great retail and mom and pop shops, and this incredible energy. I remember Senator [Frank] Padavan waxing on about [what] used to be Queens and the potato fields. I wanted to hear him out and recognize that there was this wonderful bucolic history but with all due respect we need[ed] to be clear-eyed about where we were and the future. Potato fields aren't coming back.

[City Planning Commission Chair] Amanda Burden always insisted on walking the entire span of the rezoning and I remember walking through Downtown Jamaica many times. It was fraying. A lot of the buildings were shabby or falling apart. It seemed like an area that needed a wholesale restructure and a new vision for bringing it back — but bringing it back in a thoughtful way. Not saying, "Okay, people want big box retail so we're going to bring in Bed, Bath and Beyond." There was a desire to retain the character of Jamaica and the diversity of the people who lived there.

You have artisanal bakers and butchers and fishmongers that depend on this community of residents. But there was also a recognition that this is prime real estate. It's central, it's accessible to the airports, and it was a real neighborhood. There could be far more small to medium size enterprises that could locate in Jamaica; meetings and gatherings and summits that could take place in Jamaica. Here was a hub where the transportation corridor naturally lent itself to becoming a central business district in a borough outside of Manhattan.

It was a very complex rezoning, so it needed the administration to bring everybody to the table. We needed to consider sanitation, parks, schools, transportation, housing — every agency had a part to play. [We] would parse out these 60-page PowerPoints so that every single agency had their platform to talk about their contribution because every single agency

Right: Potato farmers near Jamaica, Queens, 1916.

Below: Jamaica, Queens. Covering 368 blocks, the Jamaica rezoning was the largest by area in New York City history. It created the capacity for three million square feet of commercial space, almost 10,000 jobs, and more than 5,000 residential units.

mattered given the scale. [The meetings were] standing room only. One staffer once remarked incredulously: "How many agencies does it take to do a rezoning?!" Answer: all of them!

The Community Board meetings were also [thorny]. There was a recognition that this was not going to be a rezoning that's going to breeze through the City Council. There were many late night, long meetings that went way over time. There were strong voices not necessarily opposing the idea of revitalization, but more skepticism — what was the motive of the City? Are people going to be left behind? Is this paving the way for bigger conglomerates?

We went block by block. [The final plan has] higher density housing that coalesces around the transportation hubs, but you also have very convenient access to shops and restaurants and parks. Where the community had a fair point, there were adjustments made. That's why it took four years. It was a negotiation but it was one that made the plan defensible and durable. It's the reason why it got overwhelming support in the City Council. It was nearly unanimous.

As with many things in the Bloomberg administration, you created the blueprint, you created the catalyst, and you set the efforts in motion so that things can happen, not quite organically, but in a supported way, where there's a clear, detailed plan and a vision behind it.

FLUSHING

The Bloomberg administration recognized that stabilizing New York's economy would require revitalizing neighborhoods beyond Lower Manhattan. Deputy Mayor Dan Doctoroff immediately identified Flushing, Queens as one of the priority sites for his five-borough economic development plan, which looked to create lively, mixed-use communities and business hubs across the city. In 2003, a joint task force including Doctoroff and his team, state officials, and local leaders released the *Development Framework for Downtown Flushing*, which presented a broader vision for linking Downtown Flushing, the Flushing River waterfront, and Willets Point. To advance these goals, the plan called for rezoning a five-acre municipal parking lot into a mixed-use development that would include housing, hotel rooms, retail, and open space. The project, known as Flushing Commons, finally broke ground in 2014 and will ultimately include 600 new residential units, office and retail, a 1.5-acre "town square" including a plaza for cultural events, and a new YMCA.

Above: In 2003, a joint City–State–community task force led by Dan Doctoroff released the *Development Framework for Downtown Flushing*, which offered a vision for linking downtown Flushing, the Flushing River waterfront, and Willets Point. The plan called for rezoning a five-acre municipal parking lot into Flushing Commons, a mixed-use development that would include 600 units of housing, hotel rooms, retail, a 1.5-acre "town square," and a new YMCA. Flushing Commons finally broke ground in 2014.

Left: Main Street, the commercial center of Flushing, Queens.

THOMAS MCKNIGHT | New York City Economic Development Corporation, 2001–2019
CECILIA KUSHNER | New York City Economic Development Corporation, 2015–Present

NEW STAPLETON WATERFRONT

New Stapleton Waterfront is a 35-acre property on Staten Island's North Shore, situated between the St. George Ferry Terminal and the Verrazzano-Narrows Bridge along the Staten Island Railway. In 1990, the property was partially developed as a naval home port, but was closed four years later as part of a nationwide base realignment effort and handed over to the City of New York.

Deputy Mayor Daniel Doctoroff came into office after several unsuccessful efforts to develop the Homeport property. He convened a mayoral task force in 2003 with a mandate to create a new vision for the property within the context of the larger North Shore community. The task force was a success, overcoming political challenges to craft the New Stapleton Waterfront vision and a framework for the site's redevelopment, consisting of sustainable mixed-use development set within a network of esplanades, new bike lanes, and public open space close to the Stapleton Staten Island Railway station.

Since the task force completed its work in 2004, the City approved a rezoning to support its vision of mixed-use development. The City is investing over $200 million to transform the New Stapleton Waterfront into a vibrant new neighborhood that will include nearly 2,100 new housing units, around 50,000 square feet of retail, and 12 acres of new parkland, creating a waterfront attraction on Staten Island's North Shore.

New Stapleton Waterfront is a 35-acre development in Downtown Staten Island with public open space, housing, and new transportation access.

JERILYN PERINE | Commissioner, Department of Housing Preservation & Development, 2000-2004

AN UNLIKELY PARTNERSHIP TO CREATE THE NEW HOUSING MARKETPLACE PLAN

Two extremely diverse and unlikely roads led myself and Dan Doctoroff into the brand new Bloomberg administration. I was reappointed Commissioner for the Department of Housing Preservation & Development (HPD) shortly before Dan was announced as a new deputy mayor, meaning that — at least for the short term — he was saddled with a "leftover" commissioner responsible for a topic that was not what lured him into public service.

Dan's road was armed with a Harvard education, a successful private sector career, and a strong, almost unbreakable belief in his ability to apply those lessons to city government. My road began the lucky day that Open Admissions coincided with my high school graduation, transporting me most improbably into the entering 1970 class of the City College of New York's architecture school. That led me into a lifetime career in municipal government — the one place where someone like me could be put to work on our city's most dire problems. Dan and I were both proud of our experiences, convinced that we could add value (his confidence was certainly greater than mine in that regard!), and committed to applying our skills to have the most impact.

This was a formula for disaster! When a housing commissioner learns that they will report to the deputy mayor for economic development it drives a stake through her heart. Invariably it means a conflict between economic development and housing, with housing being the loser. Dan was also tasked with rebuilding after 9/11, both physically and economically. That became our first joint task — for him to bring New York City back from the many losses of 9/11 and for me to convince him that housing, in fact, could be the key.

Our partnership resulted in much compromise, discussion (and struggle sometimes), a growing mutual respect and affection, and most importantly, an understanding that we could accomplish our best work together. It was a unique opportunity that neither of us expected. We shared thoughts about the loss of our beloved fathers and book suggestions. (I must admit now that I never found the time to read his recommendations and he was the only person who actually read one of mine — Tony Judt's epic nearly 1,000 page book, *Postwar: A History of Europe Since 1945*).

But first I had to survive the ignominy of not being his pick for HPD commissioner. He thoughtfully and kindly relieved my anxiety upon our first meeting, asking me to stay behind. I, of course, resigned myself to being fired. Instead, he told me he was looking forward to working together in his overly polite Midwestern speak and I translated that into working-class Brooklyn speak as, "Whew, I am not fired today!"

One of his first assignments was quintessential Doctoroff: Search the world for the best examples and practices in housing policies. I then embarked on a campaign to prove that he already had all

that at his disposal, that New York City's two agencies devoted to affordable housing — HPD and the Housing Development Corporation (HDC) — already had the resources and structure that were the envy of municipalities around the world, and that he could unleash them. After I convinced him, came the task: "Okay, let's make a plan we can take to the mayor."

I understood the gravity of the assignment and how lucky I was to have Dan at the helm — especially since I had absolutely no understanding of our new Mayor Mike Bloomberg. I only knew that housing was not his priority (a benefit that probably led to my appointment!). Dan was the key to being able to translate the plan into a policy that the mayor would endorse.

The 10-year *New Housing Marketplace Plan*, which called for 65,000 new affordable units, had everything we needed for success — the Office of Management and Budget's prior approval, clear goals, and, I hoped, the mayor's blessing. Dan's finance background led to the innovative unleashing of HDC's financial capacity and strategies on how to expand the impact of HDC's AAA bond rating, which became a critical financing strategy for the plan — at that point, the most ambitious affordable housing plan in American history.

Dan remembers in his book, *Greater than Ever*, that I was scared when we presented our ideas to the mayor. I would now like to correct him. I was not frightened by the meeting — rather I had started chemotherapy and realized I made a poor choice of seating at the table in the Committee of the Whole room in City Hall very far from the nearest waste bin. Since I had to forgo anti-nausea medication that day because it made me loopy, I was terrified of the potential results.

I needn't have worried. The meeting lasted all of five minutes. Armed with our presentation and Dan's eloquence, the mayor simply responded "Okay." That was that.

I, of course, unable to leave out any of our arguments, tried to continue with our carefully crafted presentation. I remember a gentle elbow nudge from Dan — signaling "quit while you're ahead." It was an important lesson for me from Dan's private sector dealings, a place where an "Okay" could finalize a deal, versus the public sector where often an "Okay" simply meant, "Okay — until attacks come from unforeseen actors after you walk out the door that unravel all of your work."

Sometime after the mayor announced the plan on December 12, 2002, Dan told me that the mayor took him aside at an event and asked for another briefing on the plan because everywhere he went people kept telling him how great it was and that it would become a keynote of his administration. We both understood that this very private comment was the best acknowledgment of our shared work we could receive. It was a small moment between us (I can still remember Dan's small smile) that was the highlight of my career.

Mayor Michael Bloomberg and Department of Housing Preservation & Development Commissioner Jerilyn Perine, propose state legislation to provide protection to Mitchell–Lama development tenants and real estate tax relief to owners, 2003.

RAFAEL E. CESTERO | Deputy Commissioner for Development, 2004-2007 & Commissioner, 2009-2012, Department of Housing Preservation & Development

HARNESSING GROWTH TO CREATE THE LARGEST U.S. AFFORDABLE HOUSING PLAN

During the bad old days of the 1970s and 80s when the Bronx was burning, people were fleeing for the suburbs, and owners were abandoning their buildings, New York City's population plummeted, dropping by nearly a million people. Mayor Ed Koch crafted what I'd consider the city's first real housing plan. He refused to give up on entire neighborhoods, like the South Bronx, East New York, and Harlem; instead, the City took ownership of tens of thousands of units of housing through tax foreclosure and committed to investing billions in renovating these vacant buildings and constructing new buildings on the land, often in partnership with the private sector. The goal was to spur the reclamation and revitalization of communities that had been scarred by disinvestment and flight, bringing people back into the city.

By 2004, when I joined the Department of Housing Preservation & Development (HPD), New York's housing crisis was vastly different. Over the preceding decades, the city had indeed made a comeback. Thanks to improved quality of life, economics, community amenities — all of it — New York City was now a place people wanted to live. People had poured back into the city, and our problem went from not enough people, to not nearly enough housing. We had a crisis of supply and demand with housing affordability as our most critical challenge.

The Bloomberg administration, which came into office a few short months after the tragic terrorist attacks of September 11, 2001, foresaw this challenge. It rolled out a huge affordable housing plan at the end of 2002, which may have seemed counterintuitive at a time when a lot of people were once again leaving New York and many were questioning the future and relevancy of big cities in a post-9/11 world. It was more common for people to invoke the spiral of the 1970s and predict its return than worry about affordable housing. However, Mayor Michael Bloomberg and his Deputy Mayor for Economic Development and Rebuilding Dan Doctoroff, always believed in the resilience of the city and understood that we'd need those affordable units as New York continued its recovery.

The New Housing Marketplace Plan

When Dan and HPD launched the New Housing Marketplace Plan (NHMP) in December 2002, with a goal of creating and preserving 65,000 affordable units, it was New York City's largest investment in housing since the Koch administration 10-year plan. I joined the department two years later. As I acclimated to my role as Deputy Commissioner for Development, it became clear to me that Dan was somebody who cared deeply about the city and the people who lived here. He didn't worry about making waves or rubbing the old system the wrong way. Inertia was our enemy and progress was how Dan measured success.

Dan was always moving forward and, at least in principle, he didn't have time for people and policies that couldn't adapt and evolve into what the city needed right now. In 2006, amid a hot market and housing boom, we expanded the plan to 165,000 units, making it the largest affordable housing plan ever undertaken by

New housing at Hunter's Point South. With 60% of the project's 5,000 units designated as affordable, the development was a key piece of the Bloomberg administration's plan to create or preserve 165,000 units of affordable housing across New York City. Dan Doctoroff initiated the City's acquisition of the site, which he had previously envisioned for the Olympic Village, from the Port Authority.

an American city. The name itself was an intentional callout to the fact that Dan and the administration had crafted a plan that was built to operate in the broader housing and development market and would be able to move and adapt as the market changed. Our housing plan wasn't just about housing — it was about creating the right tools, policies, and infrastructure to support a growing city.

That ethos underpinned the NHMP in both its iterations. To me, that's also the brilliance of Dan's thinking and it's how we created and met the goals of the largest and most ambitious municipal housing plan the nation had ever seen.

The idea was simple. Take what the economics of the time will give you. Create programs and policies that work with, and harness, the economic ebbs and flows (which are bound to happen), and you've got a plan that's nimble and agile. This also ensured that the NHMP was strong and resilient — it was a plan that could pivot when it needed to and still operate at an impressive scale, delivering the affordable units that our city needed.

Still, it was no small feat to add 100,000 units to the original plan. A large portion of the property the City had taken through tax foreclosure during the 1970s and 80s had been sold or successfully redeveloped as affordable housing by past administrations. There were still some large parcels left, but the city needed housing in every borough and neighborhood. By and large most of the low-hanging fruit was gone or committed to projects in the pipeline.

We were still building new 100% affordable projects, but it was clear that wouldn't be enough — when you're adding 100,000 units, you need to be creative and find ways to add housing everywhere. The economy was strong and the housing market was booming. We needed to harness that market and find a way to make private development and private capital work for us to create new affordable units.

Dan understood that affordable housing was key to getting his rezoning plans approved and demanded that HPD and the Department of City Planning (DCP) find a way to make it work. This was not a simple demand. Years of disagreement and distrust had built up between the two agencies around a myriad of issues. From the public approvals required for development on City-owned land, to design guidelines built into zoning that made it more expensive to build affordable housing, HPD and DCP had frequently struggled to work collaboratively. Now the success of the NHMP depended on it.

Expanding inclusionary zoning

My first experience with this culture clash came a mere five days after I had started my job at HPD. That afternoon, I was summoned to City Hall, along with my boss Commissioner Shaun Donovan, for a meeting with Dan and DCP on a little-used tool called inclusionary zoning. The nuts and bolts of the program can be complicated, but the idea is straightforward. In a hot real estate market, builders are building; this program incentivized private development to add affordable units to their rental projects. If developers made 20% of the units in their new, market-rate rental building affordable/income-restricted, they would get a zoning bonus. That bonus would allow them to build a larger project, or they could sell that bonus at whatever the market would bear within a given geographic area.

But the program had never caught on in New York. HPD viewed this zoning tool as outside its mission and expertise. DCP had

never seen affordable housing as part of its work and key players in the department had concerns about the legality of stronger inclusionary zoning — not to mention height and density concerns. The agencies were at loggerheads. But luckily, unsticking the stuck is one of Dan's great specialties.

At this meeting, DCP presented a detailed analysis of height and density and massing diagrams showing how inclusionary zoning would impact the built environment. But Dan had a different question. He wanted to know if anyone would actually use the program. How would the market respond — would developers add the density and create the affordable housing? Would other stakeholders support the idea?

After an hour of back and forth, we were nowhere. As DCP presented their analysis, Dan did what Dan does, which is probe deeply into the numbers. He wasn't getting answers that were believable about whether somebody would actually build. He wanted to know: What are the construction costs? Are the incremental costs of building higher worth it? Are affordable units on the top or bottom? How does that impact revenues? How is a developer going to think about it?

City Planning couldn't answer that question because they were not as close to the financing side as HPD. This was my expertise coming in — I had done equity and debt in affordable housing for 15 years prior to taking the job.

Dan erupted, and said, looking straight at me, "This is why we hired you. Go run the numbers, talk to developers and the community, build the case. We need to tell the story or no one will believe it!"

I walked back to HPD with Shaun in shock. I didn't know anything about inclusionary zoning. I was a traditional affordable housing financing expert and inclusionary zoning wasn't a program New York had ever really used before. I told Shaun, "I don't ever want a meeting like that again. I need five people and three weeks to dig in and figure this out."

And that is exactly what we did. We ran exhaustive models, found willing partners at DCP to look at different planning and massing options, spent countless evenings and weekends in neighborhoods talking to community leaders to develop the model, create the program, and tell the story. This is more or less how I spent my first month on the job at HPD, and it built the foundation for how we collaborated across agencies, crunched numbers, and found ways to make things work.

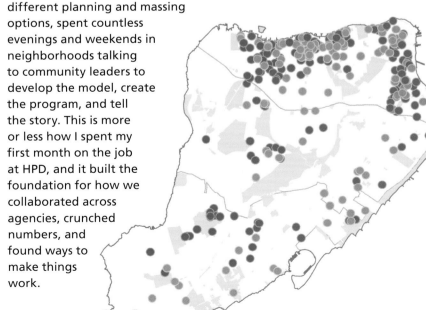

NEW HOUSING MARKETPLACE PLAN
2004–2013

Projects by Construction Type
- ● New Construction
- ● Preservation
- ■ AIRPORT
- ▨ PARK
- ☐ Community District Boundary

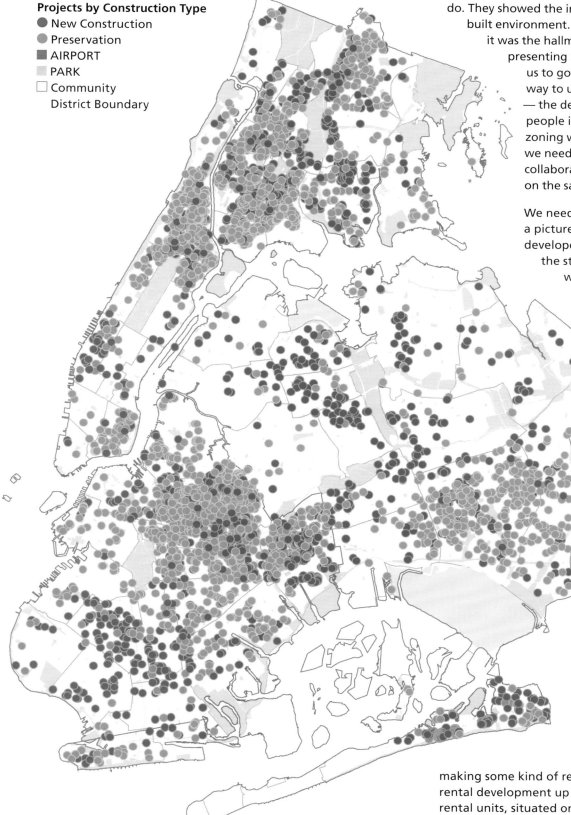

It was also a lesson for me in how Dan viewed storytelling as a key tool to achieve the outcomes he wanted.

At first glance the DCP numbers did what they were supposed to do. They showed the impact that the program would have on the built environment. Data is important. It drove Dan's thinking and it was the hallmark of the Bloomberg administration, but presenting numbers and data wasn't enough. Dan wanted us to go back, reassess that information, and find a way to use it to talk to the different constituencies — the developers, the local elected officials, and the people in the communities — about why inclusionary zoning would work for them. And if it didn't work, we needed to figure out how HPD and DCP could collaborate to make it work. It had to be both agencies on the same page, singing the same song.

We needed to find ways to use that data to paint a picture and tell the story about bottom lines for developers, positive outcomes for communities, and the stability it would bring to the people who would benefit from the housing. I learned that having stakeholders be able to find themselves and their interests in a program or policy is what creates buy-in and gets those policies to the finish line.

As a result of our efforts, inclusionary zoning went from a sleepy program in Manhattan that had created just a few hundred units over two decades to generating almost 5,000 new affordable units in Greenpoint-Williamsburg, Chelsea, and Hudson Yards — all without providing direct subsidy from the City's coffers.

Ultimately, the expansion of the Inclusionary Housing Program became one of the most enduring housing policies of the Bloomberg administration.

Creating affordable housing at Hunter's Point South

In 2006, the same year we relaunched the NHMP as a 165,000-unit plan, the looming sale of Stuyvesant Town and Peter Cooper Village put the City under immense public pressure. At the peak of the real estate boom, with seemingly every property sale making some kind of record or headline, MetLife put the iconic rental development up for sale. For almost four decades, the 11,250 rental units, situated on 80 acres near Manhattan's East River from 14th Street to 23rd Street, had been a haven of affordable rents to moderate-income families. But as the city grew, rents had begun to rise and more and more units had been converted to market rate. Tenants and local elected officials were rightly concerned that the new owners — who would almost certainly pay a record-setting sum — would try to take units out of rent stabilization in order to increase rents and drive up revenue.

There was a large, loud public call for the City to leverage its resources to purchase the complex and preserve it as affordable housing or at a minimum, use its subsidy resources to incentivize the new owner to preserve affordability. Dan's directive was to ignore the noise, stay the course, and be consistent with the pillar of our plan: Find the silver lining in the market and harness it. He asked us to think creatively about how we could preserve the complex's affordable apartments and to do an exhaustive analysis of what it would cost taxpayers.

We looked at what subsidies would be needed, how much it would cost per unit, and importantly how much it would cost to build or preserve the same number of affordable units elsewhere. After weeks of running and rerunning numbers, we presented our case to Dan, which essentially showed that intervening in the sale to support the tenant bid or to require private bidders to preserve affordability would require more than double the amount of public subsidy needed to build a new affordable unit. At the end of our presentation, Dan said, "So, if it's cheaper to build new, why not just build new?" Of course, we had a million reasons why that was easier said than done. No comparably sized land to build on was at the top of the list.

This is where Dan's creativity and his deep knowledge of every nook and cranny of New York because of his bike rides, neighborhood walks, and years of planning for the NYC2012 Olympic bid took over. He suggested we look at a long-neglected parcel of land on the Queens waterfront, called Queens West, that had been the proposed site of the Olympic Village.

Ultimately, our analysis told us that we could build new units more cheaply at that 30-acre site than preserve or purchase Stuyvesant Town. At that time, in that market environment of hyper-inflated pricing, purchasing Stuyvesant Town and Peter Cooper Village was not a move to harness the market — it was letting the market run wild.

In October 2006, the Tishman Speyer/BlackRock partnership purchased Stuyvesant Town and Peter Cooper Village for $6.3 billion, the largest price ever paid in a residential real estate sale in world history. In 2009, the partnership defaulted on its loans after their plans to remove units from rent-regulation didn't work out as planned — the value of the complexes had fallen to roughly $1.9 billion. Dan's insistence that we stick to the plan, do our homework, and not get caught up in the pressure cooker was the right move.

Today, Queens West is called Hunter's Point South. In 2013, the City broke ground on Phase I of the multiphase plan to create a new, mixed-use, mixed-income community with 5,000 units of housing in seven residential buildings, new retail space, a school, an 11-acre park, and new infrastructure like roads, sewers, and utilities. At least 60% of the total units will be permanently affordable to low-, moderate-, and middle-income New Yorkers.

Unlocking the financing power of HDC
One of Dan's least heralded accomplishments, may also be his most important: waking up the incredible potential of the New York City Housing Development Corporation (HDC), the city's housing finance agency. It was created in 1971 with the purpose of financing multifamily housing in New York, but the City had rarely used it. Prior to the NHMP, the City primarily relied on its own capital, bank financing, and other forms of subsidy to fund its affordable housing efforts. Dan understood HDC's ability to access the market and leverage its balance sheet to drive investment in affordable housing — and unleashed it.

From 2003 through 2014, HDC provided more than $8.3 billion to finance more than 70,000 units under the NHMP. In time, HDC became the largest municipal housing finance agency in the country. By its own account, from 2003 through 2022, it "has financed more than 201,000 housing units using over $28 billion in bonds and other debt obligations and provided in excess of $3 billion in subsidy from corporate reserves and other available funds held by the corporation."

It seems like a no-brainer now, considering HDC's success and stature in the industry, but in prior administrations, the agency was an afterthought. Without Dan's insight into HDC's potential, financing the creation and preservation of 165,000 units would have been impossible. I believe it's also fair to say that HDC's transformation under Dan's leadership was critical to the success of the de Blasio administration's housing plan and will continue to be a critical source of financing for subsequent administrations and their efforts to create and preserve affordable housing.

The model lives on
Roughly a decade after the completion of the NHMP, New York City still has a serious housing problem. So were we successful? I believe we were. Many of the innovations we made in practice and policy are still being used and are evolving to meet the city's current needs. Were we perfect? No. There are always things you can't control or plan for, more to be done, and things you can look back on and say "what if?" But more importantly, every one of those 165,000 units of housing represents a person or family who has a stable, secure home who may not otherwise have been able to find it or afford it. These were families living paycheck to paycheck struggling to pay rent, formerly homeless veterans, low-income senior citizens, kids aging out of foster care, nurses, teachers, cab drivers, our friends and family and fellow New Yorkers. I can't imagine what the city would look like today without it.

Ultimately, Dan rallied us around a vision of how to support a growing city and work with the market, not against it, in order to harness and drive the outcomes we needed. In doing so, he has created a legacy that goes beyond the 165,000 units created or preserved in our plan and even the hundreds of thousands of New Yorkers who now live in decent, stable, and affordable housing because of it. He advocated an entirely new approach that helped us adapt and mold our work to meet the times — a model that is the new standard for subsequent generations.

The Greenpoint-Williamsburg rezoning created 12,500 units of housing, including nearly 3,200 affordable units. Left, the Eagle + West towers, designed by OMA and Beyer Blinder Belle, where 30% of the units are designated affordable.

THE SUSTAINABLE CITY

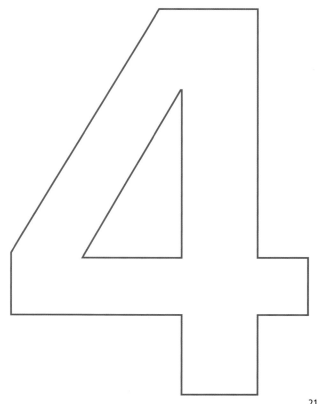

Bike path at Hunter's Point South.

"PlaNYC is the most sweeping and detailed plan to strengthen New York's urban environment in the city's modern history and create the first environmentally sustainable 21st century city."

DANIEL L. DOCTOROFF, JUNE 2007

PlaNYC oversaw the planting of one million trees across New York City to help absorb carbon and cool and purify the air. Left, sustainable plantings at Hunter's Point South Park.

ROHIT T. AGGARWALA | Founding Director, Mayor's Office for Long-Term Planning and Sustainability, 2006–2010 | Chief Climate Officer and Commissioner, Department of Environmental Protection, 2022–Present

ARIELLA MARON | Founding Deputy Director, Mayor's Office for Long-Term Planning and Sustainability, 2006–2009 | Deputy Commissioner for Energy Management, Department of Citywide Administrative Services, 2009–2012

HOW PLANYC REINVENTED URBAN SUSTAINABILITY

We released PlaNYC more than 15 years ago. Its impact is still resonating across the urban sustainability movement.

Both of us have had the opportunity to work with many cities across the country — and for Rit, the world — over the past decade and a half. We have seen firsthand the emergence of the local government sustainability field. We have experienced where it has been and how it has evolved, and now we are seeing where it might be going next.

When we released PlaNYC and New York City's first greenhouse gas (GHG) inventory in April 2007, just a handful of cities had sustainability offices or chief sustainability officers. Today, there are over 250 member cities and counties in the Urban Sustainability Directors Network, an organization that brings together local government sustainability practitioners in North America, and there are almost 300 communities that regularly track their GHG emissions.

As climate change has turned from scientific projection into the reality of each season's weather reports, the field of urban sustainability has graduated from a small movement to an established aspect of urban governance. Sustainability itself has become bigger, encompassing resilience, climate justice, and the transition to a green economy. The roles of local government sustainability offices have grown as well, and the tools they deploy have become more ambitious, interdisciplinary, and important.

In many ways, PlaNYC set the foundation for this transformation and helped shape the modern urban sustainability movement. Some of PlaNYC's impact is due simply to New York City's importance. Much is due to Mayor Michael Bloomberg's leadership. But PlaNYC was conceived and overseen by Deputy Mayor Dan Doctoroff, and a significant part of its impact is due to his personal stamp. Like Ray Anderson, the legendary CEO of Interface, who pioneered industrial ecology, Dan embraced urban sustainability not as an activist or entrepreneur, but as an executive. His oversight over a broad range of city agencies with daily operational responsibility — for water, transportation, and housing, to name just three — ensured that his support translated into action and that the approach to sustainability was "ambitious but achievable" — a phrase we heard constantly during the period in which we developed PlaNYC.

Why was PlaNYC so influential? Here are a few reasons.

New York City added nearly 400 miles of bike paths between the release of PlaNYC in 2007 and the end of the Bloomberg administration, including the city's first protected bike paths. Opposite, protected bike path, Schermerhorn Street, Downtown Brooklyn.

Dan was always willing to confront hard problems

Sustainability had posed — and continues to pose — hard questions for cities, especially in the Global North. In 2006, some of these ideas were radical: realizing how bad cars are for cities, embracing bikes, pushing those who own and manage buildings to treat efficiency as an obligation rather than a frill. But Dan was always willing to face the difficult facts and work to turn them into an actionable plan — and then into reality. Often, the initiatives to address these challenges are politically challenging. But Dan never questioned whether we were going to do something hard. It was, "How might we do it?" He always encouraged us to think big and think outside the box because the current box didn't work.

One example of this was the congestion pricing fight — a politically perilous undertaking that Dan insisted we pursue because he believed it was important.

He knew that congestion pricing, and a handful of other ideas, might prove controversial. But instead of abandoning them and going for easier wins, he embraced the effort and did everything he could to help it succeed. He led us to create a broad-based coalition of leading New Yorkers, including environmental leaders, real estate interests, environmental justice advocates, technical experts, and others on a Sustainability Advisory Board (SAB). Unlike some panels convened for press releases, Dan wanted the SAB to wield real authority in developing the plan alongside city officials, so that by the time PlaNYC was revealed, a wide set of powerful stakeholders across the city were genuinely invested in its success.

That included outreach to organizations Dan had previously battled. For instance, the Regional Plan Association had loudly opposed Dan's goal to build a stadium on the Far West Side of Manhattan and no doubt contributed to the plan's demise. Still, Dan successfully engaged them as allies on PlaNYC and congestion pricing.

Dan also used his personal relationships and credibility in the business world to win supporters at a time when business interests were not really engaged on climate. He and Rit met with developer Steve Ross of Related Companies, who was at the time the chairman of the Real Estate Board of New York (REBNY), to pitch him on congestion pricing. While many of New York's corporations had already endorsed congestion pricing, real estate had not. Dan and Steve were both board members of the World Resources Institute, and Dan explained the key connection between congestion pricing and the transit investment that was (and remains) crucial to the future of Midtown, the city's largest central business district. REBNY's subsequent support of the plan was critical, establishing congestion pricing as a joint effort of environmentalists and the business community.

Dan saw sustainability as the solution to multiple community priorities

From the outset, the initiative that eventually became PlaNYC was about meeting the needs of current and future New Yorkers through improvements to the built and natural environments. The city's chief demographer had shared projections with Dan that New York City could reach a population of 9 million people by 2030. Dan wanted to ensure that New York City had the housing and infrastructure to accommodate this population, and the clean air, water, and access to open spaces for its communities to thrive.

As a result, PlaNYC was one of the first — if not first — plan to expand and connect the work of environmental and sustainability offices to community priorities. Sustainability by definition must center people and prioritize the needs of communities most vulnerable to environmental and economic injustices. We would say, "You can't talk about land use without talking about housing, and housing without transportation, and transportation without air quality, and air quality without energy . . ." As a result, we created a plan that positions sustainability as the foundation for a healthy built environment.

For example, while not explicitly in PlaNYC, the plan helped strengthen efforts to connect affordable housing and high-performance buildings in New York City. It empowered City housing officials to prioritize the integration of healthier, climate-friendly building strategies into their efforts to preserve and expand affordable housing.

PlaNYC also prioritized improving transit access to historically underserved areas and creating open space in neighborhoods that did not have their fair share of places to play and enjoy nature. In short, it connected sustainability with affordable housing and more equitable access to transportation and open space.

We were not the first to understand the importance of this work and the need to promote more sustainable outcomes. In fact, New York City already had a number of initiatives underway, including a green building law (Local Law 86), the Staten Island Bluebelt, successful water efficiency efforts, and a history of energy efficiency upgrades to municipal buildings, to name a few.

But these were fragmented efforts. PlaNYC was the first urban sustainability plan to dare to envision a truly sustainable city, across departments, sectors, and technical specialty areas. It connected land use, housing, and open space to air and water quality, infrastructure reliability, mobility, buildings, and climate change. Dan oversaw all of the city's economic development agencies in his role as deputy mayor and integrated them all — including additional agencies like the Parks Department which were outside his purview — into the sustainability effort to create a unified response across city government.

Dan reimagined the role of local government in sustainability

Historically, the issues cities considered within their jurisdiction were limited by law and tradition. When PlaNYC was written, energy policy and brownfield remediation efforts were overseen exclusively by state governments within the United States. The few cities that did greenhouse gas inventories focused only on the emissions of municipal operations — ignoring the citywide impacts that local government can shape. Policies around green buildings were limited to establishing standards for future construction.

Under Dan's leadership, PlaNYC fundamentally changed the role of local government in transforming the built environment

under its jurisdiction to meet 21st century challenges. PlaNYC was shaped by an inventory that showed the dominant role that buildings and transportation had in citywide emissions. This led, in turn, to the 2009 *Greener, Greater, Buildings Plan*, which included benchmarking, building audit, and tune-up mandates for existing buildings; a local energy code; and the creation of the New York City Energy Efficiency Corporation to help finance this work. PlaNYC also established the nation's first city-run brownfields office — which quickly became the second-largest remediator in the United States, behind California.

Dan ensured the resources necessary for success

Beyond inspiring the plan's development, pushing us to establish bold goals, and bringing in top thinkers to support the work, Dan made sure we had what we needed to create and deliver on the plan's ambition. Dan did not stay long enough to get full credit for this, but

PlaNYC called for the creation of eight destination parks spread across all five boroughs, prioritizing under-resourced communities. The City invested more than $29 million in Far Rockaway, Queens, to create new playgrounds, sports courts and fields, a skate park, and a performance area, while integrating new trees and sustainable landscaping.

his support and leadership continues to be unprecedented in this field. He gave us his time, he leveraged his political capital, and he fought for the staffing and resources necessary to support implementation.

Dan's time was one of the most important resources we had. During the development of the plan — for more than a year — our standard PlaNYC meetings with Dan were Sunday afternoons, because, as he said, that was the only time he could devote several hours to something as complex as urban sustainability. Not only did we gain from Dan's thinking and ambition, it also ensured that he had wrestled personally with each of the issues in the plan and knew it inside and out.

That in-depth knowledge was critical because it also gave Dan the ability and willingness to invest his personal capital and relationships in the effort. Whether it was convincing

philanthropists to donate to work related to PlaNYC, working with his fellow deputy mayors, pushing the commissioners who reported to him, or building support among business, political, and cultural leaders, Dan was an active and engaged advocate.

Dan also realized that success required investment. This included the creation of a new office to develop the plan, the Mayor's Office of Long-Term Planning and Sustainability (OLTPS). That office has gone through several name changes but is now a permanent part of city government, enshrined in the City Charter. PlaNYC included funding support for the agencies tasked with implementing the work, both in the capital investment needed to create new parks, plant one million trees, repair the Delaware Aqueduct, and upgrade many city-owned buildings, and the staffing that agencies needed to implement these programs. He also wasn't timid about the oversight such efforts needed. A few weeks before the release

Rohit T. Aggarwala, Founding Director of the Mayor's Office of Long-Term Planning and Sustainability, speaking at the Operation Green Conference in Los Angeles, 2009.

of PlaNYC, Dan asked us to make a new organizational chart for OLTPS; we took a first stab, adding a few additional boxes to our team of five people. We handed it to him, and he said, "No, we need to hire at least 20 people!" Yes, that was what was needed, and New York City continues to have one of the best staffed sustainability offices in the country.

Local leadership is often not willing to do the hard work, use their political capital, and find resources from a strapped budget to support implementation. In our work with other cities, we often hear that their municipal leadership generally supports sustainability and climate initiatives in concept, but that support often does not show up when it is most needed: during budget negotiations, wrangling agencies to prioritize the work, and when it is politically inconvenient. These cities lament that the support from officials is, "a mile wide, but only an inch deep." Dan set us up to have that support — not just a mile wide and an inch deep but a mile wide and a mile deep.

Dan saw the need for PlaNYC to be a movement, not a report

Dan saw, perhaps as a lesson from the defeat of the West Side stadium and the Olympic bid, that ambitious change required not just a vision but a coalition. He saw the need for a group of leaders — from business, labor, environmentalists, and others — to give input and share in the development of the plan. He recognized the need to include environmental justice voices, and listened to them, especially on issues such as brownfields and air quality that impact their communities very differently. "I was very involved in the air quality workshop that was trying to raise issues and concerns that would really be the foundation for some of the plan," leading environmental justice advocate, Peggy Shepard, says later in this chapter. "Being able to be part of the workshops that really provided a foundation for the work, was exciting and important." With Dan, "I did find him a good listener and I found obviously that he was responsive."

One impact of this approach was that we got better, more innovative, and more effective ideas. On brownfields, the real estate executives and environmental justice advocates sat at the same table. We realized they had often talked past each other, but by making them workshop ideas, we not only found common ground but solutions that had tremendous impact. (Brownfields was one of PlaNYC's most unsung successes, sparking hundreds of cleanups — and resulting in new housing, usually in environmental justice neighborhoods — through an innovative approach to lightly-contaminated sites.)

The other impact was that the plan had tremendous support the day it came out. While most government plans are developed internally and then "sold" to advocates just prior to release, PlaNYC was genuinely co-created with a broad group of advocates. The day it was released, they saw their own ideas and impacts in the plan. As Bob Yaro, then the president of Regional Plan Association, told Rit, "you took us seriously, so we took you seriously." And that meant that the political fights over the next year were much easier because we had a strong coalition that was committed to getting PlaNYC implemented.

PlaNYC demonstrated the leading role cities can play to address climate change

All this meant that PlaNYC set the standard for other cities, at a critical time in the history of urban sustainability. A year before we started to draft PlaNYC, the U.S. Conference of Mayors committed cities to take action to reduce greenhouse gas emission in alignment with the global standards set by the Kyoto Protocol. Mayor Ken Livingstone of London, convened a global cities meeting on climate in 2005 as well, planting the seed for what is now the C40 Cities Climate Leadership Group. But urban actions were small and cities tended to think of themselves as advocates, not actors.

Through analysis and discussions with local stakeholders and national experts (many of our local stakeholders are national and global experts) it became clear that climate change was a common thread across all of PlaNYC's focus areas and there was a growing imperative to act. Dan supported the realization that his vision for New York City's built environment would need to include actions to reduce global warming emissions — and steps to adapt the built environment to handle climate impacts that were already locked in.

PlaNYC became the first municipal sustainability plan to integrate climate action, laying out specific steps to reduce greenhouse gas emissions and initiating the first annual, citywide greenhouse gas inventory to track progress. This commitment was part of a broader Bloomberg administration philosophy: "You can't manage what you can't measure." Dan and Mayor Bloomberg were both committed not just to big thinking, but following the numbers to hold themselves accountable.

PlaNYC's focus on climate, its combination of ambition and practicality, and its success in implementation made it a standard for other cities to follow. In the years since PlaNYC's release, 1,000 mayors have signed on to the Mayors Climate Protection Agreement and a growing portion now have plans for how they will meet its commitments. We now take local leadership on climate as a given. Whenever there is disappointment at the level of climate action at the federal government, we see a flurry of articles on the leadership role cities can play to fill the gap.

To be sure, we need action at every level of government — cities cannot lead alone — however, cities continue to pilot how to take building-level innovations to scale, help to grow and test new markets, and demonstrate the impacts that implementation has on residents, communities, and businesses. They continue to show what is necessary and what is possible.

Through PlaNYC, Dan drove real, lasting change for New York City and urban sustainability worldwide

The day after PlaNYC was finally announced, the culmination of nearly a year of relentless late nights and seven-day weeks, Rit opened his email at 8 a.m. to find a message from Dan. It read: "Now that you have had some time to relax, we should start thinking about implementation." It was (mostly) a joke (we think).

Dan never underestimated the work and resources it would take to achieve real, actionable change. Today, New York City has established itself as a national sustainability leader in taking chances to demonstrate what could work, what does not work, and, perhaps most importantly, de-risking ambitious action for other cities. Dan drove us to create that precedent.

From the outset of developing PlaNYC, Dan told us the plan needed to be ambitious, yet achievable. Being ambitious as a local government requires more than making big commitments. It requires making tough decisions, allocating resources to support the work, building and maintaining political capital, and expanding the fight — and the decision making — beyond City Hall. Dan made all of this possible, and we have an acute appreciation for how lucky we were to work under his leadership.

Work on New York City's third water tunnel began in 1970. Nearly 40 years later, PlaNYC listed its completion as a major infrastructure priority and the 8.5-mile Manhattan portion, which can supply 350 million gallons of water daily to the borough, was completed in 2013.

PlaNYC's MillionTreesNYC initiative pledged to plant one million trees across the city by 2017. The initiative, which mobilized thousands of New Yorkers to join in plantings, achieved its goal two years early, in 2015.

STEVE COHEN | Professor in the Practice of Public Affairs, School of International and Public Affairs & Director, Research Program in Sustainability and Management, Columbia University

STEPHEN HAMMER | Co-Founder and Co-Director, Urban Climate Change Research Network, 2007–2012 | Senior Advisor, Global Climate Policy and Strategy, World Bank Group, 2018–Present

PLANYC: ECONOMICS, QUALITY OF LIFE, AND THE ENVIRONMENT

"When I have a student do a paper comparing four or five sustainability plans from different parts of the world they all look a lot like PlaNYC."

Stephen Hammer was studying renewable energy policies in London and New York in the early 2000s just as each municipality was compiling massive future-looking plans to reshape their respective cities. As he shuttled between the two city halls, "It was amazing to watch," Hammer said.

But while London ultimately produced a series of thick, technical documents on individual urban systems, Deputy Mayor Dan Doctoroff conceived PlaNYC as a slim, 154-page document with 127 integrated initiatives spanning land, water, transportation, energy, and air under the broader framework of sustainability and climate change. Written in accessible language, PlaNYC was intended to simultaneously mobilize experts, officials, the private sector, and the general public behind a set of sweeping, but actionable proposals to secure a sustainable future for the city. "The idea of doing a sustainability plan wasn't an idea that was common," said Columbia University professor Steve Cohen, who has spent his nearly 50-year career studying sustainability. "You did an economic development plan. That was about it, if you did anything."

Today, it is common for cities to talk about climate change and develop sustainability plans. Cohen credits PlaNYC, which was subsequently taught in universities and studied by cities around the world. "I do think that everything that followed came from that very special time when this was all built," Cohen said. "You shouldn't ever underestimate how important that was and how different it was."

BACKGROUND

STEVE COHEN
At some point, Dan Doctoroff said, "We're going to get a million more people in 2030. Where are we going to put them?" And that then became a whole set of issues: How do you deal with quality of life in a city that's now a million more [people] than we have today, with deteriorating infrastructure like the third water tunnel, with parks underinvested in — a whole range of problems that would make it hard to absorb that next million people.

STEPHEN HAMMER
As the City tried to wrap its arms around, just call it the development challenges ahead, it morphed into this huge sustainability plan.

COHEN
I'd always been saying that environmental protection was actually interconnected to economic development. And yet Gallup still polls on a trade off: Can we grow the economy or can we protect the environment? And what you see here in this plan for the very first time is a government saying, "No, not only can we do both, we have to do both. The two are actually related."

DEVELOPING THE PLAN

COHEN
What PlaNYC did for New York was actually change the management paradigm of the city itself. It really was a sea change in how the development community started to think about economic development, not just in terms of their own building, but the fabric of the city around it; the idea that part of economic development is the attractiveness of the environment. I think it stems from businesses being incredibly mobile and people being incredibly mobile and that cities are now in a global competition for people in business. And what that means is, if I get off an airplane in Beijing, like I did the last time I was there, and the air is orange and I can't see in front of my hand, I'm not locating my business here. Why would I do that?

I would tie this into cultural changes, things like wellness. You get to a certain level of economic development and people start to think about physical fitness and what are my children eating and what's the air like? And you think about childhood asthma and a whole bunch of things. I grew up in Brooklyn. My mother opened up the door and said, "See you at 5:00." That was the end of parenting. Who knew what might happen to us? And lots of things happened and they never found out. But the point is that people started to pay attention to the physical wellbeing of their families and their friends and themselves in a way that was divorced from economic development before. And so you start to see a changing definition of economic development playing to higher quality of life.

Think about [the PlaNYC initiative], "You have to be within a 10-minute walk of a park." Now, Robert Moses didn't care about that. No park planner ever thought about it as being part of the economic development of the city — that everybody in the city have access to parks, because nobody had thought about, "Well, what do the parks do? How do they fit in?" That was part of this planning process.

The most incredible accomplishment, frankly, was getting real estate developers and community environmental justice people in the same room to talk about development. That's breathtaking. You never saw anything like that before.

Ditmas I.S. 62 playground in Kensington, Brooklyn, was transformed by PlaNYC's Schoolyards to Playgrounds program, which renovates school playgrounds and opens them for public use after school and on weekends. The program, a partnership between the City and the nonprofit Trust for Public Land, has opened 296 playgrounds, with more in the pipeline.

Michael Bloomberg speaks at the Global Climate Action Summit, San Francisco, 2018.

Stephen Hammer, who co-founded Urban Climate Change Research Network, presents Mayor Bloomberg with a translation of PlaNYC to share with Chinese mayors during a trip to Hong Kong.

HAMMER

My research looked at energy policymaking. There's actually this extraordinarily rich record of documents that dates back decades where people tried to put their arms around an energy strategy for New York City, but they were very narrowly focused. They didn't think in terms of emissions, they didn't think in terms of the air quality impacts, they didn't think in terms of the water quality impacts from exhausting waste heat into the waterways. PlaNYC was very multidimensional in its focus. So it wasn't just trying to link quality of life or economic growth to environmental quality — it began to link different systems together. What is the role of transportation? What is the role of energy systems? What is the role of the water system? And oh, it turns out that there are energy implications from one system to the next, and there are emission implications from one system to the next. It did change the institutional conversation.

THE EXECUTION

COHEN

What's really interesting about PlaNYC is not just the plan, but the plan to implement the plan. This wasn't just a plan for the shelf. A lot of thought was clearly given to, "How do we know if this is actually happening?" The integration of policy formulation and policy implementation is very rare. PlaNYC was very clear and very crisp on a set of practical measures that could be collected and reported on that were not beyond anybody's reach to either obtain or understand. And I think that's another unique part of this. So when you talk about subject matter integration that Steve's talking about, it's matched by the process integration of policy formulation implementation.

HAMMER

Married to that is the creation of something like [the Office of Long-Term Planning and Sustainability] and giving it such close proximity physically and operationally to City Hall. So the fact that you had a deputy mayor who was helping to steer this, the fact that [the team was] across the street and two doors down [from

City Hall], meant that the mayor was getting more engaged in this as time went on. And it really became a key part of his legacy. It became a different way of thinking within City Hall. It's been virtually impossible to walk away from that since then.

COHEN

The plan and the process that created it was transformative for New York City in so many ways and an absolutely brilliant development. Having seen what came before and having seen Bloomberg's complete transformation from a business numbers puncher, who could care less, to Mr. Climate, that all happens because of this process. It was a private sector approach in the sense that it was a startup that needed capital and needed resources and you don't resource constraint promising, important things. I sit on the board of a company and I'm watching it for the first time on the private side and I have to say, the bureaucratic constraints that I get used to in government, these guys just don't care. "We're going to get this done, here's how it happens."

THE TEAM

COHEN

Bloomberg had the A-team. This was a brilliant ensemble of people. I don't know the degree to which everybody totally understands that that group was incredibly rare in urban politics — to have that much talent in one place.

HAMMER

When I joined the World Bank, it became so clear. I was leading cities and climate for the World Bank Group when I first joined. New York City just totally stood apart.

COHEN

The historically important place that Dan established should not be overlooked because it's the human capital that makes all this happen in the end. And I think he deserves enormous credit for creating an exciting place that smart people wanted to go to. And dedicated, mission-driven, dedicated people. It's not enough to be smart. People have to really care. So I think that's clearly part of the legacy here that needs to be understood.

HAMMER

When I was teaching at [Columbia] the students who were most engaged in that class wanted to know more about New York City, what it was doing differently. And then they were going to either go to City Hall and work on that directly, that was their dream. Or they wanted to go home and do the same kind of thing in San Francisco or Denver or Seattle.

COHEN

That absolutely happened and continues to happen. There are a bunch of things going on in the world, including its potential destruction, that really is focusing the mind. And I think we saw that with PlaNYC. I think it was something that really smart, idealistic students gravitated toward and continue to, who have then spread out throughout the city, the country, the world.

GLOBAL IMPACT

HAMMER

In 2010, I left Columbia and I started working with a Chinese NGO. I said, I think we could probably translate the PlaNYC document into Chinese. And so we made that happen. And then in Hong Kong I actually had the chance to present it to Mike. And he was really excited. When he was having all those big meetings across China for the next several days, he could hand this over.

Mayors are buying into the agenda. Being able to stand up and say, "I've got this document, I've got this track record. We're updating it" — that's powerful stuff. Speaking in very practical policy terms, "Well, I needed to change the zoning rules. Well, I needed to change the tax policies. I needed to do these things so I could track this system on a regular basis." That's stuff that every mayor can relate to.

COHEN

Most of the real work of government happens at the local level. Mayors have to actually make sure things happen — the traffic lights, the buses, the picking up the garbage, getting water, getting energy, making sure the schools are okay. There are some very practical tips in PlaNYC on how to deliver a high-quality city service. It takes this vision and brings it down to the street level, which I think is really one of the signal accomplishments of Dan Doctoroff and the team that he put together.

HAMMER

The network structure of the C40 [Cities Climate Leadership Group] really picked up on a lot of the chapter headings within PlaNYC — energy, waste, water — all these issues that were considered of paramount importance in PlaNYC. When you write one of the definitive documents of its kind, you set the standard.

COHEN

When I have a student do a paper comparing four or five sustainability plans from different parts of the world they all look a lot like PlaNYC.

HAMMER

The course that I created at Columbia was called Urban Energy Systems and Policy, and then I took that to MIT. PlaNYC was a key resource for that class. And then when I started leading [urban] climate at the [World] Bank, [PlaNYC] was a resource document that I would constantly say, "Hey, you should really take a look at this."

PlaNYC has had enormous influence on city planning initiatives to reclaim and reimagine public space in cities across the U.S. and around the world, as shown in this plaza in Los Angeles.

THE LEGACY

COHEN

I really give Dan and Mike Bloomberg enormous credit for the leadership and the vision that created this. Maybe it would've happened eventually, but not in the same way and not with the same level of quality. And it's really something that they both deserve an enormous credit for.

HAMMER

It's a legacy that needs to be recognized. We're talking about system change. If you're trying to understand, how do you electrify all buildings in the city or how do you move away from gas connections in the city, there has to be an ecosystem built up. Because of what the [Office of Long-Term Planning and Sustainability] team did and Dan's leadership on that, New York City is in a very different place than it would've been otherwise.

Look at the fleet decisions. First it was natural gas vehicles and now they're moving to battery vehicles. Whether it's on the [Department of Transportation] side or whether it's on the sanitation side, New York City has the buying power to actually help move markets on some of this stuff because you give the vendors a chance to really do a lot of innovation and back it up with the size of the purchase that can sustain them for a while. So don't diminish the market-making value that New York City brings when it decides to go a new way.

COHEN

Somebody like a Dan or a Mike coming from the private sector, going into public service, you want to make something happen. It's not just chitchat at a cocktail party. You want to make something happen because you are actually sacrificing something. I come from the era of John Kennedy, "Ask not what your country can do for you." And I get the sense that's where these guys are coming from, the idea of trying to do a service to the country, which has done so much for me. And I think that's what you saw, and I think it's inspiring. I think there's no other word for it.

Opposite: PlaNYC's holistic vision for urban sustainability included expanded cycling and pedestrian options, improved mass transit, and greener, more sustainable streetscapes. Left, Queensboro Plaza.

Above: Green infrastructure such as rain gardens expanded dramatically after PlaNYC. Today, New York City has 11,000 green infrastructure projects, the most in the nation.

Right: PlaNYC's transportation plan called for New York's first dedicated bus lanes, known as Select Bus Service (SBS). By 2013, New York had 38 miles of SBS lanes. Here, an SBS lane on Madison Avenue, Manhattan.

Looking Ahead With PlaNYC

New York City has long been a place for grand urban schemes, among them the 1811 commissioners' plan that designated the street grid of Manhattan, the creation of Central Park in the 1860s, and the ambitious though controversial plans of Robert Moses in the 20th century.

Daniel L. Doctoroff

Does PlaNYC 2030, the 127-point vision of environmental sustainability announced by Mayor Michael R. Bloomberg two years ago, match those historic plans in its scope and prescience?

Daniel L. Doctoroff, the powerful deputy mayor who left the Bloomberg administration in early 2008 to run Bloomberg L.P., thinks so. In some of his most extensive public remarks since leaving city government, Mr. Doctoroff expounded on PlaNYC during a recent talk at the Museum of the City of New York.

The plan "pretty much began because of a salt pile," Mr. Doctoroff said, half joking. In 2005, he said, the city was looking for sites for the most prosaic of city necessities: "salt piles, bus garages, waste-transfer stations."

Between 2000 and 2005, the city's population grew by about 200,000, and by 2030, the city is projected to grow to nearly 9 million — the equivalent, Mr. Doctoroff said, of "cramming the entire cities of Boston and Miami into our relatively cramped boroughs."

New York Times, April 25, 2009.

Mr. Doctoroff said the plan was centered on five goals, all starting with the letter A:

ASPIRATIONAL PlaNYC was to be "a vision for the kind of city we wanted to become, and to bequeath that to the next generation," he said.

AMBITIOUS "The mayor felt that it was our responsibility to take on the tough challenges today, rather than kick them down the road to whoever was the mayor in the next term," he said. After a nervous laugh, he added, "That was a term-limits joke."

ACHIEVABLE "Everything we proposed in the plan — and there are 127 separate initiatives — had to be completely achievable," he said. "We vowed not to make a single proposal that we couldn't identify the source of funds for," he said. "This was to be a living plan that would begin implementation right after it was announced."

ACCESSIBLE "With PlaNYC this was not born as a full-fledged plan," he said. "We had a concept, but in order for the entire city to embrace it, the public needed to feel like it had a stake in it, that it was engaged — that if you wanted them to buy in, you had to ask them first."

ACCOUNTABLE "We demanded of ourselves that our progress be publicly tracked," he said.

Among the outcomes so far: The conversion of more than 15 percent of taxis in the fleet to clean-fuel vehicles; the construction of 79 new playgrounds; $100 million a year to increase the energy efficiency of government buildings; 20 pilot projects to clean up city waterways; hundreds of miles of new bike lanes. Ninety-three percent of the 127 initiatives are under way, Mr. Doctoroff said.   *SEWELL CHAN*

JOE CHAN | Senior Policy Advisor, Office of the Deputy Mayor for Economic Development and Rebuilding, 2002–2006
ANGELA SUNG PINSKY | Deputy Chief of Staff, Office of the Deputy Mayor for Economic Development and Rebuilding, 2004–2010

THE "SMART GROWTH" ORIGINS OF PLANYC

"Dan really got the fact that in order to have great and historical impact, you had to essentially force the agencies to work together, to plan together, and ultimately to spend together."

New York City had reached a turning point by the middle of 2005.

When the Bloomberg administration took office, New York was struggling to recover from the recent September 11th terrorist attacks and new Deputy Mayor Dan Doctoroff was in the midst of leading a bid for the city to host the 2012 Games.

Three years later, the city's population was growing at a startling rate and the Olympic bid had ended unsuccessfully. Although many Olympic-related projects were underway — including a series of historic rezonings that were helping to spur the growth — the deadline of the Games could no longer serve as a catalyst for action, prompting Doctoroff to begin searching for another organizing vision to guide the city's economic development. Meanwhile, longtime City demographer Joseph Salvo, shared a shocking projection: His calculations showed that New York was on pace to attract one million additional people by 2030.

The challenges Doctoroff and his team were encountering on each new rezoning — such as where to put essential neighborhood services like parks, schools, and fire stations in a land-constrained city — were about to accelerate. Without a plan to manage growth, New York risked being overrun. These challenges coalesced into a groundbreaking effort that would ultimately reshape the field of urban sustainability: PlaNYC. But initially, the plan was focused on land use.

PlaNYC "was a convergence of, 'we have to keep this machine going and we have to keep upzoning because all these people are coming, but we're running into these problems that we're having a harder and harder time solving for,'" said Angela Sung Pinsky, who rose from a City Hall intern tasked with liaising with the Olympic bid to Doctoroff's deputy chief of staff. "We were running out of land."

She and Senior Policy Advisor Joe Chan, were tasked with coordinating with agencies across city government to develop a sweeping land-use plan to accommodate and harness growth. As they developed strategies to use land more efficiently, the team realized they were actually creating a sustainability plan.

After Chan left city government in 2006, Doctoroff hired Rohit T. Aggarwala to oversee PlaNYC and make the connections between sustainability and land-use explicit. Aggarwala and his deputy, Ariella Maron, added initiatives for air quality, clean water, and climate change.

But many of PlaNYC's signature proposals, including MillionTreesNYC, converting schoolyards to community playgrounds, and congestion pricing, emerged during the initial planning phases. "One of the things that I really enjoyed was seeing these lifelong civil servants who were so committed, were so talented and passionate, but at the same time had been brushed off in the past, coming to Dan with ideas," Chan said. He could see them thinking, "'Someone gets it. Someone really powerful and important gets it. Maybe he's going to take a few of these crazy ideas we had and bring them to reality.'"

ANGELA SUNG PINSKY
It was after the Olympics [loss], and Dan did this exercise where he asked the team: What are the next generation of big ideas that we're going to work on? One of them was this idea of planning for growth. Each upzoning had similar problems. [To prepare for growth] the neighborhood was asking for things like schools or a firehouse and there wasn't a lot of land. So we were supposed to do a master planning exercise about where these things could go, citywide.

JOE CHAN
Something that factored in was [city demographer] Joe Salvo and his population projections. How do we accommodate nine million people by 2030? How, ultimately, do we make the New York City experience and quality of life better with growth?

PINSKY
His projection kind of solidified the magnitude of the growth. It was bigger than we thought.

CHAN
It was also more geographically distributed than we were originally inclined to think. Growth was not only happening in the areas that we rezoned, but was happening organically in the five boroughs — some of it through immigration, some of it through domestic migration. I think there was a realization that it's not going to only happen in these concentrated places. Commuting patterns were also diversifying. If you were to bundle that together, growth was going to be more substantial, more geographically distributed, and in some ways also more nuanced than we had originally projected.

We started going out to these different agencies, Angela and I. It was really great because it was the most amazing course on New York City government — how city government works and plans and ultimately serves the people. The Parks Department talked about the urban heat island effect. As growth happened, more of New York City's traditionally green permeable areas were getting covered. People would have to travel further and further to their neighborhood parks and playgrounds. Those were some of the initial problems when we started having discussions about the Million Trees initiative.

PINSKY

I remember the Fire Department [conversation] very well. We were saying, "How many more firehouses do you need?" They said, "It's not the firehouses and it's not the population, it's the traffic. It all depends on how quickly we can get from our place of deployment to the emergency. That's a traffic issue, not a land-use issue." [The Department of Environmental Protection (DEP)] said, "Actually our water consumption has gone down because of the toilet efficiency." You tell people, "Don't brush your teeth with the water running and don't waste water." So even though our population had grown, the water consumption had shrunk.

CHAN

DEP really seemed to have a great concern on the amount of permeable surface in New York City and the management of stormwater. As you build New York City and you cover more surface, what are you going to do with the stormwater? I think there was also just — and this predated this initiative — a great sense of consciousness that New York City was coasting off a 100-plus year old infrastructure. How much longer can we coast off that and what can we do to build new infrastructure, to accommodate future growth and to ultimately improve quality of life for New Yorkers?

There was a period of time where we became attached at the hip to Eric Kober and Sandy Hornick. I remember that they just had so many pent-up ideas. Sandy and Eric were the two senior strategic planners for the Department of City Planning. Their responsibilities entailed seeing the bigger picture on where New York City could grow, where the greatest opportunities for growth were, and where New York City's growth-related challenges would be and what they would be. They had served as counsel to planning commissioners or City Planning chairs through multiple administrations.

Dan Doctoroff initiated PlaNYC to manage and harness New York's population growth, which city demographers projected could reach nine million people by 2030. Below, Bryant Park lawn, 2002.

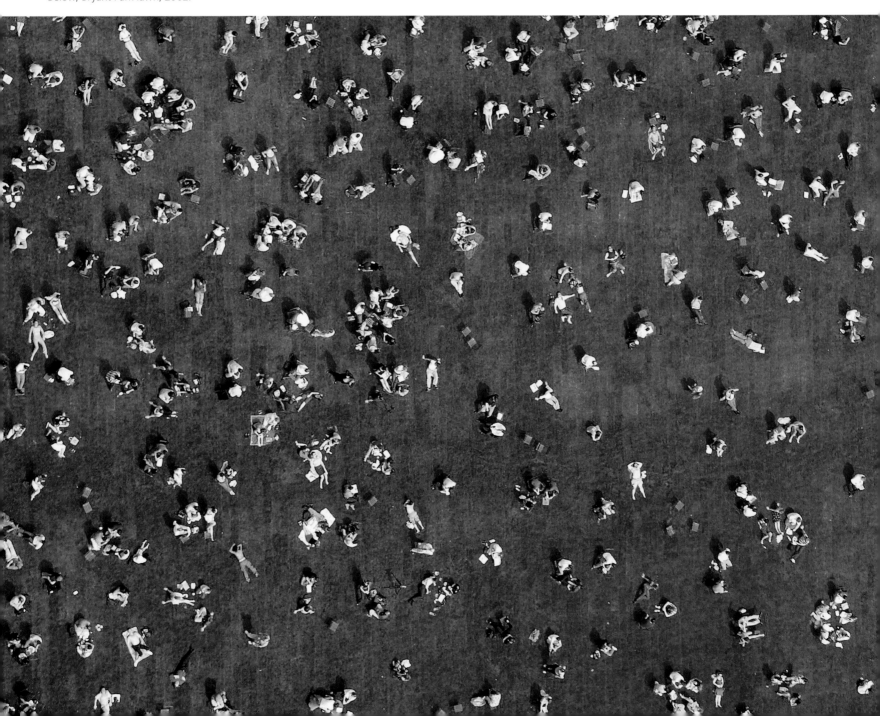

PINSKY

At that point in the administration, we had [rezoned] Greenpoint–Williamsburg. Downtown Brooklyn had been done —

CHAN

Hudson Yards. We had an incredibly ambitious plan for growth that was being realized extraordinarily quickly. If you totaled the additional residential capacity that was enabled by those rezonings, it had to be hundreds of thousands. Dan was always starting from the assumption that growth on the whole would be a good thing because it would bring the world's most talented people to New York City. Therefore, the economy would diversify and strengthen. Therefore, we would have more money to reinvest in a bigger and better city. Therefore, more talented people would come. The virtuous cycle of growth.

PINSKY

The solution for growth was, we can't just keep building proportionally, we have to live more efficiently. All of the answers were coming down to the same things. It's not just building 20% more housing across the city. It's that we had to build housing where transportation nodes were so that people could move around more efficiently. That's a sustainability solution to a land-use problem. The switch that Dan made to a sustainability plan from a growth land-use plan didn't change the answers that much.

CHAN

It didn't change the substance of the plan at all. It was just the lead-in description, really. This did not start out as an environmental plan or a sustainability plan. I think we kind of backed into that.

PINSKY

There was a new phase of it because then it became about carbon emissions and a lot of the conversations were focused around emissions. That's when it was like, okay, this is a driving force of how this is going to be constructed.

CHAN

I don't know if there has been a more far-reaching initiative that pulled in more agencies. It grew astronomically after I left. One thing that was so unique about Dan is the interagency coordination that he was able to foster. I deal with the City all the time now. Agencies don't talk to each other. City Hall also doesn't provide the same type of leadership. Obviously there's a huge element of sentimentality in all of this, but I feel like Dan really got the fact that in order to have great and historical impact, you had to essentially force the agencies to work together, to plan together, and ultimately to spend together. I think that's why he was successful.

It always bothered me when people were like, "Oh, Dan's just so heavy-handed and so ambitious." Hopefully, Sandy or Eric or many of the folks that we worked with on PlaNYC would say, Dan was a listener, Dan recognized good ideas, he was receptive. I think he also just had the intellectual capacity and bandwidth to process it. That's another thing that still amazes me about Dan to this day — just the ability that he has to recognize potential connections and the bandwidth he had to manage all this stuff and just keep it going with an incredible sense of urgency.

There was a lot of pent-up innovation and energy at the agency level where you had lifetime city employees who were incredibly talented and inspired, who never really had the opportunity or the stage to bounce their boldest ideas off of a senior level city official. Dan was able to channel a lot of that talent and commitment and pent-up innovation. It was like a joy ride for them. They're like, "This is what we've been working on our entire life and someone's taking this seriously and going to take our work to another level."

Deputy Mayor Dan Doctoroff's aggressive growth strategy included some of the largest rezonings in New York's history, such as Greenpoint–Williamsburg, West Chelsea, and Hudson Yards. The rezonings were so successful in unleashing development that planners were having trouble finding sites for essential community services, such as schools and fire stations, prompting Doctoroff to order a citywide land-use evaluation that evolved into PlaNYC. Opposite, construction of the Edge at 30 Hudson Yards.

PLANYC: A GREENER, GREATER NEW YORK

There are now 8.2 million New Yorkers — more than at any time in our history. And more are coming. They are coming because New York has renewed itself; because over the past three decades we have achieved one of the greatest resurgences of any American city. Growth is ultimately an expression of optimism; it depends on a belief in possibility — essential to New York's soul since its days as an inclusive, turbulent, tolerant Dutch colony.

That is why our recovery has not only strengthened our quality of life, but also our sense of hope. We have proven that challenges once considered insurmountable can be overcome. It is time to summon that spirit again.

Over the next two decades, more people, visitors, and jobs will bring vibrancy, diversity, opportunity — and revenue. But unless we act, they will also bring challenges; infrastructure strained beyond its limits; parks packed with too many people; streets choked with traffic; trains crammed with too many passengers. Meanwhile, we will face an increasingly precarious environment and the growing danger of climate change that imperils not just our city, but the planet.

We have offered a different vision. It is a vision of providing New Yorkers with the cleanest air of any big city in the nation; of maintaining the purity of our drinking water and opening more of our rivers and creeks and coastal waters to recreation; of producing more energy more cleanly and more reliably, and offering more choices on how to travel quickly and efficiently across our city. It is a vision where contaminated land is reclaimed and restored to communities; where every family lives near a park or playground; where housing is sustainable and available to New Yorkers from every background, reflecting the diversity that has defined our city for centuries.

It is a vision of New York as the first sustainable 21st century city — but it is more than that. It is a plan to get there.

The 127 new initiatives detailed here will strengthen our economy, public health, and quality of life. Collectively, they will add up to the broadest attack on climate change ever undertaken by an American city.

New Yorkers used to think this boldly all the time. Previous generations looked ahead and imagined how their city would grow. They built subways through undeveloped land and established Central Park far from the heart of the city. They constructed water tunnels that could serve millions when our city was a fraction of the size. Their actions made our modern city possible. Now it is our turn.

—PlaNYC, 2007

PlaNYC called for improving the quality of New York City's waterways to expand opportunities for recreation. Right, Kayak Launch, Pier 2, Brooklyn Bridge Park.

 **LAND**

As virtually every part of our city grows, one piece remains fixed: the supply of land. That's why we must use our space more efficiently to accommodate growth while preserving — and enhancing — the city's quality of life.

HOUSING GOAL: Create homes for almost a million more New Yorkers, while making housing more affordable and sustainable

CONTINUE PUBLICLY INITIATED REZONINGS
1. Use upcoming rezonings to direct growth toward areas with strong transit access
2. Continue restoring underused or vacant waterfront land across the city
3. Use transit extensions to spark growth as the subways did more than a century ago

CREATE NEW HOUSING ON PUBLIC LAND
4. Expand co-locations with government agencies
5. Seek to adapt unused schools, hospitals, and other outdated municipal sites for productive use as new housing

EXPLORE ADDITIONAL AREAS OF OPPORTUNITY
6. Develop underused areas to knit neighborhoods together
7. Examine potential of major infrastructure expansions to spur growth in new neighborhoods
8. Explore opportunities to create new land by constructing decks over rail yards, rail lines, and highways

EXPAND TARGETED AFFORDABILITY PROGRAMS
9. Develop new financing strategies
10. Expand inclusionary zoning
11. Continue to develop programs to encourage home ownership, emphasizing affordable apartments over single family homes
12. Preserve the existing stock of affordable housing throughout New York City

OPEN SPACE GOAL: Ensure that all New Yorkers live within a 10-minute walk of a park

MAKE EXISTING SITES AVAILABLE TO MORE NEW YORKERS
13. Open schoolyards across the city as public playgrounds
14. Increase options for competitive athletics
15. Complete underdeveloped destination parks in every borough

EXPAND USABLE HOURS AT EXISTING SITES
16. Convert asphalt sites into multipurpose turf fields
17. Maximize time on existing turf fields by installing additional lighting for nighttime use

REIMAGINE THE PUBLIC REALM
18. Create or enhance a public plaza in every community
19. Plant one million new trees
20. Expand Greenstreets program

BROWNFIELDS GOAL: Clean up all contaminated land in New York City

MAKE EXISTING BROWNFIELDS PROGRAMS FASTER AND MORE EFFICIENT
21. Adopt on-site testing to streamline the cleanup process
22. Create remediation guidelines for New York City cleanups
23. Establish a city office to promote brownfield planning and development

EXPAND ENROLLMENT INTO STREAMLINED PROGRAMS
24. Expand participation in the current State brownfield cleanup program (BCP)
25. Create a city program to oversee all additional cleanups
26. Provide incentives to lower the cost of remediation, including $15 million to capitalize a redevelopment fund

ENCOURAGE GREATER COMMUNITY INVOLVEMENT IN BROWNFIELD REDEVELOPMENT
27. Encourage the State to release community-based redevelopment grants
28. Provide incentives to participate in Brownfield Opportunity Area (BOA) planning
29. Launch outreach effort to educate communities about brownfield redevelopment

IDENTIFY REMAINING SITES FOR CLEANUP
30. Create a database of historic uses across New York City to identify potential brownfields
31. Limit liability of property owners who seek to redevelop brownfields

WATER

Our water system was an engineering marvel when it was created in the early 19th century. But today, growth around our reservoirs and the age of our infrastructure make it more and more challenging to maintain the quality and reliability of our supply. We must also confront the legacy of our industrial past, which treated New York's waterways as a delivery system rather than as a source of recreation or a vital ecological habitat. Today, our combined sewer system too often renders our waterways unusable. That's why we will build critical backup systems for our water network infrastructure, continue to upgrade our wastewater treatment facilities, and explore the potential of more natural solutions to cleanse and filter our waterways.

WATER QUALITY GOAL: Open 90% of our waterways to recreation by preserving natural areas and reducing pollution

CONTINUE IMPLEMENTING INFRASTRUCTURE UPGRADES
32. Develop and implement Long-Term Control Plans for all 14 New York watersheds
33. Expand wet weather capacity at treatment plants

PURSUE PROVEN SOLUTIONS TO PREVENT STORMWATER FROM ENTERING THE SYSTEM
34. Convert combined sewers into High Level Storm Sewers (HLSS) and integrate HLSS into major new developments as appropriate
35. Expand the Bluebelt program

EXPAND, TRACK, AND ANALYZE NEW BEST MANAGEMENT PRACTICES (BMPS) ON A BROAD SCALE
36. Form an interagency BMP task force to make reduction of combined sewer overflow volumes a priority for all relevant city agencies
37. Introduce 20 cubic meters of ribbed mussel beds
38. Plant trees with improved pit designs
39. Create vegetated ditches (swales) along parkways
40. Require greening of parking lots
41. Provide incentives for green roofs
42. Protect wetlands

WATER NETWORK GOAL: Develop critical backup systems for our aging water network to ensure long-term reliability

ENSURE THE QUALITY OF OUR DRINKING WATER
43. Continue the Watershed Protection Program
44. Construct an ultraviolet disinfection plant for the Catskill and Delaware systems
45. Build the Croton Filtration Plant

CREATE REDUNDANCY FOR AQUEDUCTS IN NEW YORK CITY
46. Launch a major new water conservation effort to reduce citywide consumption by 60 million gallons per day
47. Expand our supply potential through increased efficiency, better design, and updated technology at facilities
48. Evaluate 39 projects for their ability to help meet the shortfall needs of the city if a prolonged shutdown of the Delaware Aqueduct is required

MODERNIZE IN-CITY DISTRIBUTION
49. Complete stage 2 of Water Tunnel No. 3 and begin repairing Water Tunnel No. 1
50. Complete stages 3 and 4 of Water Tunnel No. 3
51. Complete backup tunnel to Staten Island
52. Accelerate upgrades to water main infrastructure to over 80 miles annually

TRANSPORTATION

Transportation has always been the key to unlocking New York's potential. From our origins as a port city to the completion of the Erie Canal, from the construction of the Brooklyn Bridge to the creation of the subway system, New York's growth has always depended on the efficiency and scale of its transportation network. But for the last 50 years we have underinvested in our most critical network: transit. Transportation is the greatest single barrier to achieving our region's growth potential. Only by strengthening transit — which uses less land and creates less pollution than automobiles — can we meet this challenge.

CONGESTION GOAL: Improve travel times by adding transit capacity for millions more residents, visitors, and workers

BUILD AND EXPAND TRANSIT INFRASTRUCTURE
53. Increase capacity on key congested routes by funding five projects that eliminate major capacity constraints

54. Provide new commuter rail access to Manhattan

55. Expand transit access to underserved areas

IMPROVE TRANSIT SERVICE ON EXISTING INFRASTRUCTURE
56. Initiate and expand Bus Rapid Transit

57. Dedicate bus/high occupancy vehicle lanes on East River Bridges

58. Explore other improvements to bus service, including completing upgrades at 22 stations by 2009

59. Expand local use of Metro-North and Long Island Rail Road trains

60. Improve access to existing transit by reducing sidewalk congestion, adding bike racks, and creating safer bus connections

61. Address congested areas around the city by creating congestion management plans for outerborough growth corridors

PROMOTE OTHER SUSTAINABLE MODES
62. Expand ferry service and improve integration with the city's mass transit system

63. Complete the City's 1,800-mile bike master plan

64. Improve cycling infrastructure with installation of 400 new racks and annually updated maps

IMPROVE TRAFFIC FLOW BY REDUCING CONGESTION
65. Pilot congestion pricing

66. Manage roads more efficiently by increasing the use of Muni meters

67. Create an integrated traffic management system for the regional transportation network

68. Strengthen enforcement of traffic violations by increasing the number of traffic enforcement agents (TEAs)

69. Empower all TEAs to give 'blocking-the-box' tickets

70. Expand the use of traffic enforcement cameras

71. Facilitate freight movements by improving access to John F. Kennedy International Airport

72. Explore potential of High-Occupancy Truck Toll Lanes

STATE OF GOOD REPAIR GOAL: Reach a full "state of good repair" on New York City's roads, subways, and rails for the first time in history

DEVELOP NEW FUNDING SOURCES
73. Establish a new regional transit financing authority, the Sustainable Mobility And Regional Transportation (SMART) Authority, funded through dedicated revenue streams (such as City and State contributions and congestion pricing fees) to advance new projects and achieve a state of good repair

ACHIEVE A STATE OF GOOD REPAIR ON OUR ROADS AND TRANSIT SYSTEM
74. Close the Metropolitan Transit Authority's state of good repair gap through a SMART Authority grant

75. Accelerate capital repairs and upgrades through a SMART Authority grant

76. Invest in bridge and tunnel upgrades

ENERGY

New Yorkers face rising energy costs and carbon emissions from an ineffective market, aging infrastructure, inefficient buildings, and growing needs. That's why we must make smart investments in clean power and energy-saving technologies to reduce our electricity and heating bills by billions of dollars, while slashing our greenhouse gas emissions by nearly 27 million metric tons every year.

ENERGY GOAL: Provide cleaner, more reliable power for every New Yorker by upgrading our energy infrastructure

IMPROVE ENERGY PLANNING
77. Establish a New York City Energy Planning Board to centralize planning for the city's supply and demand initiatives

REDUCE NEW YORK'S ENERGY CONSUMPTION
78. Commit 10% of the City's annual energy bill to fund energy-saving investments in City operations
79. Strengthen energy and building codes for New York City
80. Create the New York City Energy Efficiency Authority to oversee efforts to reach the city's demand reduction targets
81. Employ targeted mandates, challenges, and incentives to reduce energy demand in five key areas: institutional and government buildings, commercial and industrial buildings, residential buildings, new construction, and appliances and electronics
82. Expand participation in Peak Load Management programs through smart meters
83. Support expansion of real-time pricing across the city
84. Launch an energy awareness and training campaign

EXPAND THE CITY'S CLEAN POWER SUPPLY
85. Facilitate the construction of 2,000 to 3,000 MW of supply capacity by repowering old plants, constructing new ones, and building dedicated transmission lines
86. Increase the amount of Clean Distributed Generation (Clean DG) by 800 MW
87. Promote opportunities to develop district energy at appropriate sites in New York City
88. Support expansion of natural gas infrastructure
89. Create a property tax abatement for solar panel installations
90. Study the cost-effectiveness of solar electricity when evaluated on a Real Time Pricing scenario
91. Support the construction of the city's first carbon-neutral building, primarily powered by solar energy
92. Increase use of solar energy in City buildings through creative financing
93. Work with the State to eliminate barriers to increasing the use of solar energy in the city
94. Pilot one or more technologies for producing energy from solid waste
95. End methane emissions from sewage treatment plants and expand the use of digester gas
96. Study the expansion of gas capture and energy production from existing landfills

MODERNIZE ELECTRICITY DELIVERY INFRASTRUCTURE
97. Accelerate reliability improvements to the city's grid
98. Facilitate grid repairs through improved coordination and joint bidding
99. Ensure adequate pier facilities are available to Con Edison to offload
100. Support Con Edison's efforts to modernize the grid

AIR QUALITY

Despite decades of improvement, New York City still fails to meet federal air quality standards — and we have no way of measuring air quality in individual neighborhoods. That's why we will create a comprehensive program to reduce emissions from a variety of sources, including vehicles, power plants, and buildings. Natural solutions such as planting one million trees will bring us the rest of the way towards cleaner air for all New Yorkers. To track progress and help target solutions to the areas of greatest need, we will launch the largest local air quality study in the United States.

AIR QUALITY GOAL: Achieve the cleanest air quality of any big U.S. city

REDUCE ROAD VEHICLE EMISSIONS

101. Waive New York City's sales tax on the cleanest, most efficient vehicles

102. Work with the MTA, the Port Authority, and the State Department of Transportation to promote hybrid and other clean vehicles

103. Pilot new technologies and fuels, including hydrogen and plug-in hybrid vehicles

104. Reduce taxi and limousine idling

105. Work with the Taxi and Limousine Commission and the taxicab industry to double the taxi fleet's efficiency

106. Work with stakeholders to double the fuel efficiency of black cars and for-hire vehicles

107. Introduce biodiesel into the City's truck fleet, go beyond compliance with local laws, and further reduce emissions

108. Accelerate emissions reductions of private fleets through existing Congestion Mitigation and Air Quality (CMAQ) programs

109. Work with stakeholders and the State to create incentives for the adoption of vehicle emissions control and efficiency strategies

110. Improve compliance of existing anti-idling laws through a targeted educational campaign

111. Retrofit both large and small school buses and reduce their required retirement age

REDUCE OTHER TRANSPORTATION EMISSIONS

112. Retrofit the Staten Island Ferry fleet to reduce emissions

113. Work with private ferries to reduce their emissions

114. Seek to partner with the Port Authority to reduce emissions from Port facilities

115. Accelerate adoption of technologies to reduce construction-related emissions

REDUCE EMISSIONS FROM BUILDINGS

116. Lower the maximum sulfur content in heating fuel from 2000 ppm to 500 ppm

117. Reduce emissions from boilers in 100 City public schools

PURSUE NATIONAL SOLUTIONS TO IMPROVE AIR QUALITY

118. Reforest 2,000 acres of parkland

119. Partner with stakeholders to help plant one million trees by 2017

UNDERSTAND THE SCOPE OF THE CHALLENGE

120. Launch collaborative local air quality study to monitor neighborhood-level air quality across New York City

CLIMATE CHANGE

One challenge eclipses them all: climate change. We have already started to experience warmer, more unpredictable weather and rising sea levels. We have a special stake in this discussion — but also a unique ability to help shape a solution. New York emits nearly .25% of the world's total greenhouse gases; becoming more efficient will have a tangible impact. These efforts will build on the strength of the city itself. Our density, reliance on mass transit, and smaller, stacked living spaces mean that New Yorkers produce a fraction of the greenhouse gases compared to the average American. That means growing New York is, itself, a climate change strategy.

CLIMATE CHANGE GOAL: Reduce global warming emissions by more than 30%

121. Used combined initiatives from plan to achieve goal

A Avoided sprawl
Attract 900,000 new residents by 2030 to achieve an avoided **15.6 million metric tons**
— Create sustainable, affordable housing
— Provide parks near all New Yorkers
— Expand and improve mass transit
— Reclaim contaminated land
— Open our waterways for recreation
— Ensure a reliable water and energy supply
— Plant trees to create a healthier and more beautiful public realm

B Clean power
Improve New York City's electricity supply to save **10.6 million metric tons**
— Replace inefficient power plants with state-of-the-art technology
— Expand Clean Distributed Generation
— Promote renewable power

C Efficient buildings
Reduce energy consumption in buildings by **16.4 million metric tons**
— Improve the efficiency of existing buildings
— Require efficient new buildings
— Increase the efficiency of appliances
— Green the city's building and energy codes
— Increase energy awareness through education and training

D Sustainable transportation
Enhance New York City's transportation system to save **6.1 million metric tons**
— Reduce vehicle use by improving public transit
— Improve the efficiency of private vehicles, taxis, and black cars
— Decrease CO_2 intensity of fuels

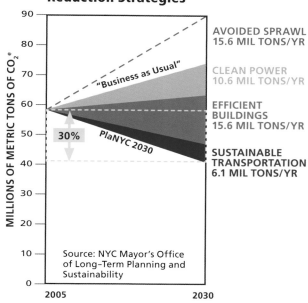

Projected Impacts of Our Greenhouse Gas Reduction Strategies

MILLIONS OF METRIC TONS OF CO_2^e

"Business as Usual"

30%

PlaNYC 2030

AVOIDED SPRAWL
15.6 MIL TONS/YR

CLEAN POWER
10.6 MIL TONS/YR

EFFICIENT BUILDINGS
15.6 MIL TONS/YR

SUSTAINABLE TRANSPORTATION
6.1 MIL TONS/YR

Source: NYC Mayor's Office of Long-Term Planning and Sustainability

2005   2030

The result will be an annual reduction of 33.6 million metric tons — and an additional 15.6 million metric tons avoided by accommodating 900,000 people in New York City.

ADAPTING TO CLIMATE CHANGE GOAL: Embark on a broad effort to adapt our city to the unavoidable climate shifts ahead

122. Create an intergovernmental Task Force to protect our vital infrastructure

123. Work with vulnerable neighborhoods to develop site-specific strategies

124. Create a strategic planning process to adapt to climate change

125. Ensure that New York's 100-year floodplain maps are updated

126. Document the city's floodplain management strategies to secure discounted flood insurance for New Yorkers

127. Amend the building code to address the impacts of climate change

PLANYC LEGACY

In 2007, PlaNYC laid out an ambitious agenda for how to create a sustainable New York City — and bequeath a cleaner, healthier, and more reliable city to the next generation of New Yorkers.

In that, it has succeeded. Two years after the plan's release, 93% of its 127 initiatives were underway, according to *The New York Times* — and the City has continued to track its progress and build on its ideas across multiple administrations, with report updates required by law every four years. In 2023, the Adams administration issued the fifth update of the plan, building on the work begun nearly two decades ago.

OPEN SPACE By 2022, the number of New Yorkers within a 10-minute walk of a park had risen to 99%, up from 70% in 2007; the City successfully planted one million new trees, 296 schoolyards had opened as community playgrounds, and more than $327 million had been invested in eight destination parks across all five boroughs. **BROWNFIELDS** New York fulfilled its PlaNYC commitment to create the first City-run brownfield program in the country and it quickly became the second-largest cleanup program in the United States, second only to California. **WATER** New York's 11,000 green infrastructure projects to filter stormwater lead the nation, helping the city achieve its cleanest water since the Civil War and attracting whales and dolphins to the Harbor; the leaking Delaware Aqueduct — highlighted as aging infrastructure — underwent a decade-long, $1 billion program to build a bypass tunnel, which is scheduled to begin service in October 2023. **AIR QUALITY** PlaNYC established the largest local air quality study in the United States which led to the elimination of one of the biggest air pollutants, No. 6 fuel oil, creating the city's cleanest air in more than a century; fuel oil No. 4 will be entirely phased out by 2026. **ENERGY** New York pioneered a way for cities to play more active roles in their own destinies; PlaNYC's *Greener, Greater Buildings Plan* included a benchmarking mandate (now a standard in most large U.S. cities) that is the foundation for Local Law 97, NYC's nation-leading mandate for building decarbonization. **TRANSPORTATION** While the signature initiative — congestion pricing — failed, as of 2023 it was on the cusp of implementation. Other initiatives, including public plazas, bike lanes, and Bus Rapid Transit, have made New York a pioneer in the people-first streets movement. **CLIMATE CHANGE** Overall, the initiatives reduced the city's greenhouse gas emissions by more than 18% (more than 25% on City-owned properties).

PlaNYC "gave all of us a north star," said Kathryn Garcia, who was the chief operating officer of the Department of Environmental Protection at the time. "It really did change the trajectory of where we were going."

"I think that's the brilliance and the magic of PlaNYC and Dan Doctoroff," said Daniel C. Walsh, the Founding Director of the Mayor's Office for Environmental Remediation. "It demonstrates that cities can do this, cities can lead. In my view, that is the next generation of the environmental revolution."

PlaNYC designated the restoration of Brooklyn's McCarren Park Pool as one of its eight destination park projects.

HOLLY LEICHT | Assistant Commissioner, 2004–2008 & Deputy Commissioner, Development, 2008–2011, Department of Housing Preservation & Development

HOUSING

Truth be told, I joined the Department of Housing Preservation & Development (HPD) during the Bloomberg administration to save community gardens. Years earlier, I had been part of a lawsuit against the Giuliani administration when the mayor announced he would auction off hundreds of community gardens — abandoned vacant lots that New Yorkers had transformed into mini urban farms and community oases, primarily in low-income communities of color. When Mayor Michael Bloomberg came into office, he quickly reversed course, and I was handed the baton to work with the Parks Department and community gardeners to determine a better path to balancing the preservation of these green spaces with the development of much-needed affordable housing.

At HPD, this was just the beginning of the Bloomberg administration's commitment to what we now call "sustainability." Like most thoughtful policies, it didn't all happen immediately; it evolved. At first, there was lingering concern that sustainability and increased housing production were at odds, that imposing green building standards would yield less affordable housing. But rather than shutting the door on sustainability, we were challenged to figure out how to achieve both goals.

What we discovered — which perhaps seems elementary today — is that it's not only possible to improve sustainability while increasing the city's supply of affordable housing, it is imperative. Sustainable housing is quality housing: It is more resilient, healthier, and more cost effective to operate. Greening New York's affordable housing stock is critical to combating asthma and other health issues related to environmental factors that have disproportionately affected low-income communities for too long. And when affordable housing is more efficient to operate, it ensures its longevity, as well as the longevity of its residents.

When Shaun Donovan became HPD commissioner in 2004, he recognized the alignment between these goals. Even before PlaNYC, he began energetically integrating sustainability into our work, with our boss, Dan Doctoroff's blessing. In June 2006, HPD joined with the American Institute for Architects (AIA) to launch a global competition to develop a site in the South Bronx that would provide "Affordable, Sustainable, Healthy and Community Living." The winning building, Via Verde, or the Green Way, by a consortium of Phipps Houses, Jonathan Rose & Co, Dattner Architects, and Grimshaw Architects won national and international awards and still sets the gold standard for modern affordable housing.

Dan's sustainability blueprint for the city, PlaNYC, released one year later, made this approach permanent and integral to HPD's mission. It paved the way for HPD to impose sustainability requirements in all City-subsidized housing, not just a few select projects. New York City led the nation in making such a sweeping change, a policy shift that would have been unthinkable before PlaNYC.

PlaNYC also reinforced HPD's goal of increasing the supply of sustainable, affordable housing, but Dan went a step further than HPD ever could have on its own. I will never forget the meeting at City Hall in the ceremonial Committee of the Whole or "COW" room at which Dan directed the commissioners of every property-owning city agency — Department of Citywide Administrative Services, Department of Transportation, School Construction Authority, New York City Housing Authority (NYCHA), Health and Hospitals Corporation, even the New York Police Department — to transfer any underutilized sites they owned to HPD for affordable housing. (If that doesn't sound like a meeting you would remember forever, you haven't tried to take land away from the Police Department.) And because it was Dan, it succeeded — every agency collaborated with us. It was government at its best.

More national models followed. We implemented the Green Housing Preservation Program, which provides low- or no-interest loans to small- and mid-sized building owners to help them improve energy efficiency and water conservation, along with lead remediation. In 2019, the City entered a new era in green building with the passage of Local Law 97, or the Climate Change Mobilization Act, which will transition New York's building stock away from fossil fuels altogether. Its targets are ambitious: Residential buildings must achieve emissions reductions starting in 2024, and by 2050, NYCHA buildings must seek to cut emissions by 80% over a 2005 baseline.

PlaNYC made sustainability the City's official platform, across every municipal system — even ones traditionally excluded from environmental plans, like housing. Today, New York City is considered a national leader in building high-quality, sustainable affordable housing — a far cry from the days before the Bloomberg administration. We set the course for an entirely new way of building affordable housing that is better for its residents, owners, and the planet.

By making sustainability integral to City operations, PlaNYC paved the way for New York to impose sustainability requirements on all affordable housing projects, building on early successes like Via Verde in the Bronx, opposite. It also led to groundbreaking legislation, such as Local Law 97, which will transition New York's building stock away from fossil fuels.

LISA W. FODERARO | Parks Beat Reporter, *The New York Times*, 2011-2015

OPEN SPACE

Across New York City, 2015 was a very good year for parks.

In June, the High Bridge, a pedestrian span evoking the grandeur of a Roman aqueduct and connecting Manhattan and the Bronx, reopened after 40 years and a $61 million restoration. A few months later, a lacebark elm was planted in Joyce Kilmer Park in the South Bronx, marking the millionth new tree in a remarkable greening campaign. And in November of that year, the $111 million Ocean Breeze Track and Field Athletic Complex made its debut on Staten Island, becoming the first indoor track facility in the nation to be certified by the International Association of Athletics Federations.

Those were just some of the fruits of PlaNYC, an ambitious blueprint launched in 2007 to make New York City more sustainable — and livable. With a strong emphasis on parks, PlaNYC was conceived and shepherded by Dan Doctoroff, Deputy Mayor For Economic Development And Rebuilding under Mayor Michael Bloomberg.

Indeed, after decades of park disinvestment and neglect, PlaNYC represented nothing less than a shot of adrenaline for the city's open spaces.

While 300 acres of new parkland were created in the five years leading up to PlaNYC, the city's growing population had outpaced the development of open space. That meant New York City had fewer acres of green space per capita than almost any other major city in the United States. Moreover, streets lacked sufficient tree canopy to keep city residents cool in a warming climate.

The list of needs continued: student athletes jockeyed for fields for practice and competition; office workers struggled to find public spaces where they could enjoy lunch; elementary students ran outside during recess only to find cracked asphalt schoolyards; and residents in forgotten corners of the five boroughs were confronted with blighted parks, or amenities that were closed all together.

Revolutionary in its scope, PlaNYC sought to address all of those challenges. It targeted eight major parks for wholesale transformation. It set out to plant one million trees. It undertook the renovation of hundreds of schoolyards in park-deprived neighborhoods, turning them into vibrant community playgrounds during non-school hours. And it pledged to expand access to athletic fields.

The plan set a high bar for making New York City greener and more resilient. Among its chief objectives was the creation of 800 acres of new parkland, a goal realized by the time Mayor Bloomberg left office. That was coupled with a commitment to put every New Yorker within a 10-minute walk of a park. Such a measurement was a novel metric for urban sustainability, with implications for public health, air quality, and climate resilience.

In July of 2007, around 2.5 million New Yorkers, or 30% of the population, lived farther than a 10-minute walk to a park or playground. According to the Trust for Public Land's 2022 ParkScore Index, which ranks the 100 largest cities for their park systems, 99%

of New York City residents now live within a 10-minute walk of a park, compared to the national average of 55%.

PlaNYC not only ramped up open-space access and improved park quality; it strategically leveraged the benefits of parks and vegetation to advance other sustainability goals. They included improving air quality, absorbing carbon dioxide (the primary greenhouse gas responsible for climate change), mitigating the so-called urban heat island effect, in which concrete and pavement retain heat, and capturing stormwater.

McCarren Park Pool opened in 1936 as one of the grandest Works Progress Administration pool projects, before falling into disrepair. Following a $50 million renovation, the pool reopened in 2012 after being shuttered for almost 30 years.

"PlaNYC was transformative for placing parks and green infrastructure at the center of an urban sustainability blueprint that created a model for cities across the globe," said Sue Donoghue, the current New York City Parks Department Commissioner who was initially hired by the City to implement the parks portion of PlaNYC.

"With its comprehensive approach, PlaNYC reoriented the public's thinking about the importance of green space while addressing resiliency planning and preparedness," she said. "It showed that sustainability in general, and parks in particular, could greatly improve quality of life. The importance of these investments were laid bare during the pandemic, when our city's parks and open spaces were the source of solace for millions of New Yorkers."

Among the eight regional park projects, which each received between $15 million and $111 million, was the restoration and reopening of McCarren Park Pool. The mammoth Brooklyn swimming pavilion, built in the 1930s, had lain fallow for years, a graffiti-scrawled, empty basin. Other big-ticket renovations transformed Soundview Park in the Bronx, Fort Washington Park in Upper Manhattan, and the Rockaway Beach and Boardwalk in Queens.

PlaNYC also involved the renovation of hundreds of asphalt schoolyards into vibrant playgrounds that became a new community resource. Before PlaNYC, these schoolyards were locked and gated after school and on weekends, despite an urgent need for recreational space for children. Nearly half of the city's

188 neighborhoods had more than 1,250 children per playground — the City's threshold for crowding. In East Flatbush alone, 12,000 children shared three neighborhood playgrounds.

At many public schools, schoolyards actually doubled as faculty parking lots. And they did nothing to inspire creative play or exercise, with asphalt surfaces baking in the hot sun.

Working with the nonprofit Trust for Public Land, the City viewed the Schoolyards to Playgrounds program as an educational opportunity. Students were enlisted to collaborate with landscape architects on the designs, learning about stormwater runoff and combined-sewer overflows in the process. In one workshop, called, "Sewer in a Suitcase," students saw how even moderate amounts of rainfall could overwhelm wastewater treatment plants. That, in turn, led to the discharge of raw sewage directly into the city's bays and rivers.

Not only were the new schoolyards filled with amenities like turf fields, yoga circles, pollinator gardens, and outdoor classrooms, they incorporated green infrastructure. Garden beds, bioswales, permeable fields, and green roofs all captured runoff and reduced flooding. Critically, the new play spaces, whose renovations ranged from $500,000 to $1 million, were opened to the community during non-school hours, expanding park access for New Yorkers.

At the outset, Mayor Bloomberg allotted $111 million in capital funding for the schoolyard renovations, and an additional $14.5 million for operations. (Trust for Public Land provided matching dollars for some of the schoolyard improvements.)

Despite budget cuts after 2008, the Schoolyards to Playgrounds program continued, with new money coming from the city's Department of Environmental Protection for projects that integrate green infrastructure to reduce stormwater runoff. In all, 296 schoolyards have participated in the program since PlaNYC's release and 30 more are planned for the next five years.

PlaNYC also expanded the number of athletic fields across the city, turning two dozen multiuse asphalt lots into green turf fields able to accommodate growing interest in soccer, cricket, and rugby. Lights were installed to extend play after dark. According to the Parks Department, by 2015, new lighting at 18 fields across a dozen sites allowed children and adults to play longer into the evening — at a fraction of the cost of a new field. The lights provided an additional two hours of competitive use for each field during the summer, and an extra four hours in spring and fall.

"The vision of PlaNYC itself, and specifically around parks, was just an unbelievably exciting moment in the city," said Adam Ganser, executive director of New Yorkers for Parks, an advocacy group. "Very rarely do you have an administration that takes the time to create a long-term vision for the city or one that is so progressive. It was galvanizing."

Then there was the MillionTreesNYC initiative, born of the realization that trees both beautify and cool neighborhoods. But that's not all: They filter air pollutants, provide wildlife habitat, store carbon, and foster stewardship. The Parks Department oversaw the planting of trees on streets and public parks, while the New York Restoration Project, the nonprofit founded by Bette Midler, assumed responsibility for private properties, including backyards, college campuses, hospital grounds, churchyards, and cemeteries.

Such was the enormity of the undertaking that the City even started its own tree farms. "We were the first city in the nation to plant a million trees," said Deborah Marton, the former director of the New York Restoration Project.

As part of its open space vision, PlaNYC called for converting excess street space into public plazas. By the end of the Bloomberg administration, the City had created 70 such plazas, with new seating, tables, and landscaping. Right, Corona Plaza, Queens, 2018.

Volunteers assisted in the planting of one million trees across the city as part of PlaNYC's MillionTreesNYC initiative.

"By emphasizing that trees are infrastructure for public health, water management, and climate-change mitigation," she added, "Million Trees stood as a large-scale testament to those connections that did not exist in a visible way before."

PlaNYC's focus on parks and nature dovetailed with a broader philosophy shared by Doctoroff and the Bloomberg administration — that parks are essential drivers of quality of life and economic development. Among the many projects funded by the City during what former Parks Commissioner Adrian Benepe, called a "golden age of parks," were the High Line, Brooklyn Bridge Park, Governors Island, and the initial stages of Freshkills Park.

Benepe, who now leads the Brooklyn Botanic Garden, placed the parks' renaissance of the Bloomberg era in the context of September 11th. After the terror attacks, many fled the city for the suburbs and points north, including the Catskills.

Parks and trees were embraced as a way to tackle a number of goals, from advancing social justice to retaining (and attracting) businesses.

"There wasn't one advocate for parks in City Hall, there were many — the mayor himself, Patti Harris and, of course, Dan Doctoroff," he said. "Dan understood parks not just as 'nice to have,' but necessary, and he saw them as key to economic development."

Donoghue was especially struck by the desire to revive abandoned pieces of infrastructure, like the High Bridge and McCarren Park Pool. Despite their enormous price tags (restoring McCarren ran to $50 million), families can once again amble high above the Harlem River or cool off in the aqua blue waters of the million-gallon pool.

"One of the goals was taking care of these incredible assets that were not only aging, but shuttered," she said. "The vision was to bring them back — rehab them, reopen them to the community, and build for resilience."

Similarly, the City under PlaNYC sought to reclaim underused stretches of roadway and turn them into public plazas. The City pledged to create or enhance such spaces in each of 59 community boards, prioritizing neighborhoods with the lowest ratio of open space to population. The people-first approach to streets sparked a national movement that yielded cleaner air and healthier lifestyles by encouraging public transportation and walking.

In the heart of Queens, Corona Plaza is less than one-tenth of one acre. But its tables and chairs, umbrellas and planters, provide a close-to-home respite in a community lacking open space. First opened in 2012, the public space — part of the Department of Transportation's Plaza Program — is now a neighborhood asset. The nearby Queens Museum has enlivened the plaza with public programs involving cultural groups and folkloric performers.

Marking the 10th anniversary of the Plaza Program in 2018, the Department of Transportation announced the completion of 74 public plazas encompassing more than 30 acres (the equivalent of nearly 23 football fields) across the five boroughs.

The approach to parks under PlaNYC, advocates say, was influenced by Doctoroff's tendency to see possibility where others saw only obstacles. "Across the board, he had a vision that was not entrenched or stuck in the failures of history," said Ganser, who was formerly vice president for planning and design at Friends of the High Line. "The entire administration, and Dan in particular, came with fresh eyes to every problem the city was facing. They thought a little bit outside the box about the generations-long issue of access to quality open space."

BROWNFIELDS

"Under Dan and Mayor Bloomberg you had the freedom to do the very best you could. It was kind of breathtaking."

Daniel C. Walsh began remediating brownfields in New York City in the late 1980s. At the time — and for the next 20 years — all brownfields programs in the country were run by states, which were far removed from the granular politics, needs, and issues of individual urban neighborhoods. "There was so much that was being left out of state and federal programs," he said. In 2007, when he saw PlaNYC had devoted an entire chapter to brownfield remediation — and recommended that the process be brought under City control, "I was shocked," Walsh said. "It's a wonky policy issue that is incredibly important," but on the radar of few government officials, he said. "The opportunity to work at the municipal level to start a cleanup program, the first city-run cleanup program in the country, probably in the world," he said, "was my dream job."

Walsh became the first director of the City's new Office for Environmental Remediation. Over the next 10 years, he oversaw the remediation of 765 properties, including the removal of 3,000 petroleum tanks and 41,000 tons of hazardous waste. By the time he left in 2018, New York City was running the second-largest cleanup program in the United States, second only to the state of California. "I think that shows the brilliance and the magic of PlaNYC and Dan Doctoroff," said Walsh, who now teaches and researches environmental history and geochemistry at Columbia University. "It demonstrates that cities can do this. Cities can lead. In my view, that is the next generation of the environmental revolution."

New York City was the most industrialized city in the U.S. right up through the 1950s. The norms were very different than they are today. It left a scar, a legacy of pollution on the land. This problem affects a giant fraction of New York's urban landscape. In New York, at least 20% of our land is pretty highly polluted.

[Before PlaNYC] cleanup programs were run by states and by the federal government, never by cities. But cities have the knowledge, they have the need, and they have the understanding of communities. They have the ability to go so much deeper in understanding the problems and solving them. Looking back, it's obvious. But at the time, nobody had ever done that. Then along came PlaNYC.

Somehow, in the brilliance of Dan Doctoroff, and the staff, and the mayor, they made brownfield remediation one of the 10 priorities. They could have easily just made the big announcement, had the press conference, and then shuffled it off to some cubicles in an agency somewhere. That's not what they did.

They put [the brownfield office] right in the heart of City Hall, gave it access to the top, lots of energy and daylight, which enabled me to get everything accomplished. I met with every commissioner that had any relevance to my work. If I was in an agency, that would never have happened. But being in City Hall, I had access and commissioners took my meetings.

When I started in City Hall, I had all these ideas. I laid out this plan. I was meeting with [Director of Operations] Jeff Kay. When I'm finished, he looks at me. I said, "Well, I'm just looking for your approval. I just assumed there was an approval process." He said, "Dan, no. That's why we hired you. That's your job. If it's a good idea, do it." A light went on for the first time in my career. "Wow. I can come up with good ideas and implement them without having to be shot down by enormous bureaucracy."

It sounds so obvious. That should happen everywhere. But I can tell you, it doesn't. In state government you couldn't do anything unless the guy above you and the guy above him, and so on, approved it. It would take a year to get something done, and mostly nothing was done because somebody would say, "Oh, no. I have a concern." With the backing I had in City Hall, I would literally tell my staff, "I want ideas. If you come to me this afternoon with a good idea, that might be a program next week." We probably built 35 or 40 different programs over the 10 years I was there.

I was doing exactly the same [environmental cleanup] for the City that I had done for years with the State, only faster and more efficiently. It was paperless. Everything was archived digitally. You had immediate access; you didn't have to find some box in a warehouse out in Queens somewhere.

Probably my favorite remediation example was a brownfield site in Williamsburg, Brooklyn. A guy who made engines for NASCAR vehicles had done work in South Carolina, but he was a Brooklyn kid and he wanted to bring [his company] back to Brooklyn. Brooklyn is not a hotbed for NASCAR. But he wanted to do it. I thought that was such a great story that married the environmental issues of cleaning up a piece of land and then bringing in some remarkable new industry right into the heart of Brooklyn. That's exactly what we did.

[We cleaned up] many sites up and down the High Line, which was heavily contaminated; it was one of the most industrialized areas in Manhattan prior to the 1940s. But I'm most proud of the interconnections that we were able to make with HPD, [the Department of Housing Preservation & Development], which led affordable housing programs. A large percentage of our cleanups occurred at affordable housing sites in all five boroughs, the Bronx being the most notable. These were formerly industrial sites, gas stations, with all sorts of historic pollution that had to be addressed before they could be redeveloped. Think about how important affordable housing is, supportive housing is, within communities. The last thing you need is to delay those projects by two, three, four years. It's unthinkable. So, we made [affordable housing cleanup] a priority for our program.

We worked collaboratively. Probably my favorite [collaboration] was a program called the New York City Clean Soil Bank, which we launched in 2013. When big development happens in New York, [excavation] goes deep and it removes not only the shallow contaminated soil, but deep pristine soils — the native soil that

PlaNYC created the nation's first city-run brownfield remediation office; among its innovations was the Clean Soil Bank, which connected construction projects in the city excavating soil with ones that needed soil. Above, the berm in Brooklyn Bridge Park was built with soil from the program.

was here before European settlement. Literally millions of tons of this soil was generated each year and shipped out of New York. A horrible idea. We need clean soil for so many uses, for community gardens, for resilience, to cover polluted landscapes, for land shaping, for creating wetlands. The soil bank was designed to find — in real time — other projects [in the city] that could use clean material. It's kind of like a Craigslist for clean soil. We gave priority to City projects, Parks projects, resilience projects. We built tidal wetlands, freshwater wetlands. We built berms. The berm in Brooklyn Bridge Park — that was built with soil from the Clean Soil Bank. It hit a nerve. There was an opportunity that made sense. It was never contemplated in PlaNYC, but it was a direct product of PlaNYC.

Under Dan and Mayor Bloomberg you had the freedom to do the very best you could. It was kind of breathtaking. On January 2, 2015, it changed. The whole philosophy of openness and communication changed. It was chilling to the whole entrepreneurial, innovative, creative process. That's not to cast aspersions on Mayor [Bill] de Blasio. It's just saying how unique and remarkable Dan was and the administration under Mayor Bloomberg. Environmental issues [were] not prioritized in the same way and the vision was not as

clear and as deep. I think those are the kinds of things that Dan and his team brought to PlaNYC.

There are so many areas where cities can accomplish so much, in a holistic way, if they assert more authority. I think the greatest value of PlaNYC is showing other cities that it's possible — and not just [with] brownfields. I've been in this field for many years. I saw the limits. I struggled with the lack of capacity that the State had. I tried to battle that and build more capacity. It was not going to happen.

I'm really thankful that we have the work of Dan Doctoroff and Mayor Bloomberg and all the staff in developing PlaNYC because it shows the path forward. This brownfield program showed a proof of concept. I've talked about this in conferences around the country. People [say], "What? You mean cities can do this? It's allowed?" Yes, it is allowed.

PlaNYC was a historical environmental moment and I think it's something that needs to be recognized more fully. Frankly, there is so much more left to be done. We've just scratched the surface.

WATER

"[Dan] wanted us to do great things . . . and he is the one who gave us the North Star."

As Chief Operating Officer of New York City's Department of Environmental Protection (DEP) from 2006 to 2014, Kathryn Garcia oversaw a major shift in the City's approach to water. Under PlaNYC, the City channeled investments away from capital-intensive "gray" infrastructure into lighter-touch "green" infrastructure, deploying strategies that work with the existing built environment and mimic natural processes to capture and filter stormwater.

DEP, more used to massive treatment plants and sprawling pipe systems than curbside rain gardens and "blue roofs," was initially somewhat resistant to a new approach. But after small pilot programs demonstrated an ability to meet the City's legal obligations with a smaller and more positive environmental footprint, a wholesale transformation began. The result is a still-growing green infrastructure program that includes more than 11,000 assets capturing and cleaning hundreds of millions of gallons of stormwater each year — the largest such program in the United States.

Garcia's time at DEP witnessed a more fundamental shift than one simply from gray to green, from large to small, or from concrete and steel to native plants and cisterns, she said. PlaNYC was "a foundational document that had a very different perspective," Garcia said, one that married quality control with quality of life, sustainability with impact, and action with vision. "This was a fundamental change in thinking about how to protect future generations to support growth and see the city continue to thrive."

DEP has a very, very long history. They date their history back to The Manhattan Company, which was actually the predecessor to J.P. Morgan. [Their approach was] very, very engineering-heavy because that was the key to being able to supply water to [ultimately] 8.5 million people. There were folks at DEP who would go visit the gravesite of the engineer of the Catskill system on their vacations. So — a real reverence for the ingenuity that had come before, but it was very, very capital intensive.

PlaNYC was a road map for how we get to a different, better place for our water and our waste water system. This is an organization that was accustomed to big, multigenerational projects, and now we were looking at it through a different lens. Rather than, "Oh, we'll put a pipe in the ground and solve our problems," [it became] "We're going to use the natural environment." There'd been some experimentation with that on Staten Island and the Bluebelt system, but this was about looking at the whole city to meet the needs of the growing population. It was very practical. It wasn't a slogan. There had to be actual real initiatives behind any goal.

Dan didn't care which way we went. But he [said], "I want a better solution." Things that were more pro-climate were better solutions. Every other option was not great. It was cars and trucks and bad air and bad water and bad everything — that, I think, is what pushed him. I don't think Dan was an environmentalist to begin with, but he became one.

I wasn't a super environmentalist when my kids were little. I didn't know any better. But when I got to government I said, "Should I spend money on building things that use a huge amount of energy [for filtering] or should we just actually keep things clean? Goodness, we should keep things clean!" Like Dan, I came to it from the practical side.

In the past, we might have built a treatment plant; instead we're going to reduce [stormwater] flows the way that nature would do it. It's much more straightforward to say you're going to put a pipe in the ground. One of the things that PlaNYC did for agencies was help to make a really coherent case with the folks in the budget office about what our goals were, how we were going to get there, and why this was important. That evolution took time. Any time you're talking about trying to make a difference in water, it's very expensive, but [the PlaNYC approach is] still cheaper than trying to build little treatment plants all over the city. You want to make the investment of a dollar now, so you're not paying $10 later.

On the drinking water side, PlaNYC articulated a lot of investments in the watershed to keep our water clean but also throughout the city to support the people who were coming. It [said] we will get [Water] Tunnel Three done before the mayor is out of office. It nearly killed us but we did it.

I always thought Dan had such vision for what we could do. He wanted us to do great things. We're all bureaucrats. We're all just trying to do what we do and he is the one who gave us the North Star. It really did change the trajectory of where we were going.

He's one of those people who wanted to be in government because it was a place where you got things done. That's why he's different. I view him as someone who looked at New York and said, "How can we do things differently? How can we make them better?" It was an amazing moment to be in public service. There's not often times where someone comes in and says, "Think totally differently — and I'm going to support you all the way." Or: "I'm going to be the best that I can be and I need you to be the best that you can be." I'm not sure I would have stayed in public service and not gone back to the private sector if it hadn't been for him. Because he was saying, do big things. Think really big thoughts.

It's hard; 18,000 people will tell you, "I don't know what you're thinking; you're stupid; that can never get done." There are 13,000 reasons why you couldn't do — ever — what you wanted to do. But creating PlaNYC — having a blueprint for what we wanted to do on climate? That wasn't crazy. It was extremely actionable.

A rain garden can be quite lovely — you have a little garden on the street. In the curb line you create a planting bed and you direct [the water that] normally would go to a catch basin into this planting bed. Then you have plants filter out any of the pollutants before [the water] is either absorbed or discharged back out. They're very engineered but they look beautiful and have the benefit of dealing with your stormwater issues but also reducing flooding, creating

Rain gardens like this one in the Bronx have become an integral part of the City's strategy to reduce stormwater runoff, which directly impacts the quality of New York's waterways. The gardens are designed to absorb and filter water to reduce flooding, while also beautifying neighborhoods.

natural parkland, cleaning the air, cooling that particular piece of cement infrastructure, and basically making your neighborhood more pleasant. So now you're getting this triple bottom line benefit.

We had the [Environmental Protection Agency] come out and look at some of the rain gardens. They loved them. What they saw was infrastructure, often in neighborhoods that had been historically underfunded, like East New York, making the neighborhood more beautiful and improving the quality of life for those neighbors — the air quality, the trees, the flowers — and still also doing the job of keeping water clean.

New York City never goes small, it's just not a thing we're good at. Of course, we were going to go big. Hundreds of millions of dollars every year has been invested in rain gardens and green infrastructure projects. As with everything, [there are] always challenges. Occasionally we took a parking spot or two; this, in New York, never makes anyone happy. But you have to be able to create the network because if you don't get enough of them in the ground, you aren't going to see the improvements in water quality. Those investments built on each other. This is making a difference and as we double down, it will continue to make a difference.

[Today, New York has] over 11,000 green infrastructure projects and assets in the ground. This is by far the largest program in the United States. And this is being done in the densest city in the United States. We are leading the way on how to support density, support greening of the city, and support keeping water quality clean.

Without PlaNYC, there wouldn't have been an organizing value structure. DEP would've had to go and think about how to fix water quality, but [without] PlaNYC, they don't think of solutions that are about greening, reducing our energy consumption, improving neighborhoods. They likely go off and do something that's not interconnected to the rest of what we are trying to achieve as a city.

The real success of PlaNYC is that it's not a book on the shelf, it's the creation of the structure to actually achieve the goals of the book. That makes it very different than other plans that I've seen. Dan [left government] pretty shortly after PlaNYC. But the people that he hired, the structure that had been created, the fact that he had convinced the mayor that this was the right thing to do, meant that you had a really lasting foundation.

TRANSPORTATION

After almost a decade in city government, I knew that PlaNYC was going to shock the institutional government, both in its breadth and detail. I also knew that for PlaNYC to succeed, we needed that same institutional government to embrace it and be held accountable for its progress.

While others focused on brainstorming new policy ideas and collecting supporting data, my job was to figure out how to get them all implemented. In order for this plan to truly succeed, it couldn't just be the Bloomberg plan — it needed to be the City's plan and it needed to outlive the Bloomberg administration. That meant support from the agencies wasn't enough — we needed to have political buy-in at all levels of government. We also needed buy-in from beyond government — from the business and real estate community, as well as the nonprofits and advocacy organizations, all of which had different priorities for the city's future.

By September 2006, after months of generating ideas internally, we decided to pause. Before we could even think about proposing such grand plans for the future, we needed to actually explain the problem. What were we solving for? And why were we the only ones with the right ideas to solve it? In retrospect, this pause was the best decision we made despite being deeply contradictory to Deputy Mayor Dan Doctoroff's initial mandate to us at the time, which was to work as fast as we could.

Slowing down is not Dan's strong suit. But he knew we needed to educate people about the real concerns of the future. We needed to create a Sustainability Advisory Board, filled with experts in green building, energy, environmental policy, urban planning, labor, environmental justice, business, real estate, and politics, and more — and build a plan together, that these leaders across the city could stand behind. We needed to invite the public to participate, laying out the problem and offering ways for them to contribute solutions. We needed the political world to realize that if we were going to propose such bold ideas, that they could not dismiss them easily. This foresight and strategic shift guided us for the next four months as we finalized the plan and prepared it for release.

The process also fundamentally changed the plan. To that point, our thinking had been set up to focus on just three problems: how do you open, maintain, and green New York City for the future. During this time, we realized that every solution was interconnected. We couldn't put these solutions into boxes because they all worked together to produce a sustainable city. The key to nearly all of our goals was the most controversial proposal of all: congestion pricing.

Congestion pricing not only reduced traffic, but also improved air quality, reduced carbon emissions, created healthier neighborhoods, potentially freed up streets for improved public space (including new plantings to help reduce stormwater), and was a major revenue source for both maintaining the transportation infrastructure and funding critical expansion projects necessary for growth.

Despite the benefits, I knew it would be an immense challenge. But giving up on it wasn't an option. We needed to be able to present congestion pricing and our other transportation initiatives in a way that would withstand its critics and prove to be a viable solution.

Strategically, we decided to focus on transportation improvements both regionally and hyperlocally. In the region, we focused on the Nassau Hub, the Access to the Region's Core and the Metropolitan Transit Authority's (MTA) Third Track plan to support reverse commuting.

We also focused on neighborhoods most impacted by congestion and limited transportation options. The day PlaNYC was announced, we simultaneously released a 166-page supplement analyzing 22 individual neighborhoods and how they would specifically benefit from congestion pricing.

What proved to be good policy — supporting your premise with an immense amount of data — also proved to be good politics. When we finally released PlaNYC in April, the Nassau County Executive expressed support for the transportation plan and none of the representatives from the outlying communities came out immediately against it. The Sustainability Advisory Board lined up in support and so did the business community. Politically, no one dared oppose the plan at its outset. Its benefits were clear to all and the plan was well received.

Congestion pricing and the overall transportation plan with its massive funding requirements could have overwhelmed all of the other initiatives. But the level of detail we presented, coupled with some very strategic planning, earned support from the majority of New Yorkers, as well as representatives in the City Council, State Senate, the MTA, the Governor's Office, and many members of the State Assembly.

The transportation initiatives could have been the downfall of the entire plan. Instead, they held it all together. The truth is, we never knew if we would actually get the green light to release it. About two weeks before releasing the plan we had set up a few briefing sessions with Mayor Michael Bloomberg. We brought binders of data and summaries and we were prepared to answer any questions the mayor and anyone else in City Hall had about PlaNYC, including the costs of implementation and the challenges we would face.

We planned to save congestion pricing for last. About three quarters of the way through the transportation presentation, Mayor Bloomberg asked one of his aides if he had any questions for us. There was one: "So is congestion pricing in here or what?" Dan responded, "Yes, and you can't take it out because then the whole thing falls apart." The mayor looked at his aide and then to Dan, the plan's director Rit Aggarwala, and me and said simply – "Well, then, I guess it is in."

After the release of PlaNYC, we spent the next two years working in Albany and with the MTA on getting the critical support we needed. We also began implementing other parts of the transportation vision — the MTA worked with us on creating Bus Rapid Transit lines and improving express bus service in outer borough neighborhoods. The Department of Transportation worked tirelessly to implement bike lanes and create open streets, pedestrian plazas, and cleaner fleets. In 2019, researchers at Columbia University and Drexel University found that between 2009 and 2015, the legislation we passed more than doubled the fuel efficiency of the city's 13,500

yellow taxis, spurring an 82% drop in nitrous oxide emissions and a 49% drop in particulate exhaust emissions.

Progress had been made, but congestion pricing was never ultimately approved under the Bloomberg administration.

How was it that the failure of congestion pricing did not unravel the entire plan as Dan had suggested to the mayor? The answer is very similar to the legacy of the 2012 Olympic bid. Just because we didn't get the Olympics doesn't mean that we didn't accomplish 80% of what we set out to do. Congestion pricing was similar in that it held everything else together and helped promote an overall message.

We still face many challenges — many of the same transportation challenges that existed in 2007. We still have an underfunded MTA capital plan and many critical expansion projects have not yet begun. Congestion is still a problem and many areas are still underserved by transit. Notwithstanding, congestion pricing is still on the table. We started a conversation that is closer than ever today. We made it clear that planning for the future will require our leaders to make hard choices. By taking the first round of hits, and making the stakes clear, PlaNYC made it a little easier.

Above: As part of its effort to strengthen the city's mass transit, PlaNYC proposed five Bus Rapid Transit routes, known as Select Bus Service (SBS), with dedicated lanes to improve speed and efficiency. By 2023, there were 17 routes in all five boroughs, with plans for more. Here, an SBS route across 14th Street in Manhattan.

Right: In 2008, the Bloomberg administration debuted the Summer Streets program, which closed some streets to traffic, sparking initial skepticism. ("Will Car-Free Summer Streets Work?" asked a *New York Times* headline.) "Summer Streets will literally turn the streets of our city into a pedestrian park," said Department of Transportation Commissioner Janette Sadik-Khan. New Yorkers agreed and the popular program continues today. Here, pedestrians and cyclists on Park Avenue South, 2017.

GIL QUINIONES | Senior Vice President of Energy and Telecommunications, New York City Economic Development Corporation, 2003-2007 | President and CEO, New York Power Authority, 2011-2021

ENERGY

"PlaNYC was when Dan basically said, 'Gil, think bigger.'"

Gil Quiniones had worked on energy efficiency initiatives for Con Edison for more than a decade when the September 11th attacks caused him to consider a career change. For months, Quiniones smelled smoke in his West Village apartment. Next door was St. Vincent's Hospital, which braced for an influx of trauma victims who never arrived. "That impacted me a lot," he said. He decided to join the public sector "to be part of the rebuilding of New York City."

At Con Edison, Quiniones had never really considered the role that energy played in the city's economy and development. But as his new boss, Deputy Mayor Daniel Doctoroff, pursued a bid to host the 2012 Olympic Games and a rezoning strategy for all five boroughs, "It clicked to me, well, this is where energy and the grid can play a role in supporting that," Quiniones said.

That meant inserting the City into energy decisions traditionally overseen by the State — including defeating a proposal to site a power plant on the Greenpoint-Williamsburg waterfront, a potential Olympic site. "The City really did not have any powers to make those kinds of decisions," he said. "Both Dan and the mayor were very good at figuring out, 'how do we do this?'" With every new rezoning, Doctoroff consulted Quiniones to develop an energy plan to support the growth and he tasked Quiniones with convening a multiagency task force — including environmental justice organizations and private business — to chart out New York's first comprehensive energy strategy. Then came PlaNYC.

That was "a bigger vision," Quiniones said. Their task was no longer "just supporting the short, medium term rebuilding of New York post 9/11. Now it's, 'Let's think about 2030. We think we're going to have nine million people. We think these are the kinds of developments that are going to happen. We need to address climate change and reduce carbon while accommodating all of this growth. How do we do that?' And it seemed impossible. To be honest with you, at the beginning I was like, "Oh my God, what ideas are we going to come up with to fast forward that far?"

I joined the administration in 2003. The City prior to the Bloomberg administration really played little to no role in energy policy. When Con Ed proposed to increase rates, it would intervene. But it never really played a role in long-term planning. [Previous administrations] never thought of using the bully pulpit.

It was really [during] the Bloomberg administration where we got a seat at the table and we proposed ideas to Con Edison, the regulators, and the state government. Making the City a big player in planning and actually driving what should happen in New York — that was a first. We always found ways to make them adopt the right policies and regulations. Once we had PlaNYC, that became the North Star.

PlaNYC was when Dan basically said, "Gil, think bigger — it's about decarbonization and addressing climate change." I wasn't even a

commissioner, but I was empowered to make decisions. When I had to build my staff, the only criteria they gave me was, "Hire the best people you can." And we did.

It was very, very clear right off the bat that if we wanted to decarbonize, we needed to address energy efficiency. Seventy percent of the [city's] emissions were from buildings. A lot of the buildings were using really polluting oil to heat buildings, causing asthma in Hunts Point, the South Bronx, and in Sunset Park. We wanted to make those buildings not burn oil anymore.

We began removing the dirty oil-based boilers that were causing a lot of asthma and pollution. It wasn't easy, because most of the buildings are privately owned. We could do it for our own portfolio, the City portfolio. But that's a fraction of all of the buildings in New York City.

We were thinking about what kind of incentives and market design and regulations — a combination of those — could spur investment in energy efficiency. We went to the State to say Con Edison, which is a [regulated] entity, should create certain incentive programs to spur those kinds of investments. And they did. When Con Edison would ask for a rate case, we would come in and say, "Yeah, we would support this plan if you do X, Y, and Z."

Cables being laid across the Hudson River to bring 660 megawatts of electricity to Midtown Manhattan from New Jersey, 2011.

When we said 70% of our emissions come from buildings and therefore we needed to focus on buildings — I thought that was a big idea. Today, it's obvious. Now every big city talks about that. The concept came from PlaNYC.

[The other big idea was that] we need to build more renewables and bring those renewables down to New York City to reduce the dependence on power plants. New York City is very unique in the sense that it doesn't have enough transmission lines feeding into the city. That's the reason why we have power plants in New York City — to make it reliable. We wanted to reduce the dependence on those power plants. We wanted to reduce the amount of hours they operate because they emit pollution, they emit carbon. Bringing renewables from upstate and from Canada will do that. That was a big idea at the time because I don't think people thought it was possible.

Dan had the foresight that we need to think big. Dan was so busy I found out the best way to talk to him was [to] ride with him [between meetings]. And so I would time it; I would call [his assistant] Marla and I said, "Marla, when is he going between point A and point B? Stick me in the car or I'll ride with him on the subway," and I would brief him during that time: "Hey, Dan, here's the status of the siting of this power plant that we're trying to

block." Or "We're putting a policy together. What do you think about this?" The most interesting thing with Dan and the mayor is that the brain capacity is just unbelievable.

The beauty of PlaNYC was that it was different sectors and it was interwoven. We knew the interactive and cumulative interactions of the various sectors. The planning and housing were inputs to my energy planning. All the rezonings, all the population growth, all the building stock, transit-oriented development — those were inputs to my energy plan. It was well put together in that way.

After PlaNYC, we did annual reports that showed concrete progress. With energy projects, by definition they're long term, but you're seeing it now. The two transmission lines being built — from upstate and Quebec to New York City — all of those were ideas that came out of PlaNYC. Local Law 97 that required energy efficiency, retrofitting buildings, was really based on PlaNYC. Now if you go to cities and local governments, that's the model.

It was a special time when we were putting that together, with probably the smartest people I've worked with ever. It was really unbelievable. A lot of cities have looked at PlaNYC. It put together the roadmap.

RUSSELL UNGER | Executive Director, Urban Green Council, 2007-2018

BUILDINGS

Much about building decarbonization may seem obvious now — that buildings and cities are essential to tackling climate change, that building codes are critical because they are the DNA of buildings, that we can't just focus on new buildings because the existing ones will still be around, that data will help us make smart policy decisions. But it wasn't evident 15 years ago when PlaNYC burst onto the scene.

The early decades of efforts to address climate change centered on international agreements, with environmental groups focused on international, national, and state policy. Cities were too small to warrant much attention and didn't control energy and climate-related issues like power plants and cars. Despite all the attention that LEED brought to buildings in the early 2000s, the focus was mainly on sparkly new construction. Existing buildings were largely the domain of weatherization experts (focused on affordability) and a small number of energy efficiency holdouts from the 1970s oil crisis.

What changed? A big part of the answer is data. For instance, McKinsey's 2007 U.S. greenhouse gas cost abatement curve illustrated the massive cost range of various climate interventions — and how building efficiency offered some of the most cost-effective approaches. Another data-centric report was released that same year: PlaNYC.

It was certainly not the first city sustainability report. But PlaNYC was different. It was for a city whose population is larger than many American states. It had far more depth than other reports. And its use of data took on special significance with buildings.

PlaNYC used data to analyze the building carbon emissions both from direct and indirect energy consumption. That is, carbon emissions from fossil fuels burned at the building for heat, hot water, and cooking *plus* fossil fuels burned at power plants to produce the electricity used by buildings. The concept was resisted by many in the real estate industry who were concerned about being evaluated by factors outside of their control like the carbon intensity of the electrical grid. And yet, the analysis revealed an inescapable truth. When you evaluated their impact holistically, buildings accounted for the lion's share of New York City's carbon emissions: about 70%.

Not every administration would have been willing to take on the real estate industry, especially in a city like New York. But the leader of the plan, Deputy Mayor Dan Doctoroff, managed something even more remarkable: PlaNYC somehow brought the key parties to the table together. There was a sense of everyone contributing to a greater whole and willingness to listen to opposition. Industry felt included, and industry leaders — particularly building owners — had the opportunity to step out from their peers and be credited. Negotiations over major legislation were not just with real estate associations, but also directly with leading owners.

Although I was only tangentially involved in the initial work — I started as the founding executive director of Urban Green Council, the year PlaNYC was released — I was not surprised by its ambition and detail. Years earlier, I had met Dan as a young legislative attorney for the New York City Council to present a Council-championed report on public markets. I assumed it would be a perfunctory meeting as he listened politely to our pitch. However, despite being a deputy mayor responsible for many of the city's most important agencies, it was evident from his questions that he had read the report closely and wanted to dig deeper. I was shocked. That was the same pattern I observed over the years in other meetings, no matter the group or context.

That same incredible curiosity and attention to detail was evident in PlaNYC, from the groundbreaking content of the plan itself to the extraordinary team that Dan assembled and empowered. The PlaNYC team reflected immense commitment and professionalism. They displayed a willingness to challenge ideas and be challenged. They respected expertise and remained open to better ideas. Over

A PlaNYC analysis revealed that buildings account for 70% of New York City's carbon emissions, leading to some of the most ambitious legislation in the country addressing building and energy codes.

time, Urban Green Council became part of this team, most notably when I was appointed Chair of the NYC Green Codes Task Force by Mayor Michael Bloomberg and Council Speaker Christine Quinn, tasked with assembling and managing a stakeholder coalition to make recommendations on greening city codes.

The buildings policies emanating from PlaNYC set the gold standard for the country. Existing buildings were front and center, with a particular emphasis on large ones, drawing from data showing that 2% of New York City's existing buildings contained about half of the city's square footage. There were laws requiring the measurement of building energy use (which laid the foundation for later regulating building carbon emissions under NYC Local Law 97) and requiring buildings to be re-tuned and to upgrade their lighting. These were emulated by other cities across the country. Following recommendations of the Green Codes Task Force, more than 50 changes were made to building and energy codes.

PlaNYC demonstrated the immense potential to advance sustainability in cities. From the strategic plans of major environmental NGOs and funders to city-dedicated organizations like C40, today cities are broadly seen as a vanguard for climate innovation. Much of that can be traced back to the example set by PlaNYC.

The last time I ran into Dan was in an elevator en route to a meeting at his urban sustainability company, Sidewalk Labs. In true form, he was the first to say hello, remembering my name, inquiring how I was doing, and asking questions. Most importantly: Now, and then, I felt he genuinely wanted to learn the answers.

AIR QUALITY

"PlaNYC represented an incredible, really proactive vision for a large city and Dan was the champion it needed."

In 1988, Peggy Shepard gathered a group of people to protest odors from a sewage plant in Northern Manhattan. That year, she founded the environmental justice group, WE ACT which has since become a national leader on establishing equity as a central concern for environmental and climate issues.

Shepard, who currently serves on the White House Environmental Justice Advisory Council, was one of two environmental justice leaders invited to join PlaNYC's Sustainability Advisory Board in 2006, participating in the brownfields and air quality workshops. She was particularly concerned about New York's asthma epidemic, which disproportionately targets communities of color, and urged the City to follow federal guidelines to monitor a tiny toxin found in diesel exhaust called PM 2.5, "that are very easy to be breathed in, but hard to be breathed out," she said. "The City embraced it."

In her meetings with Deputy Mayor Daniel Doctoroff, "I did find him a good listener and I found that he was responsive," she said. While some implementation efforts ultimately didn't go far enough, "the overall vision was great," she said, and did include some concrete steps, including establishing the largest air quality monitoring effort in the country. "These kinds of processes require a champion," she said. "Dan Doctoroff was that champion."

One of the key ways that environmental justice became very visible in the Bloomberg administration was through waterfront parks and through solid waste. That was the time when the mayor decided that every borough would take on its own waste because there were so many waste transfer stations and so many trucks trucking Manhattan's garbage out to other boroughs.

That waste transfer issue really raised the visibility of environmental justice in the administration, so that when PlaNYC was being developed, I was asked to join the advisory group as well as UPROSE. We were the two environmental justice groups on the PlaNYC board.

I was very involved in the air quality workshop. They were responsive to the concerns and issues we were raising. The administration came about at a time when we already knew that the asthma epidemic was impacting communities of color in New York City. But it was not getting recognition. I believe that PlaNYC really raised the issue of air pollution [in] city government in a way that had never happened before.

We felt that it was really important to ensure that air quality was being monitored citywide. As a result, we got the New York City Community Air Survey, called NYCCAS, which is the largest air quality survey in the country. That came out of recommendations for PlaNYC. Being able to be part of the workshops that really provided a foundation for the work was exciting and important.

In New York City, our air quality issues are exacerbated by mobile sources as well as building emissions. It's still pretty bad, especially in the Bronx. We're getting building emissions under control through PlaNYC and through the Clean Heat Program. Those were strong ways that PlaNYC began to deal with the air quality issue as well as the CO_2 issue.

I think the overall vision was great. The City is not always good in implementation, as we know. We hired a full-time person to do outreach to building managers in uptown neighborhoods to really push the adoption of the boiler retrofits because we didn't feel that there was enough attention being given to some of the lower revenue buildings uptown, which made it more difficult for landlords to retrofit.

Is everything going to roll out perfectly the way we all envision it? We know that that's not going to happen for a number of reasons — not only bureaucracy, but money as well. But the vision was important and the template that it laid down was important. PlaNYC represented an incredible, really proactive vision for a large city and Dan was the champion it needed.

Unfortunately, once you lose that champion and you go to another administration, we got OneNYC, which was nothing. They kept most of the advisory board. But instead of really being active in making recommendations, we were just sort of given PowerPoints to look at. There were a lot of lessons [in PlaNYC] that I wish were being followed.

PlaNYC has stood the test of time. It's been a model. The progress reports demonstrated that we can chart our progress and we should chart our progress. I can't tell you how many grad students have interviewed me over the years about PlaNYC and how other cities have looked to that plan.

Above: Dan Doctoroff and Peggy Shepard at the Sustainability Advisory Board.

Left: "PlaNYC really raised the issue of air pollution [in] city government in a way that had never happened before," said environmental justice leader Peggy Shepard, who served on the plan's Sustainability Advisory Board. That included acknowledging the asthma epidemic afflicting the city's communities of color and creating the largest local air quality survey in the country. Rockaway Park, shown here, was one of eight PlaNYC destination parks.

MARK WATTS | Executive Director, C40 Cities, 2013-Present

CLIMATE

When I think of Dan Doctoroff I think of PlaNYC. You can draw a direct line from the publication of PlaNYC to the mission of C40 Cities today.

I first heard of Dan when London's then-Deputy Mayor, Nicky Gavron returned from a trip across the pond to tell me that New York was doing something interesting on climate change, which meant we would have to up our game. I was then the climate and sustainability adviser to the Mayor of London, Ken Livingstone, and there was a lot of (mostly friendly) competition between city halls in London and New York. We were proud of having been the first mega-city to publish a comprehensive climate action plan. On the back of it, we had gathered together the capital cities of the G20 nations to launch what was to become the C20 (later C40) Cities Climate Leadership Group, partnering with Bill Clinton's Climate Initiative.

But that convening lent heavily on London's leadership, along with a few other pioneers like Toronto, Copenhagen, and Stockholm. Now that Mayor Mike Bloomberg and New York were entering the fray, it was going to be much more likely that mayors around the world really would step up to a leadership role in pushing climate action. Who wouldn't want to be in a club with both London and New York?

Nicky told me that PlaNYC would actually go a step further than we had by integrating a spatial, economic development, and climate plan for the city — and that it was also being led by a significant businessman who was responsible for delivering Mayor Michael Bloomberg's economic development strategy as deputy mayor. This sounded really interesting.

Today, C40's focus is to demonstrate that the faster cities cut pollution, the greater is their ability to create good jobs, keep energy bills down, and enable residents to live healthier, happier lives. When Mayor Bloomberg hosted the second C40 conference in 2007, three

dozen mayors attended. Today, nearly 100 mayors representing 700 million people and a quarter of the global economy are members, committed to halving emissions by 2030.

New York is doing its part. Since PlaNYC, the city has reduced its emissions by 19% from 2005 levels, while continuing to grow its population and economy (meanwhile, Mayor Bloomberg served as the C40 Chair between 2010-2014).

The inspiration that Dan and PlaNYC provided is still central to our thinking, and when discussing with mayors how they can make climate action the cornerstone of their city's development, I am invariably reminded of my own reaction to reading PlaNYC for the first time 15 years ago: "We need a Dan Doctoroff."

Above: Mayor Michael Bloomberg answers questions during a news conference at the C40 Large Cities Climate Summit in São Paulo, Brazil, 2011.

Opposite: PlaNYC's holistic approach marshaled all of the city's systems to simultaneously promote economic development and fight climate change. This included a transportation plan that prioritized bikes, pedestrians, enhanced streetscapes, and open space. Shown here, Herald Square pedestrian plaza and bike lanes.

Cities from New York to London End Growth in Climate–Changing Emissions

BY SEBASTIEN MALO, THOMSON REUTERS FOUNDATION   SEPTEMBER 13, 2018 6:17 PM

"More than two dozen of the world's largest cities are no longer increasing their planet–warming greenhouse gas emissions, they announced at a global climate summit in San Francisco.

The 27 cities, from New York to London, said they had reached the milestone even as their populations and economies grew.

They did so by cutting their usage of fossil–fuel–generated energy, growing their public transportation systems and reducing waste, according to C40 Cities, a network of large cities acting as leaders in combating climate change."

LONDON TO NEW YORK: HOW PLANYC BECAME THE FIRST URBAN "GREENPRINT"

No two cities on earth have more to learn from each other than London and New York. This was the basis of my collaboration (and sometimes, competition) with Dan Doctoroff as fellow deputy mayors during the 2000s.

Of all my interactions with Dan, the one I most clearly remember was a crucial meeting in May 2006 in New York.

Dan had given me 20 minutes to talk through New York's hosting of the second C20 (soon to be C40) summit. "Commiserations on the Olympic bid," I offered as I walked through the door, referencing London's recent win over New York to host the 2012 Games. "But congratulations on having hydrogen fuel cells in your city . . ."

I had set up the C20 the previous October in London as a leadership group of large cities collaborating to cut carbon emissions. It was clear even then that the battle against climate change will be won or lost in cities. New York was more vulnerable to climate change than London; we needed it to be a leader. I was already aware that Dan had an appetite for risk and thought systemically, (as depicted in his New York Olympic bid), and I wanted to capture his imagination. I knew once he was immersed in the idea, he would be an unstoppable ally.

I was still there an hour and a half later. Dan was a great listener. He quizzed me on congestion charging, how I had led on the *London Plan*, its vision of London striving to become an exemplary sustainable world city, and its focus on climate change. The *London Plan* was designed to be holistic and strategic, pulling together the spatial dimensions of all of our policies and strategies. It was complemented by a separate *Climate Change Action Plan*, being developed by Mark Watts.

Both London and New York were exploring the pressures of growth: How should our cities grow? Where should they grow? For whom should they grow? I told Dan that we saw sustainable growth — integrating social, environmental, and economic improvement — as the only way forward. Dan seemed very taken

with the idea that sustainability could be the organizing principle of the city. Sustainability had to be mainstreamed in an office under the mayor, I maintained. We parted confident that our cities would collaborate on congestion charging, strategic planning, and preparation of the second summit.

Within weeks, Michael Bloomberg announced the creation of a new office whose role would be "nothing short of formalizing policies of sustainability as integral to the future growth and development of our city," to be led by Rit Aggarwala.

They don't stand still in New York.

Dan is a deadlines man. Just a year later, at the second summit, Michael Bloomberg presented Dan's PlaNYC to an unprecedented gathering of mayors and business leaders from across the world.

It was startlingly original — not just in the context of the U.S., but globally.

A land-use growth plan had morphed into an audacious "greenprint" for the city. Unlike any other plan, PlaNYC integrated a policy document with an action plan, setting out the costings and resources needed, including those by the State and the federal government. Underpinning it was the idea that a strategy for growth, shaped and managed sustainably, is in itself a climate change strategy.

I was astonished by how candidly PlaNYC set out what had not worked and why an ambitious paradigm shift was needed to ensure that growth would not choke New York. I have yet to see a planning document, then or now, drafted in such a beautifully simple and pragmatic way. It was written to and for New York's citizens.

The quality of the plan owed everything to the quality of the process, driven by Dan's vision and vast experience. I admired its wide-ranging and diverse coalition of stakeholders. Dan had no time for siloed thinking and demanded integration across the city's systems to forge coordination and collective ownership of outcomes. This wasn't restricted to an all of government approach. It included academia, environmental justice groups, unions and, significantly, the private sector.

New York has regulatory powers to die for, enabling the plan to direct the private sector. By involving them all the way, Dan ensured that policies and initiatives were practically deliverable. The example I always single out is the exemplary brownfield initiative. Dan recognized that the plan needed to provide the private sector with certainty to drive continuity beyond political cycles.

The summit was a triumph. It presented PlaNYC to the world in spectacular fashion. One cannot overestimate the legacy of Dan's PlaNYC internationally. Major cities at that stage, if they had any kind of long-term plan (and most did not), certainly didn't include climate change. PlaNYC was used by C40 as a model for cross-city working,

London Mayor Sadiq Khan and New York City Mayor Eric Adams discuss climate change and other issues at City Hall in New York City, May 9, 2022.

New York and London were early leaders and partners in establishing cities at the forefront of the climate movement. In the past two decades, both cities have taken dramatic steps to reimagine their physical landscapes as greener, more sustainable, and more humane. Above, kayaking at Pier 2, Brooklyn Bridge Park.

Rooftop garden overlooking the River Thames, London.

galvanizing many cities to develop their own strategic plans and action plans on climate change. New York's pledge to cut carbon and measure it, had a wide-ranging influence; today over 800 cities currently disclose their emissions publicly.

Beyond C40, PlaNYC was cited, promoted and disseminated by international organizations including the Intergovernmental Panel on Climate Change (IPCC), the World Bank, the Inter-American Development Bank (IDB), the World Economic Forum (WEF), the United Nations (UN), Coalition for Urban Transition, the Organization for Economic Co-operation and Development (OECD), and United Cities and Local Governments (UCLG). As my colleague, international urbanist, Greg Clark has said, PlaNYC "became the benchmark against which other plans would be judged and it raised the ambitions and strategic thinking of multiple cities."

Collaboration and competition inspired, and fired, innovations and interactions between London and New York in those years. Sister cities, we were both racing to be the best, while also sharing a deep understanding of the relentless challenges and opportunities of governing a world city.

Today, congestion charging, for which Dan fought so hard, is nearing a reality in New York. I salute this ferociously gifted man.

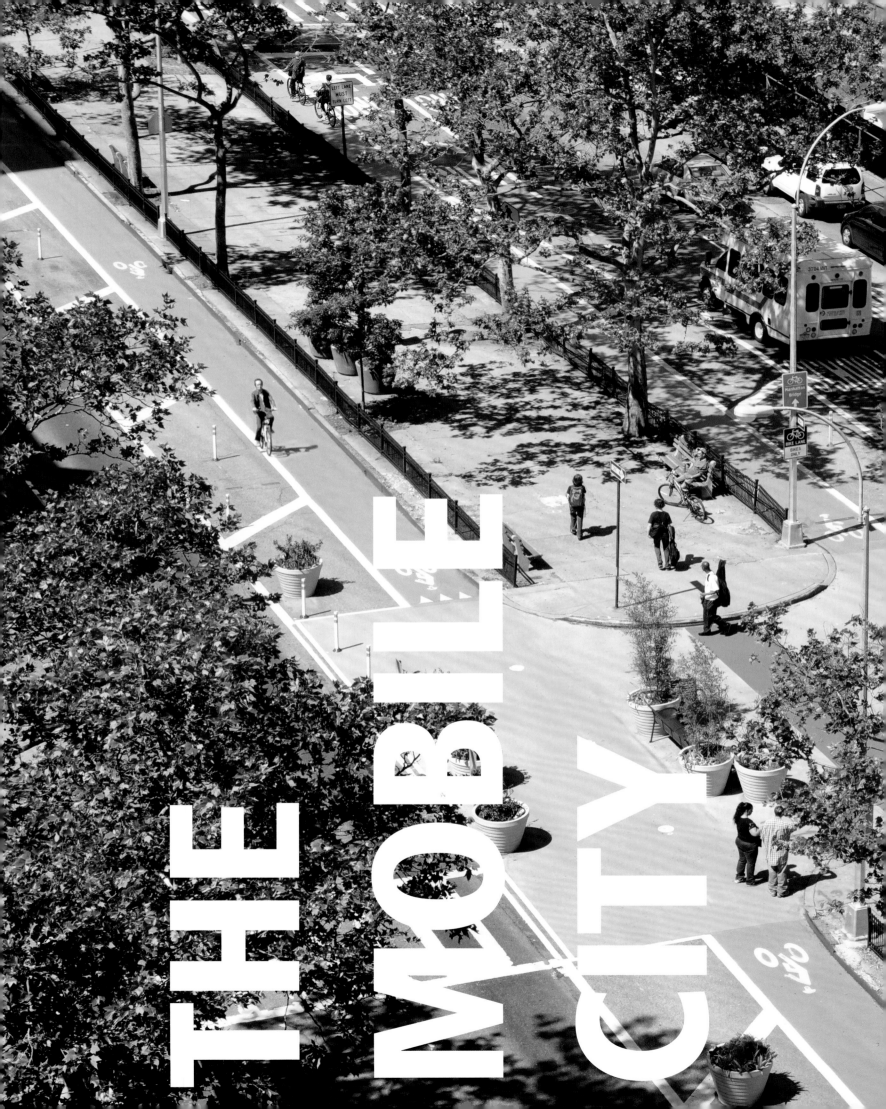

THE MOBILE CITY

Bike lanes and pedestrian plaza, Allen and Pike Streets, Lower East Side, Manhattan.

"What we've found in New York over and over again is that every time we've built mass transit, an extraordinary surge in growth has followed."

DANIEL L. DOCTOROFF, APRIL 2006

Pedestrian plaza, Flatiron District. The Bloomberg administration's sustainability report, PlaNYC, and the subsequent hiring of Janette Sadik-Khan as Commissioner of the Department of Transportation set in motion a transformation of the city's streets for greater pedestrian use.

JANETTE SADIK-KHAN | Commissioner, New York City
Department of Transportation, 2007–2013

CREATING THE PEOPLE-FIRST STREET MOVEMENT IN NEW YORK CITY

PlaNYC was a blueprint for reimagining New York's transportation network to build a more livable, sustainable city

It was not your typical job interview. I was sitting in a spacious, ornate ceremonial room, around a massive, round wooden table with a group of half a dozen questioners, most sporting neckties. But when the interview is to run the transportation department for the nation's largest city, the road runs through City Hall, and a lot of people will be at the table.

I didn't know what Mayor Michael Bloomberg might be looking for in a transportation commissioner; I had never met him before. But I knew that Dan Doctoroff had brought me to the table to represent a different vision for the city's transportation future, not to promise to maintain the status quo without controversy. I put my cards on the table: I didn't want to maintain New York City's radiating network of sidewalks, roads, and bridges, I wanted to reset and elevate them for a new era. I wanted to make cycling a safe and practical choice on New York City's streets. I wanted buses to be a premier transit option, not an unwanted stepchild of the subway. And I wanted to institute a charge for people driving into Manhattan's business district, which has great transit service, and use the proceeds to fund better transit options.

Each of these ideas were virtually unheard of in official circles at the time and I braced myself for the reaction.

The response: Crickets.

Well, at least I got to meet the Mayor, I told myself as I walked out, sure that I had blown the interview and would be able to share this anecdote for years to come. So I was surprised to receive a call a couple of weeks later inviting me to a breakfast with Mayor Bloomberg at an Upper East Side diner, where — after a deep discussion of transportation and the state of the Mets — he offered me the job.

I learned that the team hadn't reacted to my ideas because they had already been long at work on precisely this kind of people-first approach in an as-yet unreleased document called PlaNYC. What I perceived during the meeting was not indifference, but a political poker face that you get when you walk into a conversation that has been ongoing for many months.

Just a generation earlier, New York City had been famously deemed an ungovernable city. In 2007, PlaNYC outlined a path to make it a more livable, sustainable, and equitable one. Transportation was a big part of the agenda's 127 actions, with plans to build more cycle paths in

just a few years than currently existed on all of New York City's 6,300 miles of streets. It also proposed bringing every New Yorker within a 10-minute walk of open space — which would include reallocating street space for new public plazas. The six years following the plan's release were some of the most transformative for New York City's streets and public spaces since Robert Moses's massive public works and highway constructions a half-century earlier. This crucial course correction started with Dan and this document.

Through political machinations and the accumulation of power, Moses had helped transform New York City from a 19th century

PlaNYC called for reallocating street space to create new pedestrian plazas, such as this spot in the Meatpacking District, a neighborhood where pedestrians already outnumbered cars ten to one. By the end of the Bloomberg administration, the City had created 70 new plazas.

horse town into a 20th century megalopolis built around the motor vehicle. Constructing that megalopolis required the appropriation of public space and the demolition of thousands of houses and buildings, building parkways through wide swaths of the city, and repurposing the city's waterfronts as monumental highways and bridges that endure today. But modern New York outgrew and chafed at some of those megaprojects. Highways sliced through and cut off neighborhoods and disenfranchised communities, alienating Black residents and leaving immigrant communities with few parks and recreation spaces. Public transit investment stagnated and failed to grow as more people drove across the region. Somewhere

in between Moses and the modern era, New York forgot what it meant to be a city, lavishing its transportation planning model and immense resources on managing and accommodating car traffic at all costs, even though the vast majority of trips in the city are on foot or on public transportation.

Where Moses was famous for unfurling maps across tables like the one where I sat in City Hall to dazzle mayors, governors, and elected officials into supporting his vision, the future articulated by Dan in PlaNYC was a detailed action agenda that was a human-powered antidote to the overbuilt, car-forward perspective of the 20th century.

Almost every page contained a vision of the city as a collection of communities, unified by the concept of sustainable growth. Instead of designing the city's future around the motor vehicle, PlaNYC answered a question: How could New York City with one million more people work better in 2030 than it did in 2007? How could it be a place where people walked outside and liked what they saw? The document focused on neighborhoods and specific ways to improve them. The goal was to draw out street life and, with it, the economic activity that propels cities: planting one million trees to make walking endurable during the summer heat, creating community plazas, improving the efficiency of buses through street design, and making it safer and easier to walk and bike on New York City's streets.

PlaNYC articulated this vision in strong, declarative language that distinguished it from many eco-minded municipal documents of that era, envisioning a "greener, greater New York," but with so much specific policy substance that no one could accuse it of greenwashing.

To achieve these goals and operationalize PlaNYC's vision into agency actions, I directed my agency to create a strategic plan — the first in its history. It outlined overhauls of the City's approach to cycling, public space, transit, street furniture and more, while identifying ways to improve our operations and make them more sustainable.

Expanding New York City's bike lane network

New York City's bike lane network in 2007 was almost theoretical. The few bike lanes that existed were faded, disconnected, and too limited to complete any meaningful trip. Ridership and riders themselves reflected the infrastructure. The typical cyclist looked like a Zapatista mercenary, ready for battle with a shoulder-slung messenger bag, and was almost exclusively male. Encouraging people to ride with cute slogans or Ride to Work events was not going to be enough. The City needed to create a network of lanes that made cycling a safe and attractive option for women, families, and casual cyclists — not just two-wheeled mercenaries. It also required more than just a couple of white lines on the street.

We needed a new generation of bike paths that created a new sense of order on the street. I traveled to Copenhagen early in my tenure to survey the street design that helped make it one of the world's great cycling cities. I brought home the concept for a new design for a lane, one that moved the curbside parking lanes on Eighth and Ninth Avenues in Manhattan further into the street. The design was foreign, but the impact was immediately legible, with parked cars serving as a physical buffer between cruising cyclists and moving vehicles, and shortening the distances that people had to walk across traffic lanes. The parking-protected lane quickly became a standard across the city on Manhattan's north-south avenues and on avenues in Brooklyn like Kent Avenue and Prospect Park West.

With Mike and Dan's support, we embarked on one of the largest expansions of cycle paths of any big city in the world, creating nearly 400 miles of bike lanes across the city. The connected network that emerged linked the boroughs over the East River bridges and reached deeply into neighborhoods: the Bronx along Grand Concourse, in Queens on 34th Avenue, and in Brooklyn, extending on Fifth Avenue all the way into Sunset Park. Once known for its mean streets, New York became a national cycling model, with women and families coming out in large numbers, doubling the number of cyclists in just a few years, without more traffic congestion or crashes on city streets. Critics cried, "We're not Amsterdam!" claiming that New York was too New York to support a cycling culture.

Cyclists using the Queens Plaza Greenway.
During the Bloomberg administration,
the city added 470 miles of bike lanes,
including nearly 400 miles in the six years
after the release of PlaNYC.

But most people got the message. Cycling increased, crashes abated, and the streets felt calmer and easier to live, work, and play along. Studies found that the new lanes not only reduced injuries to all street users, but also increased retail sales along their corridors by as much as 49%, challenging the notion that livable streets and car traffic were an either-or proposition. *Bicycling* magazine named New York as the top American city for cycling for the first time and dozens of American cities adopted our designs along with our rapid-implementation tactics. In some cities, residents would protest proposed bike lanes claiming that, "We're not New York."

Creating new public space

In a city where a fire hydrant qualified as public seating, a hot dog stand counted as an outdoor amenity, and a sun-baked expanse of limestone outside a Midtown office building passed for a public plaza, we saw in our streets the footprint of the open space that PlaNYC sought to put within a 10-minute walk of every New Yorker.

To get this done, the New York City Department of Transportation (DOT) launched more than 70 pedestrian spaces across the city built atop former car lanes, starting with a plaza on Pearl Street below the Manhattan Bridge in Brooklyn's historic and artsy DUMBO district. While most plazas would take years of planning and iterative design processes, visualizations and community meetings, we marked the outline of Pearl Street plaza in a triangle of asphalt where a dozen cars used to park over a single weekend. We used only the materials we had on hand: Paint to mark the plaza's borders and formidable granite slabs and heavyweight planters to line the perimeter and keep cars out. We dotted the interior of the new space with tables and chairs that one might find in a world-class piazza — comfortable enough to enjoy sitting at for lunch or a cup of coffee, durable enough to withstand the outdoor elements. The plaza was an immediate sensation, drawing people during lunchtime and also after hours when the neighborhood swelled with nightlife.

We quickly adapted similar designs in the Meatpacking District, where pedestrians often outnumber cars by ten-to-one and at Madison Square, where three busy roads meet and where people were forced to cross an intersection the length of a ball field. Each time, we created public space out of the existing roadway, consolidating and more clearly defining traffic lanes to keep traffic moving safely, but leaving more than enough room for people to sit comfortably and enjoy the pulse of the city.

Even after Dan left City Hall in 2007, we kept the program going. The most famous of the new pedestrian plazas were in Times Square and Herald Square. Using the same toolbox of flexible, temporary materials, we diverted car traffic from Broadway north of Times Square onto Seventh Avenue, which we widened by one lane. This left enough capacity to process Midtown traffic while opening up five massive pedestrian spaces in Broadway's roadbed from 42nd to 47th Streets. Reporters counted down the hours until the project opened, forecasting that closing Broadway would create "carmageddon." But what happened instead is one of the great stories in modern urban design: Hundreds of thousands of people came out to the street, experiencing Times Square in a way that had never before been possible, and using only the street space that was already there. And traffic moved better than it had before, confounding the skeptics.

Above: A dozen parking spaces on Pearl Street in DUMBO were converted into one of the first PlaNYC plazas, creating a welcoming public seating area that became instantly popular.

Opposite: Pearl Street plaza before and after.

Left: Dancing at Herald Square Plaza.

Dan Doctoroff called Department of Transportation Commissioner Janette Sadik-Khan's attention to the launch of the Paris bike-share system just two months after she began her tenure in 2007. Above, Citi Bike riders in Chinatown.

Championing congestion pricing

Within weeks of my fateful interview with Mike and Dan at the big table in the Committee of the Whole (COW) room in City Hall that resulted in my appointment as commissioner, I found myself sitting at that same room at the same table, attending Dan's standing weekly strategy meetings for congestion pricing — every Monday. At 7 a.m.

I was no stranger to City Hall politics, having worked in and around City Hall during the Dinkins administration for many years. But neither then, nor in my time as Deputy Administrator for the Federal Transit Administration, nor with a global engineering firm, had I attended a standing 7 a.m. meeting. It was the mark of a different approach to government and action that we convened in those early morning hours.

Congestion pricing was a way to rationalize traffic management, setting a fee that would balance the different tolls that people paid — or didn't — to drive into the city center during rush hour.

Today, drivers over the region's bridges run by the Metropolitan Transportation Authority (MTA) pay one toll at spans like the Triborough Bridge or the Queens-Midtown Tunnel, while the Port Authority charges tolls to drivers entering Manhattan across its spans like the George Washington Bridge and through the Holland and Lincoln tunnels. But New Yorkers who drive can avoid tolls by using City-owned bridges across the East River, with no charge at all for entering Manhattan below 60th Street from Upper

Manhattan or via the Brooklyn, Manhattan, Williamsburg, and Queensboro bridges. This turns Lower Manhattan into a traffic-free-for-all that people can enter for free while riders pay a toll to cram onto unreliable buses and subways to reach the same destinations. Congestion pricing was a way to charge Peter, driving in his car to work, to pay for expanded and more reliable subways and buses for Pauline, clutching a pole on a crowded subway.

Charging people more for something that they currently pay little or nothing for is political hemlock for most leaders, whether it's tolling or parking. It smacked of social engineering to some, leading some suburban lawmakers to object that a charge was too much for the limited means of some New Yorkers who already had to drive long distances for their commutes. The only thing more challenging than the public communication was the political choreography. Implementing congestion pricing required a political campaign from within. Surmounting the political hurdles required City Council approval and ratification by the State Legislature, two bodies not known for their nimbleness and ability to reach agreement on critical issues. It would require buy-in of agency heads, staffers, legislative aides, and power brokers over a period of months and spanning neighborhood, local, regional, state, and federal agencies and constituencies.

If PlaNYC created a guidebook to chart the city's future, the early morning meetings in the COW were a physical manifestation of that process. Dan set up a face-to-face policy space, where agency heads shared ideas and data, and where they were held to account.

It was a remarkable period of insider and public interaction, political maneuvering, and process management. The congestion pricing campaign marked one of the very few times that all major daily newspapers — including the *New York Daily News* and *New York Post* — supported a major mayoral proposal. The mayor, the City Council, the city's business communities, major institutions, and advocates all stood together behind the proposal to charge cars to enter central Manhattan during peak hours. While Dan and his team did a masterful job navigating the politics, winning key legislative victories in the city, the plan ultimately foundered in Albany, with then-Speaker Sheldon Silver refusing to allow the proposal to advance to a vote in the State Assembly.

Congestion pricing's demise, without even a transparent vote in the Legislature, deprived New York of an opportunity to invest in transit and dial down traffic congestion. But the political and conceptual realignment of PlaNYC and congestion pricing did open the door to a golden age for the city's public realm, even though we are still awaiting the passage of congestion pricing some 10 years later. When it does succeed, Dan will be remembered for helping New York take those difficult first steps.

Reimagining public street furniture
Dan understood that the public sector didn't have all of the answers or expertise needed to be successful. Just as he partnered with outside authorities and advocates, he had a strong hand in leading private-sector partnerships, including a contract with the advertising company, Cemusa, to pay the City $1 billion over 20 years to erect and maintain bus shelters, newsstands, and to build the city's first-ever system of public restrooms.

Dan joined us at the ribbon-cutting for the first toilet, in Madison Square Park. The "ribbon" was actually a long slip of toilet paper, one of numerous scatological allusions that Dan resisted at first. "We're No. 1!" I told the assembled media at the press conference. Parks Commissioner Adrian Benepe said that passersby could use the toilets "in loo of" sneaking into a fast-food restaurant bathroom. Dan couldn't take it anymore, deadpanning the line that the strict siting criteria for public toilets ensured that a toilet's location won't "block pedestrian movement."

Creating the nation's largest bike share
In July 2007, barely two months into my six-and-a-half-year tenure at DOT, I arrived at the office to find an article clipped from the *Financial Times* on my desk.

A note paper-clipped to the article bore a single, handwritten sentence: "What do we think about this?"

The article announced the launch of the Vélib' bike-share system in Paris, which had gone live the day before, bringing 7,000 bikes to city streets for public use. The note was written by Dan Doctoroff.

I thought it was a great idea. But answering Dan's six-word question would become a years-long interagency question of traffic and economic management, land-use and technology, and public policy and community engagement — sparking a volley of questions, research, negotiations, and administration that extended well beyond the 4,500-person agency that I was just starting to reshape.

If New York City's streets were to accommodate a bike share system, its streets would require extensive, safe cycling infrastructure. Creating that infrastructure would require a citywide rethinking of road space, parking policy, and traffic safety. Winning public approval in New York's tabloid culture would require media acumen. Designing the system to achieve the scale and infrastructure to be successful would require political and administrative skill. Achieving it within the remaining two and a half years of what we thought was Mike Bloomberg's final term as mayor would require pure political will.

Drawing on Dan's influence, we reverse-engineered a process and created a contract model that would withstand the city's contradictory political pressures. By classifying the bike share partnership as a revenue contract, the bike share system would remain less vulnerable to politicization in the land-use process. By creating an online portal to crowdsource potential bike share locations, the DOT could identify multiple, community-identified alternate locations, helping ensure that station locations reflected local will and that we also had ample alternatives should one location not work out.

Many locations for new stations to dock thousands of Citi Bikes were sited on former parking spaces, sidewalk space or plazas, helping activate existing but underused space. Two dozen bikes could be docked and undocked in a single hour in the time a car would sit parked unused. By using private funding, we also avoided the criticism that taxpayer money would be used to fund the nascent program (heaven forbid!). And by operating the private contract with strict service requirements, the City could make sure that Citi Bike maintained minimum standards for station density, equity, and safety.

The project faced intense challenges long before the first ride. Critics forecast that the program would lead to increased traffic crashes, injuries, and deaths. They said that bike share stations would impede deliveries, sanitation trucks, and emergency vehicles. Others insinuated that terrorists might somehow use the bikes to plant explosives. Wealthy residents filed lawsuits claiming that the program, which was vetted in hundreds of public meetings in dozens of communities, was conducted in secret. Not all the obstacles were based on fantasy. The system's operating technology was buggy in early tests, requiring technical workarounds, and the historic storm surge caused by Superstorm Sandy in 2012 severely damaged hundreds of bikes and stations stored in a Brooklyn Navy Yard warehouse.

The process culminated in 2013 with the launch of Citi Bike, New York City's first new transportation system in the more than half a century since the MTA took over the city's private bus routes. When Dan wrote his note in 2007, few New Yorkers dared to ride on the city's mean streets. Now, a decade later, there have been more than 178 million Citi Bike trips since the system launched and the public-private system is expanding to 40,000 bikes across all five boroughs, making it one of the world's largest and most successful programs — as integral to the New York streetscape as yellow taxis.

Bike share in 2007 was exactly the kind of big idea that risk-averse civil servants seek to avoid. It was also exactly the kind of civic space that Dan was most interested in managing: identifying an ambitious goal and reverse-engineering the strategies to achieve it, all the way down the idea chain to a set of actionable policies that could be done immediately. Within barely a year, all lawsuits had been dismissed by the courts, the critics faded into the streetscape, and elected officials changed their tunes, demanding that the system expand into more neighborhoods.

Dan returned to the scene as part of the group that set up Motivate, which bought out Citi Bike's original operator. They recruited a new leader and tech team, which righted the system and helped spur the evolution of the entire North American bike share industry from its start-up origins.

A legacy of transformation

Politics is a long game. The bike lanes, pedestrian plazas, and transit projects, controversial and criticized just a few years earlier in the city's newspapers, proved to be extremely popular. In the last months of the Bloomberg administration, a *New York Times* poll found that 73% of New Yorkers supported bike share, 72% supported the plazas and 66% supported bike lanes. New Yorkers loved the changes that just a few years earlier were foreign ideas clipped from a newspaper. Congestion pricing died in 2008 but remains very much alive as New York struggles to rein in congestion and increase funding to maintain, modernize, and expand its buses and subways.

Using the PlaNYC playbook, we published benchmarks to measure our progress: Was DOT reducing harmful greenhouse emissions in its operations? By converting to recycled asphalt and opening a second asphalt plant, DOT avoided sending 174,000 tons of milled asphalt to landfills, eliminating 321,000 truck trips that would have been needed to carry it, and reducing the use of oil in asphalt production by 840,000 barrels. Was DOT maintaining its infrastructure? Yes, by our last year in office, the agency had brought each of its 788 bridges into a state of good repair or had projects underway to rehabilitate them. Was DOT reducing traffic deaths? The number of people killed in car crashes would drop to its lowest level in a century of record keeping, and still lower at locations where we had implemented safety fixes. In addition to creating nearly 400 miles of new bike lanes and 70 new public plazas, by the end of 2013, we calculated that we had created 38 miles of Select Bus Service lanes to improve transit options in every borough.

Most importantly, to me, Dan's greatest legacy from PlaNYC lives on in my work in cities around the world. We've turned parking spaces in Milan and in Bogotá into people places using the same strategies and palette of quick-build materials that built our first plazas in DUMBO, the Meatpacking District, and Times Square.

We created safer, more sustainable streets in Mexico City and in Los Angeles drawing from the same, people-first designs we brought to Main Street in Flushing and The Hub in the Bronx.

We worked with Athens to pedestrianize a commercial district in the city center to spur new storefronts to open, created an extensive network of protected bike paths in Detroit and in Oakland, and helped write visionary strategic plans in Los Angeles, Chicago, and Atlanta, drawing directly from PlaNYC and the projects it inspired.

In almost every city, the most ambitious projects start with a plan, and a statement of imagination. In New York and, by extension, in cities around the world, that plan, and that vision, started with Dan.

As the city's transportation commissioner, Janette Sadik-Khan executed on PlaNYC's transportation vision, creating 70 pedestrian plazas, nearly 400 bike lanes, and 38 miles of new Select Bus Service routes in all five boroughs. Above, a pedestrian plaza, along with dedicated bike and bus lanes along 23rd Street, opposite Madison Square Park.

THE DOCTOROFF DOCTRINE FOR FUNDING TRANSPORTATION

Doctoroff's vision for a sustainable city invested in mass transit to attract growth while lowering carbon emissions and improving quality of life

Michael Bloomberg became the 108th mayor of New York City immediately after the crisis of 9/11. He brought with him a new team to City Hall to confront the extraordinary challenges facing the city and region, especially the rebuilding of Lower Manhattan and the need to restore optimism, confidence, and a feeling of safety to New Yorkers. He turned to Dan Doctoroff for the position of Deputy Mayor for Economic Development and Rebuilding to lead these efforts. To succeed, Doctoroff would have to address a problem that had plagued the city and region for decades: chronic underinvestment in the transit infrastructure that was critical to economic growth.

It hadn't always been that way. In the decades immediately after the creation of greater New York City on New Year's Day in 1898, the rapidly growing metropolis built the largest transit network in the nation. The network included bridges and tunnels that connected automobiles, buses, and trains in Manhattan to Westchester and points north, to Long Island, and across the Hudson River to the mainland, subways that stretched across four of the five boroughs, and rail links that extended across three states. In 1950, the Port Authority of New York and New Jersey constructed a new bus terminal on 42nd Street and later it purchased and maintained the PATH system, preserving transit connections to New Jersey. But as the 1950s progressed, highways became ascendant. During the highway-building era of the 1950s to 1970s, when the region was building over 25 miles of new limited access highway every single year, this majestic system was allowed to sink into disrepair and decline.

In 1968, New York State created the Metropolitan Transportation Authority (MTA) to begin addressing some of the damage; 11 years later, New Jersey founded NJ Transit to begin repairing connections between the states. Through the leadership of MTA chairmen like Richard Ravitch and Robert Kiley, Metro-North and the Long Island Rail Road were able to stabilize their services and the subway system was brought back to a relative state of good repair in the 1980s. But by the end of the century, there still had been no significant expansion of the city or region's transit system for several generations. If New York City's economy was going to grow again, it would need an expanded transit system to support that growth.

In the aftermath of 9/11, planners, business leaders, and civic advocates agreed that the rebuilding of Lower Manhattan would need to address the problems that existed prior to the terrorist attacks — foremost among them the lack of connectivity and capacity. Lower Manhattan was also already in the process of becoming a more complete community, with housing and services. The redevelopment of the World Trade Center site needed to complement this transition, while also memorializing the tragic events of 9/11 and sustaining one of the largest business districts in the nation.

While Lower Manhattan could count on over $20 billion in federal support for rebuilding — funding that could be used to help rebuild the broken PATH system and fix the neighborhood's subways — New York's overall infrastructure needs were much greater and its other resources were much less. Repairs and modest improvements to the subway system had been financed by issuing MTA-backed debt, which was starting to take up an unsustainable portion of the authority's operating budget. More and more of the fares paid by the riding public were being used to pay back the bonds from earlier capital plans, rather than pay for operations or continued expansion. Many groups and planners had identified priority investments that would support future growth, such as a subway extension to Manhattan's Far West Side, a new tunnel under the Hudson River, the Second Avenue subway, and connecting the Long Island Railroad to Grand Central Terminal. In particular, Senator Chuck Schumer had convened a "Group of 35" business and civic leaders the year before the attacks that identified the Far West Side of Manhattan, along with Downtown Brooklyn and Long Island City, as opportunities for future growth and development. But there was no viable funding strategy for the billions of dollars in public investment that would be required.

Over 60 years earlier, Robert Moses had found an innovative way to raise money: building highways and bridges for cars and charging them tolls, then diverting those revenues to new projects instead of retiring the debt. As long as the bonds were never fully repaid, his Triborough Bridge and Tunnel Authority could keep collecting tolls. However, by the 2000s, the bonding capacity for existing tolls had been exhausted. Public authorities such as the MTA and the Port Authority no longer had the political independence to raise tolls in the face of public opposition, and the driving public's pocketbooks had been tested to such a degree that some toll increases turned out to be revenue negative: the higher tolls depressed driving almost as much as they generated additional income.

The "Doctoroff Doctrine"

During his extraordinary term in public service as deputy mayor, Doctoroff developed a theory of beneficial urban growth, which posited that growing cities can sustain a "virtuous cycle" where they invest in vital infrastructure systems — such as housing, parks, and transit — which generates more growth which, in turn, can be used to finance the next cycle of investment. As opposed to Robert Moses' model of investing in highways and bridges exclusively for automobiles, Doctoroff developed a vision for a sustainable city that attracted growth while lowering carbon emissions and improving quality of life.

Mayor Michael Bloomberg celebrates the impending opening of the No. 7 subway line extension to Hudson Yards, December 20, 2013. Dan Doctoroff, who drove the extension and the innovative financing model that enabled it, can be seen standing on the side, having left City Hall six years earlier.

Nowhere did this "Doctoroff Doctrine" have a greater impact than on mass transit, which experienced a rebirth under the Bloomberg administration that continues today. Thanks to Doctoroff, the City began thinking much more creatively about the connections between investment and growth and found new opportunities to merge them.

No. 7 train extension
The first great implementation of the Doctoroff Doctrine was the extension of the No. 7 subway line from Times Square to Hudson Yards. Under Doctoroff's direction, the City had prepared an ambitious plan for redeveloping the area by decking over the rail yards. The plan included rezoning an entire district for new activities and growth; constructing a new boulevard between 10th and 11th Avenues to create better public spaces and marquee addresses; investing in waterfront amenities and parks; and converting the dilapidated High Line into a new, modern elevated parkway system. (It also included a controversial football stadium that would serve as the opening and closing venue for the 2012 Olympics, but the plans had to evolve after rejection from a state board.)

Transit access was the critical piece to make this all happen. Within the extraordinary network of Manhattan subways, the Far West Side was isolated from the city's subway network. Planners had talked for decades about extending subway lines to the neighborhood, but nobody had figured out how to finance such a costly undertaking while there were so many other competing needs for the rest of the city and region. The MTA made it clear they had other priorities for the capital planning process, since a

subway expansion would be serving a population and businesses that, at the time, didn't yet exist. And with so many stalled projects such as East Side Access and the Second Avenue subway, there was little confidence that any extension could be done competently or within a reasonable timeframe.

Doctoroff's team, including the Department of City Planning, the New York City Economic Development Corporation, the Office of Management and Budget, and City Hall, developed a strategy to marry the redevelopment of what Dan named the Hudson Yards district to the expansion of the subway and develop them simultaneously. Rather than advocate for the project to be included in the MTA capital plan or apply for federal funds — which might ultimately become available but would add years of delay and billions in cost to the project — the City led the project itself, issuing the bonds, preparing the plans, and driving the project forward.

The subway extension made the neighborhood attractive for large-scale investment and redevelopment, even before the project was completed. The City became the long-term investor in the district, and is now reaping the benefit of increased revenues which not only pay for the capital costs, but will provide future revenue streams to support public services. It was a great example of the Doctoroff Doctrine in practice.

Congestion pricing
Perhaps an even greater example of this philosophy at work was the Bloomberg administration's support of congestion pricing. Following the plans for the Far West Side and Hudson Yards, Doctoroff and Mayor Bloomberg turned their sights to the entire city, and

questioned what kind of long-term plans New York had in place for housing, commercial development, public services, and the threat of climate change and sea level rise. The answer was: not much.

Planners and historians still debate whether New York should have a comprehensive plan more akin to the London Plan of 2004, which laid out detailed strategies for the city's physical development. The last mayor of New York to attempt to address the issue was John Lindsay in 1969, which became a cautionary tale. Rather than continue to update land-use plans, Doctoroff and Bloomberg decided that the City needed a strategic plan to provide guidance on its land use and public investments, especially in the face of climate change. The result was the historic PlaNYC report published in 2007, which set out to prepare the city for nearly one million more residents by the year 2030, while strengthening the economy, combating climate change, and enhancing quality of life.

PlaNYC included 10 goals and 127 initiatives for a sustainable future addressing land-use, water, transportation, energy, air quality, and climate change. The one idea that stood out above the rest was charging a toll on all drivers into the Manhattan central business district, as London and Stockholm had recently begun doing with great success.

Congestion pricing had been talked about for decades in New York City. Economists, planners, environmentalists, and policy experts all fundamentally agreed that making drivers pay more of the cost that their activities imposed on the rest of society would be a good thing, both reducing traffic congestion in the core of the region and generating revenues to pay for more investments in mass transit. In 1996, the Regional Plan Association made congestion pricing a centerpiece of its *Third Regional Plan* and Columbia University economist, William Vickrey, won the Nobel Prize in part for his work on the concept. But nobody had figured out how to make the political argument that it was worthwhile in the face of enormous opposition from residents who would have to pay the

new charge. Taxes and tolls are never popular, and even residents who rarely drove into Manhattan were assumed to be opposed to a new fee.

The genius of the Doctoroff Doctrine was to put congestion pricing in a new context. No longer was the discussion simply about tolling drivers, but the framework was — appropriately — elevated to consider the future of the entire city in the face of climate change. By making congestion pricing a key component of PlaNYC, Doctoroff changed the perspective and made the logical connection between proposing ambitious plans for transit, parks, and community development and actually coming up with a strategy to pay for them.

There's a story I've heard that during the intense internal discussions, when the final components of PlaNYC were being debated in City Hall, everyone agreed that congestion pricing was the right policy, but nobody had confidence it could be achieved. Instead of shying away from the fight, I've heard that Doctoroff said, "this may not get approved the first time someone tries, but if nobody is willing to try that first time, then it will never happen. Let's do it."

Congestion pricing, not surprisingly, became the flash point of the entire PlaNYC 2030 proposal. Transit, environmental, and business advocates all launched campaigns to support the policy under the banner of the "Campaign for New York's Future," along with Governor Eliot Spitzer, Senate Majority Leader Joseph Bruno, City Council Speaker Christine Quinn, and many others. The New York City Council approved the plan by a vote of 30 to 20, with all the opposition coming from Brooklyn, Queens and Staten Island. But the Democratic caucus of the State Assembly, led by Sheldon Silver, rejected the proposal in a closed-door session and never brought it to a full vote. One could argue that while so much attention was being paid to congestion pricing, a dozen other controversial proposals were able to move ahead precisely because so much

Located within the Hudson Yards rezoning area, the Moynihan Train Hall was able to attract the necessary private contribution to supplement public investment as a result of new development on the Far West Side. As the neighborhood became more desirable, developers contributed hundreds of millions of dollars to help fund the train hall in exchange for the right to lease the office and retail space in the building.

The NYC2012 Olympic X plan envisioned ferrying athletes and spectators to venues up and down the East River. After the bid ended, the City pursued ferries to connect workers and residents to new housing and parks along the river. Above, NYC Ferry now carries nearly 20,000 riders daily.

attention was being focused on one issue. But advocates were furious that such a powerful policy with the potential to improve the city had been rejected in Albany without so much as a vote.

However, the New York State Legislature approved congestion pricing as part of the 2019 budget and today we are in the middle of public hearings and debate about the policy. This time it looks like it will finally come to pass. Everyone involved in the fight knows that without the leadership of Dan Doctoroff and his team, who championed the proposal over 15 years ago, we would never be where we are today.

Bold visions and "sheer chutzpah"

Not every one of Doctoroff's transportation infrastructure ideas came to life, but his relentless pursuit of them illustrates how he married financial sophistication, creativity, and sheer chutzpah to drive them forward. The *Vision for Lower Manhattan* plan Doctoroff developed for Mayor Bloomberg sought to imagine the rebirth not only of the World Trade Center site, but also to accelerate the transformation of the rest of downtown into a vibrant mixed-use district. One key element of the plan was a proposal to create a direct connection from Lower Manhattan to both JFK Airport and Long Island, once again relying on transit infrastructure to drive economic growth.

Working with the city's Washington, D.C. office, Doctoroff developed an extraordinary proposal to "trade" an estimated $2 billion of unused tax credits granted by the federal government to New York, in exchange for an equivalent amount of cash to redeploy to the rail link. The proposal relied not only on a detailed analysis to prove the tax credits had not in fact been used, but also a never-before-used mechanism to convert those tax credits into cash for use by state and local entities. In the wake of repeated trips by Doctoroff and staffers to Washington, the plan received the support of then-President George W. Bush and was included in the president's official budget before ultimately failing at the last minute when a Republican senator from Arizona objected. His

reasoning? The financing plan represented such an innovative use of the tax code to send cash to New York, the senator feared it would open up the floodgates for other states and cities to follow the same approach.

Even in defeat, Doctoroff's creativity was unmatched — and he applied that creativity relentlessly in trying to use investments in transportation to accelerate development. For example, when the City and State released a Request for Proposals for the development of Governors Island in 2006, the release was accompanied by renderings of a Santiago Calatrava-designed gondola connecting the Island to Manhattan. Doctoroff had commissioned the undertaking both to attract attention to the process and to indicate the City's willingness to invest in transportation to make development feasible.

The legacy of Doctoroff's support for funding infrastructure through his beneficial growth theory has been deep and impactful. In the past decade, New York City has opened the downtown PATH terminal, Moynihan Train Hall, a new LaGuardia Airport, and the first phase of the Second Avenue subway. Recently, the Long Island Rail Road began running trains directly to Grand Central Terminal. While these projects used a wide range of funding strategies, they all relied on the argument that Dan Doctoroff so brilliantly articulated during his tenure in City Hall — the beneficial cycle of investment, improvement, growth, and further investment.

The example of Hudson Yards is driving an array of major projects forward, including major improvements to the Long Island Rail Road concourses at Penn Station and the Gateway Program to expand rail service across the Hudson River. Without Dan's vision and example, it is hard to imagine the city would ever have gotten on this positive trajectory. All these improvements can be traced back to his leadership in City Hall, which set a new course for infrastructure investing. New Yorkers will benefit from this legacy for the rest of the century, if not longer.

BOB FORAN | Head of Public Finance, Bear Stearns, 1994-2008 | Chief Financial Officer, Metropolitan Transportation Authority, 2010-2021

FINANCING THE NUMBER 7 TRAIN EXTENSION

In 2000, I was sitting in my office near Grand Central Terminal, working as a municipal finance banker at Bear Stearns. My primary job was to help governmental entities borrow money from investors at the lowest possible cost in order to pay for critical investments in infrastructure, schools, housing, and more. The government would then promise to repay those bonds using its tax revenues. When the phone rang in my office, it was often an official in the budget office of an entity such as the State or the City of New York or the Metropolitan Transportation Authority (MTA), calling to talk about one of their projects that needed financing.

But on that day, I took a call unlike any I had ever received.

The caller was a man named Dan Doctoroff, and he identified himself as the founder of NYC2012, the bid for New York City to host the 2012 Summer Olympic Games. He told me that he was working on a plan to finance an extension of the No. 7 subway to an underdeveloped area on the West Side, owned by the MTA and used as a rail yard for the Long Island Rail Road. He called the district Hudson Yards, and wanted to use it to accommodate both an Olympic Stadium and a much larger mixed-use neighborhood surrounding it. He knew that I served as a close advisor to the MTA and wanted my advice — specifically on how to pay for an extension of the No. 7 subway line from Times Square along 41st Street and then down 11th Avenue to a new station at 34th Street. The extension of the No. 7 subway and ancillary investments in the surrounding areas were projected to require more than $2 billion in new investment.

It wasn't common to receive a call from a private citizen trying to figure out how to pay for a public project. In fact, I'm confident this was the only such call I had received in my 18 years in municipal finance banking. And the obvious approach from the perspective of my business was to get off the phone as quickly as possible. After all, private citizens have no ability whatsoever to implement ideas such as the one Dan was describing. Given my long-standing relationship with the MTA, I certainly did not want to give them the impression of going behind their backs on something potentially so significant. But Dan's vision was intriguing, and after discussing his idea with the MTA, I agreed to meet with him. The very next day I found myself sitting with Dan in his Park Avenue office along with his advisor, Jay Kriegel, a former chief of staff to Mayor John Lindsay.

Our conversation began with generalities, but soon turned to the challenges of financing this particular project. On its face, the obvious way to pay for a subway extension should have been the resources available to the MTA — including rider fares and tax revenues. Unfortunately, this project faced two seemingly insurmountable obstacles. The first was the reality that the MTA hadn't funded or built an extension of the subway system in decades. The second was the fact that the Speaker of the State Assembly had made it clear that no state funding would be available, for fear that it would compete with the Second Avenue subway extension, his priority project. As a public entity relying on significant funding from the State, the Speaker's position could not be ignored. Also, the

MTA prioritized the continued restoration of the system to a state of good repair and relief of congestion on existing subway lines, over a project such as the No. 7 line extension, the purpose of which was primarily economic development.

Our conversation quickly turned to a specific idea that Dan wanted to discuss. As a knowledgeable financier (and perhaps from his time earning his law degree at the University of Chicago), Dan was aware of a technique used extensively in Chicago called "tax increment financing" (or "TIF"). The concept is that *existing* property taxes/assessments in a defined geographic area continue to flow to the municipality's general fund at the then-current level, and any *increase* in future revenues are used to finance new infrastructure investments through the issuance of new bonds, secured only by the incremental revenue with no recourse to the municipality's other funds. In other words, the new investments are funded by the incremental value that they are anticipated to create: If the new investments do not generate incremental revenues, the bonds default. In effect, the bond investors bear the risk of the project's success, sparing public finances from the risk of failure.

Given my experience advising the MTA and financing a number of large, complicated, and protracted projects in New York and around the nation, Dan asked me to consider the feasibility of a TIF for Hudson Yards and the No. 7 line extension. As I considered Dan's request, a few thoughts came immediately to mind. On its face, the idea made perfect sense in that I considered it likely that the introduction of transportation to a woefully underdeveloped area adjacent to Midtown Manhattan would unlock enormous new revenues to the public sector.

But there were also several significant obstacles. First, while TIFs had been used extensively in Chicago and elsewhere, the tool had never before been used in New York. In fact, at the moment I wasn't even sure the tool would be legal in the state. Second, at more than $2 billion, this financing would be far, far larger than the typical TIF, which was measured in the tens of millions of dollars. In fact, this would be by far the largest TIF in U.S. history. Lastly, it wasn't at all clear how Dan, this lone individual sitting in his office on Park Avenue, could possibly make real progress on this idea.

But somehow, I just couldn't say no. I was impressed with Dan's vision and enthusiasm for not only the NYC2012 proposal, but also for his understanding of the long-term impact of these investments on the city, the state, and the region. With Bear Stearns' support, I was able to offer Dan a *pro bono* study of the feasibility of this approach.

Throughout 2000 and 2001, I participated in numerous 6 a.m. meetings with Dan and others at his townhouse. It was unlike any process I had ever been a part of in my career: A private citizen convening a close group of unpaid advisors in an otherwise dark home, his children asleep upstairs, trying to advance a creative financing of new public infrastructure. Over the 28 years I spent in public finance investment banking, I have never seen such an ongoing display of energy and commitment as Dan evidenced.

Dan Doctoroff began developing a financing model for the No. 7 train extension in 2000 as a private citizen, when he was leading New York's Olympic bid.
He enlisted Bob Foran, head of public finance at Bear Stearns, to help craft a feasible plan, which Doctoroff executed upon once he entered City Hall as deputy mayor.

As we studied the details and modeled and reviewed myriad scenarios, I became convinced that, while such an approach would not be easy and would definitely be more expensive than a traditional government-backed financing, it was indeed feasible because of the enormous economic potential of the Hudson Yards area. Working together, we developed a preliminary financing plan.

Once we had a plan, we started presenting it in innumerable meetings with public officials and private influencers. We typically received a positive response, but we still faced the same obstacle we had faced from the start: With no governmental authority, Dan's ability to put this plan into action faced the steepest of uphill climbs.

All of that changed with Dan's 2002 appointment as Deputy Mayor for Economic Development and Rebuilding under Mayor Michael Bloomberg. With a credible preliminary financing plan, Dan was able to direct and guide city agencies such as the Department of City Planning and the Office of Management and Budget, and banks such as Bear Stearns and others to refine the proposal. Now with the credibility of the City behind him, Dan was able to get the MTA on board with the idea of the City writing a check to the MTA to cover the full cost of a subway extension.

In December 2006, a newly created municipal entity called the Hudson Yards Infrastructure Corporation (HYIC) issued $2 billion of 40-year bonds secured only by revenues to be generated by new development in the area (and with the City agreeing to pay only any interest shortfall on the bonds until those incremental revenues were sufficient to cover the full debt service payments). The interest rate was well below what I initially thought we would have to pay investors to assume this risk, thanks to the City's initial funding of interest payments but more importantly to the compelling vision that the City and its bankers presented to investors.

Now, more than two decades after that cold call from Dan, it's amazing to reflect on the unalloyed success of the undertaking we began together in his office, and continued at those early morning meetings in his home. While ultimately New York was not selected to host the 2012 Olympics, the effort sparked a meaningful redevelopment of the Far West Side that continues to this day.

The extension of the No. 7 line and the creation of new open space in the area has catalyzed the construction of some 34 million square feet of development, according to former city officials. That the HYIC has been able to issue more than $3 billion of bonds, outstanding bonds of which continue to trade at reasonable market levels, show that investors are confident that they will be repaid. Although the City had to cover interest payments for the first few years, since then the HYIC has repaid those funds and made additional payments to the general fund of nearly $700 million. The MTA got its first new subway extension in nearly half a century at no cost to itself and, thanks to the City's investment in the area, was able to sell its own air rights for more than $1 billion — funds dedicated to new MTA capital investments system-wide. As chief financial officer of the MTA from 2010 to 2021, I saw the transformative impact of these investments.

As impossible as it is for me to believe that all of these impacts emerged from that one phone call from Dan, it's even more impossible for me to believe that these results could have been achieved without Dan's energy and leadership. Working with Dan on this project was a privilege and pleasure and I consider having the opportunity to participate to be a highlight of my 40-year career in banking and government service.

TYLER DUVALL | Under Secretary (Acting), 2008-2009 & Assistant Secretary for Transportation Policy, 2005-2009, U.S. Department of Transportation

THE FIGHT FOR CONGESTION PRICING

As the New York region once again debates congestion pricing, the city's former deputy mayor, Dan Doctoroff, was on the case more than 15 years earlier.

In 2007, New York City had one of the most congested and poorly performing urban road systems in the world (and it remains so to this day). Of all large counties in the United States, 13 out of the 25 longest commutes were in the New York region — and the four worst counties were Queens, Staten Island, the Bronx, and Brooklyn. One study estimated that congestion cost New York $13 billion every year. The gridlock also had climate costs: the City estimated that 20% of New York's greenhouse gas emissions came from cars and trucks.

Things were about to get worse. In its sustainability blueprint, PlaNYC, New York projected that by 2030, the city would gain 900,000 residents, 20 million annual visitors, and 750,000 more jobs. Without significant interventions, the resulting congestion would extend rush hour conditions to 12 hours per day.

New York was by far the most extreme case. But when I worked as Assistant Secretary of Transportation Policy under President George W. Bush, we saw transportation meltdowns happening in metropolitan areas across the United States.

We decided we needed much bolder national action to support state and local leaders that were willing to exercise strong leadership and courage to tackle the problem of roadway supply and demand imbalance (aka "congestion") much more systematically.

We rolled out a controversial national program at the end of 2006 that we called the "Urban Partnership Program" that combined multiple federal programs for transit, roads, and even ferries with a more singular policy objective — fighting gridlock at a structural, not project level. That meant promoting an idea that had been successfully implemented in Europe, but had yet to migrate to the United States: congestion pricing.

Congestion pricing is focused on addressing a problem with a very basic cause: When people drive more cars, buses, and trucks into crowded central business districts than the roadway capacity can accommodate, it results in gridlock. In addition to the massive costs of delays from people who can't get to their jobs, goods that can't be delivered on time, and missed social and family events, it also imposes enormous environmental, health, and development impacts.

Congestion pricing, which had been successfully implemented in London, Stockholm, and Singapore, levies a small fee on drivers who take cars into the most crowded places in a city at the most crowded times. This can significantly improve traffic flows and safety while also reducing the other societal costs referenced. The revenue generated from the fee can be reinvested in a wide range of transportation solutions, including improving the performance of public transportation.

We believed the moment for congestion pricing had come in the United States. There was a consensus among academics and urban planners on the left and right in favor of the idea, and the technology

By 2007, when the Bloomberg administration began pushing for congestion pricing, one study estimated that congestion cost New York $13 billion every year, while the City estimated that 20% of New York's greenhouse gas emissions came from cars and trucks. Below, traffic congestion on Canal Street at Broadway, 2013.

to facilitate smooth implementation was finally widely available. Above all, successful programs in other countries and on specific roadways in the U.S. had proven the technology in the real world.

We used to say congestion is the easiest public policy problem to solve, but generating the political will to do it is the hardest. We needed a politician or a set of politicians willing to take the risk. So far, no one had stepped forward even though congestion pricing was not a new idea. In 1954, an economist won the Nobel Prize writing about the concept. But 50 years later, no city in America had done it.

We determined that the federal government was uniquely positioned to support state and local leaders brave enough to test the idea, by providing funding, regulatory approvals, research, support, and a bully pulpit to promote the program.

We decided to use our discretionary funding power to award $1.1 billion to three or four cities with the most ambitious plans. Allocating that much money to so few cities was unprecedented and controversial — even within our department. "Spread the peanut butter" had been the operating policy for years. But we insisted — and prevailed — by arguing that these cities would be taking extraordinary risks — and we should, too.

We had our eyes on three cities with dense downtowns, where congestion pricing could have citywide effects: New York, Seattle, and San Francisco.

When we received initial expressions of interest, New York's proposal, led by Dan, was by far the boldest and most developed. We quickly determined that New York should receive the largest award. We proposed awarding New York nearly a third of the entire budget — $354 million. This received pushback from some of my colleagues, who asked, "Why do we need to help New York?"

New York deserves it, we always said, because they are taking the most chances to get something done. In fact, we used New York's proposal to prod other cities. "They've got the courage," we said to other applicants, "Where's yours?"

New York created a hybrid of Stockholm — where you are charged for crossing the line — and London, where you are charged for moving within the zone. PlaNYC proposed a pilot

program for three years: Passenger vehicles entering or leaving Manhattan below 86th Street on weekdays between 6 a.m. and 6 p.m. would pay $8 a day, while trucks would pay $21, with exceptions for emergency vehicles, cars with handicapped plates, taxis, and other for-hire vehicles. Vehicles circulating exclusively within the zone would pay half price. The system would be run with well-established *E-ZPass* technology. The revenues would exclusively feed back into the transportation network to fund transit improvements.

But the truth is that it wasn't simply the plan that set New York apart — it was the team. The city's transportation commissioner, Janette Sadik-Khan, was an expert and a believer. She dug into the details of implementation with us and used her indefatigable energy to champion the plan. I've never met a politician more impervious to public opinion than Mayor Michael Bloomberg — once he was convinced of the merits, he publicly supported the plan regardless of any political pushback. He would become the most prominent American mayor on the issue.

But Dan was the connector pulling it all together. Dan understood the role congestion pricing played in the success of the entire city — a public policy solution that accomplished multiple objectives simultaneously, including efficiency, sustainability, and support for badly needed transit expansions. Dan understood well the relationship between transportation, economic growth, and a vibrant city. He contextualized congestion pricing as the key to building a city that was healthier to live in, more prosperous, and easier to navigate — which in turn would improve quality of life, fight climate change, and support sustainable growth.

I always viewed Dan as the cartilage holding everything together. Dan is an increasingly rare figure in public life, who can translate subject matter expertise into practical policies. Together, New York presented an extraordinarily unique team, where exceptional expertise (Janette), unprecedented political courage (Mayor Bloomberg), and visionary thinking and formidable will power (Dan), combined in one crew.

Still, neither side could quite believe the other's commitment. In our first meeting, we continually asked New York: Are you really going to do this? And they asked back: Are you really going to give us all this money? Yes, we assured each other. We will.

Congestion Pricing Proposal Races Ahead

BY RAY RIVERA
THE NEW YORK TIMES — JUNE 7, 2007

[U.S. Transportation Secretary Mary] Peters heaped lavish praise on the mayor's plan, calling it brave, bold and long overdue.

Ray Rivera, "Congestion Pricing Proposal Races Ahead,"
The New York Times, June 7, 2007

"It cannot be easy for a politician to propose charging commuters more money to enter Manhattan, but the mayor's plan is sound, and the mayor's plan will work," Ms. Peters said."

Ray Rivera, "Congestion Pricing Proposal Races Ahead," *The New York Times*, June 7, 2007

Mayor Michael Bloomberg, Deputy Mayor Dan Doctoroff, and Founding Director of the Mayor's Office of Long-Term Planning and Sustainability Rohit T. Aggarwala testify in front of a State Senate committee on congestion pricing, June, 2007. New York was the first U.S. city to propose a congestion pricing plan.

I believed this was our shot to change transportation in the United States forever. Everyone at the U.S. Department of Transportation, including Secretary Mary E. Peters, also understood the stakes: If we tried, and it didn't work because of poor structure or implementation, it would doom congestion pricing in America, possibly for decades.

That's why our confidence in New York's plan and team was so critical. Unfortunately, the real problem was yet to fully reveal itself: the New York State Legislature. Despite an extraordinary alliance of New York's civic and political leadership, including the business community, transit activists, environmental justice groups, politicians across the spectrum and across the state, and more, the plan died in the New York State Assembly without even a vote.

If you've ever been to Los Angeles or Atlanta, the $354 million we intended to allocate to New York funded projects in those cities instead, which explored successful single-roadway congestion

pricing pilots. Today, New York's congestion remains among the worst in the nation, costing the city billions of dollars and contributing to climate change.

Still, although we didn't get congestion pricing over the line in 2008, through the leadership and courage of Dan and others in the region, we changed the national transportation policy conversation forever.

By connecting congestion pricing to the health of the city in 2007, Dan helped forge a framework we all use today. When congestion pricing finally is implemented in New York, experience in other cities suggests a permanent and sustained improvement in transportation outcomes. Many won't know or remember the pivotal role of PlaNYC and Dan Doctoroff. And as we zip through Midtown, even those of us who do remember won't have time to think about it.

JUSTIN GINSBURGH | General Manager, Citi Bike, 2013-2014 | Vice President of Business Development, Motivate (Citi Bike Parent), 2014-2017

SAVING CITI BIKE

It was spring 2014, and I was working as the first General Manager of Citi Bike. One year after launch, our ridership numbers were impressive, with 105,000 members and up to 40,000 rides per day, nearly three times the number of rides per bike than any other system in the United States. The zeitgeist in New York went from: "Don't take my parking space" to "When is my neighborhood getting Citi Bike?"

The demand was clearly there, but the company had been plagued by a series of mishaps from the start that was causing us to hemorrhage money. Superstorm Sandy destroyed our warehouse and most of our initial equipment, forcing us to delay the launch by three months — and with 1,000 fewer bikes than we had planned.

Our software and hardware (which was provided by the same company) barely functioned — there was no way to track bikes and the bike docks were unreliable. As a result, around 1,000 bikes were stolen within the first couple months of opening. When we stopped paying software fees in protest, the company refused to supply spare parts for our continually breaking stations and bikes.

The contract, agreed to by the company's inexperienced and undercapitalized Portland-based owners, tied our hands from implementing important fixes to pricing and operations, like allowing single-use rides to capture more users.

After reviewing our cash flow with my controller that spring, it was clear we would go bankrupt by the fall.

I started reaching out to potential investors to save the company. Many were curious about the opportunity, but as they learned about the flawed contract, buggy software, and our supplier problems, they smelled a dog. The Portland owners were ready to declare bankruptcy and shut the program down. But then came Dan Doctoroff, formerly the city's deputy mayor.

I knew Dan from early in my career at the New York City Economic Development Corporation. One of his qualities is eternal optimism.

Dan's son, Jacob was working for us at Citi Bike. Through Jacob, Dan learned about our financial situation and my flailing efforts to raise money. With a passion for biking and an early role in supporting the city's Transportation Commissioner, Janette Sadik-Khan to pursue bike share, Dan was a true believer and knew that the model could work if we properly capitalized the business and had the right ownership team in place.

Dan invested considerable time with potential investors and the Citi Bike leadership team to build a business plan that reflected the program's potential. He approached Jeff Blau at Related Companies and Harvey Spevak at Equinox — two people who had rejected my initial pitch as too risky. Dan was able to communicate

a road to profitability and a bold vision of Citi Bike as an equitable, ubiquitous, and indispensable form of sustainable, low-cost transit that would ultimately operate at four times the size of the system's then-6,000 bikes.

Once Jeff and Harvey were on board with buying the company, Dan also decided to invest, but his true value was knowing how to get a complex, public-private partnership deal done in the no-holds barred environment of New York City. Beyond convincing the Portland owners to sell, this bold endeavor would require earning the confidence of former deputy mayor, Ed Skyler at Citibank, Deputy Mayor Alicia Glen at City Hall, our lenders at Goldman Sachs, and the broader team at Related Companies who would become part owners. Only Dan had the ability to get everyone to the table and craft a deal with the necessary compromise (and attendant pain) from all parties, to put the company on the path to growth.

Dan then helped recruit Jay Walder, the former Metropolitan Transportation Authority chairman, as CEO, to turn the company around. Under the new ownership and leadership team, Citi Bike thrived, growing from 6,000 bikes to 12,000 in three years and increasing membership by nearly 50%. As an active board member, investor, and advisor, Dan continued to steer the company through its expansion into challenging and complex public-private partnerships. He understood the critical role of shared mobility and alternative transportation in building sustainable cities. Today, there are more than 20,000 bikes in the system.

I firmly believe that without Dan, Citi Bike would have collapsed and would not be here today. There were clear indications from the de Blasio administration that they would let the program end rather than provide additional public support.

Dan's role in saving Citi Bike was never publicized, making it one of his lesser known accomplishments. But I think it is one of his biggest. My daily life, and the lives of the other 100,000 New Yorkers who use Citi Bike each day, are immensely better for it.

THE BILLION DOLLAR BUS STOP SHELTER

I'm sure that Dan Doctoroff never thought that something as mundane as a bus stop shelter could have any material impact on New York City when he became Deputy Mayor of Economic Development and Rebuilding. Before I worked for the City, I certainly did not.

But with tens of millions of residents, commuters, and tourists passing through the city each year, Dan understood that New York had an opportunity to take advantage of its world-famous status to generate more revenue for the city — and that it needed to present a more polished public image.

I had first met Dan when he was a private citizen, pitching his vision for the Olympics in New York and I was overseeing another global powerhouse, the New York Yankees. When I interviewed for the role of the city's first chief marketing officer and Dan outlined his grand vision for capitalizing on the global power of New York's brand, I got the same feeling: anything was possible. Dan believed there was tremendous untapped value in the City's inventory of outdoor media, particularly with what is commonly called "street furniture." He urged me to take a look.

There are 3,500 bus stop shelters and 600 newsstands in the five boroughs, making New York's street furniture franchise the largest in the country and among the biggest in the world. Each shelter has two billboard advertisements and each newsstand has three. Private outdoor billboard companies competed to win the contract to manage the shelters on behalf of the City. They maintained the shelters and the newsstands, sold the ad space,

and shared the revenue with taxpayers. In 2003, New York earned $13 million from street furniture ads. Working with Dan and my team, we estimated that their real value was probably double or triple that.

It wasn't just the money. The dilapidated shelters and graffiti-laden newsstands were an eyesore, cluttering the public realm of one of the world's great cities. Dan's global travels as part of the Olympic bid drove home to him just how much these outdated structures impacted New York's streets and sidewalks — and therefore the experience and impressions of visitors.

Among government insiders, the street furniture franchise had an unsavory reputation. I learned that previous administrations had avoided tackling the problem because it was too difficult of an issue: too big, too complex, and had historically been marked by corrupt deals that no one wanted to touch. In his book, *Greater than Ever*, Dan reports that a former city official told him of an effort to replace the shelters and newsstands . . . in 1979. As Dan wrote, "It was so hard because the stakes were so large."

But Dan and Mayor Michael Bloomberg were not deterred. When the contract to manage this vast media empire came due, Dan initiated a new bidding process to re-shape how our streets look, generate revenue, and promote the city.

The selection was a grand undertaking. Global firms hired world-famous architects who created unique designs offering both aesthetic and functional improvements. Rather than mere

As deputy mayor, Dan Doctoroff led the effort to redesign and negotiate a new contract for bus shelters and newsstands to generate more revenue and better reflect the emphasis of the Bloomberg administration on the quality of the public realm. The contract was projected to generate $1 billion in new revenue over 25 years.

prototypes, they built actual structures to illustrate how their proposals would look on sidewalks.

The fear of a leak that could threaten the integrity of the bidding was so intense that the members of the selection committee (of which I was one) had to maintain all franchise-related documents in separate, locked file cabinets. Only we had the key in order to maintain secrecy. Despite the bureaucracy, Dan was clearheaded and stuck to the mission. His persistence inspired me and others on the committee to ensure we held the process to the highest standards.

The result was an unprecedented deal for an American city. Cemusa, the winning firm from Spain, paid for all of the construction, installation, and maintenance costs for thousands of bus stop shelters and hundreds of newsstands. Revenue to the City from the franchise nearly quadrupled (exceeding even our own ambitious forecasts), and the franchisee agreed to provide us with 20% of the ad inventory to promote public services, and an additional $15 million per year of global ad inventory to drive tourism. Overall, we estimated the deal would generate over $1 billion for the City in the first 25 years alone.

Dan and I were thrilled. This landmark deal achieved our goal of cleaning up the streets with modern structures befitting a

premiere global city and generating much-needed funds to pay for promoting New York.

This agreement helped fund the efforts of NYC Marketing, which I modeled on a kind of league office, inspired by the great sports leagues like the National Football League and the National Basketball Association, to protect the value of New York City trademarks, like NYPD and FDNY. Within three years, we had deals and licensing agreements totaling $100 million, which we used to support causes for over 35 different agencies including the Parks Department, the Landmarks Preservation Commission, the Mayor's Office of Film, Theatre & Broadcasting, the Department of Transportation, and others.

Revenues from our new street furniture franchise also helped fund efforts to restore landmarks and support Little League baseball, while the ad space promoted high-profile events and locally filmed productions, attracting new business to New York. All of this contributed to a multiagency effort that enabled the city to reach the goal Dan and the mayor articulated of "50 by 15": 50 million visitors by 2015 (a goal the city reached four years early, in 2011).

Working with Dan was one of the highlights of my career. He always expected and inspired the best from you. My team and I worked so hard because we loved New York — but mostly because we loved Dan.

Brooklyn Bridge Park.

"We have embarked on the most ambitious waterfront reclamation effort in our city's history. And it's not just on water that we are adding to parkland across the city."

DANIEL L. DOCTOROFF, NOVEMBER 2003

Pilates class, Pier 1, Brooklyn Bridge Park.

ADRIAN BENEPE | Commissioner, Department of Parks & Recreation, 2002-2012

NEW YORK'S NEW GOLDEN AGE FOR PARKS

Doctoroff and the Bloomberg administration ushered in the third great age of New York City's parks system

Early in the Bloomberg administration, I was invited to participate in a monthly series of meetings with something called the "Economic Development Agencies Council" or "EDAC" as it came quickly to be known. These meetings were convened by Deputy Mayor for Economic Development and Rebuilding Dan Doctoroff and his staff, and the participants included the commissioners of about 40 city agencies and mayoral offices. Most of the participating agencies reported to Dan, but some, including the Parks Department, reported to others such as First Deputy Mayor Patti Harris. I didn't know at the time that these meetings would be a key element of the largest and most creative expansion and rebuilding of the New York City park and open space system since the 1930s, when the Works Progress Administration (WPA) and then-Parks Commissioner Robert Moses oversaw a "Golden Age" of park expansion.

By the time the Bloomberg administration left office in 2013, it had created or set in motion plans for more than 3,000 acres of new or refurbished parks, converted 229 barren schoolyards into green community playgrounds, upgraded or created world-class athletic facilities, and built hundreds of acres of waterfront parks and greenways.

This historic addition of new and renovated parks was fueled by an investment of over $6 billion over 12 years. And many of those achievements — including now world-famous parks such as the High Line, Brooklyn Bridge Park, and Governors Island, along with hundreds of neighborhood and regional parks, playgrounds, and sports fields in all five boroughs — were driven or substantially assisted by Dan, who technically had no formal role in the Parks Department, but who deeply understood the multiple benefits that parks bring to people, neighborhoods, and the current and future financial viability and livability of New York City.

Left: The Water Lab at Pier 6, Brooklyn Bridge Park. The Bloomberg administration prioritized transforming industrial waterfront sites into stunning new parks and public spaces, including Brooklyn Bridge Park.

Opposite: Dan Doctoroff's Olympic plan located the Olympic Village in a new development at Hunter's Point South in Queens. Today, the site hosts housing and an award-winning park.

The Granite Prospect at Brooklyn Bridge Park, built from more than 300 pieces of granite stones salvaged from the Roosevelt Island Bridge reconstruction, leads to the waterfront.

An innovative administration

It is the kind of story that might only have been possible in the Bloomberg administration, which was among the most innovative mayoral administrations in New York City history, and perhaps one of the most inventive mayoral administrations in any American city. One of its hallmarks was collaboration. In the very first week, the commissioners and deputy mayors were summoned by Mayor Bloomberg to a meeting in the room called "Committee of the Whole," known colloquially as, "the COW."

Using the COW for large meetings was part of an overall reimagining of City Hall as a place where everyone worked in one room. The first floor was reconceived by Mayor Bloomberg as "The Bullpen" where everyone, including the mayor, the deputy mayors, and everyone from senior advisors to administrative assistants all worked in an open-plan office, with no one having a bigger work space than anyone else.

At this initial meeting, with workers still laboring a few blocks away to clear the horrific pile of debris at Ground Zero, the site of the World Trade Center attacks that threatened the city's current and future prospects, Mayor Bloomberg laid out the ground rules of his incoming administration. A principal commandment was, "you must work together," and from that flowed others, such as "creative collaboration," which would be a linchpin of the Bloomberg era. All the deputy mayors hewed to that credo, including Patti, who oversaw the "fun" agencies such as Parks & Recreation and Cultural Affairs.

This spirit of collaboration also produced the essential ingredient in the secret sauce of the Bloomberg administration: the combination of longtime city government apparatchiks (like me and Sanitation Commissioner John J. Doherty, who together had a combined 81 years of government service) with technocrats and others from the private sector whose backgrounds had been exclusively or principally corporate or nonprofit/academic/advocacy. That combination of diverse backgrounds and expertise yielded an extraordinary series of inventive and historic projects and programs that would define New York City for generations.

Parks and the 9/11 rebuilding effort

The EDAC meetings brought all of these diverse perspectives together. The purpose, it appeared to me, was for agencies formally charged with economic development and rebuilding responsibilities to interface with other agencies who might play key roles in many of the projects and programs that would be essential to recovery from the physical and financial tolls of 9/11.

Those "other" agencies included Parks & Recreation, Transportation, Environmental Protection, and Cultural Affairs, based on Dan's understanding that creative, holistic collaborations could enable much greater accomplishments than individual silos. I think he also realized that there was a lot of what I called, "Other People's Money" — funding streams that could be used or augmented and combined with funding streams under his control to make more imaginative projects possible.

Dan also was inspired by a sense of urgency in the "rebuilding" part of his portfolio. He knew there were federal recovery funds available and that while rebuilding the World Trade Center (WTC) might take a decade or more, immediate wins were needed to give New Yorkers — especially those who lived and worked in the Financial District and Lower Manhattan — hope that the area and the city would not only survive the horrific blows of 9/11, but might someday thrive again. Dan understood that it would take "all hands on deck" to show these immediate, tangible signs of progress, while also accomplishing the huge long-term task of rebuilding and recovery.

That meant using $25 million of the WTC recovery funds to quickly build new and restored parks in Lower Manhattan. Park construction and design could proceed much faster than the vastly more complicated, expensive, and time-consuming buildings and transportation facilities needed for a complete recovery. In some ways, the initial burst of activity to revive New York, funded by the federal government, was a reprise of the WPA in the 1930s, meant to jumpstart a recovery of the nation from the ravages of the Great Depression.

In addition to the sense of urgency fueling these projects, Dan had larger visions. They sprung from his innate understanding of the value of clean, safe, parks to the success of New York and all its neighborhoods, which is why his quest to bring the 2012 Olympics to New York was framed around a comprehensive transportation and open space/recreational resource master plan. They were further informed by his own experiences as a resident and parent in the city. Dan spent his days riding his bicycle, taking his children to parks for fun and sports, and he chose to live sandwiched between two of the grandest parks in United States history — Riverside Park and Central Park. These were two of the masterworks of Frederick Law Olmsted and Calvert Vaux, who led the city's first "Golden Age" of parks development (of course, Central Park and Riverside Park also boast WPA overlays from Moses and his designers).

A waterfront transformation

The collaboration ethos of the Bloomberg administration as evinced in the EDAC meetings extended not only across the panoply of city agencies and offices, but also extended outward to other levels of government (state and federal) and to nonprofit and private sector partnerships. The reach was all across the city, from the South Shore of Staten Island and Far Rockaway to Van Cortlandt Park in the northern Bronx. It was particularly focused on the waterfront, where Dan understood the potential and urgency of transforming the blight of the collapsing, disused, and abandoned maritime and industrial infrastructure into waterfront parks and greenways.

I would argue that the completion of the long-planned and desired Hudson River Greenway and its adjacent parks was the most significant change to Manhattan in 70 years. The Moses *West Side Improvement* plan included the massive extension of Riverside Park and the building of the Henry Hudson Parkway, which covered waterfront railroad tracks with a huge "box" layered with trees, grass, esplanades, and waterfront ballfields and playgrounds. For all his many achievements, however, Moses failed to connect the south end of Manhattan with the north end. He could not have fully anticipated how quickly the piers full of ocean liners would become redundant and fall into ruin — creating the potential for what would later become Hudson River Park.

Dan directed his agencies and colleagues to fast-track the completion of Hudson River Park (started under earlier leaders, including Mayor Rudy Giuliani and Governor George Pataki), which was key to completing a seamless edge of parks and a greenway along the Hudson. But he also stepped in personally when a key missing greenway link needed to be filled. The Parks Department had a plan to build a connector uptown known as "River Walk" — a vital half-

mile stretch linking the WPA-era waterfront that terminated at 83rd Street with a similar path that began at 91st Street. The lane needed to be built on a free-standing pier structure in the river, which, though a scant half-mile, would be extremely costly — at least $17 million. I mentioned our opportunity and the huge shortfall to Dan (knowing he was a cyclist and would understand the enormous importance of this key connection), and in a matter of days the money was in our budget.

That expedited waterfront improvement was a microcosm for the work that Dan and the administration would go on to do by way of eliminating and transforming the industrial barriers that had walled off New Yorkers from their waterfront for more than a century. Working with City Planning, the Economic Development Corporation

(EDC), Parks, Transportation and many other agencies, and often using the city's Waterfront Zoning text to compel developers to create waterfront parks in front of their residential buildings, Dan led the transformation of the waterfront from ruins to beautiful, useful recreational amenities.

The waterfront projects, many of them fully fledged parks, included not just the completion of ongoing or planned efforts such as Hudson River, Brooklyn Bridge, and West Harlem Piers Park, but boldly imaginative new landscapes including Hunter's Point South in Queens, the reimagining of Governors Island as a massive new destination park, the East River Waterfront Esplanade from the Battery to South Street, Bushwick Inlet Park in Brooklyn, and the creation of a series of new parks completely funded for both construction and

perpetual maintenance by developers of residential housing along the Greenpoint–Williamsburg and western Queens waterfronts.

A spirit of "adaptive reuse"

One of the commissioners who reported to Dan was my colleague Amanda Burden, Chair of the City Planning Commission. We worked together on many of these projects, especially those that involved rezoning and collaboration with developers. No project was more dynamic than the reimagining of the rusting hulk of the High Line into one of the world's most admired and replicated parks. Progress on the High Line was reported both in ongoing multiagency meetings and also in EDAC, and Amanda and I worked with the designers, advocates/leaders Robert Hammond and Joshua David, and EDC, which took on the complex construction.

Dan Doctoroff and Olympic planners identified Bushwick Inlet, an abandoned waterfront site, as a potential location for Olympic swimming competitions. Despite losing the bid, the City moved ahead with plans to convert the site into a park as part of a broader reclamation of the Brooklyn waterfront.

The spirit of "adaptive reuse" of postindustrial architecture and landscape extended on a massive scale to the transformation of the world's largest garbage dump (Fresh Kills landfill) into what will ultimately become the city's second-largest park at more than 2,000 acres.

That spirit also infused the restoration and reopening of the historic but long-shuttered High Bridge, originally built in the 1840s as an aqueduct to bring fresh water to the city. That project, spearheaded by Dan's colleague, Patti Harris and included in Dan's visionary sustainability blueprint, PlaNYC, now connects the Highbridge neighborhood of the South Bronx to the Washington Heights neighborhood and Highbridge Park in Manhattan, adding a key bike and pedestrian link.

An Olympic sports legacy

Dan's leadership of EDC would prove invaluable, as we relied on its more flexible bidding and construction management abilities for the most complex projects. This included building more than $165 million worth of new parks in the neighborhood surrounding the new Yankee Stadium, all facilitated by the Olympic bid. To build the new stadium, almost 30 acres of existing (and somewhat run down) parks would have to be "alienated." But the City kept its promise to make sure the new parks would be far better and larger than the

parks they replaced, including a vast new complex of natural grass and synthetic turf playing fields, with a soccer field encircled by a 400-meter competition running track with a Mondo surface — the same as used for Olympic Games.

Shortly after the new Macombs Dam Park was completed, I ran into Congressman José Serrano, who was running on the new track, which was alive with activity — neighbors running, playing soccer and touch football, and using the new outdoor fitness facilities. He told me then: "I was staunchly opposed to the removal of the old parks, but I have to tell you that you kept your promise and gave this community much better parks."

Among the "children" of the unrealized plan to lure the 2012 Olympics to New York was a new $66 million indoor aquatic center and skating rink in Flushing Meadows Corona Park, Queens, the state-of-the-art indoor track & field center in Ocean Breeze, Staten Island, and the completion of the new Icahn Stadium on Randall's Island in partnership with the Randall's Island Sports Foundation (now Randall's Island Park Alliance), which also features the same Olympic surfacing material.

So while Dan's Olympic dreams may not have come to life, suddenly the people of New York City, especially its public high school athletes,

finally had world-class sports facilities on which to get exercise and engage in high-level competition. These new competitions included something I started that had never been done before in the city: A "Mayor's Cup" in track and field and another in cross-country running, in which the top athletes from public, parochial, and private schools would compete in a unified event to see who were the truly the best athletes in the city.

PlaNYC: a visionary master plan

Of all of Dan's many contributions to the improvement of the cityscape of New York, and especially to its parks and open spaces, none was more important, all-encompassing, and transformative as the cumulative impact of PlaNYC and its park elements.

PlaNYC, detailed in this chapter and elsewhere, was arguably the most comprehensive and visionary master plan for New York in the city's history that could actually be delivered. It grew in part out of the ambitious, transit-centered rezonings Dan oversaw which had spurred massive growth in the city's population and was fueled by the increasingly urgent necessity of acting on climate change to make a more sustainable, resilient, greener city.

PlaNYC included eight major regional park projects that stretched to far flung neighborhoods, including the High Bridge project as well as parks in the South Bronx, Washington Heights/West Harlem, Far Rockaway and Gravesend in Queens, Ocean Breeze in Staten Island, and Canarsie and Red Hook in Brooklyn.

Another key element was borrowed from the Trust for Public Land, which for several years had been converting barren asphalt schoolyards into green community playgrounds used by schoolchildren by day and by neighbors after school and on weekends. This model was put on steroids to fast-track the conversion of more than 200 low-functioning yards to amenity-rich playgrounds that would be open to the community outside of school hours in order to dramatically increase access to play spaces for neighborhoods that had lacked sufficient open space for decades.

Other elements of PlaNYC included converting asphalt Parks Department's "playing fields" into safe, usable, synthetic turf sports fields and adding night lighting to increase usable hours in order to meet the surging demand for organized sports for children, teens, and adults.

But the most dramatic and impactful element of the parks and open space segment of PlaNYC was born in one of those early EDAC meetings. One day, when it was my turn for "Show & Tell," I presented a recent study by the U.S. Forest Service and University of California, Davis, which had documented the impact of public investment in planning and maintaining street trees in New York City.

According to a *New York Times* article in April 2007, "Factoring in the costs associated with planting and upkeep, New York City's street trees provide an annual benefit of about $122 million, according to the Parks Department. The study concludes that New York receives $5.60 in benefits — including environmental benefits such as carbon absorption, cooling, and air pollution reduction, as well as increased property values for every dollar spent on trees."

In a roomful of technocrats and experts in finance, a 560% return on investment seemed like a good bet, and with that we had Dan's backing and collegial endorsement to launch the MillionTreesNYC project as a centerpiece of PlaNYC.

A golden age for New York City parks

In my 11 years serving as Parks Commissioner in the Bloomberg administration in the early 2000s, I understood that this was a unique time in the city's history, with an unprecedented half-billion dollars allocated each year over more than a decade to build new parks and restore old ones. I referred to this as a new "Golden Age" of parks, following the transformations of Olmsted and Vaux in the mid-1800s and Moses and the WPA in the early 1900s. I urged our staff to work as hard as possible to get "shovels in the ground" and the money spent, understanding we might never have such an era again in our lifetimes.

Dan's vision, leadership, partnership, and the spirit of collaboration he infused in all of his agencies and collaborators, was key to realizing the promise of the golden age and making a greener, healthier, and more sustainable New York City for all.

Dan Doctoroff oversaw the purchase of Governors Island from the federal government for $1, envisioning it as the heart of a new Harbor District, which included waterfront parks in Brooklyn and Manhattan.

CARTER STRICKLAND | Commissioner, Department of Environmental Protection, 2011–2014 | Vice President, Mid-Atlantic Region & Director, New York State, Trust for Public Land, 2017–2023

THE ECONOMIC IMPACT OF NEW YORK CITY'S PARKS

According to a Trust for Public Land analysis, the city's parks generate billions of dollars annually

It may seem counterintuitive to maximize value by declaring some land non-developable — but Dan Doctoroff has never been a conventional thinker.

At the Trust for Public Land (TPL), our research consistently showed that parks are vital infrastructure for healthy, flourishing communities and economies. With thoughtful design, they can clean and cool the air, capture carbon, foster community and more active lifestyles, reduce stormwater runoff, and beautify neighborhoods. These multiple benefits make parks a critical tool for advancing equity, creating livable cities, and generating economic opportunity. But too many civic officials consider parks to be "nice to have" amenities and their budgets become the first in line for cuts, a self-fulfilling strategy that undervalues and undermines open space.

More than 20 years ago, New York City Deputy Mayor Dan Doctoroff followed his instinct that parks were central to the quality of life — and therefore the economic success — of the city, making parks central to his sweeping vision of a revitalized New York in the wake of 9/11.

When Doctoroff and the Bloomberg administration took office in January 2002, they changed the value proposition of New York City to include creating a public realm that was attractive to the companies and employees of the creative and information economy, while also making the city more livable for all residents. Real estate developers understand that a successful building requires a full range of amenities within or near the building as well as access to interesting public spaces; Doctoroff took this concept citywide at a scale and ambition that city leaders had not dared to think about since the Robert Moses era. New York staked its claim to being the world's leading city through a design approach that interwove new residential, commercial, and clean manufacturing zones with new parks, plazas, complete streets, and green infrastructure.

Doctoroff viewed parks as critical components to a virtuous cycle of growth where quality-of-life improvements would make the city more appealing, which in turn would attract more people and businesses who would expand the tax base and generate more revenue to invest back in municipal services. When the federal government disbursed its first $25 million to help fund the rebuilding effort after 9/11, Doctoroff ensured that the City spent the money on a series of parks in Lower Manhattan to begin attracting people back to the public sphere. He reversed the Giuliani administration's

decision to destroy the High Line and used the new park to drive the rezoning of West Chelsea. The revitalization of the East River waterfront into parks and recreation spaces became the catalyst for the rezoning in Greenpoint-Williamsburg.

If the 2004 opening of Millennium Park in Chicago helped usher in a new era of signature park building and a renewed appreciation that every great city needs a great park, the Bloomberg administration took that philosophy beyond the central business districts. Under Doctoroff's leadership of economic and quality-of-life initiatives in all five boroughs, New York City not only built signature parks like the High Line, Brooklyn Bridge Park, and Governors Island, but also developed a broad-based strategy to create destination parks in every borough, build new public plazas, enhance the network of neighborhood parks, make the most of existing public assets by opening 229 schoolyards into community playgrounds, and extend park hours by installing lights. Doctoroff enshrined many of these goals into his landmark sustainability blueprint, PlaNYC.

Restaurants, retail shops, and galleries in the Meatpacking District and West Chelsea have flourished since the opening of the High Line in 2009, which by some estimates has catalyzed more than $2 billion in new development.

As deputy mayor, Doctoroff's portfolio included both economic development and the operational group of agencies that design, build, and run the streets, water, sanitation, and other infrastructure that shapes city life. This gave him a unique vantage point on how the city's systems worked together — and could be treated holistically to achieve greater efficiencies. One outgrowth of this insight was that he came to suspect that parks were more than just a way to improve quality of life or improve the city's revenues — they could become a critical tool for making the city healthier, more efficient, and sustainable. In PlaNYC, new and renovated parks were cited as strategies that appeared in the water chapter, the air quality chapter, the climate change chapter, and more.

When there was data, Dan listened. After a presentation from the Parks Department that each dollar spent on planting and caring for trees returned over five dollars in benefits, Doctoroff didn't just support planting more trees — he challenged the

Parks Department and its partners to plant one million of them, expanding the tree canopy in every neighborhood at an unprecedented scale, with priority given to underserved neighborhoods. The MillionTreesNYC campaign became a signature PlaNYC initiative — and a national model.

At the time of PlaNYC's release in 2007, more than 2.5 million New Yorkers — 3 out of every 10 New Yorkers — did not have access to a park within a 10-minute walk of their home. Today, the number is 75,000 — less than 1% off of PlaNYC's goal to achieve 100% by 2030. Overall, the Bloomberg administration created, refurbished or set in motion more than 3,000 acres of parks — a staggering scale of non-developable parcels in a land-starved city — driven in no small part by Doctoroff's suspicion that the investment would pay off.

Now we have the receipts to prove that he and the Bloomberg administration were right. In 2022, I oversaw an analysis by TPL that showed billions in benefits are generated annually by the New York City parks system. While each category stands alone because of different methodologies used, our analysis found that parks in New York City annually generate $9.1 billion in recreational value for residents. Parks also generate $1.14 billion in health care savings, including reduced costs associated with heat stress illnesses due to the ability of the city's tree canopy to cool the air. According to the report, the city's greenery also contributes significant savings by filtering the air to make it healthier and cleaner.

PlaNYC revolutionized the City's approach to sustainable water management, integrating two agencies — Parks and the Department of Environmental Protection (DEP) — who had previously been largely separate. Before I joined TPL as the New York State Director, I was recruited by Doctoroff to join the City's sustainability team to lead the water and air initiatives in PlaNYC. There I saw firsthand how powerful that collaboration could be. When I started, the agencies had only a historical relationship based on the repurposing of water infrastructure like the Receiving Reservoir into Central Park's Great Lawn or the old Croton Reservoir into Bryant Park, and didn't have a strategic approach to future collaboration. Today, DEP is a main funder of the Schoolyards to Playgrounds program, integrating green infrastructure into the redesigns to assist with stormwater management. The agency has committed $1.5 billion to natural stormwater management and already has built 11,000 separate green infrastructure projects — the most in the United States, and growing.

The more than 52,000 acres of parkland in the city managed by city, state, and federal park agencies complement this effort by absorbing stormwater that would otherwise be discharged to sewers, streets, and waterways. TPL calculates that the associated cost savings of this partnership have yielded $2.43 billion in avoided treatment costs.

Economically, the annual benefits from New York's park investments are even greater — TPL estimated that proximity to parks, even with conservative assumptions of a 500-foot benefit zone, creates $15.2 billion in increased property value for New Yorkers and $101 million in annual property tax revenues for homes within 500 feet of parks. By another calculation, $17.9 billion in the city's tourism spending is attributable to outdoor activity. These different measures quantify what New Yorkers know: Parks are where a significant portion of urban life takes place and are essential to experiencing the joy of a summer picnic with friends and family, the excitement of a pickup basketball game, the refreshment of a lunch break, and the calm immersion in nature to observe plants and wildlife.

Indeed, cities around the world are coalescing around the idea that successful urban centers require significant amounts of land to be set aside for open space. The pandemic accelerated this recognition — but New York had no need to pivot. Instead, during the Bloomberg administration and with Doctoroff's leadership, New York City established a model for how 21st century cities can — and must — include intentionally integrated open space to flourish.

The revitalized Brooklyn waterfront has hosted the Smorgasburg outdoor market and food festival since 2011; it claims to be the largest weekly open-air food market in America.

Following Spread: The U.S. Coast Guard Cutter *Eagle* docked at Pier 5, Brooklyn Bridge Park.

RIC BURNS | Documentary Filmmaker | Director, *New York: A Documentary Film*

ON THE WATERFRONT: DAN DOCTOROFF AND NEW YORK

New York City is a really big place. With 520 miles of waterfront within the city limits proper, it's also a very watery place, with more shoreline than Boston, Miami, Los Angeles, and San Francisco — combined. It's also by (non-indigenous) American standards a really old place, even though most people don't tend to think about it that way, because it always spends so much of its time with its elbows out brashly inventing the future. But it was founded in 1624, making it the oldest city in America. That means it's also about to be 400 years old.

With that milestone approaching, I've been thinking about that remarkable cohort of visionary people who over the course of the last four centuries have had a real impact on the city at scale — people who have changed the way we live in it and think about it and imagine its future. It's a small group, really. There's DeWitt Clinton, who gave us the street grid and the Erie Canal, and in the process transformed Manhattan into the greatest port city in the Western Hemisphere. There's Andrew Haswell Green, who gave us Central Park, the New York Public Library, and the Metropolitan Museum of Art — and who in 1898, as the prime mover behind Consolidation, gave us Greater New York itself — the gigantic five-borough 302-square-mile megalopolis we've been ever since. There's Fiorello LaGuardia and his billions of New Deal dollars, and Robert Moses, the great hero-villain of urban movers and shakers who did more to make, in some ways unmake, and all told reshape the contours of the city and its environs than anyone else in the 20th century. And there's Jane Jacobs, of course, who helped stop Moses in his tracks, and revealed more to us about the death and life of Great American Cities than anyone before or since.

And then there was a kind of pause — as the port faded away, and manufacturing declined, and people retreated to the suburbs — and the city kind of held its breath for the final decades of the 20th century, waiting to be reborn. Accustomed to ignoring its riverine patrimony during those Ford to City: Drop Dead years, people didn't really think much about those 520 miles of waterfront — lined with crumbling piers and rusting warehouses and belts of highway going somewhere else. And then Dan Doctoroff got an idea in his head.

In part, it was a vision of New York and the Olympics, and of bringing all the peoples of the world to the place where — more than any other city in the world — all the peoples of the world had already found a home. But it was more than that. It was a vision of a city that took a deep breath, and let its shoulders drop, and turned back again with joy and exhilaration to the endless miles of riverfront and coastline and waterway that had been its birthright and patrimony from the very start, and that were still in many respects its greatest wonder and glory.

From that great unrealized Olympian dream, came the Olympic X: Dan's luminous vision of the city jubilantly turning back — at first for competition, sport, and play — to its magnificent waterways

Dan Doctoroff made reclaiming New York's industrial waterfront a centerpiece of his urban revitalization efforts, including new waterfront parks, cleaner water that could support recreation, and an expanded ferry network. Below, promenade and viewing platforms, Hunter's Point South Park.

stretching from the far reaches of the Bronx, down the island of Manhattan and the coastlines of Queens and Brooklyn, all the way out to Staten Island, and ultimately Coney Island and the Rockaways far beyond. It was a vision that was always meant to long outlive and outlast the majestic Olympic moment that was to have been its ostensible starting point and raison d'être. It was a plan for a vast city newly integrated to itself and reunited with its waterways. It was a vision of New York City for the 21st century.

The Olympics were not to be. But to an astonishing degree, Dan's vision of the city has come to pass. No one in, say, 1975 — the year I moved to New York from the hinterlands of Michigan, where Dan, as it happens, also grew up — could possibly have imagined what would become of New York City across the first two decades of the new millennium.

During Michael Bloomberg's extraordinary three-term mayoralty, in which Dan served as Deputy Mayor for Economic Development and Rebuilding, parks, districts, and amenities in and around so many of the city's waterfront zones were gloriously, stunningly reimagined and reborn — the spectacular improvements at Brooklyn Bridge Park, Governors Island, the High Line, Hudson Yards, and Lower Manhattan only the most conspicuously triumphant among the hundreds of projects that remade the city from one end to the other over the last 20 years. No newly awakened, disco-era Rip Van Winkle riding his or her bike along the Hudson River shoreline in Manhattan could do anything but fall off his or her bike in wonder, at the prospect of such a transformation.

For nearly 30 years now I've been working on a documentary series about the history of New York City, eight episodes of which came out between 1999 and 2003, and another two episodes of which are currently on the way. One day in the spring of 2000, Dan Doctoroff and Jay Kriegel — another great New York public servant and wonder-worker, now, alas, no longer with us — came to our offices on the Upper West Side to talk with me and my colleague, James Sanders, about their plan for bringing the Olympics to New York (they wanted us to write an historical essay to accompany the official Olympic bid book submission to the United States Olympic Committee, which we did).

Jay that day played a kind of impish, infinitely urbane Sancho Panza to Dan's tall, courtly, Midwestern Don Quixote. With his curly head of hair, disarming smile, and trademark backward tilt of the head, Dan began to talk to us about what he had in mind — and James and I, two longtime students of New York, were immediately, completely spellbound. No one lets the power and plausibility of what he has to say speak for itself more plainly — or with more simple, uninsistent and, in the end, infinitely compelling matter-of-factness — than Dan Doctoroff. He has a way of making plain and simple sense out of the most complicated, multifarious, and ambitious plans and projects — and making people come together around them in the most unpretentious, uncoercive way. He's a *city-whisperer* — a visionary, and a passionately committed advocate of New York City.

That's why for the new episodes of our documentary which discuss the creation of our modern city, we sought out Dan again. We spoke to him on camera about his remarkable experiences in city life over the past many decades. He spoke calmly and passionately about so many of the challenges and opportunities facing New York: about climate change and the fiscal crisis, about sustainability and

planning, about infrastructure, rezoning, tourism, housing, diversity, Superstorm Sandy, the High Line, City Hall, 9/11, and the waterfront.

He talked about how his understanding of the waterfront had evolved — from the initial instinct that New York needed to take it back and reclaim its power, into an understanding that it was more than the city's birthright — it was the key to its future. To give New Yorkers a respite, an escape, and a salve for their health, for resilience against climate change, as the spark to ignite a torrent of new, brilliant neighborhoods around all of its edges that could offer housing, job opportunities, and generate economic growth to power the city — reclaiming the waterfront was the key to it all.

Hunter's Point South Park transformed 30 acres of postindustrial waterfront into a series of lush and sustainable public spaces, including a central green designed to absorb floodwaters.

At the very end of the interview, with one last thoughtful tilt of the head, he paused a moment, and told us why he was so committed to this wondrous, water-bound, infinitely striving miracle of a city, inadvertently echoing what its other visionaries have understood across generations.

"I just believe in the idea of New York," Dan said. "I believe that New York, at a time when the world is growing closer together, largely through technology, really represents the best — yes, imperfectly, but the best, of what the world can actually be. Where people are tolerant of each other. Where you're going to see Pakistanis and Bangladeshis and Indians working side by side. Where people basically get along, because they are bound together by this idea that it's really about openness and opportunity. I find that incredibly powerful, and I really see New York as a model for the world, as the world grows closer together."

Whenever it's needed it, New York has always found visionary citizens who can help us see and show us the way towards the future. In the city's new unrecognizable waterfront, with its jumble of cultures, games, cyclists, gardens, and grand vistas, the New York Dan spoke of is more than an idea. It's the city that Dan, through his will and his vision, made real.

BROOKLYN BRIDGE PARK

When the Bloomberg administration took office in 2002, Brooklyn Bridge Park was a vacant port area, its decaying piers walled off by chain link fences and padlocked to the public. The piers held concrete parking lots and a series of storage sheds that housed random uses, including coffee beans, lumber, and parking for the U.S. Secret Service.

Although the community had been clamoring for a park for almost two decades, the barriers seemed daunting and little progress had been made. The land was separated from the neighborhood by the Brooklyn-Queens Expressway, making the area loud and difficult to access. The 13,000 piles holding up the piers were made out of wood, meaning that they rotted easily and would be expensive to maintain (although no one had dared analyze just how expensive a restoration would be). The Port Authority owned the land and had historically managed the piers, but once cargo operations shifted to New Jersey in the 1980s, it had largely ignored the ongoing need for pier maintenance, putting the entire site at risk.

The park would be expensive to build, including extensive pile repair, and ultimately maintain — at a moment when the city's budget shortfall was in the billions and its attention focused across the river on the recovery effort in Lower Manhattan.

Dan Doctoroff, the new deputy mayor charged with the city's economic development and rebuilding, assessed the risks, the costs, the competing priorities and came to an immediate answer: Do it.

Twenty years later, the 85-acre park, which stretches along 1.3 miles of Brooklyn shoreline, now draws more than five million visitors a year from all areas of New York City and beyond to bike, kayak, play pickleball and picnic, celebrate kite festivals, food festivals, outdoor film nights, and more.

Brooklyn Bridge Park became a microcosm for the new five-borough vision Doctoroff and our Upper East Side mayor brought to City Hall — and represented a sea change for New York City.

A five-borough vision for New York

The dilapidated state of the waterfront pre-2002 was indicative of a broader attitude toward Brooklyn and the outer boroughs during previous administrations. I joined the Department of City Planning in 1984 and became director of the Brooklyn office in 1999. When I arrived in Brooklyn, the borough's potential was clear to many of us and we spent three years developing plans for rezoning the rotting waterfront at Greenpoint-Williamsburg, identifying investments that could unleash the potential of Downtown Brooklyn, and more. We had plenty of time to develop these plans because we weren't allowed to do any of them. Every time I pitched an idea, I was told the politics weren't right or the administration simply wasn't interested. When I finally coaxed senior officials to Brooklyn during the Giuliani administration, they dutifully arrived in a van, but returned to Manhattan unimpressed.

By contrast, Dan had spent years studying all five boroughs and looking for opportunities as part of his Olympic bid planning. When he and the Bloomberg administration came into office, I didn't have to convince him to visit Brooklyn — he knew many of the sites already. Dan didn't need a van — he was known for organizing bike rides through all the boroughs on weekends and holidays, and included city staff who could lead the way. I'm not a jock, but even I joined one ride that started in Downtown Brooklyn, traveled up to Red Hook, through Park Slope and Crown Heights, and back.

In the first months of the Bloomberg administration, a key staff member, Howard Slatkin and I dusted off our rejected plans for the Greenpoint-Williamsburg rezoning and steeled ourselves to try again. To our joy, Dan immediately embraced the idea, and simultaneously began moving forward with projects across the borough — Downtown Brooklyn, Coney Island, Atlantic Yards, a new cultural district surrounding the Brooklyn Academy of Music (BAM). For the first time in my career, I attended a standing weekly interagency meeting at City Hall to track our progress. It was clear something new was going to happen in Brooklyn — finally.

For decades, a series of fenced-off warehouses and rotting piers blocked off the Brooklyn waterfront. Today, Brooklyn Bridge Park is an urban oasis that draws more than 5 million visitors annually.

The 85-acre Brooklyn Bridge Park stretches along 1.3 miles of Brooklyn waterfront. The park includes beaches, rocky promenades, active recreation, and lawns that attract visitors of all ages. The City assumed sole control of the park in 2010.

The key to the puzzle

Dan embraced Brooklyn Bridge Park because he understood instantly that it was a key piece in the puzzle — a stretch of waterfront that could link our efforts in Greenpoint-Williamsburg and Downtown Brooklyn. Although the area's feisty community activists had killed Dan's initial hopes to locate Olympic diving there (their pastoral vision for the park didn't include swimming competitions), he didn't let the defeat dampen his enthusiasm for the site's potential.

Only four months into the administration, Dan convinced the City to join with the State to take the piers from the Port Authority and work on the park together. The deal reflected Dan's early optimism — and naïvete. The Memorandum of Understanding outlined that the State would pay 60% of the projected costs ($85 million), while the City covered the remaining 40% ($65 million). The State's greater funding commitment allowed it to appoint the Brooklyn Bridge Park Development Corporation chair and executive director and have an additional board member. Dan and Josh Sirefman, his chief of staff, assumed this was a reasonable agreement. They were wrong.

"The State outfoxed us," Dan writes in his book, *Greater Than Ever*, noting that the State appointees would show up at meetings and then refuse to share design drawings, information, or collaborate on the plan in any way. "It was insanity."

Some government officials might have been pleased to pay less money, hold less responsibility, and have some other entity manage the headache of an expensive waterfront park with rotting infrastructure. Dan hated it. He had a vision for Brooklyn and the park and wanted to protect it at all costs.

That is why the City team had cleverly insisted on an unusual provision in the agreement with the State: If the City could increase its funding commitment, its representation on the board would also grow. This is exactly what happened the year after Dan left City Hall — the City contributed an additional $75 million, and then demanded and received equal representation on the board.

In part thanks to Dan's foresight to include a path to increase its control, the City became the sole owner of the park in 2010. It was a costly decision: The initial agreement to fund the park covered only capital investment — not operating expenses. And the costs were steeper than anticipated. In the end, every single one of the 13,000 piles needed to be repaired or reinforced — and maintained in perpetuity.

Dan was determined to leverage the investment of the private sector by including private residences on the edge of the park, despite some community opposition. He also boldly decided that the City should forego the real estate taxes from such development to explicitly support the park, which was not a popular decision from a budgeting perspective. But it provided a unique revenue stream that proved essential to the park's construction and daunting maintenance requirements.

The five building parcels — which constitute 10% of the park area — generated $200 million in upfront payments and upwards of $20 million annually for ongoing park maintenance and improvement, or 90% of the ongoing maintenance costs. Although this approach of generating dedicated park revenue through real estate development was vital to the financing and operations of the park, it proved highly controversial in the neighborhood and generated four lawsuits over 12 years. The park ultimately prevailed and this model has proven to be extremely successful.

A transformed Brooklyn waterfront

After three years of planning and vigorous community discussion, there was finally a path forward by 2005. Two years later, I became president of the Brooklyn Bridge Park Corporation. My first task was to make the park real; developing a construction schedule, restoring the piers, and proving to the community that the park would happen. After years of advocacy, they were skeptical, but the phased park worked. We started by targeting the parking lots around Pier 1 near Fulton Ferry and Pier 6 and transformed them into welcoming entrances to the park.

Then I had to make Brooklyn fall in love with this park. Over the next decade, we opened five piers, and introduced park programming that included active recreation like basketball, soccer, sand volleyball, and plenty of wonderful paths and vistas.

We established unique destinations such as Jane's Carousel and St. Ann's Warehouse at the waterfront, and created lasting partnerships with children's sports leagues, arts organizations, schools, and other community groups.

I often say that building a park is the job of a lifetime, and looking back, the success of Brooklyn Bridge Park had its roots in the decisions Dan made at the outset and the team he built to execute the vision. None of this would have been possible without his passion for its development as a New York City park and his recognition that such investments would not only add new open space and recreation for residents, but just as importantly, aid in the city's much needed economic recovery.

Recreation areas at Brooklyn Bridge Park.

Top: One of five basketball courts, Pier 2.
Middle: Swing Valley, Pier 6.
Bottom: Water spray, Pier 2 Uplands.

Brooklyn Bridge Park, an award-winning
park designed by Michael Van Valkenburgh
Associates, at sunset.

ANDREW WINTERS | Founding Director, Mayor's Office of Capital Project Development, 2005–2012

BUSHWICK INLET PARK

Revitalizing the East River waterfront was one of the defining elements of the Olympic X plan developed by Alex Garvin and Dan Doctoroff. As part of the Olympic planning effort, they identified a series of waterfront sites where formerly industrial land could be redeveloped for use as a competition venue during the Olympics, and then opened to the community for recreational use after the Games.

A large site between North Seventh and North 12th Streets in Greenpoint-Williamsburg presented a prime opportunity for this approach. Located just a few blocks from the subway and framing spectacular views of Manhattan, NYC2012 proposed the site for the swimming competition. Partly abandoned, partly contaminated, and partly occupied by non-water dependent warehouses, this site had long been identified by the local community as a way to begin reclaiming the waterfront for neighborhood use. In the early 2000s, this neighborhood was experiencing dramatic growth, with an influx of new residents, and needed both additional housing as well as expanded open space.

As part of the Olympic effort, Dan made sure that the City moved forward with a plan to rezone this area to meet these twin needs of a growing neighborhood. The resulting 2005 Greenpoint-Williamsburg rezoning established the park along with additional density for housing.

Despite the loss of the Olympics, plans that had already been set in motion for the park continued to move forward and were embraced by New York State, which owned adjacent property.

On the blocks between North Seventh and North Ninth Streets, a new seven-acre state park opened in 2007, now known as Marsha P. Johnson State Park. Although the initial park included minimal landscaping or amenities, this new recreational area expanded on the overall vision for transforming the waterfront into a public space, and became very popular as the site of open-air concerts and the food festival, Smorgasburg. In 2021, significant improvements were made with the addition of lighting, landscaping, and event space.

The first 4.5 acres of New York City's Bushwick Inlet Park opened between 2010 and 2013, including the waterfront esplanade and picnic area, a multipurpose sports field, and an award-winning community building with a green roof. Adjacent to the state property, these combined parks provide more than 11 acres of open space.

Additional parcels have been purchased by the City — the full park will be more than 35 acres — but progress has been slow due to the high cost of land and the heavy contamination of the sites due to years of industrial use. Despite the slow progress, the 2005 rezoning designates this area as a park with no other use permitted, locking in the original vision for the transformation of this unique part of the East River waterfront.

The creation of Bushwick Inlet Park was accelerated by the city's Olympic bid, which identified the then-derelict and contaminated site as a location for swimming competitions. Today, the 4.5-acre park is a key link in the ongoing transformation of the Brooklyn waterfront.

JOSH WALLACK | Senior Policy Advisor, Office of the Deputy Mayor for Economic Development and Rebuilding, 2006–2010 | Chief Operating Officer, New York City Economic Development Corporation, 2010–2012

HUNTER'S POINT SOUTH PARK

Dan Doctoroff originally imagined the 2012 Olympic Village at Hunter's Point South, where athletes would live in buildings designed by the winners of a worldwide design competition in the "spiritual heart" of the Games just a quick boat or subway ride away from events in Manhattan or Queens. But after the Games, he said, the Village would become one of the largest social housing developments since Stuyvesant Town, forming a new community of thousands of families on the Queens waterfront, with a park that would open onto a view of Midtown Manhattan over the East River, one of the most beautiful cityscapes in the world. That astonishing vision animated the work of countless teams of people throughout City government, even years after Dan left the administration.

Of course, he somehow managed to ensure the City got control of the parcel from the Port Authority, whose own redevelopment plans had stalled for years. (Dan's then-chief of staff Marc Ricks remembers sitting next to Dan in the City Hall bullpen, when suddenly, out of the blue, Dan spun around in his chair and said, "Do you know what we should do? We should buy the Olympic Village site from the Port Authority for $100 million and turn it into middle-income housing." In 2009, that's exactly what happened, down to the dollar.)

Dan's ability to see those opportunities when no one else could and move them through the City's process at a critical moment is still unmatched. Dan originally hired me in 2006 to help move forward key parts of the administration's *Vision for Lower Manhattan*; that's where I first witnessed his combination of vision, tenacity, and strategic opportunism. Later, I saw firsthand how the key move of securing the Hunter's Point South site enabled three key parts of the administration's vision for the city to move forward.

First, to create unparalleled public space that connected people to the water. Dan helped select a design team in SWA/Balsley and Weiss/Manfredi that would navigate complex design and approval processes and the unpredictable consequences of building completely new infrastructure under a New York City waterfront parcel. They emerged with an award-winning design that gives New Yorkers a chance to exercise, celebrate, stroll, meditate, and even

fish together on the East River. Crucially, the designers incorporated elements to protect the coastline from flooding, which was put to the test when the storm surge from Superstorm Sandy hit just as Phase 1 was completed in 2012. The design worked, allowing the site to drain without straining the storm infrastructure, and construction resumed just days later.

Second, to make the city affordable for those that keep it running. The City followed through on Dan's vision of social housing, insisting that developers make 100% of the units built on the site affordable to middle- and moderate-income New Yorkers. Local activists involved in the planning spoke of how important it was that what we now call essential workers — teachers, firefighters, childcare staff, nurses, retail workers, and others — be able to remain in a community they supported and helped build. It was essential not only that they stay, but that they have pride of place, in apartments sitting high above the East River looking over Midtown. As one community board member put it, "These apartments have million-dollar views, but you don't need to be a millionaire to afford them."

And third, to create new infrastructure for the next century of the city's growth. Hunter's Point South had what at the time was viewed as a quirky amenity: We renovated a rotting pier to create a "Water Taxi," or ferry stop. As the City wrestled with how to transport the community's thousands of new residents, water transport became one of the answers. The East River Ferry service grew as Hunter's Point South and other waterfront communities did, demonstrating that the parallel growth of transit and housing could be more than a theory, along with a renewed, daily, lived connection between New York City and its waterfront.

Hunter's Point South came to life because Dan Doctoroff set out an animating vision of how city government could make space for a new community — a vision that placed a public park at its heart. Then he created an opportunity for talented engineers, planners, designers, developers, and community members to come together and shape that space in ways that serve us all.

Right: Hunter's Point South was a postindustrial site when Dan Doctoroff and Olympic planners proposed transforming it into the Olympic Village for the 2012 Games; Doctoroff used that vision to catalyze the area's transformation into a new community with a park at its heart.

Opposite: The park's award-winning design by SWA/Balsley and Weiss/Manfredi was featured in an exhibition at the Museum of Modern Art. Here, flowers in bloom with Gaston Lachaise's sculpture *Floating Woman,* in the background.

EAST RIVER WATERFRONT ESPLANADE

"It was almost like when we said, "Well, this hasn't really ever been done before, [Dan would] be more interested."

AN EDITED ORAL HISTORY

The 1.5-mile, $135 million East River Waterfront Esplanade, which stretches from the Battery Maritime Building to Pier 35 on the Lower East Side, transformed a collection of garbage strewn lots, salt piles, parking, and other municipal uses under the hulking shadow of the FDR Drive into a series of striking new public spaces along the shores of the East River. Deputy Mayor Dan Doctoroff envisioned the park as part of the rebuilding of Lower Manhattan in the aftermath of the September 11th terrorist attacks, using funds from the Lower Manhattan Development Corporation (LMDC).

To build the unusual park, scraped together from bits of forgotten and derelict land, the City selected SHoP Architects, a young New York-based firm with only three major projects under its belt. "It was a huge leap of faith," said Founding Principal Gregg Pasquarelli, who with his partners had decided to move the firm to Lower Manhattan to support the rebuilding. SHoP teamed with architect Richard Rogers on the master plan, then collaborated on the design with landscape architect Ken Smith. "The East River Waterfront was

a really significant and tricky project because it had been such a neglected area for so long."

The unusual site, which threads through multiple diverse neighborhoods, meant the project couldn't lean on the English garden tropes that inform the design of many New York City parks; it needed to innovate a new kind of urban postindustrial public space. "We were born and raised New Yorkers," Pasquarelli said, something he believes appealed to Doctoroff. "There was an understanding of how the neighborhoods worked that he respected."

The relocation of the Tin Building in 2022 completed the last element of the master plan, developed nearly 20 years ago. "I think it's just a testament to what great politics and leadership are about," Pasquarelli said. Doctoroff offered "a phenomenal vision" and established conditions that empowered the team to keep moving forward.

Dan Doctoroff secured funding for and championed the creation of the 1.5-mile, $135 million East River Waterfront Esplanade as part of the rebuilding of Lower Manhattan after 9/11; he helped to select the then little-known firm SHoP Architects to lead the design.

The whole place just felt like a lost opportunity. Because of the way the island bends, it's the only truly south-facing waterfront property in Manhattan. In most global capitals, that's the most expensive property in the city. And yet South Street had the highway above it. It was dark and scary to get under. You got across and it was a shitty esplanade with broken fences and parking lots and salt piles and garbage dumps. And then there were places, especially in Community Board 3 in the Lower East Side, where there were up to eight or nine layers of chain link fences keeping the public from actually accessing the waterfront.

You could just see people wanted to get out to that waterfront. It was like, if we just give it a little love, this thing is going to bloom. And I think Dan [Doctoroff] understood that very clearly from all the work he did with the Olympic bid.

We looked at all the failed projects proposed there for the previous 40 years. The original World Trade Center was supposed to be on that site. The Port Authority of New York and New Jersey wouldn't agree to the project unless it connected to New Jersey and the PATH Station — that was when they flipped it to the other side. There was a proposal to put the Stock Exchange there. Frank Gehry did a plan to put a Guggenheim Museum there. There were crazy plans.

We realized that every one of the projects that failed was clipping an object onto the side of Manhattan. And we said, "Why don't we just think about it the other way around? Let's be in the city and think about how you move out and extend towards the water."

The [project] money really came out of LMDC with the rebuilding of Lower Manhattan. Dan was a huge cheerleader [for the idea that] 'It's not just about rebuilding the Trade Center site, it's thinking holistically about Lower Manhattan.' We couldn't just put all the money into the 16 acres. You had to make everything else around it more vibrant and vital and 24/7 to make the 16 acres work. Here was this moment where we had all this waterfront property that most people weren't taking advantage of.

[The esplanade] went through six or seven neighborhoods, distinct areas, from the Battery to the Financial District, to the Seaport, to the Civic Center, to Chinatown, to the Lower East Side. Very different neighborhoods, very different socioeconomic and cultural

The Esplanade travels from the Battery Maritime Building through multiple neighborhoods including Chinatown and the Lower East Side, culminating in swings at Pier 35 that offer majestic views of New York Harbor.

bases. And then this giant piece of infrastructure — the FDR — running right through the middle of it.

Our whole concept was: narrow South Street, put crosswalks in with signals, light the FDR, paint it, get people to see these ways to get across, build things under the FDR so it mitigates the presence of this highway, and wherever we can grab any kind of space, build out into the water and just open it up.

So often you hear, "Oh, you can't do that." And then you go, "Why?" And they go, "Because we haven't done it before." That's just such a refrain mostly from construction executives and politicians. And then with Dan, it was the opposite. It was almost like when we said, "Well, this hasn't really ever done before," he'd be more interested.

[There were] factions with different goals. There had to be a tiebreaker, there had to be someone to lead. Dan was really good at that. And you always felt like the right decision would be made and that everyone wasn't going to be happy, but it would move the project in the right direction. By definition, that's leadership.

[An example] is Pier 15. There were piers all along [the waterfront] until the 90s. And then as they were becoming more and more dilapidated, the City knocked them all down. Pier 15 was one of the last ones left. The pier was falling into the water and it was dangerous. So they took it down, but they kept the permit open because once you remove the pier, you can't rebuild it. There was a huge battle over whether it should be rebuilt or not. Dan was in support of rebuilding the pier. And now it's a wildly successful public park. Without Dan as the tie breaker, I don't know if it ever happens.

We had to build up the soil wherever we could to get plantings in there because you didn't have any soil below. And so we did these precast concrete walls with embedded lighting, and we calculated how far the light would go underneath the FDR to allow things to grow. We created these planters up and down to give green space. You meander past Pier 11 with the ferries, and then there's a dog run.

Then you get to Industry Kitchen, this fantastic restaurant. Everyone was like, "Who would ever rent a space underneath a highway?" It's a magical space. We designed a canopy that's a sound attenuation piece that takes [away] the sound of the highway above, and you're literally in one of the shittiest pieces of property you could imagine [with] a magical view and it's beautiful. And you have no idea that there's this crappy 70-year-old highway right above you.

Top: Dan Doctoroff supported rebuilding Pier 15 and transforming it into a public amenity. Today, the two-level 50,000 square-foot structure is a popular public park.

Bottom: The designers used precast concrete walls to build up soil for plantings and landscaping, creating lush public seating areas along the waterfront.

Then there's Pier 15 on the right: a double-deck pier with passive recreation on the top and active maritime and revenue generating things on the bottom. Then you get to the South Street Seaport and Pier 17. We moved the Tin Building from under the FDR, got it all out of the floodplain, got the Esplanade through.

You keep going north, and there starts to be more community things. There's basketball courts, there's workout areas, there's outdoor weightlifting, almost like Muscle Beach in Venice. There's fishing platforms because the Chinatown community loves to fish in that area.

Eventually it gets up to Pier 35 and the Esplanade turns and it creates this big trellis that blocks the view of the sanitation shed. The vines are growing up. They're only about a third of the way there. It'll probably take another five to 10 years.

We put mussel reefs in [at the foot of the pier] and [ways] to get students down to study the river and the ecologies. Then you get out to the end of the pier. Now you're looking back, all the way down towards the Statue of Liberty and under the bridges. We put these giant swings in there. It all ends up on these lawns and swings and trellises, but very urban, looking at this magnificent view of the harbor.

This summer is going to be the first summer where it's all done and we're going to watch it operate. It's so clearly going to be a giant success. It's like it happened overnight in 20 years. Without Dan's support at City Hall, none of it happens. None of it happens. He was able to help unite people in the vision.

The upper viewing platform and lower plaza at Pier 15 provide opportunities to enjoy the previously inaccessible East River waterfront.

SHoP Architects designed a sound attenuating canopy over the restaurant Industry Kitchen that buffers noise from the highway above.

BETTY Y. CHEN | Vice President for Planning, Design, and Preservation, Trust for Governors Island, 2005-2011

GOVERNORS ISLAND

The metamorphosis of Governors Island was certainly not inevitable.

A 172-acre island in the heart of New York Harbor, Governors Island offers a sublime 360-degree vista of the New York skyline, city waterfront, Statue of Liberty, and the Brooklyn Bridge. When the Bloomberg administration came into office, the Island had been closed to New Yorkers for more than 200 years. For most of that time, it had served as a United States military base which decreased in use over the decades. In 1996, the U.S. Coast Guard, the last tenant, moved its operations, leaving the Island abandoned.

By 2002, the island's infrastructure was missing or in disrepair — no potable water, no Internet, a crumbling seawall, a failing electrical network, limited ferry-only access, deteriorating historic buildings full of asbestos and lead paint, acres of cracked asphalt, and no public services for sanitation or public safety. Having been off-limits to the public for so long, the island was no longer on anyone's mental map of New York City.

Deputy Mayor Dan Doctoroff had visited Governors Island when scouting sites for New York's Olympic bid. He ruled it out as an athletes' housing venue but was struck by its incredible beauty and setting. So, when the federal government signaled it would be willing to sell the property to New York, Doctoroff leapt at the opportunity. The agreement they signed committed that the island would be redeveloped for public benefit and prohibited casinos, power plants, and private residences. New York bought the island in 2003 for $1, which Doctoroff pulled out of his wallet and stuck in the file when the transfer papers arrived for his signature.

The City and State initially had joint ownership and rotated board leadership (and therefore, decision-making) every two years. For the first two years under State leadership, efforts were focused on establishing baseline maintenance and ferry operations.

By 2005, when Doctoroff assumed board leadership of Governors Island, initial groundwork had given way to a pressing question, "What should the Island become?"

I was working on rebuilding efforts in Lower Manhattan when Doctoroff's chief of staff, Josh Sirefman, reached out to see if I would be willing to come on board as the director of planning for the Island. I agreed on one condition: I wanted to meet with Doctoroff first. Josh arranged it, and I went to City Hall. I posed my one question: "What do you have in mind for Governors Island?"

"I have no idea," Doctoroff replied. "Just make it great."

It was exactly what I needed to hear, and I had had enough experience watching him and the Bloomberg team in action to know he meant it. As long as we met a standard of greatness and presented something civic-minded, bold, and beautiful, we would have a receptive audience. It was a license to be creative and ambitious. We got to work.

Later, as I got to know Doctoroff and Mayor Michael Bloomberg better, I saw how they complemented each other. Bloomberg's infamous directive to new hires was, "Don't fuck it up." Together, they established a perfect mandate for Governors Island — "Don't fuck it up" and "Make it great." With such a beautiful site, both needed to be said — it was an immense challenge to bring the Island back to life without ruining it.

Doctoroff insisted the mission wasn't merely to reawaken a forgotten island but to develop a plan worthy of the site's vast potential. He foresaw that Governors Island could have global impact and become one of the great urban places of New York City: "Imagine a place that could help inspire the world — and bring it together," read one of his pitches in the Island's promotional materials. "A place that could help define future solutions to some of our most urgent global challenges."

Right: While scouting potential Olympic sites, Dan Doctoroff visited Governors Island, a 172-acre former military base in the middle of New York Harbor that had been abandoned since 1996. Recognizing its potential, Doctoroff later orchestrated the purchase of the Island from the federal government for $1. Nearly one million people now visit Governors Island via ferry annually.

Opposite: Doctoroff helped oversee a new public space master plan for the island, including The Hills, far right, which provide spectacular views of Lower Manhattan.

Doctoroff posited a range of possibilities for a new campus on Governors Island: a home to some of the world's top scientists pioneering research in global health, technology, engineering, and the environment; a place for think tanks, convening national and global thinkers and leaders engaged in sustainability or public health; or a center for applied research and innovation.

We issued a national Request for Proposals with the goal of attracting partners to the venture. Unfortunately, submissions were … underwhelming — a minimum-security drug rehabilitation center, a feral cat sanctuary, a neon-colored theme park featuring a giant animated sponge, an outdoor shooting range. There was no way we would approve any of those; it would have been the most squandered opportunity in New York history.

From the disappointing open call results, we realized too few people knew what Governors Island was or could be. We had underestimated the inherent psychological barriers which, combined with the poor physical condition of the Island's infrastructure, made our proposition too risky for investors. So we pivoted.

We focused on the one viable submission that served the Island's civic potential, a proposal for the New York Harbor School. We brought them to Governors Island and today the Harbor School serves 520 students in grades 9-12 with a maritime and environmental stewardship curriculum.

Doctoroff brought in Leslie Koch to be president of the redevelopment agency. She was an unconventional choice with a background outside real estate but was known to be smart, effective, tireless, and tenacious. She spearheaded a multipart strategic plan which the Bloomberg administration not only embraced but prioritized.

We realized we needed to catalyze development by first creating new world-class parks and public open space that would introduce people to the Island. In 2005, we opened the Island to the public. Even then, success was not assured until we demonstrated meaningful change — preserving historic buildings and making deep investments in operations and utilities, transportation, and marine infrastructure to prepare the Island to welcome more visitors and attract tenants.

To that end, the Bloomberg administration committed $260 million for park construction and a long-term infrastructure capital program. We launched an international design competition to develop a master plan for the Island's public spaces.

In 2007, Doctoroff unveiled the park and public space master plan from the acclaimed landscape architect, Adriaan Geuze of West 8, delivering on the idea that quality public space is essential infrastructure.

West 8 envisioned a new 87-acre sustainable waterfront park for the 21st century, serving as the centerpiece of Doctoroff's plan for a reactivated Harbor District, which linked to the waterfront development on the Brooklyn and Manhattan shorelines along the East River.

The design included thousands of trees and plantings to turn seas of asphalt into lush green lawns, meadows, gardens, and forested areas for recreation and play. It addressed rising sea levels by transforming the Island with new topography. Demolition debris was incorporated into new hills to provide visitors with breathtaking vantage points of the harbor and the Statue of Liberty. Long before public bikeshare, Geuze introduced the idea of public bikes in New York City at Governors Island.

The West 8 plan created a vibrant world apart from New York City, a playground oasis of car-free biking, strolling, climbing, sliding, ball sports, outdoor movies, relaxing in a hammock, picnicking, and grilling. Outdoor spaces were activated with music, sound art, visual art, and festivals of all sorts. Visitors could enjoy the sounds and smells of a peaceful green island surrounded by water, indulging in the delight of fresh salty air, sunlight, waves, wind, and birdsong.

By the end of the Bloomberg administration, most of the park was complete or underway. The Island had an identity and had become a beloved destination for New Yorkers embracing recreation on the revitalized New York waterfront.

Together with new parkland, the significant infrastructure investments laid the foundation for responsible development. They succeeded in generating enough meaningful interest from not-for-profit and private partners that, in 2022, the City committed to establishing a global Center for Climate Solutions on Governors Island, fulfilling the vision Doctoroff outlined nearly two decades ago. With the future climate center, Governors Island takes its place as a centerpiece of the Bloomberg administration's mission to make New York greener, healthier, and greater than ever.

Above: As part of the deal for a new Yankee Stadium, the City agreed to build parks to replace the ones displaced by the new facility, resulting in 55 acres of new sports fields, tracks, and areas for passive recreation.

Right: The 11-acre Mill Pond Park transformed decayed industrial land into a waterfront esplanade, picnic and play areas, and 16 tennis courts.

Far Right: The 44-acre Macombs Dam Park, built over a parking garage, includes three grass ballfields and a 400-meter running track that uses the same surfacing as the Olympics.

MICHAEL KALT | Senior Policy Advisor, Office of the Deputy Mayor for Economic Development and Rebuilding, 2003–2006

YANKEE STADIUM PARKS

After Mayor Michael Bloomberg and Deputy Mayor Dan Doctoroff took office, they immediately struck down a deal by their predecessors to give the Mets and the Yankees $400 million each to construct new stadiums. In response, the Yankees agreed to fund their own stadium across 161st Street — if the City agreed to build a new park to compensate for the one displaced by the new facility.

Doctoroff agreed and tasked his team with finding an acceptable site within the community. But land parcels of that size in that neighborhood were hard to find. The situation was complicated further when the Yankees asked for more than 2,000 new parking spaces, presenting a classic, "12 pounds of salami in a 10-pound bag" problem.

The team finally identified a clever solution: The topography immediately south of 161st Street allowed for a new parking garage to be constructed with a large park on its roof. There were other advantages to this site: For the first time, the community would have direct access to the park from 161st Street (the previous park was 10 feet below grade and could only be reached via a steep step-down).

The new 44-acre Macombs Dam Park and Heritage Field was an upgrade over the original park, with three championship-quality grass ballfields built for softball, baseball and Little League against the dramatic backdrop of the historic Yankee Stadium facade, a state-of-the-art 400-meter track with the same surfacing used at the Summer Olympic Games, and a new all-weather turf field with seating for 600 spectators, along with courts for basketball and handball. It was a terrific example of the sensible urban planning and creative solutions to intractable problems that was at the core of Doctoroff's approach to economic development.

In addition, an abandoned 11-acre site along the Bronx River waterfront was identified as an additional new park, later named Mill Pond Park. Today it contains 16 tennis courts, recreational lawns and trails, a playground, and a renovated power station that now contains the Bronx Children's Museum.

The $20 million West Harlem Piers Park replaced a parking lot with a two-acre waterfront park as part of the *West Harlem Master Plan*.

WEST HARLEM PIERS PARK

West Harlem Piers Park transformed a parking lot between 125th and 135th Streets into an inviting waterfront park designed to connect visitors with the water and strengthen the neighborhood's connections with the surrounding city. A series of refurbished piers now offer fishing, recreational boating, and docks, while the park's new bike paths connect West Harlem to the Hudson River Greenway, creating a continuous ride from the Battery to Upper Manhattan. New walking paths enlivened by public art weave through the landscaped park.

The $20 million, two-acre park was conceived as part of the *West Harlem Master Plan*, a 125-page study released in 2002 that outlined a vision for waterfront renewal, transportation improvements, and economic development in West Harlem. The study was a joint project between Deputy Mayor Dan Doctoroff as part of his five-borough development plan, multiple state entities, the City Council, and local community and environmental justice groups. The park opened fully in 2009 and quickly became host to film festivals, community events, cyclists, and boaters.

JOSHUA LAIRD | Assistant Commissioner for Planning and Parklands, Department of Parks & Recreation, 1997–2013

LOWER MANHATTAN POCKET PARKS

Prospects for the New York City Parks Department seemed dim when Mike Bloomberg took office as mayor. We were all still in shock from the September 11th attacks, but to the extent we could wrap our heads around the overwhelming tasks of recovery, it seemed very likely that public open space would not be a priority for the foreseeable future. Only months earlier, an energetic campaign by the Parks Council, an advocacy group (later renamed New Yorkers for Parks), seemed to have momentum to convince the City to allocate 1% of its annual budget to the Parks Department. By September 12th, it was off the table.

Everyone in the department expected that Parks was in for a tough slog while City Hall's attention turned to rebuilding Lower Manhattan. Nobody knew what Mayor Bloomberg would be like and how the city would be run. But the new administration quickly revealed itself to be focused and organized. It also demonstrated very quickly the type of management approach that would become a signature of the Bloomberg years: Find smart people, offer them opportunities for input, and empower them to pursue and carry out good ideas.

We got an early encouraging sign when Parks was invited to join the Lower Manhattan Task Force. I quickly found myself working beside colleagues from many other agencies, all of us engaged in regular meetings with top City Hall officials to comprehensively discuss recovery plans. During a previous administration, a deputy mayor had literally closed a heavy oak door in my face as I tried to accompany the Parks commissioner into a meeting at City Hall. This was a dream come true.

Deputy Mayor Dan Doctoroff was at the center of it all. He chaired those meetings, was the most significant asker of questions, challenger of ideas, and booster for getting things done. As far as Dan was concerned, our goal wasn't just to stagger back onto our feet, but to seize an opportunity to make New York City better. He set a mandate that the redevelopment of Lower Manhattan was not just about bringing back a business district, but about promoting residential development, open space, and schools. He made it clear parks were central to that vision.

To that end, he embraced our idea that now was a good time to finally close the gaps in the lower portions of the Manhattan Waterfront Greenway, which had been planned — but unfinished — for years.

We also began discussing more neighborhood parks to serve a growing residential population the City planned to encourage. Dan made it clear that he saw residential growth as critical to bringing 24-hour life to a revitalized district and as a strategy for adaptively reusing older "Class B" office buildings. He understood that residential growth would only be successful with enhanced public open spaces and directed Parks and the Department of City Planning to come up with proposals.

We embarked on multiple walking tours of Lower Manhattan, followed by meetings around a conference table laden with maps and various property records. We soon focused our attention on Lower Manhattan's old "slip streets" — locations where 18th and 19th century waterfront boat slips carved into the shoreline had been filled in, creating flared street ends as Manhattan expanded into the rivers. These spaces, with an overabundance of asphalt and jammed with parking spaces, held potential for the creation of pocket parks.

The plan that emerged called for the creation of new parks at Coenties Slip, Old Slip, Wall Street, John Street, and Peck Slip. Opportunities were also identified to expand existing green spaces at Titanic Memorial Park, Pearl Street Playground, DeLury Square on Fulton Street, and at Drumgoole Plaza under one of the Brooklyn Bridge approach ramps.

Dan was enthusiastic. Our proposed pocket parks concept seemed to fit right in with other planning objectives that were coming into focus, such as streetscape improvements along Water Street and the growing notion that Fulton Street was critical as one of the few streets to fully traverse Lower Manhattan from the East River to the World Trade Center site.

Dan was intensely interested in how the pieces would fit together and kept us all focused on the agenda before us, while leaving the details of how each park would be designed to others. He recognized that our proposed park improvements made use of land that was already City-owned and therefore had the potential to function as early wins for a larger rebuilding effort that would take many years. Rather than be treated as superfluous to an effort with so many big things seemingly at stake, a $25 million plan for Lower Manhattan pocket parks was pushed forward and funded by the Lower Manhattan Development Corporation.

Of course, nothing is that simple. Turning streets into parks meant that the Department of Transportation would need to get behind changes to its domain. Utilities located under the streets would need to be moved or otherwise addressed. Catch basins and stormwater runoff would need to be figured out. Dan's leadership was invaluable in overcoming these obstacles. I can recall multiple instances of Dan standing up at meetings to insist that the agencies work together, sometimes in a benevolent tone, sometimes in angry exasperation. He also chose a group of talented policy advisors to carry out his mission. With Dan's imprimatur behind them, they kept things moving, made agencies work cooperatively, and cleared the way of many obstacles.

The first of the projects, at Drumgoole Plaza, was completed in November 2003 — slightly more than two years after the World Trade Center attack. The new and expanded parks that came into existence over the next few years happened because Dan understood it was important for them to happen and was willing to exert the leadership necessary to overcome obstacle after obstacle. Many of these parks are now fixtures of a rejuvenated Lower Manhattan, whether as a place for children to play like Imagination Playground on John Street (completed in 2010), or as a lunchtime hangout for the business community like Mannahatta Park on Wall Street (completed in 2007). Although many were finished after Dan's departure from City Hall, all got started thanks to the vision and leadership of Dan and the Bloomberg administration.

Opposite: Imagination Playground at Burling Slip, Lower Manhattan.

JOSHUA DAVID | Co-Founder, Friends of the High Line, 1999-Present
ROBERT HAMMOND | Co-Founder, Friends of the High Line, 1999-Present

THE HIGH LINE

"Dan is a vision guy. When it began to look like one piece of a much bigger planning vision, that's where I saw him tip to our side."

When young Chelsea residents Joshua David and Robert Hammond began lobbying the Giuliani administration to save the rusting 1934 elevated railway in their neighborhood from destruction by developers, they were bluntly shot down. "'All the two of you guys know how to do is make a brochure,'" David recalled an official telling them. "Which was correct," he added. By the time the Bloomberg administration came into office, the High Line was one court decision away from being torn down.

Although Bloomberg had supported the High Line as a mayoral candidate, that was before the terrorist attacks on September 11th. When he came into office, "the City had a lot on its plate," David said, including a budget shortfall of $5 billion. Given the complexity and cost of saving the High Line, and the intensity of opposition, "some light support wasn't going to cut it," he said.

The High Line's history as an active railroad and its winding 1.5-mile route through city streets, City-owned and State-owned property, and private property along the West Side created a tangle of jurisdictions, agencies, and regulations blocking its preservation. It was owned by the railroad, CSX Transportation, which had already made plans to destroy it.

Converting it into a park would require transferring easements from CSX to the City under a federal program known as "Rails to Trails" — in addition to other federal and state approvals; each of the 22 private property owners whose land touched the High Line needed to reverse their position and sign agreements supporting its preservation; the design had to navigate bizarre regulations for elevated parks (one, the Frozen Turkey Rule, was written to require fences because some teenagers had once thrown a frozen turkey off a bridge); it required a funding and long-term management strategy at a time of dire city budget shortfalls; and it needed to be situated within a broader rezoning for the neighborhood that had to allay the concerns of property owners, create affordable housing, preserve the growing art gallery scene, and appease the preservation-minded neighborhood. "Without the expertise and determination and knowledge that the team that Dan assembled brought to the project, we could never have waded through all of that," David said.

Doctoroff tasked his staff and the Law Department with overseeing the negotiations with the railroad and the property owners, and assigned design and construction as the first project for the newly created Office of Capital Projects, which he founded to oversee complex, interagency projects. "Everyone working on the project at every agency knew that this was a particular priority for Dan, and that fact alone did an immense amount to ensure that it did not get delayed or caught in bureaucratic hell," said Andrew Winters, the founding director of the Office for Capital Project Development.

But first David and Hammond, who co-founded Friends of the High Line, had to win Dan over. On the advice of a consultant, they commissioned an economic impact analysis from the same firm Dan had hired to assess the economic impact of the Olympic bid. It predicted that the park would take $65 million to build and generate $140 million in incremental tax revenue over 20 years. That was "the central argument that we all latched onto, both Friends of the High Line and the City for carrying this project forward," David said, even though, Hammond admitted, privately "we thought those numbers were sort of laughable." Dan was "not convinced," either, said Hammond. But "Dan is a vision guy," said David. "He understands and gets behind big vision projects. The more we talked about it, the more that he saw the piece that it could play in a very large vision."

As it turned out, the numbers were wrong: As of 2022 the High Line has cost around $300 million — and is projected to generate nearly $2 billion in revenue over those 20 years, drawing eight million visitors annually and inspiring a slew of striking elevated parks around the world.

Above: 10th Avenue Square and Overlook. Dan Doctoroff overruled other City staffers in granting Friends of the High Line time to raise additional funds to include the now-iconic feature.

AN EDITED ORAL HISTORY

Left: Dan Doctoroff and Congressman Jerrold Nadler at the groundbreaking ceremony for the High Line, April, 2006.

CONTEXT

JOSHUA DAVID

There was a movement to get the High Line torn down by a group of real estate owners. They had brought a lot of allies into the fold of, "the High Line was the worst thing in the world. It was separating Chelsea from the waterfront. It was falling down. It was going to kill people." They would send these flyers to all of our supporters. During the period post 9/11 when people were freaked out about anthrax attacks, they actually mailed [City Planning Chair] Amanda Burden an envelope with dust that was supposed to be concrete dust that had fallen from the declining High Line. So, that was what we were up against.

All of Chelsea was different then. I've lived there since '86, '87. It was an industrial area on reclaimed swamp land that had been filled with all sorts of terrible things. If you dug down there, you'd find God knows what. [After] manufacturing slowed down, there were a lot of underused or unused spaces. A bunch of nightclubs went in, which the neighborhood was really upset about. The local community was actually very supportive of there being a rezoning west of 10th Avenue because it was seen that zoning for residential would take care of this nightlife problem.

The rezoning of West Chelsea was going to happen, but it was going to happen without the High Line. And we were saying, "This will be a better rezoning, this will be a better neighborhood. This will deliver a greater financial return to the city with the High Line in it than without it."

WINNING OVER DOCTOROFF

ROBERT HAMMOND

When [Mayor Bloomberg] got into office and appointed Dan as the deputy mayor, we realized this is the guy that we were going to have to convince. Dan was skeptical. Before he ever talked to us, he went up on a tour of the High Line. Amanda [Burden] reported back that he was unimpressed and just thought it was a railroad with a whole bunch of weeds growing on it.

DAVID

That first meeting with Dan, the city was in a very tough economic situation. I was a freelance magazine writer, so I worked by myself. I didn't do a lot of full on sales pitches to powerful people — I did little written pitches to magazine editors. So this was frankly terrifying to me.

HAMMOND

We gave our pitch and it was a pretty stony faced, polite response. He very expressly conveyed to us that he needed to understand the economic benefits to the city of doing this. It was a pretty clearly phrased challenge to us.

DAVID

There wasn't a concrete precedent to look at. There was Central Park, which created extraordinary value all around its borders. But Central Park is Central Park, it's huge. Looking at linear parks and small parks, the data was pretty spotty. You were really grasping at straws. The big thing that we argued was that it was going

to create value all through the neighborhood. I can't say I fully believed it when I was arguing it.

If you had just taken it in isolation and said, 'You've got this rusty metal structure and there are these people who want to build a park on it!' that might not have flown. But Dan is a vision guy. He understands and gets behind big vision projects. The more we talked about it, the more that he saw the piece that it could play in a very large vision, which included the Jets Stadium/Olympics/Hudson Yards/West Chelsea, against the backdrop of a movement to rezone large areas all across New York City that were previously manufacturing. When it began to look like one piece of a much bigger planning vision, that's where I saw him tip to our side.

HAMMOND
A theme also for Dan and the High Line is taking huge risks. We didn't have a design, we didn't even know what we were going to build. And we were two relatively young guys that had zero experience in raising money, building a park, or operating a park. And so it was a pretty gutsy risk.

DAVID
There were people who called us two guys and a logo. There were people who called us neighborhood nobodies.

HAMMOND
And those were our friends.

DAVID
As much as we bristled against those descriptions, they weren't wrong.

NEGOTIATIONS

DAVID
We couldn't have done it without Dan's team. The people that he assigned to the High Line and said, "Make this happen" were extraordinary. What they had to navigate to get this through — we needed a federal approval of something called a Certificate of Interim Trail Use, which had already gone very far down the track in the opposite direction to demolish. The State was very not on board with this idea. There were 22 underlying property owners that all had to be dealt with individually.

HAMMOND
Now people are like, "Well, no shit. How hard could it have been to get property owners to make money?" But this was really difficult.

Opposite: View over the Hudson River from the High Line.

Below: Aerial view of the 10th Avenue Square and Overlook.

DAVID

The property owners we're talking about weren't the big real estate developers that we all think of as being associated with the High Line now. This was a very diverse group, some of whom had held their properties since the time they sold the easement to the railroad in 1930. A lot of them were mom-and-pop concerns that were difficult to reach and difficult to negotiate with. It was not a standard issue New York City real estate negotiation.

HAMMOND

We had to have a rezoning and it was special rezoning. It was a transfer of development rights, which had only been done twice before. These things are so difficult and complicated. [We succeeded because] Dan attracted smart talent that normally would not be interested in coming to government. He was able to find these people, who were some of the best people I've worked with in my whole career, and empower them to get things done. It would not have happened if they had not gotten all the properties. If they had not gotten the MTA, if they had not done a deal with CSX.

DESIGN AND CONSTRUCTION

DAVID

Now we have so many new parks that are of a very high level of design. You've got Little Island, you have the new Brooklyn waterfront parks. It was a little bit less so at the time. There were voices who were pushing to do [the High Line] completely in the vocabulary of "a standard New York City park" with hex pavers and standard New York City benches. Dan and the administration more broadly was very supportive of our place at the table in the design. Their trust in our sense of what would be right for the High Line from a design perspective ultimately made the High Line a much more ambitiously designed park.

HAMMOND

We had this working group. We would decide everything with this committee. The testimony to the people that Dan found is [that it] never came down to votes. It was really collaborative.

ANDREW WINTERS

Dan assigned the project to the Office of Capital Project Development for coordination. At the first few design meetings we attended, there were about four agencies in attendance, plus Friends of the High Line, and each provided separate notes/responses to the design team, frequently contradictory. Our office coordinated all of the City responses and brokered solutions to all issues.

DAVID

Always there was some kind of consensus reached, which I think is pretty extraordinary.

WINTERS

As design progressed, one of the developers designing a major building along the High Line — Related — put pressure on the design teams and agencies to add a private entrance to the High Line, which was absolutely not permitted by the plan. This went all the way up to Dan, and I attended the meeting at City Hall where [CEO] Steve Ross himself, along with his team, made the case to Dan. Dan said "no."

HAMMOND

He was so sure, even after Dan said no, that Dan would let him do it or someone would let him do it. If you walk along the High Line and you go to the Caledonia, there's a glass door, there's

advertising on it, there's a handle, there's a little micro thing where you would put your key card. This is where we were so dependent on [Dan]. If he said, "Look, you have to do this," we would've screamed and yelled but we would've rolled on it. Ultimately, he listened to his staff. He was protecting the experience of the High Line so it didn't feel like a private entrance.

DAVID

In fact, virtually every single developer next to the High Line came to us with that same request. Every single one. We've had this conversation, I would say, 20 times. And because this precedent has been set, we have a policy. If that policy had not been developed, virtually every building alongside the High Line would have retail space directly opening onto the High Line. It ended up being something that was very important to preserving the special quality of the High Line because otherwise it would be a mall.

WINTERS

Josh and Robbie wanted to raise money for the 10th Avenue Overlook which would be $4 million. The city had no more money for the project. The City team recommended we go ahead without it, but Dan argued for a short delay while Josh and Robbie worked to raise the funds. They somehow raised the money very quickly and it happened. Everyone loves it!

DAVID

[Dan] could have said, "We're just going forward. Cut it. You're done. We don't have time to mess around with this." Giving us the chance to come up with that money was such an important thing that Dan did for us. The whole physical environment of the High Line was changed. The 10th Avenue [feature] is part of the audacity of building something like the High Line.

[Dan] appreciates a great vision. I think you see it in the gondola proposal for Governors Island, the idea that a really dramatic gesture has the ability to capture the public imagination in a way that can drive something forward. Dan gets that.

Below: Apple trees on the High Line.

Opposite: The High Line, which now attracts more visitors than the Statue of Liberty, has helped spur a revitalization of West Chelsea and Manhattan's West Side.

Transition from day to night along the High Line as
seen from 17th Street and 10th Avenue.

FRESHKILLS PARK

"Taking a big old garbage dump and making it into an Olympic facility — it has the kernel of making the impossible possible and that's what he liked."

For more than 50 years, New York City's garbage marred the landscape of Staten Island, filling marshland with mountains of trash that sent stenches circulating through nearby neighborhoods. Robert Moses founded Fresh Kills in 1948, with visions of using garbage to fill in the soggy land, which could then be covered and converted into a new community. By 1955, those plans had faded and Fresh Kills had become the largest landfill in the United States.

During peak operations, at the end of the 1980s, barges brought nearly 30,000 tons of garbage to the landfill every day; a decade later, Fresh Kills was the last operating landfill within city limits, with 2,200 moldering acres. As neighborhood protests grew, the City finally closed the facility in 2001, capping its five massive mounds. The Giuliani administration initiated a design competition to develop a master plan for the site's transformation into a park.

As a private citizen in the 1990s, Dan Doctoroff, then in the midst of planning a potential Olympic Games in New York City, identified the vast site as a potential host for equestrian and mountain biking events. When he entered city government, Doctoroff prioritized the site's transformation into a park (to be named Freshkills Park), overseeing the process to select a master plan in 2003 by then-little known landscape architect, James Corner (who would later design the High Line). Over the next three years, Doctoroff and his team refined the plan and in 2006, they hired Eloise Hirsh to oversee the project full time.

Hirsh, who had worked in the mayoral administration of Ed Koch and was fresh from overseeing waterfront reclamation projects in Pittsburgh, PA, embraced the challenge. "There was just so much to do," she said. The 17 years since the release of the plan have seen the slow but steady realization of its vision, acre by acre, as people, plants, and wildlife have found their way back to a landscape meticulously transformed through engineering, ecological management, and careful public programming.

Hirsh credits Doctoroff and his team for clearing the way for progress on the project, which, when completed, will be three times the size of Central Park.

"He set up the guideposts and he gave it the energy it needed to get through the first blocks that any project — especially one that complicated — has to get through," Hirsh said.

Fresh Kills* opened in 1948. It's a Robert Moses story. Robert Moses came to the people of Staten Island and said 'We're going to fill in these marshes — they're filled with pestilential mosquitos, it's not good for your health. We're going to fill them in and we're going to come back in three years and then we will build residential communities and light industry.' Three years turned into five years turned into 10 years turned into 50 years. These people were very pissed off.

My husband actually happened to be a sanitation commissioner in the Lindsay administration and [Fresh Kills] was loathed. It was hated. The main thing that people remember to this day is the smell. There's a major mall in Staten Island across the street from the site. People have memories of running into Macy's holding their noses.

But at the same time the Sanitation Department went about it in completely conscientious ways and the edifice of it, the immensity of the project, in a way, was their pyramids. It actually is incredibly important in the world of waste management. People come from all over the world to understand the systems.

Staten Island being the only reliable Republican borough in the city is therefore the least powerful. The landfill kept building and getting bigger and it kept growing until [the 1980s]. Eventually Fresh Kills was taking all the city's garbage. [In 2001] there was a political confluence of Republican leadership. There was [Republican Rudy] Giuliani [as] mayor, [Republican George] Pataki [as]

*The landfill is known as Fresh Kills; the park is Freshkills.

AN EDITED ORAL HISTORY

Dan Doctoroff and his Olympic planning team identified Fresh Kills, once the world's largest landfill, as a potential site for Olympic equestrian and mountain biking competitions. Once in City Hall, Doctoroff prioritized the landfill's ongoing transformation into a 2,200-acre park. In recent years, Freshkills Park has attracted grassland birds long absent from New York City, including the Grasshopper Sparrow, Bobolink, and Sedge Wren.

governor and of course, all the Staten Island elected officials. So that political moment in time allowed the action that the State had to take to close the landfill.

The Municipal Art Society went to then-Mayor Giuliani and said, 'This is the last time the city is going to get this much vacant land, you must not lose this opportunity, you should do an international competition for how to develop this land.'

There were actually entrants from all over the world and the winner of the competition was James Corner Field Operations, who eventually did the High Line. But this was pre-High Line. This was an early project in his career and it was basically a draft master plan.

When [Mayor Michael] Bloomberg came into office in 2002, he had Dan come in. Before the park planning began there was a history of the site potentially being used for an Olympic bid. There were two sites at Fresh Kills that could possibly have been used. The fact that Dan was already working on it really meant that there was energy behind it, and people paying attention to Fresh Kills, which is invaluable because it is really hard for people to keep their mind on Staten Island. It was critical that there actually was energy from the very beginning around Freshkills [Park] and around all the big projects.

Freshkills [Park] is the kind of project that totally depends on mayoral will. People were still making attempts at the beginning, 'Let's put a bus garage there. Let's put a correctional high school for kids there.' Uses that they didn't want in their neighborhood. People were still thinking about it as a dump. That's what could have happened. It would have been nibbled to death in strange little projects at the edges.

Even today you have to hang on to the political will. De Blasio, for example — we didn't make a lot of progress during that administration.

The most important thing that [Dan and City Planning Chair Amanda Burden] did was make sure that this place remained the kind of park that people would walk in, people would relate to nature in ways of wonder.

There was a lot of very beautiful land, what we now understand to be an important ecological benefit from wetlands, and it was destroyed. Taking something this compromised and giving it back to the public is a very important thing for the City to demonstrate that it can do. It's a message: "We can fix what we broke." It puts New York in a position as an environmental leader. It also puts sustainability as a principle front and center for a big project, for something that's going to take a lot of resources.

I was hired by the Parks Department because Parks was going to be the implementer of the *Draft Master Plan*. I had a good background for it, having just returned to New York from Pittsburgh, where I'd done a lot of work on taking the riverfronts back.

Thanks to Dan and the mayor, it was such a high profile project, people from all over the country and all over the world came to see it. The project was enthralling to people whose field this is. It's famous in landscape architecture schools for the potential of the design. Pipes all over the landfill are connected to a gas processing plant on site that [has] heated the equivalent of 30,000 homes.

Grasslands is a very threatened habitat, particularly in the eastern part of the country. We now have a thousand acres of grasslands, which means we are attracting threatened species of birds; about 200 different species have been sighted there. There's deer, opossums. We have tons of foxes, groundhogs, snakes. The waters are clean enough for fish. The State has ruled that the waterways are good for recreation, for boating and catch-release fishing, but not for swimming. Our kayak programs are totally sold out all the time because people love to kayak and there's only so many places in the city that you [can] do it.

A big piece of what we tried to do from the beginning was to create as many experiences as we could for people to come on the site and see the reality, the beauty of it. Once it is built, it can give New Yorkers access to big outdoor activities on a scale that isn't available anywhere else in the city.

Pre-pandemic, twice a year we opened about 800 acres of the site. That's about the size of Central Park. It was staffing intensive, but it was really important because people got to come and see what had been a very mysterious place to them. People walk around saying, "It doesn't smell. It doesn't smell. Look at this." One guy burst into tears saying he thought he'd never live to see the day. Visitors constantly asked, "When can we be here all the time?"

Elected officials want to see things happen within their term. From the beginning, the full build out was anticipated to take until 2036. One of the things that made Dan Doctoroff different from really all the other officials, was that he just wanted to get it going. He wanted to make sure that it was started, because he believed in the potential of the project enough that it didn't matter so much to him that he himself carried [it] through.

[Dan had a] drive to show the world that New York City was back, doing big, challenging projects. So an outsize project like Freshkills — taking a big old garbage dump and making it into an Olympic facility — it has the kernel of making the impossible possible and that's what he liked. It would not have happened really without his drive and his dedication to the starring role of all five boroughs in the City of New York.

Above: The Schmul Park playground at Freshkills Park includes a spray shower, swings, and a sand box in addition to brightly colored play equipment.

Opposite and Top Right: The seasonal changes at Freshkills Park provide a colorful backdrop for kayakers navigating the park's waterways.

LISA W. FODERARO | Parks Beat Reporter,
The New York Times, 2011-2015

THE HIGH BRIDGE

For more than 100 years, the High Bridge transported fresh water from Westchester County to a burgeoning New York City. Soon after its debut in 1848, the bridge also doubled as a pedestrian walkway that linked the Bronx and Manhattan, providing a scenic stroll high above the Harlem River for everyone from high-style New Yorkers parading back and forth to writers like Edgar Allan Poe, who loved using the span to travel to and from his Bronx cottage.

Then, after a century of operation, it closed. The 1,450-foot span, whose arches evoke the grandeur of a Roman aqueduct, stopped carrying water in the 1950s, as new water sources from the Catskills came online. By the 1970s, after construction of the Major Deegan Expressway and the Harlem River Drive, access to the public walkway ceased, a move that coincided with increased water pollution, as well as rising crime and poverty in the area. The closure severed Bronx residents from Manhattan's Highbridge Park and its large Works Progress Administration (WPA)-era public pool, depriving them of access to recreation just across the river.

And so for 40 years, the civil engineering marvel — so famous for its elegance that Edith Wharton had a heroine traverse it in one of her novels, so essential that for decades it offered safe passage for children to playgrounds and swimming — stood dormant. Then the Bloomberg administration targeted its revival under PlaNYC, and a restoration project nearly as monumental as the bridge's construction got underway.

In 2012, a small army of workers began to apply mortar to the stone joints, fix the dilapidated brick walkway, repaint steel supports, and restore the original handrails. They also installed new lighting, ramps, and safety fencing. Bronze medallions set into the walkway tell the story of the High Bridge's history, explaining, for instance, that from 1861 to 1864, "public demand for water outpaced the capacity of the two original 3-foot pipes." A new pipe embedded in the High Bridge was a capacious 7.5 feet, by contrast.

Finally, after undergoing a $61 million renovation, the High Bridge reopened on June 9, 2015 amid much fanfare, including marching bands and speeches by city officials and historians. The bridge was one of eight signature park projects contained in PlaNYC, all chosen for their ability to deliver equitable access to the outdoors in marginalized communities.

New York City's sustainability blueprint, PlaNYC, called for the $62 million restoration of the High Bridge, New York City's oldest standing bridge, which had been shuttered for decades. The High Bridge reopened in 2015, enabling pedestrians and cyclists to cross between the Bronx and Manhattan over the Harlem River.

In addition to restoring and reopening the High Bridge, the City subsequently poured $10 million into renovating the adjacent Highbridge Park. With a new connection to Manhattan, residents of the South Bronx can now walk across the pedestrian span to access a wide range of recreational amenities: playgrounds, ballfields, a mountain biking course, a skate park, walking paths, and the newly restored Highbridge Recreation Center and swimming pool.

"Highbridge Park went from being literally a dumping ground for thousands of tires and cars to being near pristine in many sections," said Adrian Benepe, who served as Parks commissioner in the Bloomberg administration.

But it was the High Bridge itself that garnered the most attention on opening day, as visitors gazed out from the 123-foot-tall walkway to take in the Harlem River below and the city's skyline to the south. As Rubén Díaz Jr., then–Bronx borough president, said during the festivities, "Downtown may have the High Line, but Uptown we have the High Bridge."

SUE DONOGHUE | Assistant Commissioner for Communications and Strategic Initiatives, 2007-2013 & Commissioner, 2022-Present, Department of Parks & Recreation

PLANYC'S DESTINATION PARKS

"Seeing the effort to make use of every single open and vacant space — that's an amazing thing."

In 2007, over two million New Yorkers lived more than ten minutes away from open space. PlaNYC, the city's landmark sustainability plan, sought to reduce that number to zero by prioritizing the creation of new parks and open spaces across New York. This included expanded access to local neighborhood playgrounds — and the creation of eight destination parks distributed throughout the five boroughs. These new major parks would transform sites that had languished, in some cases for decades, and transform them into regional attractions that offered New Yorkers varied experiences and amenities.

PlaNYC's massive, multifaceted parks effort involved an almost $1.3 billion initial commitment by the administration, making it collectively one of the largest capital investments in the Parks Department's recent history. Deputy Mayor Dan Doctoroff, who initiated and led the PlaNYC effort, insisted that every initiative in the report had funding and appropriate staffing. This enabled the Parks Department to hire Sue Donoghue as a dedicated project manager for the PlaNYC projects.

Donoghue had just completed a masters in public administration at New York University and was looking to transition out of her private sector job in finance. "I wasn't, as you might imagine, getting the psychic gratification from my work," she said. Still, she harbored some "unfortunate stereotypes" about the public sector. But the Parks Department, with PlaNYC as a guiding star, was less different from the high-intensity corporate world than she might have imagined. "Seeing initiatives move aggressively forward was incredibly eye-opening to me," she said. PlaNYC was "incredibly well thought out and well implemented and had so much force behind it. It was gratifying to see how effectively city government could work and does work when there's a good plan."

Today, all eight destination parks are open to the public, and many have spurred revival in the surrounding neighborhoods. "Seeing the effort to make use of every single open and vacant space — that's an amazing thing," she said.

It was an enormous opportunity. There was all this open space that just hadn't had the investment that it needed. In each borough there were opportunities to take underutilized, under-resourced parks and open space and transform them. It fit into what PlaNYC was looking to address overall: The city was going to grow by a million people and we needed to plan for that. We needed to address aging infrastructure, but also how are we going to accommodate that growth?

I was hired mainly because [PlaNYC represented] such an enormous investment for Parks — $1.3 billion in new capital for the Parks Department. What happens so often is that people in government will just get another project, another thing put on them and there's a bandwidth issue. You're juggling so many things. City Hall knew this couldn't be just someone within Parks. It needed to be a designated individual who was solely focused on managing the implementation.

The thing about PlaNYC was what a good plan it was from the outset. There were clearly identified milestones, there were deliverables, there was accountability — people who were passionate and committed to seeing it work. So much of what I was able to set up comes from the fact that it was a really good, solid plan to begin with. It had the attention of the highest levels of City Hall. To have both— to have the plan and the backing of capital — is really extraordinary.

Ocean Breeze Park, Staten Island   **Project size: 10 acres**   **Budget: $111 million**

The Ocean Breeze Athletic Complex added an elite track and field facility with seating for 2,500 spectators around a 200-meter running track to Ocean Breeze Park on Staten Island, set within nearly 140 acres of seagrass meadow. The 135,000 square-foot complex is the first indoor facility certified by the International Association of Athletic Federations (IAAF) and includes space for long and high jump, pole vaulting, and shot put. By 2022, 18 national records had been set on its courses. "There was no facility there before, now it's a world-class facility that attracts people from all over the country and beyond," Donoghue said. The complex also incorporated PlaNYC's sustainability goals, with geothermal heating and cooling, stormwater systems to support the surrounding wetlands, and natural ventilation and lighting.

Top: Invitational track meet at Ocean Breeze Athletic Complex.

Left: The site prior to the PlaNYC intervention.

I used to say, when I was in the thick of it, "We're not building prisons, we're building parks." And yet, there are challenges. There were neighborhoods where people didn't want a lot more people coming, didn't want to share the resources that they had, didn't want to be a destination. There was concern about safety and security. There were competing uses. I think about McCarren [Park] — not only did we bring back to life this enormous, beautiful public pool, but also [created] this incredible new year-round facility; it's really extraordinary. But [the empty pool] had been utilized for concerts and people loved that. It didn't serve all in the community, but people were sad about that going away. In Ridgewood [reservoir], there is actually a full-on forest [in the basins]. There was concern; the most extreme was, you're going to put in synthetic turf fields. We were never intending to put some synthetic fields in the reservoir. But that was part of what was put out there. So we just did the walking paths on the outside of the reservoir, which are phenomenal and so well utilized now and people love them. But because of that opposition, we never got into the basins.

You don't think these kinds of transformations are going to cause concern or opposition, but they certainly do — from concertgoers to environmentalists. In a sense, it was beneficial that I didn't come out of city government. That I came to it with a different perspective, that I had run big projects.

At the time I had young kids. Having my kids come along with me and plant trees — I think that was what was so appealing for New Yorkers writ large; to get involved in something really hands-on. You get your hands dirty and you say, "I'm making an impact. This is my tree. I'm planting it, I'm making a difference." That's what we're looking to build here at the Parks Department — that kind of stewardship.

Parks are a quality-of-life issue. With New York being so diverse, the destination parks allow for a wider range of uses. They mirror New York: big and constantly evolving and changing. We needed to adapt our green spaces to meet that demand — more activities, more people, more trees, more greening.

It was a very conscious decision looking at where these investments would make the most difference, looking at historically under-resourced communities. I think so much of the plan was looking at: Where is density increasing? How can we make sure we're providing the amenities that are needed? Where are these parks going to have the most impact for a growing population?

The idea of making an investment in creating these destinations for New Yorkers was so critical. To rally thousands of New Yorkers behind a cause — it's an amazing thing to do. That stewardship on a local level is a critical output of the work that PlaNYC started and the work that we continue to do today.

Top: Opening of the renovated McCarren Park Swimming Pool, June 28, 2012.
Above: McCarren Park Swimming Pool before improvements made through PlaNYC.

McCarren Park, Brooklyn

Project size: 5.5 acres   **Budget: $50 million**

The restoration of McCarren Park in Williamsburg, Brooklyn reclaimed a distinctive, historic outdoor swimming pool and enclosed bathhouse, which had been shuttered for nearly three decades. Built under the Great Depression-era Works Progress Administration (WPA), McCarren Pool opened in 1936, featuring vaulted ceilings reminiscent of Roman architecture. But over the decades it fell into disrepair. Though the empty pool basin was used by some members of the surrounding community for outdoor concerts, the site was officially closed to the public in 1984.

The whole complex was designated as a New York City landmark in 2007 and the structure underwent a major renovation, reopening

in 2012 with a smaller-footprint swimming pool, an expanded poolside deck, and larger community spaces that can be used year-round, including a fitness center and an indoor basketball court. "Taking something that is just a summer amenity and being able to create a year-round destination for a community that has taken off — it's really extraordinary," Donoghue said. "Once you make that kind of investment it really can be transformative." The Parks Department recently renovated an adjacent building and opened a cafe to support the growing neighborhood. "Williamsburg has just skyrocketed," Donoghue said. "I believe it's because of anchor investments like this one."

Far Rockaway, Queens

Project size: 18.5 acres
Budget: $29 million

Though the expansive beaches of the Rockaways have a global reputation that draw New Yorkers and tourists alike during the summer months, less known are the neighborhoods at the far end of the peninsula — densely populated and historically under-resourced, and organized around large public housing complexes. "There was a real interest in making sure we were investing in this area" at the farthest end of the Rockaways, Donoghue said, "and providing amenities and upgrades that would be important to the community." That included transforming underutilized spaces like a parking lot and paved concrete picnic areas into sports courts, playgrounds, a comfort station, a skateboard park, and performance space with an amphitheater — "a gathering space for communities," said Donoghue. "It took an area that had historically been underinvested in, and dramatically transformed it."

Soundview Park, Bronx
Budget: $15 million

Built on former landfill and marshland in the South Bronx — and embedded in an historically under-resourced neighborhood with significant public housing — Soundview Park was "in dire need of investment," Donoghue said. The park, which sits along the Bronx River, was "a growing and busy neighborhood; lots of kids and families." But the park "didn't feel welcoming or accessible," she said. The PlaNYC investment "really took into account, how do we accommodate and provide for all ages, for kids and families, as well as community gathering?" Improvements included track and field facilities, an amphitheater, and a brand-new playground. The family-friendly redesign, which reflected community priorities (including an onsite bathroom), has been able to "engage kids and families and make the park feel safe and accessible" for concerts, movie nights, and other community events, reflecting the importance of "intergenerational places for the community to gather," she said.

The High Bridge, Bronx/Manhattan

Budget: $61 million

In 2007, the High Bridge, New York City's oldest standing bridge, had been fenced off behind barbed wire for almost 40 years. The closure cut off communities in the Bronx from a large park and public pool on the Manhattan side of the bridge. "Kids would jump the fence and cross over to get to the public pool," Donoghue said. PlaNYC resolved to make the bridge safe and accessible again, while knitting the communities back together. "It was an incredible opportunity to reconnect the Bronx and Manhattan, reconnect families," Donoghue said. Through a combination of renovation and historic preservation, the Parks Department brought the bridge back to life. The project included new lighting, including along the pathways and entrances, to "highlight this incredible asset, but also make it safer for people who are utilizing it," Donoghue said. They installed benches for people to sit and enjoy the river views and a new bike lane. "The best way to make something safer is actually to have it be busy," Donoghue said, noting that on a recent visit she saw the span filled with pedestrians and cyclists. "It's now a really busy thoroughfare," she said. "It's beautiful. It's a masterpiece."

Ridgewood Reservoir/Highland Park, Queens

Project size: 3 acres   **Budget: $18 million**

Highland Park, formed by ancient ice sheets, was converted into a reservoir in the 19th century. In 1990, the Department of Environmental Protection decommissioned the site, leaving two empty basins which quickly became overgrown. PlaNYC targeted the reservoir for a sustainable restoration and recreation destination, but the project encountered some challenges from environmental advocates, who objected to any interventions in the forested basins. This was a misunderstanding of the Parks Department's intent, Donoghue said. "Forests aren't maintained on their own," Donoghue said. "That was part of what we wanted to do, was get in there and further restore and sustain what was there." Despite the pushback, the PlaNYC project made significant investments in restoring the park area around the reservoir basins themselves, investing $18 million in a network of paths, essential lighting, and access points. "The paths are so well utilized now," Donoghue said. "It's such a destination for people walking their dogs, jogging, and biking."

Fort Washington Park, Manhattan

Project size: 11.5 acres   Budget: $19 million

Fort Washington, which features attractions like the Little Red Lighthouse, "is a beautiful, beautiful park, but because of the West Side Highway, it was really cut off to the public," Donoghue said. "And so, our work here was adding amenities, bringing more people in, making it more accessible." The project strengthened connections to the existing Greenway and upgraded the park entrances to make them more welcoming. The renovation introduced new amenities, including a playground, basketball courts, handball courts, and turf ball fields. The renovated park also boasts new concession spaces to support the vibrant surrounding neighborhood. "We knew that it was big, open, expansive, green space in an area that really needed it," Donoghue said. "You're making it a destination for kids and families."

Calvert Vaux Park, Brooklyn   Project size: 10 acres   Budget: $23 million

Calvert Vaux Park was named after the famed landscape designer who worked with his junior partner, Frederick Law Olmsted, to create some of New York's most iconic parks. But for years, his namesake park, which stretches along waterfront in southern Brooklyn abutting Gravesend Bay, provided limited benefit to the surrounding community. Though PlaNYC's intended restoration faced some initial opposition, by 2013 Parks had earned community support to respond to "a lot of demand for baseball fields and active recreation," Donoghue said. In addition to two synthetic turf fields, the project included new perimeter landscaping, as well as more parking, creating new accessible resources for more people, Donoghue said. The project also restored aquatic and coastal habitats and built a main entry rain garden, a field house and a district headquarters. PlaNYC influenced the park's sustainable design which includes recycled materials and new permeable green space to aid in stormwater capture.

MARY ALICE LEE | Director, NYC Playgrounds Program, Trust for Public Land, 2002–Present
JOAN KEENER | Deputy Director, NYC Playgrounds Program, Trust for Public Land, 2008–Present

SCHOOLYARDS TO PLAYGROUNDS

"More than four million New Yorkers live within a 10-minute walk of one of our playgrounds. That's half of our city, which is amazing."

A barren stretch of asphalt — that's what thousands of New York City schoolchildren faced when they went out to play in the 1990s. When the nonprofit Trust for Public Land (TPL) inventoried the city's schoolyards, it found most "were really parking lots," recalled Mary Alice Lee, Director of TPL's New York City Playgrounds Program. In 1996, TPL started renovating them. But progress was slow — and the problem was about collide with another citywide challenge. By the Bloomberg administration's second term, New York's resurgence had led to projections that the city's population would grow by a million more people by 2030, making the search for usable open space in neighborhoods even more urgent.

In response, Deputy Mayor Dan Doctoroff oversaw PlaNYC, a master plan to accommodate growth while improving quality of life, combating climate change, and creating a sustainable 21st century city. PlaNYC vowed to put open space within easy reach of every New Yorker. The team quickly identified schoolyards as a potential solution, noting that 81% locked their gates when school ended, depriving neighborhoods of significant recreational space.

PlaNYC proposed updating a program that originated during the Great Depression, whereby New York City opened school playgrounds to the community through a partnership between the Parks Department and the Department of Education. Working with TPL, the City launched the new Schoolyards to Playgrounds

program in 2007, which renovated playgrounds with greenery and safe play equipment then opened them to the public outside of school hours.

The team identified three categories of interventions: Category I schoolyards were ready to open to the public. Category II schoolyards needed new equipment, and Category III schoolyards also required capital improvements. Meetings were held with schools and local residents, where the children made playground "wish lists."

Kids dream big. They wished for swimming pools and soft ground, chocolate fountains — and drinking fountains. They even asked for garbage cans, so they could keep their playground clean. Sometimes, adults dream big, too. Since PlaNYC, the Schoolyards to Playgrounds program has invested nearly $210 million in opening 296 playgrounds, and 30 more are in the pipeline.

Today, 99% of New Yorkers live within a 10-minute walk of open space. The Schoolyards to Playgrounds program was essential to reaching that goal. "That is something PlaNYC gave to four million New Yorkers, that gift of being able to play in their own neighborhood," said Lee. "The plan has fulfilled its vision," agreed Deputy Director Joan Keener. "We want to continue doing it until there's no schoolyard that doesn't have a beautiful place for kids to play."

AN EDITED ORAL HISTORY

Above: Since the release of PlaNYC in 2007, a partnership between New York City and Trust for Public Land has opened nearly 300 playgrounds to the surrounding neighborhood on weekends and after school hours. Here, students at P.S. 156 / I.S. 392, Brooklyn, celebrate the opening of the new playground in 2019.

Opposite: A renovated playground at P.S. 176 in Bay Ridge, Brooklyn.

BACKGROUND

MARY ALICE LEE
There [were] over 1,000 schools in New York City, and [many] of their yards were really parking lots. Teachers were constantly seeing kids getting their knees scraped or getting hurt because there were cracks in the asphalt. There wasn't that much to do. Kids would sit by the fence, and it was just—

JOAN KEENER
Depressing. They were barren asphalt lots.

LEE
TPL realized they could function as neighborhood parks. Also, because they were school property, you had a built-in maintenance crew, the school custodians. Mayor [Michael] Bloomberg and Dan Doctoroff came into office and said, "We're looking around for the good ideas nonprofits are doing, because we want to be forward-thinking about when a million more residents are living in the city." TPL came in and spoke about our program. We were linked up [as] the nonprofit partner for the Schoolyards to Playgrounds project.

The idea Dan came up with was extremely ambitious. At that point, 69 yards were [Category] I sites that could be opened immediately to the public, which was revolutionary. Schoolyards are in everyone's neighborhood. You're radically increasing the amount of park space around the city. [For renovated playgrounds] we put in trees, green roof gazebos, gardens, for [kids] to have one-on-one experiences with nature. That's a really important step for their self-esteem: that no matter where they live in New York City, they have a nice place to play, that they're worthy of that.

PROCESS AND PROGRAM

KEENER
In the beginning, we show a slideshow to the school [outlining the participatory design process] and invite parents to see it. We show them other schoolyards that we've designed. The kids come up with a wish list, and then the whole school votes. We've done sensory gardens for special needs populations, game tables and benches, outdoor classrooms with seating. Play equipment. Basketball, volleyball, tennis courts. Whatever the kids can imagine. The sky's the limit, except there's a budget.

LEE
A lot of them really wanted to have swimming pools. We'd have to explain that swimming pools are fantastic, but most of the time that you're swimming, it's July and August when school is not in session. Kids also were really interested in chocolate fountains, and we tried to explain that that was not possible either. [But] if you can't have a roller coaster or a rocket ship, maybe we're putting in the moon and stars on the ground.

KEENER
Some of the inventions are particular to certain schools. One that always stands out to me is [a] school in Harlem. The girls wanted a hair braiding station, so the landscape architects invented this very cute setup of benches where girls could braid each other's hair during recess.

Another was in a school in the Bronx. The girls felt like the boys dominated the basketball courts. So, they decided that they would paint one of the practice courts pink and that would deter the boys. In fact, it did. They have a dedicated girls' basketball practice hoop. We can make play equipment that looks like a spaceship or a boat. In Midwood, the theme was Coney Island, so there is a roller coaster piece of artwork.

LEE
The kids are the ones who are drawing those things. So, there's a chance to do art, as well, in the playgrounds. There was one playground [where] we did a rainbow track. It just looks so stunning.

KEENER
The themes are really great. One of them is aliens and humans —

LEE
Living together —

KEENER
Together as friends. There are all these adorable pictures of aliens and humans holding hands and helping each other.

The program helped create community spaces to connect to other people — neighborhood merchants or grandparents or older friends. So, they became these spaces for multigenerational interaction that contributed to the health of communities.

LEE
Some people were upset that we were opening up the schoolyards to the community. They were worried about things like noise. One of the great things about the community process was we were able to talk to those people and find out what their issues were. Then, through the design process, we were able to address that as much as possible. If they were worried about noise, we would put trees in front of their apartment window and move the basketball courts away from the window.

Custodial funding for PlaNYC projects was really the linchpin in creating this program. We were able to negotiate with the union for them to get paid to open up these yards to the community after school and on weekends. You need to have someone who's there opening, closing, and maintaining it and keeping it safe for the kids to use.

KEENER
When we would approach [the custodians], they were like, "I'd love to be in that program. Please bring your playground here." They take pride in something beautiful that they help keep clean and safe for the kids in the community.

SUSTAINABILITY

LEE
PlaNYC [was] bringing greenery into playgrounds where there hadn't been. It also adds, in a small way, to helping lower temperatures. Something that used to be just an asphalt lot now has shady areas and greenery, which are also good for mental health.

Our partnership with DEP [the Department of Environmental Protection] started once PlaNYC ended. DEP [was] able to start funding green infrastructure amenities in the playgrounds. With the increased storms that we're having in New York City, green infrastructure playgrounds are more important than ever. We're able to pitch [the playground surface] toward the turf fields, capturing millions of gallons of stormwater every year. One of our sites was underwater during Hurricane Ida. The custodian saw that because we had green infrastructure there, all the water went straight down into the turf field and into the —

KEENER
Gravel bed [underneath]. No puddles the next day. The partnership with DEP was kind of an extension of making city areas more sustainable. Making them more resilient to climate change, resilient to floods.

THE LEGACY

KEENER
With Schoolyards to Playgrounds, every neighborhood has a little pocket of green. A little oasis for the people who live near that school, where they can have a better quality of life.

LEE
Dan Doctoroff thought about how to make this city even better. More than four million New Yorkers live within a 10-minute walk of one of our playgrounds. That's half of our city, which is amazing.

Before and after photos of the playground at I.S. 192, the Piagentini-Jones School in the Bronx. As part of a participatory design process, students were invited to share ideas for the redesign.

FIONA WATT | Chief of Forestry, 2001–2008 & Assistant Commissioner of Forestry, Horticulture and Natural Resources, 2008–2010, Department of Parks & Recreation

ONE MILLION TREES

The launch of MillionTreesNYC on October 9, 2007, featuring city officials wielding shovels alongside Big Bird, Bette Midler, and the cast of the Broadway show, *Wicked*, was a splashy, public milestone for trees in our city. Behind the scenes, it was also the culmination of a long, uphill struggle for recognition of the importance of trees — and our agency — within the larger city government thanks to new allies in the Bloomberg administration like Deputy Mayor Dan Doctoroff.

When I joined the Parks Department in 1996, tree planting and care was at a low point. Much of the agency's forestry staff had been laid off in the budget crises of the early 1990s. A modest street tree planting budget serviced constituent requests and trees in parks were rarely replaced. Pleas for more funding were largely ignored by City Hall. Despite the impassioned efforts of our small cadre of arborists, larger agencies ran roughshod over trees growing in the way of their street reconstruction projects. We were loath to allow tree removals and demanded ample replacements when it was unavoidable. In late 2000, this practice landed us in the office of a furious budget director, who, red in the face, screamed at the Parks commissioner that we were costing other city agencies millions of dollars with such frivolous policies. This attitude even persisted into the early days of the Bloomberg administration. But in urban forestry circles, researchers were proving that taking a stand for trees was anything but frivolous.

In fact, trees could advance an astonishing range of urban priorities: ecological functions such as reducing air pollution and greenhouse gases, cooling air temperatures, and capturing stormwater runoff; economic benefits such as increasing property values, reducing energy costs from shading buildings, and encouraging pedestrian activity in business districts; public health benefits such as lowering stress and anxiety, reducing hospital stays, and reducing asthma hospitalizations; and social benefits such as increasing civic pride, reducing violence, and even improving learning outcomes. We were hungry to apply the science of quantifying tree benefits to New York City. In 2006, we completed our second-ever count of New York City's trees (result: 592,130 trees) and initiated studies to assess our tree canopy, its potential benefits, and gaps in coverage.

Knowing that Dan and Mayor Michael Bloomberg thrived on data-driven arguments, we calculated the exact rate of return on investment in trees ($5.60 for every $1 spent). Parks Commissioner Adrian Benepe presented these findings to an interagency group convened and run by Dan called the Economic Development Agencies Council (EDAC) which met regularly so agencies could share their most compelling projects with each other.

It turned out Dan was in the middle of developing a comprehensive sustainability plan to guide New York's development through 2030 called PlaNYC. Our call to significantly increase New York City's tree canopy to combat urban climate challenges advanced nearly every PlaNYC goal and merged with actress Bette Midler's public campaign to plant one million trees (as Los Angeles had recently declared). MillionTreesNYC was born.

Unlike some politicians who might have been pleased with the catchy headline, Dan always demanded details. He didn't want to announce anything we didn't have a plan to fully fund and execute. This would prove prescient as other cities subsequently made their own flashy million trees announcements — then ultimately failed to deliver.

The PlaNYC report called for planting one million trees across New York City to advance multiple sustainability priorities, including improving air quality, reducing temperatures, improving community health and quality of life, and fighting climate change. Governors Island was one of the planting sites.

Top and Above: Thayer Street in Inwood, Manhattan in 2009, before tree planting. By 2022, tree plantings had transformed Thayer Street into a lush streetscape.

Above: Former Mayor Michael Bloomberg at Joyce Kilmer Park in the Bronx, 2015, with Bette Midler, Mayor Bill de Blasio, and others to celebrate planting the one millionth tree, two years ahead of schedule.

Opposite: Trees under the Brooklyn Bridge, part of the MillionTreesNYC initiative.

A "radical and systemic" change

Once Dan was behind the plan, things changed immediately. Planting one million trees in New York City demanded radical and systemic changes to business as usual. Dan and the mayor fought for the funding we needed for tree care and planting and helped us break through the bureaucratic challenges. We could finally get meetings with decision makers, and our first stop was the city's counsel to discuss the tree supply chain. We had previously argued with various city procurement offices over whether we could enter into our own growing contracts directly with nurseries. "It can't be done," they said. Once PlaNYC was in progress, we described the problem to Dan. He issued a mandate to the city's legal and budgeting team: You have to figure it out. And they did.

So we became tree farmers. The scale of trees required to meet New York's goals was vast, and even if we had pursued privately available trees, they weren't the kinds we needed. Nurseries typically specialize in the same handful of varieties because they need guaranteed sales. But we were hoping for 100 different varieties — or more — that could thrive in New York City's range of habitats — from forests to coastal landscapes to city streets. One of our contracted nurseries grew saplings from seeds we gathered from local native tree specimens. Another nursery shaped trees especially for the streets, with high limbs to ease sidewalk passage, a strong central branching system, and particular resilience to soil compaction, winter de-icing salt, heat, drought, and other urban stressors. This is why on New York City streets today you can see unusual species such as Fragrant Snowbell (*Styrax obassia*), Eastern Hop-hornbeam (*Ostrya virginiana*) and Kentucky Coffeetree (*Gymnocladus dioicus*).

Dan also elevated tree planting within other city agency mandates, supporting a major amendment to the city's zoning resolution that required street tree planting as part of private construction projects, and long-term agreements to fund robust tree replacement and planting as part of major road and bridge reconstruction projects. Dan and the mayor also provided firm back-up when we dealt with regular folks who did not like or want street trees — it's New York City, after all! His unbridled enthusiasm and support for the campaign ultimately helped draw in 64 partner organizations, more than $30 million in private and matching funds, and over 50,000 New Yorkers to plant and steward one million trees in their neighborhoods, parks, yards, and other public and private spaces between 2007 and 2015 (we finished two years early!).

An equitable and sustainable approach

MillionTreesNYC had equity in its DNA. It transformed entire communities, especially in underserved areas, at a time when few initiatives were doing so. Between 2010 and 2017, New York City gained 3,252 acres of overall tree canopy, an increase of 1.7% citywide. But street tree canopy increases in neighborhoods such as East Harlem (6.2%), East New York, Brooklyn (4.8%), Morrisania, Bronx (6.4%), South Jamaica, Queens (5%), and Stapleton, Staten Island (4.4%) far exceeded this gain.

And thanks to their ability to clean the air — New York City's trees now remove 1,100 tons of air pollution each year — these trees are improving human health. Stunning new research from the U.S. Forest Service shows that because of this lower exposure to air pollution, there are 16,500 fewer adverse health conditions — including acute respiratory symptoms, exacerbated asthma, emergency room visits, hospital admissions, and mortality — experienced by New Yorkers each year. It's hard to put a dollar value on that, but if it would get us a million more trees, I bet Dan would encourage us to try.

THE CULTURAL CITY

The worldwide premiere of Björk's *Cornucopia*, performed at The Shed, May 6, 2019.

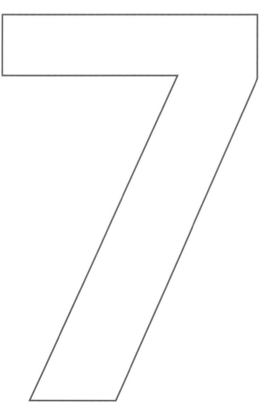

"The arts draw millions of visitors here every year, fuel creative industries like film and television production, and are at the heart of the revivals of some of our most exciting neighborhoods."

DANIEL L. DOCTOROFF, DECEMBER 2003

The Polonsky Shakespeare Center, designed by Hugh Hardy to house Theatre for a New Audience, is part of the Downtown Brooklyn Cultural District.

UNITING FIRE AND ICE IN NEW YORK

Dan Doctoroff understood that supplementing the city's traditional Financial, Insurance, and Real Estate (FIRE) strengths with growth in the Intellectual, Cultural, and Educational (ICE) economy was the key to maintaining New York's competitive global advantage

I have been blessed with Dan Doctoroff's friendship for more than three decades and, over those years, I have had the opportunity to observe his many virtues and talents (they are legion). In this brief introduction to the chapter on the Cultural City, however, I will focus on just one: Dan's uncanny ability to see before others do both the essence of the matter and the possibilities flowing from it.

Scholars of urban life have offered various explanations of New York's uniqueness. Our city, from its birth as a Dutch harbor to the construction of the Erie Canal, was first a gateway economy for the importing, manufacturing, and distribution of goods. When other cities surpassed New York as a port and manufacturing center, New York became America's preeminent location for more modern forms of commerce, focused on three crucial industries: Finance, Insurance, and Real Estate — what urbanologists came to call the FIRE sector of the economy.

Like the gateway economy, the FIRE sector flourished because of New York's locational advantage. In an economy fueled by the stock market, businesses found real opportunity in being situated near the trading floor, allowing entrepreneurs to conduct daily, and even hourly, transactions. Insurance followed finance and real estate thrived. The impact of the FIRE sector, together with the high-paying jobs the sector provided, propelled the city's growth, amplified its importance, and validated its claim as the world's commercial capital.

Yet, as the 21st century dawned and the Bloomberg administration (with its dynamic new Deputy Mayor for Economic Development and Rebuilding, Dan Doctoroff) began to gain traction, the number of city jobs in finance, insurance, and real estate was dwindling. As I noted in a reflection I wrote during my presidency at New York University (NYU) called *Fire and Ice: The Knowledge Century and the Urban University*, those jobs were down 9% from 1990 to 2005. Looking ahead, it was clear that cyberspace would increasingly deny oxygen to New York's FIRE sector, as chief executives conducted business from Aspen or made deals from the Caribbean. Rather than depending on physical proximity for their effectiveness, the channels of commerce were becoming fiber-optic cables and network servers (a trade by a specialist takes an average of 12 seconds longer than an identical trade in cyberspace, and even milliseconds can translate into many millions of dollars).

Dan saw that the consequence of this change to New York was potentially profound. Although FIRE would remain important for some time, it seemed unlikely to be viable as a long-term, solitary strategic base. Yet to find a replacement for this sector was not at all simple: The solution did not lie in relative tax and cost advantages, whether measured against Route 128 in Boston or the Research Triangle in Raleigh-Durham. Instead, Dan saw New York as reinventing itself once again, drawing on a different source of advantage, the unique assets that, regardless of the FIRE sector's future, could sustain it as a leading world city.

He saw our Intellectual, Cultural, and Educational (ICE) strengths — already among the world's greatest — becoming the newly visible essence of New York's identity. He saw the creative industries of New York repositioning the city as yet a different kind of gateway economy, a city where creative initiatives and ideas are born or showcased that influence and shape the world. And, of course, the city's unique inclusive nature — captured in Dan's Olympic slogan describing it as "the world's second home" — only amplified its gateway capacity in that regard, making it a welcoming place for what urbanist Richard Florida would call "the creative class."

It was a lesson that New York had been teaching anyone willing to listen for four centuries. In 1609, Henry Hudson sailed into New York Harbor for the Dutch East India Company, dreaming that he would discover a northwest passage to connect Europe and Asia. At the time, Amsterdam was the world's center of commerce, home to the most progressive and culturally diverse society in Europe. Small but remarkably vital and adventurous, Amsterdam was the source of half the world's published books throughout the 17th century.

Its citizens embraced difference and viewed encounters with other cultures as enriching. Reflecting these origins, New Amsterdam would become New York, the prototype for the American

Deputy Mayor Dan Doctoroff cultivated the city's Intellectual, Cultural, and Educational (ICE) sectors as part of the Bloomberg administration's efforts to diversify New York's economy. This included supporting Columbia University's most ambitious expansion in a century to a new Manhattanville campus. Below, Lenfest Center for the Arts, Jerome L. Greene Science Center, and The Forum at Columbia University.

experiment: open to immigrants, strengthened by many cultures, and always striving. In his marvelous history of Dutch Manhattan, *The Island at the Center of the World*, Russell Shorto reports that New Amsterdam was restless, ambitious, and polyglot; it was, in a profound way, the New York City of today right from the start. Dan Doctoroff recognized that foundational character of our city long before he became deputy mayor and began developing his theory on the crucial role culture played in the city's virtuous cycle of growth.

Though I am certain that Dan's conversations with others had a different flavor, his conversations with me emphasized the centrality of colleges and universities in this process. He saw, for example, that New York State already was the lead destination for first-year college students leaving their home state. He saw that our state ranked with California as home to more of the top 50 universities and top 50 liberal arts colleges than any of the other states, and that seven of our universities housed medical schools that rank among the nation's top 50.

Dan saw immediately that New York City's universities fueled and enhanced much of its ICE sector. There are more college students in New York than in any other city in the country. New York City is a global leader in academic fields as diverse as applied math and fine arts, soft-condensed-matter physics and philosophy. As of 2007, it was home to 128 Nobel Laureates in science and 146 members of the National Academy of Sciences, and the city had the highest concentration of science students and postdocs of any city. And those students and faculty naturally were both creators and consumers of the broader cultural life of the city. Former New York Senator Daniel Patrick Moynihan once was asked what it takes to build a world-class city; he answered, "Create a world-class university and wait 200 years." Dan saw that New York could focus on cementing its position by using its universities to take the city to a new level.

Most of all, Dan understood that this nucleus of creative energy within our universities and colleges sits synergistically amidst an extraordinary array of cultural and artistic assets — a wealth of museums, libraries, theaters, concert halls, workshops, galleries, and studios. From its historic settlement houses on the Lower East Side to the United Nations headquarters to the New York Botanical Garden, a cornucopia of institutions presented cultural riches that, in Dan's eyes, served not only as a natural backdrop for a newly invigorated film industry but also as the substance of an ICE sector. When highlighted, these would combine with the city's strength in the FIRE sector to secure New York's place as not just a commercial capital, but one of the world's greatest cities. Armed with this insight, Dan marshaled his formidable background in management and finance to move a litany of cultural projects from the dream board to reality, from the impractical to the feasible, from the periphery to the center.

Of course, Dan's focus as deputy mayor for economic development and rebuilding meant it was relevant that the ICE sector provided jobs at a wide range of income and experience levels, including many that required a high degree of expertise and training. Indeed, from 1990 to 2005 (the year when Dan began consciously to frame the city's strategy in terms of FIRE and ICE), the number of jobs in this sector rose 17%. But, in Dan's view, the ICE sector was essential to the city's future not simply for the employment that it created; ICE could keep FIRE from being extinguished. He saw that New York's unique mixture of FIRE with its ICE assets could serve as a magnet attracting talented people in other fields and anchoring them here.

The ICE assets influence those who decide where to locate businesses. In turn, the magnetic force of the ICE sector attracts the gifted and knowledgeable workforce that businesses of every stripe increasingly need. And a virtuous circle of talent invigorates the ICE sector, thereby creating the next cycle of growth. Real estate, too, has come

to depend on ICE, on the desire of people to live here when they don't have to do business here — but choose to. In short, Dan saw that elements of the FIRE sector could survive and prosper in New York, but the city would maintain its status only if it intentionally cultivated its ICE-sector advantage. From that insight, he created a strategy that fully integrated the Cultural City and the Commercial City to establish and maintain New York's global preeminence.

Dan understood that the ICE sector is crucial to the definition of New York, to the city's economic health, to maintaining its competitive advantage, and to creating rich, attractive lives for its residents and its visitors alike. Only he would grasp so completely that the deputy mayor for economic development should make supporting the city's cultural institutions — and thereby shaping its culture — a foundational part of an agenda for growing jobs and the tax base. Of course, Dan did not oversee the Department of Cultural Affairs (which was ably run by Kate Levin as commissioner in partnership with First Deputy Mayor Patti Harris), but he understood the importance of their work, coordinated seamlessly with them, and often put crucial wind behind the sails of their work that helped them cross the finish line.

So it is that his mark is on cultural projects throughout our town. From the Whitney Museum of American Art on the High Line to the Downtown Brooklyn Cultural District, from Yankee Stadium to Citi Field to the Barclays Center, from Coney Island to Long Island City, from the ubiquitous appearances of film crews around the city to the innovative performances at The Shed, and of course, from Columbia's Manhattanville to NYU's Greenwich Village, Dan's legacy exceeds even the descriptions that follow.

I would be remiss if I closed without mentioning Dan's impact on NYU, on my professional life as part of the University, and (more deeply) on me personally.

I remember as if it were yesterday, the breakfast about 30 years ago with Dan and Jay Kriegel, the executive director of the city's Olympic bid, where Dan explained: "New York is the first city in the world that has a neighborhood for every country in the world populated by immigrants who were born in that country."

For Dan, this yielded what would become the motto for the Olympic bid: "Come to New York, the World's Second Home, where every team will have a neighborhood cheering it on." For me, it prompted a profound hope: If the neighborhoods of New York could synchronize (like elements of a fine watch) to create a community wherein each element remained identifiable, even as a greater whole was created, then perhaps humankind could create an integrated world beyond the divisions of the day. From that day forward, this hope became the unifying teleology of NYU's Global Network of campuses.

Thus it was Dan who provided the template that is NYU's network of campuses on six continents, anchored by principal campuses in New York, Abu Dhabi, and Shanghai. It was Dan who suggested the word "network" become part of the base language used to describe this new version of a university, since it was to be a circulatory system through which faculty and students could move seamlessly rather than a "branch campus" system with a hub and spokes. And, it was Dan who, in monthly breakfasts or lunches in the Village, encouraged us to continue forward, even in the face of largely uninformed opposition by a relatively small but very vocal group of critics. Today, this network is recognized as a transformative move for NYU and higher education generally and as a huge success. Of course, there are many who are responsible for that result; but Dan was a key, though largely publicly invisible, member of the team.

So, it would be accurate to say that it was Dan who created today's NYU — just as over decades of devotion to our city he has created, or at least shaped in important ways, its cultural landscape.

Opposite: Filming of *Law & Order* on location in New York, 2006. The film and television industry employed 30,000 more New Yorkers in 2012 than it did in 2004.

Left: The Whitney Museum of American Art relocated from the Upper East Side to a city-owned site at the southern end of the High Line in 2015.

Below: Citi Field, the new Mets stadium, opened in Flushing, Queens, in 2009.

PATRICIA E. HARRIS | CEO of Bloomberg Philanthropies and former First Deputy Mayor of New York City

A VOCAL ADVOCATE FOR THE ARTS

Dan Doctoroff partnered across agencies and jurisdictions to help advance one of the most profound cultural transformations in New York City's recent history

I first met Dan Doctoroff during the fall of 2001. Mayor-elect Mike Bloomberg was recruiting him for a newly created position in city government, one that reflected the unprecedented challenges we faced after the 9/11 attacks. In New York's history, there had been many mayoral deputies responsible for overseeing economic development. Dan would be the city's first Deputy Mayor for Economic Development *and Rebuilding*.

I remember a conversation we had that fall, after he decided to accept the job and our boss decided that an underused public hearing chamber would become our everyday, open office — "the bullpen." Dan was a little concerned that the volume of his voice might be distracting to others. But even though he occasionally did, let's say, *project* his voice just a bit, it didn't distract us at all: It reminded us of how deeply passionate he was about the work we were doing together — passion that helped bring out the best in all of our teams.

To understand how Dan approached the job, it helps to remember the event that sparked his entry into the city's civic life. As Dan often tells it, a visit to the World Cup semifinals at Giants Stadium, and the energy and excitement of so many people of different backgrounds cheering together, inspired his quest to bring the Olympics to New York. But while the Olympics would have brought enormous new investment in construction projects, Dan's work for the bid was never about building athletic facilities — it was always about the people who would fill them.

Dan recognized that for our city to rebound from 9/11, we needed more public places that would bring people together and make the city more of a magnet for talent and tourists from around the world. Creating those places, and the energy and excitement they generate, meant changing the way people inside and outside government viewed the relationship between the creative sector — arts, culture, parks, great design — and economic development.

It's easy to forget how unconventional it was back then for economic development leaders to focus on this kind of investment in the public realm. Government officials charged with economic development tended to see "the arts" as a secondary issue, at best. And the economic impact of arts and culture rarely affected public policy. Especially after 9/11, with New York City facing steep budget deficits and so many pressing needs to address, it would have been easy for our economic development agencies to push the creative sector aside. Instead, Dan took the opposite approach. He made them a central part of his team's work, even though most of the agencies directly involved in arts and culture didn't fall into his portfolio. He didn't oversee the Department of Cultural Affairs, or the Parks Department, or the Design Commission, or the Department of Design and Construction, or the Landmarks Preservation Commission. That was my job. But together, we shared a mission: creating places that are full of beauty, energy, and creativity, where people would want to live, work, and visit.

That shared mission is why our partnership worked so well. Our relationship was forged over the course of many extraordinarily

Tony Award–winner Julie Taymor directed *A Midsummer Night's Dream* as the inaugural production at the Theatre for a New Audience's Polonsky Shakespeare Center, located in the Downtown Brooklyn Cultural District.

The Bloomberg administration believed that the emerging Hudson Yards neighborhood needed a cultural anchor, in addition to its commercial and residential development. Dan Doctoroff continued to champion the idea even after leaving City Hall, becoming The Shed's founding board chairman. Above, a performance at The Shed in the building's iconic venue, The McCourt, formed when the building's movable outer shell is deployed over an adjoining plaza.

difficult projects, and none was more challenging and complex — and so personal, sensitive, and emotional for so many people — than rebuilding the World Trade Center.

Dan was our administration's lead point of contact for the Port Authority and the Lower Manhattan Development Corporation, spending long hours making sure our interests were represented in the mix of state and federal agencies involved — including preserving space for the 9/11 Memorial & Museum, which now attracts millions of visitors to the area. The work of building a bright future for Lower Manhattan after 9/11 centered on creating a more vibrant residential community, and part and parcel of that work was art, culture, and public space. When critics argued against our administration's insistence on including space for the performing arts in the redevelopment of the World Trade Center, Dan helped ensure we prevailed. And now, a new Performing Arts Center at the site is taking its place among the city's most dynamic public spaces.

Dan understood the power of the arts, and time and again, he fought for them. He worked with people through disagreements, made numbers work, and helped different sides understand one another's objectives and interests. He combined a

brilliant ability to imagine the future and develop long-term goals, with a careful, methodical ability to work, one step at a time, through the small hurdles that can derail big projects — and get things done.

Over the years, our teams worked together to turn an abandoned stretch of elevated railroad track, called the High Line, into one of the world's great parks — and to bring two incredible cultural institutions to anchor it: on the south end, a new home for the Whitney Museum of American Art, and on the north end, The Shed: an adaptable cultural space like no other. Along 42nd Street, we worked to bring the Signature Theatre into a major housing development, fulfilling a community wish. Together with the new office and residential buildings that would rise over and around the rail yards, the West Side became a powerful example of how the arts and parks, when stitched together, can attract visitors, drive economic development, and strengthen neighborhoods.

We applied that strategy to neighborhoods across the city to fulfill Mayor Michael Bloomberg's vision of rebuilding areas that had been long neglected. On Governors Island and the Brooklyn piers, for instance, our redevelopment plans centered on parks, art, and culture — and the

Dan Doctoroff and Patti Harris at the construction site of The Shed, 2017. Harris served as first deputy mayor during the Bloomberg administration, including acting as the mayor's top advisor and overseeing major agencies such as the Department of Cultural Affairs and the Department of Parks & Recreation.

results have been truly spectacular. In Downtown Brooklyn, we teamed up to create a new cultural district that has enhanced and attracted dozens of dynamic arts organizations, along with new housing and businesses. On Staten Island, restoration of the Old St. George Theater was a centerpiece of our efforts to bring more people and investment to the borough's north shore. In Queens, we worked together on a variety of projects around Flushing Meadows Park, including renovations and expansions of the Queens Museum, Queens Theatre, Queens Botanical Garden, and the New York Hall of Science. In the Bronx, we brought together major institutions including the Bronx Zoo/Wildlife Conservation Society, The New York Botanical Garden, Fordham University, and Montefiore Medical Center to collaborate on park and streetscape improvements, including removing graffiti and illegal dumping — all part of the investments we made across the borough that helped strengthen neighborhoods, create jobs, and attract new residents and businesses.

In all five boroughs, Dan helped bring our community and government partners on board for investments in parks and arts. And even though Dan earned a well-deserved reputation for his relentless drive, his other character qualities were no less essential to his success, including one that isn't always associated with him, but should be: patience. He understood that successfully overcoming the biggest obstacles takes time and requires extensive dialogue and painstaking compromise.

Dan combined his passion and patience with a mastery of facts and statistics that strengthened our administration's hand in negotiations. He put agencies under his purview to work crunching numbers and providing data and analysis showing the economic

impact that the arts and culture have on our city, including the thousands of small cultural organizations in communities all around the five boroughs. At the same time, he appreciated how large temporary art installations, like *The Gates* and *The Waterfalls*, could be economic drivers for the city — and by sharing their economic impact publicly, we helped inspire other cities to embrace public art as an economic engine.

Over the years, more and more cities have come to recognize the critical role that the creative sector plays in economic development, a change that Dan helped accelerate. And now, as part of the Bloomberg Foundation's board, he's helping more cities invest in the arts and harness their power to bring people together, build energy and excitement, and strengthen the communities where people live and work. All of those benefits are more important than ever as cities continue to grapple with the devastation caused by the pandemic.

Countless city leaders around the world have learned from the work that Dan helped lead. And more than any single project, or any one aspect of the city's economic development, it is always Dan's approach that makes all the difference: thinking big, being creative, working relentlessly, putting people first, and always — always — believing that the best is still ahead.

Neither of us could have known that the partnership we forged in the early days of the administration would grow into two decades of collaboration and friendship. But working in the bullpen will do that. And even though we no longer sit just a few seats away, I can always hear the passion in his voice — and always will.

Opposite: In his role as Deputy Mayor for Economic Development and Rebuilding, Dan Doctoroff represented the City's interests at the World Trade Center site, including advocating for an appropriate 9/11 Memorial and Museum.

Left: First Deputy Mayor Patti Harris, Deputy Mayor Dan Doctoroff, and Cultural Affairs Commissioner Kate Levin worked to bring the Signature Theatre into a new housing development on 42nd Street.

DOWNTOWN BROOKLYN CULTURAL DISTRICT

Dan Doctoroff and I have always seen eye-to-eye. Though at the start of the Bloomberg administration, that was more about us being the same height than agreeing on policies or projects.

That's because historically, my agency — the New York City Department of Cultural Affairs — has had an uneasy relationship with Dan's policy area. The priorities and tools of economic development don't always align well with the nonprofit arts sector. While marquee cultural organizations with an obvious role in the city's tourism industry are acknowledged, artists often create and innovate at small and midsize organizations that aren't recognized for their essential contribution to New York's identity as the creative capital of the world. On top of that, their economic impact can be hard to quantify through traditional means.

The Downtown Brooklyn Cultural District exemplified all those tensions. However, the project also made clear to me Dan's extraordinary ability to go big *and* get home: Embrace a transformative vision, and make it real by turning impossible obstacles into solvable problems.

This initiative started as the BAM Local Development Corporation (BAM LDC), a brainchild of Harvey Lichtenstein, the legendary President of the Brooklyn Academy of Music — New York's oldest performing arts center — from 1967 to 1999. During that time, Harvey came to believe that Brooklyn's rebirth as a cultural epicenter could be deepened by using BAM to anchor a critical mass of organizations. While a handful of nonprofit cultural organizations had made their homes near BAM, could there be more? In a neighborhood sprinkled with surface parking lots and underutilized City-owned buildings, could New York deliberately plan a cultural district?

After leaving BAM in 1999, Harvey and his colleague Jeanne Lutfy secured a $50 million matching grant from the City, commissioned a master plan, purchased a building to house arts groups, and cultivated two projects: an Enrique Norten-designed branch of the Brooklyn Public Library and a new home for the modern classical Theatre for a New Audience (TFANA), by architects Frank Gehry and Hugh Hardy.

Then things got difficult. Local community concerns about gentrification, especially in the context of the nearby Atlantic Yards sports, retail, and housing development, raised questions about inclusivity and affordability. And the underlying mechanics of the BAM LDC relied on revenue generation from underground parking to be built on a City-owned "south site" — which was especially costly (and questionable) given multiple subway lines serving the Atlantic Avenue transit hub one block away.

In addition, the financing model asked cultural organizations to cover 80% of their capital costs, with the remaining 20% coming from the BAM LDC. This just wasn't feasible for the kinds of artistically adventurous organizations the Cultural District needed.

Plans for the Downtown Brooklyn Cultural District had been stalled for years when Deputy Mayor Dan Doctoroff embraced the project's potential to create a "left bank" cultural destination in Brooklyn. He oversaw a successful restructuring that has since led to a slew of arts organizations locating in the district.

Opposite: The Theatre for a New Audience produces Shakespeare, classic, and contemporary plays.

Left: BRIC House is the new permanent home of BRIC, a 40-year-old Brooklyn arts organization. It includes exhibition space, two performance spaces, a television studio, and artist work spaces. UrbanGlass, founded in 1977, uses their new space to advance glass as a creative medium.

So the project inherited by the Bloomberg administration had big ideas, some strong potential partnerships, and a financing set-up that looked good . . . but only on paper.

Patti Harris, the deputy mayor I reported to, strongly supported the BAM LDC's goals. But our colleagues at the New York City Economic Development Corporation (EDC), which controlled the City's funding, weren't seeing deal terms that made sense in terms of cost or return on investment.

By 2004, things were really stuck. The Brooklyn Public Library decided a major new branch wasn't viable — so the south site needed rethinking. That meant TFANA's project was also frozen, leading to fundraising challenges and mounting skepticism about the organization's future home. Two groups already in the District who shared a City-owned building long overdue for a renovation — Brooklyn Information and Culture (BRIC), a multifaceted arts and media organization, and UrbanGlass, a major studio center and gallery space for glass art — were stymied by an increasingly tangled real estate transaction.

Then Dan got involved. His approach was to distill the key elements of the project and solve for each one.

He found Harvey's vision compelling: Brooklyn had become the generative "Left Bank" alternative to Manhattan's cultural establishment. And that catalytic value deserved a considered place in the city's economic recovery and expansion. By framing nonprofit culture as a strategic advantage, Dan set the guardrails that protected and made possible everything that followed.

Second, Dan insisted on a mixed-use approach that respected the existing residential and retail character of Fort Greene and didn't try to imitate another cultural campus — à la Lincoln Center. Because Dan was committed to giving the project its own spatial vocabulary, the district's streetscapes, view corridors, and street furniture became City-funded priorities.

Third, the financing got real. Below-grade parking went away, and the ratio flipped so that the City provided 80% of funding for cultural capital projects, with our nonprofit partners raising 20%. It was still a high bar given the complexities and costs of the District sites, but possible. And the amount of City investment through EDC rose from $50 million to $100 million.

Fourth, Dan insisted on coordinated oversight. His Office of Capital Project Development, headed by Andrew Winters, was the quiet hero in delivering a range of projects with different players, timeframes, and regulatory issues across city agencies. EDC, the Department of Housing Preservation & Development (HPD), the Department of City Planning (DCP), and the Office of Management and Budget (OMB) continued to raise concerns, some of which were major (and to me, excruciating): EDC and OMB arguing to demolish an arts building in the District and sell the site; or HPD leaving out the cultural tenant requirement from a Request for Proposals (RFP).

Everyone got their say, but there was always a commitment to get past the problem du jour and take the next step. Bureaucratic nimbleness — the jumbo shrimp of government! — even flourished. When a sudden opportunity arose for BAM to build the smaller, flexible Fisher Theater, my agency secured the capital funding and worked with the Landmarks Preservation Commission, while EDC handled complex reciprocal negotiations with Two Trees, the developer ultimately selected for the south site.

And when it became clear to Dan that the BAM LDC itself wasn't sufficiently integrated into the overall project machinery, he combined it into a larger consolidated business improvement district covering all of Downtown Brooklyn.

Bumps and bruises along the way — to egos, blueprints, operating budgets? Many. But things got done because Dan understood the long-term value of culture alongside the short-term bottom line. He broke relentless complications into acceptable units of risk by embracing both the unquantifiable upside of creativity and the finely honed spreadsheet. Dan's successors, Bob Lieber and Bob Steel, brought their own excellent insights and tactics to the mix — while never questioning the underlying rationale or processes put in place early on. I took that as a massive endorsement of Dan's rigor and generosity as a partner, not just to me, but in laying compelling groundwork for his future colleagues.

The District has since been expanded, dropping the "Downtown" to include the adjacent DUMBO neighborhood and the Brooklyn Navy Yard. The most recent count is 46 nonprofit cultural venues that continue to complement, attract, and sustain volumes of housing, retail, and office space. The embrace of the "Brooklyn" brand around the world has everything to do with this concentration of authentic, visionary organizations, and the artists, audiences and ideas they nurture.

I've had the privilege of working with Dan on a lot of projects, including the World Trade Center site, the Whitney Museum of American Art, and The Shed. Of them all, the Downtown Brooklyn Cultural District is the Essential Dan: He bought the dream, inspired the team, and shaped ideas into realities.

Brooklyn Academy of Music, Downtown Brooklyn.

KAREN BROOKS HOPKINS | President, Brooklyn Academy of Music, 1999–2015

Brooklyn Academy of Music

The making of the Brooklyn Cultural District, today one of New York City's most successful creative neighborhoods powered by the arts, was a long and complicated path to completion.

Today the District is home to 46 cultural institutions, with nine at the core, including BRIC and the BAM Harvey Theater. This remarkable collection of world-class organizations sits on top of the Atlantic Avenue subway terminal, one of the largest transportation hubs in New York City.

But its evolution as a District is a 40-year tale of government appropriations followed by funding cuts, leadership transitions, and a parade of architects and planners who came and went over the decades.

As deputy mayor, Dan Doctoroff saw the potential of the project and moved heaven and earth to get the ball rolling. Dan brought leadership and passion, as well as government capital funding, finally breaking the logjam that had crawled on for decades. He never wavered in his belief that Brooklyn had the "chops" to be a major destination of a five-borough cultural city.

Ultimately, BAM, with its four buildings and audience of over 750,000 people annually, plus the inclusion of several smaller, but incredibly powerful arts groups (including Theatre for a New Audience, the Mark Morris Dance Group, 651 ARTS, The Center for Fiction, and the Museum of Contemporary African Diasporan Art (MoCADA), among others), gave the District its character. Collectively, these institutions cemented Brooklyn's reputation as a formidable cultural hub and extended the impact of the "Brooklyn brand" worldwide.

The Brooklyn Cultural District has succeeded because of the innovative concept at the core of the enterprise. Rather than constructing large, monolithic marble palaces of culture built away from the street, which had been the custom for performing arts areas for years, the Brooklyn Cultural District embraces the local vibe and neighborhood life. The organizations are both small and large, racially diverse, and with visual and performing arts all connected to each other — in other words — a metaphor for 21st century New York.

Right: The plaza at 300 Ashland sits in the heart of the Downtown Brooklyn Cultural District. The District is now the cultural heart of Brooklyn, with 46 nonprofit cultural groups that complement, attract, and sustain housing, retail, and office space.

MARTY MARKOWITZ | Brooklyn Borough President, 2002–2013

KINGS THEATRE

Kings Theatre opened in 1929 as one of five Loew's "Wonder Theaters" in the New York area with an interior inspired by the Palace of Versailles and the Paris Opera house. As a teenager, "I would take my first dates there, spending hours with friends," former Brooklyn Borough President Marty Markowitz said. "You not only had two full-length movies, but you also had comics, travelogs, world news."

But with the rise of television and multiplexes, Kings Theatre shuttered in 1977 and deteriorated for decades. In 2015, it reopened as a performing arts center after a $95 million renovation, thanks to years of advocacy by Markowitz and Flatbush community activists, who finally found a receptive partner in Deputy Mayor Dan Doctoroff.

Kings Theatre had significant roof breakages, people stealing brass, [it was] totally abandoned. The City was debating whether or not to knock it down and build a mini mall. A lot of us in the community in the 1970s and 80s and 90s fought to prevent the theater from being knocked down because it would destroy the beauty of how they did things in those days.

Even though I was a state senator in the Flatbush district for 23 years, we needed Dan Doctoroff to make it happen. And he got it done. Dan was receptive. [He assigned] members of his economic development team who were able to launch it from concept. How

do you do the financing? How do you select the right developer? I wouldn't know how to do it, to tell you the truth. That was what he was extremely talented in. Through the Bloomberg administration, the City negotiated to totally renovate the theater back to the way it looked in the 1920s. It restored its grandeur. My focus was restoring the theater for live concerts and preserving it and [Dan's] thing was what it would do as a catalyst for economic activity. Today, I'm happy to say that the theater is open as a live venue for concerts and other major events. It preserved a landmark and it accelerated economic development on Flatbush Avenue — his vision.

WHITNEY MUSEUM OF AMERICAN ART

"Dan recognized that this was something that would be transformative for the Whitney as well as the city of New York."

With more than a million visitors each year flocking to the Whitney Museum of American Art's iconic Renzo Piano building before the pandemic, it's easy to imagine that the museum has always overlooked the Hudson River in Manhattan's Meatpacking District. But in fact, the move to this now-booming neighborhood was controversial — even among its own board members.

When the Whitney opened its new doors in 2015, it claimed its part in a radical transformation of the West Side — a transformation envisioned, championed, and ultimately secured through the persistence of Deputy Mayor Dan Doctoroff and his colleagues under Mayor Michael Bloomberg.

It was an intuitive match between an institution devoted to the adventurousness and vision of American art and a team at City Hall determined to reshape the landscape of America's boldest, most creative city. "They understood that the Whitney was about the future," said Adam Weinberg, who was director of the Whitney at the time. "This was a bold, vibrant, exciting, visionary stroke of understanding that a combination of parks, cultural centers, new businesses, and university facilities would fundamentally change the view of the West Side forever. We were very proud to be a part of it."

The Whitney was originally going to build an addition to its famous Marcel Breuer building on 75th Street and Madison Avenue. We worked for years on a design and it was quite wonderful, but very small. The only way we could get anywhere close to the full amount [of space] was to go vertical. The problem was that museums are horizontal spaces, not vertical spaces. So after several years, we decided it was not best to build on that site.

I had known that the DIA Foundation had been in discussions with the City through [Commissioner of Cultural Affairs] Kate Levin and

Dan Doctoroff about a site on the south end of the High Line. I thought to myself, "This is very interesting because Michael Govan [then the director of DIA] just announced that he was going to become the director of the Los Angeles County Museum of Art." And so, I called Michael and he said, "Realistically, the likelihood of something getting built there is not that great."

This was at a time when the whole West Side corridor, essentially from the Meatpacking District up all the way up to Columbia, was underutilized. I'm an old-time New Yorker, and I remember, my grandparents would ask me when I [would be] moving back from the West Side, as if I had gone to another country.

Dan recognized that this side of New York could be a place, not just for a handful of New Yorkers who either lived here or knew about it, but for a much larger world. It was [about] reminding people that [Manhattan] island is an island. The development of boat transportation and parks on the river was all part of the planning. All of a sudden, people were going to the art Frieze by boat, they were taking boats to work. The Whitney [could be] part of taking back the waterfront.

To be part of this vision about the future [of New York] was a total match for the Whitney, as opposed to a more historical institution. The Whitney is a museum about the present and the future. Our number one commitment is to the artists of our time. And this was a homecoming — the Whitney was on Eighth Street for almost 30 years. This was a neighborhood where dozens and dozens of artists live and work.

So I went to Kate and I said, "I hear that the DIA Foundation has this site and there's a chance that they may not go into it." And she said, [if they back out] "we would be thrilled to have the Whitney,

Opposite: The new Whitney Museum of American Art building along the Hudson River is over three times the size of the museum's former home on the Upper East Side. The expansion led to growth in annual visitorship from about 400,000 people a year to well over a million.

Right: The building, designed by Renzo Piano, offers 50,000 square feet of indoor galleries and an additional 13,000 square feet of outdoor exhibition space.

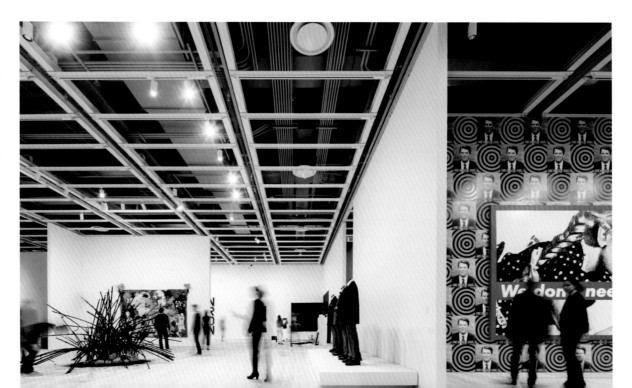

AN EDITED ORAL HISTORY

because Dan and I feel that it is absolutely critical that at the south end of the High Line, there be a [cultural] anchor." The thinking was also there would be something in the north end which would [ultimately] become The Shed. One of the great things about Dan is he understands that good culture makes for good business.

We felt really pioneering, but my board was not so anxious for us to move the entire museum.

You have to remember, this is before the opening of the High Line. I remember [a Whitney trustee] saying, "Excuse me, can you tell me what the High Line is?" Now, that's almost unthinkable. But in those days, it wasn't open yet. I thought either I would lose my job or people would say, "What a brilliant move." And I didn't know which one it would be.

I remember calling Dan, and I said, "I need somebody who's a peer with my trustees, who will come in and say that this is not just a vision without any legs — [that it was] a vision that the mayor stood behind, that not only were they supportive, but they would do everything they could to help us for the greater good of New York."

He came to a board meeting and he gave a very passionate, moving talk. Dan gave a sense of the history and of the future and of the larger project on the whole West Side. The [trustees] saw there was a possibility the Whitney could be part of something so much larger that was absolutely transformational.

I would say that was the turning point in the project — the first time where our board leadership said, "We'll give this young

director a chance, especially if he has somebody like Dan behind him." I don't think [the vote] was taken that day, but it was unanimous when it happened, and it would not have happened had it not been for Dan.

[In the years that followed] we had the Trials of Job. First the convincing of the board, then the raising of the money. We had very long negotiations with poultry merchants and beef merchants and had to buy out a number of the meatpackers. We had to do all kinds of remediation on our site [including] abandoned factory spaces. Then we had [the] 2008 [financial crash], and Hurricane Sandy. Millions of dollars of HVAC had just been installed, and water destroyed all the equipment.

But the support of the City was always steadfast. [First Deputy Mayor] Patti Harris was key throughout this entire process. She was really the quarterback and the one who made sure that everything

The decision to relocate the museum was controversial, even among the Whitney's own board members. The High Line had yet to open and the neighborhood was filled with abandoned warehouses and meatpacking operations. "I thought I would either lose my job or people would say, 'what a brilliant move,'" said Director Emeritus Adam Weinberg, who oversaw the relocation. "The Whitney's presence on the river was essential. We're a museum of American art. We should look out to America."

was on track. I met almost weekly with Kate. [City Planning Chair] Amanda Burden was extraordinary in this process. And Dan was always obviously just a phone call away if we needed him as well. They really put their shoulders to the wheel and made sure that it moved forward.

Mayor Bloomberg once asked me, "How did you have the nerve to move the Whitney downtown?" I said, "Mr. Mayor, it's the two Ns: naïveté and necessity." Naïveté in that, if I knew what I was doing, I never would've done it. But we absolutely needed the space. We had about 2,500 works in 1966, when we opened the Whitney uptown. By the time we came downtown, we had over 20,000 works in the collection, of which a very large number were very large works.

The [new] building was over three times the size of our building uptown. Our audience went from about 400,000 people a year to well over a million. Our membership base went from about 12,000 people to closer to 55,000. Our endowment grew tremendously. Dan recognized that this was something that would be transformative for the Whitney as well as New York City.

When you're up on the Whitney [roof deck], you see the Empire State Building, the Statue of Liberty, the World Trade Center. People see us from 360 degrees as opposed to being buried in the middle of an uptown block. The whole West Side project was about that sense of visibility. The Whitney's presence on the river was essential. We're a museum of American art. We should look out to America, not just across Madison Avenue.

[Dan] was willing to take risks for things that he believed in, and the Whitney was about risk-taking; that's where his values, my values, the city's values, and the institutional values all lined up.

HOLLY HOTCHNER | Founding Executive Director, Museum of Arts and Design (Formerly American Craft Museum), 1997–2013

MUSEUM OF ARTS AND DESIGN

When I became the Director of the American Craft Museum in 1997, the museum was in its third location in 40 years, in the lower levels of the Deutsche Bank building across from the Museum of Modern Art.

I was tasked with taking a floundering organization and reinventing the museum. Over the next eight years, we took a niche museum that focused narrowly on craft objects to a new kind of interdisciplinary museum focused on materials and process across the fine arts, decorative arts, and design. We renamed ourselves the Museum of Arts and Design (MAD) and began developing a strategic plan to execute on this new vision. One of our top priorities was more functional space. After extensive study, it became clear that renovating our current site would be exorbitantly expensive — and still inadequate. We began our search for a new home.

We heard that the long-abandoned 2 Columbus Circle might be available. It had opened as the Huntington Hartford Gallery of Modern Art in 1964 — with Salvador Dali and Huntington Hartford greeting guests on opening night — but closed due to a lack of funding five years later. The building was reinvented for use multiple times until finally serving as the home for the city's Department of Cultural Affairs. But after the agency left, the building stayed vacant. By 1998, homeless people had moved in and the facade was visibly cracking.

With the construction of the Time Warner Center, the rest of Columbus Circle was becoming a hub — appropriate for the literal epicenter of New York (when distances are measured from New York City, the starting point is Columbus Circle). The abandoned building no longer fit with the area's emerging image and in 2000, the Giuliani administration issued a Request for Proposals (RFP) for the building's redevelopment. We were one of many developers and not-for-profits to submit an application.

Given the extensive renovations that would be required, we proposed a purchase price of $10 million and argued that our bid would generate economic benefit by strengthening the city's cultural sector and increasing tourism. However, it was not to be. On the eve of Rudy Giuliani's departure as mayor, he awarded the site to Donald Trump to create a boutique hotel.

Enter the Bloomberg administration and Dan Doctoroff, the new Deputy Mayor for Economic Development and Rebuilding. A few early decisions — like revoking major taxpayer subsidies for the New York Stock Exchange and two new baseball stadiums, among them — had shown that they were open to reevaluating deals made by the Giuliani administration. In early 2002, our lobbyist, Suri Kasirer flagged this project and asked Dan for reconsideration. Dan, like many people at the time, hadn't really heard of the American Craft Museum. But he was intrigued enough to put the sale to Trump on hold and rebid the building. Trump, Dan writes in his book, *Greater Than Ever*, was not pleased (an understatement).

When we presented to Dan, the idea that seemed to resonate with him the most was that our museum could introduce talented but little-known artists to new audiences. Our mission was also unique among the city's existing cultural institutions. Frankly, our proposal came with enormous risks — Trump had offered more money, including cash up front, and Dan was aware that we had few resources and would need years to pay the debt we would likely have to take on to build the project. We had only raised $4 million — far short of the $115 million we would need (the number later ballooned

to $130 million) — and had virtually no fundraising experience on this scale. This was one of the Bloomberg administration's first cultural projects, on a high-profile site, with the potential to set a tone for the next four years. We were a small team with big ideas, and no proof that we could pull it off. Dan, however, recognized our potential. In June 2002, the City selected us as the winner to develop the site. Then the lawsuits began.

Although our plans bypassed the opportunity to build additional stories, a new ceramic facade and the addition of windows was too much for some preservationists who believed the building should have been designated a landmark. Four different groups launched separate lawsuits to delay the project and filed seven appeals. Everything was on hold as we spent almost six years fighting in court, and fending off attacks that sometimes became personal.

Petitioners claimed that changing the exterior of the building would "compromise their quality of life." One of the most amusing letters was from a neighbor who said his bathroom faced our building and that his bowel movements would be hampered by a change. A "shame cam" was installed across the street to monitor the building and record our progress and there were weekly protests.

Dan remained our cheerleader. Despite his overwhelming portfolio of other projects, he showed up at every deposition and never wavered in his support, giving me, the board, and staff the courage that we would prevail.

In 2006, we did exactly that and opened 18 months later in the fall of 2008. Miraculously, given the economic climate in 2008, we raised all of the funds and opened with no debt. The new building allowed us to completely transform the museum. We had our first collections galleries and space for temporary exhibitions. Importantly, we had an auditorium for educational programs, open artist studios for public demonstrations, and space for a significant shop and a restaurant that generated revenue to support the mission.

In our first three years, our attendance went from 40,000 annually to 500,000 — ranking us just behind the Museum of Modern Art, the Metropolitan Museum of Art, and the Whitney Museum of American Art. Today, MAD is an icon of Columbus Circle and contributes to the cultural landscape of the city.

Dan loved solving problems and moving things forward that had been stuck forever. It was the urban story he cared about — not just buildings and landscape, but the people. He cared about our mission, he cared about me, and he cared about the people who would come to our museum and have an exciting experience.

When I reflect on the obstacles we faced and what Dan had on his plate — the obvious answer was that we weren't worth the headache. But Dan stuck with us. When I expressed doubt, he reassured me, "This is just part of it, we're going to get through it. We're not leaving you."

The faith Dan showed in me still helps me today. He taught me that a leader must be willing to endure doubters, possess the patience and skill to convert some of them into believers, and the courage to move forward even when there is no clear path. His loyalty, kindness, and tenacity kept us going. MAD would not be there without him.

Dan Doctoroff halted a sale of 2 Columbus Circle to Donald Trump in favor of the former American Craft Museum, later renamed the Museum of Arts and Design. In its first three years, the museum's annual attendance increased from 40,000 to 500,000.

GLENN D. LOWRY | Director, Museum of Modern Art, 1995–Present

THE ORIGINS OF THE SHED

I first met Dan Doctoroff in the late 1990s when he began to think about New York hosting the Olympic Games and was exploring how culture might play a role in strengthening the city's bid. Even then, Dan understood that culture was one of New York's greatest differentiators — and therefore, one of its best competitive advantages.

He didn't know that I was also a jock who skied competitively in my youth and who was passionate about the Olympics. While the bid did not pan out, our friendship did, and over the years we met episodically to discuss the city and how the arts, and museums in particular, could contribute to making New York an even better place.

In more than 20 years as the Director of the Museum of Modern Art (MoMA), across four mayoral administrations, the number of economic development deputy mayors who have reached out to discuss how culture fits into an overall economic agenda for the city remains the same: precisely one. Dan understood that the cultural infrastructure of New York created jobs, served as a magnet for tourism, and, most importantly, improved the quality of life for people in the city.

That's why when Dan began contemplating a new neighborhood on Manhattan's Far West Side, he recognized that it couldn't simply be a development of high-rise apartments and office towers. There needed to be one — or more — cultural

institutions that could enliven the community and enrich the city's cultural life more broadly. The question was: What should it be?

Jay Kriegel, a mutual friend whom Dan and I both considered a mentor, and who served as the executive director of the Olympic bid, suggested we talk. In 2006, Dan asked if I would convene a group of leaders in the arts to help the City think through cultural options for the development of Hudson Yards. This led to an intense brainstorming session at MoMA that included, among many others, Thelma Golden, director of the Studio Museum in Harlem; Karen Brooks Hopkins, then Executive Director of the Brooklyn Academy of Music; the gallerist Jeffrey Deitch; Jerry Speyer, chair of the MoMA board of trustees; Kate Levin, Commissioner of the city's Department of Cultural Affairs; and Alanna Heiss, then–director of MoMA PS1.

What did New York need? Where were the gaps in its cultural scene? And Dan's favorite question: What could we do here that would be different?

The group was adamant that the city didn't need another museum or experimental theater — especially one that could draw funding away from some of our vital but more precarious institutions. But there was something missing. It became apparent over the course of the conversation that New York City lacked a state-of-the-art, multipurpose space that could be programmed on relatively short notice for cultural events ranging from exhibitions of art, to performances, to theater, and much more. Participants used the German word, *Kunsthalle* frequently, and pointed to the Centre Pompidou in Paris as a reference point, albeit one that was slightly dated. We imagined that a space like this — a kind of cultural all-purpose "shed" — could ensure that important projects that would otherwise not come to New York City because of a lack of space, or not enough time to plan for them, would suddenly have a potential home in the heart of a resurgent West Side of the city.

At the time, I was somewhat skeptical that anything would actually happen as a result of the conversation, which after all, was designed to be wholly speculative with none of us responsible for executing on any of it. What we were talking about was going to cost several hundred million dollars that did not exist and was going to require a massive effort on the part of the City to realize. But once Dan got excited about the idea and decided to run with it, he was unstoppable — he knew how to mobilize the necessary city agencies, how to work with the developers of the site, and how to galvanize public opinion and private support, not the least of which was Michael Bloomberg's enthusiastic endorsement. And, so the Culture Shed, later just The Shed, was born, and is now a vital part of the city cultural ecosystem under the able direction of Alex Poots.

Above: Installation *Free the Air: How to hear the universe in a spider/web* by Tomás Saraceno at The Shed, 2022. The installation included a feature that suspended visitors 40 feet in the air on a synthetic web.

Opposite: The idea for The Shed grew out of a working session organized by Glenn Lowry at the Museum of Modern Art in response to Dan Doctoroff's vision for a cultural institution to anchor major new development in Hudson Yards. Here, The Shed, as seen from the High Line.

ELIZABETH DILLER | Founding Partner, Diller Scofidio + Renfro, 1979–Present

A CULTURAL START-UP

My history with The Shed began in 2008. I was intrigued by a Request for Proposals (RFP) released by the City of New York soliciting ideas for a contemporary arts venue on a site at the southern edge of the Hudson Yards development that was reserved for cultural use. The prospect of a new building for the arts seemed improbable at the time given the financial downturn and an acute philanthropic drought. Who could realistically contemplate building a new cultural facility in such a cash-strapped economy? Besides, the site was far too small for a contemporary arts building. But I admired the foresight to set aside civic space in this massive commercial development and saw the open-ended nature of the prompt as an opportunity to think big about the cultural future of New York. In a chance encounter with David Rockwell at the Venice Biennale, with my skepticism drowned out by several Bellinis, David and I decided to join forces.

We put forward an aspirational proposal for a ground-up institution we dubbed, "Culture Shed" that would unite all artistic disciplines and cultural industries under one roof. We asked ourselves, "What will artists care about in 10 years? 20 years? 30 years? What media will they be using? Will they be working at a large scale or intimate?" The answer was — we cannot possibly know. By definition,

Dan Doctoroff, seated, with (left to right): Alex Poots, founding artistic director of The Shed, and project architects David Rockwell and Elizabeth Diller.

contemporary art is always in flux. Architecture, on the other hand, is slow, geo-fixed, and static from the time of its completion. This new venue would have to be a machine responsive to perpetual change. It would be so flexible that it could accommodate work in any medium, in any size. It would overcome the physical limitations of its site by doubling its footprint on demand: a fixed building with an expandable outer shell.

Our scheme was selected and we were encouraged to continue working on the design. However, there was no definitive program, budget, timeline, client or fee. With a sense of naïve optimism, we continued developing this theoretical institution, effectively acting as our own client for the next two years. Throughout this period, there was an inexplicable momentum propelling the project from behind the scenes. It seemed to defy the financial crisis and the conventional obstacles of building an institution from scratch.

When I first met Dan face-to-face in 2010, these hazy formative years came into sharper focus. The release of the RFP coincided with

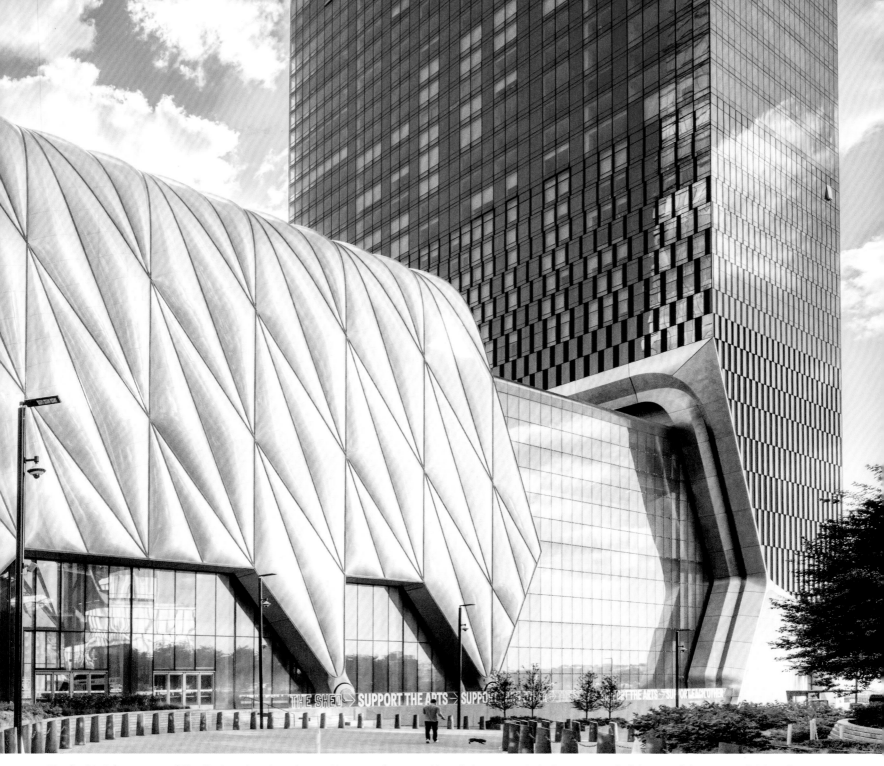

The flexible infrastructure of The Shed can be adapted to a wide range of event and installation spaces, including an outer shell that can slide over an adjoining plaza, doubling the venue's footprint and creating The McCourt.

Dan's transition from city government to the private sector. It became clear that Dan, along with Cultural Affairs Commissioner Kate Levin, had conceived the idea of a City-owned cultural footprint on this predominantly commercial site, which he had continued to champion from the sidelines over the previous years. As we began our dialogue, I realized how strongly Dan felt about bringing a civic dimension to Hudson Yards — a conviction fueled by the desire to fill this last huge tract of underutilized land in Manhattan with an integrated approach to development. The commercial and residential expansion of the city had to be balanced by the proportional growth of its public assets, especially culture. Dan had a passion for the project and was determined to get it built. The next step was to persuade others, including Mayor Michael Bloomberg, community boards, the public, cultural leaders, and diverse stakeholders.

In the years that followed, the project started to gain traction. As a cultural start-up, we had to move beyond building a building to building the institution itself. The hardware was evolving but it still needed human software. Dan's genius was to expand the team to include strategists, cultural advisors, managers, lawyers, contractors, and cost consultants. He created a remarkably democratic process that gave each member an equal voice at the table. It was a master class in leadership, inspiring everyone to perform at their very best doing something no one was individually qualified to do.

When Culture Shed was finally incorporated as an independent nonprofit entity in 2013, it was time for Dan to start building a board. We had to produce materials to show prospective board members but had different instincts about how to pitch the project. My point of view was that of a New Yorker educated in the 1970s, who witnessed the city's slow transition from an experimental breeding ground of countercultural production to an expensive playground of overconsumption. I saw Culture Shed as a critique of traditional art institutions increasingly defined by predictable and static content. The project would be an antidote to New York's fading creative edge, one that would provide a range of indoor and outdoor opportunities for artistic cross-pollination in a city starved of flexible space. In short, for me, it was about reviving New York's interdisciplinary effervescence.

For Dan, the project wasn't so much about reclaiming a past. He saw Culture Shed in a lineage of "firsts." Just as MoMA was the first museum devoted to the modern era and Lincoln Center was the first to co-locate all the performing arts onto a single urban site, Culture Shed would be the first to bring the visual arts, performing arts, and creative industries under one roof in an ultra-flexible building defined by an era of breakneck technological progress. Establishing this historical parallel helped position the project as a game changer for New York — an argument that converted many skeptics into believers.

I was often with Dan as he went door to door armed with a PowerPoint presentation that explained the historical argument, urban approach, precedent analysis, programming scenarios, and economic rationale — all brought to life through his exuberant civic pride for New York City. Dan leveraged his deep ties to the business community and persuaded many courageous entrepreneurs to step into the unknown. At the same time, he launched a search for the artistic director, or, in Dan's language, a "cultural impresario." From a long list of candidates and exhaustive interviews, the board selected Alex Poots, whose vision was in perfect alignment with the Culture Shed's experimental ethos. For the first time in its six years of development, the cultural start-up had a creative director. Alex's first act was to extract the word "culture" from the institution's name, which he found self-evident and pretentious. "The Shed" was officially born. His second act was to challenge our claim of total flexibility by asking us to accommodate a rock concert at a noise level of 110 decibels. A series of successive challenges led to a higher level of flexibility than we had ever imagined. Alex started to build a staff while commissioning the first years of programming with a brilliant roster of blue-chip and emerging artists.

Project development continued with years of value engineering, construction timelines, and legal fine print. Without fail, Dan attended every weekly coordination meeting with the team he built until the opening day in April 2019. His leadership continued post-occupancy, carrying the fledgling institution through numerous challenges, including the pandemic. Dan's almost childlike optimism — coupled with his civic-minded vision, entrepreneurial spirit, empathy, infectious enthusiasm, unyielding perseverance, and attention to every last detail — were crucial in willing this most improbable project into existence. Looking back, it was a miraculous achievement to build a new institution from conception to reality in 11 years. But the beauty of The Shed is its ability to respond dynamically to a changing world, ensuring that it remains definitively unfinished.

DAVID ROCKWELL | Founder and President, Rockwell Group, 1984–Present

Designing The Shed

I first met Dan in 2001, soon after he joined the Bloomberg administration as deputy mayor for economic development and rebuilding. My studio was trying to launch what would become Imagination Playground, a five-year research and development project with the goal of inventing a new kind of playground that would allow children to create their own worlds. We brought our idea to Dan, who immediately became the key to making the playground a reality by connecting us to all the right people.

I found Dan to be a rare combination of insight, curiosity, and openness. He also knew how and when to take action — when the talking needed to end so the *doing* could begin. I realized then that Dan was going to help define the future of New York City.

Architect David Rockwell speaking at the dedication ceremony for The Shed, 2019.

Multidisciplinary artists, DRIFT, transform The Shed in *Fragile Future*, 2021. The exhibit took place in The McCourt, a 17,000-square-foot light-, sound-, and temperature-controlled hall with a ceiling height of 110 feet, enabling it to accommodate installations that could not otherwise come to New York.

Then came Hudson Yards, a city within a city on Manhattan's Far West Side. Dan had a vision for creating the world's most flexible cultural institution as the new neighborhood's beating heart — what would become The Shed. When Liz Diller and I submitted a proposal in 2008 and were awarded the project, Dan gave us the confidence to flip the script on the normal paradigm of a performance center. He insisted that we project ourselves into the future and imagine what the demands of creativity, presentation, and performance might look years from now — that the building be future-facing and also solve for the years and decades to follow. He was adamant that The Shed should not only accommodate, but also encourage invention.

There were so many players with a stake in The Shed, from the City to the entire arts community, whose needs we had to consider. Then there were the physical constraints of the site itself. With his uncanny ability to synthesize everyone's needs and points of view, Dan got obstacle after obstacle out of the way by always finding the human-centered way forward.

I always found Dan to be open to new ideas, mostly expressed during one-on-one walks filled with rich conversation. He answers questions by asking another question, constantly digging deeper. And, more than anyone I've ever worked with, he exudes an incredible spirit of hope, curiosity, and optimism. The Shed would not exist as an idea, as a building, or as a program were it not for Dan's driving passion for marrying the demands of the present with the potential of the future.

Ralph Fiennes as Robert Moses in David Hare's *Straight Line Crazy*, which sold out its three-month run at The Shed, October 2022.

DARREN WALKER | President, Ford Foundation, 2013–Present

Dan Doctoroff's Big Vision

The great architect Daniel Burnham famously said, "Make no little plans" — a perfect title block for the blueprint of Dan Doctoroff's life and life's work.

Dan's legacy looms large, amidst the great skyline of America's greatest city. Like Robert Moses or Fiorello La Guardia or John Lindsay, he belongs to that pantheon of New Yorkers who dare to eschew the small in favor of the big and bold — who challenge convention in service of righteous progress.

Indeed, Dan's *big* plans have stirred the souls of millions. His ambition and imagination laid the foundations of Brooklyn Bridge Park, the High Line, and of course, The Shed, which the Ford Foundation is proud to support.

Together, we honor shared commitments to open, inclusive public space; to art, not only as a vessel for beauty, but as a vehicle for social change. For all of us at the Ford Foundation, supporting The Shed's artistic programming has been a great joy — one enabled and sustained by Dan's creative genius.

Every time I walk through Brooklyn Bridge Park or gaze up at the preposterously brilliant structures of Hudson Yards, I think of Dan and his vision. It will endure in perpetuity, long after we all are gone, for future generations of New Yorkers — a living monument, as Burnham wrote, for all who "aim high in hope and work."

Darren Walker, president of the Ford Foundation, which has supported innovative programming at The Shed.

The Building

The Shed comprises a fixed building and a telescoping outer shell that slides into an adjoining plaza, doubling its footprint to accommodate large performances, installations, and events. The fixed building houses a stack of column-free spaces: two are museum-quality galleries and the third is a black box theater. Its topmost-floor is a skylit event space augmented with power and rigging to host events.

When deployed, the telescoping outer shell can be light, sound, and climate-controlled. The entire ceiling is a walkable, riggable theatrical deck that can accommodate two-ton loading from any point across its surface. The kinetic systems that move the shell are adapted from gantry-crane technology. Propelled by a rack-and-pinion drive system located on the roof of the fixed building, the

shell sits on wheel assemblies that roll on rails. The shell can be deployed or nested in five minutes using the horsepower of one Toyota Prius engine. Guillotine doors on three sides can open to create a seamlessly indoor/outdoor space. You can drive a truck right in. The structure is an exposed lightweight steel diagrid clad in translucent Teflon-based ethylene tetrafluoroethylene cushions. This material is filled with low-pressure air and provides the thermal properties of glass at 1/100 of the weight. It does not need to be heated or cooled when there is no show or event; it can simply be nested, opening up a public space. The spatial elasticity of The Shed allows it to be spontaneous and responsive to the ever-changing needs of artists and audiences.

Elizabeth Diller

A STAGE FOR NEW YORK'S FUTURE

"[Dan] has that magic to effect change, which is what artists do as well. They can change the way people feel and think."

The Shed — a new arts facility on Manhattan's Far West Side — was designed to host an unprecedented range of artistic endeavors from around the world.

In 2014, Alex Poots agreed to become the institution's artistic director on one condition: The Shed needed to create art itself.

Poots found an ally in Founding Chairman Dan Doctoroff.

"He didn't only have the vision, but he had the history with key people to turn an idea into a reality," said Poots, who had previously been artistic director at the Manchester International Festival and the Park Avenue Armory. "He has that magic to effect change, which is what artists do as well. They can change the way people feel and think. I'd not really met someone who had that power."

Since The Shed's opening night in April 2019, and through the challenges of the COVID-19 pandemic, the venue has played host to artistic visions from filmmaker Steve McQueen and composer and singer Björk, a revival of a classic one-woman play starring Cecily Strong, new commissioned theatrical works, traditional art exhibitions, and immersive experiences that leverage the building's unique spaces, including a 120-foot-tall canopy with geodesic-style facets that can expand and retract on 6-foot-wide wheels.

The Shed's taste for bold ideas, interdisciplinary shows, and unabashed experimentation reflects the melding of minds behind the project: namely, Poots and Doctoroff. "We needed each other," Poots said. "Without a place, it's all talk from my end. Without a function, then the building lies empty, ready to be activated."

But first, Poots needed to be convinced to say yes.

When I was asked if I would apply for the post, I didn't. Then, I was asked again and I didn't apply. Then, the third time they said, "Dan Doctoroff would like to meet you." [From our first meeting] I just knew he was a titan. He had this reputation of having helped New York back on its feet after 9/11; people trust him because he has an amazing track record. But he was not that [well] known in the cultural sector. I said, "I have a show coming to New York in three weeks, so I could arrange tickets for Dan and his wife, and then we could meet the next day." Then there'd be something to talk about.

The show was *Macbeth*, starring Kenneth Branagh at the Park Avenue Armory. It was a very immersive show. It rained and there was mud and sword fights. In fact, the first few rows would get mud and blood on themselves.

We met the next day, in his office. He said, "We absolutely loved it." I said, "Great. That show costs $4 million to make, and if it sells out, it would only generate $3.1 million. My question to you is: is the $900,000 an investment in the arts or a loss?" He said, "I've been warned about you." We were laughing.

I laid out how I work. From my perception, the outline of The Shed and the job read like a rental space, which was not where my head was at. I was a commissioning, producing type of leader. He talked about wanting to keep New York on the cutting edge. Then he said, "Look, you've convinced me about becoming a place that makes the future, rather than just hosts it. Will you convince this nascent board that I'm putting together?" Within two or three meetings they had evolved their way of thinking and their approach to

Right: As Founding Chairman of The Shed, Dan Doctoroff led a successful $636 million capital campaign. Here, Doctoroff presiding over a preview of The Shed, 2019.

Opposite: Performance of *An Audience with Kelsey Lu*, The Shed, 2019.

Björk's *Cornucopia*, performed in The McCourt at The Shed in May 2019.

The Shed. They said they would be interested in that mission and in that vision. I think that's a sign of the greatest intelligence, when you're open to a different direction.

The fact that The Shed is on [public] land helped considerably, because it meant a civic purpose. It couldn't all be about financial goals, it had to also be about, "Well, is this good for society?" We've not built a cultural center [in New York] since Lincoln Center, and yet we are in a new century. Don't we need places for art forms that we don't even know exist yet?

Dan's instinct was that flexibility would be very important. It meant that in COVID we could pivot. We could lay out seats six feet apart because there's no fixed seating. The stage could be moved back, because it's a flexible stage. Because we don't have a permanent collection, we can pivot between performing arts and visual arts and popular culture.

We've actually reimagined The Shed two times in three years. We've gone from being purely a commissioning-producing house, to being a hybrid, where we commission and produce some work and we receive other works. There's nothing like it in terms of the intersection of performance, visual, and pop. No one has that breadth.

We had challenges. The building went over budget, then it was [six] months late. Just as we were getting out of that, we hit COVID. Dan has had my back the whole way, because the different things that we brought to The Shed were aligned and because he's an honorable human being. Even when we've been weeks away from having no money left, Dan will lift the world up in his arms and make it happen. He has the brain power to create a strategy that will be woven into a story to create the desired outcome. Every time we hit an insurmountable roadblock or challenge, Dan says, "We're

As a nonprofit organization built on public land, The Shed has sought to make its programming accessible and affordable, including $10 exhibition tickets and free entry for visitors 18 and under. Above, *Summer on the Plaza*, The Shed, May 2019.

In 2022, The Shed presented *Tomás Saraceno: Particular Matter(s)*, giving the Argentine artist three of its four public spaces. Above, *Museo Aero Solar*, a grounded balloon made out of plastic grocery bags.

going to sit down, we're going to make a plan, and we're going to make it happen." Just that indomitable ability to succeed, every time.

When you make a show with someone, their true self comes out. When you sit down with them in the first few meetings, you kind of know what traits are going to either help or hinder along that journey. I trusted Dan's integrity. I believed in his strength and ability to effect change.

We opened with no electricity in the theater, with a generator outside piping in electricity. I mean, there was nothing that was going to stop us. The opening night of The Shed was conceived by Steve McQueen, Quincy Jones, and Maureen Mahon. When Jon Batiste comes in with the recreation of the Harlem Hellfighters the whole vision came to life. The joy that was emanating from the two of us was incredible, because we'd actually made it happen. It was real for the first time.

I'll give you a line from William Blake: "Great things happen when men and mountains meet." That's Dan at The Shed.

MISTY COPELAND | Female Principal Dancer, American Ballet Theatre, 2015-Present | Member of the Board of Directors, The Shed, 2020-Present

Modeling an Inclusive Approach to the Arts

When Dan invited me to join the Board of Directors I instantly felt his warmth and openness. Dan and his invitation made me feel seen and heard as both a Black woman and an artist respectively and I know that he was instrumental in providing me an actual seat at the table.

Sustainable and lasting change begins from working within and by being a part of making decisions that have lasting institutional impact — I cannot thank Dan enough for allowing me to be a part of this process. And who better to have led that charge than Dan himself as the founding board chair. His thoughtfulness has been at the forefront of several impactful organizations that will stand the test of time and I'm more encouraged than ever by his leadership and what we're doing here at The Shed.

Thank you, Dan, for helping The Shed to provide an inclusive and engaging performance space for artists across all forms of creativity. Because of your leadership, we are building a cultural institution that we hope will be a model that other organizations will be inspired to follow.

Misty Copeland, Principal Dancer at the American Ballet Theatre and board member at The Shed, is committed to advancing inclusivity in the arts.

LEE C. BOLLINGER | President, 2002–2023 & Seth Low Professor of the University, 2002–Present, Columbia University

COLUMBIA UNIVERSITY EXPANSION

When I delivered my inaugural address as Columbia's president in 2002, I said that chief among my priorities was expanding the institution's constrained physical footprint in New York. I knew that for a great research university like Columbia to thrive in the 21st century, it needed space to grow.

After lengthy discussions, we settled on a proposal for a campus extending from 125th Street to 133rd Street along Broadway to the Hudson River, in a former industrial area called Manhattanville. We worked with two architectural firms, Renzo Piano Building Workshop and Skidmore, Owings & Merrill, on a master plan to develop a campus that was open and welcoming, connecting Columbia to its neighbors and the broader city. The new campus would be the university's most ambitious expansion in more than a century.

The proposal was a bold endeavor, but it was also rife with seemingly insurmountable obstacles. We all knew that many residents in Upper Manhattan were wary of Columbia and would have concerns about the expansion, stemming in large part from an aborted attempt to build a gymnasium in Morningside Park in 1968. We also knew that this plan was essential for the university's future and would be of enormous benefit to the City of New York by investing in a new generation of innovators, scientists, and

cultural leaders. In 2003, my senior executive vice president Robert Kasdin and I met with Deputy Mayor Dan Doctoroff and Mayor Michael Bloomberg to ask for their support. For many politicians, the meeting would have ended there given the difficult community history, scope, and complexity of the project. Without flinching, they agreed.

We knew success would depend on creating a collaborative approach that brought residents, business owners, community leaders, and elected officials together with Columbia administrators. Dan and his team were instrumental in helping us develop such a process. The goal was to make sure that the university's plans addressed the needs of both Columbia and its neighbors. In this, Dan's leadership proved invaluable.

He and his colleagues worked with partners in government and in the community to incorporate an independent body, the West Harlem Local Development Corporation, that would negotiate on behalf of the community. The upshot was a monumental agreement that committed the university to $150 million in community benefits and services, including support for local nonprofits, funds for affordable housing, access to university

facilities, and guarantees to hire minority-, women-, and locally-owned businesses and workers for construction.

Running parallel to the community benefits agreement was the lengthy and complex rezoning process required for the project to proceed, which included an extensive environmental impact statement requiring contributions from multiple city agencies. It was not atypical for such processes to drag on for years, as agencies attended to other more urgent matters. Luckily, in this case all of the relevant agencies reported to Dan. He made sure they understood this project was a priority, ensuring that the process stayed on track.

From the beginning, Dan made it clear that he would help us in whatever ways he could, that the economic, cultural, and intellectual advancements that the new campus would bring to the city made this project a top agenda item for his office. I will never forget how tirelessly he and his team labored to advise us and to bring together the necessary city agencies to see this through.

In 2007, the New York City Council approved the rezoning plans. Ten years later, we opened the first two buildings in Manhattanville: the Jerome L. Greene Science Center, home of the Zuckerman Mind Brain Behavior Institute, and the Lenfest Center for the Arts. The Forum, a multiuse gathering venue, followed in 2018. In January 2022, we completed the first phase of the 17-acre expansion with the opening of Henry R. Kravis Hall and David Geffen Hall, the new home for Columbia Business School.

As I reflect on the two decades that have passed since that meeting in 2003, I am in awe of the magnitude of our collective achievement. What we accomplished should not have been possible, yet we succeeded beyond our wildest expectations. That triumph was thanks in large part to Dan. He brought to this project an unbridled optimism and an unyielding faith in the power of smart and thoughtful people to come together to do great things and serve the public good. He knew the risks, he understood that he would likely get little public credit for the rewards, and he stood by us the whole time. Columbia owes Dan Doctoroff an enormous debt. I simply cannot imagine how we would have gotten this project done without him.

When Henry R. Kravis Hall, which houses Columbia University's business school, opened in 2022, it completed the first phase of the university's 17-acre Manhattanville campus expansion plan. Then–Columbia president Lee Bollinger says of Dan Doctoroff, "I simply cannot imagine how we would have gotten this project done without him." Opposite and below, Henry R. Kravis Hall interior and exterior.

KATHERINE L. OLIVER | Commissioner, Mayor's Office of Film, Theatre & Broadcasting, 2002-2013

FILM & TELEVISION PRODUCTION

When the Bloomberg administration took office in January 2002, there were only nine television shows still filming in New York City — and three of them were *Law & Order* variations, showcasing new violent crimes every week.

That spring, I flew to New York from London, where I was running media operations for Bloomberg LP, to meet with the new deputy mayor for economic development, Dan Doctoroff, who oversaw the city's film and television office. After discussing our favorite New York movies, we talked about how the creative community could help lure the film and television industry back to New York — and play a big role in the city's resurgence. We had our work cut out for us.

The Mayor's Office of Film, Theatre & Broadcasting (MOFTB) had been born out of a similar challenge. Mayor John Lindsay founded it in 1966 — the first agency of its kind in the world. Its mission was to reinvigorate the film and television industries, which, though born in New York, had largely moved away, drawn to the sunnier weather in California. During the late 1960s through the early 1980s, MOFTB helped spark a dramatic increase in film and television production giving rise to a vibrant industry throughout the five boroughs. New York film production during this period changed the face of American filmmaking. In iconic movies from *Rosemary's Baby* and *Midnight Cowboy*, to *Taxi Driver*, *The Godfather* and *Ghostbusters*, New York City served not only as a backdrop, but as a leading character. These films gave the world a sense of New York's grit and determination, a city where cops hurtled through bustling streets chasing bad guys beneath the Brooklyn El, where iconic skyscrapers set the stage for a greedy Wall Street tycoon's fall from grace, and where humor and romance hovered over every block.

But by 2002, the gains of the previous decades had been lost. Film and TV production had grown ever more competitive and focused on the bottom line, with producers becoming cautious of the logistics and costs of production in New York City. I would later speak to a producer who told me that when he saw New York City as the setting for a film or TV script he often crossed it out and insisted the film be shot elsewhere. The industry perception was that the cost was simply too high, the logistics nearly impossible to overcome. And the economic downturn of the time, compounded by the aftereffects of September 11th, did not help the city's image.

The film industry may have largely written off New York by the time we took office, but 9/11 cracked the door back open, because advertisers and filmmakers wanted to show support to New York. Mayor Bloomberg and Dan recognized the opportunity. They both understood the need to find new ways to diversify the economy, create good middle class jobs, improve New York's image, and attract people back to the city. Film and television production could help do all of that.

We had a glimpse of the possibilities: *Sex and the City* was one of the other few shows still filming on the streets of New York. With its glamor, friendship, Jimmy Choo shoes, and pink Cosmopolitans, the show was inspiring people around the world to come to the city to experience the New York they saw on screen. That was advertising you couldn't buy.

Improving customer service

Upon taking the job, I learned that the agency was still using electric typewriters and processing permits by hand, a system that could take as long as several days. Within one month, people in my office had computers and we put the applications online. For a city agency generally characterized by bureaucracy and labyrinthine systems, this was groundbreaking.

We made the office a one-stop shop so that filmmakers could spend more time doing what they wanted to do: Be creative and make a film or a TV show in our city. During the 2003 blackout, City Hall shut down along with much of New York. But film crews continued shooting with backup generators, so we set up permitting stations on the sidewalk using battery-powered laptops to keep pace.

We also put out the word that New York was "willing to pull out all of the stops" to attract producers. That meant that when *The Interpreter*, a Sydney Pollack film starring Sean Penn and Nicole Kidman, had difficulty securing rights to film inside the United Nations, we invited Secretary-General Kofi Annan to City Hall to meet with Mayor Bloomberg and smooth the way.

When the Will Smith film, *I am Legend* promised to shoot the entire production in New York City, we agreed to close the Brooklyn Bridge overnight for filming. The newspapers covered it — we didn't want people to be alarmed at the scene depicting military evacuation from a zombie apocalypse — but the articles also showed the industry that a new day had dawned here. We had a strategic plan, but Dan and I both understood the need for a story. The industry needed to know

In 2002, only nine television shows still filmed in New York; two decades later, close to 100 television and feature films are filmed in the city annually. Right, Kristin Davis, Sarah Jessica Parker, and Cynthia Nixon film a scene from *And Just Like That . . .* on Crosby Street in SoHo, Manhattan in July 2021.

After multiple expansions, Silvercup Studios now has production complexes in Queens and the Bronx. In 2023, a City analysis estimated that New York's film industry generates $81.6 billion in economic output annually and supports 185,000 jobs.

that things were different and so our marketing and communications plan became just as essential to our success.

Dan understood this wasn't simply about a better permit process, but something bigger. At the time, in addition to being deputy mayor, he was leading the city's bid for the Olympic Games. I quickly realized this meant three things: First, he wasn't afraid of crazy ideas. Second, he was already engaged with the city's creative marketing and film community to showcase New York for the bid. And finally, pitching New York City on the world stage gave him deeper insight into New York's advantages and obstacles. It made him appreciate culture as foundational to the city's appeal and shifted his perspective beyond any single initiative or office. We needed to figure out the image of New York after 9/11 and position the city to thrive.

Made in New York

One of my most memorable days in city government came early on, when we worked with Dan and his team and some of the city's top ad agencies and production companies on short films for the Olympic bid. We shut down the Brooklyn Bridge at 5 a.m. on a glorious August morning so RadicalMedia could recreate a torch relay. That day, their CEO, Jon Kamen and I sketched out a marketing plan to help promote New York and tap into the

industry's creative pride called, "Made in NY." We took it to Dan and he loved it.

Radical designed an iconic logo that harkened back to New York City's subway token design that would be prominently displayed in production credits. Our "Made in NY" program ensured that the world would know when movies, dramas, and documentaries were created in New York.

The "Made in NY" logo quickly became a symbol of homegrown talent and pride. Radical created a line of apparel featuring the logo. We launched official walking tours of famous film locations, published a book with Rizzoli commemorating the 40th anniversary of the agency, and inaugurated an awards program to honor actors, producers, and executives in the industry who had supported New York with a garden party at Gracie Mansion.

As part of this outreach to the industry, we invited every major studio head, all 14 entertainment unions, and industry leaders to Gracie Mansion for a summit with me, Dan, and the mayor. They all came. For many, it was the first time they had ever met with the mayor of New York City. We asked their advice and developed a strategic plan from their feedback. They were clear about the biggest problem: Filming in New York just cost too much.

Increasing our competitiveness

Dan suggested I work with Seth Pinsky, who worked in the city's Economic Development Corporation, to explore the viability of a film tax credit that could keep productions — and the strong blue collar jobs they created on soundstages, carpentry, catering, and more — in the city.

Seth and I worked with industry executives, union leaders and legislative affairs. We delivered an innovative tax credit plan to Governor George Pataki in 2004 which included a provision for a first-ever city tax credit. The Made in NY tax credit was born.

At the same time, we explored ways to modernize the city's production infrastructure to meet the needs of an evolving industry. Shortly upon arriving in City Hall, Dan closed a deal with Doug Steiner to found a new film studio in the Brooklyn Navy Yard, jumpstarting a major creative services industry in an underused

formal naval warship production complex. It was a bold move that unleashed a cascade of new or expanded film studios concentrated in Brooklyn and Queens.

When the tax credit passed, we had a press conference at the new Steiner Studios, which were built at the Navy Yard with the City's support. Mel Brooks joined us at the event and announced that his new version of *The Producers* would be filmed in the studio, in his hometown of Brooklyn.

By the end of 2013, three major film studios — Steiner Studios in the Brooklyn Navy Yard, Silvercup Studios in Long Island City, and Kaufman Studios in Astoria, Queens — were undergoing or planning major multimillion dollar modern expansions.

Left: Mel Brooks's *The Producers*, starring Nathan Lane and Matthew Broderick, was the first major film shot inside Steiner Studios, then a 280,000-square-foot, 15-acre complex inside the Brooklyn Navy Yard. The studio, which has since undergone multiple expansions, opened during the Bloomberg administration.

Above: A student in the "Made in NY" Production Assistant Training Program, which was launched during the Bloomberg administration to bring diversity to the film and television production industry. The program model is now expanding to other cities with growing film industries, including Chicago and Atlanta.

The legacy

That growth continues today. There are now close to 100 television and feature films made in New York on an annual basis. The "Made in New York" logo remains in closing credits of shows and is proudly displayed on Haddad's trucks that line the streets of our city.

As we grew the industry, we also worked to diversify its workforce. With the mayor's backing, Dan and I teamed up with union leaders to create new job training programs to give more New Yorkers a pathway to these good careers. Today, more than 15 years later, the program is still in place and expanding to other cities that have growing film industries, including Chicago and Atlanta.

By the end of the Bloomberg administration in 2013, New York had the second-most film jobs of any state in the country. The industry was generating $7 billion a year in economic impact to the city, an increase of over $2 billion from 2002, while providing jobs for 150,000 New Yorkers. Productions benefited thousands of ancillary businesses.

And it's only gotten stronger. According to a City analysis completed in 2023, the film and television industry now generates approximately $81.6 billion in total economic output, supports 185,000 total jobs, and $18.1 billion in total wages. Additionally, the industry's output, jobs, and wages have outpaced the growth of citywide equivalents.

Dan played a central role in driving this growth. His support for our office was crucial to its success. The day I knew we had crossed a threshold came at the end of our first term. Before we took office, Martin Scorsese had shot *Gangs of New York* on a soundstage in Italy. But in 2005, he decided to film *The Departed* in New York — even though it was set in Boston. It went on to win four Academy Awards, including Best Picture. New York had become so appealing that producers were coming here to shoot other locations. We had made it. In New York.

ANGELA SUN | Senior Policy Advisor, Office of the Deputy Mayor for Economic Development and Rebuilding, 2006–2008

FASHION INDUSTRY

"Dan understood that . . . fashion has the power of creativity, of innovation, of imagination, of fantasy — and of creating jobs."

In the 19th century, New York stood at the intersection of trains carrying raw materials from across the country and boats carrying immigrants from Europe looking for factory work; the combination established the city as the center of the national garment industry. But after World War II, deindustrialization drove the majority of clothing manufacturing away from New York, even as the city established its status as a fashion hub.

In 2006, Diane von Furstenberg was elected President of the Council of Fashion Designers of America (CFDA) and made it her mission to create a more permanent base for the industry in New York that could uplift younger, more diverse designers and bolster American leadership on the runway.

She found partners in the Bloomberg administration, especially with Dan Doctoroff and his team, who saw the fashion industry's potential to differentiate New York as a cultural force and strengthen the city's economy.

It was a "multipronged agenda," said Angela Sun, Doctoroff's senior policy advisor who spearheaded the initiative from City Hall. In partnership with von Furstenberg, they focused on preserving the city's historic Garment District, securing new spaces to support the industry's growth, and "incubating and cultivating an emerging generation of new designers" who "also represented the fabric of the city" and the ways it was changing, she said.

That included "not just young designers, but also diverse designers," Sun said. Asian, African American, and Hispanic designers emerged as new forces in the field, including New York designer Jason Wu, who would go on to outfit Michelle Obama at her husband's first inaugural ball.

Economically the efforts also succeeded: Today, the fashion industry employs 4.6% of the city's workforce, while generating $11 billion in wages and $3 billion in tax revenue. It all underscores "the importance of fashion for the city and the country," Sun said.

The mayor and Dan [were] meeting with Diane von Furstenberg, and I thought, "This is like a rock star coming to City Hall." I wrote a memo for Dan and Mike called "*DVF, or Michael Jordan for Girls.*" It was about the iconic wrap dress that started it all, but it was also about her [business] failure and her ultimate comeback. Dan always loves a story about rebirth and resurgence. [Doctoroff's chief of staff] Marc [Ricks] called me and said, "Dan and the mayor read your memo. You should be at this meeting. But there's a catch: If you take this meeting, then all things Garment District and fashion will be in your portfolio as well." And I said, "Well, Marc, that's like telling me that in order to eat a spoonful of caviar, I need to wash it down with a glass of champagne. Yeah, I can do that. I'll take it on."

Diane had just taken the mantle as [president] of the Council for Fashion Designers of America, an organization that supports American design. She felt strongly that we [needed] to focus on placemaking for American fashion — we need[ed] to have a home, a physical space, an archive, and a center point for fashion in America, which is Donna Karan, Ralph Lauren, Tommy Hilfiger — all the greats — but also a space where the designers of the future could access resources, mentorship, and produce and show their work. We need[ed] to build a community that helps New York continue to advance fashion as a major industry and a cultural force. That was her mission. Dan, of course, asked for many, many things: a real plan, financials, a programmatic vision, and details on how the space would be used year-round and into the future — A Dan Plan.

New York's fashion industry employs nearly 5% of the city's workforce and generates $11 billion in wages and $3 billion in tax revenue annually. Above, New York Fashion Week, Lincoln Center, 2010.

That was the beginning of aligning Diane's goal for the CFDA with Dan's goal of prompting more economic development. Dan recognized the importance of fashion, not just as an economic generator, but [its role in] the history of New York and the evolution of New York [beyond] an international center for commerce. The city's history is punctuated not just by finance, but also by culture. Culture is what put New York City on the global map.

We worked with the organizers in securing a new home for New York Fashion Week; it was a multiagency effort. Ultimately, [Fashion Week landed] at Damrosch Park in Lincoln Center, a bigger space that already represented New York City as a cultural innovator. The process also allowed Fashion Week more organic growth. It expanded to being much more inclusive. [Now] there are many places where emerging designers show [their collections]. You don't need to be at Bryant Park or Lincoln Center; you can be in a fifth floor walk-up and that's all part of the big biannual event that is New York Fashion Week.

We also [explored] a rezoning of the Garment District to allow the neighborhood to be sustainable. The Garment District was seen as a

place that was slowly dying, a relic of what fashion was in the past. Manufacturing, as much as we'd like it to, isn't going to come back in the same way. But that doesn't mean that there shouldn't be a vibrant district that's focused on fashion. Many designers, especially emerging designers, were opting to make their collections locally to get [their work] out on the runway quickly. There was also the hub effect of having the most prominent design schools in the country — FIT [Fashion Institute of Technology] and Parsons located here. [Today] there are lots of very specialized makers and suppliers of fabrics, trims, tools, and workshops that still support designers in New York. Anything you need as a designer, you can access here.

The city, in fact, has grown as a global center for fashion. You need only look at the annual Met Gala — the "Oscars of the East"— to see the outsize influence that fashion has and the economic impact it generates: 4.6% of New York's workforce is employed in fashion. It generates over $11 billion in wages and it brings over $3 billion in tax revenue for the city, not to mention millions of dollars in tourism.

Dan's an eternal optimist. People have said many, many times in the history of New York, "the city's dead." One of the conclusions that [Dan] made is that the growth of New York happened, not just because of financial markets [establishing] New York as a capital of finance, but also because of our cultivation of culture. Dan always recognized that a big part of economic development isn't just, "How do we keep New York City a financial capital in the world?" but "What makes the city attractive to people?" We always talked about making New York a place where people want to live, work, and visit. Fashion is a big part of that story: It's aspirational, it's inspiring. Fashion has the power of creativity, of innovation, of imagination, of fantasy — and of creating jobs. Dan understood that and understood the importance of the industry to New York.

MARTY MARKOWITZ | Brooklyn Borough President, 2002-2013

LYNN KELLY | President, Coney Island Development Corporation, 2007-2010

CONEY ISLAND

"We have to still keep Coney Island funky and weird and edgy and cool . . . [Dan] got that immediately."

By 1905, Coney Island was the most famous amusement destination in the world, annually drawing 20 million visitors who marveled at its thrill rides, wild sideshows, and hundreds of thousands of lights, earning it the nickname, "The Electric Eden."

A century later, the district had withered to a single block of seasonal amusements, with shabby, crime-ridden side streets, limited infrastructure, and a community of 60,000 residents angry at decades of neglect reaching back to the days of Robert Moses, when he designed the Belt Parkway to bypass Coney Island and carry beachgoers to Jones Beach instead.

"Coney Island was limping along until the Bloomberg administration and Dan Doctoroff, along with his able colleagues like Lynn Kelly and Josh [Sirefman] and others, began to focus their attention on Coney Island," said former Borough President Marty Markowitz.

In 2001, Kelly, then a young staffer at the city's Economic Development Corporation (EDC) who had grown up visiting Coney Island every year with her grandfather, was assigned the task of overseeing the development. It was a daunting task, including ethnic separations between the large concentrations of public housing and Mitchell Lama housing that bordered the amusement district.

"This is so New York, this is the impossible dream, this has to work," Kelly remembered thinking. "In a place that had so many systemic issues, at the brink of losing an entire chunk of New York City's history — we had to find a way."

Along with tenacious Brooklyn boosters like Markowitz, Council Member Domenic Recchia, community leaders, and backing from Doctoroff and City Hall, Kelly helped form the Coney Island Development Corporation to develop a multiyear plan to revive the historic district. Since then, the public and private sector have invested nearly $3 billion in reviving the neighborhood. In 2009, the City passed a rezoning that created a 27-acre amusement and entertainment district, along with plans for new housing, parks, infrastructure upgrades, and other improvements.

That ultimately included more than $20 million preserving and restoring some of the neighborhood's most iconic features, including the Parachute Jump, world-famous boardwalk, and historic B&B Carousell — the last surviving Coney Island carousel featuring 36 hand painted horses — which was nearly auctioned off and destroyed in 2005. Instead, the City purchased the carousel for $1.8 million, spent another $1.7 million for the restoration, and housed it in a state-of-the-art pavilion as the centerpiece of a newly renovated 2.2-acre Steeplechase Plaza.

At Kelly's urging, the City made other local investments, including funding that allowed Coney Island USA, an arts organization that

As the 20th century began, Coney Island was the most famous amusement destination in the world, drawing 20 million visitors annually. A century later when the Bloomberg administration came into office, the area was a shell of its former self.

runs the Mermaid Parade and Burlesque at the Beach, to purchase and renovate its building. "Bloomberg cares about this so much he's saving the last remaining wooden carousel and he's making sure that we can all wear mermaid pasties in perpetuity," Kelly remembers thinking. "Think about what the City is doing to make sure that Coney Island can stay freaky and thrilling and fun."

There were other investments: $168 million in a new shark exhibit at the aquarium and, perhaps, the biggest and most controversial purchase: spending $98 million to purchase land from Thor Equities to

In 2009, the City passed a rezoning that created a 27-acre amusement and entertainment district, along with plans for new housing, parks, infrastructure upgrades, and other improvements.

protect the amusement area. "Coney Island would have been gone forever if the City had not stepped in," Kelly said.

By 2017, there were 51 rides run by 10 separate operators helping to draw more than 5 million people to Coney Island each year. In 2022, a *New York Times* parenting newsletter declared the reinvigorated Coney Island, "the epitome of pure childhood joy."

"Today Coney Island is certainly vital for this city," Markowitz said. "The People's Playground thrives."

BACKGROUND

LYNN KELLY

[Coney Island is] a peninsula that was created largely by landfill. Over the years the population grew and the infrastructure did not keep up. In large portions of Coney Island there was literally no infrastructure. No outfall systems for flood mitigation, no sewers. On any given day the lightest rainstorm would completely flood western sections of Coney Island. It just was a mess.

MARTY MARKOWITZ

I experienced Coney Island throughout my youth and adult years. I remember when Coney Island was the gathering space for most everyone in Brooklyn; Nathan's was a must-visit. Gargiulo's was the place for dinner. It was our getaway, especially during the summer. It was teeming with folks of every ethnicity, nationality. And it was an exciting place to be. And then I remember in the mid-60s when it became very dirty. You could see it aging. It became seedy.

KELLY

I grew up in New York. So every year my grandpa would take me — this would've been the 70s and the 80s when it had fallen apart. But it was very important to my grandpa and to our family to continue that tradition. We'd ride the Cyclone and we'd get a hot dog at Nathan's — in that order. Even as a kid, I can remember thinking, "This place must have been magical" but it was completely run down. You would see debris everywhere, burnt out cars, dilapidated buildings, blighted lots.

MARKOWITZ

Coney Island under the City administration and Robert Moses became a depository of low-income housing because the land was cheap.

KELLY

So you have a huge concentration of public housing, with public transportation mediocre at best, an amusement area that survived on sweat equity of the generations of owners barely keeping it together, you had thousands more residents that lived in Mitchell Lama [Housing] right up against the amusement district, you had only one really major point of egress by public transportation a good mile and a half or more from one end [of the neighborhood]. And crippling infrastructure problems. And we haven't even talked about crime.

THE REDEVELOPMENT

KELLY

Fast forward to 2001 and the Giuliani administration wanted a minor league ballpark. The Bloomberg administration realized very quickly we can't just build a stadium and leave. That's not economic development. That's like the equivalent of an Atlantic City; you build a casino and you walk away. What have you actually done for the community? What have you actually done for the residents that have been through those decades of disinvestment and hard times? That was when the concept of a strategic plan for Coney Island was born.

I started at EDC in February 2001. I was a lowly project manager and they basically said, "Okay, you're assigned [to] Coney Island." I barely knew where the bathroom was.

Going back [to Coney Island] in my role at EDC, I remember getting off the subway at Stillwell, walking up to the boardwalk, looking around and thinking, "What a shame." Not a lot had changed. You had this beautiful stadium being built but everything else around it — it just looked like a movie star that had seen their better years.

As we got to know the neighborhood the overwhelming reaction was: We want to be able to stay here. We want to get jobs. We need a community center. We don't want Coney Island to only be known as the amusement district because it's not. That's the truth — there were 60,000 residents that lived there.

The Bloomberg administration really took that concept to heart. How do we figure out what the plan is going forward for the next 15 years? And how do we make sure that not just the business owners

benefit from the investment, but also the neighborhood? That's my memory of how this birthed the renaissance of Coney Island.

CHALLENGES

KELLY

A lot of the area was condemned out or destroyed during the Moses era but people spoke about that as if it happened yesterday. There was an inherent distrust of the City — immediate, inherent distrust.

I was literally knocking on [New York City Housing Authority] doors trying to get tenant leaders to talk to us. They had every right to be like, "Who's this white lady coming to my door from the City of New York?" The only ice breaker was that they would hear my [Staten Island accent] and say, "Hey, she's local." And they cut me some slack.

I learned an important lesson about working in New York, which is that you have to move at the speed of trust. That was interesting because Dan [and] Bloomberg are very timeline oriented. We all

Above: The Zenobio ride, located in the "Scream Zone" at Luna Park, Coney Island. The ride is named after Tricia Zenobio, who helmed the redevelopment for the Office of Capital Project Development, created by Dan Doctoroff to ensure high-quality execution of complex multiagency capital projects.

Opposite and Below Left: The restored Parachute Drop, boardwalk, and amusement district at Coney Island were beneficiaries of hundreds of millions of dollars of public investment during the Bloomberg administration.

Above Left: Coney Island hosts the annual Mermaid Parade, the nation's largest art parade.

learned you can't put a timeline on generations of community members that have a natural distrust of authority figures. It was good for us. It made us go back and do our homework.

The ULURP [public approval process] was probably one of the more contested and controversial ULURPs that the Bloomberg administration had seen at that point.

The base of the whole plan was a rezoning that would allow for the protection and expansion of the amusement district, in addition to changing the zoning on some lots to allow for affordable housing with amenities. It increased the density to achieve more housing, but not housing within the amusement area.

There were factions of amusement supporters that felt that we were trying to eradicate the amusement area which was completely wrong but once a message gets momentum, perception is often harder to fight than reality. We had one of the bigger public ULURP hearings for the rezoning and one [person] dressed up as a mermaid in a wheelchair and went on a hunger strike; another dressed up as a priest against the corporate taking of the amusement district. Looking back, we had starving mermaids. We had people singing folk songs. It was insane. But it was Coney Island.

Historically, the community hasn't always worked with the amusement districts. That was part of the deal we struck. Some of those 17-year-olds who got their jobs serving cotton candy at Luna Park became general managers of the park years later.

DELIVERING THE PLAN

MARKOWITZ

Dan Doctoroff, he's a tough guy who wants to get things done. I think because of the force of his personality, his brilliance, and the tactician that he was, he really brought together a great team of folks with Lynn Kelly quarterbacking to make this dream, in part, become true.

KELLY

[Dan's] pace drove others to work at his speed and pace. And frankly, if you didn't, you didn't last long. You were moved to another project. He had a vision. He handpicked the team of people he wanted. He saw inefficiencies in government very quickly and had no tolerance for it.

We pitched a $2 billion — with a B — need for infrastructure. Cas [Holloway, Deputy Mayor for Operations] and Dan pulled together a meeting of every single agency head — [Department of Transportation], Parks, you name it. Dan [said] you better all work together to figure this out. But it was a huge lift.

The City had to pay big bucks to Thor Equities, a developer. [The owner] got in there, he assembled land, and so it meant the City then had to find a way to either work with him or buy him out. We knew we were overpaying. But we weren't willing to erase 100 years of history.

Dan came from the private sector. He had developed so many good relationships with people in real estate, in banking, and finance, that when it came time to do these megaprojects that required public-private initiatives and cooperation, he was able to speak both languages fluently. He could transition out of talking to a hedge fund CEO, and then still convey to a commissioner at HPD what he wanted.

MARKOWITZ

He wasn't a Brooklyn guy. I forgave him. But he did have the ability to impart some of his Midwest manners to smooth me out, let me put it that way, when I was talking with him. He wasn't in your face, but he got more done. And I was able to understand where he was coming from and bought into the fact that he had far more experience, in many ways, than I did.

I don't want to paint the picture here that Dan and I were holding hands all the time. The role of a borough president is, if there was a way that 95% of the city budget can go to Brooklyn and 5% to the other four boroughs, I would've been okay with it. My attitude is whatever we got, it's not enough. I had to fight with others to make sure that the goals that I set for Brooklyn were being paid attention to by Mayor Bloomberg.

KELLY

Marty used his tenacity, his chutzpah, his leadership to go out there and say things and demand things for his borough that, at that time, were really bold. "I want a world-class amphitheater. I want indoor, outdoor amusements. We need hotels. We need a community center. We need a revived Asser Levy Park. We need a Parachute Jump that's the Eiffel Tower of Brooklyn."

Once you put it out as an elected official into the ethos and the press picks it up and the community picks it up, it puts the administration and the legislative branch of government in a tough position where they either have to address it, solve it, or work to make it happen. And that's the power of the pulpit.

MARKOWITZ

The Parachute Jump did become our Eiffel Tower. It didn't become a ride, but it did become a tourist attraction and a beacon of welcome to Coney Island. Manhattan's got its Empire State Building and in Brooklyn we've got our Parachute Jump.

By 2017, there were 51 rides run by 10 separate operators helping to draw more than five million people to Coney Island each year, with infrastructure upgrades and amenities to support the neighborhood's 60,000 residents.

KELLY

There was a fear that because Bloomberg was mayor and Bloomberg [LP] was this big corporation — were we going to come in and sanitize and ruin Coney Island?

A pivotal moment in my career [was when] I was asking the mayor to approve — which means you had to go through Dan — $2.2 million [for] Coney Island USA, a small arts organization in Coney Island responsible for the creation of the Mermaid Parade. Full disclosure, I'm on their board now years later. At the time, their building was falling apart and their landlord was looking to sell the building but was willing to sell to them if they could come up with the cash.

There were lots of reasons why it made no sense for the City to spend $2.2 million on this in advance of all the other big ticket items that we had to do in Coney Island. But I sat down with Dan.

I was this lowly project manager at EDC. He was intimidating. I had to explain to him why it was so important that we spent $2.2 million preserving burlesque, sword swallowing, eating glass light bulbs, the tradition of the Mermaid Parade.

There are a few things in American culture that are truly American, but the sideshow is one of them. I had this whole thing worked up in my head of how I'm going to convince him that this $2.2 million is going to save America, save the world. For us, it was a key way of putting an olive branch out to the amusement district to show that we [weren't] looking to create a Coney Island that no one recognizes.

So, I'm sitting down with Dan, he's in his typical blue shirt, sleeves rolled up. Imagine telling this guy, "Yes, they do burlesque." I'm picturing the Saturday night shows with the pasties on the stage and all the craziness that's Coney Island. And I'm just like, "There's

no way he's going to approve this." And I didn't even finish. You basically always had 20 minutes with Dan; that was it. If you didn't get your thing [across] in 20 minutes, it didn't happen. I might have only gotten through the first five or seven minutes, and he was like, "This is great. Done."

It was such a small thing, but it was one of my first encounters with Dan. And it showed me that he was going to respect what we were saying, which is we have to still keep Coney Island funky and weird and edgy and cool. And it can't be a great adventure plopped in Brooklyn, it's got to be authentic; he got that immediately.

That led to a series of other investments shortly thereafter, like the saving of the B&B Carousell, all these small capital items that were olive branches to the community but also showed commitment to the quirkiness that was Coney Island.

THE OPENING

KELLY

We built Luna Park literally in under 100 days. I kid you not, the night before the mayor was supposed to be there to open it up, we were hoping, watching, praying the asphalt was going to dry in time. [That morning] we had a few sections, unbeknownst to Marty or any of the other dignitaries and leaders that were there, that we had cordoned off. We said, "Oh, it's for VIP." No, it's because you would've put your foot in the asphalt.

We had publicly committed to open by Memorial Day, which was the kickoff of the amusement season. We didn't want to lose that first summer. That was really important. Getting all those agencies

— Parks Department, DOT, City Hall, DEP, Department of Buildings, the list goes on and on — to move at the same pace took some time. By the time we got a shovel in the ground, it was a 24/7 operation.

If it wasn't Coney Island, I don't think people would have worked as hard as they did. The electrician who would be on the job at 10:00 at night, calling his wife, "I'm sorry, I'm going to be here till midnight," calling at midnight, "I'm sorry, it's going to be an overnight job," would be the same [person] that would say to me, "I remember this place." People put their hearts into it. If it was any other job, they would've said, "100 days, not happening." But because it was Coney Island, people made it happen.

HIDDEN AMUSEMENT ZONE SECRETS

KELLY

The Zenobio is the second ride to be named after one of the team members. I have the first: "Lynn's Trapeze." I go back every summer and there's always some young teenager running the ride. I always say, "I'm that Lynn." And they're like, "Yeah lady, come on. Next."

I worked closely with Tricia [Zenobio, who oversaw implementation through the Office of Capital Project Development, which Doctoroff created to accelerate multiagency projects]. The Zenobio is a super thrill ride. She got the big bang. You know what? She deserved it.

THE LEGACY

MARKOWITZ

I still don't think Coney Island has reached its potential, but it's a hell of a lot better than it was before Lynn Kelly and before Dan and before Michael Bloomberg, for sure. It's a tourist attraction, number one. Number two, it provides jobs for low- and moderate-income folks — and let's not forget the other part of it; housing. And it is affordable for income diverse families — just about everyone can afford to summer in Coney Island. [Dan] really brought together a great team to restore Coney Island's legacy.

NEW SPORTS VENUES: YANKEE STADIUM, CITI FIELD, AND BARCLAYS CENTER

Sitting today in Citi Field, the new Yankee Stadium, or the Barclays Center, it is easy to forget that at the time Mike Bloomberg took office in January 2002, there hadn't been a new major professional sports facility constructed in New York City in over three decades. As cities across the country opened new facilities, New Yorkers were stuck with mid-century sports infrastructure, with the City largely footing the tens of millions of dollars in annual upkeep expenses for its two aging baseball stadiums.

The almost complete turnover of New York's professional stadium infrastructure in less than a decade was a result of several factors — the NYC2012 Olympic bid, the realization that these facilities could be significant drivers of bold, but sensible, economic development goals, the Bloomberg administration's commitment to judging each project through its potential return on investment — but at the center of all these initiatives was Dan Doctoroff.

Dan arrived at City Hall with the mandate for a new stadium on his agenda. Ironically, that stadium, the New York Sports and Convention Center, which was the centerpiece of the NYC2012 Olympic bid and was to serve as a new home for the New York Jets, turned out to be the only proposed major sports facility of the Bloomberg administration not to get done. Its impact on the other facilities was profound, however, as its demise ultimately led directly to the deal for Citi Field, helped expedite the Yankee Stadium project, and established a template the City would follow on subsequent deals to reject empty government subsidies to wealthy sports teams in favor of real economic development. (In the case of the West Side, simply planning for the stadium project catalyzed the development of Hudson Yards, arguably the crown jewel of Dan's accomplishments during his time as deputy mayor.)

At the end of the day, the City wound up spending less on two stadiums, an arena, 55 acres of new parkland, and anchors for two massive mixed-use developments than most places have spent on one isolated stadium or arena project. That we were able to yield so much for such a relatively modest investment, in such a short amount of time, was due almost exclusively to Dan's ingenuity, vision, and perseverance.

Yankee Stadium and Citi Field

Plans for new stadiums for the Yankees and Mets were, to put it politely, going nowhere when Mike Bloomberg was sworn into office on New Year's Day 2002. The Giuliani administration, in its waning days, had announced new $800 million stadiums for each club, with the City footing half the bill. But the proposed Giuliani deals were so lacking in any economic development rationale that it took the new mayor less than a week into his new term to reject them outright.

Left to start over in their respective quests for a new building, the Yankees and Mets took dramatically different tacks in their approach to the incoming Bloomberg administration. Whereas the Mets were primarily focused on the workaday issues of who was responsible for what when it came to maintaining the City-owned Shea Stadium, the Yankees aggressively pushed a revised proposal for a new stadium in the Bronx. Their new plan came with one significant advantage: The club was offering to privately finance the entire construction. But it also came with two massive disadvantages: First, the Yankees initially proposed to replace the parkland that would be eliminated by the new stadium on a site

Opposite: Dan Doctoroff envisioned Barclays Center in Downtown Brooklyn as part of the broader Atlantic Yards project, which involved decking over exposed rail yards to build residential, commercial, cultural, and entertainment space.

Left: The New York Mets paid for construction of Citi Field, relieving the City of millions of dollars of annual maintenance obligations for the dilapidated Shea Stadium.

The new Yankee Stadium opened in 2009. The City replaced the site of the former stadium with the new 44-acre Macombs Dam Park and Heritage Field, including grass ballfields, a state-of-the-art 400-meter track, a new all-weather turf field, and courts for basketball and handball. The City also transformed an abandoned 11-acre site along the Bronx River into Mill Pond Park, with 16 tennis courts, recreational lawns and trails, a playground, and the Bronx Children's Museum, housed in a former power station.

almost a mile away, in an entirely different community; and second, the club wanted the City to pay for maintenance and upkeep of the new building, as it did with the old City-owned stadium, which at the time was costing the City $7-10 million annually to operate, with the maintenance cost rising every year.

Dan hired me in 2003, primarily to oversee City Hall's relationship with the Economic Development Corporation (EDC) and charged me with handling the City's negotiations with sports teams. To the Yankees' credit, the club quickly capitulated on the maintenance request. This was essential, as we had absolutely no interest in signing up for four more decades of eight-figure annual upkeep expenses on depreciating stadium infrastructure. Just as importantly, being relieved of this annual expense burden enabled us to justify the investment of city capital in new and improved parkland to replace what was being lost to the new stadium site. In essence, we were trading an annual upkeep obligation on a crumbling, old stadium for a new and enhanced park — and getting a new, privately financed stadium in the bargain.

While the Yankees and the City had a new deal by the end of 2004, by that time progress on the West Side stadium had stalled. We decided to hold off on the Yankees announcement while the delicate political negotiations over the West Side proceeded, acutely aware that we had less than a year before the International Olympic Committee would make its decision on the 2012 host city.

As the weeks turned into months, the frustration of Yankees President Randy Levine boiled over into almost daily calls, with threats of calling the governor of New Jersey about building the new stadium across the Hudson River. Of course, Levine's ability to execute on these threats was severely limited by the four million fans the club was drawing annually to the Bronx, a fact I finally pointed out by telling him, "Look, you can call the mayor and say you're moving to Jersey, but he's just going to laugh."

They wouldn't have to wait much longer. The end of the West Side Stadium saga came on a quiet Sunday morning in June 2005. While Mayor Bloomberg and the leader of the State Assembly Sheldon Silver, caucused downstairs, my colleague, Marc Ricks and I kept Dan company in the City Hall bullpen, trying, and largely failing to engage him in small talk. The atmosphere upstairs was eerily

First thing Monday morning, I found myself in a windowless conference room with Andrew Winters, the Olympic planning director, and the staff at EDC, separating wheat from chaff.

It quickly became apparent that there was a lot of chaff, and not a lot of wheat. The site had to be available and accessible — a significant challenge when you are trying to identify 25 to 50 acres in New York City. It also needed to have a long-term tenant and we knew it couldn't be the Jets, who were clear they would only relocate to Manhattan. So out went potential options like Aqueduct, Willets Point, and my initial favorite, Randall's Island. In the end, the survey of potential options took us right back to where we found ourselves on the day that the mayor was sworn in, Shea Stadium.

While the proposed Giuliani deals were dead-on-arrival when Mike Bloomberg arrived at City Hall, they nevertheless brought with them a few key advantages that survived. First and foremost, there was an approved environmental review on the Shea Stadium site that could relatively easily be transferred to a new project. Second, the Mets were obviously a long-term tenant who had expressed interest in a new stadium. Finally, we had already negotiated a new deal with the Yankees, providing a template for the offer to Mets owners Fred and Jeff Wilpon.

Luckily for all parties, the Mets were highly responsive and fully understood the stakes. Discussions moved remarkably fast, especially for a project of this magnitude. The memorandum of understanding for Citi Field was announced within a week of the West Side stadium's demise — and was largely the result of a find-and-replace on the Yankees' memorandum of understanding that had been on ice for months.

We had our Olympic Stadium and, as a *New York Times* headline declared the day after the announcement, "The Mets Finally Get Their New Stadium, but They Have to Pay For It." For the Yankees' part, they refused to play into the feel-good optics of both of our baseball teams working together for the good of the Olympic bid (if New York was awarded the 2012 Olympics, the Yankees would have to host the Mets for the 2012 season), instead insisting on their own announcement, which took place later the same week.

From a financial perspective, the two stadiums were a clear boon for the city, handing us two new privately-financed stadiums (as contrasted to the $800 million total public contribution that the prior administration had negotiated), with deals that relieved the City of almost $20 million in annual maintenance obligations. The Yankee Stadium project also yielded brand-new parkland that featured state-of-the-art ball fields and a world-class running track, while Citi Field could serve as an anchor for the eventual redevelopment of Willets Point.

That the latter project has yet to fully materialize is less about any shortcomings of Citi Field, and more an object lesson in the difficulty of large-scale planning in New York City — today, more than a decade later, the development is finally moving forward, with plans for new affordable housing, the city's first soccer-specific stadium, a hotel, and new retail. If anything, the lessons from Willets Point make what we were able to accomplish so quickly at Hudson Yards and the rail yards surrounding Atlantic Terminal, even more impressive.

reminiscent of a hospital waiting room. After an hour or so, the mayor came upstairs. "We have good news and bad news," he declared as he entered the room. "The good news is that we're building a stadium." We immediately perked up. We were getting the West Side stadium. Silver had capitulated. Unfortunately, our hopefulness lasted only moments, as the mayor continued, "the bad news is that we're going to have to build it on the World Trade Center site." That was Mike Bloomberg in a nutshell. Incredibly sharp wit, perhaps a little harsh in the moment, but also tinged with an underlying faith that the world would keep turning, and Dan would figure something out.

I had planned to spend the afternoon working with Marc and Dan on a West Side stadium victory announcement. Instead, I wound up walking with Dan uptown through Hudson River Park after the meeting. Again, my attempts at small talk fell flat. Dan was clearly not in the mood for my casual observations.

But it did not take long for Dan to find his focus. By later that afternoon, he was already emailing me with instructions to begin cataloging every other conceivable Olympic Stadium site, setting off a frantic 72-hour scramble to find a suitable Olympic stadium for the NYC2012 bid.

Barclays Center

The push to construct the Barclays Center as part of a new mixed-use development over 22 acres of rail yards and largely underutilized property in the heart of Brooklyn reflected much more than the nuts-and-bolts economic analysis of a typical development project. It was about what Brooklyn meant, had once meant, and could mean again. And the emotions that the project sparked, both in favor and against, reflected that as well.

For my part, having grown up in Brooklyn in the 1980s, it was almost unthinkable that such a project would ever be considered. Brooklyn was almost a synonym for all the postwar trends in development that so negatively impacted American cities. The Dodgers decamping to Los Angeles in 1957 summarized many of them in one nice, neat package — a preference for cars over public transportation, the Sunbelt to the Northeast and Midwest, lower scale development to New York-style density. Even as the tide began to turn in the

mid-90s, as a native Brooklynite, I still could not quite shake lingering skepticism about the borough's revival. It seemed like in my lifetime, Brooklyn would always be known as a place people were from, never a destination where they aspired to go.

Viewed from that lens, bringing a National Basketball Association team to the streets of Downtown Brooklyn — away from a comfortable home in suburban New Jersey — was a big deal. It was a palpable, physical manifestation of the borough's rebirth, one that perfectly complemented the many transformative initiatives that Dan was already spearheading via rezonings in Downtown Brooklyn, along the Greenpoint-Williamsburg waterfront, and through the construction of Brooklyn Bridge Park. And it made obvious economic development sense, covering a massive scar in the heart of the borough created by the rail yards while leveraging one of the largest mass transit hubs in the city.

Of course, not everyone agreed. The pushback was intense, even if it often spoke in the name of a small, and rather insular, minority of the borough's residents who raised concerns, like traffic, that were ultimately proven to be almost complete non-issues. Lawsuits, particularly regarding the use of eminent domain, led to delays, ultimately pushing the opening of the arena almost to the very end of the mayor's third term.

But Dan never wavered in the face of this intense opposition. He understood the need for the Atlantic Yards project because he is a unique amalgam of a banker and a visionary. The visionary intuitively understood the optics, that having a major professional sports franchise back in Brooklyn would transform the narrative and remove any of those lingering doubts about the borough's revival. The banker, though, needed to see a return on investment and maintained the conviction that we needed to demand favorable terms from the developers to make it happen. I still smile thinking about his reaction after almost every meeting (and there were many) we had with the developer Forest City Ratner and its leader Bruce Ratner over the more than year and half it took to negotiate the original memorandum of understanding. "It's a great project," he'd tell me on the way to his next appointment, "but Bruce needs to pay for it." And by the time Barclays Center opened in 2012, almost three quarters of a billion dollars of private money had gone into its construction.

Left: As part of the Atlantic Yards project, the Nets, a National Basketball Association team, moved from suburban New Jersey to the heart of Downtown Brooklyn, giving the borough its first professional sports team in nearly half a century.

Above: A crowd gathered outside of Ebbets Field, home of the Brooklyn Dodgers, in 1920. Barclays Center is built on nearly the same spot where owner Walter O'Malley wanted to build a stadium for the Brooklyn Dodgers. When plans fell through, he relocated the team to Los Angeles before the 1958 season.

THE FUTURE CITY

Sidewalk Labs rendering of proposed mass timber buildings at Quayside, Toronto.

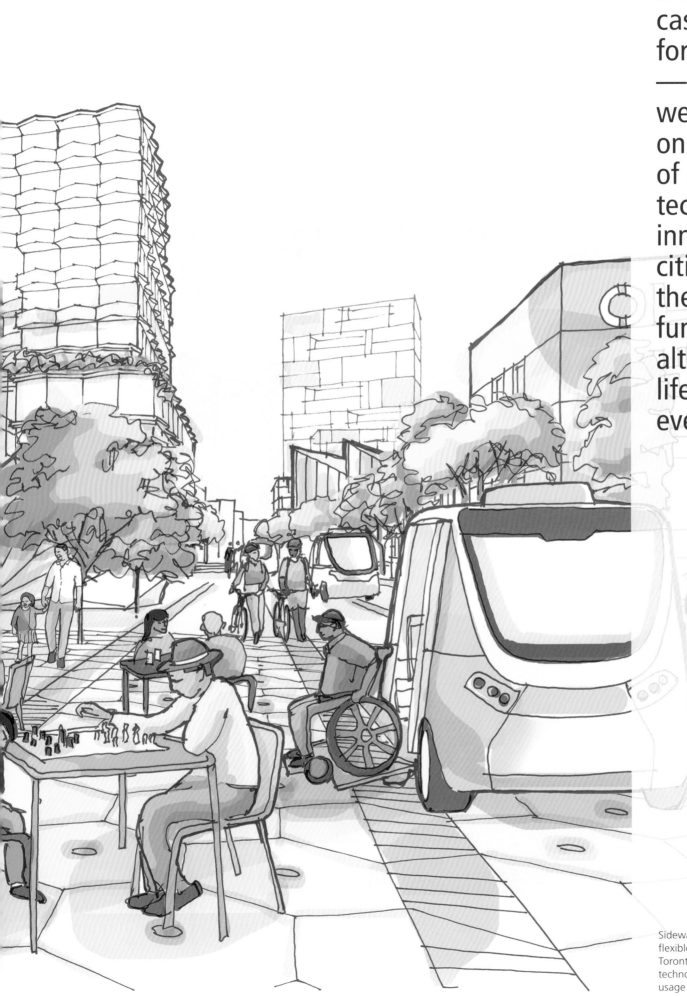

"I believe there is a very powerful case to be made for optimism — I think that we're actually on the threshold of a rare era of technological innovation in cities that has the potential to fundamentally alter quality of life across almost every dimension."

DANIEL L. DOCTOROFF, JANUARY 2017

Sidewalk Labs sketch showing a flexible street proposed for the Toronto waterfront that utilizes digital technology to maximize pedestrian usage on a weekend.

RICHARD FLORIDA | University Professor, Rotman School of Management and School of Cities, University of Toronto

SIDEWALK LABS AND THE FUTURE OF CITIES

Between Jacobs and Moses: Dan Doctoroff as visionary urbanist

Two things stick in my mind about the first time I met Dan Doctoroff. The first is that I thought there was little we would agree on. The second is that he was onto something big.

When it comes to the economic development of cities, Dan is a true visionary, whose ideas have always been far ahead of their time. And this is why, even though these ideas may have met with resistance at times, they have opened our eyes and the proverbial playing field to the future of cities and urban development.

I had heard about Dan long before we actually met — and it was clear that people didn't expect us to get along. Colleagues and other urbanists described to me how Dan was leading a bid to bring the Olympic Games to New York City — could you imagine? I guess they thought we occupied separate corners in the field of urban development. In my book, *The Rise of the Creative Class*, I argued that cities were wasting their time and money on big ticket items like stadiums. Like many urbanists, I had come to see hosting the Olympics as a burden on local taxpayers that rarely paid off. How exactly would a new stadium here or there draw

in the entrepreneurs, artists, designers, tech workers, and other knowledge workers who made up the creative class? These groups wanted walkable neighborhoods, green spaces, and access to a wide array of social and cultural amenities.

When we eventually met, it was quickly apparent that we shared a common interest in cities and city-building. We bonded immediately over being from hard-pressed industrial cities struggling to revive their glory years: Dan from Detroit, me from Newark. For someone who was able to shape the development trajectory of the world's greatest and most powerful city, he was incredibly open, willing to talk, engage and listen, and truly interested in new and different ideas. When I asked him about the city's failed Olympic bid, he didn't miss a beat. He said the strategy was less about actually winning the Games per se, and much more about garnering the political will to invest in the infrastructure, create the density, and establish a development template for the city's future. Today, that notion is so conventional that it's a plot line in the TV show, *Billions*. Back then, I hadn't heard anything like it. For the first time — but not the last — I realized just how far ahead of the curve Dan was.

A step ahead of his time

I got to know Dan a lot better when he started the brainstorming process for Sidewalk Labs, a Google-backed company he founded in order to bring together technologists and urbanists to tackle some of the most urgent challenges facing cities in the 21st century. The conversation surprised me: It was less about technology and much more about city-building — about how to create vibrant, interactive, mixed-use, sustainable, and inclusive neighborhoods. It was about how to build Jane Jacobs kinds of neighborhoods, using technology to support and advance the goals.

We talked about density — the right kind of density for great neighborhoods. We talked about building heights. We talked about walkability and bikeability — how to get beyond the use of the car. We talked about new, greener building technologies and materials like mass timber. We talked about how to create more environmentally sustainable neighborhoods. We talked about how to create more affordable housing; and much, much more. Most of all we talked about how to do this at a scale that matters. Not by developing a single building, but by creating a neighborhood or "district" which could serve as a template or test site for innovating and creating a new model for urban development.

Sidewalk Labs proposed mass timber commercial buildings on Villiers Island as part of the reimagined Toronto waterfront. The rendering shows the new lively commercial district, which would have been served by an extended streetcar line on Cherry Street.

Sidewalk Labs proposed a new design for Cherry Street that prioritized pedestrians, bicycles, and public transit, while utilizing digital technologies to minimize the impact of cars.

Like New York's Olympic bid, it was a vision that was far ahead of its time — one that will continue to shape our urban future for decades to come. Dan's vision for Sidewalk Labs catalyzed the new field of urban innovation, seeing the city as a platform for creativity and invention and transforming urban development from real estate and atoms to digital technology and bits.

All of this was possible because Dan's unique background and skill sets enable him to understand three things that most traditional urbanists, mayors, economic developers, and real estate developers cannot.

First, he understands how cities actually work. Not how they're supposed to work, or how activists want them to work, or how theorists expect them to work — he knows how municipal leadership actually drives change. He was deputy mayor of the most important city in the world, after all, and under a mayor who empowered his deputies more than any New York City administration in recent history. He knows that urban change is never easy but can be approached in many ways, whether that's visioning, like PlaNYC, public–private partnerships like the High Line, pilot programs like the Times Square pedestrian space, and more. He also understands that sometimes even the best ideas in cities must simply wait for their time to arrive, as in the case of congestion pricing.

Second, he understands how financial markets work and their centrality to urban development. Finance was his first career, after all. While many urbanists deceive themselves into thinking that only government has the resources, or mandate, to solve the problems facing cities, Dan recognizes that market interest in innovation is essential to scaling urban solutions. The public–private partnership approach he took when establishing New York's successful Citi Bike program is perhaps the best example — and it's no surprise that the model has been adopted and replicated by dozens of cities around the world. As a former deputy mayor of New York City, he also knows that there are times where markets must be reined in and that the public sector has an essential role in protecting the public good.

Third, he has a unique understanding of the power of digital technology. This partly stems from his tenure as CEO of the information tech and media company, Bloomberg LP, where he went after leaving city government. While many urbanists see digital technology as a danger to cities, Dan understands that it is inevitable. Instead of simply trying to block it, the key is to shape it and harness it in ways that promote better city-building. In the case of Bloomberg, that meant having a front-row seat for how real-time information can drive new products and industry investment. In the case of cities, which already operate as engines of innovation thanks to the density of new ideas, Dan quickly realized you could supercharge that potential by creating a new layer of digital infrastructure.

It is that remarkable trio of skill sets that led Google to bet on Dan as the best person capable of realizing Larry Page's vision to build a city of the future. I remember hearing Google's CEO at the time, Eric Schmidt, talk about this on economist Tyler Cowen's podcast.

After outlining the enormous challenges facing cities, he said, "The most interesting thing about city-building is city-building is extremely rare. Even in cities where they go bankrupt or they get in big trouble, it's almost impossible to change the planning assumptions about a city." And he zeroed in on Dan's unique capabilities to do just that. "We were able to hire Dan Doctoroff, who'd done a lot of work in New York, to lead that. What he's been doing is, he first assembled all of the new ideas about cities, and everyone has lists of complaints about cities a mile long, right? The traffic is bad, the air is bad, I can't get a taxi ... There's a long list of people's complaints about cities. They're not safe, the education system isn't strong enough. The idea is to come up with urban settings where you can address a multiplicity of those."

Sidewalk Toronto: a living laboratory for urban innovation

This unique approach to urban innovation was on display from the very start at Sidewalk Labs. In 2015, as Dan was getting Sidewalk off the ground, he and his original team convened some of the world's brightest urban thinkers to brainstorm ideas for tackling the biggest problems facing cities: traffic, clean energy, housing, sustainability, mobility, affordability, and economic opportunity.

All of it was rooted in urban innovation — the use of digital technology as a new tool in city-building and neighborhood development. Dan defined urban innovation broadly and deeply, and he wanted us to overcome our normal silos to do the same. That's when he called me and asked if I would be part of an economic development working group with people like Bruce Katz, who then ran the Metropolitan Policy Program at the Brookings Institution, and Edward Glaeser, the eminent urban economist at Harvard. I recall suggesting that whatever we did, it should be more than just a development or even a district, that we should create some kind of a living laboratory to forge and continuously evaluate new approaches to urban development. We all agreed that urbanism needed a global think tank or institute that could bring together the leading thinkers and doers in the field to generate and test new ideas at scale and in real-time conditions. To my surprise, it was an idea that resonated with Dan and the group, and we pledged to do just that.

In short, we needed a new place that functioned as a laboratory of urban innovation. Existing cities aren't places where it's appropriate to experiment — they're homes where people live. But if we developed a new place from the ground up, we could create the conditions and partnerships to see what worked and what did not and adjust according to a shared set of goals. We needed this type of place when President Barack Obama identified innovative "Urban Development Districts" as a priority in his *2016 President's Council of Advisors on Science and Technology* report. We needed it when Dan first talked about Sidewalk Labs. And we still need it today.

The upshot, embodied in Sidewalk's proposal for the Toronto waterfront, was a path-breaking systems approach to the theory and practice of urban innovation unlike anything I'd ever seen. This was far beyond the construct of the "smart city," which, to my mind, was about bolting technologies like sensors onto pieces of cities. Central to Dan's vision of urban innovation was the core idea that real change doesn't happen at the individual level of a building or a road or a park. There needed to be a holistic approach that involved and integrated various layers of digital and physical infrastructure.

Cities as holistic systems

I had seen this kind of change before. It had surfaced in my earliest research on the modernization of manufacturing back in the 1980s and 1990s. The successful companies took this kind of systems approach — along with involving workers and tapping their intelligence fully as part of teams that redesigned the production process. The unsuccessful companies adopted random innovations and practices and failed to involve their workers. I subsequently used that research to argue in my published work that in the new knowledge-based economy, cities were replacing the corporation as the essential platforms of innovation and productivity.

Dan and his team were the very first city-builders who saw the opportunity to build communities at the system level and to do so by tapping into the collective intelligence of their residents. The innovations did not come from on high, they came from the cluster of companies, start-ups, residents, and workers who would create a truly open system for urban innovation.

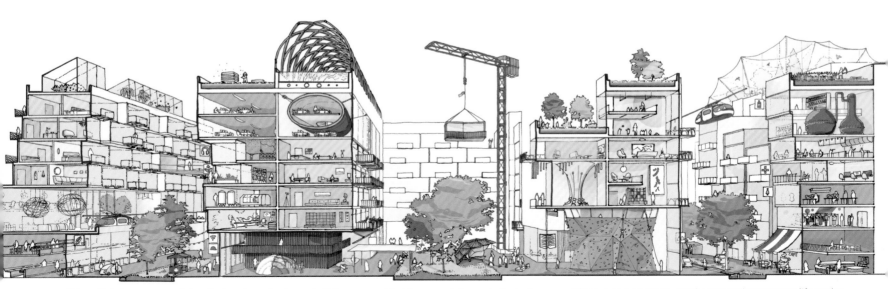

A Sidewalk Labs conceptual sketch showing mixed-use buildings assembled from modular parts (note the crane lifting a new section), emphasizing vibrant street life at the ground level of a neighborhood.

One of the clearest examples, which we talked about early on, was the potential impact of autonomous vehicles, or AVs, on urban life. When people look at AVs as the next big car technology, they are missing their ability to transform an entire, broader system. By removing the need for parking, AVs enable cities to repurpose street space and help developers cut housing costs — parking garages are expensive. By following careful rules, AVs enable traffic engineers to route vehicles onto certain streets, opening up others to pedestrians, cyclists, and pop-up shops. By providing a shared mobility option, AVs enable residents to give up car ownership and save money. By operating through open data, AVs enable ongoing innovation by entrepreneurs looking to build the next great transportation service. In doing so, this basic technology alone has cascading benefits to affordability, mobility, community, economic opportunity, and more — and it has to be thought through and planned from the outset.

The Master Innovation and Development Plan (MIDP) for the Toronto waterfront that Sidewalk published in 2019 was the culmination of all this thinking. If you clear away all the controversy around the project — a conversation that reflected a place and time but that didn't really engage with the plan itself — it's a remarkable vision. Here was a strategy to use technology to underpin a dense, diverse, Jane Jacobs-style neighborhood. It was a blueprint for reinventing urban development for the 21st century. And this is exactly why I supported it in my hometown of Toronto.

A new trajectory for urban innovation

The Toronto plan was, like Dan himself, so incredibly far ahead of its time that even though it ultimately did not pan out, it set the tenor and trajectory for urban development for years to come.

For one, it created the new field of urban innovation or what I dubbed urban tech. My own research finds that urban tech is now the single biggest area of venture capital investment, accounting for nearly a quarter of all venture capital funding of high-tech start-ups in 2017 — and it has surely grown since then. Venture capital funds like Fifth Wall to Andreessen Horowitz, URBAN-X,

As part of its Toronto proposal, Sidewalk Labs envisioned tree-lined pedestrian walkways through modular mass timber residential buildings. Above, a rendering shows ground floor spaces with roll-up doors that would provide easy access to retail and community facilities, and low balconies to create a more intimate scale.

MetaProp, and 2150, which I am part of in Europe, have populated this space. Google itself has taken on and funded Sidewalk products Delve, Mesa, and Pebble. And it has integrated many of these technologies and ideas in its new mixed-use urban campus being developed in downtown San Jose in close collaboration with city government, residents, and labor and community activists. The diaspora of Dan's hires and disciples at Sidewalk Labs is a part of many of these efforts and keeps their spirit alive.

Academic research is following suit. If you search the term "urban innovation" on Google Scholar, you find just 4,200 citations for all time prior to 2015, the year Sidewalk Labs launched. In the seven years since, there are already 10,000-plus references — and rising. Cornell Tech has made urban innovation part of its academic mission and the University of Chicago has created a center for research on the topic as well. The emerging field has shaped our own thinking about the new School of Cities at the University of Toronto.

Real estate is recognizing the importance of urban innovation, too. Major firms from RXR to Lendlease to Related Companies are using technology in all kinds of new ways — in some cases, even setting up dedicated innovation units. On the flip side of that coin, tech companies remain increasingly interested in the built environment. Google's real estate division has an R&D Lab that explores advances like mass timber and a district development team that uses a large-scale systems approach to deploy innovations that wouldn't be feasible within a single building. Toyota's Woven City development project strongly echoes Sidewalk's language, all the way down to the "living laboratory" description. Sidewalk Labs isn't solely responsible for this industry movement, but the process Dan initiated surely helped to set it in motion.

Last but not least are the conversations happening in cities themselves. Municipal innovation offices and agency-led innovation challenges have become commonplace, covering every pillar of urban life. For transportation, there are self-driving car pilots in Phoenix,

New housing, renovated industrial buildings, and a
public walkway along Keating Channel would create new
recreational space and significant economic development
opportunities, as shown in this Sidewalk Labs sketch.

car-free neighborhoods in Tempe, a mobility innovation hub in Detroit, an urban consolidation center in Nijmegen. For energy, there's a climate-positive development in Stockholm, a climate innovation campus in development on Governors Island in New York City, a push for Vancouver to calculate full life-cycle emissions. For housing, there are modular initiatives in San Francisco, middle-income pilot programs in Los Angeles, new mass timber models in San Jose, robotic furniture in Buffalo and Durham. For infrastructure, there are advanced stormwater systems in Kansas City, vacuum waste tubes in London, digital electricity in Fort Worth, a lifelong learning hub in South Bend. For digital layers, there's Barcelona's cutting-edge sensor platform, Taiwan's data commons — even the embrace of local crypto by Miami and other cities, which, while perhaps misguided, reflects an open mind toward data innovation. This list is hardly exhaustive. And again, all of them are descendants of (or at least accelerated by) the new field Dan catalyzed at Sidewalk Labs.

An urban visionary

As for me, I continue to be inspired by Dan's vision in my academic work as an advisor to cities, philanthropic foundations, real estate companies, venture capital funds, and urban innovation companies.

Dan ultimately occupies that rare middle ground between Jane Jacobs and Robert Moses. Most urbanists are far to the left of Jacobs. They repel any attempt to create new places that aren't stuck in 1960s activism. They have a reflexive aversion to private markets and new technology that Jacobs herself never had. Dan embraces the Jacobs ethos of promoting local innovation to solve local problems, sees the value of public-private partnership, wants to create the conditions for bottom-up urbanism while recognizing it might take some top-down infrastructure to get there.

Most practitioners and developers, meanwhile, have the deal-driven mentality of Moses but lack his appreciation for systems-level thinking. Dan is a systems-level city builder who comes at city-building with a notion that it must still support neighborhoods and people. He knows the power of a sweeping vision, but also the catastrophe of digging a highway through the center of a community. He sees the importance of cities as platforms of innovation and economic opportunity but respects the need to build them in a democratic way.

And that's ultimately the true legacy of Dan Doctoroff — a man who saw the future of cities and urban innovation, and in doing so, opened the door for our collective effort to realize it.

JUSTIN DAVIDSON | Architecture Critic, *New York Magazine*, 2007–Present | Winner of the Pulitzer Prize

LESSONS FROM QUAYSIDE

Sidewalk Labs had a plan to test how technology could advance old–fashioned urban virtues along the Toronto waterfront. Its defeat was a lost opportunity for the future of cities.

To urban visionaries, cities can be frustrating reminders of what their predecessors screwed up. All those vast parking lots, multi-level interchanges, and wide boulevards that oblige us to drive from an office tower to the mall next door — all the myopia, opportunism, and corruption — makes retrofitting the world we live in a pain in the ass. Hence the lure of the blank-slate city, designed to avoid not just the mistakes of the past but also the pitfalls of the present. In practice, though, new cities are rarely an improvement over old ones. Depending on how you count them,

half the world's metropolitan centers were built within the last four decades and many are already shabby and charmless, with all the same strip malls, slums, and traffic jams as their elders. Technology stirs new fantasies and promises fresh disappointments. Saudi Arabia is pitching Neom, a 100-mile-long, ultra-wired, high-density ribbon of Edenic urbanism sandwiched between mirrored towers. You'd have to be an awfully early adopter for that to seem like a plausible, let alone appealing, version of the next model megalopolis.

Yet when Sidewalk Labs proposed to erect a new neighborhood, called Quayside, on a stretch of Toronto waterfront, it chipped away at my skepticism. The new zone would be fused to a large, existing metropolis, not plunked on a distant plain. And the plan, a nearly 1,600-page, multivolume opus bristling with detail, placed advanced technology at the service of old-fashioned urban virtues. A network of plazas and pedestrian-first streets would be sprinkled with "lightweight, adjustable street furniture" — sort of like the peddlers' carts and bicycle-powered knife-sharpening stations that are staples of improvised urban life across the developing world.

In the Sidewalk vision, all this Copenhagenish coziness would be laced with sensors and processors chewing through data and feeding it to a committee of artificially intelligent decision-makers. Messages would fly through the network, ordering sidewalks to melt snow, robots to deliver packages from central sorting facilities, streetlights to wait until a slow-trudger has finished crossing, automatic vehicles to yield, electronic beacons to guide the blind. Walking around wouldn't be the high-stakes rodeo it is today.

The presumptive output of this computerized system is safer, cleaner, and more pleasant urban living — not exactly an agenda for futuristic revolution. Compare that chorus of quasi-invisible gizmos to the technological shocks that transformed late 19th century New York or London into the metropolis we recognize today. Elevators, electric lights, subways, steel-frame towers, internal combustion engines, standardized trash bins, suspension bridges — these things made urban life faster, brighter, richer, noisier, more prosperous, and more democratic. Well into the 21st century, we're still living off the Victorian era's investments and imagination, as well as the huge disruptions and displacement they caused.

The Sidewalk Labs proposal for Quayside featured a major car-free pedestrian plaza with water features, market stalls, and restaurants to anchor the public space of this newly created neighborhood.

A car-free internal courtyard provides green space and community gathering areas in this Sidewalk Labs sketch, part of the company's proposal for the creation of a new neighborhood along the Toronto waterfront.

By those standards, the Quayside proposal was modest, but its goal was the same: to multiply the value of small efficiencies by combining them into a vast and interdependent system. In our day, that streamlining project aspires not only to improve the lives of individuals, but also to reduce their environmental impact — an essential ingredient of Sidewalk-style ambitions. (Quayside would have included a collection of towers framed in structural mass timber, for instance, decreasing the need for carbon-spewing processes that yield concrete and steel.) Cities contribute disproportionately to greenhouse gases, which means they can contribute disproportionately to reducing them. And the same digital technologies that have contributed disproportionately to fragmentation, polarization, and isolation can help nurture the glorious jangle of urban living.

And yet the vision of the city as motherboard spooked Torontonians, who saw Quayside as a Trojan horse, a scheme for sucking up its residents' private business and selling surveillance for profit. To me, the Trojan horse was a red herring. Corporate snoops already have a range of cheap and effective techniques for violating the privacy of billions; putting up a whole waterfront complex for a few thousand people seems like a cumbersome and expensive way to do the same thing on a tinier scale. Focusing on the threat of an intrusive city is a distraction from the real world's global arsenal of cookies, bots, malware, cameras, trackers, facial recognition algorithms, metadata, and social media polls. If a boardroom's worth of evil overlords wants to know your taste in shoes or when you raid the refrigerator at midnight, they don't need to build so much as a smart garden shed to find out.

In fact, the prospect of Quayside, and the debate it engendered, had begun to move the surveillance-versus-privacy debate into a new arena, subjecting private technology to fresh public scrutiny. By the time Sidewalk issued its printed plan, the company had vowed not to hold the city hostage with proprietary technology, sell the data it collected, or link it to individuals. An independent urban data trust would watch over how information got handled and the public, not the company, would have the final say. The mechanism was not foolproof or final. In an article published in the journal *Surveillance and Society* after Quayside's demise, University of Toronto law professor Lisa Austin and engineering professor David Lie concluded that the trust model was so ill-defined that it "reduced accountability and oversight in relation to privacy while increasing complexity." But governing the use of data in the physical public realm remains one of the great policy challenges. It's work that urgently needs doing, because technology will continue to infiltrate cities whether we plan for it or not. Usually, the gizmos come first and the rules come panting behind them, always out of date. Quayside provided a chance to change that dynamic. When the plan collapsed, Toronto (and, by extension, all urbanites) lost an opportunity to renegotiate the relationship between technology and privacy, to open new frontiers and set new boundaries at the same time.

A "smart" city isn't categorically distinct from the old, dull-witted kind. Cities have a long track record of absorbing transformative technologies, favoring stone and steel over wood to ward off fire, laying tracks for streetcars (still among the most civilized forms of urban transit), running fiber optic cable beneath the asphalt, hooking gutters up to a centralized sewer system, sowing the streets with battery-powered bikes. All these innovations had their downsides and delays, yet we depend on them every day.

Cities of any age need to be nimble, and all make technological decisions every day, like electrifying rickshaws in Delhi, installing solar water heaters in Cairo's slums, or revamping the ancient subway signals in New York. Sometimes, massive, generational investments wind up having a short lifespan, or eventually need to be undone. Back when motor vehicles were the technology of the future, cities contorted themselves to accommodate them; now they're wrestling with ways to keep them out. Phasing out obsolete hardware implies the development of new hardware, like electronic license plate readers and automated toll systems (which, by the way, now need to be upgraded to defeat a common low-tech cheat: covering a license plate with a piece of paper).

We urbanites live in a tangle of overlapping algorithms, feeding it with our movements, habits, needs, and desires. We need not surrender to it, but we can't avoid it, either. The promise of Quayside was to master that reality, not by dictating behavior but by responding to the way people want to live. The only way to do that is to understand what urban dwellers do, how often, and, most important, why. Today's advocates of humane streets and livable public spaces often worship at the altar of William "Holly" Whyte, a sociologist who collected anonymized data about urbanites' habits with the most advanced tools at his disposal: a film camera and a notebook. His observations about where people chose to stand, sit, lunch, and converse on sidewalks and plazas, have influenced generations of planners (including those at Sidewalk). Whyte might have been delighted to have some AI help in his project, because he understood that the right data, collected in the right way and with the right intentions, is an instrument of freedom, not control.

With Quayside, Sidewalk hoped to translate Whyte's insights from the dynamics of what he called "small urban spaces" to a large urban neighborhood and beyond. (The 12-acre site would ideally have led to the redevelopment of a much wider swath of Toronto waterfront.) The company hoped to create its own precedents at that scale — to give bold mayors everywhere something to emulate, to placate lenders who insist on comps, and to demonstrate apparatuses that keep working even after suffering assaults from buffeting winds and peeing dogs.

Equally important, the development would have allowed technologies to fail and grow old. Conduits and pavers were designed for easy access, so that workers could rip out one kind of cable and install another. Despite all the dewy renderings and high-flown tech, the plan grappled with an important limitation: A slightly above-average-intelligence city that can take plenty of punishment is a far better place to live than a hyper-intelligent city that swoons at the first heat wave.

It's a shame that Quayside never got far enough to test those propositions. The project came up against the one ancient barrier inherent to almost all urban planning: inertia. Opposition to systemic novelty isn't just the concern of a few ignorable cranks; it's a fundamental force. Fighting it requires patience, humility, and an appreciation for the virtues of incremental change. Those are hard lessons for would-be revolutionaries to absorb. At the same time, Quayside's opponents should be chastened by their victory, or at least spare a pang for the futures they chased away.

Right: This aerial view of the proposed Quayside development shows sustainable mass timber buildings extending along Queens Quay and a major new public plaza celebrating waterfront recreation and providing new levels of access where Parliament Street meets Lake Ontario.

Following Spread: An aerial rendering of the Toronto Portlands, with Downtown Toronto in the background, showing an imagined future urban landscape dominated by natural shorelines and waterfront access, green spaces mixed with sustainable mass timber buildings, and a series of mixed-use, pedestrian-oriented neighborhoods built at a traditional city scale.

Parliament St

Gardiner Expy

Lake Shore Blvd

Trinity St

Parliament Plaza

Parliament Cove

MASTER INNOVATION AND DEVELOPMENT PLAN (MIDP)

In June 2019, Sidewalk Labs released its *Master Innovation and Development Plan* (MIDP), a 1,524-page, four-volume vision for inclusive urban growth. The MIDP had two core purposes. First, it proposed a comprehensive development plan for Toronto's waterfront with the potential to create over 93,000 jobs, achieve climate-positive status, provide an unprecedented 40% below-market housing, enable 77% of trips to be made without a car, and establish a responsible new approach to data governance.

More broadly, the MIDP was intended to provide a global blueprint for urban innovations that make it possible to address some of the toughest challenges facing

high-growth cities around the world. The plan outlined more than 50 innovations across six key areas of urban life — mobility, public realm, housing, sustainability, social infrastructure, and digital innovation — representing a powerful toolkit of solutions capable of delivering significant quality-of-life improvements.

The following pages provide an overview of these ideas, many of which have already been put into practice for the benefit of people living and working in cities around the world.

The Quayside proposal by Sidewalk Labs prioritized public waterfront access and recreational opportunities. Below, rendering of a proposed dynamic public plaza along the shores of Lake Ontario.

MOBILITY

The MIDP's mobility innovations were designed to support a transportation system that reduces the need to own a car by providing safe, convenient, connected, and affordable options for every trip.

Initiatives

1. Expand public transit through innovative self-financing
Expanding transit options is the most efficient way to transport the most people in the most sustainable way — an investment that can also spur development along the new routes. But limited budgets frequently make such expansions all but impossible. By borrowing against future revenues, municipalities can self-finance expansions to connect residents and workers to new job hubs and accelerate existing plans without relying solely on public funding. This mirrors the strategy Dan Doctoroff successfully used to finance the extension of the No. 7 subway in New York City to the new Hudson Yards neighborhood, which has already enabled billions of dollars of development on Manhattan's Far West Side.

2. Redesign streets to prioritize pedestrians and cyclists
Incorporating wider sidewalks, wider and heated bike lanes, and accessibility elements into an interconnected citywide transportation system can encourage walking and cycling by making it a more inviting and more efficient way to travel.

3. Offer new mobility services
Developing a network of ride-hail, bike-share, electric vehicle car-share, and e-scooters can provide affordable alternatives to private car trips.

4. Design unique street types to serve different users
Thoughtfully varied street designs can better recognize and reflect the different speeds and needs of travelers, including faster, bigger "Boulevards" and "Transitways" for vehicle and public transit traffic, "Accessways" designed specifically for cyclists, and "Landways" for pedestrian-only experiences.

Digital tools embedded in the street can transform how the space is used during the day, permitting more pedestrian usage during non-peak hours.

5. Improve accessibility
A wide set of accessibility initiatives, including curbless street design, wider sidewalks, heated pavement, wayfinding beacons, and accessible ride-hail vehicles can support people using wheelchairs or other assistive devices.

6. Leverage technology to help travelers make smarter choices
An integrated mobility subscription package can establish a new pricing model that enables residents and workers to see all their trip choices in real time, including transit, bikeshare, rideshare and other options, and pay in one place.

7. Reduce freight congestion via underground delivery tunnels
A freight logistics hub featuring a consolidated shipping center with underground delivery can reduce truck traffic on local streets and improve convenience.

8. Develop smarter tools for managing traffic
A mobility management system can use real-time information to coordinate travel modes, traffic signals, and street infrastructure, and apply pricing to curb and parking spaces — reducing congestion and encouraging shared trips.

9. Implement more sustainable, centralized parking
A district parking management system can incorporate high-density on- and off-site parking, on-demand vehicle retrieval, and electric-vehicle charging.

10. Create dynamic curbs to improve street flexibility
Flexible street spaces known as dynamic curbs can provide passenger loading zones during rush hour and public spaces in off-peak times.

11. Develop more responsive traffic signals
Adaptive traffic signals can prioritize pedestrians who need more time to cross a street or transit vehicles running behind schedule.

PUBLIC REALM

The MIDP's public realm innovations supported a system of streets, parks, plazas, and open spaces designed to encourage people to spend more time outdoors, together.

Initiatives

1. Build flexible open spaces for year-round use
Dynamic water features, adaptable performance spaces, multisport fields, and more can make spaces flexible and appropriate for year-round use.

2. Install an innovative outdoor comfort system
Sidewalk Labs developed an innovative outdoor comfort system featuring "Raincoats" that can extend over sidewalks in inclement weather, free-standing "Fanshells" to cover open spaces, and "Lanterns" designed to block wind; collectively this toolkit can dramatically increase the amount of time it is comfortable outside.

3. Create "Stoa" spaces to enliven streets
Flexible ground-floor "Stoa" spaces designed to accommodate a wide range of uses beyond traditional retail can ensure that communities have a lively mix of shops, restaurants, cafes, art installations, gathering spaces, and maker studios.

4. Generate more diverse leasing options for small businesses
A digital leasing platform can help small businesses and other retailers book a wide range of Stoa sizes, from anchor-tenant spaces to micro-stalls, for short- or long-term use to ensure a diverse mix.

5. Develop people-first streets to encourage time outdoors
People-first street designs can eliminate curbside parking, widen sidewalks, and increase tree plantings to improve safety and activate street life.

6. Install innovative modular pavement to make streets more flexible and easier to repair
Modular pavement — hexagonal pavers that can be replaced or repaired in hours by a single person with a handheld machine — can dramatically reduce the amount of time streets are closed for road or utility work and increase the flexibility of street use.

7. Centralize open space management
An "Open Space Alliance" entity can coordinate programming, operations, and maintenance across a community's parks, plazas, streets, and water spaces for a more responsive public realm.

8. Create a real-time public realm maintenance map
A real-time map of public realm assets — including park benches and landscaped gardens — can enable proactive maintenance and keep spaces in good condition.

9. Improve utility access for easier repairs and infrastructure upgrades
Open access channels located under removable pavers can allow for easy utility access and greater flexibility to incorporate new infrastructure systems as they are developed over time.

A car-free Parliament Plaza would provide a wide range of recreational and commercial uses, serving the local community and the broader city.

BUILDINGS AND HOUSING

The MIDP's building innovations included more sustainable development approaches that supported faster and more adaptable construction, while its housing innovations featured financial and design tools to improve affordability and expand living options.

Initiatives

1. Create an affordable housing program targeting all levels of need

Communities succeed best when people of all backgrounds can live there and thrive; that's why an ambitious housing affordability program should feature affordable housing units for low-income households and middle-income households who still can't pay market rate, as well as purpose-built rentals that help sustain long-term affordability.

2. Pioneer the use of mass timber for tall buildings

By embracing the emerging construction material known as mass timber, we can create sustainable tall buildings that work well in dense urban environments.

3. Build a mass timber factory to accelerate production

A mass timber factory can produce building parts for fast assembly, making construction quicker and more affordable, while catalyzing a new industry that supports sustainable forests.

4. Create flexible building floor plates

New construction can include adaptable loft spaces, featuring flexible floor plates to accommodate evolving residential, commercial, and light manufacturing uses that enable a true live-work community.

Modular mass timber buildings can be built faster, with less waste and fewer negative impacts on the local community.

5. Integrate movable wall panels for easier renovations

A system of flexible wall panels — enabled by new advances such as low-voltage power and mist sprinklers — can make it possible for renovations to occur much faster than normal, reducing vacancies and helping neighborhoods adapt to changing market conditions.

6. Institute outcome-based building codes

Monitoring noise, nuisances, and structural integrity in real time can inform more responsive building and zoning codes that help a mix of residential and non-residential uses thrive without sacrificing public safety or comfort.

7. Innovate shared equity housing options to make home ownership accessible to a broader range of people

"Shared equity" housing options can help households build value in their home without the high up-front cost of a traditional mortgage down payment.

8. Create affordability by design

"Affordability by design" packages enable the creation of additional housing units, unlocking development value that can be applied to support below-market options. For example, ultra-efficient unit designs can reduce the size of apartments to improve affordability while remaining livable through features such as space-saving furniture, shared building amenities, and on-demand delivery of off-site storage.

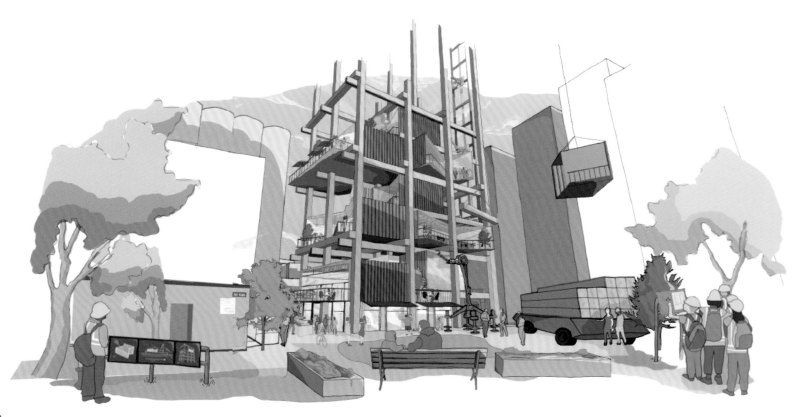

SUSTAINABILITY

The MIDP's sustainability innovations created a blueprint for truly "climate-positive" communities, meaning places that generate an excess of clean energy that can be shared with the rest of the city.

Initiatives

1. Implement low-energy building designs

Inspired by the passive house movement, more sustainable building designs can feature substantial wall insulation, airtight facades, and higher-quality windows to maintain a consistent, comfortable interior temperature without the need for heating or cooling.

2. Leverage digital tools to manage energy use more efficiently

Digital active energy management tools can optimize energy systems for residents, businesses, and building operators, ensuring that buildings operate in the most energy efficient way possible.

3. Build a more sustainable district thermal grid

A district energy system called a "thermal grid" can provide heating, cooling, and domestic hot water by drawing on clean energy sources such as geothermal energy, excess building heat, and wastewater heat.

4. Install a smart power grid that prioritizes clean energy

An advanced power grid can use solar energy, battery storage, and time-based energy pricing to reduce reliance on the main electricity grid during periods of peak demand and make all-electric communities more affordable.

5. Revamp utility bills to incentivize clean energy use

An innovative utility bill structure — tied to the advanced power grid — can enable residents and businesses to set monthly budgets for energy costs, similar to the way people pay for mobile phone plans.

6. Improve recycling through real-time feedback

A smart disposal chain can use real-time feedback to improve waste sorting and recycling, while "pay as you throw" chutes can levy individual charges based on actual waste disposal, discouraging household and business waste.

7. Create cleaner recycling streams

An underground pneumatic tube system can separate waste streams to reduce contamination and centralize trash hauling.

8. Establish an anaerobic digestion facility to reduce waste and generate clean energy

An anaerobic digestion facility can convert organic food waste into a clean energy source called biogas.

9. Integrate smart, green infrastructure to reduce stormwater runoff

An active stormwater management system incorporates green infrastructure to capture and retain stormwater and digital sensors to empty storage containers in advance of storms.

Sustainable infrastructure can support a healthy city with clean air, clean water, new green spaces, and extensive recreational opportunities.

SOCIAL INFRASTRUCTURE

The MIDP's social infrastructure innovations embedded social considerations into the foundation of neighborhood design, creating a community that could support health services, civic life, learning, and workforce initiatives more naturally and effectively to help all residents thrive.

Initiatives

1. **Co-locate health care and community services in a Care Collective**

   A "Care Collective" can enhance health and well-being by co-locating the delivery of health care and community services alongside proactive health programming in a dedicated community space.

2. **Establish a Civic Assembly space to facilitate community engagement**

   A "Civic Assembly" in the heart of a neighborhood can provide central access to community programs, civic engagement, and cultural events.

3. **Provide more integrated childcare**

   Co-locating an elementary school and childcare center can ensure that families in the neighborhood have access to basic education and childcare needs across age groups.

4. **Extend and expand public library services**

   A public library collaboration can integrate the library's presence throughout a neighborhood, resulting in pop-up lending services or library-developed classes in community spaces.

5. **Create easy digital ways to facilitate community participation**

   An online resource called "Collab" can empower community members to help shape public space programming.

6. **Establish workforce programs within the neighborhood**

   A local jobs program can bring together employers and educators to prepare workers to acquire in-demand skills, connecting companies with a diverse and talented community workforce.

Accessible and highly visible community spaces built into flexible ground floor sites can provide opportunities to connect people with each other and serve the needs of a diverse population.

462

DIGITAL INNOVATION

The MIDP's digital innovations established a new standard for the responsible collection and use of data in cities.

Initiatives

1. Create ubiquitous connectivity
A ubiquitous connectivity network — powered by a new "Super-PON" technology that reaches faster speeds with less equipment — can provide households and businesses with a secure personal network across an entire neighborhood.

2. Equip the urban environment to make technology upgrades faster and easier
Standardized physical "Koala" mounts can dramatically reduce the cost of deploying new digital innovations by serving as a sort of "urban USB port" for the physical environment.

3. Make it easier to create useful digital services to improve quality of life
Open, published standards can make properly protected urban data accessible to the community in real time, and make it easy for third parties to build new digital services or competitive alternatives to existing ones.

4. Build world-class digital security
A best-in-class approach to digital security and resiliency can prevent most disruptions, rapidly detect the rest, and quickly restore functionality.

5. Establish an independent Urban Data Trust to ensure privacy standards are met
An independent "Urban Data Trust" can oversee the review and approval of all digital innovations that propose to use or collect urban data in a neighborhood, complementing existing privacy laws.

6. Develop Responsible Data Use Guidelines to protect privacy and support innovation
"Responsible Data Use Guidelines" can safeguard the public good while enabling innovation, including by making de-identified or non-personal data publicly accessible by default.

7. Create a transparent Responsible Data Use Assessment for ongoing accountability
A publicly transparent "Responsible Data Use Assessment" can ensure that companies or community members who use urban data do so in a way that has a beneficial purpose and protects privacy.

A digitally enabled "raincoat" would provide shelter and opportunities for comfortable sidewalk use and social interaction during cold or rainy weather, and open space on nicer days.

FOUNDING SIDEWALK LABS: GOOGLE'S BOLD BET

"[Dan] believes that a sizable opportunity exists to transform cities with technology — making them more livable, more sustainable, more equitable . . . There is no wall he would not go through. Nothing was impossible."

When Ruth Porat arrived at Google in 2015 as the Chief Financial Officer for Google (before the formation of Alphabet), she had less than two months before her first earnings call. Porat said, "I assumed I knew what my main event was — I had to figure out Google in a very short period of time, analyze the financials and the outlook, and identify the key opportunities and issues to review on the earnings call."

But she soon learned that Larry Page, the CEO of Google, was spearheading a major new project to reimagine the future of cities. Page already had a leader for the initiative in mind: former New York City Deputy Mayor Dan Doctoroff. Porat and Doctoroff had crossed paths when he led Bloomberg LP and she was the chief financial officer at Morgan Stanley. "He was a formidable personality. He was imposing, brilliant, opinionated, energetic, in a very positive way — just his sheer strength, the fortitude, the conviction," Porat said. She immediately warmed to the idea. "My view was: We've got a guy who understands the public sector, private sector, and is an amazing human being. This is intriguing."

Over the next seven years, Porat watched Doctoroff advance the vision of leveraging technology to improve life in cities. Although Sidewalk Labs ceased to be a stand-alone business in 2022 when it was folded into Google after Doctoroff's announcement of his ALS diagnosis, it had already spun out three companies valued at billions of dollars combined, while three additional initiatives were absorbed into Google, where development and commercialization continues today. Doctoroff's "ability to bring together the public and private sector to work together is invaluable," Porat said. His legacy is "trying to meld the two in a way that's supportive of people who live in cities in a really beautiful way."

As the work initiated at Sidewalk Labs continues, she said, "it'll be important over the years to see how broad and embedded" these ideas become.

I showed up at Google in May of 2015. Very quickly, our CEO, Larry Page told me how focused he was on using technology to transform cities. He even had someone who he thought would be great to lead this work: Dan Doctoroff.

It was still an idea, very much in formation. Google has always been focused on how we can use technology to make a difference in the lives of people and businesses and communities around the world. The goal was to find ways to use technology to improve the quality of life in cities, to make them more sustainable, to make them more equitable.

Dan brought a unique skill set, having been a leader in one of the most important, complex cities on the planet and a leader in the private sector. The whole notion of bringing the private and public sector together to work to improve lives is at the crux of what became Sidewalk Labs.

The specific priorities and approach to transforming cities evolved over months of debate and analysis. It started with the goal to create a model for what cities could be — some sort of prototype, something that others could then build off of, benefit from, use as a template. If you can make cities more livable, just think how many people can benefit. Their view was that cities were designed and built hundreds of years ago, in an obviously different time. The thesis was that knowing what we know now, we can think about the application of technology to improve quality of life, quality of experience, equitable access to things that we all take for granted.

There was a lot of iteration. In fact, there was an early, oversized, very dense book that was rich with ideas. Dan and Larry [Page] would meet on a regular basis to go through the ideas, literally brainstorming back and forth about the application of technology

---

ERIC SCHMIDT | Co-Founder, Schmidt Futures | Former CEO & Chairman, Google

Reimagining the Future of Cities with Dan Doctoroff

Dan Doctoroff is a brilliant visionary in many areas, but what is most impressive is his vision for cities. After many years at Bloomberg LP and as deputy mayor of New York City, he developed a real feel for what a city should be like — he led one. We hired Dan to build a new kind of city, and he delivered in spades. His vision for timber buildings, lowering building costs, and making mobility systems run like electricity grids are good examples of his incredibly popular ideas. But what Dan really did is create a different kind of feeling for a city: safe, inclusive, intelligent, and extremely interesting. Dan and I met with municipal leaders and after initial success, the tech backlash ultimately made it impossible to proceed with his ideas. Over the course of this experience, Dan created the blueprint for many future cities, whose residents will never know how hard-fought his visions were. All of this is due to the vision of Dan Doctoroff, a hero of mine.

Eric Schmidt, pictured, reached out to Dan Doctoroff, leading to the creation of Sidewalk Labs.

Ruth Porat, Chief Financial Officer of Alphabet/Google, served on the Sidewalk Labs board from its inception as a stand-alone company owned by Alphabet until its integration into Google after Dan Doctoroff announced his illness and stepped down as Chief Executive Officer.

to cities — how to improve sustainability, the quality of the built environment, increasing mobility in a way that is both supportive of health and quality living. They identified that there is an opportunity for creating large-scale urban development that can serve as a model for sustainable inclusive growth. What problem would be solved, in what way, that showed respect for what cities are trying to do and how they can work with the private sector?

I would say one of my very favorite examples from New York City was in the Bloomberg administration, when Dan, serving as deputy mayor, helped the mayor realize his vision to transform the way we use city streets. At the time, my Morgan Stanley office was right at the center of Times Square and the concept that the roads would be shut down in Times Square seemed impractical. Yet, what actually happened? It brought everybody out into the streets in a joyful way — dramatically more foot traffic. It quickly became apparent that rethinking long-held principles for this city's historic places could energize the city.

Dan was never afraid to take on big challenges. He personified my view that leadership is having a point of view about the right thing to do. Even though it may not (in the moment) be the most popular thing to do, it's the responsibility of leaders to take it on. When I look back on the Bloomberg administration and the work they did, it was clearly the right thing to do. In the moment, it was not necessarily the most popular thing to do, but then many of those policies became models for the rest of the world. Sometimes the toughest calls that leaders make can be the most important and the most valuable.

[Dan] believed firmly that there is a sizable opportunity to transform cities with technology, making them more livable, more sustainable, more equitable. That goal guided his work at Sidewalk Labs. But then there were many branches on the tree to deliver it.

Just to name a few: [Sidewalk's initiative] Mesa, enables energy efficiency in buildings; Pebble helps address the search for parking lots, which is a major share of vehicle emissions. These projects were not random ideas but the end product of the team's broader thematic work. Dan and his team systematically went through each of the major components of city infrastructure and asked if technology could improve the experience, decrease the impact on the planet, or both. The sum of these ideas returned to the overall vision for transforming cities through technology.

I remember being with Dan at a demo in Toronto and the level of exuberance was palpable. Seeing the ideas begin to translate into mock-ups and functioning prototypes excited us all, and I know Dan was proud to see some of his vision coming into physical reality. Those early prototypes were just a few of the many different ways you can apply technology, from outdoor space, to indoor space design, to city curbs and street infrastructure.

Dan was clearly very committed, passionate about the work, given the impact that he had in New York City. [His] relentless impatience just raised the bar for everyone. Nothing was off limits. There is no wall he would not go through. Nothing was impossible.

PREM RAMASWAMI | Head of Product, 2018-2021 & President of Urban Products, 2021-2022, Sidewalk Labs | Head of Sidewalk Labs, Google, 2022-Present

AT GOOGLE, SIDEWALK LABS IS CONTINUING TO SHAPE AN URBAN FUTURE

In technology, there is a concept called an impedance mismatch. If two signals run at different frequencies and then mix, it results in a ton of noise.

Technologists think disruption is a good thing because their innovation cycles are every six months and if you need to fix something, it's as simple as pushing a line of code. Regulation is largely derided. On the other hand, urbanists think in charrettes, in democratic decision-making down to the base level. They work in five-year cycles, and to them, disruptions are earthquakes, hurricanes or riots. It's a very different language.

Dan Doctoroff, Founder and CEO of Sidewalk Labs, a company that brought together urbanists and technologists, was obsessed with the clash of ideas and resultant creation that occurs when these two signals collide. Dan's vision was to bridge that urbanist and technologist divide, building an organization whose true secret sauce was human API (an Application Programmable Interface, or a way for two different computer programs to speak to one another).

In 2016, I was firmly on the technologist side. I had my dream job at Google, leading Search Social Impact, which provides Search users with health, civics, education, crisis response, social good, and arts information. I had the world's largest, most targeted megaphone at my lips. But then, in 2016, a confluence of events made me feel powerless. The 2016 election made the Internet look like a glass house, with trolls throwing stones at it. In addition, the life expectancy in the U.S. had gone down after I had spent five years focused on Health Search. The world also crossed 400 parts per million of carbon dioxide in the environment. I have two young boys, and I was worried about the world I would one day leave for them.

I wasn't going to solve these issues sitting behind a digital search box. Craig Nevill-Manning, a technology guru and early leader at Google who had become a founding executive at Sidewalk Labs, urged me to join Sidewalk saying, "If you want to move the world, you have to stop twiddling around in bits and bytes and start trying to move atoms." At his urging, I met with Dan on a personal trip to the East Coast. We spent an hour discussing cities, his time as deputy mayor, politics, the climate, and the two billion humans who were urban dwellers. By the end of that hour, I wanted to be a member of Dan's team building a "City of the Future."

Dan, similar to stellar technology product managers, was able to dive deeply into a topic very quickly, understand it intimately — dissecting the issues at hand and breaking them down into fundamentals — and then hire the experts needed to deliver solutions. Visionaries like Dan are able to assemble high performance teams who solve grand challenges. To quote architect Daniel Burnham, "Make no little plans."

Within a few months, I joined Dan and Craig, moved my family to the East Coast, and started as Head of Product at Sidewalk Labs, ultimately becoming President of Sidewalk Urban Products. I was tasked with being the conduit between urbanists and technologists — to speak both languages and bridge the unique needs and asks of each to build commercial products. But fundamentally, I was a technologist. And all along, Dan was my tutor. He was teaching me how to be more of an urbanist.

Our mission was to show the world a climate-positive, inclusive way to build cities. Dan's aspiration for Sidewalk Labs was based on his New York experience. He strongly believed that cities are wonderful because of their inherent heterogeneity: the range of incomes, the diverse people, and the cornucopia of thoughts that come from them. He didn't want to live in a dystopian, uber wealthy, perfectly polished city. A prime example of this commitment was Dan's vision that 40% of housing in our model city be below market rate. He wanted an entire workstream focused on social infrastructure. It's not something all urbanists, and especially technologists, think about.

My team of technologists was charged with figuring out how to build commercial, scalable products around our ideas and objectives. Delve was one such product at the intersection of urban planning, cloud computing, and machine learning — designing better urban plans that could squeeze out more affordable housing, more park space, and more profit (to make those better plans commercially viable). Our goal was to use machines where they exceeded human capability, but to pair them in a user experience with the human judgment and aesthetic sense needed for urban design.

DELVE

Delve is a software tool that uses machine learning to help development teams discover the best neighborhood design for their project, based on the priority outcomes that they care about most. The Delve team has built a model of the core components of a neighborhood that include buildings, open spaces, amenities, streets, and energy infrastructure. By applying machine learning to that model, Delve explores millions of design possibilities for a given project, measuring the impact of these designs to help development teams arrive at the one that's right for them. By revealing the optimal design option, Delve helps development teams exceed their project economic goals while improving quality-of-life outcomes for residents and businesses.

Ultimately, we didn't succeed at building out the futuristic city we imagined along the Toronto waterfront, but the idea and approach continues to shape our work today. Dan pushed us to not fear failure. He taught me that the biggest failure is just limping along and wasting time. There was only "Go big!" for Dan. His rallying cry of "F the odds" stays with me, the attitude of, "Why can't we? What do you mean, no? This is doable and we're going to run against it as hard as possible until we can't run anymore, and then … we'll run harder."

With products such as Mesa, which automates building controls to save energy and cost, Delve, which applies generative design and artificial intelligence to real estate development, and Pebble's mobility solutions, we wanted to improve the ways we have designed and live in our built environment. Additionally, we were building businesses because capitalism is the only thing (other than government) that scales. Can there be successful businesses that marry carbon and capitalism? That's the question that intrigued Google, as they invited Sidewalk to join in their goal to accelerate climate action at Google and beyond.

Google is in its third decade of climate work. But when Google execs traveled to COP, the United Nations' primary annual climate-focused conference, in November 2022, they were gravely disappointed that the world was not acting in an urgent way that would prevent the positive feedback loop of carbon.

After Dan stepped away from the company, the Sidewalk Labs team joined the Maps and Earth groups of Google, because although those are digital products, they interact in the real world. As part of our joining, Google has set up a company-wide practice focused on sustainability, and we are lucky to continue to work on the Sidewalk Labs mission: We build products that will radically improve the quality of life in cities, for now and for generations to come.

Today, it is Delve, Mesa, and Pebble. My goal is to make one of these seminal Sidewalk products a gangbuster success, and thus to prove Dan's theory that we can marry carbon and capitalism to effect great change. Time will tell what outcomes these — and other initiatives — may yield, but I know one thing for certain: Once we've accomplished this, I'll go back and say, "Let's go bigger." After all, to quote Dan, "Why can't we?"

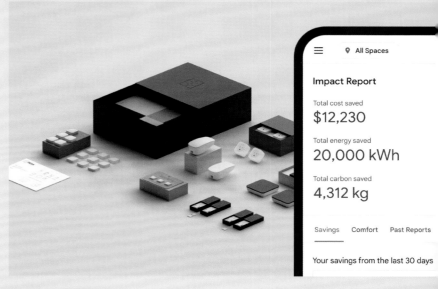

PEBBLE

Pebble is designed to reduce the need for parking, freeing up more street space for the public realm. Pebble uses technology to show drivers (starting with trucks) information about available and appropriate parking spaces, reducing emissions and frustration from circling. It also allows them to book spaces in advance for extra reliability. Pebble also provides real-time information to cities that allow them to plan, manage, and enforce parking spaces through dashboards and apps that allow them to allocate curb space, set rules and rates for those spaces, and ensure the spaces are being used properly. These tools allow cities to maximize public uses such as transit, biking, and green space.

MESA

Mesa's connected sensors and smart devices use artificial intelligence to automatically adjust heating, ventilation, air conditioning systems, and outlets based on occupancy level, predicted weather, humidity, and more. This unprecedented responsiveness enables commercial buildings to achieve automated energy savings of 20% when using Mesa. Customers can also track their savings in real time using Mesa's digital dashboard.

SIDEWALK LABS SPINOUT COMPANIES

Sidewalk Labs incubated three companies that ultimately spun out to become independent businesses. Today, they are collectively valued at billions of dollars and are pioneering new connections between technology and urban challenges such as mobility and public health.

Cityblock Health, a company incubated and spun out of Sidewalk Labs in 2017, combines technology with high-touch healthcare to improve outcomes for low-income populations that have historically been marginalized by the healthcare system.

Replica, a company incubated and spun out of Sidewalk Labs in 2019, provides powerful mobility data visualization tools to enable governments and others to make investments in transportation infrastructure that are more likely to achieve the intended outcomes.

TOYIN AJAYI | Co-Founder, 2017-Present & CEO, 2022-Present, Cityblock Health
IYAH ROMM | Co-Founder, 2017-Present & CEO, 2017-2022, Cityblock Health

NICK BOWDEN | Co-Founder and CEO, Replica, 2019-Present

CITYBLOCK HEALTH

REPLICA

TOYIN AJAYI

Cityblock provides high-quality, integrated primary care, mental health, and social services to low-income populations that have historically been marginalized by the healthcare system. We deliver an experience that is respectful, that's dignifying, and that enables us to close gaps in their care and improve their health and well-being.

Dan was the visionary and leader behind unlocking the investment in us and recruiting myself and Iyah to the team. He's served on the board of Cityblock since its inception. He's been deeply committed to the mission, to seeing outcomes improve for the members we serve, and to supporting the team.

IYAH ROMM

Dan is by far the toughest investor and negotiator I sat across from in my years of building Cityblock (and in my career prior). He held investment discipline as a matter of deep pride, and in so doing, pushed us to be better and better in our earliest days. Dan's exacting methods were crucial to building and telling a very tight story, and bringing the early focus in moving from a vision held by four intrepid founders to a fledgling business. I carried the skills learned from negotiating with Dan throughout every conversation throughout Cityblock's strong capital trajectory.

Cityblock Health spun out of Sidewalk Labs in 2017.

Replica is a data platform for the built environment. We provide privacy-friendly data about how people move to public agencies to inform policy making. We work with four of the five biggest transit agencies in the U.S. Before Replica, a public agency could either have really detailed data, or they could have data that had privacy protections, but they couldn't have both.

Replica just wouldn't exist without Dan. Dan had this ambitious long-term vision about what was possible. He set this really far-off destination that felt like a near impossibility to reach. And then it was our job to figure out how to build the ship to get there.

Rendering of Cavnue's first proposed project, linking Detroit and Ann Arbor. The project — a joint undertaking with the Michigan Department of Transportation — will result in a first-of-its-kind connected and autonomous vehicle corridor that will bring together technology and infrastructure to improve safety, congestion, and accessibility in the local community. Cavnue is a spinoff of Sidewalk Infrastructure Partners, which was incubated and spun out of Sidewalk Labs in 2019.

BRIAN BARLOW | Co-Founder and Co-CEO, Sidewalk Infrastructure Partners, 2019–Present

SIDEWALK INFRASTRUCTURE PARTNERS (SIP)

Dan has been particularly interested in how [to] make streets safer. If you want to target intersections with higher rates of low-income minority populations using this route to take their kids to school that also coincide with high rates of traffic volumes at certain speeds, how do we pick the [riskiest] to prioritize? The only way is to have very detailed data.

[Dan's] got an insatiable impatience for wanting stuff to happen faster, better. That rubs off on everybody. You want to continue to push when you're around him. He's wildly impatient in the very best way.

Replica spun out of Sidewalk Labs in 2019.

I was recruited to help Dan think about how we get innovation into infrastructure. I said what would be impactful is an investment platform that could catalyze innovation through investment in early-stage companies, but then also be the partner to bring them to market quicker. We identified the Ontario Teachers' Pension Plan as our launch partner and created SIP in the summer of 2019.

[Later], Dan, [co-founder and co-CEO Jonathan Winer], and I were sitting around, "Why don't we have smarter roads?" About six to nine months later we're scratching our heads like, "Holy cow, there's nothing to invest in. Nobody's working on this problem."

Jonathan and I proposed that we should start this company from scratch. Most boards would tell you you're crazy. Dan said, "This is a fantastic idea. What if we can create smart

roads? Wouldn't that be amazing as to the sustainability and safety benefits?"

Cavnue is the name of the business. It's already won its first project, building the first connected and autonomous vehicle laneway from the University of Michigan to downtown Detroit. Access to public transportation for the most underserved communities has been one of the downfalls of the greater Detroit area. We're hoping to go directly at those inequities built into the infrastructure system and reverse some of those trends using technology.

It was really Dan's will and force and vision that made [SIP] happen. It just would have never been done if Dan wasn't a force of nature.

Sidewalk Infrastructure Partners spun out of Sidewalk Labs in 2019.

RICHARD R. BUERY, JR. | Deputy Mayor for Strategic Policy Initiatives, 2014-2018 | CEO, Robin Hood, 2021-Present

CREATING A "NEW" NEW YORK DRIVEN BY EQUITABLE GROWTH

"[Dan] loves New York . . . His desire to make sure that the city rebuilds in a way that speaks to equity and racial and economic justice is a distillation of his love for the city."

Richard R. Buery, Jr. and Dan Doctoroff were on separate paths that converged at City Hall. When Doctoroff joined the Bloomberg administration in the aftermath of the September 11th attacks as Deputy Mayor for Economic Development and Rebuilding, he left a career in finance and was in the middle of a quest to bring the Olympic Games to New York.

When Buery joined the de Blasio administration as Deputy Mayor for Strategic Policy Initiatives in 2014, he brought his nonprofit sector experience to bear on the city's challenges of equity in education, justice, and opportunity. A mutual friend introduced him to Doctoroff. "It was just a friendly and kind conversation to give me some counsel as I started this new journey," Buery said. "I just felt connected to him and we stayed in touch."

Then the COVID-19 pandemic hit New York. The two former deputy mayors began long discussions about how the city had recovered from past crises — and what would need to change this time. "Productively, the Bloomberg administration took an approach to recovery that was about investing in the future of the city as opposed to cutting costs and trying to balance the budget during a crisis," Buery said. "You could see a city that was growing, but that growth was not something the entire city shared in."

Doctoroff "realized that had to be different about this recovery," Buery said. The two even explored forming a new nonprofit, the Coalition for Equitable Growth, to shape the city's recovery agenda. Instead, in 2022, Buery and Doctoroff served as co-chairs of the "New" New York Panel, a 59-person committee of civic leaders convened by Mayor Eric Adams and Governor Kathy Hochul, to develop a set of actionable proposals to drive another recovery for New York's economy — but this time with equity at the center.

Dan "loves New York," Buery said. "His desire to make sure that the city rebuilds in a way that speaks to equity and racial and economic justice is a distillation of his love for the city."

I met Dan at the beginning of my tenure at City Hall; he was running Bloomberg [LP]. I had never worked in city government before, much less at such a senior role. A colleague of mine at the Children's Aid Society, Josh Wallack, had worked with Dan in the Bloomberg administration. [He] respects Dan a lot and was like, "You should meet Dan."

It was a "get to know you" meeting, frankly with no real purpose other than to be nice to someone who was terrifyingly entering City Hall to take on a big project, in much the way that Dan joined City Hall to take on some big projects.

Richard R. Buery, Jr. co-chaired the "New" New York Panel formed to guide New York's economic recovery after the COVID-19 pandemic, alongside Dan Doctoroff.

One of the things that I worked on was OneNYC, the next iteration of PlaNYC. So, even in that distant way, [I had] an opportunity to help continue work that he launched. I think [Dan] understands that if you want changes to last, those changes have to have a broad constituency. They have to reflect the wisdom and the will of the people. It's a good idea to organize the government around a clear set of quantifiable and trackable initiatives that are designed to help build a more sustainable city. We wanted to expand that vision and put the question of equity at the center.

When I was thinking of leaving City Hall, he was one of the first people I spoke to, including about potentially coming to join Sidewalk [Labs]. The appeal was being a part of this innovative, really groundbreaking approach to rethinking this part of Toronto. It [wound] up not working out, but we stayed in touch.

During the pandemic, Dan called me. We were all thinking about this fundamental question, how does the city recover? Look at the history of New York City — crises from Spanish flu, to the Depression, to 9/11, to [Superstorm] Sandy. The city actually [came] back stronger after those challenges. I think Dan's personal reflection [was] that despite the successes of the post–Sandy and post–9/11 recoveries, those recoveries did not benefit all New Yorkers.

In Dan Doctoroff fashion, [he] thought to pull together like-minded folks, with different disciplines and perspectives, to think about how we as citizens could offer a vision of equitable growth. A vision that, first of all, made the case for growth — because with growth comes jobs, with growth comes tax revenue, with growth comes resources. But you could do that and put equity in the center.

Many times in policy rooms I am the only Black person in the room and often feel [the weight] of carrying that. [This project] was exciting because we were trying to do the same thing and that idea was central to all of us. We tried to articulate a plan for equitable growth that we could use as a rallying cry for the city.

For a range of reasons, that organization didn't happen, but then [came] the "New" New York Panel. The focus [was] specifically around central business districts across the five boroughs. Central business districts continue to drive much of what allows us to be a vibrant city: economic activity, creating jobs not just for the wealthy but for the food carts, retail, building cleaners, and all the working folks who depend on the economy.

We pulled together this panel of experts across sectors to try to develop actionable goals, in the way that we envisioned in our

AN EDITED ORAL HISTORY

The Association for a Better New York (ABNY) breakfast conference on December 14, 2022, announcing the release of the "New" New York Panel report, which proposed 40 initiatives designed to revive New York's economy and enliven its central business districts while centering equitable growth.

Left to right:
ABNY CEO Melva Miller, Panel Co–chairs Dan Doctoroff and Richard R. Buery, Jr., Governor Kathy Hochul, Mayor Eric Adams.

Coalition for Equitable Growth, and in the way that I think Dan pioneered with PlaNYC. [The panel was] an opportunity to drive some of those ideas forward.

Because his career has spanned such a variety of sectors, [Dan] is a good spokesman for [the] vision that equity and growth are not enemies. As somebody said to me the other day, "You can't love jobs and hate businesses." You can have an economy that is pro-growth, that is focused on ensuring that all people have access to that growth, that ensure[s] that growth is not rapacious, and in fact,

supports the core value of the community. In fact, you have to do all that, because without growth, you can't have the tax revenue that you need for great schools or the economic activity that allows the young Black entrepreneur to grow their business, or that allows [a] family to have a job that stabilizes their income.

Whenever you're doing a project, it gets very easy to get watered down in the tactics. Because we're all human beings, we all bring our professional bias and interests to the conversation. But I think [Dan helped] us keep in mind that big picture. [It's] very easy to just move onto the next thing. We can't take our foot off the gas

and assume everything is going to be fine. If we see that we are redoing the traditional sins of our country, then that would be a failure.

Dan has deep experience as an operator and an executor, but those things are centered in a very clear vision. In all the work that I've been doing with him on the future of the city, that has always been the anchor for him — that in order to get to execution and plans, you have to articulate a clear and compelling vision that everybody can rally around. You have to be able to tell a story. Stories create urgency in a way that can drive accountability.

[Dan] loves New York. He loves cities. If you look at his career, few people can claim as much impact on the state of the city right now as he does. [But] cities are like sharks, they have to move forward. The job for us is to reimagine the next version of the city. You look at his great work, in some way, the city is his masterpiece. I think he wants to continue to see that through.

DAN DOCTOROFF AND THE MAKING OF NEW YORK'S FUTURE

New York City would not be what it is today without Dan Doctoroff. Dan is one of the great New Yorkers of our era, a man whose vision and energy have done so much to shape the city we live in now. From Lower Manhattan to Hudson Yards, the Brooklyn waterfront to Atlantic Yards, and so much more — Dan saw possibility and promise where others only saw defeat and decline.

One of the most significant parts of his legacy came in the earliest days of his public service to our city, as new Mayor Michael Bloomberg's Deputy Mayor for Economic Development and Rebuilding. When we think about September 11th, we often focus on the tragedy of the day — but it's equally important to think about September 12th. On that day, our city was faced with a choice. Do we allow ourselves to be defeated by terrorism, or do we get up and start rebuilding our city?

Dan led the way, understanding that we could not simply rebuild and that government, business, and civic leaders would have to work together to go beyond recovery and actively reinvent and re-energize the city for the future. The impact of those decisions can be seen in the 24/7 community that Lower Manhattan has now become, and in the way our city's economy has evolved and strengthened.

Dan showed us that transformation is not only possible, but essential. He left his mark on important developments like the Coney Island rezoning, and the reactivation of the Brooklyn Navy Yard — places that are now hubs of job creation, economic power, and civic pride.

Mayor Eric Adams and Dan Doctoroff.

He has always been driven by a mission to make this city better, and his leadership has inspired a generation of forward-thinking public servants, including many that hold senior roles in my own administration.

When I was running for mayor, Dan was generous with his time and advice, and when I was elected, he was an advisor on my transition team. His work for our city in the wake of 9/11 remains the blueprint for navigating crises and coming back stronger, and our city called on him once again after the COVID-19 pandemic.

The "New" New York Panel, co-chaired by Dan Doctoroff and Richard R. Buery, Jr., recommended significant improvements to the public realm in New York's central business districts in order to help attract commuters and tourists in greater numbers. Below, a rendering of a potential new pedestrian experience along Fifth Avenue, New York's premier shopping district and a significant generator of economic activity.

As co-chair of the "New" New York panel, Dan helped shape our administration's plan for the city's economic recovery after untold grief and devastation. His collaborative spirit and ambitious vision have helped lay the groundwork for major changes in everything from transit to housing to the reimagining of a newly vibrant Midtown Manhattan.

And it has been inspiring to watch him turn his personal pain into purpose as the founder of Target ALS, dedicated to eradicating this disease once and for all. His mission has always been to transform the world around him, and New York City was extremely fortunate that he chose to make his home here.

There isn't a day that goes by that New Yorkers don't benefit directly from the work he did for our city; and everything we do going forward will build on his incredible legacy of public service.

Thank you, Dan, for making the greatest city in the world even stronger, more livable, and more resilient.

Building a city & legacy

Doctoroff leaving gov't for Bloomberg L.P.

BY KIRSTEN DANIS and WILLIAM SHERMAN
DAILY NEWS STAFF WRITERS

DEPUTY MAYOR DANIEL Doctoroff, the brilliant and often imperious city master planner, is leaving government, Mayor Bloomberg said yesterday — coming close to tears as he made the announcement.

"He leaves an extraordinary record of accomplishment," Bloomberg said.

Doctoroff, who has firmly stamped how the city will change and grow in the next 20 years, isn't going far.

Starting with the new year, the mayor's most trusted aide will become president of Bloomberg L.P., the mayor's giant media company, headquartered in Manhattan.

"I'm thrilled to remain part of the Bloomberg family," said Doctoroff, who for six years has worked 18-hour days away from the many- or the open bullpen office in City Hall.

Doctoroff's exit is a major one for the Bloomberg administration as it heads into its final two years because Doctoroff was the architect of many of the mayor's biggest initiatives.

They include the development of Hudson Yards, a vision for a new Coney Island; 70 neighborhood rezonings to provide for new housing and commercial ventures; the extension of the Number 7 subway line west to 34th St. and 11th Ave.; and the construction of 66,897 units of affordable housing.

"Every one of these initiatives and dozens and dozens more bear Dan's fingerprints," Bloomberg said.

For all his plans, most of which are in production, Doctoroff has had two colossal and stunning losses.

The first was the failure two years ago to land the 2012 Olympics for the city, a project he had worked on for 11 years, even before he entered government.

The second was his failure to gain state legislative approval for a new football stadium for the Jets on the far West Side at 33rd St. He lost a shutout to Assembly Speaker Sheldon Silver (D-Manhattan) and Senate Majority Leader Joseph Bruno (R-Rensselaer); neither would comment about Doctoroff or his legacy.

Doctoroff, in a 90-minute interview with the Daily News, found a silver lining in those defeats.

"We're buying the site for the Olympic Village [in Queens] for the city and turning it into 5,000 units, the vast majority of which will be middle income housing which was the purpose of the Olympic Village to begin with," he said. "So I had opportunity to actually achieve the legacy of the Olympics without actually having the Olympics."

The same holds true for the once purported site of the Jets stadium.

"We rezoned the entire area [Hudson Yards]. We invested billions of dollars to produce what I think is the single most important development and project in the city's post-World War II history," he said referring to the 26 acres of commercial and residential buildings along with parks that will be developed.

Congestion pricing — charges for trucks and cars entering Manhattan south of 66th St. has not received state legislative approval. Doctoroff said he expects that will turn around with a new session in March.

At his shoes will be hard to fill, but at least two City Hall insiders, Housing Preservation and Development Commissioner Shaun Donovan and Small Services Commissioner Robert Walsh are interested in the job, sources said.

Bloomberg is just as likely to turn to his vast network of friends and contacts in the financial sector to fill the job, just as he turned to Doctoroff through an intermediary when he was mayor-elect in 2001, just after 9/11.

Doctoroff and Bloomberg have much in common. Both are self-made men who made tremendous fortunes in the private sector at a relatively young age. Both also believe in cutting through the inertia of governmental bureaucracy with apolitical logic and tough, take-no-prisoners, management skills.

Doctoroff's detractors describe him as temperamental, impatient and a bully in his dealings with politicians, community boards and the state Legislature.

"Impatient, that's fair. I don't deny that. I am impatient,but I don't think I'm a bully," Doctoroff said. He is imposing at 6-feet-2 with a Harvard College and University of Chicago honed intellect and a memory for details that is nonpareil.

Many have compared him to Robert Moses, who for 44 years ending in the 1960s dominated building in New York with $27 billion in public works, including highways and parks.

Doctoroff is uneasy with the comparison, saying, "I don't think it's apt. The time periods are completely different. If what people mean is we get a lot done, I'll take the comparison and take it as a compliment."

kdanis@nydailynews.com

Deputy Mayor Dan Doctoroff explains his leaving City Hall while an emotional Mayor Bloomberg looks on. Photos by Michael Appleton/Daily News

WILLIAMSBURG

NETS ARENA

LINDA ROSIER / DAILY NEWS

HUDSON YARDS

Doctoroff is a key player behind several major projects. Clockwise from above, the new arena for the Nets at Atlantic Yards in Brooklyn along with the planned Hudson Rail Yards on the West Side and development in the Williamsburg-Greenpoint area.

EDITORIAL SEE PAGE 54

Man with a plan leaves huge void

STEVE CUOZZO

WHAT happens now? That's the question about a batch of giant, public-private land-use schemes that Dan Doctoroff either set in motion or decisively kick-started.

They're all deals yet to be settled down. But it's unclear whether anyone else at City Hall has the brains, technical skills and persuasive power to see them through before Mayor Bloomberg leaves office at the end of 2009.

Most proposals you've read about — such as the West Side rail yards, Atlantic Yards, Moynihan Station, Ground Zero rebuilding and the JPMorganChase tower — have a long way to go before shovels can go into the ground.

Renderings and preliminary agreements are fine — but the grunt work to seal deals and push them through tortuous public review has barely begun.

Real-estate players agree the proposals couldn't have gotten as far as they have without Doctoroff, who led the city in complex negotiations and sparked some of the ideas in the first place.

He brought to the often tedious deputy mayor's job a rare combination of intellect, hands-on skills and what Mary Ann Tighe, regional CEO of the real-estate concern CB Richard Ellis, called "energy, passion and intensity."

In early 2000, long before Bloomberg's election, Doctoroff came to The Post to present his pitch to bring the 2012 Olympic Games to the city.

Many of us who saw his images of Olympic villages thought he was nuts. But a few years later, the city came close to getting the nod — losing out mainly because Albany killed plans for a stadium above the West Side rail yards.

But the failed stadium dream began the MTA's monumental decision to sell development rights at the Hudson Yards site.

Doctoroff spearheaded Bloomberg's ambitious rezoning of neglected parts of the city so they could be used for modern office space and housing.

He propelled plans for the High Line park off the drawing board. The park, set to open next year, has catalyzed nearly $1 billion in development nearby.

Robert Hammond, who helped dream up the idea of turning the former elevated train line into an urban oasis, said of Doctoroff, "He got the deal done and he's getting the job done on time."

RIGHT HAND DAN QUITS

Lorenzo Ciniglio

THE 'DOCTOR' IS OUT: Mayor Bloomberg gives Deputy Mayor Dan Doctoroff a farewell handshake at City Hall yesterday.

Mike's deputy to be Bloomberg LP prez

By DAVID SEIFMAN
City Hall Bureau Chief

In a stunning development, the senior mayoral aide overseeing some of the city's largest and most ambitious projects announced yesterday that he was resigning to become president of Bloomberg LP, the mayor's information-services company.

"The city's loss will be the private sector's gain," declared Mayor Bloomberg as he disclosed both the resignation and hiring of Deputy Mayor Dan Doctoroff.

The situation was certainly unusual.

On one hand, the mayor said he had "done everything he could" to keep his trusted longtime aide from leaving.

On the other hand, Doctoroff couldn't have been hired by Bloomberg LP without the mayor's blessing.

"It's sort of a bittersweet moment for us," the mayor conceded.

Doctoroff, a wealthy investment banker working for just $1 a year, was long rumored to be job hunting after serving nearly six years as the deputy mayor for economic development and rebuilding.

"Peter said this is the kind of guy we really need, and I checked with the Conflicts of Interest Board as to whether I could have a general conversation with him. They said yes."

Mindful of the city's strict mistake of letting Dan go to Korea with Peter to give a speech," the mayor recalled.

Unfinished business

Selected projects and initiatives in Deputy Mayor Doctoroff's portfolio:

1. **Congestion pricing** — Administration wants to charge motorists $8 to enter Manhattan on weekdays between 6 a.m. and 6 p.m. Commission studying the proposal.

2. **Hudson Yards** — Five developers vying for rights.

3. **Javits Center** — Expansion stalled by arguments over projected cost overruns.

4. **Governors Island** — Grandiose plan that includes gondola connections to mainland stalled.

5. **Willets Point** — City pushing ahead with $3 billion development of 62 acres in the face of opposition by longtime businesses.

6. **Off-Track Betting** — City's only legal bookie will be broke by June 30 unless the state Legislature comes to the rescue with a revenue-sharing formula.

7. **Coney Island Redevelopment** — Elected officials don't support rezoning of 47 acres that impacts local businesses.

Through a spokesman, Silver declined comment on Doctoroff's departure.

Doctoroff made no apologies for thinking big, and even a fierce critic acknowledged that he brought a visionary eye to the city's landscape.

"While we've had disagreements on the specifics, Mr. Doctoroff deserves credit for his role in the ethos of innovation we've seen at City Hall," said Rep. Anthony Weiner, a vocal opponent of the administration's congestion-pricing proposal.

With numerous projects still in development, from Willets Point to the West Side rail yards, some officials questioned the timing of Doctoroff's resignation, which takes effect at year's end.

"Why is he leaving now?" asked City Councilman Leroy Comrie (D-Queens). "It's going to be a big loss to me. There's a lot of heavy stuff in the pipeline, and he's very knowledgeable."

Councilman Mike McMahon (D-SI) raised another issue: Since Bloomberg isn't supposed to be running his company from City Hall, how could he have helped engineer the deal that landed Doctoroff?

"It certainly seems like a close call," McMahon said. "If this was football, they'd order...

He was also at the helm of New York's urban environment since the days of Robert Moses.

Doctoroff is credited with overseeing 289 separate projects, from the expansion of the No. 7 subway line to the rezoning of vast parts of the five boroughs.

Well done, Dan

Deputy Mayor Dan Doctoroff, who announced yesterday that he is stepping down, may be the least well-known member of the Bloomberg cabinet who has had the most sweeping impact on New York. He performed superbly — at $1 a year.

Neighborhoods across the city are being transformed; Yankees, Mets and Nets fans will enjoy new arenas; subway riders are gaining an extension of the No. 7 line; families have, or will soon find, homes in 65,000 affordable apartments, and the transit system may soon secure the financing for major improvements — all thanks to Doctoroff's six years of work as Mayor Bloomberg's economic development pointman.

The mayor is fond of saying that Doctoroff "has done more to change the face of this city than anyone since Robert Moses," and it's hard to argue the point.

By rezoning 6,000 blocks in the five boroughs to unlock their development potential, Doctoroff helped spark a historic building boom. Major commercial and residential growth is happening on Manhattan's far West Side, in downtown Brooklyn and on the Greenpoint-Williamsburg waterfront in Brooklyn, as well as in Willets Point and Jamaica, Queens.

It was also under Doctoroff that City Hall crafted a plan for meeting the challenges of transportation, housing, recreation and more over the coming decades, when the population is projected to grow by 1 million people. Included is congestion pricing, a plan that would dramatically boost mass transit and revolutionize commuting patterns.

Doctoroff thought big. Sometimes a bit too big, as in his failed crusade to bring the Olympics to New York along with a stadium for the Jets. But he won far more than he lost by marrying business skills with vision — and the city is far the better for it.

Chairman & Publisher **Mortimer B. Zuckerman**
Chief Executive Officer **Marc Z. Kramer**
Deputy Publisher & Editor-in-Chief **Martin Dunn**
Senior Executive Editor **Robert Sapio**   Executive Editor **David Ng**
Managing Editor/News **Stuart Marques** Managing Editor/Features **Orla Healy**
Sports Editor **Leon Carter**   Editorial Page Editor **Arthur Browne**

Doctoroff Departs

Mayor Bloomberg yesterday announced that Dan Doctoroff, his long-time deputy for economic development, will depart at year's end to run the media company the mayor founded, Bloomberg L.P.

Doctoroff, the mayor correctly noted yesterday, has "done more to change this city than anyone since Robert Moses."

Just as Rudy Giuliani disproved the notion that New York City was ungovernable, the Bloomberg-Doctoroff team transformed the city in the area of economic development.

More sections of New York — the equivalent of 6,000 city blocks across *all* five boroughs — have been rezoned in the last six years than under the tenure of the last six mayors combined.

That translates to the creation of up to 40 million square feet of new commercial development and as many as 45,000 new houses and apartments (enough to house 120,000 people).

Doctoroff's highlights include:
● Helping spark the residential, commercial and retail renaissance in post-9/11 Lower Manhattan — despite multiple bureaucratic Ground Zero obstacles.
● Rezoning downtown Brooklyn, with 10,000 residential units being built.
● Negotiating construction of new stadiums for the Yankees and Mets.
● Developing financing for the No. 7 line extension.

These achievements are all the more remarkable in a city notorious for "NIMBY"-ism and an intractable bureaucracy.

Even when Doctoroff didn't succeed — such as the West Side Stadium/New York Jets complex or bringing the 2012 Olympics here — it certainly wasn't for lack of vision or effort.

And Doctoroff — who knew that New York City is all about big goals and big projects — succeeded far more often than not.

The city will benefit from his vision and hard work for decades to come.

Building the New New York

The Bob *and* Jane Way.

WE ARE A CITY of 8 million people, give or take a few hundred thousand. But we are building a ... million. Literally. Right now. That will ... k City's total population just a couple ... hence, and politicians, bureaucrats, ... architects, and engineers are, as you ... words, figuring out how to fit another ... people onto the collection of islands ... ulas we call home. We can't just build ... ap up some towers — we've learned ... ns from the sixties — and it isn't just ... on new homes that we need. Those ... d offices, factories, labs to work in. ... nd ferries and trams) to commute in. ... places to play, plus the power to light ... can't sprawl.

... new city, a city larger than San Francisco ... we know. In ten years, New York City ... s we can only guess at. But in the ... plore our best guess, based on the ... stones, and the rising steel in nine ... over all five boroughs. In 2016, we ... chial anymore—one Times Square ... fill the entertainment needs of that ... se population, and you'll be talking ... street. Fresh Kills will be three times ... ou imagine the city as a play—every ... lot of understudies are finally going

When New York didn't get the Olympics or the Jets, there were lots of pitying articles about how Mayor Bloomberg's (and Deputy Mayor Dan Doctoroff's) big dreams had died. But that was a complete misperception. City agencies went right on ahead with their plans. Greenpoint-Williamsburg rezoning, check. East River waterfront, check. Soon, Governors Island, Willets Point. Eventually, something new on those West Side rail yards.

And New York is—finally—getting greener. Mandated green city buildings, new sustainable towers in Battery Park City. Community groups dream of more green buildings on the ruins of the Sheridan Expressway. What is fascinating is the recovery and recycling of the works of the city's greatest bogeyman, Robert Moses. He was responsible for the last great era of park building in the city, but he also sliced apart neighborhoods with highways and towers. Today's mini-Moseses are combining his initiatives, building parks on the neighborhoods his roadways isolated, transforming infrastructure into landscape architecture. It is on the long-ignored waterfront that the most amazing transformation is occurring.

Sprinkled like jewelry across this new city fabric are projects, some fabulous, some already outdated, by both the dinosaurs and fledglings of the architectural pantheon. Yes, we're getting our Gehry (one, two, three, four, maybe more), but also our Morphosis, our ShoP, our TEN Arquitectos.

But often in some peculiar locations. Piano across from the Port Authority? Gehry in Brooklyn? Viñoly by the Williamsburg Bridge? The New York of 2016 doesn't husband all the new design ideas in Manhattan but spreads them out. (One can't help but get a little giddy with all the big names, but there is a dark side to hiring all these out-of-towners. Too often they serve as ambassadors

AS MASSIVE BROOKLYN REDEVELOPMENT PROJECT GETS GO-AHEAD, NEWS LOOKS AT PLANNERS' FUTURE DREAMS
THE FACE OF NEW YORK CITY 2025

BY CELESTE KATZ
DAILY NEWS STAFF WRITER

IF WE COULD look into the future, and see New York City two decades from now, what would we see?

For starters, in 2025, the city will probably be home to well over 8.5 million people — a half a million more than today — not to mention those who flock here daily and nightly to work and play.

"I see the city right now in an era of dramatic transformation," says Dan Doctoroff, deputy mayor for economic development.

"I do believe when we look back on this period of time, the post-9/11 decade, people will view this as one of the most significant building periods in the city's history."

As the city grows, Planning Department chief Amanda Burden and Doctoroff say they envision a future New York that is laid out more reasonably, is more attractive and doesn't force out all but the richest.

There are a handful of tenets driving the new New York:

■ Increasing the amount of waterfront space available, and having more water taxis, marinas and other new recreational uses, such as parks and playing fields.

■ Creating more mixed-use areas that seamlessly weave together business, shopping and residential areas.

■ Bringing streets back to life with bustling outdoor cafes and better pedestrian access, and vastly expanding the amount of public green space for people to enjoy.

■ Responding to community concerns so their specific areas are preserved and maintained rather than remade.

The spirit of rejuvenating the waterfronts wouldn't be limited to Brooklyn, Doctoroff said.

"All over the city, there's a recognition that many of the old uses of lands along the waterfronts, in many of the old industrial areas, [can] be put to use with other things that are more appropriate for this century," Doctoroff said.

In open space, a perfect example of innovative new park space planned for the future is Manhattan's High Line, an abandoned railroad track that runs for 22 blocks high above west Chelsea.

Business and residential districts would blossom around public transportation hubs such as Long Island City in Queens and downtown Brooklyn, as well as Hudson Yards on the West Side.

Much of that development is intended to keep crucial jobs from bleeding into New Jersey.

Doctoroff sees a 2025 city with an array of new sports stadiums — the Jets in Manhattan, and new homes for both the Yankees and Mets.

He also speaks of a New York with enough new housing for 200,000 to 250,000 people, a good deal of it in formerly distressed areas like the South Bronx, Bedford-Stuyvesant and the Rockaways.

"There will be many more options for everyone at different income levels, different kinds of jobs, to live, work and visit," Doctoroff said.

But some places will resist change as much as others cry out for it, Burden noted.

"Those neighborhoods you grew up in and your grandmother grew up in will look a lot the same," she said.
ckatz@nydailynews.com

Amanda Burden

Dan Doctoroff

THE HIGH LINE/CHELSEA

The elevated freight rail line that snakes across Manhattan's West Side will, they say, one day become what one designer called "a mile-and-a-half of surreal gardens in the sky."

Right now, the site — owned by CSX Transportation — is off limits to the average hiker. There are plans to convert it to public land.

The city already has committed upwards of $43 million in planning and construction money to transform the High Line into a ribbon of suspended parkland running between the hip Meatpacking District and W. 34th St.

"By preserving and reusing a fantastic piece of our industrial heritage, we will create an innovative public open space unlike any other in the world," said Joshua David of the nonprofit group Friends of the High Line.

Plans for West Chelsea also foresee more development of the area's burgeoning art gallery scene and the inclusion of more affordable housing.

FRESH KILLS/STATEN ISLAND

Covering 2,200 acres on Staten Island, the former Fresh Kills landfill is ultimately envisioned as a sprawling park that encompasses any number of activities and landscapes.

"[Parks Commissioner] Adrian Benepe has already said it's going to be greater than Central Park — it'll be much more naturalistic ... something we don't have anywhere in the metro region," said Planning Department Director Amanda Burden.

There have been any number of suggestions as to what the Fresh Kills site — which is 2.5 times the size of the 840-acre Central Park — could accommodate: Biking, golf, ballfields, canoeing, tennis, bridle paths, a wildlife refuge and even a dude ranch.

Fresh Kills also is projected to include miles of car paths, a mountain biking course, horse trails and a running track. The various habitats for wildlife will include marshes, woodlands and prairies.

Although decomposition of the trash at Fresh Kills won't be complete for decades, work on some parts of the new parkland can begin in 2007, after the master plan undergoes public scrutiny.

Parts of the refurbished park could be created and opened to the public between 2008 and 2012, with new stages opening about every five years.

NEW JERSEY — BRONX — MANHATTAN — QUEENS — BROOKLYN — STATEN ISLAND — DOWNTOWN

GREENPOINT/WILLIAMSBURG

In these immigrant neighborhoods that have become renowned centers for hipsters, there will be a renaissance of activity centering on two miles of waterfront.

"There will be ... water taxis, boat launches, fishing, ways for people to finally access that waterfront," Burden said.

There would be a long public esplanade to stroll, and a mixture of light manufacturing and residential areas.

Importantly, thousands upon thousands of new housing units would be built, although limits would be set to keep building heights down near the water.

Several new parks would open to the public, including the Newtown Barge Park at the end of Greenpoint Ave., a park at the end of Manhattan Ave. and a state park on the waterfront between Williamsburg's N. Seventh and Ninth Sts.

If the city won the 2012 Olympics, the waterfront between N. 9th St. and the edge of the Bushwick inlet would become parkland. On that land and the state land, Olympians would compete in events such as archery and beach volleyball.

ARTIST RENDERINGS COURTESY OF N.Y.C. DEPARTMENT OF

(AND DON'T FORGET GR[OUND] ZERO), DOWNTOWN WIL[L] A REAL NEIGHBORHOOD

GROUND ZERO will be re[built] perhaps. That's the date th[at] ciled powers-that-be have [...] goal. Port Authority [...] Charles Gargano bristles [at the sugges]tion that nothing has happ[ened ...] just that most of the work [...] derground. "You need [...] everything. Abraham Linc[oln ...] don't have consensus, you [...] thing done,'" says Gargano [...] has begun on Santiago Cal[atrava's] hub and what is now the P[...]

middle class for owners with an agenda [...] ers in a park.

[...]ng phrase on everyone's lips is "eyes on [...] bsurdum of the argument of the late [...] nd Life of Great American Cities. Jaco[bs ...] of her then-threatened neighborho[od ...] pkeepers and homeowners and stoo[d ...] sidewalks and parks for free. Under [...] r Amanda Burden, neighborhoods are [...] o preserve their "special character." [...] sion was lovely but limited, with little [...] w neighborhoods. Rereading her a[...] eaking admiration for the size of Mos[es ...] o grow, it needed major change. Unde[r ...] s happening again. What we have is a [...] alliance of Bob and Jane. Exaltation [...] upled with the idea of building ne[w ...] Bloomberg administration still lags in [...] ery economic-development initiative [...] e? (Note to gadflies: Many of these p[...] ne. If you hate it, you can still change [...] t also start imagining an alternative—[...]

[...] Majora Carter, executive director [...] stands on the newly green rooftop of the historic [...]nknote Company Building and quotes Daniel Burn[ham ...] t help but get a little chill. "Make no little plans," [...] ave no magic to stir man's blood," goes the rest of the [...] orrowland, little plans haven't been made.

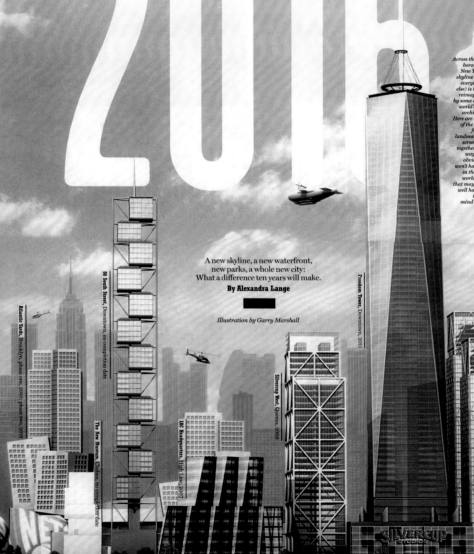

NEW YORK 2016

A new skyline, a new waterfront, new parks, a whole new city: What a difference ten years will make.

By Alexandra Lange

Illustration by Garry Marshall

Across the five boroughs, New York's skyline (and everything else) is being reimagined by some of the world's best architects. Here are a few of the city's future landmarks—assembled together in a way that obviously won't happen in the real world, but that may very well happen in the mind's eye.

2016 NEW YORK
JUNE 5, 2006

TOMORROWLAND

New York is radically transforming itself before our eyes. Inside, what the city will look like in just 10 years.
BY ALEXANDRA LANGE

CLOSING REFLECTIONS: MAKE IT BOLDER

For more than 20 years, Dan and I have collaborated on projects to remake cities. Each time the work is different, but the approach is always the same: Past all reason, he never stops pushing for projects to be bigger, better, more ambitious, and above all, bolder.

As the closing voice I have the last word, a role for which I feel confident I am qualified. Dan and I are approaching over 20 years of professional collaboration and partnership, as well as friendship, mentorship, and sometimes even combat. This includes five years working closely with Dan in the Bloomberg administration, starting in 2002, where I spent several years as his chief of staff. Almost two decades later, in 2015, we co-founded Sidewalk Labs, a company we built to reshape the future of cities by leveraging technological breakthroughs to solve long-standing challenges of urban life.

These two professional forays bookended a stretch where we went different directions professionally but remained close personally. In many ways, our relationship has most resembled that of a younger and older sibling (he's the older one!), affording me a unique vantage point from which to witness the force of nature that is Dan Doctoroff.

Nevertheless, it's still no easy task to follow the remarkable stories, testimonials, and comprehensive insights throughout this volume. In true Doctoroff fashion, I've been in a painful wrestling match with the narrative for this essay. I've been there before on projects with Dan — that dark place that deep down you know you're in but that Dan affirms through loud, angry declaration: "We're nowhere! The story is all wrong!"

So, back to the drawing board to dig a little deeper: to really understand the message, the story that wants to be told. And lo and behold, as I think back to what we did, and where I am now, it hits me: He's with me all the time. That is the story — the sheer impact the man has had on how I can have impact in the world. Not because it's about me, but because that is where I find him.

Dan Doctoroff and Joshua Sirefman on their way to meet with Schoharie County officials to review the Gilboa Dam stabilization. At the onset of Mayor Michael Bloomberg's second term, Doctoroff was tasked with overseeing the Department of Environmental Protection, which manages New York City's water supply.

Especially these days, with time and distance from our most recent collaboration at Sidewalk Labs, I can see more clearly the influence, the teaching, the lessons learned, and how I've internalized and unwittingly applied so much of what he's taught me.

There are the easy lessons, the low-hanging fruit, if you will.

Understanding the power of the story, and the ability to craft it — and tell it — in ways that compel the audience. And its twin sibling, the power of a vision, substantiated with the hard work that's deep in the details — visionary but credible. And the faith in that vision to carry the day, all as described by Eric Jaffe in his essay, "The Storyteller," in the introductory chapter of this book.

My first foray deep into this with Dan was the *Vision for Lower Manhattan*, early in our days in city government, a document we used strategically to gain the upper hand, the high road, when the governor controlled the World Trade Center site and we had to make sure the rebuilding was a part of something bigger. It gave the mayor a story to tell, a platform, and became the blueprint for a larger transformation Downtown, as chronicled by Roy Bahat in "The Resilient City" chapter.

Since then, there have been so many other examples. The pattern remained the same — always push the thinking deeper, bolder, work to the bone to do the analyses and the homework, ultimately find the narrative that captures it, tell it in a compelling way. Big things will follow. Through the years, this approach has been the foundation, enabling so much to be accomplished. At Sidewalk Labs, we even wrote a 400-page book, yes, an old-school, bound, publisher-quality book, to convey our vision for the city of the future to the founders of Google, two of the world's most successful tech pioneers. And it worked — Larry Page came into our presentation carrying his copy of the book, overflowing with easily over 100 post-its with his comments. He'd even read the 200-page financial appendix.

The circumstances around us in City Hall and those at Sidewalk Labs could not have been more different. Working for the City of New York brings a clear underlying mission, sense of purpose, and parameters, even before factoring in the intense loyalty to the mayor. This gave us all a framework, clarity around objectives, a structured canvas within which we could shape our agenda — a crash course on the complexities and challenges of city shaping and development.

At Sidewalk Labs, the construct was entirely different — it was a blank canvas. Whereas City Hall was completely structured, here we were making it all up as we went along. We were driven by the knowledge that we know how to effect change in cities, a belief that we were on to something, and a conviction that technology was dramatically changing the tools at our disposal, yet not being utilized. Our confidence driving us to always be one step ahead of the sheriff as we built the plane while we flew it, through progress and mistakes.

Yet these two experiences are tied together by a belief in the conviction of a vision, the ability to substantiate it with rigor, and to translate it into a compelling story.

Sirefman and Doctoroff worked together at City Hall to revitalize decaying, postindustrial piers into Brooklyn Bridge Park, which now attracts five million visitors a year. Movie Night, Brooklyn Bridge Park, 2014.

When combined with an almost superhuman ability to keep driving at the answer and to constantly push for more, well, we've seen the results. Does The Shed exist without that? Would the Olympic bid have become a city-changing effort? Does Alphabet (and then Google) invest at scale in an idea? Does the search for a new location for a salt pile become the groundbreaking PlaNYC? No way whatsoever.

There are, however, additional layers that matter.

The ability to handle, even to outright choose, maybe even seek, extreme pressure. To have courage and take risks, and sometimes to double down on that risk by going even further. To live with uncertainty and ambiguity, to break down and systematically work through complexity. The vision and the ability to articulate it to others is great, but absent these capabilities, big things, things that are hard to do, won't be achieved.

The understanding of — one could even argue the embrace of — the role of conflict. I laugh writing this, thinking about my deeply calloused scars from years of Doctoroff combat. A favorite anecdote for both of us is how often at City Hall I became the basis for Dan to

start a famous streak of consecutive days without yelling, and the cause for him to break the streak! Whether because the work isn't there yet, or it's frustrating that it doesn't reflect the clarity needed, or maybe even because of stress having nothing to do with the situation at hand, conflict is a part of the day-to-day work with Dan.

Yet, what is underlying that tendency also matters. To be able to address tough issues head on, to bend the dynamic to your will, to expose wherein the weakness lies (unless someone else has worked hard enough to push back and prevail — in which case, ultimately, the idea was Dan's anyway!). Absent the ability to confront, it's difficult to push people, push ideas, to constantly strive for a better answer.

The consumption of information and the analytics, and an understanding of how to use it. Sounds simple, but it differentiates. The quest to understand, and then to leverage the data, anchors the pursuit of the big idea. It's not a coincidence that most of Dan's speeches include historical references and context, or clever data points that reveal deep insight. As the New York historian Kenneth

T. Jackson, writes in the introduction, Dan tests ideas against the city's 400 years of history, not election cycles.

The deep, relentless discipline. It's what channels the drive, turns belief in ideas into sustained action and results. The discipline to give every subject the same level of effort, the same rigor — to never compromise the standard, whether the stakes are modest or great. There's no on or off, the expectations never diminish, whatever the content of the work. He is just as angry about Maria Torres-Springer's small, subpar brochure on Coney Island, as she details in her introductory essay, as mistakes on high-profile endeavors like Hudson Yards. It's the only mode of functioning: always on.

There are additional layers, ones that I appreciate even more these days.

It's too simple to say one should live with and learn from failure. Rather, it's an inherent conviction that the only acceptable path is to try and give it everything. We were way ahead of our time in Toronto, and the impact from our work there has been profound, on a global scale. We opened the door for urbanism to embrace new technologies and presented a new approach to urban planning that is studied by academics and implemented by practitioners alike around the world, as noted by Richard Florida in his "Future City" essay.

Few people know what it took and what we gave to make that effort possible. Or that it reflected an extraordinary body of work from a phenomenal team that is now having impact in a myriad of ways — leading cities, scaling start-ups, managing investment funds, building new products. Or the inherent capabilities, conviction, and strength that it took to sustain.

Dan is always building — teams, organizations, strategies, to travel from idea to reality, to pull and push others along to worthy outcomes. And he has learned how to cope when those outcomes are very different than hoped.

Then there is the impatience. Ah, the impatience. I've also been at the receiving end on that one, more than a few times. Yet, for city-shaping work at scale, the impatience is paramount. Dan and I have both always believed that this work requires a mastery of functioning at all times with equal doses of patience and urgency, but the impatience is something different. It's a constant race against something unseen, an anxiety, a pace, coupled with a disdain for the path of least resistance. It will grind you down, but it underpins impact and gets tough things done. Dan's body of work in government — even with the extraordinary leadership and empowerment from Mike Bloomberg — just doesn't happen if you accept the status quo or don't push harder.

Ultimately, though, the people. Those close to Dan know that he may well be most proud of his people, that his analysis of your personal life may actually be even more rigorous than that of your work. That even though you're having shadow conversations with him in your head about how wrong he is about, oh, everything, you'd still run through the next wall for, or with him. The built legacy around New York is one thing, but the network of people within the Dan universe, and their ongoing collective impact on New York and cities around the world will be the next volumes.

It's not easy to do justice to Dan's impact in 2,000 words, though I have the benefit of the broad commentary throughout this book. I will confess, however, that I can't help thinking that when Dan reads this, he's going to find the missing piece, the spot where it doesn't quite hold together. I can't quite shake the feeling that when reading this, despite having changed New York City, having dramatically advanced the global movement around urban innovation, and having inspired an army of extraordinary people who are out creating their own impact, Dan will declare, "It could be even more bold."

Joshua Sirefman

New York
June 2023

Joshua Sirefman and Dan Doctoroff, working side by side at an open table at Sidewalk Labs. After the leaders of Google reached out to Doctoroff about a potential partnership, he quickly brought in Sirefman to join him in founding the company. Its mission was to bring together urbanists and technologists to improve the quality of life in cities.

During their time together in government, Sirefman and Doctoroff advanced an array of landmark projects, including the acquisition of Governors Island from the federal government, the creation of Brooklyn Bridge Park, the rebirth of Coney Island, and more.

Opposite: They jointly spearheaded the Sidewalk Toronto proposal to build a "neighborhood of the future" on the Toronto waterfront.

ACKNOWLEDGMENTS

This project is a result of discussions among a group of Dan's longtime colleagues, friends, and advisors about how best to preserve and honor his legacy: Sharon Greenberger, Nate Jenkins, Jonathan Rosen, Joshua Sirefman, Angela Sung Pinsky, Jed Walentas, and Jim Whelan.

After aligning on this book, the next step was to secure funders. Friends of Dan stepped forward readily. While we do not name them here, we are grateful for their contributions and their confidence in us to complete a worthy product.

With funding in hand, we sought to build a world-class team to deliver on our commitment. Jed Walentas made the critical first recommendation: Pulitzer Prize-winning architectural critic Paul Goldberger. Paul — another longtime friend and admirer of Dan's — provided an eloquent introduction to this work, ongoing wise counsel, and also led us to extraordinary people who executed on our vision: namely, Brad Collins and his team at Group C.

Brad, who has worked with Paul many times over three decades, was our guide and counselor from the very beginning, both responding to and improving upon our ideas. His colleague Lynne Talbot was the indefatigable executor, wrangling an extraordinary volume of content into a clean and compelling aesthetic.

With input from both Paul and Brad, we filled out the rest of the team — most critically our photography editor Melissa Goldstein. Having recently played the same role for a Pulitzer Prize-winning book on Susan Sontag, Melissa embraced the project, which ultimately required securing the rights for some 450 images. Despite a herculean work ethic, even Melissa required support. Thankfully, she was able to deputize Caroline Hirsch, who stepped in seamlessly and quickly became a valued member of the team, and Nia Lowe, who helped in securing rights. Ben Oldenburg completed our image team, creating the book's new content-rich maps.

We set ourselves a high standard of accuracy. Fortunately, Bill Shaffer — another referral from Paul — used his detailed research to help us meet it. Bill also assisted with the captions in the book. His wife Christine, served as our copy editor, reviewing nearly 180,000 words in manuscript and layout. N2 Communications provided additional support for our contributors.

The entire team delivered a project that was of far greater breadth and depth — and words, pages, and images — than any of us expected. We are so very grateful.

In our search of the right publisher, Joshua David and Robbie Hammond, co-founders of Friends of the High Line, pointed us to Keith Fox at Phaidon. Keith actually knew Dan well from the sale of *BusinessWeek* to Bloomberg LP, and readily took on the project under the Monacelli imprint with the enthusiastic support of his owners. Keith tasked Philip Ruppel and Michael Vagnetti with shepherding the project, which they did with great skill and tremendous care.

Of course, this book is the product of the contributors who lent their time and remembrances to celebrate Dan. We thank them for working with Dan's preferred combination of urgency and patience — the former when we placed deadlines on them, the latter when we failed to meet our own, self-imposed deadlines.

Some individuals assisted beyond their own essays, including most especially Andrew Winters (practically a deputy editor), Joe Chan, Regina Myer, Michael Kalt, Sue Donoghue, Seth Pinsky, Angela Sung Pinsky, Eric Jaffe, and Ariella Maron, who helped guide the Sustainable City chapter. Others provided invaluable behind-the-scenes-support, including Howard Slatkin, Seth Solomonow, Michael Meola, Marvin Markus, Anthony Hogrebe, and Jeremy Soffin. Two Twelve dug deep in their archives to find the original Olympic X map.

We and our photography team are grateful to the extraordinary photographers and archivists who helped tell this New York story in the most beautiful way possible, and very often with pricing below their usual rates. Our photography team offers special thanks to the following individuals and organizations:

Suzanne Tóth-Pál and Iwan Baan
Bill Kalis, Bloomberg Philanthropies
Sigurjon Gudjonsson and Chris Browne, New York City Department of Transportation
David Sundberg and Albert Vecerka, Esto
Kristina Fetkovich, New York City Department of Environmental Protection
Eloise Hirsh, Freshkills Park Alliance
Etienne Frossard for his landscapes of Brooklyn Bridge Park
Harish Bhandari and Erika Harvey, Friends of the High Line
Frank Oudeman
Malcolm Pinckney and Meghan Lalor, New York City Department of Parks & Recreation
Lori Reese Redux
Angela Glass, Related Companies
Jeff Levine, The Shed
SHoP Architects
Tim Kau, Google/Sidewalk Labs
David Lloyd, SWA/Balsley
Seth Solomonow, Bloomberg Associates
Arissa Lahr and Mary Alice Lee, The Trust for Public Land
Hufton + Crow Photography and Sophia Gibb, VIEW Pictures Ltd.
Paul Warchol
Weiss/Manfredi
Stephen and Bette Wilkes

Bloomberg Philanthropies contributed in a wide variety of ways under the leadership of CEO Patti Harris, who also provided a beautiful remembrance of her partnership with Dan on cultural projects. Special thanks to Howard Wolfson, Kevin Sheekey, Tarara Deane-Krantz, Jamie Staugler, Frank Barry, Gabe DeVries, Bill Kalis, Page Meredith, and Suzanne Foote.

Marla Pardee was our secret weapon — a familiar role during her long years of service to Dan — helping to uncover documents, contact information, and more without Dan's knowledge.

We reserve our biggest thanks for our spouses and children, for their infinite patience and unyielding support as we often substituted "book time" for "family time" for more than 18 months. Dan would be the first to tell us to return to family time.

DAN DOCTOROFF

CREDITS

Edwine Seymour
p. 63 top portrait

Brett Beyer, courtesy The Shed
Dust Jacket, front cover, top right; p. 401

Christopher Garcia Valle, courtesy The Shed
p. 407

Jasdeep Kang, courtesy The Shed
p. 409 top

Nicholas Knight. Courtesy the artist and
Tanya Bonakdar Gallery, New York/Los
Angeles; Neugerriemschneider, Berlin;
Andersen's, Copenhagen; Ruth Benzacar,
Buenos Aires; and Pinksummer Contemporary
Art, Genoa. Photo courtesy The Shed.
p. 399

Nicholas Knight, courtesy The Shed
p. 409 middle

Ed Lederman, courtesy The Shed
p. 37 top

Simon Luethi, courtesy The Shed
Dust Jacket, back flap

Tori Mumtaz, courtesy The Shed
p. 409 bottom

Jonno Rattman, courtesy The Shed
p. 402

Scott Rudd Events, courtesy The Shed
p. 406

Artwork ©Tomás Saraceno. Commissioned by
The Shed. Photo: Nicholas Knight. Courtesy
the artist and Tanya Bonakdar Gallery, New
York/Los Angeles; Neugerriemschneider,
Berlin; Andersen's, Copenhagen; Ruth
Benzacar, Buenos Aires; and Pinksummer
Contemporary Art, Genoa. Photo courtesy
The Shed.
p. 399

Ahad Subzwari, courtesy The Shed
p. 403

Walter Wlodarczyk, courtesy The Shed
p. 405

©Scott Shigley
p. 320 top

SHoP Architects
p. 329 (2)

quiggyt4/Shutterstock
p. 273

Daniel W/Shutterstock
p. 287

Kamira/Shutterstock
p. 425 bottom

Jason Szenes/EPA/Shutterstock
p. 99 top right

Delve by Sidewalk Labs
p. 466

Pebble by Sidewalk Labs
p. 467 left

Mesa by Sidewalk Labs
p. 467 right

Sidewalk Labs, Part of Google
p. 480 (2)

Beyer Blinder Belle Architects/
Sidewalk Labs, Part of Google
p. 453

Heatherwick Studio/
Sidewalk Labs, Part of Google
438, 442, 443, 446, 450, 458, 459, 460, 461,
462, 463

Picture Plane for Heatherwick Studio/
Sidewalk Labs, Part of Google
p. 30, 436, 440, 444, 448, 454, 456, 481

Joshua Simpson
p. 57 top right, 81, 86 bottom, 336 bottom

Kristin Sisley/"Made in NY"
Production Assistant Training Program
p. 417

SkyCamUSA
p. 175 top

Marielle Solan
p. 243, 247

Courtesy of Steiner Studios
p. 188

©George Steinmetz
Dust Jacket, back cover, middle left; p. 369

Street Lab
p. 248

Ajay Suresh https://commons.wikimedia.
org/w/index.php?curid=80250889
Brooklyn_Academy_of_Music_(BAM)_
(48228024996).jpeg
p. 386

©SWA/Balsley Photo: David Lloyd
Dust Jacket, front cover, bottom left; Dust Jacket,
back cover, top left; p. 55 top right, 75, 209, 214,
Back Endpaper

©SWA/Balsley Photo: Jonnu Singleton
p. 9 middle bottom, 174, 336 top, 337

Courtesy of Mike Szpot,
The Howard Hughes Corporation
p. 137 top

T

34bp.org
p. 275 bottom

Thomson Reuters Foundation,
September 13, 2018
p. 262 bottom

Trust for Public Land
p. 365, 367 (2)

Mike Tschappat
p. 71

Two Twelve
p. 54

V

Lexi Van Valkenburgh
p. 299

©Hufton+Crow/VIEW
p. 110, 112, 115, 116, 119, 120, 122, 192

Grant Smith Collection/View Pictures
p. 150

W

Paul Warchol Photography
p. 322 right, 323 top

Julian Wass
p. 13, 382

Weiss/Manfredi
Dust Jacket, front flap; p. 160, 313, 324

Stephen Whitehouse/Starr Whitehouse
Landscape Architects and Planners
p. 303, 323 bottom

https://commons.wikimedia.org/wiki/
File:New_York_Stock_Exchange_
09-2018.jpg
p. 147

https://commons.wikimedia.org/wiki/
File:USA-NYC-Pier_15_Esplanade.JPG#file
p. 129

The Highline, NYC, Day to Night TM,
2009, by Stephen Wilkes
p. 348

Coney Island Boardwalk, Day to Night TM,
2011 by Stephen Wilkes
p. 428

Barbara Wilks
p. 338

Andrew Winters
p. 55 middle left

Filip Wolak
p. 425 top left

Y

Michael Young
p. 135 bottom

Z

Connie Zhou
p. 197

Wade Zimmerman
p. 216

If any of the projects in this book have inspired you or changed your life for the better, please consider making a donation at **TargetALS.org** in Dan's honor.

Editors: Sophia Hollander and Marc Ricks

Photography Editor: Melissa Goldstein, with assistance from Caroline L. Hirsch and Nia Lowe.

Design: Group C Inc: Brad Collins, Lynne Talbot

Printed in China

Dust Jacket Front Cover
Portrait: Brad Trent/Redux
The Shed: Brett Beyer. Courtesy The Shed
U.S. Coast Guard Cutter Docked at Pier 5: ©Etienne Frossard
Hunter's Point South: ©SWA/Balsley Photo: David Lloyd

Dust Jacket Front Flap
Hunter's Point South: Weiss/Manfredi

Dust Jacket Spine
Coney Island Parachute Jump: ©Eduard Hueber/archphoto

Dust Jacket Back Cover
Hunter's Point South: ©SWA/Balsley Photo: David Lloyd
The High Line: Timothy Schenck
Governors Island: ©George Steinmetz
City Point Development, Brooklyn: ©David Sundberg/Esto
Movie Night in Brooklyn Bridge Park: ©Etienne Frossard

Dust Jacket Back Flap
Dan Doctoroff: Simon Luethi. Courtesy The Shed

Monacelli

A Phaidon Company

65 Bleecker Street

New York, New York 10012

Pages 482–483: Central Lawn, Pier 3, Brooklyn Bridge Park.

Opposite: Brooklyn Bridge Park.

Closing Image: Hunter's Point South Park.